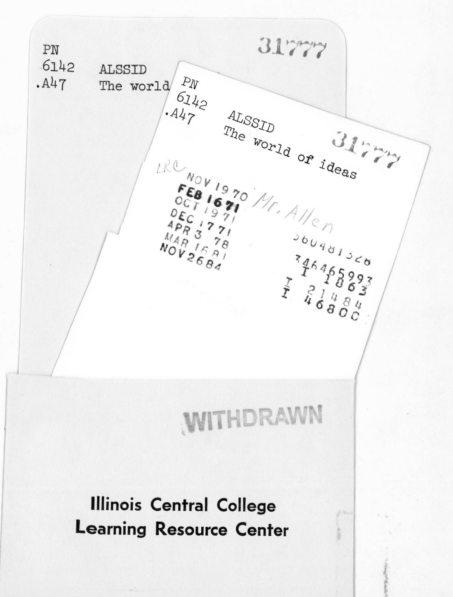

THE WORLD OF IDEAS:
ESSAYS FOR STUDY

THE WORLD OF IDEAS:

ESSAYS FOR STUDY

THE WORLD OF IDEAS:
ESSAYS FOR STUDY

EDITED BY

MICHAEL W. ALSSID, *1927 –*   *ed.*

Boston University

WILLIAM KENNEY

State College at Boston

Holt, Rinehart and Winston, Inc.

NEW YORK   CHICAGO   SAN FRANCISCO   TORONTO

June, 1966

PREFACE

This collection of essays is unique because it includes topics that are basic to almost all of the liberal arts. Our assumption is that such a collection, used for example in a freshman composition course, could serve as an introduction to the world of ideas. The essays contain stimulating subject matter and, at the same time, are challenging from a rhetorical-stylistic point of view. They are intellectually demanding without being abstruse; they represent various levels of complexity, from the popularizing account of the earth's composition in Peter Farb's "The Placenta of Life" to the comparatively heavily abstract discussion of religion in Paul Tillich's "Man and God."

For the instructor who wants to emphasize problems of rhetoric, the essays provide a great variety of styles. Each area or discipline is subject to its own particular problems of diction, of "voice," of arrangement of ideas. The man of science has a different frame of reference that expresses itself in a slightly different "voice" from that of the literary critic, the musician, or the economist. Needless to say, the essays do not have to be studied solely in terms of subject matter; they may be studied according to the conventional categories of exposition, logical and persuasive argument, description, and narration. Any one of the essays can be subjected to the analytical approach. The historical range of the selections allows the instructor to discuss and to evaluate style from a chronological point of view, from Bacon to Mencken, from Jefferson to Kennedy, from Gibbon to Max Lerner.

The essays, eighty-two items in all, are arranged under nine categories: A Liberal Education (essays attempting to define the purpose and scope of learning); Language and Literature (opinions ranging from Plato to Joseph Wood Krutch and Allen Ginsberg); The Nature of Man (essays in biology); The Life Within (essays on psychology, philosophy and religion); Creative Man (essays on art, architecture, music, and the aesthetic experience); Civilization in Perspective (ideas concerning history and government); Man in the Market Place (economics); Man in Society (essays on sociology and anthropology); and The Environment of Man (essays on physics and mathematics).

In each of these sections, the emphasis is placed upon recent trends, but not to the disadvantage of the great thinkers of the past. For example, in the section "Language and Literature," five classics (Plato, Aristotle, Reynolds, Wordsworth, and Hazlitt) are included together with recent statements on the function of criticism and poetry by T. S. Eliot and Allen Ginsberg and, in addition, an article by Bergen Evans on the recent controversy over *Webster's New International Dictionary* 3d. ed. In the sections entitled "The Nature of Man" and "The Environment of Man" appear essays on the scientific method by Thomas H. Huxley, on the planetary system by Shapley, on cybernetics by Wiener, on oceanography by McElroy and, in addition, an article by C. P. Snow on the contributions of Rutherford. In the section entitled "Man in the Market Place," there is an effort to contrast and to heighten distinctions between classical and modern thought in essays by Smith, Veblen, Marx and Engels, on the one hand, and Becker, Galbraith, and Theobald on the other.

Finally, there are a number of "interrelationships" in subject matter among the essays in the different sections. Thus Reynolds's essay on the universality of taste may be contrasted with concepts of cultural relativism held by the anthropologist Ruth Benedict. Kandinsky's "The Spiritual in Art," essentially an aesthetic statement, may be contrasted with the theological ideas of Martin Buber and Paul Tillich. Ultimately, then, this collection of essays not only illustrates distinctions between the various disciplines, but also demonstrates areas of similarity. Thus one may recognize that these authors are describing essential aspects of the human condition.

The editors want to express their thanks to Professor Richard Beal of Boston University for his invaluable advice and to Rebecca Alssid for her great patience and technical assistance.

M. W. A.

W. K.

Boston, Massachusetts
1964

TABLE OF CONTENTS

IX. THE ENVIRONMENT OF MAN

I
A LIBERAL EDUCATION

MORTIMER J. ADLER

•

WHAT IS AN IDEA?

What *is* an idea?

Ideas are my business. I've been at it forty years now, and I have not yet found a new idea. But the old ones—and I am just getting started on some of them—have kept me going. And in all this time I have come to some conclusions and, I believe, a clearer notion not only of what an idea is but of what it is not.

It is not just a word, nor is it a string of words. Words are performing their highest function when they express ideas, but they do not constitute the ideas they express. This is clearly shown by the fact that different persons all using the same word may not have the same comprehension of the idea which that word expresses.

Consider the word "love." It has many meanings which we recognize as soon as we consider the difference between romantic love and conjugal love, the difference between love of country and love of God, or the difference between the love that parents readily bestow upon their children and the love that children slowly develop for their parents. All these meanings of the word—all these kinds of love—have something in common. All are related aspects of a single, very large idea—the idea of love. But as most people employ the word in ordinary speech, they have only a small part of this idea in mind; and when young people use it, they seldom have in mind the same part that older people have. Few who use the word ever have the whole idea in mind, for it takes a lifetime of experience and thought to comprehend it fully.

An idea is not a fact of any kind, nor a collection of facts, no matter how massive or recondite. The telephone book is full of facts, but it

From the *Saturday Review*, November 22, 1958. Reprinted by permission of the *Saturday Review* and of the author.

doesn't contain a single idea. A history book is full of facts, none of which is an idea, though if the writer is given to philosophizing about history he may illuminate the facts with some basic idea, such as the idea of progress, the idea of chance, or the idea of fate. Suppose we are dealing with the idea of "progress," in itself abstract and general. To grasp it, we consider one example after another, each a concrete or particular instance of the essential idea. We look at the changes that have been made in transportation to increase comfort and speed. We call attention to the advances that have been made in the conquest of disease. We may even point to improvements in certain social or political institutions, such as the treatment of criminals or the protection of human rights. But none of these things is the idea of progress, though each may exemplify it. Moreover, if we did not have some idea of progress in the first place, we would not have chosen these examples to illustrate what we have in mind and to hold that idea before us.

Ideas influence our actions no less than feelings, desires, emotions, and purposes do, but not in the same way. Our particular passions or desires determine the attitudes we take and move us to the things we do. But if we ever recognize the discrepancy between what we do and what we ought to do, we are moved by ideas, not passions. Particular loves and hates may lead us to befriend certain minority groups and persecute others. But if we ever question such discrimination—our own or someone else's—we do so in virtue of ideas about love and man (especially insights about the fraternity and equality of men) that move us to judge our attitudes, and even perhaps to overcome our prejudices.

Some of the positive attributes of an idea have already been indicated by the difference between ideas and words, facts, examples, and emotions or desires. An idea alters and grows. Having a life, it can have a history—a past, present, and future. Each of the great ideas is a complex and organic whole, a dissectible structure of related parts. It has an interior, and in this sense it is like a domain which can be probed, pried into, explored, approached from many angles, taken apart in many ways.

Ideas may look alike from the outside, but the more we look into them the more we find that each is a world of its own, with its own special history and its own special structure. Yet each also belongs to a vaster world or universe of thought in which ideas group themselves as so many constellations or galaxies. In themselves and in relation to one another they comprise the configurations of the human mind, as intricate and varied in their criss-crossing patterns as the starry heavens. And like each individual star, every idea is a source of life and light which animates and illuminates the words, facts, examples, and emotions that are dead—or deadly—and dark without them. The idea of Government, for example, moves in the orbit of such other ideas as State, Law, Constitution, Citizen, Democracy, Revolution. The idea of Virtue not only has such ideas as Wisdom, Temperance, Justice, Prudence, and Courage as its satellites, but it also is one of the focal points in a group of ideas that includes Desire, Duty, Sin, Happiness, and Pleasure and Pain. The more fully one investigates any great idea, the more one has to delve into others. The pursuit is endless—and fascinating.

None of these things would be true if ideas were words, or facts, or examples, or feelings. Nor would words, facts, examples, or feelings play the roles that they do in human life if ideas did not intervene to give them meaning and direction. Apart from ideas, great or small, they would not be discussable, interpretable, or even relateable. But while all ideas have the properties mentioned, the nature of ideas is most clearly seen in the case of the relatively small number of great ideas which are the main points of reference in the universe of human thought.

What are these "great ideas?"

Working with a large research staff, I spent eight years directing the construction of a reference work entitled "The Great Ideas" or "Syntopicon," which aimed at a systematic and comprehensive inventory of the fundamental ideas to be found in the great books of the Western world. In the beginning, we drew up a list of some 700 possible candidates for inclusion in our encyclopedic catalogue of great ideas. Then we started to examine them. After two years we found that most of these notions were parts or bits of more inclusive ideas. When we came to count up the really big and independent ideas that could stand by themselves, we determined that the irreducible minimum numbered 102.

The "Syntopicon" was published in 1952 as an adjunct to the fifty-four-volume "Great Books of the Western World." Since then I have been continuously at work on ideas with my colleagues at the Institute for Philosophical Research, and so far we have not found any ideas of a magnitude comparable to the 102. Nor has further study suggested dropping any from the list.

None of the 102 great ideas is a recent discovery in the sense in which there are really new inventions in every age. The ancient Greeks had a name for every one of them. All have been objects of speculation and inquiry since the beginning of thought. They have always been the common stock of the human mind. Innumerable men have engaged in the discussion of each one of them. The vast literature which exists on every great idea reflects not only the continuity of human thought about them, but also the wide diversity of opinions to which such thought inevitably gives rise. In the sphere of the great ideas we can find all the fundamental disagreements—and agreements—of mankind.

When I say that there are no new ideas—or no great ones that are new—I do not mean that there is nothing new in the world of ideas. On the contrary, most of the great ideas have kept on changing and growing in substance and scope, to whatever extent thinking men have been at work on them century after century. Unlike facts, which remain fixed for all time once they are established, the great ideas, once discovered in the dim past, remain the same in the way in which living organisms remain the same while developing.

In every epoch, intellectual geniuses have added not new ideas but new facets to the same enduring ones. Some of the great ideas have been more energetically or creatively pursued at certain periods or places than at others. Ideas like Prophecy or Angel have had a livelier history in antiquity or the Middle Ages than in modern times. The opposite is true of such ideas as Progress and Evolution. But the lineage of these goes back to antiquity. As Mark Twain wryly observed, "The ancients stole all our ideas from us."

Even more important than the living presence of a great idea is its future. Each is still unfinished business; each is still imperfectly understood. For six years the staff of the Institute for Philosophical Research has worked on a single idea—Freedom. We studied its past by trying, so far as possible, to read through all the major writings on the subject. We explored the whole range of differing conceptions and theories which eminent thinkers have advanced or held about freedom, assessing this idea's present significance by taking stock of all that has been thought about it in the past and is being thought about it now. This stocktaking, we hope, will reveal the fundamental agreements and disagreements which unite and divide men, together with the arguments by which they have carried on the debate of the issues.

Later we plan to undertake similar inquiry and investigation of such fundamental ideas as Justice, Law, Love, Wealth, Knowledge, and Government. The venture is a formidable one. Taking four or five years for the exploration of an idea, it will require much more than several lifetimes to examine human thought on all 102 of the great ideas, each of which has a future larger and more interesting than its past.

One thing we know from the experience we have had in constructing the "Syntopicon" and in examining the idea of freedom. Every one of the great ideas is a unique adventure. Each has an interior structure and life of its own, not to mention its difference from others in size and complexity. Some great ideas—God, State, Man, Knowledge, and Wealth —involve as many as forty or fifty different topics. Some, like Fate, Element, and Honor, require only ten or fifteen. Some have a relatively simple order of parts. Some have a complex and intricate structure. But all have enough scope and variety to deserve a fuller treatment than could be given in a short essay. In the "Syntopicon," the treatment of liberty took about twenty-one pages. When "The Idea of Freedom," the first volume of which has recently been published, is completed, it will run to about 1,500 pages.

Whether we know it or not, we are all philosophers. We all think—well or sloppily, enthusiastically or inattentively. The slightest sense-perception—a falling leaf, a twinkling star, a smiling child—awakens our minds as well as arouses our feelings, and forces us to ask: Why? What? Whence? Whither?

Not to engage in this pursuit of ideas is to live like ants instead of like men. The ant can live without ideas because the whole course of its life is fixed. But man has the freedom—and therefore the necessity—to choose and to choose in terms of ideas.

We often think of ourselves as living in a world which no longer has any unexplored frontiers. We speak of pioneering as a thing of the past. But in doing so we forget that the greatest adventure of all still challenges us—what Mr. Justice Holmes called "the adventure of the human mind." Men may be hemmed in geographically, but every generation stands on the frontiers of the mind. In the world of ideas, there is always pioneering to be done, and it can be done by anyone who will use the equipment with which he is endowed. The great ideas belong to everyone.

• Questions for Study

1. What methods does Adler use to organize his essay and to define the word "idea"?
2. What is he trying to illustrate in his discussion of the word "love"?
3. How does he show that an idea is not a fact, a word, an emotion, or a feeling?
4. How does he define the word "idea"?
5. Comment on the statement "There are no new ideas." How does Adler qualify it?
6. Compare Adler's use of the ant-man contrast in the penultimate paragraph with the similar one in Einstein's essay "On Education." Which writer is more effective in his use of the contrast? Why?

EDMUND S. MORGAN

•

WHAT EVERY YALE FRESHMAN SHOULD KNOW

The world does not much like curiosity. The world says that curiosity killed the cat. The world dismisses curiosity by calling it idle, or *mere* idle, curiosity—even though curious persons are seldom idle. Parents do their best to extinguish curiosity in their children, because it makes life difficult to be faced every day with a string of unanswerable questions about what makes fire hot or why grass grows, or to have to halt junior's investigations before they end in explosion and sudden death. Children whose curiosity survives parental discipline and who manage to grow up before they blow up are invited to join the Yale faculty. Within the university they go on asking their questions and trying to find the answers. In the eyes of a scholar, that is mainly what a university is for. It is a place where the world's hostility to curiosity can be defied.

Some of the questions that scholars ask seem to the world to be scarcely worth asking, let alone answering. They ask about the behavior of protons, the dating of a Roman coin, the structure of a poem. They ask questions too minute and specialized for you and me to understand without years of explanation.

If the world inquires of one of them why he wants to know the answer to a particular question, he may say, especially if he is a scientist, that the answer will in some obscure way make possible a new machine or weapon or gadget. He talks that way because he knows that the world understands and respects utility and that it does not understand much else. But to his colleagues and to you he will probably not speak this language. You are now part of the university, and he will expect you to understand that he wants to know the answer simply because he does

---

From the *Saturday Review*, January 23, 1960. Reprinted by permission of the *Saturday Review* and of the author.

not know it, the way a mountain climber wants to climb a mountain simply because it is there.

Similarly a historian, when asked by outsiders why he studies history, may come out with a line of talk that he has learned to repeat on such occasions, something about knowledge of the past making it possible to understand the present and mold the future. I am sure you have all heard it at one time or another. But if you really want to know why a historian studies the past, the answer is much simpler: he wants to know about it because it is there. Something happened, and he would like to know what.

All this does not mean that the answers which scholars find to their questions have no consequences. They may have enormous consequences: they may completely alter the character of human life. But the consequences seldom form the reason for asking the questions or pursuing the answers. It is true that scholars can be put to work answering questions for the sake of the consequences, as thousands are working now, for example, in search of a cure for cancer. But this is not the primary function of the scholar. For the scholar the consequences are usually incidental to the satisfaction of curiosity. Even for the medical scholar, the desire to stamp out a dreaded disease may be a less powerful motive than the desire to find out about the nature of living matter. Similarly Einstein did not wish to create an atomic bomb or to harness atomic energy. He simply wanted to find out about energy and matter.

I said that curiosity was a dangerous quality. It is dangerous not only because of incidental effects like the atomic bomb but also because it is really nothing more or less than a desire for truth. For some reason this phrase sounds less dangerous than curiosity. In fact, the desire for truth sounds rather respectable. Since so many respectable people assure us that they have found the truth, it does not sound like a dangerous thing to look for. But it is. The search for it has again and again overturned institutions and beliefs of long standing, in science, in religion, and in politics. It is easy enough to see today that these past revolutions brought great benefits to mankind. It was less easy to see the benefits while the revolutions were taking place, especially if you happened to be quite satisfied with the way things were before. Similarly it is not always easy today to see that the satisfaction of a scholar's curiosity is worth the disruption of society that may result from it. The search for truth is, and always has been, a subversive activity. And scholars have learned that they cannot engage in it without an occasional fight.

You may therefore find them rather belligerent toward any threat to the free pursuit of curiosity. They are wary of committing themselves to institutions or beliefs that might impose limitations on them or deliver ready-made answers to their questions. You will find them suspicious of loyalty oaths, religious creeds, or affiliations with political parties. In particular they will try to preserve their university as a sanctuary within whose walls *any* question can be asked.

This wariness of commitment can sometimes degenerate into a scholarly vice, a vice that paralyzes curiosity instead of preserving it. A scholar at his worst sometimes seems to be simply a man who cannot make up his mind. Every classroom from here to Melbourne has echoed with the feeble phrases of academic indecision: "There are two schools of thought on this question, and the truth probably lies halfway between them." When you hear this sentence repeated, or when you are tempted to repeat it yourself, remember that the truth may lie between two extremes, but it assuredly does not lie halfway between right and wrong. Don't short-circuit your curiosity by assuming you have found the answer when you have only made a tidy list of possible answers.

Dedication to curiosity should not end in indecision. It should, in fact, mean willingness to follow the mind into difficult decisions.

A second quality that makes a scholar has no apparent relation to the first and yet is inseparably connected to it. It is a compulsion to communicate. A scholar is driven by a force as strong as his curiosity, that compels him to tell the world the things he has learned. He cannot rest with learning something: he has to tell about it. Scholarship begins in curiosity, but it ends in communication. And though scholars may in a university take refuge from the world, they also acknowledge responsibility to the world, the responsibility to communicate freely and fully everything that they discover within the walls of their sanctuary. The search for truth needs no justification, and when a man thinks he has found any part of it, he cannot and ought not to be silent. The world may sometimes not care to listen, but the scholar must keep telling it until he has succeeded in communicating.

Now, there are only two methods of communication for scholars, writing and speaking. The scholar publishes his discoveries in books and articles and he teaches them in the classroom. Sometimes one or the other method will satisfy him, but most of us feel the need for both. The scholar who merely writes books falls into the habit of speaking only to the experts. If he works at his subject long enough, he reaches the position where there is no one else quite expert enough to understand him, and he winds up writing to himself. On the other hand, if he writes not at all, he may become so enamored of his own voice that he ceases to be a scholar and becomes a mere showman.

Communication is not merely the desire and the responsibility of the scholar; it is his discipline, the proving ground where he tests his findings against criticism. Without communication his pursuit of truth withers into eccentricity. He necessarily spends much of his time alone, in the library or the laboratory, looking for the answers to his questions. But he needs to be rubbing constantly against other minds. He needs to be tested, probed, and pushed around. He needs to be made to explain himself. Only when he has expressed himself, only when he has communicated his thoughts, can he be sure that he is thinking clearly.

The scholar, in other words, needs company to keep him making sense. And in particular he needs the company of fresh minds, to whom he must explain things from the beginning. He needs people who will challenge him at every step, who will take nothing for granted. He needs, in short, you.

You may have various purposes in coming here, and you may fulfill them: you may play football or tennis or the trombone; you may sing in the glee club, act in plays, and act up on college weekends. But what the faculty expects of you is four years of scholarship, and they will be satisfied with nothing less. For four years we expect you to join us in the pursuit of truth, and we will demand of you the same things we demand of ourselves: curiosity and communication.

Curiosity, of course, is not something you get simply by wishing for it. But it is surprisingly contagious. The curiosity we expect is more than a passing interest. We will not be satisfied by your ability to ask an occasional bright question, nor yet by your assimilation of a lot of predigested information. The accumulation of information is a necessary part of scholarship, and unfortunately the part most likely to be tested on examinations, especially those wretched ones called "objective examinations" where the truth is always supposed to lie in answer space A, B, C, D, or E, but never apparently in X, Y, or Z. But the curiosity we expect of you cannot be satisfied by passing examinations or by memorizing other people's answers to other people's questions. We do not wish to put you through a mere course of mental gymnastics. We want you to be content with nothing less than the whole truth about the subject that interests you. Which means that we want you to be forever discontent with how little you know about it and how little we know about it. We want you to back us into corners, show us up, make us confess we don't know. Does this sound formidable? It is not. We may tell you what we know with great assurance, but push us and you will find the gaps.

Follow your own minds into the gaps. Follow your minds where curiosity takes them. You will not get the whole truth, not about protons, not about the structure of a poem, not even about a Roman coin. Nobody does. But if you learn anything, it ought to change your minds, and hopefully it will change ours too. It will be a sign that we have both wasted four years if you leave here thinking pretty much the same way that you do now or if you leave us thinking the same way *we* do now.

We expect of you, then, that you will be curious for the truth. We also expect that you communicate whatever truth you find, and that you do it both in speech and in writing. Many people suppose that they know something if they can stammer out an approximation of what they mean in speech. They are mistaken. It is extremely unlikely that you have thought clearly if you cannot express yourself clearly, especially in writing. Writing is more than an instrument of communication. It is an instrument of thought. You should have acquired some competence in its use by now. I suspect from past experience that you have not. But even if you have, you have a great deal more to learn about it. And if you do not know much more about it four years from now, it will again be a sign that we have failed in part of our job, the job of making you communicate clearly.

Communication is a two-way process, and a university is a community of scholars, where questions are asked and the answers communicated, your answers to us, ours to you. For the next four years we will be engaged as scholars together in this community. After the four years are over, most of you will leave Yale, but if our community is a successful one, if we really do communicate with each other, I believe that you will continue to be in some sense scholars, asking new questions, looking for new answers, and communicating them to the world.

• Questions for Study

1. Morgan was addressing an incoming freshman class at Yale. What influence does the occasion for which the talk was delivered have on the tone, style, and content?
2. What does he mean when he says, "The search for truth is, and always has been, a subversive activity"?
3. Around what two qualities of the scholar does Morgan organize his essay? Point out the similarities between this essay and Learned Hand's "Freedom of Dissent."
4. How do Morgan's ideas concerning knowledge relate to the concepts expressed by Bacon in "Of Studies" and "The End of Knowledge," and by Newman in "The Pursuit of Knowledge"?

MARK TWAIN

•

CONTINUED PERPLEXITIES

Now I had often seen pilots gazing at the water and pretending to read it as if it were a book; but it was a book that told me nothing. A time came at last, however, when Mr. Bixby seemed to think me far enough advanced to bear a lesson on water-reading. So he began:

"Do you see that long, slanting line on the face of the water? Now, that's a reef. Moreover, it's a bluff reef. There is a solid sand-bar under it that is nearly as straight up and down as the side of a house. There is plenty of water close up to it, but mighty little on top of it. If you were to hit it you would knock the boat's brains out. Do you see where the line fringes out at the upper end and begins to fade away?"

"Yes, sir."

"Well, that is a low place; that is the head of the reef. You can climb over there, and not hurt anything. Cross over, now, and follow along close under the reef—easy water there—not much current."

I followed the reef along till I approached the fringed end. Then Mr. Bixby said:

"Now get ready. Wait till I give the word. She won't want to mount the reef; a boat hates shoal water. Stand by—wait—*wait*—keep her well in hand. *Now* cramp her down! Snatch her! snatch her!"

He seized the other side of the wheel and helped to spin it around until it was hard down, and then we held it so. The boat resisted, and refused to answer for a while, and next she came surging to starboard, mounted the reef, and sent a long, angry ridge of water foaming away from her bows.

"Now watch her; watch her like a cat, or she'll get away from you. When she fights strong and the tiller slips a little, in a jerky, greasy sort of way, let up on her a trifle; it is the way she tells you at night that the

From *Life on the Mississippi*, 1883.

water is too shoal; but keep edging her up, little by little, toward the point. You are well up on the bar now; there is a bar under every point, because the water that comes down around it forms an eddy and allows the sediment to sink. Do you see those fine lines on the face of the water that branch out like the ribs of a fan? Well, those are little reefs; you want to just miss the ends of them, but run them pretty close. Now look out—look out! Don't you crowd that slick, greasy-looking place; there ain't nine feet there; she won't stand it. She begins to smell it; look sharp, I tell you! Oh, blazes, there you go! Stop the starboard wheel! Quick! Ship up to back! Set her back!"

The engine bells jingled and the engines answered promptly, shooting white columns of steam far aloft out of the 'scape-pipes, but it was too late. The boat had "smelt" the bar in good earnest; the foamy ridges that radiated from her bows suddenly disappeared, a great dead swell came rolling forward, and swept ahead of her, she careened far over to larboard, and went tearing away toward the shore as if she were about scared to death. We were a good mile from where we ought to have been when we finally got the upper hand of her again.

During the afternoon watch the next day, Mr. Bixby asked me if I knew how to run the next few miles. I said:

"Go inside the first snag above the point, outside the next one, start out from the lower end of Higgins's woodyard, make a square crossing, and—"

"That's all right. I'll be back before you close up on the next point."

But he wasn't. He was still below when I rounded it and entered upon a piece of the river which I had some misgivings about. I did not know that he was hiding behind a chimney to see how I would perform. I went gaily along, getting prouder and prouder, for he had never left the boat in my sole charge such a length of time before. I even got to "setting" her and letting the wheel go entirely, while I vaingloriously turned my back and inspected the stern marks and hummed a tune, a sort of easy indifference which I had prodigiously admired in Bixby and the other great pilots. Once I inspected rather long, and when I faced to the front again my heart flew into my mouth so suddenly that if I hadn't clapped my teeth together I should have lost it. One of those frightful bluff reefs was stretching its deadly length right across our bows! My head was gone in a moment; I did not know which end I stood on; I gasped and could not get my breath; I spun the wheel down with such rapidity that it wove itself together like a spider's web; the boat answered and turned square away from the reef, but the reef followed her! I fled, but still it followed, still it kept—right across my bows! I never looked to see where I was going, I only fled. The awful crash was imminent.

Why didn't that villain come? If I committed the crime of ringing a bell I might get thrown overboard. But better that than kill the boat. So in blind desperation, I started such a rattling "shivaree" down below as never had astounded an engineer in this world before, I fancy. Amidst the frenzy of the bells the engines began to back and fill in a curious way, and my reason forsook its throne—we were about to crash into the woods on the other side of the river. Just then Mr. Bixby stepped calmly into view on the hurricane-deck. My soul went out to him in gratitude. My distress vanished; I would have felt safe on the brink of Niagara with Mr. Bixby on the hurricane-deck. He blandly and sweetly took his toothpick out of his mouth between his fingers, as if it were a cigar—we were just in the act of climbing an overhanging big tree, and the passengers were scudding astern like rats—and lifted up these commands to me ever so gently:

"Stop the starboard! Stop the larboard! Set her back on both!"

The boat hesitated, halted, pressed her nose among the boughs a critical instant, then reluctantly began to back away.

"Stop the larboard! Come ahead on it! Stop the starboard! Come ahead on it! Point her for the bar!"

I sailed away as serenely as a summer's morning. Mr. Bixby came in and said, with mock simplicity:

"When you have a hail, my boy, you ought to tap the big bell three times before you land, so that the engineers can get ready."

I blushed under the sarcasm, and said I hadn't had any hail.

"Ah! Then it was for wood, I suppose. The officer of the watch will tell you when he wants to wood up."

I went on consuming, and said I wasn't after wood.

"Indeed? Why, what could you want over here in the bend, then? Did you ever know of a boat following a bend up-stream at this stage of the river?"

"No, sir—and *I* wasn't trying to follow it. I was getting away from a bluff reef."

"No, it wasn't a bluff reef; there isn't one within three miles of where you were."

"But I saw it. It was as bluff as that one yonder."

"Just about. Run over it!"

"Do you give it as an order?"

"Yes. Run over it!"

"If I don't, I wish I may die."

"All right; I am taking the responsibility."

I was just as anxious to kill the boat, now, as I had been to save it before. I impressed my orders upon my memory, to be used at the inquest, and made a straight break for the reef. As it disappeared under our bows I held by breath; but we slid over it like oil.

"Now, don't you see the difference? It wasn't anything but a *wind* reef. The wind does that."

"So I see. But it is exactly like a bluff reef. How am I ever going to tell them apart?"

"I can't tell you. It is an instinct. By and by you will just naturally *know* one from the other, but you never will be able to explain why or how you know them apart."

It turned out to be true. The face of the water, in time, became a wonderful book—a book that was a dead language to the uneducated passenger, but which told its mind to me without reserve, delivering its most cherished secrets as clearly as if it uttered them with a voice. And it was not a book to be read once and thrown aside, for it had a new story to tell every day. Throughout the long twelve hundred miles there was never a page that was void of interest, never one that you could leave unread without loss, never one that you would want to skip, thinking you could find higher enjoyment in some other thing. There never was so wonderful a book written by man; never one whose interest was so absorbing, so unflagging, so sparklingly renewed with every reperusal. The passenger who could not read it was charmed with a peculiar sort of faint dimple on its surface (on the rare occasions when he did not overlook it altogether); but to the pilot that was an *italicized* passage; indeed, it was more than that, it was a legend of the largest capitals, with a string of shouting exclamation-points at the end of it, for it meant that a wreck or a rock was buried there that could tear the life out of the strongest vessel that ever floated. It is the faintest and simplest expression the water ever makes, and the most hideous to a pilot's eye. In truth, the passenger who could not read this book saw nothing but all manner of pretty pictures in it, painted by the sun and shaded by the clouds, whereas to the trained eye these were not pictures at all, but the grimmest and most dead-earnest of reading-matter.

Now when I had mastered the language of this water, and had come to know every trifling feature that bordered the great river as familiarly as I knew the letters of the alphabet, I had made a valuable acquisition. But I had lost something, too. I had lost something which could never be restored to me while I lived. All the grace, the beauty, the poetry, had gone out of the majestic river! I still kept in mind a certain wonderful sunset which I witnessed when steamboating was new to me. A broad expanse of the river was turned to blood; in the middle distance the red hue brightened into gold, through which a solitary log came floating, black and conspicuous; in one place a long, slanting mark lay sparkling upon the water; in another the surface was broken by boiling, tumbling rings, that were as many-tinted as an opal; where the ruddy flush was faintest, was a smooth spot that was covered with graceful circles and radiating lines, ever so delicately traced; the shore on our left was densely wooded, and the somber shadow that fell from this forest was broken in one place by a long, ruffled trail that shone like silver; and high above the forest wall a clean-stemmed dead tree waved a single leafy bough that glowed like a flame in the unobstructed splendor that was flowing from the sun. There were graceful curves, reflected images, woody heights, soft distances; and over the whole scene, far and near, the dissolving lights drifted steadily, enriching it every passing moment with new marvels of coloring.

I stood like one bewitched. I drank it in, in a speechless rapture. The world was new to me, and I had never seen anything like this at home. But as I have said, a day came when I began to cease from noting the glories and the charms which the moon and the sun and the twilight wrought upon the river's face; another day came when I ceased altogether to note them. Then, if that sunset scene had been repeated, I should have looked upon it without rapture, and should have commented upon it, inwardly, after this fashion: "This sun means that we are going to have wind to-morrow; that floating log means that the river is rising, small thanks to it; that slanting mark on the water refers to a bluff reef which is going to kill somebody's steamboat one of these nights, if it keeps on stretching out like that; those tumbling 'boils' show a dissolving bar and a changing channel there; the lines and circles in the slick water over yonder are a warning that that troublesome place is shoaling up dangerously; that silver streak in the shadow of the forest is the 'break' from a new snag, and he has located himself in the very best place he could have found to fish for steamboats; that tall dead tree, with a single living branch, is not going to last long, and then how is a body ever going to get through this blind place at night without the friendly old landmark?"

No, the romance and beauty were all gone from the river. All the value any feature of it had for me now was the amount of usefulness it could furnish toward compassing the safe piloting of a steamboat. Since those days, I have pitied doctors from my heart. What does the lovely flush in a beauty's cheek mean to a doctor but a "break" that ripples above some deadly disease? Are not all her visible charms sown thick with what are to him the signs and symbols of hidden decay? Does he ever see her beauty at all, or doesn't he simply view her professionally, and comment upon her unwholesome condition all to himself? And doesn't he sometimes wonder whether he has gained most or lost most by learning his trade?

• Questions for Study

1. This essay may be divided into two parts. The first is a dramatic recreation of an event; the second is a comment on Twain's "studies" of the river. What stylistic characteristics distinguish each part? Do the parts form a coherent whole?
2. Twain likens the river to a book. In what ways is the analogy appropriate? Is it defective in any way? Explain.
3. The process of education is usually divided into stages connected with the formal learning acquired in schools and colleges. Describe the ways in which Morgan and Twain broaden the definition, both of them recognizing that formal learning is only one aspect of the larger meaning of the term "education."
4. What does he mean when he says that "the romance and beauty were all gone from the river"? Does a thorough knowledge of a subject lessen our enjoyment of it?

SIR FRANCIS BACON

•

OF STUDIES

Studies serve for delight, for ornament, and for ability. Their chief use for delight is in privateness and retiring; for ornament, is in discourse; and for ability, is in the judgment and disposition of business; for expert men can execute, and perhaps judge of particulars, one by one; but the general counsels, and the plots and marshaling of affairs come best from those that are learned. To spend too much time in studies is sloth; to use them too much for ornament is affectation; to make judgment wholly

From *Essays and Counsels, Civil and Moral*, 1625.

by their rules is the humor of a scholar. They perfect nature, and are perfected by experience; for natural abilities are like natural plants, that need pruning by study; and studies themselves do give forth directions too much at large, except they be bounded in by experience. Crafty men contemn studies, simple men admire them, and wise men use them; for they teach not their own use; but that is a wisdom without them and above them, won by observation. Read not to contradict and confute, nor to believe and take for granted, nor to find talk and discourse, but to weigh and consider. Some books are to be tasted, others to be swallowed, and some few to be chewed and digested; that is, some books are to be read only in parts; others to be read but not curiously, and some few to be read wholly, and with diligence and attention. Some books also may be read by deputy, and extracts made of them by others; but that would be only in the less important arguments and the meaner sort of books; else distilled books are, like common distilled waters, flashy things. Reading maketh a full man; conference a ready man; and writing an exact man. And, therefore, if a man write little, he had need have a great memory; if he confer little, he had need have a present wit; and if he read little, he had need have much cunning, to seem to know that he doth not. Histories make men wise; poets, witty; the mathematics, subtle; natural philosophy, deep; moral, grave; logic and rhetoric, able to contend: *Abeunt studia in mores!*[1] Nay, there is no stand or impediment in the wit but may be wrought out by fit studies; like as diseases of the body may have appropriate exercises. Bowling is good for the stone and reins, shooting for the lungs and breast, gentle walking for the stomach, riding for the head, and the like. So if a man's wit be wandering, let him study the mathematics; for in demonstrations, if his wit be called away never so little, he must begin again. If his wit be not apt to distinguish or find differences, let him study the schoolmen; for they are *cymini sectores!*[2] If he be not apt to beat over matters, and to call up one thing to prove and illustrate another, let him study the lawyers' cases. So every defect of the mind may have a special receipt.

---

[1] Studies develop into habits.
[2] Hair-splitters.

THE END OF KNOWLEDGE

The greatest error of all the rest is the mistaking or misplacing of the last or furthest end of knowledge. For men have entered into a desire of learning and knowledge, sometimes upon a natural curiosity and inquisitive appetite; sometimes to entertain their minds with variety and delight; sometimes for ornament and reputation; and sometimes to enable them to victory of wit and contradiction; and most times for lucre and profession, and seldom sincerely to give a true account of their gift of reason to the benefit and use of men; as if there were sought in knowledge a couch, whereupon to rest a searching and restless spirit; or a terrace, for a wandering and variable mind to walk up and down with a fair prospect; or a tower of state, for a proud mind to raise itself upon; or a fort or commanding ground, for strife and contention; or a shop, for profit or sale; and not a rich storehouse, for the glory of the Creator and the relief of man's estate. But this is that which will indeed dignify and exalt knowledge, if contemplation and action may be more nearly and straitly conjoined and united together than they have been, a conjunction like unto that of the two highest planets, Saturn, the planet of rest and contemplation, and Jupiter, the planet of civil society and action. Howbeit, I do not mean, when I speak of use and action, that end beforementioned of the applying of knowledge to lucre and profession, for I am not ignorant how much that diverteth and interrupteth the prosecution and advancement of knowledge, like unto the golden ball thrown before Atalanta, which while she goeth aside and stoopeth to take up, the race is hindered,

Declinat cursus, aurumque volubile tollit.[1]

Neither is my meaning, as was spoken of Socrates, to call philosophy down from heaven to converse upon the earth; that is, to leave natural philosophy aside, and to apply knowledge only to manners and policy.

From *The Advancement of Learning*, 1605.
[1] "She [Atalanta] swerves from the course and picks up the golden ball."

But as both heaven and earth do conspire and contribute to the use and benefit of man, so the end ought to be, from both philosophies to separate and reject vain speculations and whatsoever is empty and void, and to preserve and augment whatsoever is solid and fruitful, that knowledge may not be as a curtesan, for pleasure and vanity only, or as a bondwoman, to acquire and gain to her master's use, but as a spouse, for generation, fruit, and comfort.

• Questions for Study

1. Bacon first popularized the essay as a literary type in England, and "Of Studies" is an example of what he conceived the type to be—an "attempt" at treating a subject. In what ways is this essay merely an "attempt"? In what other ways could this subject be approached?
2. A modern educator, writing on the same subject for a modern audience, would most likely employ specific examples and even perhaps statistics to convey his ideas. At what points in Bacon's essay would such examples or statistics have helped to make his ideas clearer? Select any single sentence and illustrate it from your own experience.
3. What is Bacon's concept of the use of knowledge in "The End of Knowledge" and in what ways does he qualify this concept? Can you illustrate some misuses of knowledge (which Bacon describes generally or by means of metaphor) with examples from your own experience?
4. Bacon is a famous stylist. From these selections can you deduce five or six characteristics of his style?
5. Analyze carefully the metaphoric structure of the most famous sentence of "Of Studies," "Some books are to be tasted. . . ." How appropriate are the metaphors to the basic idea?

JOHN HENRY NEWMAN

•

THE PURSUIT OF KNOWLEDGE

Cicero, in enumerating the various heads of mental excellence, lays down the pursuit of Knowledge for its own sake, as the first of them. "This pertains most of all to human nature," he says, "for we are all of us drawn to the pursuit of Knowledge; in which to excel we consider excellent, whereas to mistake, to err, to be ignorant, to be deceived, is both an evil and a disgrace." And he considers Knowledge the very first object to which we are attracted, after the supply of our physical wants. After the calls and duties of our animal existence, as they may be termed, as regards ourselves, our family, and our neighbors, follows, he tells us, "the search after truth. Accordingly, as soon as we escape from the pressure of necessary cares, forthwith we desire to see, to hear, to learn; and consider the knowledge of what is hidden or is wonderful a condition of our happiness."

This passage, though it is but one of many similar passages in a multitude of authors, I take for the very reason that it is so familiarly known to us; and I wish you to observe, Gentlemen, how distinctly it separates the pursuit of Knowledge from those ulterior objects to which certainly it can be made to conduce, and which are, I suppose, solely contemplated by the persons who would ask of me the use of a University or Liberal Education. So far from dreaming of the cultivation of Knowledge directly and mainly in order to our physical comfort and enjoyment, for the sake of life and person, of health, of the conjugal and family union, of the social tie and civil security, the great Orator implies, that it is only after our physical and political needs are supplied, and when we are "free from necessary duties and cares," that we are in a condition for "desiring to see, to hear, and to learn." Nor does he contemplate in the least degree the reflex or subsequent action of Knowledge, when ac-

From "Discourse V," *The Idea of a University*, 1873.

quired, upon those material goods which we set out by securing before we seek it; on the contrary, he expressly denies its bearing upon social life altogether, strange as such a procedure is to those who live after the rise of the Baconian philosophy, and he cautions us against such a cultivation of it as will interfere with our duties to our fellow-creatures. "All these methods," he says, "are engaged in the investigation of truth; by the pursuit of which to be carried off from public occupations is a transgression of duty. For the praise of virtue lies altogether in action; yet intermissions often occur, and then we recur to such pursuits; not to say that the incessant activity of the mind is vigorous enough to carry us on in the pursuit of knowledge, even without any exertion of our own." The idea of benefiting society by means of "the pursuit of science and knowledge," did not enter at all into the motives which he would assign for their cultivation.

This was the ground of the opposition which the elder Cato made to the introduction of Greek Philosophy among his countrymen, when Carneades and his companions, on occasion of their embassy, were charming the Roman youth with their eloquent expositions of it. The fit representative of a practical people, Cato estimated everything by what it produced; whereas the Pursuit of Knowledge promised nothing beyond Knowledge itself. He despised that refinement or enlargement of mind of which he had no experience.

• Questions for Study

1. Newman uses the argument from tradition to support the points which he is making and he cites Cicerco, the great Latin orator, as his authority. Is this use of Cicero effective in convincing you of the accuracy of his argument?
2. Explain precisely what Newman means by "knowledge for its own sake."
3. Consider Bacon's remarks in "The End of Knowledge" and explain in what ways Newman's ideas differ from Bacon's.
4. Do you think that the knowledge of an ancient language is as important as the knowledge that leads to the discovery of a new life-prolonging drug? Explain your remarks. What do you think Newman's opinion would be?
5. Examine Newman's diction. Would you classify it as formal or informal? Explain the reasons for your classification.

ALBERT EINSTEIN

•

ON EDUCATION

The school has always been the most important means of transferring the wealth of tradition from one generation to the next. This applies today in an even higher degree than in former times for, through modern development of the economic life, the family as bearer of tradition and education has been weakened. The continuance and health of human society is therefore in a still higher degree dependent on the school than formerly.

Sometimes one sees in the school simply the instrument for transferring a certain maximum quantity of knowledge to the growing generation. But that is not right. Knowledge is dead; the school, however, serves the living. It should develop in the young individuals those qualities and capabilities which are of value for the welfare of the commonwealth. But that does not mean that individuality should be destroyed and the individual become a mere tool of the community, like a bee or an ant. For a community of standardized individuals without personal originality and personal aims would be a poor community without possibilities for development. On the contrary, the aim must be the training of independently acting and thinking individuals, who, however, see in the service of the community their highest life problem. As far as I can judge, the English school system comes nearest to the realization of this ideal.

But how shall one try to attain this ideal? Should one perhaps try to realize this aim by moralizing? Not at all. Words are and remain an empty sound, and the road to perdition has ever been accompanied by lip service to an ideal. But personalities are not formed by what is heard and said, but by labor and activity.

The most important method of education accordingly always has

From *Out of My Later Years*, New York: Philosophical Library, Inc., 1950. Reprinted by permission of the Estate of Albert Einstein.

consisted of that in which the pupil was urged to actual performance. This applies as well to the first attempts at writing of the primary boy as to the doctor's thesis on graduation from the university, or as to the mere memorizing of a poem, the writing of a composition, the interpretation and translation of a text, the solving of a mathematical problem or the practice of physical sport.

But behind every achievement exists the motivation which is at the foundation of it and which in turn is strengthened and nourished by the accomplishment of the undertaking. Here there are the greatest differences and they are of greatest importance to the educational value of the school. The same work may owe its origin to fear and compulsion, ambitious desire for authority and distinction, or loving interest in the object and a desire for truth and understanding, and thus to that divine curiosity which every healthy child possesses, but which so often early is weakened. The educational influence which is exercised upon the pupil by the accomplishment of one and the same work may be widely different, depending upon whether fear of hurt, egoistic passion or desire for pleasure and satisfaction are at the bottom of this work. And nobody will maintain that the administration of the school and the attitude of the teachers does not have an influence upon the molding of the psychological foundation for pupils.

To me the worst thing seems to be for a school principally to work with methods of fear, force and artificial authority. Such treatment destroys the sound sentiments, the sincerity and the self-confidence of the pupil. It produces the submissive subject. It is no wonder that such schools are the rule in Germany and Russia. I know that the schools in this country are free from this worst evil; this also is so in Switzerland and probably in all democratically governed countries. It is comparatively simple to keep the school free from this worst of all evils. Give into the power of the teacher the fewest possible coercive measures, so that the only source of the pupil's respect for the teacher is the human and intellectual qualities of the latter.

The second-named motive, ambition or, in milder terms, the aiming at recognition and consideration, lies firmly fixed in human nature. With absence of mental stimulus of this kind, human cooperation would be entirely impossible; the desire for the approval of one's fellowman certainly is one of the most important binding powers of society. In this complex of feelings, constructive and destructive forces lie closely together. Desire for approval and recognition is a healthy motive; but the desire to be acknowledged as better, stronger or more intelligent than a fellow being or fellow scholar easily leads to an excessively egoistic psychological adjustment, which may become injurious for the individual and for the community. Therefore the school and the teacher must guard against employing the easy method of creating individual ambition, in order to induce the pupils to diligent work.

Darwin's theory of the struggle for existence and the selectivity connected with it has by many people been cited as authorization of the encouragement of the spirit of competition. Some people also in such a way have tried to prove pseudo-scientifically the necessity of the destructive economic struggle of competition between individuals. But this is wrong, because man owes his strength in the struggle for existence to the fact that he is a socially living animal. As little as a battle between single ants of an ant hill is essential for survival, just so little is this the case with the individual members of a human community.

Therefore one should guard against preaching to the young man success in the customary sense as the aim of life. For a successful man is he who receives a great deal from his fellowmen, usually incomparably more than corresponds to his service to them. The value of a man, however, should be seen in what he gives and not in what he is able to receive.

The most important motive for work in the school and in life is the pleasure in work, pleasure in its result and the knowledge of the value of the result to the community. In the awakening and strengthening of these psychological forces in the young man, I see the most important task given by the school. Such a psychological foundation alone leads to a joyous desire for the highest possessions of men, knowledge and artist-like workmanship.

The awakening of these productive psychological powers is certainly less easy than the practice of force or the awakening of individual ambition but is the more valuable for it. The point is to develop the childlike inclination for play and the childlike desire for recognition and to guide the child over to important fields for society; it is that education which in the main is founded upon the desire for successful activity and acknowledgment. If the school succeeds in working successfully from such points of view, it will be highly honored by the rising generation and the tasks given by the school will be submitted to as a sort of gift. I have known children who preferred schooltime to vacation.

Such a school demands from the teacher that he be a kind of artist in his province. What can be done that this spirit be gained in the school? For this there is just as little a universal remedy as there is for an individual to remain well. But there are certain necessary conditions which can be met. First, teachers should grow up in such schools. Second, the teacher should be given extensive liberty in the selection of the material to be taught and the methods of teaching employed by him. For it is true also of him that pleasure in the shaping of his work is killed by force and exterior pressure.

If you have followed attentively my meditations up to this point, you will probably wonder about one thing. I have spoken fully about in what spirit, according to my opinion, youth should be instructed. But I have said nothing yet about the choice of subjects for instruction, nor about the method of teaching. Should language predominate or technical education in science?

To this I answer: In my opinion all this is of secondary importance. If a young man has trained his muscles and physical endurance by gymnastics and walking, he will later be fitted for every physical work. This is also analogous to the training of the mind and the exercising of the mental and manual skill. Thus the wit was not wrong who defined education in this way: "Education is that which remains, if one has forgotten everything he learned in school." For this reason I am not at all anxious to take sides in the struggle between the followers of the classical philologic-historical education and the education more devoted to natural science.

On the other hand, I want to oppose the idea that the school has to teach directly that special knowledge and those accomplishments which one has to use later directly in life. The demands of life are much too manifold to let such a specialized training in school appear possible. Apart from that, it seems to me, moreover, objectionable to treat the individual like a dead tool. The school should always have as its aim that the young man leave it as a harmonious personality, not as a specialist. This in my opinion is true in a certain sense even for technical schools, whose students will devote themselves to a quite definite profession. The development of general ability for independent thinking and judgment should always be placed foremost, not the acquisition of special knowledge. If a person masters the fundamentals of his subject and has learned to think and work independently, he will surely find his way and besides will better be able to adapt himself to progress and changes than the person whose training principally consists in the acquiring of detailed knowledge.

Finally, I wish to emphasize once more that what has been said here in a somewhat categorical form does not claim to mean more than the personal opinion of a man, which is founded upon *nothing but* his own personal experience, which he has gathered as a student and as a teacher.

• *Questions for Study*

1. Does the fact that Einstein was the greatest scientist of his age automatically make him an authority on education?
2. To which levels of education do Einstein's ideas primarily apply (elementary, secondary, or university)?
3. Is his analogy relating physical exercise to mental exercise a good one? Is a person who has a "trained" mind automatically proficient in all subjects? Explain your answers with specific references to the essay.
4. What function in terms of style or content does his brief concluding paragraph serve?

JOHN DEWEY

•

MY PEDAGOGIC CREED

———

ARTICLE I—*What Education Is*

I Believe that

—all education proceeds by the participation of the individual in the social consciousness of the race. This process begins unconsciously almost at birth, and is continually shaping the individual's powers, saturating his consciousness, forming his habits, training his ideas, and arousing his feelings and emotions. Through this unconscious education the individual gradually comes to share in the intellectual and moral resources which humanity has succeeded in getting together. He becomes an inheritor of the funded capital of civilization. The most formal and technical education in the world cannot safely depart from this general process. It can only organize it or differentiate it in some particular direction.

From *Education Today* by John Dewey. © 1940 John Dewey. Reprinted by permission of G. P. Putnam's Sons.

—the only true education comes through the stimulation of the child's powers by the demands of the social situations in which he finds himself. Through these demands he is stimulated to act as a member of a unity, to emerge from his original narrowness of action and feeling, and to conceive of himself from the standpoint of the welfare of the group to which he belongs. Through the responses which others make to his own activities he comes to know what these mean in social terms. The value which they have is reflected back into them. For instance, through the response which is made to the child's instinctive babblings the child comes to know what those babblings mean; they are transformed into articulate language, and thus the child is introduced into the consolidated wealth of ideas and emotions which are now summed up in language.

—this educational process has two sides—one psychological and one sociological—and that neither can be subordinated to the other, or neglected, without evil results following. Of these two sides, the psychological is the basis. The child's own instincts and powers furnish the material and give the starting-point for all education. Save as the efforts of the educator connect with some activity which the child is carrying on of his own initiative independent of the educator, education becomes reduced to a pressure from without. It may, indeed, give certain external results, but cannot truly be called educative. Without insight into the psychological structure and activities of the individual, the educative process will, therefore, be haphazard and arbitrary. If it chances to coincide with the child's activity it will get a leverage; if it does not, it will result in friction, or disintegration, or arrest of the child nature.

—knowledge of social conditions, of the present state of civilization, is necessary in order properly to interpret the child's powers. The child has his own instincts and tendencies, but we do not know what these mean until we can translate them into their social equivalents. We must be able to carry them back into a social past and see them as the inheritance of previous race activities. We must also be able to project them into the future to see what their outcome and end will be. In the illustration just used, it is the ability to see in the child's babblings the promise and potency of a future social intercourse and conversation which enables one to deal in the proper way with that instinct.

—the psychological and socal sides are organically related, and that education cannot be regarded as a compromise between the two, or a superimposition of one upon the other. We are told that the psychological definition of education is barren and formal—that it gives us only the idea of a development of all the mental powers without giving us any idea of the use to which these powers are put. On the other hand, it is urged that the social definition of education, as getting adjusted to civilization, makes of it a forced and external process, and results in subordinating the freedom of the individual to a preconceived social and political status.

—each of these objections is true when urged against one side isolated from the other. In order to know what a power really is we must know what its end, use, or function is, and this we cannot know save as we conceive of the individual as active in social relationships. But, on the other hand, the only possible adjustment which we can give to the child under existing conditions is that which arises through putting him in complete possession of all his powers. With the advent of democracy and modern industrial conditions, it is impossible to foretell definitely just what civilization will be twenty years from now. Hence it is impossible to prepare the child for any precise set of conditions. To prepare him for the future life means to give him command of himself; it means so to train him that he will have the full and ready use of all his capacities; that his eye and ear and hand may be tools ready to command, that his judgment may be capable of grasping the conditions under which it has to work, and the executive forces be trained to act economically and efficiently. It is impossible to reach this sort of adjustment save as constant regard is had to the individual's own powers, tastes, and interests—that is, as education is continually converted into psychological terms.

In sum, I believe that the individual who is to be educated is a social individual, and that society is an organic union of individuals. If we eliminate the social factor from the child we are left only with an abstraction; if we eliminate the individual factor from society, we are left only with an inert and lifeless mass. Education, therefore, must begin with a psychological insight into the child's capacities, interests, and habits. It must be controlled at every point by reference to these same considerations. These powers, interests, and habits must be continually interpreted—we must know what they mean. They must be translated into terms of their social equivalents—into terms of what they are capable of in the way of social service.

ARTICLE II—*What the School Is*

I Believe that

—the school is primarily a social institution. Education being a social process, the school is simply that form of community life in which all those agencies are concentrated that will be most effective in bringing the child to share in the inherited resources of the race, and to use his own powers for social ends.

—education, therefore, is a process of living and not a preparation for future living.

—the school must represent present life—life as real and vital to the child as that which he carries on in the home, in the neighborhood, or on the playground.

—that education which does not occur through forms of life, forms that are worth living for their own sake, is always a poor substitute for the genuine reality, and tends to cramp and to deaden.

—the school, as an institution, should simplify existing social life; should reduce it, as it were, to an embryonic form. Existing life is so complex that the child cannot be brought into contact with it without either confusion or distraction; he is either overwhelmed by the multiplicity of activities which are going on, so that he loses his own power of orderly reaction, or he is so stimulated by these various activities that his powers are prematurely called into play and he becomes either unduly specialized or else disintegrated.

—as such simplified social life, the school life should grow gradually out of the home life; that it should take up and continue the activities with which the child is already familiar in the home.

—it should exhibit these activities to the child, and reproduce them in such ways that the child will gradually learn the meaning of them, and be capable of playing his own part in relation to them.

—this is a psychological necessity, because it is the only way of securing continuity in the child's growth, the only way of giving a background of past experience to the new ideas given in school.

—it is also a social necessity because the home is the form of social life in which the child has been nurtured and in connection with which he has had his moral training. It is the business of the school to deepen and extend his sense of the values bound up in his home life.

—much of present education fails because it neglects this fundamental principle of the school as a form of community life. It conceives the school as a place where certain information is to be given, where certain lessons are to be learned, or where certain habits are to be formed. The value of these is conceived as lying largely in the remote future; the child must do these things for the sake of something else he is to do; they are mere preparations. As a result they do not become a part of the life experience of the child and so are not truly educative.

—the moral education centers upon this conception of the school as a mode of social life, that the best and deepest moral training is precisely that which one gets through having to enter into proper relations with others in a unity of work and thought. The present educational systems, so far as they destroy or neglect this unity, render it difficult or impossible to get any genuine, regular moral training.

—the child should be stimulated and controlled in his work through the life of the community.

—under existing conditions far too much of the stimulus and control proceeds from the teacher, because of neglect of the idea of the school as a form of social life.

—the teacher's place and work in the school is to be interpreted from this same basis. The teacher is not in the school to impose certain ideas or to form certain habits in the child, but is there as a member of the community to select the influences which shall affect the child and to assist him in properly responding to these influences.

—the discipline of the school should proceed from the life of the school as a whole and not directly from the teacher.

—the teacher's business is simply to determine, on the basis of larger experience and riper wisdom, how the discipline of life shall come to the child.

—all questions of the grading of the child and his promotion should be determined by reference to the same standard. Examinations are of use only so far as they test the child's fitness for social life and reveal the place in which he can be of the most service and where he can receive the most help.

ARTICLE III—*The Subject-Matter of Education*

I Believe that

—the social life of the child is the basis of concentration, or correlation, in all his training or growth. The social life gives the unconscious unity and the background of all his efforts and of all his attainments.

—the subject-matter of the school curriculum should mark a gradual differentiation out of the primitive unconscious unity of social life.

—we violate the child's nature and render difficult the best ethical results by introducing the child too abruptly to a number of special studies, of reading, writing, geography, etc., out of relation to this social life.

—the true center of correlation on the school subjects is not science, nor literature, nor history, nor geography, but the child's own social activities.

—education cannot be unified in the study of science, or so-called nature study, because apart from human activity, nature itself is not a unity; nature in itself is a number of diverse objects in space and time, and to attempt to make it the center of work by itself is to introduce a principle of radiation rather than one of concentration.

—literature is the reflex expression and interpretation of social experience; that hence it must follow upon and not precede such experience. It, therefore, cannot be made the basis, although it may be made the summary of unification.

—once more that history is of educative value in so far as it presents phases of social life and growth. It must be controlled by reference to social life. When taken simply as history it is thrown into the distant past and becomes dead and inert. Taken as the record of man's social life and progress it becomes full of meaning. I believe, however, that it cannot be so taken excepting as the child is also introduced directly into social life.

—the primary basis of education is in the child's powers at work along the same general constructive lines as those which have brought civilization into being.

—the only way to make the child conscious of his social heritage is to enable him to perform those fundamental types of activity which make civilization what it is.

—the so-called expressive or constructive activities are the center of correlation.

—this gives the standard for the place of cooking, sewing, manual training, etc., in the school.

—they are not special studies which are to be introduced over and above a lot of others in the way of relaxation or relief, or as additional accomplishments. I believe rather that they represent, as types, fundamental forms of social activity; and that it is possible and desirable that the child's introduction into the more formal subjects of the curriculum be through the medium of these activities.

—the study of science is educational in so far as it brings out the materials and processes which make social life what it is.

—one of the greatest difficulties in the present teaching of science is that the material is presented in purely objective form, or is treated as a new peculiar kind of experience which the child can add to that which he has already had. In reality, science is of value because it gives the ability to interpret and control the experience already had. It should be introduced, not as so much new subject-matter, but as showing the factors already involved in previous experience and as furnishing tools by which that experience can be more easily and effectively regulated.

—at present we lose much of the value of literature and language studies because of our elimination of the social element. Language is almost always treated in the books of pedagogy simply as the expression of thought. It is true that language is a logical instrument, but it is fundamentally and primarily a social instrument. Language is the device for communication; it is the tool through which one individual comes to share the ideas and feelings of others. When treated simply as a way of getting individual information, or as a means of showing off what one has learned, it loses its social motive and end.

—there is, therefore, no succession of studies in the ideal school curriculum. If education is life, all life has, from the outset, a scientific aspect, an aspect of art and culture, and an aspect of communication. It cannot, therefore, be true that the proper studies for one grade are mere reading and writing, and that at a later grade, reading, or literature, or science, may be introduced. The progress is not in the succession of studies, but in the development of new attitudes towards, and new interests in, experience.

—education must be conceived as a continuing reconstruction of experience; that the process and the goal of education are one and the same thing.

—to set up any end outside of education, as furnishing its goal and standard, is to deprive the educational process of much of its meaning, and tends to make us rely upon false and external stimuli in dealing with the child.

ARTICLE IV—*The Nature of Method*

I Believe that

—the question of method is ultimately reducible to the question of the order of development of the child's powers and interests. The law for presenting and treating material is the law implicit within the child's own nature. Because this is so I believe the following statements are of supreme importance as determining the spirit in which education is carried on:

—the active side precedes the passive in the development of the child-nature; that expression comes before conscious impression; that the muscular development precedes the sensory; that movements come before conscious sensations; I believe that consciousness is essentially motor or impulsive; that conscious states tend to project themselves in action.

—the neglect of this principle is the cause of a large part of the waste of time and strength in school work. The child is thrown into a passive, receptive, or absorbing attitude. The conditions are such that he is not permitted to follow the law of his nature; the result is friction and waste.

—ideas (intellectual and rational processes) also result from action and devolve for the sake of the better control of action. What we term reason is primarily the law of orderly or effective action. To attempt to develop the reasoning powers, the powers of judgment, without reference to the selection and arrangement of means in action, is the fundamental fallacy in our present methods of dealing with this matter. As a result we present the child with arbitrary symbols. Symbols are a necessity in mental development, but they have their place as tools for economizing effort; presented by themselves they are a mass of meaningless and arbitrary ideas imposed from without.

—the image is the great instrument of instruction. What a child gets out of any subject presented to him is simply the images which he himself forms with regard to it.

—if nine-tenths of the energy at present directed towards making the child learn certain things were spent in seeing to it that the child was forming proper images, the work of instruction would be indefinitely facilitated.

—much of the time and attention now given to the preparation and presentation of lessons might be more wisely and profitably expended in training the child's power of imagery and in seeing to it that he was continually forming definite, vivid, and growing images of the various subjects with which he comes in contact in his experience.

—interests are the signs and symptoms of growing power. I believe that they represent dawning capacities. Accordingly the constant and careful observation of interests is of the utmost importance for the educator.

—these interests are to be observed as showing the state of development which the child has reached.

—they prophesy the stage upon which he is about to enter.

—only through the continual and sympathetic observation of childhood's interests can the adult enter into the child's life and see what it is ready for, and upon what material it could work most readily and fruitfully.

—these interests are neither to be humored nor repressed. To repress interest is to substitute the adult for the child, and so to weaken intellectual curiosity and alertness, to suppress initiative, and to deaden interest. To humor the interests is to substitute the transient for the permanent. The interest is always the sign of some power below; the important thing is to discover this power. To humor the interest is to fail to penetrate below the surface, and its sure result is to substitute caprice and whim for genuine interest.

—the emotions are the reflex of actions.

—to endeavor to stimulate or arouse the emotions apart from their corresponding activities is to introduce an unhealthy and morbid state of mind.

—if we can only secure right habits of action and thought, with reference to the good, the true, and the beautiful, the emotions will for the most part take care of themselves.

—next to deadness and dullness, formalism and routine, our education is threatened with no greater evil than sentimentalism.

—this sentimentalism is the necessary result of the attempt to divorce feeling from action.

Article V—*The School and Social Progress*

I Believe that

—education is the fundamental method of social progress and reform.

—all reforms which rest simply upon the enactment of law, or the threatening of certain penalties, or upon changes in mechanical or outward arrangements, are transitory and futile.

—education is a regulation of the process of coming to share in the social consciousness; and that the adjustment of individual activity on the basis of this social consciousness is the only sure method of social reconstruction.

—this conception has due regard for both the individualistic and socialistic ideals. It is duly individual because it recognizes the formation of a certain character as the only genuine basis of right living. It is socialistic because it recognizes that this right character is not to be formed by merely individual precept, example, or exhortation, but rather by the influence of a certain form of institutional or community life upon the individual, and that the social organism through the school, as its organ, may determine ethical results.

—in the ideal school we have the reconciliation of the individualistic and the institutional ideals.

—the community's duty to education is, therefore, its paramount moral duty. By law and punishment, by social agitation and discussion, society can regulate and form itself in a more or less haphazard and chance way. But through education society can formulate its own purposes, can organize its own means and resources, and thus shape itself with definiteness and economy in the direction in which it wishes to move.

—when society once recognizes the possibilities in this direction, and the obligations which these possibilities impose, it is impossible to conceive of the resources of time, attention, and money which will be put at the disposal of the educator.

—it is the business of every one interested in education to insist upon the school as the primary and most effective instrument of social progress and reform in order that society may be awakened to realize what the school stands for, and aroused to the necessity of endowing the educator with sufficent equipment properly to perform his task.

—education thus conceived marks the most perfect and intimate union of science and art conceivable in human experience.

—the art of thus giving shape to human powers and adapting them to social service is the supreme art; one calling into its service the best of artists; that no insight, sympathy, tact, executive power, is too great for such service.

—with the growth of psychological service, giving added insight into individual structure and laws of growth; and with growth of social science, adding to our knowledge of the right organization of individuals, all scientific resources can be utilized for the purposes of education.

—when science and art thus join hands the most commanding motive for human action will be reached, the most genuine springs of human conduct aroused, and the best service that human nature is capable of guaranteed.

—the teacher is engaged, not simply in the training of individuals, but in the formation of the proper social life.

—every teacher should realize the dignity of his calling; that he is a social servant set apart for the maintenance of proper social order and the securing of the right social growth.

—in this way the teacher always is the prophet of the true God and the usherer in of the true kingdom of God.

• *Questions for Study*

1. Dewey calls his thoughts on education a creed and he organizes these thoughts accordingly. Is this unusual method of organization effective? Explain.
2. In Dewey's opinion, should the school be primarily a social institution? Is education a social process? What other purposes of education can you think of? It may be useful to consider the ideas of other essayists in this section in forming an answer.
3. From your reading of Bacon's "The End of Knowledge" and Newman's "The Pursuit of Knowledge" what do you think their attitudes toward vocational training as a major aspect of the educational process would be?
4. Write an essay in which you define your own pedagogic creed, considering the four aspects which Dewey provides.

II
LANGUAGE AND LITERATURE

LEWIS MUMFORD

•

THE MIRACLE OF LANGUAGE

The growth of conscious purpose and self-direction—all that is implied
in the historic concepts of the soul and the person—was made possible
by man's special skill in interpreting his own nature and working his
experiences into a meaningful and valuable whole, upon which he could
draw for future actions and operations. That skill rests upon a special
aptitude, embedded in man's very physiology: the ability to form and
transmit symbols. Man's most characteristic social trait, his possession of
an extra-organic environment and a super-organic self, which he trans-
mits from generation to generation without using the biological mechanism of heredity, is dependent upon his earlier conquest of the word.

During the last century this essential fact about man's nature has
been obscured by the false assumption that man is primarily a "tool-using
animal." Carlyle called him that long before Bergson suggested that the
term Homo Faber, Man the Maker, should replace Homo Sapiens. But
man is not essentially distinguished from his animal relatives either by
the fact that he lives in groups or performs physical work with tools.
Man is first and foremost the self-fabricating animal: the only creature
who has not rested content with his biological form or with the dumb
repetitions of his animal role. The chief source of this particular form
of creativity was not fire, tools, weapons, machines, but two subjective
instruments far older than any of these: the dream and the word.

Without dwelling on the function of symbolization, one cannot begin
to describe the nature of man or plumb the deepest spring of his creativeness. That is why I pass over many other attributes, fully taken into
account today by anthropology and psychology, to dwell on man's role

as interpreter. Language, the greatest of all human inventions, is the most essential key to the truly human. When words fail him, as we find in the few authenticated cases of wild children reared without the benefit of human society, man is an animal without a specific life-plan, compelled to imitate the wolfish habits of the animal in whose brood he has been suckled and reared.

One can, of course, only speculate on the way in which man invented and perfected the various tools of symbolization. But in the primary instance of speech, the word was made possible by changes in the bodily organs including the larynx, the tongue, the teeth, and not least the creation of mobile lips: in the earliest skulls identifiable as man, the anatomists find the speech centers already relatively well developed. The enlargement of man's powers, through his quicker ability to learn by trial and correction, demanded a special instrument for dealing with the multitude of sensations and meanings, suggestions and demands, that impinged upon him. Every sensation, as Adelbert Ames has experimentally demonstrated, is a prognostic directive to action: hence even the simplest stimulus must be interpreted, for whether we accept it or reject it depends not only upon its own nature but upon our purposes and predispositions and proposals. Even the purest sensation must be translated and re-ordered, before the organism will in fact see it, hear it, or answer it. In that response, the entire organism co-operates; and what is actually seen or heard or felt is only what makes sense in terms of the organism's immediate purpose or its historic plan of development.

At every moment of his waking existence, man senses, interprets, proposes, acts in a single unified response: but between the starting point and the end, the intermediate steps of interpretation and planful reorganization are critical, for it is here that error, miscalculation, and frustration may intervene. With the development of language, man created an instrument of interpretation that gave him a way of traversing the largest possible field of life. What he took in of the world expressed his own nature: what he expressed of himself partook of the nature of the world; for it is only in thought that organism and environment can be separated.

Now other creatures than man respond to immediate signals: the snarl of a dog has meaning for another dog, and the upraised white tail of a doe tells the fawns, as plainly as words, "Follow me!" But man, at a critical moment in his development, began to invent signs, in the form of audible words, which represent an event or a situation even when they are not present. By this act of detachment and abstraction, man gained the power of dealing with the non-present, the unseen, the remote, and the internal: not merely his visible lair and his daily companions, but his ancestors and his descendants and the sun and the moon and the stars: eventually the concepts of eternity and infinity, of electron and universe: he reduced a thousand potential occasions in all their variety and flux to a single symbol that indicated what was common to all of them.

Similarly, by kindred means, man was able to give form to and project his inner world, otherwise hidden and private: by words, images, related sounds, it became part of the public world, and thus an "object." This extraordinary labor-saving device, for extracting, condensing, and preserving the most complicated kinds of events, was perhaps another manifestation of the creative uses of his exuberance and vital proliferation. Man's possession of a "useless instrument," his special voice-producing organs, with their wide range of tones, plus a love of repetition, which one observes in the fullest degree in infants, opened up playful possibilities. If man is an inventor or an artist, the first object of his interest is his own body: he falls in love with his own organs long before he seeks to master the outside world.

"We must never forget," the distinguished philologist Jespersen once observed, "that the organs of speech . . . are one of mankind's most treasured toys, and that not only children but also grown people in civilized as well as savage communities, find amusement in letting their vocal cords and tongue and lips play all sorts of games." Out of this original organic overflow, man found too a way to shape a meaningful, orderly world: the world realized in language, music, poesy, and directed thought. The gift of tongues is the greatest of all gifts: in the beginning was the Word.

Speech, human speech, affected a miraculous transformation in human society: by such magic Prospero tamed Caliban and released Ariel. Speech, at first probably inseparable from gesture, exclamatory, disjointed, structureless, purely emotive, laid the foundation for a more complex mechanism of abstractions, the independent structure of language itself; and with language, human culture as an extra-organic activity, no longer wholly dependent upon the stability and continuity of the physical body and its daily environment, became possible. This broke through the boundaries of time and place that limit animal associations.

In the behavior of that perpetual primitive, the human infant, we can follow the original transition from babble to the involuntary reproduction of facial movements, from private gurglings for self-satisfaction to public demands in which a particular tone will be evoked to bring forth a particular response from the mother: the offer of a breast, the production of a dry diaper, the removal of a pricking pin, the reassurance of human companionship. Much of the intercourse between mother and child is the expression, on both sides, of feeling: tenderness, joy, rage, anxiety. Beyond doubt, the introjection and projection of feeling were basic to the whole achievement of language; a point often overlooked by pragmatic or rationalist interpretations.

In the instances of wild children nurtured by animals, we can verify this interpretation: for the ability to form words seems to disappear altogether when the infant's earliest vocalizings are not encouraged by similar vocalizing on the part of those who look after him. With the loss of language man also loses the facility for more complex forms of human behavior: though some of his organic capacities become intensified to animal sharpness, in an extra-sensitive nose or in muscular endurance, the veritably human touch remains absent: above all, the wild child forfeits the capacity to understand or communicate human feeling, thus becoming inferior, not only to other human beings, but to the dog or cat, who have had the benefit of human association, and who have learned the gestures and tones by which human feelings are expressed. Negatively, there is still another way of understanding the specifically human role of language: for psychologists have found that deaf-mutism, even when combated with skillful care, is a greater handicap to intelligence than blindness. Speech, even though accompanied by blindness, opens the path of social co-operation.

In his attempt to associate intelligence with the special faculty for dealing with the geometrical, the mechanical, the non-living, Henri Bergson curiously underestimated the formative effect of language and over-stressed the part played by physical tools and mechanical aptitudes, for he perversely interpreted speech as being lamed by man's rational preoccupation with static objects. On the contrary, language developed far more rapidly and effectively than mechanical tools; and it was probably in origin primarily a means of representing labile feelings and attitudes, the least geometrical part of man's experience. The most important thing for a human being to know, from infancy onward, is whether he is welcome or unwelcome, whether he is being loved and cherished and protected or hated and feared; and the give-and-take of speech, with all its modulation of color and tone, provides these essential clues. Language was not invented by philosophers seeking truth or by scientists seeking to understand the processes of nature, nor yet by mechanics seeking to shape a more adequate tool; nor was it created by methodical bookkeepers seeking to make an inventory of the contents of the world. Language was the outcome of man's need to affirm solidarity with his own kind. Because it was a prime organ, not only of social co-operation, but of sympathetic and dramatic insight, it helped to control and direct all human behavior.

In time, no doubt, language lent itself to many other uses besides communion and fellowship: it gave rise to a sense of "thatness" as well as "we-ness" and furthered causal insight into processes and relationships. Not least, language was a means whereby subjective reactions became externalized, and objective facts became internalized: thus it favored constant intercourse and traffic between the public world and the private world. In every sense, then, speech was man's prime instrument for sharing his private world with his fellows and for bringing the public world home to himself, though in time it was supplemented by the symbols and significants of the other arts. He who could speak the language could be trusted: every word was a password, indicating friend or foe, in-group or out-group; and these practices linger on in establishing identity right down to our own day. The practical and rational offices of language, which now seem to us all-important, must for long have been purely incidental.

The complicated structure, the grammatical and logical subtlety, and the immense variety of even primitive languages drive one to believe that a large part of man's creative activity, perhaps for hundreds of thousands of years, must have concerned itself almost exclusively with the development of intelligible speech, and with secondary means of symbolization through the visual arts; for painting, too, in the Aurignacian caves, shows an exquisite perfection that argues a prolonged period of unremitting effort. No machine that man invented before the twentieth century compares in complexity and refinement with the simplest of human languages. No wonder this superorganic structure transformed the terms of man's self-development.

Beavers can build dams: bees can construct efficient dwellings: the meanest bird has still a surer mechanism for flying and landing than man has yet achieved. But no other creature has come within sight of man in the arts of symbolic communication. Mainly through language man has created a second world, more durable and viable than the immediate flux of experience, more rich in possibilities than the purely material habitat of any other creature. By the same agent, he has reduced the vastness and overpowering multiplicity of his environment to human dimensions: abstracting from its totality just so much as he could handle and control. The very formal qualities of words served as an instrument for understanding and directing the everlasting flow of things: it is because the structure of language and logic is relatively static (Parmenides and Plato) that the unceasing changes and processes of the natural world

(Heraclitus) can be interpreted. If meanings changed as quickly as events, no event would have a meaning.

Let us make no mistake then: language is far more basic than any other kind of tool or machine. Through man's overdeveloped forebrain and his overflowing sensory-emotional responses, he came into contact with an ever-enlarging field of action; and through language, he found an economic way of dealing with this complexity and turning every state and activity to the service of meaning. So essential is language to man's humanness, so deep a source is it of his own creativity, that it is by no means an accident in our time that those who have tried to degrade man and enslave him have first debased and misused language, arbitrarily turning meanings inside out. Civilization itself, from the most primitive stage onward, moves toward the continuous creation of a common social heritage, transcending all the peculiarities of race and environment and historic accident, shared over ever wider reaches of space and time. This heritage, apart from environmental modifications, such as roads, canals, and cities, is transmitted largely in symbolic form; and by far the greater part of its symbolization is in spoken and written language. Contrary to the proverb, words make a greater difference than sticks and stones: they are more durable, too.

• Questions for Study

1. Discuss Mumford's principle intention in this essay. Is he attempting to inform us or to persuade us of the significance of language? Cite specific instances in the selection to prove your answer.
2. Mumford, like many other writers, uses a number of allusions to emphasize or to explain his points. In this essay, he alludes to Bergson, Parmenides, Caliban, and Ariel, among others. Where would a reader unfamiliar with these names go for information about them? To what extent is a knowledge of them necessary for an understanding of Mumford's remarks?
3. What does the author mean when he says: "Mainly through language man has created a second world, more durable and viable than the immediate flux of experience, more rich in possibilities than the purely material habitat of any other creature"? To what extent do you agree or disagree with him?

C. S. LEWIS

•

AT THE FRINGE OF LANGUAGE

Language exists to communicate whatever it can communicate. Some things it communicates so badly that we never attempt to communicate them by words if any other medium is available. Those who think they are testing a boy's "elementary" command of English by asking him to describe in words how one ties one's tie or what a pair of scissors is like, are far astray. For precisely what language can hardly do at all, and never does well, is to inform us about complex physical shapes and movements. Hence descriptions of such things in the ancient writers are nearly always unintelligible. Hence we never in real life voluntarily use language for this purpose; we draw a diagram or go through pantomimic gestures. The exercises which such examiners set are no more a test of "elementary" linguistic competence than the most difficult bit of trick-riding from the circus ring is a test of elementary horsemanship.

Another grave limitation of language is that it cannot, like music or gesture, do more than one thing at once. However the words in a great poet's phrase interanimate one another and strike the mind as a quasi-instantaneous chord, yet strictly speaking, each word must be read or heard before the next. That way, language is as unilinear as time. Hence, in narrative, the great difficulty of presenting a very complicated change which happens suddenly. If we do justice to the complexity, the time the reader must take over the passage will destroy the feeling of suddenness. If we get in the suddenness we shall not be able to get in the complexity. I am not saying that genius will not find its own ways of palliating this defect in the instrument; only that the instrument is in this way defective.

One of the most important and effective uses of language is the emo-

---

From *Studies in Words*, New York: Cambridge University Press, 1960. Reprinted by permission of Cambridge University Press.

tional. It is also, of course, wholly legitimate. We do not talk only in order to reason or to inform. We have to make love and quarrel, to propitiate and pardon, to rebuke, console, intercede, and arouse. "He that complains," said Johnson, "acts like a man, like a social being." The real objection lies not against the language of emotion as such, but against language which, being in reality emotional, masquerades—whether by plain hypocrisy or subtler self-deceit—as being something else.

All my generation are much indebted to Dr. I. A. Richards for having fully called our attention to the emotional functions of language. But I am hardly less indebted to Professor Empson for having pointed out that the conception of emotional language can be very easily extended too far. It was time to call a halt.

We must obviously not call any utterance "emotional" language because it in fact arouses, even because it must arouse, emotion. "It is not cancer after all," "The Germans have surrendered," "I love you"—may all be true statements about matter of fact. And of course it is the facts, not the language, that arouse the emotion. In the last the fact communicated is itself the existence of an emotion but that makes no difference. Statements about crime are not criminal language; nor are statements about emotions necessarily emotional language. Nor, in my opinion, are value-judgements ("this is good," "this is bad") emotional language. Approval and disapproval do not seem to me to be emotions. If we felt at all times about the things we judge good the emotion which is appropriate, our lives would be easier. It would also be an error to treat "I am washed in the blood of the Lamb" as emotional language. It is of course metaphorical language. But by his metaphor the speaker is trying to communicate what he believes to be a fact. You may of course think the belief false in his particular case. You may think the real universe is such that no fact which corresponded to such a statement could possibly occur. You may say that the real cause which prompts a man to say things like that is a state of emotion. But if so, an emotion has produced erroneous belief about an impossible fact, and it is the fact erroneously believed in which the man is stating. A man's hasty belief that the Germans had surrendered (before they did) might well be caused by his emotions. That would not make "The Germans have surrendered" a specimen of emotional language. If you could find a man nowadays capable of believing, and saying, "The Russians have all been annihilated by magic," even this would not be emotional language, though his belief in magic might be a belief engendered by emotion.

All this is fairly plain sailing. We reach something harder in the things said by poets. For there the purpose of the utterance would be frustrated if no emotion were aroused. They do not merely, like the sentences cited above, arouse emotion in fact; it is their purpose—at any rate, part of their purpose—to do so. But we must be very careful here. Having observed that a poetical utterance in fact arouses emotion, and is intended to arouse emotion, and that if taken as a statement about reality—or even about the make-believe "realities" of the fictitious narrative—it would be nonsensical or at least false, can we conclude that it communicates nothing but emotion? I think not.

Nothing will convince me that "My soul is an enchanted boat" [Shelley, *Prometheus Unbound*] is simply a better way—however much better—of doing what might be done by some exclamation like "Gee!" Asia has risen from the dark cave of Demogorgon. She is floating upwards. She is saluted as "Life of Life!" The reversed temporal process in ll. 97–103 ("We have passed Age's icy caves" etc.), borrowed from Plato's *Politicus* (269ᶜ *sq.*), marks the fact that at this moment the whole cycle is reversed and cosmos begins anew. She is undergoing apotheosis. What did it feel like? The poet says to us in effect "Think of going in a boat. But quite effortless" ("Like a sleeping swan gliding with the current," he adds in the next line), "Like a boat without sail or oar; the motive power undiscoverable. Like a magic boat—you must have read or dreamed of such things—a boat drawn on, drawn swiftly on, irresistibly, smoothly, by enchantment." Exactly. I know now how it felt for Asia. The phrase has communicated emotion. But notice how. By addressing in the first instance my imagination. He makes me imagine a boat rushing over waves, which are also identified with sounds. After that he need do no more; my emotion will follow of itself. Poetry most often communicates emotions, not directly, but by creating imaginatively the grounds for those emotions. It therefore communicates something more than emotion; only by means of that something more does it communicate the emotion at all.

Burns compares his mistress to "a red, red rose"; Wordsworth his to "a violet by a mossy stone Half hidden from the eye." These expressions do communicate to me the emotion each poet felt. But it seems to me that they do so solely by forcing me to imagine two (very different) women. I see the rose-like, overpowering, midsummer sweetness of the one; the reticent, elusive freshness, the beauty easily overlooked in the other. After that my emotions may be left to themselves. The poets have done their part.

This, which is eminently true of poetry, is true of all imaginative writing. One of the first things we have to say to a beginner who has brought us his MS. is, "Avoid all epithets which are merely emotional. It is no use *telling* us that something was 'mysterious' or 'loathsome' or 'awe-inspiring' or 'voluptuous.' Do you think your readers will believe you just because you say so? You must go quite a different way to work.

By direct description, by metaphor and simile, by secretly evoking power-ful associations, by offering the right stimuli to our nerves (in the right degree and the right order), and by the very beat and vowel-melody and length and brevity of your sentences, you must bring it about that we, we readers, not you, exclaim 'how mysterious!' or 'loathsome' or whatever it is. Let me taste for myself, and you'll have no need to *tell* me how I should react to the flavor."

In Donne's couplet

> *Your gown going off, such beautious state reveals*
> *As when from flowry meads th'hills shadow steales*

beautious is the only word of the whole seventeen which is doing no work.

There are exceptions to this principle. By very successful placing, a great author may sometimes raise such words to poetic life. Wordsworth's lines are a specimen:

> *Which, to the boundaries of space and time,*
> *Of melancholy space and doleful time,*
> *Superior—*

Here we have almost the reverse of the process I have been describing. The object (space and time) is in one way so familiar to our imaginations and in another so unimaginable—we have read so many tedious attempts to exalt or over-awe us with mere superlatives or even with simple arith-metic—that nothing can be made of it. This time, therefore, the poet with-draws the object (the ground for emotion) altogether and appeals directly to our emotions; and not to the quite obvious ones. Another exception is naturally to be found in drama or very dramatic lyric, where the poet—with discretion and a proper use of illusion—imitates the speech of people in some highly emotional situation—even, at need, their inarticulate cries. This in its purity, which purity a good poet never sustains for long, be-longs to poetry not in so far as poetry is a special use of language but in so far as poetry is *mimesis*. In themselves the "Ah! Ah!" or "Otototoi" or "Iou! Iou!" of characters in a Greek tragedy are not specimens of poetry any more than the "Bé, bé" of the lamb or the "Au! Au!" of the dog in Aristophanes.

In general, however, the poet's route to our emotion lies through our imaginations.

We must also exclude from the category "emotional language" words such as I have taken *supernatural* to be. The class of things which they refer to may be bound together chiefly by a common emotion; but the purpose of using the words is to assign something to that class, not merely to communicate the emotion which led to the classification.

Having thus narrowed the field, we can now make a new start. It will be noticed that I have throughout used the word *emotional* rather than *emotive*. This is because I think the latter word applicable to only one aspect of emotional language. For an "emotive word" ought to mean one whose function is to arouse emotion. But surely we ought to distinguish utterances which arouse, from those which express, emotion? The first is directed towards producing some effect on a (real or imagined) hearer; the second discharges our own emotion, cleanses our stuffed bosom of some perilous stuff.

The distinction will seem straw-splitting if we have in mind the language of love. For, as Samson says, "love seeks to have love," and it would be hard to say whether endearments serve more as expressions of love in the speaker or incitements to it in the beloved. But that tells us more about the nature of love than about the nature of language. One of my old headmasters once wisely said it was a pity that *amare* was the first Latin verb we all learn. He thought this led to an imperfect grasp of the difference between the active and the passive voice. It might be better to begin with *flagellare*. The difference between flogging and being flogged would come home to the business and bosoms of schoolboys far more effectively than that of loving and being loved. On the same principle, we can best see the distinction between the stimulant and the expressive functions of emotional language in a quarrel; and best of all where the same word performs both. The man who calls me a low hound both expresses and (actually or intentionally) stimulates emotion. But not the same emotion. He expresses contempt; he stimulates, or hopes to stimulate, the almost opposite emotion of humiliation.

Again, in the language of complaint we often find the expressive without the stimulant. When two people who have missed the last train stand on the silent platform saying "Damn" or "Bloody" or "Sickening," they neither intend nor need to stimulate each other's disappointment. They are just "getting it off their chests."

The vocabulary of endearment, complaint, and abuse, provides, I think, almost the only specimens of words that are purely emotional, words from which all imaginative or conceptual content has vanished, so that they have no function at all but to express or stimulate emotion, or both. And an examination of them soon convinces us that in them we see language at its least linguistic. We have come to the frontier between language and inarticulate vocal sounds. And at that frontier we find a two-way traffic going on.

On the one hand we find inarticulate sounds becoming words with a fixed spelling and a niche in the dictionary. Thus English *heigh-ho* and Latin *eheu* are clearly formalised imitations of the sigh; *ah,* of the gasp;

tut-tut, of the tongue clicked against the hard palate. These are general. In particular situations the "verbification" of the inarticulate may occur *ad hoc.* A voluntary scream may become a cry for mercy. A voluntary groan, from a wounded man, uttered to attract the attention of the stretcher-bearers, may be the equivalent of a sentence ("There is a wounded man in this ditch").

But we also see the frontier being crossed in the opposite direction. In the vocabulary of abuse and complaint we see things that once were words passing out of the realm of language (properly so called) and becoming the equivalents of inarticulate sounds or even of actions; of sighs, moans, whimperings, growls, or blows.

The "swear-words"—*damn* for complaint and *damn you* for abuse— are a good example. Historically the whole Christian eschatology lies behind them. If no one had ever consigned his enemy to the eternal fires and believed that there were eternal fires to receive him, these ejaculations would never have existed. But inflation, the spontaneous hyperboles of ill temper, and the decay of religion, have long since emptied them of that lurid content. Those who have no belief in damnation—and some who have—now damn inanimate objects which would on any view be ineligible for it. The word is no longer an imprecation. It is hardly, in the full sense, a word at all when so used. Its popularity probably owes as much to its resounding phonetic virtues as to any, even fanciful, association with hell. It has ceased to be profane. It has also become very much less forceful. You may say the same of *sickening* in its popular, ejaculatory, use. There are alarms and disappointments which can actually produce nausea, or, at least, emotions which we feel to be somehow similar to it. But the man who says *sickening!* when he has missed the train is not thinking about that. The word is simply an alternative to *damn* or *bloody.* And of course far weaker than it would be if it still carried any suggestion of vomiting.

So with abusive terms. No one would now call his schoolfellow or next door neighbour a *swine* unless someone had once used this word to make a real comparison between his enemy and a pig. It is now a mere alternative to *beast* or *brute* or various popular unprintable words. They are all interchangeable. *Villain,* as we know, once really compared your enemy to a *villein.* Once, to call a man *cad* or *knave* assigned to him the status of a servant. And it did so because, earlier still, these words meant "boy" or "junior" (you address a slave as "boy" in Greek and a waiter as *garçon* in French).

Thus all these words have come down in the world. None of them started by being *merely* abusive, few of them by being abusive at all. They once stimulated emotion by suggesting an image. They made the enemy odious or contemptible by asserting he was like somebody or something we already disliked or looked down on. Their use was a sort of passionate parody of the syllogism: pigs (or servants or my juniors) are contemptible—John is like a pig (or servant or adolescent)—therefore John is contemptible. That was why they really hurt; because hurting was not the whole of what they did. They stimulated emotion because they also stimulated something else; imagination. They stimulated emotion in the particular case because they exploited emotions which already existed towards whole classes of things or persons. Now that they are nothing whatever but emotional stimulants, they are weak emotional stimulants. They make no particular accusation. They tell us nothing except that the speaker has lost his temper.

And even this they do not tell us linguistically, but symptomatically; as a red face, a loud voice, or a clenched fist, might do equally well. The fact of the other person's anger may hurt or frighten us; hurt us if we love him, or frighten us if he is larger and younger than ourselves and threatens violence. But his language as such has very little power to do the only thing it is intended to do. It would have been far more wounding to be called *swine* when the word still carried some whiff of the sty and some echo of a grunt; far more wounding to be called a *villain* when this still conjured up an image of the unwashed, malodorous, ineducable, gross, belching, close-fisted, and surly boor. Now, who cares? Language meant solely to hurt hurts strangely little.

This can be seen clearly when we catch a word "just on the turn." *Bitch* is one. Till recently—and still in the proper contexts—this accused a woman of one particular fault and appealed, with some success, to our contempt by calling up an image of the she-dog's comical and indecorous behavior when she is in heat. But it is now increasingly used of any woman whom the speaker, for whatever reason, is annoyed with—the female driver who is in front of him, or a female magistrate whom he thinks unjust. Clearly, the word is far more wounding in its narrower usage. If that usage is ever totally lost—as I think it will be—the word will sink to the level of *damn her*. Notice, too, how *cat* (of a woman) is still strong and useful because the image is still alive in it.

An important principle thus emerges. In general, emotional words, to be effective, must not be solely emotional. What expresses or stimulates emotion directly, without the intervention of an image or concept, expresses or stimulates it feebly. And in particular, when words of abuse have hurting the enemy as their direct and only object, they do not hurt him much. In the field of language, however it may be in that of action, hatred cuts its own throat, and those who are too "willing to wound" become thereby impotent to strike. And all this is only another way of saying that as words become exclusively emotional they cease to be words and therefore of course cease to perform any strictly linguistic function. They operate as growls or barks or tears. "Exclusively" is an important adverb here. They die as words not because there is too much emotion in them but because there is too little—and finally nothing at all—of anything else.

In this there is not much to be lamented. If a mother with a baby, or lovers in each other's arms, use language so emotional that it is really not language at all, I see no ground for shame or offence; and if men in an orgy of resentment, though (in the physical sense) they articulate, are no more speaking—are saying no more—than a snarling animal, this is perhaps all for the best. The real corruption comes when men whose purpose in speaking is in fact purely emotional conceal this from others, and perhaps from themselves, by words that seem to be, but are not, charged with a conceptual content.

We have all heard *bolshevist, fascist, Jew,* and *capitalist,* used not to describe but merely to insult. Rose Macaulay noticed a tendency to prefix "so called" to almost any adjective when it was used of those the speaker hated; the final absurdity being reached when people referred to the Germans as "these so-called Germans." *Bourgeois* and *middle class* often suffer the same fate.

A literary man of my acquaintance, on reading an unfavourable reference to his own words, called it *vulgar.* The charge brought against him was one that only highly educated people ever bring; the tone of the passage not otherwise offensive than by being unfavourable; the phrasing perfectly good English. If he had called it false, unintelligent, or malicious, I could have understood, though I might have disagreed. But why *vulgar?* Clearly, this word was selected solely because the speaker thought it was the one that the enemy, if he could hear it, would most dislike. It was the equivalent of an oath or a growl. But that was concealed from the speaker because "This is vulgar" sounds like a judgement.

When we write criticism we have to be continually on our guard against this sort of thing. If we honestly believe a work to be very bad we cannot help hating it. The function of criticism, however, is "to get ourselves out of the way and let humanity decide"; not to discharge our hatred but to expose the grounds for it; not to vilify faults but to diagnose and exhibit them. Unfortunately to express our hatred and to revenge ourselves is easier and more agreeable. Hence there is a tendency to select our pejorative epithets with a view not to their accuracy but to their power of hurting. If writing which was intended to be comic has set our teeth on edge, how easily the adjectives *arch* or *facetious* trickle out of the pen! But if we do not know exactly what we mean by them, if we are not prepared to say how comic work which errs by *archness* and *facetiousness* differs from comic work which errs in any other way, it is to be feared that we are really using them not to inform the reader but to annoy the author—*arch* or *facetious* being among the most effective "smear-words" of our period. In the same way work which obviously aspires and claims to be mature, if the critic dislikes it, will be called *adolescent;* not because the critic has really seen that its faults are those of adolescence but because he has seen that adolescence is the last thing the author wishes or expects to be accused of.

The best protection against this is to remind ourselves again and again what the proper function of pejorative words is. The ultimate, simplest and most abstract, is *bad* itself. The only good purpose for ever departing from that monosyllable when we condemn anything is to be more specific, to answer the question "Bad in what way?" Pejorative words are rightly used only when they do this. *Swine,* as a term of abuse is now a bad pejorative word, because it brings no one accusation rather than another against the person it vilifies; *coward* and *liar* are good ones because they charge a man with a particular fault—of which he might be proved guilty or innocent. As applied to literature, *dull, hackneyed, incoherent, monotonous, pornographic, cacophonous,* are good pejoratives; they tell people in what particular way we think a book faulty. *Adolescent* or *provincial* are not so good. For even when they are honestly used, to define, not merely to hurt, they really suggest a cause for the book's badness instead of describing the badness itself. We are saying in effect "He was led into his faults by being immature" or "by living in Lancashire." But would it not be more interesting to indicate the faults themselves and leave out our historical theory about their causes? If we find words like these—and *vulgar,* and others—indispensable to our criticism, if we find ourselves applying them to more and more different kinds of things, there is grave reason to suspect that—whether we know it or not—we are really using them not to diagnose but to hurt. If so, we are assisting in verbicide. For this is the downward path which leads to the graveyard of murdered words. First they are purely descriptive; *adolescent* tells us a man's age, *villain,* his status. Then they are specifically pejorative; *adolescent* tells us that a man's work displays "mawkishness and all the thousand bitters" confessed by Keats, and *villain* tells that a man has a churl's mind and manners. Then they become *mere* pejoratives, useless synonyms for *bad,* as *villain* did and as *adolescent* may do if we aren't careful. Finally they become terms of abuse and cease to be language in the full sense at all.

As this book is now almost done, what would otherwise be a digression—for it carries us beyond the subject of vocabulary—may perhaps be excused as a sort of *coda*. In the last few paragraphs we have had to touch on criticism. I would be very glad if I could transfer to even one reader my conviction that *adverse* criticism, far from being the easiest, is one of the hardest things in the world to do well. And that for two reasons.

Dr. I. A. Richards first seriously raised the problem of badness in literature. And his singularly honest wrestling with it shows how dark a problem it is. For when we try to define the badness of a work, we usually end by calling it bad on the strength of characteristics which we can find also in good work. Dr. Richards began by hoping he had found the secret of badness in an appeal to stock responses. But Gray's *Elegy* beat him. Here was a good poem which made that appeal throughout. Worse still, its particular goodness depended on doing so. This happens again and again. The novel before you is bad—a transparent compensatory fantasy projected by a poor, plain woman, erotically starving. Yes, but so is *Jane Eyre*. Another bad book is amorphous; but so is *Tristram Shandy*. An author betrays shocking indifference to all the great political, social, and intellectual upheavals of his age; like Jane Austen. The solution of the problem is, I suspect, still far away.

The other difficulty lies within. As I said before, what we think thoroughly bad, we hate. If, besides being bad, it enjoys great popularity and thereby helps to exclude works that we approve from their "place in the sun," hatred of a somewhat less disinterested sort will creep in. Lower and still lower levels of hatred may open; we may dislike the author personally, he and we may belong to opposed literary "parties" or factions. The book before us becomes a symbol of *l'infâme*. Hence a perpetual danger of what is called criticism (judgement) becoming mere action—a blow delivered in a battle. But if it does, we are lost as critics.

Everyone who remembers Arnold's "Literary Influence of Academies" will see why we are lost. But its lesson has been forgotten. There has been in our time a determined, and successful, attempt to revive the *brutalité des journaux anglais*. Reviews so filled with venom have often been condemned socially for their bad manners, or ethically for their spite. I am not prepared to defend them from either charge; but I prefer to stress their inutility.

They can, no doubt, be enjoyed if we already agree with the critic. But then, you know, we are not reading them to inform our judgement. What we enjoy is a resounding blow by our own "side." How useless they are for any strictly critical function becomes apparent if we approach them with an open mind. I had this forced upon me when I read some unusually violent reviews lately which were all by the same man. My mind could not but be open. The books he reviewed were not by me nor by any close friend of mine. I had never heard of the critic. I read (at first—one soon learned to skip his productions) to find out what the books were like and whether I should consider buying them. But I found I could learn nothing about the books. In the first hundred words the critic had revealed his passions. What happened to me after that is, I think, what must happen to anyone in such circumstances. Automatically, without thinking about it, willy-nilly, one's mind discounts everything he says; as it does when we are listening to a drunk or delirious man. Indeed we cannot even think about the book under discussion. The critic rivets our attention on himself. The spectacle of a man thus writhing in the mixed smart and titillation of a fully indulged resentment is, in its way, too big a thing to leave us free for any literary considerations. We are in the presence of tragi-comedy from real life. When we get to the end we find that the critic has told us everything about himself and nothing about the book.

Thus in criticism, as in vocabulary, hatred over-reaches itself. Willingness to wound, too intense and naked, becomes impotent to do the desired mischief.

Of course, if we are to be critics, we must condemn as well as praise; we must sometimes condemn totally and severely. But we must obviously be very careful; in their condemnations great critics long before our time have exposed themselves. Is there any way in which we—lesser men than they—can avoid doing the same? I think perhaps there is. I think we must get it firmly fixed in our minds that the very occasions on which we should most like to write a slashing review are precisely those on which we had much better hold our tongues. The very desire is a danger signal. When an author whom we admire in general, writing in a *genre* we thoroughly enjoy, produces a disappointing work, we may proceed with tolerable safety. We know what we had hoped for. We see, and would have relished, what he was trying to do. By that light we may possibly diagnose where the book has gone wrong. But when an author we never could stand is attempting (unsuccessfully—or, worse still, successfully) "exactly the sort of thing we always loathe," then, if we are wise, we shall be silent. The strength of our dislike is itself a probable symptom that all is not well within; that some raw place in our psychology has been touched, or else that some personal or partisan motive is secretly at work. If we were simply exercising judgement we should be calmer; less anxious to speak. And if we do speak, we shall almost certainly make fools of ourselves.

Continence in this matter is no doubt painful. But, after all, you can always write your slashing review now and drop it into the wastepaper basket a day or so later. A few re-readings in cold blood will often make this quite easy.

• *Questions for Study*

1. Describe in your own words the three limitations of language which Lewis discussses.
2. Why do you think that Lewis focuses attention upon the vocabulary of endearment, complaint, and abuse in his effort to describe the "fringe" of language? What exactly does he mean by the "fringe" of language?
3. What special problems, according to the author, are presented by the language of poetry?
4. What does Lewis believe to be the proper function of criticism? Why must the mature critic choose words which "diagnose" rather than "hurt" the author? In what ways does a critic who uses merely abusive words to "hurt" the author reveal his inadequacy as a critic while, at the same time, he tells us "everything about himself"?
5. Compare and contrast the style and content of this selection with Mumford's "The Miracle of Language." Which essay did you find more informative? Why?

BERGEN EVANS

•

BUT WHAT'S A DICTIONARY FOR?

The storm of abuse in the popular press that greeted the appearance of *Webster's Third New International Dictionary* is a curious phenomenon. Never has a scholarly work of this stature been attacked with such unbridled fury and contempt. An article in the *Atlantic* viewed it as a "disappointment," a "shock," a "calamity," "a scandal and a disaster." *The New York Times*, in a special editorial, felt that the work would "accelerate the deterioration" of the language and sternly accused the editors of

From the *Atlantic*, May 1962. Reprinted by permission of the *Atlantic* and the author.

betraying a public trust. The *Journal* of the American Bar Association saw the publication as "deplorable," "a flagrant example of lexicographic irresponsibility," "a serious blow to the cause of good English." *Life* called it "a nonword deluge," "monstrous," "abominable," and " a cause for dismay." They doubted that "Lincoln could have modelled his Gettysburg Address" on it—a concept of how things get written that throws very little light on Lincoln but a great deal on *Life*.

What underlies all this sound and fury? Is the claim of the G. & C. Merriam Company, probably the world's greatest dictionary maker, that the preparation of the work cost $3.5 million, that it required the efforts of three hundred scholars over a period of twenty-seven years, working on the largest collection of citations ever assembled in any language—is all this a fraud, a hoax?

So monstrous a discrepancy in evaluation requires us to examine basic principles. Just what's a dictionary for? What does it propose to do? What does the common reader go to a dictionary to find? What has the purchaser of a dictionary a right to expect for his money?

Before we look at basic principles, it is necessary to interpose two brief statements. The first of these is that a dictionary is concerned with words. Some dictionaries give various kinds of other useful information. Some have tables of weights and measures on the flyleaves. Some list historical events, and some, home remedies. And there's nothing wrong with their so doing. But the great increase in our vocabulary in the past three decades compels all dictionaries to make more efficient use of their space. And if something must be eliminated, it is sensible to throw out these extraneous things and stick to words.

Yet wild wails arose. The *Saturday Review* lamented that one can no longer find the goddess Astarte under a separate heading—though they point out that a genus of mollusks named after the goddess is included! They seemed to feel that out of sheer perversity the editors of the dictionary stooped to mollusks while ignoring goddesses and that, in some way, this typifies modern lexicography. Mr. Wilson Follett, folletizing (his mental processes demand some special designation) in the *Atlantic*, cried out in horror that one is not even able to learn from the Third International "that the Virgin was Mary the mother of Jesus"!

The second brief statement is that there has been even more progress in the making of dictionaries in the past thirty years than there has been in the making of automobiles. The difference, for example, between the much-touted Second International (1934) and the much-clouted Third International (1961) is not like the difference between yearly models but like the difference between the horse and buggy and the automobile.

Between the appearance of these two editions a whole new science related to the making of dictionaries, the science of descriptive linguistics, has come into being.

Modern linguistics gets its charter from Leonard Bloomfield's *Language* (1933). Bloomfield, for thirteen years professor of Germanic philology at the University of Chicago and for nine years professor of linguistics at Yale, was one of those inseminating scholars who can't be relegated to any department and don't dream of accepting established categories and procedures just because they're established. He was as much an anthropologist as a linguist, and his concepts of language were shaped not by Strunk's *Elements of Style* but by his knowledge of Cree Indian dialects.

The broad general findings of the new science are:

1. All languages are systems of human conventions, not systems of natural laws. The first—and essential—step in the study of any language is observing and setting down precisely what happens when native speakers speak it.

2. Each language is unique in its pronunciation, grammar, and vocabulary. It cannot be described in terms of logic or of some theoretical, ideal language. It cannot be described in terms of any other language, or even in terms of its own past.

3. All languages are dynamic rather than static, and hence a "rule" in any language can only be a statement of contemporary practice Change is constant—and normal.

4. "Correctness" can rest only upon usage, for the simple reason that there is nothing else for it to rest on. And all usage is relative.

From these propositions it follows that a dictionary is good only insofar as it is a comprehensive and accurate description of current usage. And to be comprehensive it must include some indication of social and regional associations.

New dictionaries are needed because English has changed more in the past two generations than at any other time in its history. It has had to adapt to extraordinary cultural and technological changes, two world wars, unparalleled changes in transportation and communication, and unprecedented movements of populations.

More subtly, but pervasively, it has changed under the influence of mass education and the growth of democracy. As written English is used by increasing millions and for more reasons than ever before, the language has become more utilitarian and more informal. Every publication in America today includes pages that would appear to the purist of forty years ago, unbuttoned gibberish. Not that they are; they simply show that you can't hold the language of one generation up as a model for the next.

It's not that you mustn't. You *can't*. For example, in the issue in which *Life* stated editorially that it would follow the Second International, there were over forty words, constructions, and meanings which are in the Third International but not in the Second. The issue of *The New York Times* which hailed the Second International as the authority to which it would adhere and the Third International as a scandal and a betrayal which it would reject used one hundred and fifty-three separate words, phrases, and constructions which are listed in the Third International but not in the Second and nineteen others which are condemned in the Second. Many of them are used many times, more than three hundred such uses in all. The Washington *Post,* in an editorial captioned "Keep Your Old Webster's," says, in the first sentence, "don't throw it away," and in the second, "hang on to it." But the old Webster's labels *don't* "colloquial" and doesn't include "hang on to," in this sense, at all.

In short, all of these publications are written in the language that the Third International describes, even the very editorials which scorn it. And this is no coincidence, because the Third International isn't setting up any new standards at all; it is simply describing what *Life,* the Washington *Post,* and *The New York Times* are doing. Much of the dictionary's material comes from these very publications, the *Times,* in particular, furnishing more of its illustrative quotations than any other newspaper.

And the papers have no choice. No journal or periodical could sell a single issue today if it restricted itself to the American language of twenty-eight years ago. It couldn't discuss half the things we are interested in, and its style would seem stiff and cumbrous. If the editorials were serious, the public—and the stockholders—have reason to be grateful that the writers on these publications are more literate than the editors.

And so back to our questions: what's a dictionary for, and how, in 1962, can it best do what it ought to do? The demands are simple. The common reader turns to a dictionary for information about the spelling, pronunciation, meaning, and proper use of words. He wants to know what is current and respectable. But he wants—and has a right to—the truth, the full truth. And the full truth about any language, and especially about American English today, is that there are many areas in which certainty is impossible and simplification is misleading.

Even in so settled a matter as spelling, a dictionary cannot always be absolute. *Theater* is correct, but so is *theatre.* And so are *traveled* and *travelled, plow* and *plough, catalog* and *catalogue,* and scores of other variants. The reader may want a single certainty. He may have taken an unyielding position in an argument, he may have wagered in support of his conviction and may demand that the dictionary "settle" the matter. But neither his vanity nor his purse is any concern of the dictionary's; it must record the facts. And the fact here is that there are many words in our language which may be spelled, with equal correctness, in either of two ways.

So with pronunciation. A citizen listening to his radio might notice that James B. Conant, Bernard Baruch, and Dwight D. Eisenhower pronounce *economics* as ECKuhnomiks, while A. Whitney Griswold, Adlai Stevenson, and Herbert Hoover pronounce it EEKuhnomiks. He turns to the dictionary to see which of the two pronunciations is "right" and finds that they are both acceptable.

Has he been betrayed? Has the dictionary abdicated its responsibility? Should it say that one *must* speak like the president of Harvard or like the president of Yale, like the thirty-first President of the United States or like the thirty-fourth? Surely it's none of its business to make a choice. Not because of the distinction of these particular speakers; lexicography, like God, is no respecter of persons. But because so widespread and conspicuous a use of two pronunciations among people of this elevation shows that there *are* two pronunciations. Their speaking establishes the fact which the dictionary must record.

Among the "enormities" with which *Life* taxes the Third International is its listing of "the common mispronunciation" *heighth*. That it is labeled a "dialectal variant" seems, somehow, to compound the felony. But one hears the word so pronounced, and if one professes to give a full account of American English in the 1960s, one has to take some cognizance of it. All people do not possess *Life's* intuitive perception that the word is so "monstrous" that even to list it as a dialect variation is to merit scorn. Among these, by the way, was John Milton, who, in one of the greatest passages in all literature, besought the Holy Spirit to raise him to the "highth" of his great argument. And even the *Oxford English Dictionary* is so benighted as to list it, in full boldface, right alongside of *Height* as a variant that has been in the language since at least 1290.

Now there are still, apparently, millions of Americans who retain, in this as in much else, some of the speech of Milton. This particular pronunciation seems to be receding, but the *American Dialect Dictionary* still records instances of it from almost every state on the Eastern seaboard and notes that it is heard from older people and "occasionally in educated speech," "common with good speakers," "general," "widespread."

Under these circumstances, what is a dictionary to do? Since millions speak the word this way, the pronunciation can't be ignored. Since it has been in use as long as we have any record of English and since it has been used by the greatest writers, it can't be described as substandard or slang. But it is heard now only in certain localities. That makes it a dialectal pronunciation, and an honest dictionary will list it as such. What else can it do? Should it do?

The average purchaser of a dictionary uses it most often, probably, to find out what a word "means." As a reader, he wants to know what an author intended to convey. As a speaker or writer, he wants to know what a word will convey to his auditors. And this, too, is complex, subtle, and forever changing.

An illustration is furnished by an editorial in the Washington *Post* (January 17, 1962). After a ringing appeal to those who "love truth and accuracy" and the usual bombinations about "abdication of authority" and "barbarism," the editorial charges the Third International with "pretentious and obscure verbosity" and specifically instances its definition of "so simple an object as a door."

The definition reads:

a movable piece of firm material or a structure supported usu. along one side and swinging on pivots or hinges, sliding along a groove, rolling up and down, revolving as one of four leaves, or folding like an accordion by means of which an opening may be closed or kept open for passage into or out of a building, room, or other covered enclosure or a car, airplane, elevator, or other vehicle.

Then follows a series of special meanings, each particularly defined and, where necessary, illustrated by a quotation.

Since, aside from roaring and admonishing the "gentlemen from Springfield" that "accuracy and brevity are virtues," the *Post's* editorial fails to explain what is wrong with the definition, we can only infer from "so simple" a thing that the writer takes the plain, downright, man-in-the-street attitude that a door is a door and any damn fool knows that.

But if so, he has walked into one of lexicography's biggest booby traps: the belief that the obvious is easy to define. Whereas the opposite is true. Anyone can give a fair description of the strange, the new, or the unique. It's the commonplace, the habitual, that challenges definition, for its very commonness compels us to define it in uncommon terms. Dr. Johnson was ridiculed on just this score when his dictionary appeared in 1755. For two hundred years his definition of a network as "any thing reticulated or decussated, at equal distances, with interstices between the intersections" has been good for a laugh. But in the merriment one thing is always overlooked: no one has yet come up with a better definition!

Subsequent dictionaries defined it as a mesh and then defined a mesh as a network. That's simple, all right.

Anyone who attempts sincerely to state what the word *door* means in the United States of America today can't take refuge in a log cabin. There has been an enormous proliferation of closing and demarking devices and structures in the past twenty years, and anyone who tries to thread his way through the many meanings now included under *door* may have to sacrifice brevity to accuracy and even have to employ words that a limited vocabulary may find obscure.

Is the entrance to a tent a door, for instance? And what of the thing that seals the exit of an airplane? Is this a door? Or what of those sheets and jets of air that are now being used, in place of old-fashioned oak and hinges, to screen entrances and exits. Are they doors? And what of those accordion-like things that set off various sections of many modern apartments? The fine print in the lease takes it for granted that they are doors and that spaces demarked by them are rooms—and the rent is computed on the number of rooms.

Was I gypped by the landlord when he called the folding contraption that shuts off my kitchen a door? I go to the Second International, which the editor of the *Post* urges me to use in preference to the Third International. Here I find that a door is

> The movable frame or barrier of boards, or other material, usually turning on hinges or pivots or sliding, by which an entranceway into a house or apartment is closed and opened; also, a similar part of a piece of furniture, as in a cabinet or bookcase.

This is only forty-six words, but though it includes the cellar door, it excludes the barn door and the accordion-like thing.

So I go on to the Third International. I see at once that the new definition is longer. But I'm looking for accuracy, and if I must sacrifice brevity to get it, then I must. And, sure enough, in the definition which raised the *Post's* blood pressure, I find the words "folding like an accordion." The thing *is* a door, and my landlord is using the word in one of its currently accepted meanings.

We don't turn to a work of reference merely for confirmation. We all have words in our vocabularies which we have misunderstood, and to come on the true meaning of one of these words is quite a shock. All our complacency and self-esteem rise to oppose the discovery. But eventually we must accept the humiliation and laugh it off as best we can.

Some, often those who have set themselves up as authorities, stick to their error and charge the dictionary with being in a conspiracy against them. They are sure that their meaning is the only "right" one. And when the dictionary doesn't bear them out they complain about "permissive" attitudes instead of correcting their mistake.

The New York Times and the *Saturday Review* both regarded as contemptibly "permissive" the fact that one meaning of one word was illustrated by a quotation from Polly Adler. But a rudimentary knowledge of the development of any language would have told them that the underworld has been a far more active force in shaping and enriching speech than all the synods that have ever convened. Their attitude is like that of the patriot who canceled his subscription to the *Dictionary of American Biography* when he discovered that the very first volume included Benedict Arnold!

The ultimate of "permissiveness," singled out by almost every critic for special scorn, was the inclusion in the Third International of *finalize.* It was this, more than any other one thing, that was given as the reason for sticking to the good old Second International—that "peerless authority on American English," as the *Times* called it. But if it was such an authority, why didn't they look into it? They would have found *finalize* if they had.

And why shouldn't it be there? It exists. It's been recorded for two generations. Millions employ it every day. Two Presidents of the United States—men of widely differing cultural backgrounds—have used it in formal statements. And so has the Secretary-General of the United Nations, a man of unusual linguistic attainments. It isn't permitting the word but omitting it that would break faith with the reader. Because it is exactly the sort of word we want information about.

To list it as substandard would be to imply that it is used solely by the ignorant and the illiterate. But this would be a misrepresentation: President Kennedy and U Thant are highly educated men, and both are articulate and literate. It isn't even a freak form. On the contrary, it is a classic example of a regular process of development in English, a process which has given us such thoroughly accepted words as *generalize, minimize, formalize,* and *verbalize.* Nor can it be dismissed on logical grounds or on the ground that it is a mere duplication of *complete.* It says something that *complete* doesn't say and says it in a way that is significant in the modern bureaucratic world: one usually *completes* something which he has initiated but *finalizes* the work of others.

One is free to dislike the word. I don't like it. But the editor of a dictionary has to examine the evidence for a word's existence and seek it in context to get, as clearly and closely as he can, the exact meaning that it conveys to those who use it. And if it is widely used by well-educated, literate, reputable people, he must list it as a standard word. He is not compiling a volume of his own prejudices.

• Questions for Study

1. What tone does Evans adopt toward those who dislike the *Webster's New International Dictionary*, 3d ed.? What words and phrases reveal this tone?
2. Do you find any justification for the attacks against the dictionary? What assumptions about lexicography are held by those who have attacked the work?
3. What has been the influence of the new science of descriptive linguistics on the making of the dictionary? How does Evans answer the question raised by the title?
4. How does Evans use the words *door* and *finalize* to illustrate the problems of definition? Choose one of the following words and consult the *Oxford English Dictionary*, the *Webster's New International Dictionary*, 3d ed., and your own desk dictionary for etymology and meaning: nice, contact, goof, dilapidated, hysteria, worm.

SIR JOSHUA REYNOLDS

•

ON TASTE

I shall now say something on that part of *taste,* which as I have hinted to you before, does not belong so much to the external form of things, but is addressed to the mind, and depends on its original frame, or, to use the expression, the organization of the soul; I mean the imagination and the passions. The principles of these are as invariable as the former, and are to be known and reasoned upon in the same manner, by an appeal to common sense deciding upon the common feelings of mankind. This sense, and these feelings appear to me of equal authority, and equally conclusive. Now this appeal implies a general uniformity and agreement in the minds of men. It would be else an idle and vain en-

From the *Seventh Discourse,* 1776.

deavour to establish rules of art; it would be pursuing a phantom, to attempt to move affections with which we were entirely unacquainted. We have no reason to suspect there is a greater difference between our minds than between our forms; of which, though there are no two alike, yet there is a general similitude that goes through the whole race of mankind; and those who have cultivated their taste, can distinguish what is beautiful or deformed, or, in other words, what agrees with or deviates from the general idea of nature in one case, as well as in the other.

The internal fabric of our minds, as well as the external form of our bodies, being nearly uniform; it seems then to follow of course, that as the imagination is incapable of producing anything originally of itself, and can only vary and combine those ideas with which it is furnished by means of the senses, there will be necessarily an agreement in the imaginations, as in the senses of men. There being this agreement, it follows, that in all cases, in our lightest amusements, as well as in our most serious actions and engagements of life, we must regulate our affections of every kind by that of others. The well-disciplined mind acknowledges this authority, and submits its own opinion to the public voice. It is from knowing what are the general feelings and passions of mankind, that we acquire a true idea of what imagination is; though it appears as if we had nothing to do but to consult our own particular sensations, and these were sufficient to ensure us from all error and mistake.

A knowledge of the disposition and character of the human mind can be acquired only by experience; a great deal will be learned, I admit, by a habit of examining what passes in our bosoms, what are our own motives of action, and of what kind of sentiments we are conscious on any occasion. We may suppose an uniformity, and conclude that the same effect will be produced by the same cause in the mind of others. This examination will contribute to suggest to us matters of inquiry; but we can never be sure that our own sentiments are true and right, till they are confirmed by more extensive observation. One man opposing another determines nothing; but a general union of minds, like a general combination of the forces of all mankind, makes a strength that is irresistible. In fact, as he who does not know himself, does not know others, so it may be said with equal truth, that he who does not know others, knows himself but very imperfectly.

A man who thinks he is guarding himself against prejudices by resisting the authority of others, leaves open every avenue to singularity, vanity, self-conceit, obstinacy, and many other vices, all tending to warp the judgment, and prevent the natural operation of his faculties. This submission to others is a deference which we owe, and indeed are forced involuntarily to pay. In fact, we never are satisfied with our opinions, whatever we may pretend, till they are ratified and confirmed by the suffrages of the rest of mankind. We dispute and wrangle for ever; we endeavor to get men to come to us, when we do not go to them.

He therefore who is acquainted with the works which have pleased different ages and different countries, and has formed his opinion on them has more materials, and more means of knowing what is analogous to the mind of man, than he who is conversant only with the works of his own age or country. What has pleased, and continues to please, is likely to please again: hence are derived the rules of art, and on this immoveable foundation they must ever stand.

This search and study of the history of the mind, ought not to be confined to one art only. It is by the analogy that one art bears to another, that many things are ascertained, which either were but faintly seen, or, perhaps, would not have been discovered at all, if the inventor had not received the first hints from the practices of a sister art on a similar occasion. The frequent allusions which every man who treats of any art is obliged to make to others, in order to illustrate and confirm his principles, sufficiently show their near connection and inseparable relation.

All arts having the same general end, which is to please; and addressing themselves to the same faculties through the medium of the senses; it follows that their rules and principles must have as great affinity, as the different materials and the different organs or vehicles by which they pass to the mind, will permit them to retain.

We may therefore conclude, that the real substance, as it may be called, of what goes under the name of taste, is fixed and established in the nature of things; that there are certain and regular causes by which the imagination and passions of men are affected; and that the knowledge of these causes is acquired by a laborious and diligent investigation of nature, and by the same slow progress as wisdom or knowledge of every kind, however instantaneous its operations may appear when thus acquired.

It has been often observed, that the good and virtuous man alone can acquire this true or just relish even of works of art. This opinion will not appear entirely without foundation, when we consider that the same habit of mind, which is acquired by our search after truth, in the more serious duties of life, is only transferred to the pursuit of lighter amusements. The same disposition, the same desire to find something steady, substantial, and durable, on which the mind can lean, as it were, and rest with safety, actuates us in both cases. The subject only is changed. We pursue the same method in our search after the idea of beauty and perfection in each; of virtue, by looking forward beyond ourselves to society, and to the whole; of arts, by extending our views in the same manner, to all ages and all times.

Every art, like our own, has in its composition, fluctuating as well as fixed principles. It is an attentive enquiry into their difference, that will enable us to determine how far we are influenced by custom and habit, and what is fixed in the nature of things.

To distinguish how much has solid foundation, we may have recourse to the same proof by which some hold that wit ought to be tried; whether it preserves itself when translated. That wit is false, which can subsist only in one language; and that picture which pleases only one age or one nation, owes its reception to some local or accidental association of ideas.

We may apply this to every custom and habit of life. Thus, the general principles of urbanity, politeness, or civility, have been the same in all nations; but the mode in which they are dressed is continually varying. The general idea of showing respect, is by making yourself less; but the manner, whether by bowing the body, kneeling, prostration, pulling off the upper part of our dress, or taking away the lower, is a matter of custom.

Thus, in regard to ornaments,—it would be unjust to conclude, that, because they were at first arbitrarily contrived, they are therefore undeserving of our attention; on the contrary, he who neglects the cultivation of those ornaments, acts contrary to nature and reason. As life would be imperfect without its highest ornaments, the Arts, so these arts themselves would be imperfect without *their* ornaments. Though we, by no means, ought to rank with these positive and substantial beauties, yet it must be allowed, that a knowledge of both is essentially requisite towards forming a complete, whole, and perfect taste. It is in reality from their ornaments, that arts receive their peculiar character and complexion; we may add, that in them we find the characteristical mark of a national taste; as, by throwing up a feather in the air, we know which way the wind blows, better than by a more heavy matter.

• *Questions for Study*

1. Does Reynolds clearly define what taste is? Using a dictionary and your own experience, attempt to define this difficult word.
2. What do you think the author means by the "general law of nature"? Reynolds assumes a "uniformity of nature's laws" and "a general union of minds" that give us a basis for developing taste. Do you agree with his assumptions? Are there certain rules and regulations common to all people

at all times upon which standards of taste and morality can be based? Explain your answers.

3. How does the author use argument by analogy? Are the relations among the arts as inseparable as he assumes? Does a person who has taste in music necessarily have taste in literature?

4. Discuss Reynold's style with emphasis on his manner of generalizing, his sentence structures, and his development of transitional devices between and within paragraphs.

WILLIAM   HAZLITT

•

ON FAMILIAR STYLE

It is not easy to write a familiar style. Many people mistake a familiar for a vulgar style, and suppose that to write without affectation is to write at random. On the contrary, there is nothing that requires more precision, and, if I may say so, purity of expression, than the style I am speaking of. It utterly rejects not only all unmeaning pomp, but all low, cant phrases, and loose, unconnected *slipshod* allusions. It is not to take the first word that offers, but the best word in common use; it is not to throw words together in any combinations we please, but to follow and avail ourselves of the true idiom of the language. To write a genuine familiar or truly English style is to write as any one would speak in common conversation who had a thorough command and choice of words, or who could discourse with ease, force, and perspicuity, setting aside all pedantic and oratorical flourishes. Or, to give another illustration, to write naturally is the same thing in regard to common conversation as to read naturally is in regard to common speech. It does not follow that it is an easy thing to give the true accent and inflection to the words you utter, because you do not attempt to rise above the level of ordinary

From *Table Talk*, 1822.

life and colloquial speaking. You do not assume, indeed, the solemnity of the pulpit, or the tone of stage-declamation; neither are you at liberty to gabble on at a venture, without emphasis or discretion, or to resort to vulgar dialect or clownish pronunciation. You must steer a middle course. You are tied down to a given and appropriate articulation, which is determined by the habitual associations between sense and sound, and which you can only hit by entering into the author's meaning, as you must find the proper words and style to express yourself by fixing your thoughts on the subject you have to write about. Any one may mouth out a passage with a theatrical cadence, or get upon stilts to tell his thoughts; but to write or speak with propriety and simplicity is a more difficult task. Thus it is easy to affect a pompous style, to use a word twice as big as the thing you want to express: it is not so easy to pitch upon the very word that exactly fits it. Out of eight or ten words equally common, equally intelligible, with nearly equal pretensions, it is a matter of some nicety and discrimination to pick out the very one the preferableness of which is scarcely perceptible, but decisive. The reason why I object to Dr. Johnson's style is that there is no discrimination, no selection, no variety in it. He uses none but "tall, opaque words," taken from the "first row of the rubric"—words with the greatest number of syllables, or Latin phrases with merely English terminations. If a fine style depended on this sort of arbitrary pretension, it would be fair to judge of an author's elegance by the measurement of his words and the substitution of foreign circumlocutions (with no precise associations) for the mother-tongue. How simple is it to be dignified without ease, to be pompous without meaning! Surely it is but a mechanical rule for avoiding what is low, to be always pedantic and affected. It is clear you cannot use a vulgar English word if you never use a common English word at all. A fine tact is shown in adhering to those which are perfectly common, and yet never falling into any expressions which are debased by disgusting circumstances, or which owe their signification and point to technical or professional allusions. A truly natural or familiar style can never be quaint or vulgar, for this reason, that it is of universal force and applicability, and that quaintness and vulgarity arise out of the immediate connection of certain words with coarse and disagreeable or with confined ideas. The last form what we understand by *cant* or *slant* phrases.—To give an example of what is not very clear in the general statement. I should say that the phrase *To cut with a knife,* or *To cut a piece of wood,* is perfectly free from vulgarity, because it is perfectly common; but to *cut an acquaintaince* is not quite unexceptionable, because it is not perfectly common or intelligible, and has hardly yet escaped out of the limits of slang phraseology. I should hardly, therefore, use the word in this sense without putting it in italics as a license of expression, to be received *cum grano salis*. All provincial or bye-phrases come under the same mark of reprobation—all such as the writer transfers to the page from his fireside or a particular *coterie,* or that he invents for his own sole use and convenience. I conceive that words are like money, not the worse for being common, but that it is the stamp of custom alone that gives them circulation or value. I am fastidious in this respect, and would almost as soon coin the currency of the realm as counterfeit the King's English. I never invented or gave a new and unauthorised meaning to any word but one single one (the term *impersonal* applied to feelings), and that was in an abstruse metaphysical discussion to express a very difficult distinction. I have been (I know) loudly accused of revelling in vulgarisms and broken English. I cannot speak to that point; but so far I plead guilty to the determined use of acknowledged idioms and common elliptical expressions. I am not sure that the critics in question know the one from the other, that is, can distinguish any medium between formal pedantry and the most barbarous solecism. As an author I endeavour to employ plain words and popular modes of construction, as, were I a chapman and dealer, I should common weights and measures.

The proper force of words lies not in the words themselves, but in their application. A word may be a fine-sounding word, of an unusual length, and very imposing from its learning and novelty, and yet in the connection in which it is introduced may be quite pointless and irrelevant. It is not pomp or pretension, but the adaptation of the expression to the idea, that clenches a writer's meaning:—as it is not the size or glossiness of the materials, but their being fitted each to its place, that gives strengh to the arch; or as the pegs and nails are as necessary to the support of the building as the larger timbers, and more so than the mere showy, unsubstantial ornaments. I hate anything that occupies more space than it is worth. I hate to see a load of bandboxes go along the street, and I hate to see a parcel of big words without anything in them. A person who does not deliberately dispose of all his thoughts alike in cumbrous draperies and flimsy disguises may strike out twenty varieties of familiar everyday language, each coming somewhat nearer to the feeling he wants to convey, and at last not hit upon that particular and only one which may be said to be identical with the exact impression in his mind. This would seem to show that Mr. Cobbett is hardly right in saying that the first word that occurs is always the best. It may be a very good one; and yet a better may present itself on reflection or from time to time. It should be suggested naturally, however, and spontaneously, from a fresh and lively conception of the subject. We seldom succeed by trying at improvement, or by merely substituting one word for another that we are not satisfied with, as we cannot recollect the name of a place or person by merely plaguing ourselves about it. We wander farther from the point by persisting in a wrong scent; but it starts up accidentally in the memory when we least expected it, by touching some link in the chain of previous association.

There are those who hoard up and make a cautious display of nothing but rich and rare phraseology—ancient medals, obscure coins, and Spanish pieces of eight. They are very curious to inspect, but I myself would neither offer nor take them in the course of exchange. A sprinkling of archaisms is not amiss, but a tissue of obsolete expressions is more fit *for keep than wear*. I do not say I would not use any phrase that had been brought into fashion before the middle or the end of the last century, but I should be shy of using any that had not been employed by any approved author during the whole of that time. Words, like clothes, get old-fashioned, or mean and ridiculous, when they have been for some time laid aside. Mr. Lamb is the only imitator of old English style I can read with pleasure; and he is so thoroughly imbued with the spirit of his authors that the idea of imitation is almost done away. There is an inward unction, a marrowy vein, both in the thought and feeling, an intuition, deep and lively, of his subject, that carries off any quaintness or awkwardness arising from an antiquated style and dress. The matter is completely his own, though the manner is assumed. Perhaps his ideas are altogether so marked and individual as to require their point and pungency to be neutralised by the affectation of a singular but traditional form of conveyance. Tricked out in the prevailing costume, they would probably seem more startling and out of the way. The old English authors, Burton, Fuller, Coryate, Sir Thomas Browne, are a kind of mediators between us and the more eccentric and whimsical modern, reconciling us to his peculiarities. I do not, however, know how far this is the case or not, till he condescends to write like one of us. I must confess that what I like best of his papers under the signature of Elia (still I do not presume, amidst such excellence, to decide what is most excellent) is the account of "Mrs. Battle's Opinions on Whist," which is also the most free from obsolete allusions and turns of expression—

A well of native English undefiled.

To those acquainted with his admired prototypes, these *Essays* of the ingenious and highly gifted author have the same sort of charm and relish that Erasmus's *Colloquies* or a fine piece of modern Latin have to the classical scholar. Certainly, I do not know any borrowed pencil that has more power or felicity of execution than the one of which I have here been speaking.

It is as easy to write a gaudy style without ideas as it is to spread a pallet of showy colours or to smear in a flaunting transparency. "What do you read?" "Words, words, words."—"What is the matter?" "Nothing," it might be answered. The florid style is the reverse of the familiar. The last is employed as an unvarnished medium to convey ideas; the first is resorted to as a spangled veil to conceal the want of them. When there is nothing to be set down but words, it costs little to have them fine. Look through the dictionary, and cull out a *florilegium*, rival the *tulippomania*. *Rouge* high enough, and never mind the natural complexion. The vulgar, who are not in the secret, will admire the look of preternatural health and vigour; and the fashionable, who regard only appearances, will be delighted with the imposition. Keep to your sounding generalities, your tinkling phrases, and all will be well. Swell out an unmeaning truism to a perfect tympany of style. A thought, a distinction is the rock on which all this brittle cargo of verbiage splits at once. Such writers have merely *verbal* imaginations, that retain nothing but words. Or their puny thoughts have dragon-wings, all green and gold. They soar far above the vulgar failing of the *Sermo humi obrepens*—their most ordinary speech is never short of an hyperbole, splendid, imposing, vague, incomprehensible, magniloquent, a cento of sounding common-places. If some of us, whose "ambition is more lowly," pry a little too narrowly into nooks and corners to pick up a number of "unconsidered trifles," they never once direct their eyes or lift their hands to seize on any but the most gorgeous, tarnished, threadbare, patchwork set of phrases, the left-off finery of poetic extravagance, transmitted down through successive generations of barren pretenders. If they criticize actors and actresses, a huddled phantasmagoria of feathers, spangles, floods of light, and oceans of sound float before their morbid sense, which they paint in the style of Ancient Pistol. Not a glimpse can you get of the merits or defects of the performers: they are hidden in a profusion of barbarous epithets and wilful rodomontade. Our hypercritics are not thinking of these little fantoccini beings—

That strut and fret their hour upon the stage—

but of tall phantoms of words, abstractions, *genera* and *species,* sweeping clauses, periods that unite the Poles, forced alliterations, astounding antitheses—

And on their pens Fustian *sits plumed.*

If they describe kings and queens, it is an Eastern pageant. The Coronation at either House is nothing to it. We get at four repeated images—a curtain, a throne, a sceptre, and a footstool. These are with them the wardrobe of a lofty imagination; and they turn their servile strains to servile uses. Do we read a description of pictures? It is not a reflection of tones and hues which "nature's own sweet and cunning hand laid on," but piles of precious stones, rubies, pearls, emeralds, Golconda's mines, and all the blazonry of art. Such persons are in fact besotted with words, and their brains are turned with the glittering but empty and sterile phantoms of things. Personifications, capital letters, seas of sunbeams, visions of glory, shining inscriptions, the figures of a transparency, Britannia with her shield, or Hope leaning on an anchor, make up their stock-in-trade. They may be considered as *hieroglyphical* writers. Images stand out in their minds isolated and important merely in themselves, without any groundwork of feeling—there is no context in their imaginations. Words affect them in the same way, by the mere sound, that is, by their possible, not by their actual application to the subject in hand. They are fascinated by first appearances, and have no sense of consequences. Nothing more is meant by them than meets the ear: they understand or feel nothing more than meets their eye. The web and texture of the universe, and of the heart of man, is a mystery to them: they have no faculty that strikes a chord in unison with it. They cannot get beyond the daubings of fancy, the varnish of sentiment. Objects are not linked to feelings, words to things, but images revolve in splendid mockery, words represent themselves in their strange rhapsodies. The categories of such a mind are pride and ignorance—pride in outside show, to which they sacrifice everything, and ignorance of the true worth and hidden structure both of words and things. With a sovereign contempt for what is familiar and natural, they are the slaves of vulgar affectation—of a routine of high-flown phrases. Scorning to imitate realities, they are unable to invent anything, to strike out one original idea. They are not copyists of nature, it is true; but they are the poorest of all plagiarists, the plagiarists of words. All is far-fetched, dear-bought, artificial, oriental in subject and allusion; all is mechanical, conventional, vapid, formal, pedantic in style and execution. They startle and confound the understanding of the reader by the remoteness and obscurity of their illustrations; they soothe the ear by the monotony of the same everlasting round of circuitous metaphors. They are the *mock-school* in poetry and prose. They flounder about between fustian in expression and bathos in sentiment. They tantalise the fancy, but never reach the head nor touch the heart. Their Temple of Fame is like a shadowy structure raised by Dulness to Vanity, or like Cowper's description of the Empress of Russia's palace of ice, "as worthless as in show 'twas glittering"—

It smiled, and it was cold!

• *Questions for Study*

1. To what extent are Hazlitt's ideas on "true" or "pure" style applicable to modern prose? In what ways are the abuses which Hazlitt deplores still evident in modern writing? Explain specifically why Hazlitt objects to Johnson's style?
2. Consider his reservations concerning certain phrases such as "to cut an acquaintance"? Do his reservations still have validity today? Discuss.
3. According to Hazlitt, what is a "hieroglyphical writer"?
4. What similes and examples does he use to vivify his own style? Which of these are the most effective? Which the least effective? Why?
5. Would you call Hazlitt's style in this essay a "familiar" style? Why or why not?

CHARLES W. FERGUSON

•

A SANE APPROACH TO STYLE

———————————

Everyone who uses the wealth of language wants to use it in some way that is characteristically his own. He wants it, in a sense, as his private property. This desire is the most genuine tribute we pay to our heritage because it is unspoken and often unacknowledged, but it is steady.

Henry Seidel Canby said that style is like happiness: "Everyone recognizes it, everyone describes it, but no two people agree as to its exact nature." There are many views and many mysteries into which the student can delve, but for working purposes style may be looked upon as our personal appearance in print, our self-image given speech. When we become personal about the language we become conscious of style, for it

Reprinted from *Say It With Words* by Charles W. Ferguson, by permission of Alfred A. Knopf, Inc. Copyright © 1959 by Charles W. Ferguson. David McCord's "Gloss" from *Odds and Ends* reprinted by permission of Little, Brown and Co.

is through style that we make the language our own. A style, representing the sum total of choices made in daily speech and writing, expresses our individual connection with that vast and confusing body of knowledge known as language.

Thus no definition of style will satisfy. Swift said, "Proper words in proper places make the true definition of style." There is wisdom here that we all might heed, but the fact remains that what is proper for one person would not be proper for another. Any person who writes even a post card wants it inwardly or openly to be his own. It must bear his hallmark. It is one of our surest and most creative conceits that the way we write and talk must have features that mark us off from the mass.

Two reasons exist why most of us want a manner of writing considered peculiarly our own. One is the healthy and inherent satisfaction provided; writing may be the last stronghold of individuality, the place where within reason a man may be himself without being odd or losing status. Indeed, he may gain status if he has a novel as well as a persuasive way of putting ideas. With all our ironclad conformity, most of us still give a man or woman rein when it comes to speech.

The very origin of the word *style* emphasizes choice. When writing began to be common on tables of wood covered over with colored wax, men used "a sort of bodkin, made of iron, or brass, or bone; which in Latin is called stylus." Significantly, the instrument was sharp on one end, but the other end was "blunt and broad to scratch out what was written, and not approved of, to be amended; so that 'vertere stylum,' i.e. *to turn the style,* signifies, in Latin, to blot out."

Certainly there can be no accomplished style without a good deal of blotting out, of giving consistent attention to terms and constructions that do or do not adequately represent the thought within. "Style is organic," writes J. Middleton Murry, "not the clothes a man wears, but the flesh, bone, and blood of his body. Therefore it is really impossible to consider styles apart from the whole system of perceptions and feelings and thoughts that animate them."

In my own case, for example, the style of writing and speaking natural to me is rotund and centrifugal, for it is my nature to take a point and roam in ever wider elliptical orbits from it. This tendency leads often to tedious reiteration if not to turgid repetition and the rhythmical monotony of a big bass drum. I tend to tantalize the reader. I fancy sesquipedalian words and shambling ambiguities that cover confusion with the semblance of profundity. The sound of words interests me more than their meaning, and I prefer a noisy obscurity to a simple truth. What I seek, if left alone, is to create an effect with words, not to convey meaning with them.

The total of these qualities constitutes my natural style. Perhaps I ought to go unashamedly ahead and write naturally. And, in point of fact, I do. I consciously modify some traits, correct others, accommodate myself to an imagined reader, try to break up long periods and put in breathing spaces. When all is said and done, I write the way I write. But a steady and unrelenting effort to consider the principles of styles other than my own, if only for exercise, makes my style less obscure and still leaves it essentially mine.

Your style will remain you, no matter what you do. You won't change it markedly by trying to improve it. You may not improve it, but you will become jovially conscious of your writing and the many faces it may wear while remaining an expression of the inner self.

So an attentive analysis of various pronounced styles (or stylized forms of expression) current in our time will not be amiss for the student. The study of these forms is even more important to the writing non writer than it is to the professional, whose tasks and literary preoccupations incline him to observe the cause of prose effects. The businessman who writes a letter, the professor who fashions a lecture, the student who prepares a theme, needs style and covets style as much as the man who writes an editorial for the *Times.*

Purely as an exercise in attentiveness, consider some of the current patterns of writing, the salient features of their weave and how they are achieved. Then apply these patterns to an office memorandum, say, and note the results and the differences.

First and foremost, of course, comes the casual style. As brilliantly delineated by William H. Whyte, Jr., it exhibits several obvious and re-current features. One is studied understatement, as in such phrases as "something less than good." Not downright bad. Just less than good. It combines folksiness with sophistication, for it uses the terms of familiarity encountered on a village street to convey impressions of a city cocktail party. It marks our day, which is chatty. It affects informality, being full of slick contrivances to make café society seem like a hamburger joint. To this end it drops articles and verbs and pronouns and starts sentences in the middle, thus aiming at a clipped conversational effect.

The casual style reaches its apex in the better sequences of "The Talk of the Town" in *The New Yorker* and its nadir in columnists and bored writers here and there who make less than interesting things that were not interesting to begin with. Used well or ill, it is the *Zeitgeist:* its influence creeps into all of us, for we love at times to be *dégagé* and tweedy and full of threat and right on the verge of saying something. It accommodates itself either to the momentous or to the trifling, for it touches upon the momentous with artistic restraint and upon the trifling in a tone altogether appropriate. It is the language of the tired literary man, of all the sad young men. It brings to mind Gamaliel Bradford's description of Theodore Roosevelt: he killed lions as if they were mosquitoes and mosquitoes as if they were lions.

Next in influence, especially on college moppets by whom the writing pace of the near future may be set, is the celebrated *Time* style. As Mencken pointed out: "*Time* likes to begin sentences with adjectives and it deals heavily in compounds of the Homeric variety, e.g., *hot-eyed, Maine-born, moon-placid, Yankee-shrewd*." *Time* insists that it has no style, "only tempo and attitude." But it has added scores of phrases to the language, thrown captions into people's eyes, truncated and agglutinated words, proliferated neat inversions, kept the hyphen in the language, and turned sentences topsy-turvy, giving Wolcott Gibbs in his profile of Henry Luce a chance to end the whole lampoon with the classic line: "What he will do next, knows God." The manner of writing is sharp and crisp, with effects often sought after like fugitives, and the total effect is to make even the humdrum lively and readable and to show that any subject, however dull, can be made to glow, at least for a time, like a Lone Ranger ring.

Whatever one thinks of the *Time* manner, it stays with us. It has put itself right there at the back of the American mind, and of the several manners of speaking that thrust themselves forward in any piece of writing, the *Time* style is likely to be among the chief. It is both old and up to date, for Briton Hadden, a co-founder of *Time,* is said to have underlined all the compound epithets in the "Iliad" he owned, such as "wine-dark sea" and "far-darting Apollo." With his addiction to Homer and the classics, Hadden set in the early days of *Time* a tradition for writing, for conscious and unflagging attention to the alchemy of words.

In noting the casual and the stentorian, one must not overlook the prosaic, the inescapable style of the government expert. This sort of writing confronts us more than any other, and it stands to reason that it has some influence, if only an inverse one, upon us. I find on my desk, as an example, the second annual report of the Secretary of Agriculture on the Rural Development Program. I pick a paragraph at random and I can type it in my sleep. It happens to fall on page twenty-two.

Through the work of government agencies, private organizations, businesses, and other groups contributing to the Rural Development program, we have been able to gain new insights into the problems of low-income rural areas, and to better understand what these areas have to work with and what they need if their levels of living are to move upward with other areas in the Nation. . . . On the basis of preliminary work in pilot counties and areas and the considerable body of information gathered in studies already made there, we can attempt to draw certain general conclusions about programs and services affecting these areas. . . .

So it seems to me that alertness to the values and dangers in stylized forms of writing—stereotypes of style—can help us. But stylized writing offers no substitute for style. There are certain components all good writing needs. These components and the attitude that must guide their use were never better set forth, to my knowledge, than they are by F. L. Lucas, Fellow of King's College, Cambridge, in his remarkably helpful book, "Style."

The first is clarity. And how is clarity to be achieved? "Mainly," says Lucas, "by taking trouble and by writing to serve people rather than to impress them."

This point has special sharpness in the English-speaking world. A Frenchman once told a friend of Lucas: "In France it is the writer that takes the trouble; in Germany, the reader; in England it is betwixt and between." A piece of writing in our day must above all else be readable, so beveled that it will pass almost unnoticed through the eye into the mind. One reads it without thinking and reflects on it, if at all, *after* he has read it.

Think what an illuminating difference it would make all around if those now using, say, business dialect or pedagogical patois would control their expression by this principle of service to the reader. Certain hefty terms become the signs of learning, and a great deal of the turgid prose in the field of education, for example, comes about simply because words are used to show that the writer belongs to the *cognoscenti*. Thus we get in education and social work an *underprivileged preadolescent,* meaning a poor child.

Nor is ostentation by any means confined to persons who aim at scholarly attainments. One finds it also in business and in the professions, where men, often for reasons touching their livelihood and advancement, write or speak to show that they have mastered the mumbo jumbo of the initiated instead of seeking to pass along either ideas or information. Bankers, both in talking to stockholders and in ordinary conversation, seem possessed by their specialized vocabularies. They will speak casually of a "fiduciary," whatever that is, or of a "funded debt" without adding or explaining that it is a debt that matures in more than one year. "Interest in arrears" is a totally confusing term to those not behind the cages or rails of a bank. It does not mean that you are behind in your interest: it refers to interest that is collected at the end of the period instead of at the beginning.

Schopenhauer likens a man's style to "the dough out of which all the contents of his mind are kneaded." He goes on to observe that, instead of really revealing these contents, many writers "try to make the reader believe that their thoughts have gone much further and deeper than is really the case. They say what they have to say in long sentences that wind about in forced and unnatural ways. . . . They tremble between the two separate aims of communicating what they want to say and of concealing it. Their object is to dress it up so that they may look learned or deep, in order to give people the impression that there is more in it than for the moment meets the eye. . . . Authors should," he concludes, "use common words to say uncommon things."

Of a further essential ingredient of good style, which is brevity, it would appear that the less said the better! This at least is the theory, but not the case. Brevity is not briefness. There are occasions when, almost by way of retort, a single pungent line may be spoken or written. Such an occasion was provided by Philip of Macedon when he threatened the Laconians: "If I enter Laconia, you shall be exterminated." The inhabitants of Laconia wrote back one word: "*If.*"

Since then *laconic* has been the classic term for pithiness. But there are few moments when the stage is so beautifully set for brevity. Generally it must be achieved, and, like all services to the reader, it is to be wrought by effort and not simply by intent. Brevity is not a virtue; it is a result. In a word, if you would be brief, first be long. To make a telephone conversation short, think it over and rehearse it, and anticipate as far as possible what is likely to be said and what needs to be said. To make a business letter short or an annual report pointed, let it first be written in fullness or at least outlined in some luxuriance of detail. Only then will it be possible to make it brief.

Shortness must not be confused with brevity. If a telegram is short to save costs or a letter short to have the look of brevity, it may not spare the recipient at all. Indeed, the ambiguities of omission may waste the reader's time and cause him more aches and pains than a long letter which he could read with a selective eye. Brevity thus ought to be thought of as tied up inextricably with clarity, and if there happens to fall an unhappy choice between brevity and clarity, let brevity be sacrificed. If brevity becomes an end in itself, it becomes an irrelevance. But if it is achieved by a full mind out of sympathy for the reader, it becomes a joy as well as an accomplishment.

A man will reveal his manners as well as his thoughts in what he writes. Let him know this, and he will write in such a way that the reader will meet him more than halfway. A good spirit must be reckoned with as an essential of a pleasing style. The person who would commend himself to Americans in particular, who rate ability as naught without affability, will see to it that his manner of writing comes from a genial nature and one that has the reader's entertainment as well as enlightenment at heart. A feeling of warmth and kindness toward any audience will supply a resilience of spirit which no brilliance of mind can make up for. Peevishness can be detected as easily as a glaring error in grammar.

Theories of style vary with the teacher. Seeing that style is personal, reactions to suggestions about style are subjective and always fraught with emotion. No other phase of writing offers so much substance for disagreement and controversy—a further sign that style, in the last analysis, is a personal affair and not one to be ruled by rules. We may be willing to observe the minimum requirements set forth by such a thoughtful mentor as Lucas, but sooner or later we want to return to experiments with our own views.

Experiments can help us immensely, for they increase our awareness and, even if they are not successful, do us no permanent harm. Trying to attain various effects with differing styles can keep us from striving for a fixed style or for style as such. The best style, we may find, can be the absence of any style at all.

Not one style, but an awareness of many, so that the one best suited to the subject can be chosen—this should be the controlling principle of one who seeks to improve self-expression. The best craftsmen will be found to follow this principle. In the heyday of *The American Mercury* and in his "Prejudices," H. L. Mencken showed himself a master of protest, dealing with Dr. Coolidge, the Bible Belt, the Sahara of the Bozart, mountebanks, and charlatans, and lashing out against hocus-pocus. In "The American Language" he showed an occasional flash of humor, but for the most part he wrote with smooth regard for reader and subject, and he respected the dignity of both. He was not the same Mencken. And in his reminiscent book, "Happy Days," being the recounting of his Baltimore childhood, his prose was properly benign, his mood mellow, and his style quiet. There was no need to whambang. In "The American Language" he was a scholar and he wrote in an appropriate manner. In his "Prejudices" he was the Bad Boy of Baltimore, in "Happy Days" an old man recalling. In each case he adapted his writing to the requirements of the job.

Determining the fitness of a particular piece of prose to a particular occasion seems to me the first step toward thinking clearly about style. I realized this afresh when an airliner steward tried to be funny about a delay in take-off that came from a motor failure. What is the appropriate tone? This is the question we must forever ask ourselves. If one can decide on the tone happily, we have a head start on any audience.

One can study the style of a man or a magazine without either imitating it or parodying it. Rather, the important thing at all times is an ear and an eye for style, a perceptive awareness, a conviction that a style should be suited to subject matter and audience, and express the mind of him who uses it. It seems to me that this sense of style, rather than any particularly cultivated style, frees the mind and lends confidence. We have Robert Louis Stevenson's assurance that he often played the ape to Hazlitt. Yet Stevenson's style was his own.

"There is," says Schopenhauer, "no quality of style that can be gained by reading writers who possess it; whether it be persuasiveness, imagination, the gift of drawing comparisons, boldness, bitterness, brevity, grace, ease of expression or wit, unexpected contrasts, a laconic or naïve manner, and the like. But if these qualities are already in us, exist, that is to say, potentially, we can call them forth and bring them to consciousness; we can learn the purpose to which they can be put; we can be strengthened in our inclination to use them, or get courage to do so. . . . The only way in which reading can form style is by teaching us the use to which we can put our own natural gifts."

Whatever the larger complexities of style, in day to day use style means "that idiosyncrasy of expression by which one recognizes a writer." And while it may be true that "to say that a writer has style is not necessarily to praise him," still it does mean that we recognize him as a distinct person. And when we in our common writing achieve style, it brings us a certain satisfaction because it means that we have discovered and put to use our own peculiarities.

Both *idiom* and *idiosyncrasy* take their cue from the Greek word meaning personal, private, peculiar. So does the word *idiot*. In the process of discovering one's idiom and exercising one's idiosyncrasies without being an utter idiot, it surely does no harm to follow Mario Pei's advice: "If you come across an author that you particularly like, try to imitate him in your own writing, using the words and combinations of words he uses. Since there will be more than one such author, after a time you will come out with a style of writing which, while it is a compromise or merger of all your favorites, will really be your own."

The endlessly fascinating problem which the amateur writer shares with the professional is that of discovering the real mental self and giving it voice. This means not only that we must experiment, but also that we must have enough courage to venture with words and enough honesty to use the words we like.

We reach a point sooner or later at which style ceases to be a matter of form and becomes a matter of substance, revealing the content and habits of the mind. The way we write reveals our bent, our inclinations, our inner drives. Thus if we are to cultivate any manner of writing, it should reflect what we are—and let the consequences go hang. We should not attempt to express ourselves in the modern boogie-woogie manner if we are not modern and not hep. Not the form that is popular, but the form that is honest—this is our hope of effectiveness.

Such counsel still gives plenty of range for studying forms of speech and choice of words. Let us say that, for good or ill, a person finds or knows or admits that he is of a negative turn of mind. His manner of writing ought advisedly to reflect it. I know one young man who achieved a good conversational style by prefixing a *de* or *dis* to many commonplace terms. His own use was natural and effective, and one finds support of the practice in words that some of the learned men have approved and added to the language, such as *decontaminate* and *derequisition* and *derestrict*.

As Gowers warns us, we might as well be prepared for such terms. "If to affect with gas is to contaminate, to enforce a speed limit is to restrict, and to commandeer a house is to requisition, then the cancellation of these things will inevitably be decontaminate, derestrict, and derequisition, whether we like it or not, and it is no use saying that they ought to be *cleanse, exempt* and *release*."

The prefix *non* has an amazing record. Take the term *nonfiction*. It has been in use for at least fifty years and shows no sign of being replaced. Even with the decline of fiction and the increase of a vast body of serious literature in magazine and book publishing, there still is no real term to designate it save by a prefix that shows it is not something else. Gowers cites other strong and apparently permanent *non* words: *nonappearance, noncombatant, nonconformist, nonexistent.* He deplores the excessive use of the prefix and instances the rise of "institutions for the care of the non-sick." But the word is no more ridiculous than the fact.

I do not suggest that a person build his style on words beginning with *de, dis,* or *non.* I am suggesting that such words may be found to represent him, however, and that if they do it is fair that he sprinkle his writing with them, at least as an exercise. More to another's taste (as to mine) would be to cultivate terms that accent the positive.

It is odd how many words in the language today are accepted and used only in their negative form. Their darker side has been the more useful and has triumphed, which must be some kind of cultural commentary. Leland Stowe once said that he planned to use the word *ruthless;* it occurred to him that there must also be a word *ruth.* There is. It means kind, considerate. But if the use for it has not disappeared, the more dramatic term of *ruthless* has all but obliterated it.

David McCord, executive secretary of the Harvard Fund Council, and a writer of light verse, has been making, over a period of years, a real campaign to get positive forms of common words (such as *inept*) back into the language. If a person is *uncouth,* another one can be *couth;*

if a man is *unkempt,* another one may be *kempt;* if one is *incorrigible,* one can be *corrigible* too; if a woman's hair is *disheveled* or if her clothes are, as they almost always are in the scandal sheets, she may be *sheveled* when she is well coifed or neatly attired. Weather can be *clement* as well as *inclement.* So it goes in McCord's view, and he has summed the case up neatly:

> *I know a little man, both ept and ert,*
> *An intro? Extro? No, he's just a vert.*
> *Shevelled and couth and kempt, pecunious, ane;*
> *His image trudes upon the captive brain.*
> *When life turns sipid and my friend is traught*
> *The Spirit soars as I would sist it ought.*
> *Chalantly then, like any gainly goof,*
> *My digent self is sertive, choate, loof.*[1]

There are great bodies of neglected words, some of them archaic, some forgotten, which any person might study and sensitize himself to if he sought to flavor a style that would really reveal his own sentiments. We still use, as Ivor Brown notes, the word *gruesome* but we have dropped for some unaccountable reason the verb to *gruve,* meaning to shudder.

Think for a moment of what might be done with the body of phrasal verbs we are adding to the language, to the pardonable distress of the grammarians, who would like to keep prepositions in their place. These verbs are formed by simply adding a preposition (or, in some cases, an adverb) and thereby creating, in an instant, a world of difference.

By the same practice of turning a trouble into an asset, deliberate repetition of words may be made a *leitmotif* of style. Half of one's time in writing must be spent in avoiding the repetition of words or repenting it. If this is enough of a problem in writing, let repetition be conspicuously deliberate. One need not go as far as Gertrude Stein, but one could study her effects with profit and with consolation:

It's funny about honey, you always eat honey during a war, so much honey, there is no sugar, there never is sugar during a war, the first thing to disappear is sugar, after that butter, but butter can always be had but not sugar, no not sugar, so during a war you always eat honey, quantities of honey, really more honey than you used to eat sugar, and you find honey so much better than sugar, better in itself and better in applesauce, in all desserts so much better and then peace is upon us and no one eats honey any more . . .

And style is like that because that's the way style is, it ought to be clear. but once it's clear it ought to be peculiar because we are all peculiar

---

[1] Copyright 1954 by David McCord.

and being peculiar in some way we ought not to disguise it but admit it
and show it and be peculiar in some peculiar way, some way that is
peculiarly our own, but not so peculiar that people will call us peculiar,
just peculiar enough to be ourselves, remembering that *peculiar* comes
from and old Latin term meaning *private property,* and our style is our
private property.

• *Questions for Study*

1. Compare and contrast the ideas in this essay with those of Hazlitt in "On
   Familiar Style."
2. Consider Ferguson's types of modern style. Is he drawing overly minute
   distinctions between styles? Explain. In what other ways is it possible to
   classify style?
3. What does Ferguson consider the central aspect of style? What are the
   primary characteristics of a good style?
4. Explain the author's idea that a good style should be "peculiar." Do you
   agree? Evaluate Ferguson's style in the light of his own comments on style.

PLATO

•

ON POETRY AND POETS

Can you tell me what imitation is? for I really do not know.

A likely thing, then, that I should know.

Why not? for the duller eye may often see a thing sooner than the
keener.

Very true, he said; but in your presence, even if I had any faint notion, I could not muster courage to utter it. Will you inquire yourself?

Well then, shall we begin the inquiry in our usual manner: Whenever

---

From *The Republic,* c. 355 B.C.

a number of individuals have a common name we assume them to have also a corresponding idea or form:—do you understand me?

I do.

Let us take any common instance; there are beds and tables in the world—plenty of them, are there not?

Yes.

But there are only two ideas or forms of them—one the idea of a bed, the other of a table.

True.

And the maker of either of them makes a bed or he makes a table for our use, in accordance with the idea—that is our way of speaking in this and similar instances—but no artificer makes the ideas themselves: how could he?

Impossible.

And there is another artist,—I should like to know what you would say of him.

Who is he?

One who is the maker of all the works of all other workmen.

What an extraordinary man!

Wait a little, and there will be more reason for your saying so. For this is he who is able to make not only vessels of every kind, but plants and animals, himself and all other things—the earth and heaven, and the things which are in heaven or under the earth; he makes the gods also.

He must be a wizard and no mistake.

Oh! you are incredulous, are you? Do you mean that there is no such maker or creator, or that in one sense there might be a maker of all these things but in another not? Do you see that there is a way in which you could make them all yourself?

What way?

An easy way enough; or rather, there are many ways in which the feat might be quickly and easily accomplished, none quicker than that of turning a mirror round and round—you would soon enough make the sun and the heavens, and the earth and yourself, and other animals and plants, and all the other things of which we were just now speaking, in the mirror.

Yes, he said; but they would be appearances only.

Very good, I said, you are coming to the point now. And the painter too is, as I conceive, just such another—a creator of appearances, is he not?

Of course.

But then I suppose you will say that what he creates is untrue. And yet there is a sense in which the painter also creates a bed?

Yes, he said, but not a real bed.

And what of the maker of the bed? were you not saying that he too makes, not the idea which, according to our view, is the essence of the bed, but only a particular bed?

Yes, I did.

Then if he does not make that which exists he can not make true existence, but only some semblance of existence; and if any one were to say that the work of the maker of the bed, or of any other workman, has real existence, he could hardly be supposed to be speaking the truth.

At any rate, he replied, philosophers would say that he was not speaking the truth.

No wonder, then, that his work too is an indistinct expression of truth.

No wonder.

Suppose now that by the light of the examples just offered we inquire who this imitator is?

If you please.

Well then, here are three beds: one existing in nature, which is made by God, as I think that we may say—for no one else can be the maker?

No.

There is another which is the work of the carpenter?

Yes.

And the work of the painter is a third?

Yes.

Beds, then, are of three kinds and there are three artists who superintend them: God, the maker of the bed, and the painter?

Yes, there are three of them.

God, whether from choice or from necessity, made one bed in nature and one only; two or more such ideal beds neither ever have been nor ever will be made by God.

Why is that?

Because even if He had made but two, a third would still appear behind them which both of them would have for their idea, and that would be the ideal bed and not the two others.

Very true, he said.

God knew this, and He desired to be the real maker of a real bed, not a particular maker of a particular bed, and therefore He created a bed which is essentially and by nature one only.

So we believe.

Shall we, then, speak of Him as the natural author or maker of the bed?

Yes, he replied; inasmuch as by the natural process of creation He is the author of this and of all other things.

And what shall we say of the carpenter—is not he also the maker of the bed?

Yes.

But would you call the painter a creator and maker?

Certainly not.

Yet if he is not the maker, what is he in relation to the bed?

I think, he said, that we may fairly designate him as the imitator of that which the others make.

Good, I said; then you call him who is third in the descent from nature an imitator?

Certainly, he said.

And the tragic poet is an imitator, and therefore, like all other imitators, he is thrice removed from the king and from the truth?

That appears to be so.

Then about the imitator we are agreed. And what about the painter? —I would like to know whether he may be thought to imitate that which originally exists in nature, or only the creations of artists?

The latter.

As they are or as they appear? you have still to determine this.

What do you mean?

I mean, that you may look at a bed from different points of view, obliquely or directly or from any other point of view, and the bed will appear different, but there is no difference in reality. And the same of all things.

Yes, he said, the difference is only apparent.

Now let me ask you another question: Which is the art of painting designed to be—an imitation of things as they are, or as they appear—of appearance or of reality?

Of appearance.

Then the imitator, I said, is a long way off the truth, and can do all things because he lightly touches on a small part of them, and that part an image. For example: A painter will paint a cobbler, carpenter, or any other artist, though he knows nothing of their arts; and, if he is a good artist, he may deceive children or simple persons, when he shows them his picture of a carpenter from a distance, and they will fancy that they are looking at a real carpenter.

Certainly.

And whenever any one informs us that he has found a man who knows all the arts, and all things else that anybody knows, and every single thing with a higher degree of accuracy than any other man—whoever tells us this, I think that we can only imagine him to be a simple creature who is likely to have been deceived by some wizard or actor whom he met, and whom he thought all-knowing, because he himself was unable to analyze the nature of knowledge and ignorance and imitation.

Most true.

And so, when we hear persons saying that the tragedians, and Homer, who is at their head, know all the arts and all things human, virtue as well as vice, and divine things too, for that the good poet can not compose well unless he knows his subject, and that he who has not this knowledge can never be a poet, we ought to consider whether here also there may not be a similar illusion. Perhaps they may have come across imitators and been deceived by them; they may not have remembered when they saw their works that these were but imitations thrice removed from the truth, and could easily be made without any knowledge of the truth, because they are appearances only and not realities? Or, after all, they may be in the right, and poets do really know the things about which they seem to the many to speak so well?

The question, he said, should by all means be considered.

Now do you suppose that if a person were able to make the original as well as the image, he would seriously devote himself to the image-making branch? Would he allow imitation to be the ruling principle of his life, as if he had nothing higher in him?

I should say not.

The real artist, who knew what he was imitating, would be interested in realities and not in imitations; and would desire to leave as memorials of himself works many and fair; and, instead of being the author of encomiums, he would prefer to be the theme of them.

Yes, he said, that would be to him a source of much greater honor and profit.

We may state the question thus:—Imitation imitates the actions of men, whether voluntary or involuntary, on which, as they imagine, a good or bad result has ensued, and they rejoice or sorrow accordingly. Is there anything more?

No, there is nothing else.

But in all this variety of circumstances is the man at unity with himself—or rather, as in the instance of sight there was confusion and opposition in his opinions about the same things, so here also is there not strife and inconsistency in his life? Though I need hardly raise the question again, for I remember that all this has been already admitted; and the soul has been acknowledged by us to be full of these and ten thousand similar oppositions occurring at the same moment?

And we were right, he said.

Yes, I said, thus far we were right; but there was an omission which must now be supplied.

What was the omission?

Were we not saying that a good man, who has the misfortune to lose his son or anything else which is most dear to him, will bear the loss with more equanimity than another?

Yes.

But will he have no sorrow, or shall we say that although he can not help sorrowing, he will moderate his sorrow?

The latter, he said, is the truer statement.

Tell me: will he be more likely to struggle and hold out against his sorrow when he is seen by his equals, or when he is alone?

It will make a great difference whether he is seen or not.

When he is by himself he will not mind saying or doing many things which he would be ashamed of any one hearing or seeing him do?

True.

There is a principle of law and reason in him which bids him resist, as well as a feeling of his misfortune which is forcing him to indulge his sorrow?

True.

But when a man is drawn in two opposite directions, to and from the same object, this, as we affirm, necessarily implies two distinct principles in him?

Certainly.

One of them is ready to follow the guidance of the law?

How do you mean?

The law would say that to be patient under suffering is best, and that we should not give way to impatience, as there is no knowing whether such things are good or evil; and nothing is gained by impatience; also, because no human thing is of serious importance, and grief stands in the way of that which at the moment is most required.

What is most required? he asked.

That we should take counsel about what has happened, and when the dice have been thrown order our affairs in the way which reason deems best; not, like children who have had a fall, keeping hold of the part struck and wasting time in setting up a howl, but always accustoming the soul forthwith to apply a remedy, raising up that which is sickly and fallen, banishing the cry of sorrow by the healing art.

Yes, he said, that is the true way of meeting the attacks of fortune.

Yes, I said; and the higher principle is ready to follow this suggestion of reason?

Clearly.

And the other principle, which inclines us to recollection of our troubles and to lamentation, and can never have enough of them, we may call irrational, useless, and cowardly?

Indeed, we may.

And does not the latter—I mean the rebellious principle—furnish a great variety of materials for imitation? Whereas the wise and calm temperament, being always nearly equable, is not easy to imitate or to appreciate when imitated, especially at a public festival when a promiscuous crowd is assembled in a theatre. For the feeling represented is one to which they are strangers.

Certainly.

Then the imitative poet who aims at being popular is not by nature made, nor is his art intended, to please or to affect the rational principle in the soul; but he will prefer the passionate and fitful temper, which is easily imitated?

Clearly.

And now we may fairly take him and place him by the side of the painter, for he is like him in two ways: first, inasmuch as his creations have an inferior degree of truth—in this, I say, he is like him; and he is also like him in being concerned with an inferior part of the soul; and therefore we shall be right in refusing to admit him into a well-ordered State, because he awakens and nourishes and strengthens the feelings and impairs the reason. As in a city when the evil are permitted to have authority and the good are put out of the way, so in the soul of man, as we maintain, the imitative poet implants an evil constitution, for he indulges the irrational nature which has no discernment of greater and less, but thinks the same thing at one time great and at another small—he is a manufacturer of images and is very far removed from the truth.

Exactly.

But we have not yet brought forward the heaviest count in our accusation:—the power which poetry has of harming even the good (and there are very few who are not harmed), is surely an awful thing?

Yes, certainly, if the effect is what you say.

Hear and judge: The best of us, as I conceive, when we listen to a passage of Homer, or one of the tragedians, in which he represents some pitiful hero who is drawling out his sorrows in a long oration, or weeping, and smiting his breast—the best of us, you know, delight in giving way to sympathy, and are in raptures at the excellence of the poet who stirs our feelings most.

Yes, of course I know.

But when any sorrow of our own happens to us, then you may

observe that we pride ourselves on the opposite quality—we would fain be quiet and patient; this is the manly part, and the other which delighted us in the recitation is now deemed to be the part of a woman.

Very true, he said.

Now can we be right in praising and admiring another who is doing that which any one of us would abominate and be ashamed of in his own person?

No, he said, that is certainly not reasonable.

Nay, I said, quite reasonable from one point of view.

What point of view?

If you consider, I said, that when in misfortune we feel a natural hunger and desire to relieve our sorrow by weeping and lamentation, and that this feeling which is kept under control in our own calamities is satisfied and delighted by the poets;—the better nature in each of us, not having been sufficiently trained by reason or habit, allows the sympathetic element to break loose because the sorrow is another's; and the spectator fancies that there can be no disgrace to himself in praising and pitying any one who comes telling him what a good man he is, and making a fuss about his troubles; he thinks that the pleasure is a gain, and why should he be supercilious and lose this and the poem too? Few persons ever reflect, as I should imagine, that from the evil of other men something of evil is communicated to themselves. And so the feeling of sorrow which has gathered strength at the sight of the misfortunes of others is with difficulty repressed in our own.

How very true!

And does not the same hold also of the ridiculous? There are jests which you would be ashamed to make yourself, and yet on the comic stage, or indeed in private, when you hear them, you are greatly amused by them, and are not at all disgusted at their unseemliness;—the case of pity is repeated;—there is a principle in human nature which is disposed to raise a laugh, and this which you once restrained by reason, because you were afraid of being thought a buffoon, is now let out again; and having stimulated the risible faculty at the theatre, you are betrayed unconsciously to yourself into playing the comic poet at home.

Quite true, he said.

And the same may be said of lust and anger and all the other affections, of desire and pain and pleasure, which are held to be inseparable from every action—in all of them poetry feeds and waters the passions instead of drying them up; she lets them rule, although they ought to be controlled, if mankind are ever to increase in happiness and virtue.

I can not deny it.

• Questions for Study

1. What is the relation to an object (such as a bed) of God, the maker of the bed, and the artist who paints it? Does this relation explain satisfactorily why the artist who paints the bed is, in Plato's opinion, the inferior of the three? Discuss your answer.
2. This selection, translated from the Greek, obviously posed problems to its translator, Jowett. What, especially with regard to diction, do you think were some of these problems?
3. This selection provides us with an example of the Socratic dialogue—a specific method of teaching what Socrates considered ultimate truth. Using the selection as your guide, describe the method. Compare and contrast Plato's use of the dialogue with Becker's use in "The Marxian Philosophy of History."

ARISTOTLE

•

THE ART OF FICTION

_____

• Chapter 1

Let us talk of the art of poetry as a whole, and its different species with the particular force of each of them; how the fables must be put together if the poetry is to be well formed; also what are its elements and their different qualities; and all other matters pertaining to the subject.

To begin in the proper order, at the beginning. The making of epics and of tragedies, and also comedy, and the art of the dithyramb, and most flute and lyre art, all have this in common, that they are imitations.

From _Aristotle: On the Art of Fiction,_ translated by L. J. Potts, New York: Cambridge University Press, 1953. Reprinted by permission of the Cambridge University Press.

But they differ from one another in three respects: the different kinds of medium in which they imitate, the different objects they imitate, and the different manner in which they imitate (when it does differ).

Just as some people imitate many things in color and outline, depicting them either by a deliberate technique or by trial and error, and others imitate by the voice, so the arts I have mentioned all do their imitating in one or more of the following media—rhythm, language, and music. The arts of the flute and lyre use only music and rhythm, and so does any other art that has a similar force, for example the art of the pipes. Ballet imitates by sheer rhythm, without music; for dancers too imitate characters and experiences and doings by the rhythm of their postures. Epic poetry: by language alone: prose or verse: verse either in a mixture of meters, or using only one kind (which is what it happens to have done up to the present).

(N.B. We have no term to denote the class that includes the farces of Sophron and Xenarchus, and Socratic dialogues; nor should we have one even if the imitating were done in iambic trimeters or elegiacs or any other meter. People append the term "poetry" to the meter, distinguishing for example between "elegiac poets" and "epic poets." They class them, not as poets in virtue of the act of imitating, but according to the meter used; even if some one produces a work on medicine or music in verse form, they are in the habit of calling him a poet. But Homer and Empedocles have nothing in common except their meter; and therefore, while it is correct to call the former a poet, the latter should be called a scientist rather than a poet. Again, even if some one did his imitating in a mixture of all the meters, as Chaerēmon actually did in his *Centaur*— a rhapsody in a mixture of all the meters—he would have to be classed simply as a poet. That is the way in which we ought to distinguish between writers.)

Now there are some kinds of imitation that use all the traditional media, such as rhythm, melody, and verse: dithyrambic and nomic poetry and tragedy and comedy do so. But they differ from one another in that the first two use all these media together, while the second two use them successively. So much for the differences between the arts depending on the media in which they do their imitating.

• Chapter 2

When the imitators imitate the doings of people, the people in the imitation must be either high or low; the characters almost always follow this line exclusively, for all men differ in character according to their degree of goodness or badness. They must therefore be either above our norm, or below it, or normal; as, in painting, Polygnōtus depicted superior, Pauson inferior, and Dionysius normal, types. It is clear that each variant of imitation that I have mentioned will have these differences, and as the object imitated varies in this way so the works will differ. Even in the ballet, and in flute and lyre music, these dissimilarities can occur; and in the art that uses prose, or verse without music, as Homer depicted superior types, Cleophon normal types, and Hēgēmon of Thasos (the first writer of parodies) and Nichochăres (the author of the *Deiliad*) inferior types; so also in the dithyramb and the nome imitations may vary as the Cyclopses of Timothĕŭs and Philoxĕnus varied. This is the difference that marks tragedy out from comedy; comedy is inclined to imitate persons below the level of our world, tragedy persons above it.

· Chapter 3

Again, a third difference between these arts is the manner in which each of these objects can be imitated. For given the same medium and the same object, one can imitate partly by narration and partly by dramatic dialogue (as Homer does); or one can speak invariably in one's own person; or one can use actors to imitate the whole thing as though they were living it themselves.

The imitation, then, differs in these three respects, as we said at the beginning: in medium, in object, and in manner. Thus Sophocles would be in one respect in the same class of imitators as Homer, for both imitate high people; but in another respect in the same class as Aristophanes, for they both imitate by means of actors in a performance.

(Some say this is the origin of the term *drama*, from the verb DRĀN (to perform). Hence the Dorians claim both tragedy and comedy. (The Megarians lay claim to comedy: those in the mother country on the assumption that it belonged to the date when their city became a democracy, and the Megarian colonists in Sicily because the poet Epicharmus, who was a countryman of theirs, was much earlier than Chionĭdes and Magnes. Some of the Dorians in the Peloponnese also lay claim to tragedy.) Their argument is etymological. They say their name for a satellite village is KŌMĒ, whereas the Athenian name is DEMOS; for they derive the word comedy not from KOMOS (revel), but from KOME, because the comedians left the city, where they were looked down on, and toured the villages. And their word for "act" is DRAN, whereas the Athenian word is PRATTEĪN.)

So much for the different subdivisions of imitation, and what they amount to.

• *Chapter 4*

There seem to be two causes that gave rise to poetry in general, and they are natural. The impulse to imitate is inherent in man from his childhood; he is distinguished among the animals by being the most imitative of them, and he takes the first steps of his education by imitating. Every one's enjoyment of imitation is also inborn. What happens with works of art demonstrates this: though a thing itself is disagreeable to look at, we enjoy contemplating the most accurate representations of it—for instance, figures of the most despicable animals, or of human corpses. The reason for this lies in another fact: learning is a great pleasure, not only to philosophers but likewise to every one else, however limited his gift for it may be. He enjoys looking at these representations, because in the act of studying them he is learning—identifying the object by an inference (for instance, recognizing who is the original of a portrait); since, if he happens not to have already seen the object depicted, it will not be the imitation as such that is giving him pleasure, but the finish of the workmanship, or the coloring, or some such other cause.

And just as imitation is natural to us, so also are music and rhythm (meters, clearly, are constituent parts of rhythms). Thus, from spontaneous beginnings, mankind developed poetry by a series of mostly minute changes out of these improvisations.

But a temperamental difference of character caused poetry to break sharply into two. The more serious writers imitated illustrious doings, involving illustrious persons; the lighter-minded imitated those of low people, at first in the form of flytings, while the others were writing hymns and encomiums. We cannot tell of any such light poem by any one before Homer, though it is likely that there were many who wrote them, but beginning with Homer we can: his *Margitēs*, for instance, and similar works. (It was here that the iambic meter came into use, in virtue of its appropriateness for the purpose; that is how the meter got its present name, because it was the name of the lampoons in which they attacked each other. So it came about that some of the early poets wrote in heroic verse and others in iambics.) And just as Homer was the great exemplar of high poetry, being the only poet who not only wrote nobly but also made dramatic imitations, so too he was the first to adumbrate the outlines of comedy by making his drama not vituperative but ludicrous; in fact the relationship between the *Margites* and our comedies is analogous to that between the *Iliad* and *Odyssey* and our tragedies. But as soon as tragedy and comedy had become available, those whose natural temperaments impelled them towards one or the other kind of poetry wrote comedies instead of lampoons, and tragedies instead of epics, because comedy and tragedy were grander and esteemed more highly. To examine whether or no the organic evolution of tragedy is now complete, and to settle that question both absolutely and in relation to the stage, does not belong to our present discussion.

Going back to the improvisations in which it at first consisted (and so did comedy—tragedy began with the leaders of the dithyramb, and comedy with the leaders of the phallic performances which still survive as customary practices in many of our cities), it grew up little by little as its character became clear and its form was developed. So after many transformations, tragedy settled down when its nature was formed. Aeschylus first increased the number of actors from one to two, reduced the chorus part, and put the chief weight on the speeches; Sophocles introduced three actors and scene-painting. As to its amplitude: it acquired its serious character at a late stage, when it outgrew slight fables and grotesque language in the process of transformation from satyr-drama; and at the same time the meter changed from trochaic tetrameters to iambics. At first they used the tetrameter, because their poetry was satyr-poetry and more akin to the dance; but when it began to be spoken, the very nature of the thing found its right meter, for the iambic is the best adapted of all meters to speech. For a demonstration of this: we use iambics most often in conversation with one another, but hexameters seldom, and by way of a departure from normal intonation.—(Also, division of the play into acts.) Lastly, we may pass over all the superficial graces of tragedy; for it would no doubt be a long business to go through their whole history in detail.

• *Chapter 5*

Comedy is, as I have said, an imitation of lower types; though it does not include the full range of badness, nevertheless to be ridiculous is a kind of deformity. The causes of laughter are errors and disgraces not accompanied by pain or injury; the comic mask, for instance, is deformed and distorted, but not painfully so. We know something of the stages through which tragedy passed and the men to whom they were due, but there are no early records of comedy, because it was not highly valued. It was a long time before comic dramas were licensed by the magistrate; the earlier comedies were produced by amateurs. Comedy had already acquired certain outlines by the time of the earliest comic poets whose names are known. Who added masks or prologues or extra actors, and other such matters, we have no means of knowing. The fable-structure first came from Sicily (Epicharmus and Phormis); at Athens, Crătes was the first to drop the lampoon form and make unified stories, that is to say fables.

Epic poetry coincides with tragedy in so far as it is an imitation, in metrical speech, of high people; but they differ in that the epic has the same meter throughout and is in narrative form. They also differ in length, because tragedy tends as far as possible to keep within a single day and night or thereabouts, whereas the epic has no time-limit; though at first tragic poets followed the epic in this respect. As for their elements, some are the same and some are peculiar to tragedy. Accordingly, any one who can tell a tragedy of high value from a poor one can do the same for an epic; for tragedy has everything that the epic has, but the epic has not everything that there is in tragedy.

• *Chapter 6*

Of the art that imitates in hexameters, and of comedy, we will speak later; let us now discuss tragedy, having first picked up from what has been said the definition of its essence that has so far emerged. Tragedy, then, is an imitation of an action of high importance, complete and of some amplitude; in language enhanced by distinct and varying beauties; acted not narrated; by means of pity and fear effecting its purgation of these emotions. By the beauties enhancing the language I mean rhythm and melody; by "distinct and varying" I mean that some are produced by meter alone, and others at another time by melody.

Now since the imitating is done by actors, it would follow of necessity that one element in a tragedy must be the *Mise en scène*. Others are Melody and Language, for these are the media in which the imitating is done. By Language I mean the component parts of the verse, whereas Melody has an entirely sensuous effect. Again, since the object imitated is an action, and doings are done by persons, whose individuality will be determined by their Character and their Thought (for these are the factors we have in mind when we define the quality of their doings), it follows that there are two natural causes of these doings, Thought and Character; and these causes determine the good or ill fortune of every one. But the Fable is the imitation of the action; and by the Fable I mean the whole structure of the incidents. By Character I mean the factor that enables us to define the particular quality of the people involved in the doings; and Thought is shown in everything they say when they are demonstrating a fact or disclosing an opinion. There are therefore necessarily six elements in every tragedy, which give it its quality; and they are the Fable, Character, Language, Thought, the *Mise en scène*, and Melody. Two of these are the media in which the imitating is done, one is the manner of imitation, and three are its objects; there is no other element besides these. Numerous poets have turned these essential components to account; all of them are always present—the *Mise en scène*, Character, the Fable, Language, Melody, and Thought.

The chief of these is the plotting of the incidents; for tragedy is an imitation not of men but of doings, life, happiness; unhappiness is located in doings, and our end is a certain kind of doing, not a personal quality; it is their characters that give men their quality, but their doings that make them happy or the opposite. So it is not the purpose of the actors to imitate character, but they include character as a factor in the doings. Thus it is the incidents (that is to say the Fable) that are the end for which tragedy exists; and the end is more important than anything else. Also, without an action there could not be a tragedy, but without Character there could. (In fact, the tragedies of most of the moderns are non-moral, and there are many non-moral poets of all periods; this also applies to the paintings of Zeuxis, if he is compared with Polygnōtus, for whereas Polygnōtus is a good protrayer of character the painting of Zeuxis leaves it out.) Again, if any one strings together moral speeches with the language and thought well worked out, he will be doing what is the business of tragedy; but it will be done much better by a tragedy that handles these elements more weakly, but has a fable with the incidents connected by a plot. Further, the chief means by which tragedy moves us, Irony of events and Disclosure, are elements in the Fable. A pointer in the same direction is that beginners in the art of poetry are able to get the language and characterization right before they can plot their incidents, and so were almost all the earliest poets.

So the source and as it were soul of tragedy is the Fable; and Character comes next. For, to instance a parallel from the art of painting, the most beautiful colors splashed on anyhow would not be as pleasing as a recognizable picture in black and white. Tragedy is an imitation of an action, and it is chiefly for this reason that it imitates the persons involved.

Third comes Thought: that is, the ability to say what circumstances allow and what is appropriate to them. It is the part played by social morality and rhetoric in making the dialogue: the old poets made their characters talk like men of the world, whereas our contemporaries make them talk like public speakers. Character is what shows a man's disposition—the kind of things he chooses or rejects when his choice is not obvious. Accordingly those speeches where the speaker shows no preferences or aversions whatever are non-moral. Thought, on the other hand, is shown in demonstrating a matter of fact or disclosing a significant opinion.

Fourth comes the Language [of the speeches]. By Language I mean, as has already been said, the expressive use of words. It has the same force in verse as in prose.

Of the remaining elements, Melody is the chief of the enhancing beauties. The *Mise en scène* can excite emotion, but it is the crudest element and least akin to the art of poetry; for the force of tragedy exists even without stage and actors; besides, the fitting out of a *Mise en scène* belongs more to the wardrobe-master's art than to the poet's.

• Chapter 7

So much for analysis. Now let us discuss in what sort of way the incidents should be plotted, since that is the first and chief consideration in tragedy. Our data are that tragedy is an imitation of a whole and complete action of some amplitude (a thing can be whole and yet quite lacking in amplitude). Now a whole is that which has a beginning, a middle, and an end. A beginning is that which does not itself necessarily follow anything else, but which leads naturally to another event or development; an end is the opposite, that which itself naturally (either of necessity or most commonly) follows something else, but nothing else comes after it; and a middle is that which itself follows something else and is followed by another thing. So, well plotted fables must not begin or end casually, but must follow the pattern here described.

But, besides this, a picture, or any other composite object, if it is to be beautiful, must not only have its parts properly arranged, but be of an appropriate size; for beauty depends on size and structure. Accordingly, a minute picture cannot be beautiful (for when our vision has almost lost its sense of time it becomes confused); nor can an immense one (for we cannot take it all in together, and so our vision loses its unity and wholeness)—imagine a picture a thousand miles long! So, just as there is a proper size for bodies and pictures (a size that can be kept in view), there is also a proper amplitude for fables (what can be kept well in one's mind). The length of the performance on the stage has nothing to do with art; if a hundred tragedies had to be produced, the length of the production would be settled by the clock, as the story goes that another kind of performance once was. But as to amplitude, the invariable rule dictated by the nature of the action is the fuller the more beautiful so long as the outline remains clear; and for a simple rule of size, the number of happenings that will make a chain of probability (or necessity) to change a given situation from misfortune to good fortune or from good fortune to misfortune is the minimum.

• Chapter 8

Unity in a fable does not mean, as some think, that it has one man for its subject. To any one man many things happen—an infinite number—and some of them do not make any sort of unity; and in the same way one man has many doings which cannot be made into a unit of action. It seems, therefore, that all the poets who have composed *Heracleïds*, *Theseïds*, and suchlike, made a mistake; people think that because Hēracles was one man it follows that his fable has unity. Homer, as always, is an exception; he seems to have seen this admirably well, either by art or by nature. In writing his *Odyssey* he did not include everything that happened to Odysseus (for instance, his wound on Parnassus, or his pretense of madness at the mobilization, since there was no necessity or probability that either of these events should have led to the other); but he confined the plot of the *Odyssey* to an action that has the kind of unity I mean, and he did the same with the *Iliad*. Accordingly, just as in the other imitative arts the object of each imitation is a unit, so, since the fable is an imitation of an action, that action must be a complete unit, and the events of which it is made up must be so plotted that if any of these elements is moved or removed the whole is altered and upset. For when a thing can be included or not included without making any noticeable difference, that thing is no part of the whole.

• Questions for Study

1. Aristotle's *Poetics*, from which this selection was taken, may be seen as a justification for the existence of poetry and art in the light of Plato's distrust of the poet and his function. In what ways does Aristotle find the arts useful?
2. Of what value is Aristotle's etymological digression on the word "drama"? Consult sources for the etymology of other key words in this selection ("tragedy," "comedy," "epic," "imitation"). What, according to Aristotle, are the three respects in which the arts differ concerning imitation?
3. How does the author distinguish between tragedy and comedy?
4. Examine carefully his definition of tragedy and apply it to some serious modern play. Write a theme in which you apply specific points in the definition to the play.
5. Why is "selection" in the *Odyssey*, or in any unified work of art, important? Can Aristotle's ideas of unity be applied, for example, to the writing of essays?

JOSEPH WOOD KRUTCH

•

THE TRAGIC FALLACY

I

All works of art which deserve their name have a happy end. This is indeed the thing which constitutes them art and through which they perform their function. Whatever the character of the events, fortunate or unfortunate, which they recount, they so mold or arrange or interpret them that we accept gladly the conclusion which they reach and would not have it otherwise. They may conduct us into the realm of pure fancy where wish and fact are identical and the world is remade exactly after the fashion of the heart's desire or they may yield some greater or less allegiance to fact; but they must always reconcile us in one way or another to the representation which they make and the distinctions between the genres are simply the distinctions between the means by which this reconciliation is effected.

Comedy laughs the minor mishaps of its characters away; drama solves all the difficulties which it allows to arise; and melodrama, separating good from evil by simple lines, distributes its rewards and punishments in accordance with the principles of a naive justice which satisfies the simple souls of its audience, which are neither philosophical enough to question its primitive ethics nor critical enough to object to the way in which its neat events violate the laws of probability. Tragedy, the greatest and the most difficult of the arts, can adopt none of these methods; and yet it must reach its own happy end in its own way. Though its conclusion must be, by its premise, outwardly calamitous, though it must speak to those who know that the good man is cut off and that the fairest things are the first to perish, yet it must leave them, as *Othello* does, content that this is so. We must be and we are glad that Juliet dies and glad that Lear is turned out into the storm.

Milton set out, he said, to justify the ways of God to man, and his phrase, if it be interpreted broadly enough, may be taken as describing the function of all art, which must, in some way or other, make the life which it seems to represent satisfactory to those who see its reflection in the magic mirror, and it must gratify or at least reconcile the desires of the beholder, not necessarily, as the naiver exponents of Freudian psychology maintain, by gratifying individual and often eccentric wishes, but at least by satisfying the universally human desire to find in the world some justice, some meaning, or, at the very least, some recognizable order. Hence it is that every real tragedy, however tremendous it may be, is an affirmation of faith in life, a declaration that even if God is not in his Heaven, then at least Man is in his world.

We accept gladly the outward defeats which it describes for the sake of the inward victories which it reveals. Juliet died, but not before she had shown how great and resplendent a thing love could be; Othello plunged the dagger into his own breast, but not before he had revealed that greatness of soul which makes his death seem unimportant. Had he died in the instant when he struck the blow, had he perished still believing that the world was as completely black as he saw it before the innocence of Desdemona was revealed to him, then, for him at least, the world would have been merely damnable, but Shakespeare kept him alive long enough to allow him to learn his error and hence to die, not in despair, but in the full acceptance of the tragic reconciliation to life. Perhaps it would be pleasanter if men could believe what the child is taught—that the good are happy and that things turn out as they should—but it is far more important to be able to believe, as Shakespeare did, that however much things in the outward world may go awry, man has, nevertheless, splendors of his own and that, in a word, Love and Honor and Glory are not words but realities.

Thus for the great ages tragedy is not an expression of despair but the means by which they saved themselves from it. It is a profession of faith, and a sort of religion; a way of looking at life by virtue of which it is robbed of its pain. The sturdy soul of the tragic author seizes upon suffering and uses it only as a means by which joy may be wrung out of existence, but it is not to be forgotten that he is enabled to do so only because of his belief in the greatness of human nature and because, though he has lost the child's faith in life, he has not lost his far more important faith in human nature. A tragic writer does not have to believe in God, but he must believe in man.

And if, then, the Tragic Spirit is in reality the product of a religious faith in which, sometimes at least, faith in the greatness of God is replaced by faith in the greatness of man, it serves, of course, to perform the function of religion, to make life tolerable for those who participate in its beneficent illusion. It purges the souls of those who might otherwise despair and it makes endurable the realization that the events of the outward world do not correspond with the desires of the heart, and thus, in its own particular way, it does what all religions do, for it gives a rationality, a meaning, and a justification to the universe. But if it has the strength it has also the weakness of all faiths, since it may—nay, it must —be ultimately lost as reality, encroaching further and further into the realm of imagination, leaves less and less room in which that imagination can build its refuge.

II

It is, indeed, only at a certain stage in the development of the realistic intelligence of a people that the tragic faith can exist. A naiver people may have, as the ancient men of the north had, a body of legends which are essentially tragic, or it may have only (and need only) its happy and childlike mythology which arrives inevitably at its happy end, and where the only ones who suffer "deserve" to do so and in which, therefore, life is represented as directly and easily acceptable. A too sophisticated society on the other hand—one which, like ours, has outgrown not merely the simple optimism of the child but also that vigorous, one might almost say adolescent, faith in the nobility of man which marks a Sophocles or a Shakespeare, has neither fairy tales to assure it that all is always right in the end nor tragedies to make it believe that it rises superior in soul to the outward calamities which befall it.

Distrusting its thought, despising its passions, realizing its impotent unimportance in the universe, it can tell itself no stories except those which make it still more acutely aware of its trivial miseries. When its heroes (sad misnomer for the pitiful creatures who people contemporary fiction) are struck down it is not, like Oedipus, by the gods that they are struck but only, like Oswald Alving, by syphilis, for they know that the gods, even if they existed, would not trouble with them, and they cannot attribute to themselves in art an importance in which they do not believe. Their so-called tragedies do not and cannot end with one of those splendid calamities which in Shakespeare seem to reverberate through the universe, because they cannot believe that the universe trembles when their love is, like Romeo's, cut off or when the place where they (small as they are) have gathered up their trivial treasure is, like Othello's sanctuary, defiled. Instead, mean misery piles on mean misery, petty misfortune follows petty misfortune, and despair becomes intolerable because it is no longer even significant or important.

Ibsen once made one of his characters say that he did not read much because he found reading "irrelevant," and the adjective was brilliantly chosen because it held implications even beyond those of which Ibsen was consciously aware. What is it that made the classics irrelevant to him and to us? It is not just exactly those to him impossible premises which make tragedy what it is, those assumptions that the soul of man is great, that the universe (together with whatever gods may be) concerns itself with him and that he is, in a word, noble? Ibsen turned to village politics for exactly the same reason that his contemporaries and his successors have, each in his own way, sought out some aspect of the common man and his common life—because, that is to say, here was at least something small enough for him to be able to believe.

Bearing this fact in mind, let us compare a modern "tragedy" with one of the great works of a happy age, not in order to judge of their relative technical merits but in order to determine to what extent the former deserves its name by achieving a tragic solution capable of purging the soul or of reconciling the emotions to the life which it pictures. And in order to make the comparison as fruitful as possible let us choose *Hamlet* on the one hand and on the other a play like *Ghosts*, which was not only written by perhaps the most powerful as well as the most typical of modern writers but which is, in addition, the one of his works which seems most nearly to escape that triviality which cannot be entirely escaped by any one who feels, as all contemporary minds do, that man is relatively trivial.

In *Hamlet* a prince ("in understanding, how like a god!") has thrust upon him from the unseen world a duty to redress a wrong which concerns not merely him, his mother, and his uncle, but the moral order of the universe. Erasing all trivial fond records from his mind, abandoning at once both his studies and his romance because it has been his good fortune to be called upon to take part in an action of cosmic importance, he plunges (at first) not into action but into thought, weighing the claims which are made upon him and contemplating the grandiose complexities of the universe. And when the time comes at last for him to die he dies, not as a failure, but as a success. Not only has the universe regained the balance which had been upset by what *seemed* the monstrous crime of the guilty pair ("there is nothing either good nor ill but thinking makes it so"), but in the process by which that readjustment is made a mighty mind has been given the opportunity, first to contemplate the magnificent scheme of which it is a part, and then to demonstrate the greatness of its spirit by playing a rôle in the grand style which it called for. We do not need to despair in *such* a world if it has *such* creatures in it.

Turn now to *Ghosts*—look upon this picture and upon that. A young man has inherited syphilis from his father. Struck by a to him mysterious malady he returns to his northern village, learns the hopeless truth about himself, and persuades his mother to poison him. The incidents prove, perhaps, that pastors should not endeavor to keep a husband and wife together unless they know what they are doing. But what a world is this in which a great writer can deduce nothing more than that from his greatest work and how are we to be purged or reconciled when we see it acted? Not only is the failure utter, but it is trivial and meaningless as well.

Yet the journey from Elsinore to Skien is precisely the journey which the human spirit has made, exchanging in the process princes for invalids and gods for disease. We say, as Ibsen would say, that the problems of Oswald Alving are more "relevant" to our life than the problems of Hamlet, that the play in which he appears is more "real" than the other more glamorous one, but it is exactly because we find it so that we are condemned. We can believe in Oswald but we cannot believe in Hamlet, and a light has gone out in the universe. Shakespeare justifies the ways of God to man, but in Ibsen there is no such happy end and with him tragedy, so called, has become merely an expression of our despair at finding that such justification is no longer possible.

Modern critics have sometimes been puzzled to account for the fact that the concern of ancient tragedy is almost exclusively with kings and courts. They have been tempted to accuse even Aristotle of a certain naiveté in assuming (as he seems to assume) that the "nobility" of which he speaks as necessary to a tragedy implies a nobility of rank as well as of soul, and they have sometimes regretted that Shakespeare did not devote himself more than he did to the serious consideration of those common woes of the common man which subsequent writers have exploited with increasing pertinacity. Yet the tendency to lay the scene of a tragedy at the court of a king is not the result of any arbitrary convention but of the fact that the tragic writers believed easily in greatness just as we believe easily in meanness. To Shakespeare, robes and crowns and jewels are the garments most appropriate to man because they are the fitting outward manifestation of his inward majesty, but to us they seem absurd because the man who bears them has, in our estimation, so pitifully shrunk. We do not write about kings because we do not believe that any man is worthy to be one and we do not write about courts because hovels seem to us to be dwellings more appropriate to the creatures who inhabit them. Any modern attempt to dress characters in robes ends only by making us aware of a comic incongruity and any modern attempt to furnish them with a language resplendent like Shakespeare's ends only in bombast.

True tragedy capable of performing its function and of purging the soul by reconciling man to his woes can exist only by virtue of a certain pathetic fallacy far more inclusive than that to which the name is commonly given. The romantics, feeble descendants of the tragic writers to whom they are linked by their effort to see life and nature in grandiose terms, loved to imagine that the sea or the sky had a way of according itself with their moods, of storming when they stormed and smiling when they smiled. But the tragic spirit sustains itself by an assumption much more far-reaching and no more justified. Man as it sees him lives in a world which he may not dominate but which is always aware of him. Occupying the exact center of a universe which would have no meaning except for him and being so little below the angels that, if he believes in God, he has no hesitation in imagining Him formed as he is formed and crowned with a crown like that which he or one of his fellows wears, he assumes that each of his acts reverberates through the universe. His passions are important to him because he believes them important throughout all time and all space; the very fact that he can sin (no modern can) means that this universe is watching his acts; and though he may perish, a God leans out from infinity to strike him down. And it is exactly because an Ibsen cannot think of man in any such terms as these that his persons have so shrunk and that his "tragedy" has lost that power which real tragedy always has of making that infinitely ambitious creature called man content to accept his misery if only he can be made to feel great enough and important enough. An Oswald is not a Hamlet chiefly because he has lost that tie with the natural and supernatural world which the latter had. No ghost will leave the other world to warn or encourage him, there is no virtue and no vice which he can possibly have which can be really important, and when he dies neither his death nor the manner of it will be, outside the circle of two or three people as unnecessary as himself, any more important than that of a rat behind the arras.

Perhaps we may dub the illusion upon which the tragic spirit is nourished the Tragic, as opposed to the Pathetic, Fallacy, but fallacy though it is, upon its existence depends not merely the writing of tragedy but the existence of that religious feeling of which tragedy is an expression and by means of which a people aware of the dissonances of life manages nevertheless to hear them as harmony. Without it neither man nor his passions can seem great enough or important enough to justify the sufferings which they entail, and literature, expressing the mood of a people, begins to despair where once it had exulted. Like the belief in love and like most of the other mighty illusions by means of which human life has been given a value, the Tragic Fallacy depends ultimately upon the assumption which man so readily makes that something outside his own being, some "spirit not himself"—be it God, Nature, or that still vaguer thing called a Moral Order—joins him in the emphasis which he places upon this or that and confirms him in his feeling that his passions and his opinions are important. When his instinctive faith in that correspondence between the outer and the inner world fades, his grasp upon the faith that sustained him fades also, and Love or Tragedy or what not ceases to be the reality which it was because he is never strong enough in his own insignificant self to stand alone in a universe which snubs him with its indifference.

In both the modern and the ancient worlds tragedy was dead long before writers were aware of the fact. Seneca wrote his frigid melodramas under the impression that he was following in the footsteps of Sophocles, and Dryden probably thought that his *All for Love* was an improvement upon Shakespeare, but in time we awoke to the fact that no amount of rhetorical bombast could conceal the fact that grandeur was not to be counterfeited when the belief in its possibility was dead, and turning from the hero to the common man, we inaugurated the era of realism. For us no choice remains except that between mere rhetoric and the frank consideration of our fellow men, who may be the highest of the anthropoids but who are certainly too far below the angels to imagine either that these angels can concern themselves with them or that they can catch any glimpse of even the soles of angelic feet. We can no longer tell tales of the fall of noble men because we do not believe that noble men exist. The best that we can achieve is pathos and the most that we can do is to feel sorry for ourselves. Man has put off his royal robes and it is only in sceptered pomp that tragedy can come sweeping by.

• *Questions for Study*

1. Explain Krutch's statement that "all works of art which deserve their name have a happy end."
2. According to Krutch, how does the tragedy of the great ages differ from that of the modern age? How does the contrast which Krutch notes between *Hamlet* and *Ghosts* illustrate what he wishes to emphasize? If you are familiar with these plays, can you find reasons to disagree with his conclusions concerning them?
3. In your opinion, is the author arbitrarily defining the word "tragedy"? (You may wish to consider Aristotle's remarks in your answer.) Do modern dramas illustrate other ways of defining tragedy? Upon what does the significance of Krutch's use of the word "fallacy" depend?

WILLIAM WORDSWORTH

•

WHAT IS POETRY?

The principal object, then, proposed in these Poems was to choose incidents and situations from common life, and to relate or describe them,
throughout, as far as was possible in a selection of language really used
by men, and, at the same time, to throw over them a certain colouring of
imagination, whereby ordinary things should be presented to the mind
in an unusual aspect; and, further, and above all, to make these incidents
and situations interesting by tracing in them, truly though not ostenta-
tiously, the primary laws of our nature: chiefly, as far as regards the
manner in which we associate ideas in a state of excitement. Humble
and rustic life was generally chosen, because, in that condition, the
essential passions of the heart find a better soil in which they can attain
their maturity, are less under restraint, and speak a plainer and more
emphatic language; because in that condition of life our elementary
feelings coexist in a state of greater simplicity, and, consequently, may
be more accurately contemplated, and more forcibly communicated;
because the manners of rural life germinate from those elementary feelings, and, from the necessary character of rural occupations, are more
easily comprehended, and are more durable; and, lastly, because in that
condition the passions of men are incorporated with the beautiful and
permanent forms of nature. The language, too, of these men has been
adopted (purified indeed from what appear to be its real defects, from
all lasting and rational causes of dislike or disgust) because such men
hourly communicate with the best objects from which the best part of
language is originally derived; and because, from their rank in society
and the sameness and narrow circle of their intercourse, being less under
the influence of social vanity, they convey their feelings and notions in
simple and unelaborated expressions. Accordingly, such a language, aris-

---

From the Preface to the *Lyrical Ballads,* 1800.

ing out of repeated experience and regular feelings, is a more permanent, and a far more philosophical language, than that which is frequently substituted for it by Poets, who think that they are conferring honour upon themselves and their art, in proportion as they separate themselves from the sympathies of men, and indulge in arbitrary and capricious habits of expression, in order to furnish food for fickle tastes, and fickle appetites, of their own creation. . . .

Taking up the subject, then, upon general grounds, let me ask, what is meant by the word Poet? What is a Poet? To whom does he address himself? And what language is to be expected from him?—He is a man speaking to men: a man, it is true, endowed with more lively sensibility, more enthusiasm and tenderness, who has a greater knowledge of human nature, and a more comprehensive soul, than are supposed to be common among mankind; a man pleased with his own passions and volitions, and who rejoices more than other men in the spirit of life that is in him; delighting to contemplate similar volitions and passions as manifested in the goings-on of the Universe, and habitually impelled to create them where he does not find them. To these qualities he has added a disposition to be affected more than other men by absent things as if they were present; an ability of conjuring up in himself passions, which are indeed far from being the same as those produced by real events, yet (especially in those parts of the general sympathy which are pleasing and delightful) do more nearly resemble the passions produced by real events, than anything which, from the motions of their own minds merely, other men are accustomed to feel in themselves: whence, and from practice, he has acquired a greater readiness and power in expressing what he thinks and feels, and especially those thoughts and feelings which, by his own choice, or from the structure of his own mind, arise in him without immediate external excitement.

But whatever portion of this faculty we may suppose even the greatest Poet to possess, there cannot be a doubt that the language which it will suggest to him, must often, in liveliness and truth, fall short of that which is uttered by men in real life, under the actual pressure of those passions, certain shadows of which the Poet thus produces, or feels to be produced, in himself.

However exalted a notion we would wish to cherish of the character of a Poet, it is obvious, that while he describes and imitates passions, his employment is in some degree mechanical, compared with the freedom and power of real and substantial action and suffering. So that it will be the wish of the Poet to bring his feelings near to those of the persons whose feelings he describes, nay, for short spaces of time, perhaps, to let himself slip into an entire delusion, and even confound and identify his own feelings with theirs; modifying only the language which is thus suggested to him by a consideration that he describes for a particular purpose, that of giving pleasure. Here, then, he will apply the principle of selection which has been already insisted upon. He will depend upon this for removing what would otherwise be painful or disgusting in the passion; he will feel that there is no necessity to trick out or to elevate nature: and, the more industriously he applies this principle, the deeper will be his faith that no words, which *his* fancy or imagination can suggest, will be to be compared with those which are the emanation of reality and truth.

But it may be said by those who do not object to the general spirit of these remarks, that, as it is impossible for the Poet to produce upon all occasions language as exquisitely fitted for the passion as that which the real passion itself suggests, it is proper that he should consider himself as in the situation of a translator, who does not scruple to substitute excellencies of another kind for those which are unattainable by him; and endeavours occasionally to surpass his original, in order to make some amends for the general inferiority to which he feels that he must submit. But this would be to encourage idleness and unmanly despair. Further, it is the language of men who speak of what they do not understand; who talk of Poetry as of a matter of amusement and idle pleasure; who will converse with us as gravely about a *taste* for Poetry, as they express it, as if it were a thing as indifferent as a taste for rope-dancing, or Frontiniac or Sherry. Aristotle, I have been told, has said, that Poetry is the most philosophic of all writing: it is so: its object is truth, not individual and local, but general, and operative; not standing upon external testimony, but carried alive into the heart by passion; truth which is its own testimony, which gives competence and confidence to the tribunal to which it appeals, and receives them from the same tribunal. Poetry is the image of man and nature. The obstacles which stand in the way of the fidelity of the Biographer and Historian, and of their consequent utility, are incalculably greater than those which are to be encountered by the Poet who comprehends the dignity of his art. The Poet writes under one restriction only, namely, the necessity of giving immediate pleasure to a human Being possessed of that information which may be expected from him, not as a lawyer, a physician, a mariner, an astronomer, or a natural philosopher, but as a Man. Except this one restriction, there is no object standing between the Poet and the image of things; between this, and the Biographer and Historian, there are a thousand.

Nor let this necessity of producing immediate pleasure be considered as a degradation of the Poet's art. It is far otherwise. It is an acknowledgement of the beauty of the universe, an acknowledgement the more sincere, because not formal, but indirect; it is a task light and easy to him who looks at the world in the spirit of love: further, it is a homage paid to the native and naked dignity of man, to the grand elementary principle of pleasure, by which he knows, and feels, and lives, and moves. We have no sympathy but what is propagated by pleasure: I would not be misunderstood; but wherever we sympathize with pain, it will be found that the sympathy is produced and carried on by subtle combinations with pleasure. We have no knowledge, that is, no general principles drawn from the contemplation of particular facts, but what has been built up by pleasure, and exists in us by pleasure alone. The Man of science, the Chemist and Mathematician, whatever difficulties and disgusts they may have had to struggle with, know and feel this. However painful may be the objects with which the Anatomist's knowledge is connected, he feels that his knowledge is pleasure; and where he has no pleasure he has no knowledge. What then does the Poet? He considers man and the objects that surround him as acting and reacting upon each other, so as to produce an infinite complexity of pain and pleasure; he considers man in his own nature and in his ordinary life as contemplating this with a certain quantity of immediate knowledge, with certain convictions, intuitions, and deductions, which from habit acquire the quality of intuitions; he considers him as looking upon this complex scene of ideas and sensations, and finding everywhere objects that immediately excite in him sympathies which, from the necessities of his nature, are accompanied by an overbalance of enjoyment.

To this knowledge which all men carry about with them, and to these sympathies in which, without any other discipline than that of our daily life, we are fitted to take delight, the Poet principally directs his attention. He considers man and nature as essentially adapted to each other, and the mind of man as naturally the mirror of the fairest and most interesting properties of nature. And thus the Poet, prompted by his feeling of pleasure, which accompanies him through the whole course of his studies, converses with general nature, with affections akin to those, which, through labour and length of time, the Man of science has raised up in himself, by conversing with those particular parts of nature which are the objects of his studies. The knowledge both of the Poet and the Man of science is pleasure; but the knowledge of the one cleaves to us as a necessary part of our existence, our natural and unalienable inheritance; the other is a personal and individual acquisition, slow to come to us, and by no habitual and direct sympathy connecting us with our fellow-beings. The Man of science seeks truth as a remote and unknown benefactor; he cherishes and loves it in his solitude: the Poet singing a

song in which all human beings join with him, rejoices in the presence
of truth as our visible friend and hourly companion. Poetry is the breath
and finer spirit of all knowledge; it is the impassioned expression which
is in the countenance of all Science. Emphatically may it be said of the
Poet, as Shakespeare hath said of man, "that he looks before and after."
He is the rock of defence for human nature; an upholder and preserver,
carrying everywhere with him relationship and love. In spite of difference
of soil and climate, of language and manners, of laws and customs: in
spite of things silently gone out of mind, and things violently destroyed;
the Poet binds together by passion and knowledge the vast empire of
human society, as it is spread over the whole earth, and over all time.
The objects of the Poet's thoughts are everywhere; though the eyes and
senses of man are, it is true, his favourite guides, yet he will follow where-
soever he can find an atmosphere of sensation in which to move his
wings. Poetry is the first and last of all knowledge—it is as immortal as
the heart of man. If the labours of Men of science should ever create any
material revolution, direct or indirect, in our condition, and in the impressions which we habitually receive, the Poet will sleep then no more
than at present; he will be ready to follow the steps of the Man of
science, not only in those general indirect effects, but he will be at his
side, carrying sensation into the midst of the objects of the science itself.
The remotest discoveries of the Chemist, the Botanist, or Mineralogist,
will be as proper objects of the Poet's art as any upon which it can be
employed, if the time should ever come when these things shall be
familiar to us, and the relations under which they are contemplated by
the followers of these respective sciences shall be manifestly and pal-
pably material to us as enjoying and suffering beings. If the time should
ever come when what is now called science, thus familiarized to men,
shall be ready to put on, as it were, a form of flesh and blood, the Poet
will lend his divine spirit to aid the transfiguration, and will welcome
the Being thus produced, as a dear and genuine inmate of the household
of man.—It is not, then, to be supposed that any one, who holds that
sublime notion of Poetry which I have attempted to convey, will break
in upon the sanctity and truth of his pictures by transitory and accidental
ornaments, and endeavour to excite admiration of himself by arts, the
necessity of which must manifestly depend upon the assumed meanness
of his subject.

     What has been thus far said applies to Poetry in general; but
especially to those parts of composition where the Poet speaks through
the mouths of his characters; and upon this point it appears to authorize
the conclusion that there are few persons of good sense, who would not
allow that the dramatic parts of composition are defective, in proportion

as they deviate from the real language of nature, and are coloured by a diction of the Poet's own, either peculiar to him as an individual Poet or belonging simply to Poets in general; to a body of men who, from the circumstance of their compositions being in metre, it is expected will employ a particular language.

It is not, then, in the dramatic parts of composition that we look for this distinction of language; but still it may be proper and necessary where the Poet speaks to us in his own person and character. To this I answer by referring the Reader to the description before given of a Poet. Among the qualities there enumerated as principally conducing to form a Poet, is implied nothing differing in kind from other men, but only in degree. The sum of what was said is, that the Poet is chiefly distinguished from other men by a greater promptness to think and feel without immediate external excitement, and a greater power in expressing such thoughts and feelings as are produced in him in that manner. But these passions and thoughts and feelings are the general passions and thoughts and feelings of men. And with what are they connected? Undoubtedly with our moral sentiments and animal sensations, and with the causes which excite these; with the operations of the elements, and the appearances of the visible universe; with storm and sunshine, with the revolutions of the seasons, with cold and heat, with loss of friends and kindred, with injuries and resentments, gratitude and hope, with fear and sorrow. These, and the like, are the sensations and objects which the Poet describes, as they are the sensations of other men, and the objects which interest them. The Poet thinks and feels in the spirit of human passions. How, then, can his language differ in any material degree from that of all other men who feel vividly and see clearly? It might be *proved* that it is impossible. But supposing that this were not the case, the Poet might then be allowed to use a peculiar language when expressing his feelings for his own gratification, or that of men like himself. But Poets do not write for Poets alone, but for men. Unless therefore we are advocates for that admiration which subsists upon ignorance, and that pleasure which arises from hearing what we do not understand, the Poet must descend from this supposed height; and, in order to excite rational sympathy, he must express himself as other men express themselves. To this it may be added, that while he is only selecting from the real language of men, or, which amounts to the same thing, composing accurately in the spirit of such selection, he is treading upon safe ground, and we know what we are to expect from him. Our feelings are the same with respect to metre; for, as it may be proper to remind the Reader, the distinction of metre is regular and uniform, and not, like that which is produced by what is usually called POETIC DICTION, arbitrary, and subject to infinite caprices upon which no calculation whatever can be made. In the one case, the Reader is utterly at the mercy of the Poet, respecting what imagery or diction he may choose to connect with the passion; whereas, in the other, the metre obeys certain laws, to which the Poet and Reader both willingly submit because they are certain, and because no interference is made by them with the passion, but such as the concurring testimony of ages has shown to heighten and improve the pleasure which co-exists with it.

It will now be proper to answer an obvious question, namely, Why, professing these opinions, have I written in verse? To this, in addition to such answer as is included in what has been already said, I reply, in the first place, Because, however I may have restricted myself, there is still left open to me what confessedly constitutes the most valuable object of all writing, whether in prose or verse; the great and universal passions of men, the most general and interesting of their occupations, and the entire world of nature before me—to supply endless combinations of forms and imagery. Now, supposing for a moment that whatever is interesting in these objects may be as vividly described in prose, why should I be condemned for attempting to superadd to such description the charm which, by the consent of all nations, is acknowledged to exist in metrical language? To this, by such as are yet unconvinced, it may be answered that a very small part of the pleasure given by Poetry depends upon the metre, and that it is injudicious to write in metre, unless it be accompanied with the other artificial distinctions of style with which metre is usually accompanied, and that, by such deviation, more will be lost from the shock which will thereby be given to the Reader's associations than will be counterbalanced by any pleasure which he can derive from the general power of numbers. In answer to those who still contend for the necessity of accompanying metre with certain appropriate colours of style in order to the accomplishment of its appropriate end, and who also, in my opinion, greatly underrate the power of metre in itself, it might, perhaps, as far as relates to these Volumes, have been almost sufficient to observe, that poems are extant, written upon more humble subjects, and in a still more naked and simple style, which have continued to give pleasure from generation to generation. Now, if nakedness and simplicity be a defect, the fact here mentioned affords a strong presumption that poems somewhat less naked and simple are capable of affording pleasure at the present day; and, what I wished *chiefly* to attempt, at present, was to justify myself for having written under the impression of this belief.

But various causes might be pointed out why, when the style is manly and the subject of some importance, words metrically arranged will long continue to impart such a pleasure to mankind as he who proves the extent of that pleasure will be desirous to impart. The end of Poetry is to produce excitement in co-existence with an over-balance of pleasure; but, by the supposition, excitement is an unusual and irregular state of the mind; ideas and feelings do not, in that state, succeed each other in accustomed order. If the words, however, by which this excitement is produced be in themselves powerful, or the images and feelings have an undue proportion of pain connected with them, there is some danger that the excitement may be carried beyond its proper bounds. Now the co-presence of something regular, something to which the mind has been accustomed in various moods and in a less excited state, cannot but have great efficacy in tempering and restraining the passion by an inter-texture of ordinary feeling, and of feeling not strictly and necessarily connected with the passion. This is unquestionably true; and hence, though the opinion will at first appear paradoxical, from the tendency of metre to divest language, in a certain degree, of its reality, and thus to throw a sort of half-consciousness of unsubstantial existence over the whole composition, there can be little doubt but that more pathetic situations and sentiments, that is, those which have a greater proportion of pain connected with them, may be endured in metrical composition, especially in rhyme, than in prose. The metre of the old ballads is very artless; yet they contain many passages which would illustrate this opinion; and, I hope, if the following Poems be attentively perused, similar instances will be found in them. This opinion may be further illustrated by appealing to the Reader's own experience of the reluctance with which he comes to the re-perusal of the distressful parts of *Clarissa Harlowe,* or *The Gamester;* while Shakespeare's writings, in the most pathetic scenes, never act upon us, as pathetic, beyond the bounds of pleasure—an effect which, in a much greater degree than might at first be imagined, is to be ascribed to small, but continual and regular impulses of pleasurable surprise from the metrical arrangement.—On the other hand (what it must be allowed will much more frequently happen) if the Poet's words should be incommensurate with the passion, and inadequate to raise the Reader to a height of desirable excitement, then (unless the Poet's choice of his metre has been grossly injudicious), in the feelings of pleasure which the Reader has been accustomed to connect with metre in general, and in the feeling, whether cheerful or melancholy, which he has been accustomed to connect with that particular movement of metre, there will be found something which will greatly contribute to impart passion to the words, and to effect the complex end which the Poet proposes to himself.

If I had undertaken a SYSTEMATIC defence of the theory here maintained, it would have been my duty to develop the various causes upon which the pleasure received from metrical language depends. Among the chief of these causes is to be reckoned a principle which must be well known to those who have made any of the Arts the object of accurate reflection; namely, the pleasure which the mind derives from the perception of similitude in dissimilitude. This principle is the great spring of the activity of our minds, and their chief feeder. From this principle the direction of the sexual appetite, and all the passions connected with it, take their origin: it is the life of our ordinary conversation; and upon the accuracy with which similitude in dissimilitude, and dissimilitude in similitude are perceived, depend our taste and our moral feelings. It would not be a useless employment to apply this principle to the consideration of metre, and to show that metre is hence enabled to afford much pleasure, and to point out in what manner that pleasure is produced. But my limits will not permit me to enter upon this subject, and I must content myself with a general summary.

I have said that poetry is the spontaneous overflow of powerful feelings: it takes its origin from emotion recollected in tranquillity: the emotion is contemplated till, by a species of reaction, the tranquillity gradually disappears, and an emotion, kindred to that which was before the subject of contemplation, is gradually produced, and does itself actually exist in the mind. In this mood successful composition generally begins, and in a mood similar to this it is carried on; but the emotion, of whatever kind, and in whatever degree, from various causes, is qualified by various pleasures, so that in describing any passions whatsoever, which are voluntarily described, the mind will, upon the whole, be in a state of enjoyment. If Nature be thus cautious to preserve in a state of enjoyment a being so employed, the Poet ought to profit by the lesson held forth to him, and ought especially to take care, that, whatever passions he communicates to his Reader, those passions, if his Reader's mind be sound and vigorous, should always be accompanied with an over-balance of pleasure. Now the music of harmonious metrical language, the sense of difficulty overcome, and the blind association of pleasure which has been previously received from works of rhyme or metre of the same or similar construction, an indistinct perception perpetually renewed of language closely resembling that of real life, and yet, in the circumstance of metre, differing from it so widely—all these imperceptibly make up a complex feeling of delight, which is of the most important use in tempering the painful feeling always found intermingled with powerful descriptions of the deeper passions. This effect is always produced in pathetic and impassioned poetry; while, in lighter compositions, the ease and gracefulness with which the Poet manages his numbers are themselves confessedly a principal source of the gratification of the Reader. All that it is *necessary* to say, however, upon this subject, may be effected by affirming, what few persons will deny, that, of two descriptions, either of passions, manners, or characters, each of them equally well executed, the one in prose and the other in verse, the verse will be read a hundred times where the prose is read once.

Having thus explained a few of my reasons for writing in verse, and why I have chosen subjects from common life, and endeavoured to bring my language near to the real language of men, if I have been too minute in pleading my own cause, I have at the same time been treating a subject of general interest; and for this reason a few words will be added with reference solely to these particular poems, and to some defects which will probably be found in them. I am sensible that my associations must have sometimes been particular instead of general, and that, consequently, giving to things a false importance, I may have sometimes written upon unworthy subjects; but I am less apprehensive on this account, than that my language may frequently have suffered from those arbitrary connexions of feelings and ideas with particular words and phrases, from which no man can altogether protect himself. Hence I have no doubt, that, in some instances, feelings, even of the ludicrous, may be given to my Readers by expressions which appeared to me tender and pathetic. Such faulty expressions, were I convinced they were faulty at present, and that they must necessarily continue to be so, I would willingly take all reasonable pains to correct. But it is dangerous to make these alterations on the simple authority of a few individuals, or even of certain classes of men; for where the understanding of an Author is not convinced, or his feelings altered, this cannot be done without great injury to himself: for his own feelings are his stay and support; and, if he set them aside in one instance, he may be induced to repeat this act till his mind shall lose all confidence in itself, and become utterly debilitated. To this it may be added, that the critic ought never to forget that he is himself exposed to the same errors as the Poet, and, perhaps, in a much greater degree: for there can be no presumption in saying of most readers, that it is not probable they will be so well acquainted with the various stages of meaning through which words have passed, or with the fickleness or stability of the relations of particular ideas to each other; and, above all, since they are so much less interested in the subject, they may decide lightly and carelessly.

• Questions for Study

1. This essay served as a preface to a volume of poems which was considered radically different from traditional poetry. What characteristics of older

poetry is Wordsworth attacking? Can you sum up what he has to say concerning (a) the language of poetry, (b) the function of the poet, (c) the
process of poetic creation?

2. What do you think Wordsworth means when he says that poetic language
should be the language of common men? Is the language of one class of
people, in your opinion, necessarily more poetic than the language of
another?

3. Compare Wordsworth's ideas about poetry and its function with those of
Plato and Aristotle. For example, do their ideas concerning imitation agree?

T. S. ELIOT

•

TRADITION AND THE INDIVIDUAL TALENT

I

In English writing we seldom speak of tradition, though we occasionally apply its name in deploring its absence. We cannot refer to
"the tradition" or to "a tradition"; at most, we employ the adjective in
saying that the poetry of So-and-so is "traditional" or even "too traditional." Seldom, perhaps, does the word appear except in a phrase of
censure. If otherwise, it is vaguely approbative, with the implication, as
to the work approved, of some pleasing archæological reconstruction.
You can hardly make the word agreeable to English ears without this
comfortable reference to the reassuring science of archæology.

Certainly the word is not likely to appear in our appreciations of
living or dead writers. Every nation, every race, has not only its own
creative, but its own critical turn of mind; and is even more oblivious
of the shortcomings and limitations of its critical habits than of those
of its creative genius. We know, or think we know, from the enormous
mass of critical writing that has appeared in the French language the

critical method or habit of the French; we only conclude (we are such unconscious people) that the French are "more critical" than we, and sometimes even plume ourselves a little with the fact, as if the French were the less spontaneous. Perhaps they are; but we might remind ourselves that criticism is as inevitable as breathing, and that we should be none the worse for articulating what passes in our minds when we read a book and feel an emotion about it, for criticizing our own minds in their work of criticism. One of the facts that might come to light in this process is our tendency to insist, when we praise a poet, upon those aspects of his work in which he least resembles anyone else. In these aspects or parts of his work we pretend to find what is individual, what is the peculiar essence of the man. We dwell with satisfaction upon the poet's difference from his predecessors, especially his immediate predecessors; we endeavour to find something that can be isolated in order to be enjoyed. Whereas if we approach a poet without his prejudice we shall often find that not only the best, but the most individual parts of his work may be those in which the dead poets, his ancestors, assert their immortality most vigorously. And I do not mean the impressionable period of adolescence, but the period of full maturity.

Yet if the only form of tradition, of handing down, consisted in following the ways of the immediate generation before us in a blind or timid adherence to its successes, "tradition" should positively be discouraged. We have seen many such simple currents soon lost in the sand; and novelty is better than repetition. Tradition is a matter of much wider significance. It cannot be inherited, and if you want it you must obtain it by great labour. It involves, in the first place, the historical sense, which we may call nearly indispensable to anyone who would continue to be a poet beyond his twenty-fifth year; and the historical sense involves a perception, not only of the pastness of the past, but of its presence; the historical sense compels a man to write not merely with his own generation in his bones, but with a feeling that the whole of the literature of Europe from Homer and within it the whole of the literature of his own country has a simultaneous existence and composes a simultaneous order. This historical sense, which is a sense of the timeless as well as of the temporal and of the timeless and of the temporal together, is what makes a writer traditional. And it is at the same time what makes a writer most acutely conscious of his place in time, of his contemporaneity.

No poet, no artist of any art, has his complete meaning alone. His significance, his appreciation is the appreciation of his relation to the dead poets and artists. You cannot value him alone; you must set him, for contrast and comparison, among the dead. I mean this as a principle of æsthetic, not merely historical, criticism. The necessity that he shall conform, that he shall cohere, is not one-sided; what happens when a new work of art is created is something that happens simultaneously to all the works of art which preceded it. The existing monuments form an ideal order among themselves, which is modified by the introduction of the new (the really new) work of art among them. The existing order is complete before the new work arrives; for order to persist after the supervention of novelty, the *whole* existing order must be, if ever so slightly, altered; and so the relations, proportions, values of each work of art toward the whole are readjusted; and this is conformity between the old and the new. Whoever has approved this idea of order, of the form of European, of English literature, will not find it preposterous that the past should be altered by the present as much as the present is directed by the past. And the poet who is aware of this will be aware of great difficulties and responsibilities.

In a peculiar sense he will be aware also that he must inevitably be judged by the standards of the past. I say judged, not amputated, by them; not judged to be as good as, or worse or better than, the dead; and certainly not judged by the canons of dead critics. It is a judgment, a comparison, in which two things are measured by each other. To conform merely would be for the new work not really to conform at all; it would not be new, and would therefore not be a work of art. And we do not quite say that the new is more valuable because it fits in; but its fitting in is a test of its value—a test, it is true, which can only be slowly and cautiously applied, for we are none of us infallible judges of conformity. We say: it appears to conform, and is perhaps individual, or it appears individual, and may conform; but we are hardly likely to find that it is one and not the other.

To proceed to a more intelligible exposition of the relation of the poet to the past: he can neither take the past as a lump, an indiscriminate bolus, nor can he form himself wholly on one or two private admirations, nor can he form himself wholly upon one preferred period. The first course is inadmissible, the second is an important experience of youth, and the third is a pleasant and highly desirable supplement. The poet must be very conscious of the main current, which does not at all flow invariably through the most distinguished reputations. He must be quite aware of the obvious fact that art never improves, but that the material of art is never quite the same. He must be aware that the mind of Europe—the mind of his own country—a mind which he learns in time to be much more important than his own private mind—is a mind which changes, and that this change is a development which abandons nothing *en route*, which does not superannuate either Shakespeare, or Homer, or the rock drawing of the Magdalenian draughtsmen. That this development, refinement perhaps, complication certainly, is not, from the point of view of the artist, any improvement. Perhaps not even an improvement from the point of view of the psychologist or not to the extent which we imagine; perhaps only in the end based upon a complication in economics and machinery. But the difference between the present and the past is that the conscious present is an awareness of the past in a way and to an extent which the past's awareness of itself cannot show.

Some one said: "The dead writers are remote from us because we *know* so much more than they did." Precisely, and they are that which we know.

I am alive to a usual objection to what is clearly part of my programme for the *métier* of poetry. The objection is that the doctrine requires a ridiculous amount of erudition (pedantry), a claim which can be rejected by appeal to the lives of poets in any pantheon. It will even be affirmed that much learning deadens or perverts poetic sensibility. While, however, we persist in believing that a poet ought to know as much as will not encroach upon his necessary receptivity and necessary laziness, it is not desirable to confine knowledge to whatever can be put into a useful shape for examinations, drawing-rooms or the still more pretentious modes of publicity. Some can absorb knowledge, the more tardy must sweat for it. Shakespeare acquired more essential history from Plutarch than most men could from the whole British Museum. What is to be insisted upon is that the poet must develop or procure the consciousness of the past and that he should continue to develop this consciousness throughout his career.

What happens is a continual surrender of himself as he is at the moment to something which is more valuable. The progress of an artist is a continual self-sacrifice, a continual extinction of personality.

There remains to define this process of depersonalization and its relation to the sense of tradition. It is in this depersonalization that art may be said to approach the condition of science. I shall, therefore, invite you to consider, as a suggestive analogy, the action which takes place when a bit of finely filiated platinum is introduced into a chamber containing oxygen and sulphur dioxide.

II

Honest criticism and sensitive appreciation is directed not upon the poet but upon the poetry. If we attend to the confused cries of the newspaper critics and the susurrus of popular repetition that follows, we shall hear the names of poets in great numbers; if we seek not Blue-book knowledge but the enjoyment of poetry, and ask for a poem, we shall seldom find it. In the last article I tried to point out the importance of the relation of the poem to other poems by other authors, and suggested the conception of poetry as a living whole of all the poetry that has ever been written. The other aspect of this Impersonal theory of poetry is the relation of the poem to its author. And I hinted, by an analogy, that the mind of the mature poet differs from that of the immature one not precisely in any valuation of "personality," not being necessarily more interesting, or having "more to say," but rather by being a more finely perfected medium in which special, or very varied, feelings are at liberty to enter into new combinations.

The analogy was that of the catalyst. When the two gases previously mentioned are mixed in the presence of a filament of platinum, they form sulphurous acid. This combination takes place only if the platinum is present; nevertheless the newly formed acid contains no trace of platinum, and the platinum itself is apparently unaffected; has remained inert, neutral, and unchanged. The mind of the poet is the shred of platinum. It may partly or exclusively operate upon the experience of the man himself; but, the more perfect the artist, the more completely separate in him will be the man who suffers and the mind which creates; the more perfectly will the mind digest and transmute the passions which are its material.

The experience, you will notice, the elements which enter the presence of the transforming catalyst, are of two kinds: emotions and feelings. The effect of a work of art upon the person who enjoys it is an experience different in kind from any experience not of art. It may be formed out of one emotion, or may be a combination of several; and various feelings, inhering for the writer in particular words or phrases or images, may be added to compose the final result. Or great poetry may be made without the direct use of any emotion whatever: composed out of feelings solely. Canto XV of the *Inferno* (Brunetto Latini) is a working up of the emotion evident in the situation; but the effect, though single as that of any work of art, is obtained by considerable complexity of detail. The last quatrain gives an image, a feeling attaching to an image, which "came," which did not develop simply out of what precedes, but which was probably in suspension in the poet's mind until the proper combination arrived for it to add itself to. The poet's mind is in fact a receptacle for seizing and storing up numberless feelings, phrases, images, which remain there until all the particles which can unite to form a new compound are present together.

If you compare several representative passages of the greatest poetry you see how great is the variety of types of combination, and also how completely any semi-ethical criterion of "sublimity" misses the mark. For it is not the "greatness," the intensity, of the emotions, the components, but the intensity of the artistic process, the pressure, so to speak, under which the fusion takes place, that counts. The episode of

Paolo and Francesca employs a definite emotion, but the intensity of the poetry is something quite different from whatever intensity in the supposed experience it may give the impression of. It is no more intense, furthermore, than Canto XXVI, the voyage of Ulysses, which has not the direct dependence upon an emotion. Great variety is possible in the process of transmutation of emotion: the murder of Agamemnon, or the agony of Othello, gives an artistic effect apparently closer to a possible original than the scenes from Dante. In the *Agamemnon,* the artistic emotion approximates to the emotion of an actual spectator; in *Othello* to the emotion of the protagonist himself. But the difference between art and the event is always absolute; the combination which is the murder of Agamemnon is probably as complex as that which is the voyage of Ulysses. In either case there has been a fusion of elements. The ode of Keats contains a number of feelings which have nothing particular to do with the nightingale, but which the nightingale, partly, perhaps, because of its attractive name, and partly because of its reputation, served to bring together.

The point of view which I am struggling to attack is perhaps related to the metaphysical theory of the substantial unity of the soul: for my meaning is, that the poet has, not a "personality" to express, but a particular medium, which is only a medium and not a personality, in which impressions and experiences combine in peculiar and unexpected ways. Impressions and experiences which are important for the man may take no place in the poetry, and those which become important in the poetry may play quite a negligible part in the man, the personality.

I will quote a passage which is unfamiliar enough to be regarded with fresh attention in the light—or darkness—of these observations:

> *And now methinks I could e'en chide myself*
> *For doating on her beauty, though her death*
> *Shall be revenged after no common action.*
> *Does the silkworm expend her yellow labours*
> *For thee? For thee does she undo herself?*
> *Are lordships sold to maintain ladyships*
> *For the poor benefit of a bewildering minute?*
> *Why does yon fellow falsify highways,*
> *And put his life between the judge's lips,*
> *To refine such a thing—keeps horse and men*
> *To beat their valours for her?* . . .

In this passage (as is evident if it is taken in its context) there is a combination of positive and negative emotions: an intensely strong attraction toward beauty and an equally intense fascination by the ugliness which is contrasted with it and which destroys it. This balance of contrasted emotion is in the dramatic situation to which the speech is perti-

nent, but that situation alone is inadequate to it. This is, so to speak, the
structural emotion, provided by the drama. But the whole effect, the
dominant tone, is due to the fact that a number of floating feelings, having an affinity to this emotion by no means superficially evident, have
combined with it to give us a new art emotion.

It is not in his personal emotions, the emotions provoked by particular events in his life, that the poet is in any way remarkable or interesting. His particular emotions may be simple, or crude, or flat. The
emotion in his poetry will be a very complex thing, but not with the
complexity of the emotions of people who have very complex or unusual
emotions in life. One error, in fact, of eccentricity in poetry is to seek
for new human emotions to express; and in this search for novelty in the
wrong place it discovers the perverse. The business of the poet is not to
find new emotions, but to use the ordinary ones and, in working them
up into poetry, to express feelings which are not in actual emotions at all.
And emotions which he has never experienced will serve his turn as well
as those familiar to him. Consequently, we must believe that "emotion
recollected in tranquillity" is an inexact formula. For it is neither emotion,
nor recollection, nor, without distortion of meaning, tranquillity. It is a
concentration, and a new thing resulting from the concentration, of a very
great number of experiences which to the practical and active person
would not seem to be experiences at all; it is a concentration which does
not happen consciously or of deliberation. These experiences are not
"recollected," and they finally unite in an atmosphere which is "tranquil"
only in that it is a passive attending upon the event. Of course this is not
quite the whole story. There is a great deal, in the writing of poetry,
which must be conscious and deliberate. In fact, the bad poet is usually
unconscious where he ought to be conscious, and conscious where he
ought to be unconscious. Both errors tend to make him "personal." Poetry
is not a turning loose of emotion, but an escape from emotion; it is not
the expression of personality, but an escape from personality. But, of
course, only those who have personality and emotions know what it
means to want to escape from these things.

III

ὁ δὲ νοῦς ἴσως θειότερόν τι καὶ ἀπαθές ἐστιν

This essay proposes to halt at the frontier of metaphysics or mysticism, and confine itself to such practical conclusions as can be applied
by the responsible person interested in poetry. To divert interest from
the poet to the poetry is a laudable aim: for it would conduce to a juster

estimation of actual poetry, good and bad. There are many people who appreciate the expression of sincere emotion in verse, and there is a smaller number of people who can appreciate technical excellence. But very few know when there is expression of *significant* emotion, emotion which has its life in the poem and not in the history of the poet. The emotion of art is impersonal. And the poet cannot reach this impersonality without surrendering himself wholly to the work to be done. And he is not likely to know what is to be done unless he lives in what is not merely the present, but the present moment of the past, unless he is conscious, not of what is dead, but of what is already living.

• *Questions for Study*

1. A light wittiness is brought into play in Eliot's essay, some of it depending upon sarcasm, irony, and such. Point out locutions in which this wittiness appears. What kind of effect does it have upon the tone of the essay? Does it detract from the seriousness of the essay?
2. What does Eliot mean by the "historical sense"? How does he relate it to tradition? What attitudes toward tradition does he find dangerous? How does he answer the charge that the artist would have to have too much learning to acquire this "historical sense"?
3. What does Eliot say about the relationship of personality to tradition? Can you cite any similarity between Eliot's attitude toward personality and Reynolds's "general idea of nature" in "On Taste"? Compare also Eliot's remarks on the role of the poet to those of Wordsworth on this subject.
4. Consider closely the analogy of the catalyst. Does it effectively explain Eliot's concept of depersonalization?

ALLEN GINSBERG

•

WHEN THE MODE OF MUSIC CHANGES
THE WALLS OF THE CITY SHAKE

I

Trouble with conventional form (fixed line count & stanza form) is, it's
too symmetrical, geometrical, numbered and pre-fixed—unlike to my own
mind which has no beginning and end, nor fixed measure of thought (or
speech—or writing) other than its own cornerless mystery—to transcribe
the latter in a form most nearly representing its actual "occurrence" is
my "method"—which requires the Skill of freedom of composition—and
which will lead Poetry to the expression of the highest moments of the
mindbody—mystical illumination—and its deepest emotion (through
tears—love's all)—in the forms nearest to what it actually looks like (data
of mystical imagery) & feels like (rhythm of actual speech & rhythm
prompted by direct transcription of visual & other mental data)—plus
not to forget the sudden genius-like Imagination or fabulation of unreal
& out of this world verbal constructions which express the true gaiety &
excess of Freedom—(and also by their nature express the First Cause of
the world) by means of spontaneous irrational juxtaposition of sublimely
related fact,

by the dentist drill singing against the piano music; or pure construction of imaginaries, hydrogen jukeboxes, in perhaps abstract images
(made by putting together two things verbally concrete but disparate
to begin with)—

always bearing in mind, that one must verge on the unknown, write
toward the truth hitherto unrecognizable of one's own sincerity, including
the avoidable beauty of doom, shame and embarrassment, that very area
of personal selfrecognition (detailed individual is universal remember)
which formal conventions, internalized, keep us from discovering in our-

From *The Second Coming Magazine,* July 1961. Reprinted by permission of the
author and *The Second Coming Magazine.*

selves & others—For if we write with an eye to what the poem should be (has been), and do not get lost in it, we will never discover anything new about ourselves in the process of actually writing on the table, and we lose the chance to live in our works, & make habitable the new world which every man may discover in himself, if he lives—which is life itself, past present & future.

Thus the mind must be trained, i.e. let loose, freed—to deal with itself as it actually is, and not to impose on itself, or its poetic artifacts, an arbitrarily preconceived pattern (formal or Subject)—and *all* patterns, unless discovered in the moment of composition—all remembered and *applied* patterns are by their very nature arbitrarily preconceived—no matter how wise & traditional—no matter what sum of inherited experience they represent—The only pattern of value or interest in poetry is the solitary, individual pattern peculiar to the poet's moment & the poem *discovered* in the mind & in the process of writing it out on the page, as notes, transcriptions,—reproduced in the fittest accurate form, at the time of composition. ("Time is the essence" says Kerouac). It is this personal discovery which is of value to the poet & to the reader—and it is of course more, not less, communicable of actuality than a pattern chosen in advance, with matter poured into it arbitrarily to fit, which of course distorts & blurs the matter . . . Mind is shapely, art is shapely.

II

The amount of blather & built-in misunderstanding we've encountered— usually in the name of good taste, moral virtue or (at most presumptuous) civilized value—has been a revelation to me of the absolute bankrupty of the Academy in America today, or that which has set itself up as an academy for the conservation of literature. For the Academy has been the enemy and Philistine host itself. For my works will be taught in the schools in 20 years, or sooner—it is already being taught for that matter—after the first screams of disgruntled mediocrity, screams which lasted 3 years before subsiding into a raped moan.

They should treat us, the poets, on whom they make their livings, more kindly while we're around to enjoy it. After all we are poets and novelists, not Martians in disguise trying to poison man's mind with anti-earth propaganda. Tho to the more conformist of the lot this beat & Buddhist & mystic & poetic exploration may seem just that. And perhaps it is. "Any man who does not labor to make himself obsolete is not worth his salt."—Burroughs.

People take us too seriously & not seriously enough—nobody interested in what *we* mean—just a lot of bad journalism about beatniks parading itself as highclass criticism in what are taken by the mob to be the great journals of the intellect.

And the ignorance of the technical accomplishment & spiritual interests is disgusting. How often have I seen my own work related to Fearing & Sandberg, proletarian literature, the 1930's—by people who don't *connect* my long line with my own obvious reading: Crane's *Atlantis*, Lorca's *Poet in NY*, Biblical structures, psalms & lamentations, Shelley's high buildups, Apollinaire, Artaud, Myakovsky, Pound, Williams & the American metrical tradition, the new tradition of measure. And Christopher Smart's *Rejoice in the Lamb*. And Melville's prose-poem *Pierre*. And finally the spirit & illumination of Rimbaud. Do I have to be stuck with Fearing (who's alright too) by phony critics whose only encounter with a long line has been anthology pieces in collections by Oscar Williams? By intellectual bastards and snobs and vulgarians and hypocrites who have never read Artaud's *Pour En Finir Avec Le Jugement de Dieu* and therefore wouldn't begin to know that this masterpiece which in 30 years will be as famous as *Anabasis* is the actual model of tone for my earlier writing? This is nothing but a raving back at the false Jews from Columbia who have lost memory of the Shekinah & are passing for middleclass. Must I be attacked and contemned by these people, I who have heard Blake's own ancient voice recite me the Sunflower a decade ago in Harlem? and who say *I* don't know about "poetic tradition"?

The only poetic tradition is the Voice out of the burning bush. The rest is trash, & will be consumed.

If anybody wants a statement of values—it is this, that I am ready to die for Poetry & for the truth that inspires poetry—and will do so in any case—as all men, whether they like it or no—. I believe in the American Church of Poetry.

And men who wish to die for anything less or are unwilling to die for anything except their own temporary skins are foolish & bemused by illusion and had better shut their mouths and break their pens until they are taught better by death—and I am sick to death of prophecying to a nation that hath no ears to hear the thunder of the wrath & joy to come —among the "fabled damned" of nations—& the money voices of ignoramuses.

We are in American Poetry & Prose still continuing the venerable tradition of compositional self exploration & I would say the time has not come, historically, for any effort but the first sincere attempts at discovering those natural structures of which we have been dreaming & speaking. Generalizations about these natural patterns may yet be made—time for the Academies to consider this in all technical detail—the data, the poetry & prose, the classics of original form, have already been written or are about to be—there is much to learn from them and there may be generalizations possible which, for the uninitiated, the non-poets, may be reduced to "rules & instructions" (to guide attention to what is being done)—but the path to freedom of composition goes through the eternal gateless gate which if it has "form" has an indescribable one—images of which are however innumerable.

There is nothing to agree or disagree with in Kerouac's method—there is a statement of fact (1953) of the method, the conditions of experiment, which he was persuing, what he thought about it, how he went about it. He actually did extend composition in that mode, the results are apparent, he's learned a great deal from it & so has America. As a proposed method of experiment, as a completed accomplishment, there is nothing to agree or disagree with, it is a fact—that's what he was interested in doing, that's what he did—he's only describing his interest (his passion) for the curious craftsman or critic or friend—so be it. Why get mad and say he's in "error"? There's no more error here than someone learning how to build a unicorn table by building one. He's found out (rare for a writer) *how* he really wants to write & he is writing that way, courteously explaining his way.

Most criticism is semantically confused on this point—should & shouldn't & art is & isn't—trying to tell people to do something other than that which they basically & intelligently want to do, when they are experimenting with something new to them (and actually in this case to U.S. literature).

I've had trouble with this myself, everybody telling me or implying that I shouldn't really write the way I do. What do they want, that I should write some other way I'm not interested in? Which is the very thing which doesn't interest me in their prose & poetry & makes it a long confused bore?—all arty & by inherited rule & no surprises no new invention—corresponding inevitably to their own dreary characters—because anyway most of them have no character and are big draggy minds that don't *know* and just argue from abstract shallow moral principles in the void? These people are all too abstract, when it comes down to the poetry facts of poetry,—and I have learned in the past 2 years that argument, explanation, letters, explostulation are all vain—nobody listens anyway (not only to what I say, to what I *mean*) they all have their own mental ax to grind. I've explained the prosodaic structure of *Howl* as best I can, often, and I still read criticism, even favorable, that assumes that I am not interested in, have no, form—they just don't recognize any form but what they have heard about before & expect & what they want (they, most of them, being people who don't write poetry even & so have no idea what it involves & what beauty they're violating).—And it is also tiresome

& annoying to hear K or myself or others "Beat" described because of our art as Incoherent, we are anything but. After all.

But so far we have refused to make arbitrary abstract generalizations to satisfy a peculiar popular greed for Banality. I perhaps lose some of this ground with this writing. I occasionally scream with exasperation (or giggles); this is usually an attempt to communicate with a blockhead. And Kerouac sometimes says "Wow" for joy. All this can hardly be called incoherence except by .ververbal madmen who depend on longwinded defenses of their own bad prose for a livelyhood.

The literary problems I wrote of above are explained at length in Dr. Suzuki's essay Aspects of Jap Culture (*Evergreen Review*) & placed in their proper aesthetic context. Why should the art of spontaneity in the void be so, seem so, strange when applied in the U.S. prosepoetry context? Obviously a lack of intuitive spirit and/or classical experience on the part of these provincial frauds who have set themselves up as conservators of tradition and attack our work.

A sort of philistine brainwashing of the public has taken place. How long the actual sense of the new poetry will take to filter down, thru the actual writing and unprejudiced sympathetic reading of it, is beyond my power to guess & at this point beyond my immediate hope. More people take their ideas from reviews, newspapers & silly scholarly magazines than they do from the actual texts.

The worst I fear, considering the shallowness of Opinion, is that some of the poetry & prose may be taken too familiarly, and the ideas accepted in some dopey sociological platitudinous form—as perfectly natural ideas & perceptions which they are—and be given the same shallow treatment, this time sympathetic, as, until recently, they were given shallow unsympathy. That would be the very woe of fame. The problem has been to communicate the very spark of life, and not some opinion about that spark. Most negative criticism so far has been fearful overanxious obnoxious opinionation about this spark—and most later "criticism" will equally dully concern itself with favorable opinions about that spark. And that's not art, that's not even criticism, that's just more dreary sparkless blah blah blah—enough to turn a poet's guts. A sort of cancer of the mind that assails people whose loves are eaten by their opinions, whose tongues are incapable of wild lively thought, which is poetry.

The brainwashing will continue, tho the work be found acceptable, and people will talk as emptily about the void, hipness, the drug high, tenderness, comradeship, spontaneous creativity, beat spiritual individuality & sacramentalism, as they have been talking about man's "moral destiny" (usually meaning a good job & full stomach & no guts and the necessity of heartless conformity & putting down your brother because of the inserviceability of love as against the legal discipline of tradition because of the unavailability of God's purity of vision & consequent souls angels—or anything else worthwhile). That these horrible monsters who do nothing but talk, teach, write crap & get in the way of poetry, have been accusing us, poets, of lack of "values" as they call it is enuf to make me vow solemnly (for the second time) that pretty soon I'm going to stop even trying to communicate coherently to the majority of the academic, journalistic, mass media & publishing trade & leave them stew in their own juice of ridiculous messy ideas. SQUARES SHUT UP & LEARN OR GO HOME. But alas the square world will never & has never stopt bugging the hip muse.

That we have begun a revolution of literature in America, again, without meaning to, merely by the actual practice of poetry—this would be inevitable. No doubt we knew what we were doing.

• *Questions for Study*

1. Like Wordsworth's essay, Ginsberg's essay purports to be a statement of revolutionary ideas in the writing of poetry. Compare his ideas on the process of poetic creation and his attitude toward diction with those of Wordsworth in "What is Poetry?". How does Ginsberg try to make his prose style reflect his poetic principles?
2. Can you describe Ginsberg's attitude toward the readers of poetry?
3. Defend or attack the statement that this selection is more a poem than it is an essay.

III

THE NATURE OF MAN

III

THE NATURE OF MAN

•

WHAT IS LIFE?

Before we can attempt to follow the development of life on Earth there
are two main problems to be considered. The first is to find, if we can, a
satisfactory definition of the word "life." The second is to look briefly at
the workings of organic evolution. Bound up with these questions is the
ancient enigma of life's origins and the problem of whether evolution
can be said to have any discoverable purpose or goal.

The question "What is life?" seems at first almost too obvious to
need an answer. I am alive, this book I am reading is not. A cow, and
the grass it eats, although belonging to the different groups "animal" and
"vegetable," are both alive: the pail into which the cow is milked, however, in addition to being "mineral," is very obviously "dead." Apparently,
therefore, there are two distinct categories; there is the organic, popu-
larly exemplified by the Animal and Vegetable Kingdoms, and the inorganic, exemplified by the rest of nature. It should, one would think, be
a simple matter to sort things into one compartment or the other.

Until recent years this was in fact the general opinion. A hard and
fast line was drawn between living and non-living matter. Life was regarded as a special process carried on against a background of dead rocks
and minerals, and the main problem was to discover how living things had
intruded into this inanimate scene.

It is astonishing to consider in retrospect the extent to which this
dual theory of nature has kept its place in human thought. Man seems to
have hung on to the barrier between living and non-living matter with
extreme tenacity, and apparently without any suspicion that it might be
artificially erected. As a result the question of the "origin" of life has been,

and still is, a fundamental enigma to the vast majority of mankind. In religion it has led to the many charming legends of the creation, in which God is assumed to have produced the different classes of living things by a kind of celestial conjuring trick. In science it has produced some almost equally picturesque theories, such as those of Hieronymus Richter and Lord Kelvin, which suggested that life, in the form of tiny living spores or "cosmozoans," was driven here from other planets by the radiation pressure of starlight—a theory which incidentally only served to transfer rather than to solve the problem.

During the last few years, however, a more radical approach has been made to the whole question. It is beginning to be suspected that the difference between living and non-living matter, between the animal and the vegetable on the one hand, and the mineral on the other, is less a difference in kind than in complexity. In other words, it is felt that "living" matter may have evolved from "dead" matter by as natural and uninterrupted a process as that which has seen the evolution of man via an ape-like ancestor from a Devonian air-breathing fish.

To understand this revolution in scientific thought it is necessary first of all to consider the features which distinguish organic from inorganic matter. The differences are not nearly as great as was once supposed. We will begin by cataloguing the various qualities which are normally said to characterize living things. These are, firstly, constant change—the life process can never stand still; secondly, the transformation of latent energy in the form of fuel into apparent energy in the form of work; thirdly, the replacement or repair of outworn tissues; fourthly, the ability to react to hostile influences or changes in environment; fifthly, the power of multiplication and growth; and finally, in more advanced life forms, the capacity for memory and intelligence.

Now it is a significant fact that nearly all these qualities are present also in non-living substances. The constant change of all forms of matter is a basic assumption of modern physics, and the behaviour of crystals fulfils every other item in the specification except possibly memory and intelligence. These last qualities are not, however, present in primitive forms of life, and cannot therefore be regarded as indispensable to the definition of living substance. Rather they are the outcome of a long process of evolution, and represent a complex degree of organization, not a fundamental difference in quality.

The difficulty of drawing a definite line between living and non-living matter becomes even greater when we begin to explore the strange no-man's-land revealed by the electron microscope. The electron microscope is an instrument which does not, like the ordinary optical microscope, make use of light rays. Instead it uses cathode rays, replacing a beam of light by a stream of electrons, and lenses by electromagnets. This gives it the advantage of a greatly increased resolving power, allowing far smaller objects to be studied. The only disadvantage, if such it can be called, is that as light waves are not used the objects studied by the electron microscope cannot be directly observed with the eye, but must first be registered on a photographic plate.

One of the most interesting contributions of the electron microscope to science is the knowledge it gives us of those minute substances known as filter-passing viruses, which lie on the borderlands of life. Viruses are now known to be responsible for many kinds of diseases in man, animals and plants, but their exact nature is still in doubt. Their most extraordinary property is that they behave at different times either as animate or inanimate things.

The first discovery of the existence of viruses was made by the Russian botanist Dmitry Ivanovsky in the early 1890's. He was investigating a disease of the tobacco plant which caused a mosaic-like mottling of its leaves. In one of his experiments he passed some of the juice from a diseased tobacco plant through a germ filter, thereby producing a clear liquid that was entirely free of visible germs. But when he reinjected this liquid into a healthy plant it immediately contracted the mosaic disease, thus proving the existence of some minute substance in the liquid whose nature was not known. This substance has since been identified as the tobacco mosaic virus.

During the last twenty years or so some extraordinary discoveries have been made about this and many of the other types of viruses. In 1935, for example, the American biochemist W. M. Stanley succeeded in isolating a sample of pure tobacco mosaic virus from the juice of an infected plant. To his astonishment he found that the virus was not alive in the ordinary sense of the word, but had all the attributes of a crystalline solid. Its chemical constitution could be analysed and it even formed regular shapes like the crystals of other chemicals such as salt or sugar. In its isolated form it certainly did not possess the power of reproduction so typical of living things; but—and this is the important point—when reintroduced into a healthy tobacco plant after a long period as an inanimate crystal it literally "came alive," infecting the plant with mosaic disease and rapidly multiplying like an ordinary primitive organism.

The analysis of viruses seems therefore a promising line of attack if we are to arrive at an answer to our question "What is life?" Recent research has, in fact, gone far towards confirming this opinion. It is now known, for example, that viruses are composed of the substances known as proteins, which are the fundamental constituents of all living cells. The cell material itself is called protoplasm; it is the raw material of life, and is built up in different degrees of complexity into all the varied forms of living things. But although proteins are essential to life, and in one sense actually *are* life, they are themselves strictly chemical entities. Their organization is complex, but the substances of which they are composed, known as amino-acids, are comparatively simple. Many of these amino-acids have actually been synthetically produced in the laboratory.

The implication of these facts is that the condition of matter which we call "living" does not necessarily belong to an entirely separate order of nature. Rather it could be regarded as just one of the stages in the growth of more complex substances from simpler ancestors. We nowadays accept without question the evolution of the higher forms of life from the lower, but we somehow resist the idea that life itself could have evolved just as logically from an earlier non-living stage. Yet surely there is a greater mental jump to be made from the mind of a Shakespeare or a Beethoven to a drop of primitive protoplasmic froth, than there is from this same froth to the strictly chemical stage preceding it. Science seems to be moving to the inevitable conclusion that "life" must be defined not as a unique and distinct phenomenon, but as a particular degree of organization in the basic materials of the Universe.

If this is the case we can offer a far more beautiful and satisfying account of the "origin" of life than has hitherto been possible. We can imagine the primitive life-stuff being chemically developed in the shallow water of the first seas as naturally and inevitably as the Earth had previously evolved by physical laws from a wisp of stellar gas. We can feel this great process continuing through the long ages of geological time, slowing a little here, hurrying a little there, like the different movements of a great symphony. But always through the varying rhythms we shall find the same irresistible momentum, giving evidence of a force that has organized the non-living into the living, the instinctive into the mental, and which must even now be driving us forward to new and unimaginable ends.

Of course, it may be said, this is all very romantic and attractive, but are there any scientific grounds for believing it to be true? The answer to this question may perhaps be clearer when we have considered the picture of evolutionary change which this book aims to present. Meanwhile, with regard to the first appearance of life on Earth, there is certainly good reason to believe that it resulted from some kind of chemical reaction in the oceans.

We have already tried to picture the conditions in early geological time when the waters began to run over the cooling rocks and collect in hollows to form the first seas. These seas, incidentally, would have been fresh, not salt, for the saltiness of present-day sea water has resulted from the long accumulation in the ocean basins of salts in solution washed down from the land by the great rivers. When the first seas were formed this process had not been long enough under way to produce any appreciable salinity. There may, however, have been carbohydrates dissolved in the sea, formed by the action of the water on carbon compounds in the Earth's crust; also the warm moisture-laden atmosphere would probably have contained such gases as carbon dioxide, chlorine, and nitrogen. Under such conditions additional carbohydrates would probably have formed, and these, combining with the nitrogen, would have created the typical compounds found in amino-acids and proteins. In the final stage a chemical agitator such as phosphorus may have touched off the process that we now call life.

These possibilities are still, of course, highly speculative. The final test will be made if material with the characteristic life-activity of ordinary protoplasm can be artificially produced in the laboratory. We have seen that a step has already been made in this direction with the manufacture of synthetic amino-acids. And it has been claimed recently from Germany that certain amino-acids can now be artificially combined to form albumen, a recognized protein. The production of synthetic proteins in this way is a task involving immense technical difficulties, but scientists are confident that in time all the problems can be overcome. If they are proved correct the mystery of life as a physical process will be well on the way to solution.

• *Questions for Study*

1. Upon what methods of organization—definition, classification, illustration—does Carrington heavily rely? By what method or methods does he present the crucial argument against drawing a distinct line between animate and inanimate organisms?
2. Does he invalidate in any way his argument when he writes of a "force that has organized the non-living into the living"?
3. What is Carrington's attitude toward religious explanations of the origin of life as implied, for instance, in the phrase "the many charming legends of the creation"? Would you say that his own description of the origin of life is a satisfactory one?
4. What other theories of the origin of life and the place of man in evolution are you familiar with? Which of these may be compared and contrasted to Carrington's theory?

A. C. B. LOVELL

•

CAN SCIENCE PROVE WHEN TIME BEGAN?

I suppose it would hardly be an exaggeration to say that the problem of the origin of the universe is the greatest challenge to the intellect which faces man. I cannot pretend that I have any new solution to offer you. However, the air is alive with a new hope and expectancy because our new instruments of astronomical observation, the radio telescopes (which hear rather than see and so can detect objects too distant to be visible), may be reaching out so far into space that we may soon be able to speak with more confidence. I am going to set out the problem as I see it, and I hope you will get an idea of these vast cosmological issues and of the implications of the alternative solutions which lie ahead.

The largest optical telescopes in existence today tell us about the universe as it exists out to distances of about two thousand million light years. At that distance we are seeing the universe as it existed two thousand million years ago. Within this vast area of space and time we can study several hundred million galaxies of stars. As far as we can see, the overall structure of the universe within these limits has a high degree of uniformity. There is no indication that we are seeing anything but a small part of the total universe.

To give this small part more familiar dimensions, one should recall that the Sun is eight light-minutes away from Earth, five light-hours away from the planet Pluto, and four light-years away from the next nearest star. By the standards of the cosmos, the solar system is an extremely compact unit, rotating on the edge of the Milky Way. Looking across this galaxy of ten thousand million stars, then on across the cluster of perhaps two dozen other galaxies to which we now believe the Milky Way belongs, we see thousands of millions of systems, each made up of thousands of millions of stars.

This is our present observable horizon of the universe. The radio telescopes well may push this horizon back perhaps a few thousand million light years. Then we must be content. No further strivings or inventions of man will enable us to probe the conditions which existed in epochs of history beyond. They are gone forever.

At this point we reach the second stage of our inquiry. Can we formulate a theory in terms of known physical laws whose predictions agree so well with the present observable universe that we can predict the past and future?

Several theories can explain from acceptable postulates the present observable state of the universe. These bring us face to face with the ultimate problem of the origin of the universe in ways which are startlingly different. But the new techniques in astronomy may be on the verge of producing observational data decisively in favor of one or other of them. At least one of the alternatives would, I think, present theology with a very serious dilemma. In fact, if the full implications of the theory eventually receive the support of astronomical observations it is difficult to see how certain fundamental doctrines could continue to be maintained in their present harmonious relations with our physical knowledge of the universe.

I think it would be correct to say that evolutionary models of the universe, which are a consequence of Einstein's general theory of relativity, are regarded with the most favor by the majority of contemporary astronomers. The possible types fall into three main families. One is a universe which starts from a point origin at a finite time in the past and expands continuously to become infinitely large after an infinite time. Another is a universe whose radius has a certain finite value at the initial moment of time, and thence expands to become infinite after an infinite time. A third is a universe which expands from zero radius to a certain maximum and then collapses to zero again, this process of oscillation being capable of indefinite repetition.

By far the most thoroughly studied of these is the Abbé Lemaître's model, according to which the universe originated at a finite time in the past and expands to an infinite size at an infinite future time. At present there are no known features of the observable universe which are incompatible with it. The fundamental concept of it is that the universe originated from a dense and small conglomerate which Lemaître calls the primeval atom.

If the universe was created in this manner then the conception that the creation of the primeval material was a divine act can never be attacked by scientific investigation. A set of conditions which existed over twenty thousand million years ago, and which can never return again, is forever beyond investigation.

From the initial moment of time when the primeval atom disintegrated, astronomy and mathematics can attempt to describe the subsequent history of the universe to the state which we observe today. But when we inquire what the primeval atom was like, how it disintegrated and by what means and at what time it was created we begin to cross the boundaries of physics into the realms of philosophy and theology.

The alternative to the evolutionary theory of creation is that creation of matter is taking place continuously, and that although stars and galaxies evolve from this basic material, the universe, when considered as a large scale structure, is in a steady state. Although individual galaxies recede beyond the observable horizon, others are always being created to take their place. In a million million years' time the universe will look very much as it does now. The individual galaxies will have changed, but their average spatial density remains the same, because matter is always in creation throughout all of space.

The implications of this point of view are, of course, profound. For example, there cannot have been a beginning in any scale of time at all. However far we go back, there is no stage at which we can say that the universe, as a whole, had a beginning. In the only language at our command we can say that the history of the universe on the steady-state theory extends to an infinite time in the past.

The conflict between the steady-state and evolutionary theories is of the very greatest significance to cosmology and to human thought. The evolutionary theory, I repeat, places the creation of matter beyond human investigation. But if the steady-state theory is correct, then the primeval gas is being created now, at this moment, and hence is open to human investigation. The tools of science can probe the regions of space where this creation is occurring.

If time and space had a beginning, then when the universe was only a few thousand million years old it would be much more compact than it is today. The galaxies would be in existence, but they would be packed closer together compared with their spatial density today. The spatial density today—by which I mean the number of galaxies within, say, fifty or a hundred million light years of the Milky Way—can be determined by the large optical telescopes. If we could count the number in a similar volume of space at a distance of several thousand million light years we should in effect be making a count of the galaxies as they existed several thousand million years ago. If creation is still taking place, then on the steady-state theory this number should be the same as today. If the evolutionary model is correct, then the spatial density at this distance in time and space will be much greater.

The possibility of carrying out this decisive observational test excites the imagination. Unfortunately it seems likely that the hindrances introduced by the atmosphere of the earth will prevent the great optical telescopes from penetrating to the required regions of space. It may well be that only when optical telescopes can be carried in earth satellites or erected on the Moon will it be possible to look back into the past to this extent. Before the advent of such futuristic enterprises it seems likely that the great radio telescopes will give us the answer we require. Already, we believe, we are witnessing collisions of galaxies which, for reasons not yet understood, generate radio waves easily picked up in the radio telescopes, although the light from these galaxies is so faint that they must be far beyond the range of optical telescopes. We believe that these investigations are already taking us so far out in space and so far back in time that the radio waves have been on their journey for a few thousand million years. The circumstantial evidence for this belief in the origin of many of the unidentified radio sources is very strong, and if this is confirmed we have the tools with which human beings can bring the cosmological issues to a decisive test.

As a matter of hard fact, radio astronomers in Cambridge (England) and in Sydney (Australia) claim to have made the counts of the remote galaxies which are necessary to determine the question. However, the results are in direct contradiction to each other and no satisfactory conclusion can yet be drawn. Various experiments are now in progress in an effort to throw further light on the problem. For example, we at Jodrell Bank are studying the diameters of the unidentified objects that are being measured, in hope of making some sort of classification of the objects. It is difficult to guess when these various experiments might yield results which would be generally acceptable. But it seems to me to be reasonable to expect progress within a matter of a few years.

The concept of continuous creation also presents us with another opportunity to make an even more direct and decisive test. If the theory is correct, then the hydrogen gas which forms the primeval material of the galaxies must be in creation at a considerable rate. The theory demands the appearance of hydrogen at the rate of several million million trillion tons per second in the observable universe. Although this figure is vast, by ordinary human concepts of terrestrial space the rate is exceedingly slow. It represents the creation of only a few atoms of hydrogen per cubic mile of space per year. The presence of this hydrogen in intergalactic space may well be detectable in the near future by the radio telescopes.

The method here is to listen for what we astronomers call a "twenty-one centimeter emission" from a remote galaxy. Every chemical element in nature has a characteristic wave-length in the electromagnetic spectrum, a kind of fingerprint. The identifying wave of neutral hydrogen gas is twenty-one centimeters long. This particular spectral "sound" has been very useful in radio exploration of the Milky Way. It also helped to confirm the existence of colliding galaxies in the constellation of Cygnus. With sufficiently sensitive instruments, it should be possible to find any hydrogen there may be in intergalactic space. Although any one hydrogen atom is likely to emit the twenty-one centimeter wave only once in eleven million years, the numbers of atoms in the interstellar clouds of hydrogen gas are so great that the emission should be detectable.

As individuals we must therefore face the possibility that within the next few years astronomers may be able to speak with unanimity about the ultimate cosmological problem. Only the materialist can turn aside unmoved by this prospect. For others, a settlement of this cosmological issue might mean an affirmation or rejection of deeply embedded philosophical and theological beliefs.

My present personal attitude to the scientific aspects of the problem is neutral in the sense that I do not believe that there yet exist any observational data which are decisively in favor of any particular contemporary cosmology. The optimism with which I believe that we are on the verge of producing the necessary observational data is tempered with a deep apprehension, born of bitter experience, that the decisive experiment nearly always extends one's horizon into regions of new doubts.

On the question of the creation of the primeval material of the universe it seems to me unlikely that there can ever be a scientific description, whether in terms of the evolutionary or steady-state theories. If the idea of continuous creation is substantiated, then science will have penetrated very far indeed into the ultimate processes of the universe. It might then appear that a completely materialistic framework would have been established, but it does not seem to me that this is the case. If one imagines a scientific device which is so perfect that it could record the appearance of a single hydrogen atom as demanded by the continuous creation theory, then the scientific description of the process would still be imperfect. A quite fundamental difficulty would appear in the further effort to obtain information about the nature of the energy input which gave rise to the created atom.

If I were pressed on this problem of creation I would say, therefore, that any cosmology must eventually move over into metaphysics for reasons which are inherent in modern scientific theory. The epoch of this transfer may be now and at all future time, or it may have been twenty thousand million years ago. In respect of creation the most that we can hope from our future scientific observations is a precise determination of the epoch.

I must emphasize that this is a personal view. The attitudes of my professional colleagues would be varied. Some would no doubt approve of this or a similar line of metaphysical thought. Others would not be willing to face even this fundamental limit to scientific knowledge, although an analogous limitation occurs in modern scientific theory which describes the well-known processes of atomic behavior. Some, I am afraid, will be aghast at my temerity in discussing the issue at all. As far as this group is concerned, all that I can say is that I sometimes envy their ability to evade by neglect such a problem which can tear the individual's mind asunder.

The validity of combining a metaphysical and physical process as a description of creation is the individual's problem. In my own case, I have lived my days as a scientist, but science has never claimed the whole of my existence. Some, at least, of the influence of my upbringing and environment has survived the conflict, so that I find no difficulty in accepting this conclusion. I am no more surprised or distressed at the limitation of science when faced with this great problem of creation than I am at the limitation of the spectroscope in describing the radiance of a sunset or at the theory of counterpoint in describing the beauty of a fugue.

• Questions for Study

1. According to Lovell, what are the evolutionary theories of the origin of the universe? Why do theologians favor some form of the evolutionary theory?
2. What alternative does he give to this theory? What evidence is there to support it?
3. Through what methods may the theory of continuing creation be proven correct in the next few years?
4. Consider the importance in style and content of Lovell's concluding paragraphs. Does his ability to blend philosophy and science resolve the kind of conflict which Krutch presents between philosophical and physical thought in his essay "The Meaning of Awareness"?

PETER FARB

•

THE PLACENTA OF LIFE

"The soil is the placenta of life," a scientist once wrote, and truly the earth does nourish nearly every living thing on this planet. But to the ancients, Mother Earth was an actual scientific fact. So obviously was the soil teeming with life that the Greeks regarded it as a place from which life could arise spontaneously, without benefit of sexual reproduction. The Greek Thales instructed his students that they could watch life be born from slime under the influence of heat. Other writers of about 2500 years ago attributed the birth of life to ooze or as arising from heated earth.

Spontaneous generation was asserted as a scientific fact by Aristotle, the first great naturalist whose writings remain. He observed that creatures seemed to grow in a wondrous fashion out of the earth and lifeless matter around him. The larvae of some insects appeared to be born from the morning dew settling upon the soil; mice arose, fully developed, from moist soil; crabs and frogs came from slime rained upon and heated by the sun; humus gave life to flies.

Spontaneous generation was not disproven until the middle of the last century. Although the soil itself does not give birth to life, it is the incubator for the living world. The abundance of life to be found in the soil is staggering. The organisms vary from the submicroscopic up to the relatively gigantic. The largest invertebrate animal, the earthworm, is a million times the size of the smallest one visible to the naked eye, the mite; and the mite may be a million times larger than the smallest soil animal, a protozoan, which is itself a giant alongside the bacteriophage virus. In numbers, the soil life ranges from billions to the ounce to only a handful of some species per acre. They carpet the particles of soil and weave a way through them. They make burrows and tunnels and underground nests; they honeycomb the earth with a latticework of passage-ways. They may live at the surface of the soil, like the millipedes, or dig more than 100 feet down, like some desert termites. Wherever life can exist in the soil, nature has evolved a form to fill that niche.

One of the first modern naturalists to be intrigued by soil life was Dr. William Beebe of the New York Zoological Society, the curator of the world's tropics. While he was on a bird-collecting expedition to Belem, Brazil, over forty years ago, it occurred to Dr. Beebe that the soil he had tramped on every day, while his eyes were aimed at the treetops, might also hold something of interest. So, just before heading downstream to board his steamer, he dumped handfuls of jungle earth, mold, and decay-ing leaves into an old bag.

A few days later, on the high seas en route back to New York, he began examining with a magnifying glass this thin veneer from the jungle floor. What he thought would be a shipboard diversion became a mighty labor. For the jungle soil was indeed alive, with ants, termites, beetles, scorpions and false scorpions, worms of every sort, springtails—all visible to the naked eye. With his magnifying lens, he discovered more organisms, each one hugging its grain of soil. Day after day he pored through the litter, drawn into its secret world:

Contracting the field of vision to this world where leaves were fields and fungi loomed as forests, competition, the tragedies, the mystery lessen not at all. Minute seeds mimicked small beetles in shape and in exquisite tracery of pat-terns; small beetles curled up and to the eye became minute seeds of beautiful design. Bits of bark simulated insects, a patch of fungus seemed a worm, and in their turn insects and worms became transmitted optically into immobile vegetation. . . . When we had worked with the lens for many minutes, all relative comparisons with the surrounding world were lost. Instead of looking down from on high, a being apart, with titanic brush of bristles ready to cap-ture the fiercest of these jungle creatures, I, like Alice in Wonderland, felt myself growing smaller, becoming an onlooker, perhaps hiding behind a tiny leaf or twig.

—from *Zoologica*, 1916

When his vessel reached New York City, Dr. Beebe had not yet com-pleted his examination of the jungle soil. From this section of the tropics, four square feet in area, he had collected over 500 specimens, and calcu-lated that at least twice that number remained. In fact, Dr. Beebe con-cluded, at least a thousand organisms visible to the naked eye were sheltered in this bit of jungle earth.

Nowadays one may wonder that Dr. Beebe found so few specimens, for many scientists have since made accurate counts of the soil popula-tion. The ants alone add up to tremendous numbers: in some western states, as many as twenty thriving ant cities are found to the acre. The construction of these cities requires that two tons of earth be moved by the ants. About 95 per cent of all insect species (and there are roughly a million of them) invade the soil at some stage of their life cycles; that is why a sample count of insect eggs, larvae, and adults on a single acre may total about half a billion. In addition, nearly a billion mites swarm through this same acre.

Dr. Beebe was not searching for soil microbes in his sample, but if he had counted them, he would have found unbelievable numbers. Even in a teaspoonful of soil from the temperate regions, there may be five billion bacteria, twenty million actinomycetes, a million protozoa, and 200,000 algae and fungi. These crowds of microorganisms carry on such fierce activity on each acre that they expend an amount of energy equal to 10,000 human beings living and working there.

Within the earth live strange and delicate forms, some almost aerial in their fineness. Then, too, there are algae and shrimp and familiar sea-dwellers which have somehow made homes for themselves in the soil. Many of these forms are of ancient lineage, their ancestors flourishing while man was only a promise in some tiny mammal quivering between the rocks. The slime molds, the worms, the fantasies of underground vegetation—where does man fit into that scheme?

In the soil are the preyers and the preyed-upon, the tiny links in far-reaching food chains. The stage is set for competition, yet there is much less of it than might be supposed. Regulating the multiplicity of lives is the soil itself—conservative, buffering the populations against startling changes, a complex material that resists any one form of life's becoming dominant for very long. Among the microorganisms, the very act of living keeps their numbers within bounds. For they are faced with the seeming contradiction of all life on the planet: they grow only in favorable environments, but their very act of growing removes the favorable conditions from the environment. Most microorganisms, for example, require oxygen—and when it is available, they multiply. But their increased numbers soon temporarily exhaust the supply in the soil, and their population shrinks.

A few cells, however, survive the downfall of their kingdom on a grain of sand, ready to begin again a new burst of activity when favorable conditions reappear. A single bacterial cell, producing a new generation every twenty minutes, in only two days could theoretically give rise to twenty-four trillion trillion of bacteria, an amount equal to 4000 times the weight of the earth itself. But runaway growth can never take place in the vast, and often hidden, complexities of the soil.

The soil beings are not evenly distributed as in a solution. Bacteria, for example, live in clumps or colonies. Most of the fungi are concentrated around decaying plant and animals debris. The roots of plants, in particular, swarm with microbes, and their numbers drop off sharply the further from the root that the count is made. Insects, too, often congregate in favorable places. The wild bees contruct their individual burrows only a fraction of an inch apart; there may be 100,000 nests in that crammed piece of earth, yet not another nest within miles.

Nor are the numbers of soil-dwellers a constant thing. There are definite periods of activity and growth, usually in the spring and fall, alternating with periods of dormancy during the heat of summer and the cold of winter. Underground must be a scene of considerable turmoil, for the microbes are constantly changing in numbers. A bit of garden soil was examined every two hours around the clock, for two days, and counts made. Although the temperature and moisture were kept constant, the populations of microbes on a teaspoonful of soil jumped from 2.4 billion to 3.4 billion in only a couple of hours.

The soil animals spend much of their time in restless movement, searching out favorable living conditions. Most of this movement is in the form of vertical migration—up and down in response to dryness, heat, food, and the other necessities for a successful soil life. Those forms which cannot withstand radiation from the sun burrow downward during the day, to reappear in the upper horizons at night. The ants' devotion to work has been emphasized since the days of King Solomon, yet one aspect of their labors has often gone unnoticed: a whole corps of nurse-ants do little all day but move the brood from place to place, fussing to find warmth and moisture. Even the reptiles, which also have their representatives in the soil community, migrate within the soil: a legless lizard from Spain has been reported to fashion deep underground tunnels to escape the heat.

There is no soil that has proven inhospitable to life. It is crowded to its limits. A bit of fungus, before it is fully dead, may be attacked by ravenous bacteria. A highway gash leaves the bare ribs of the earth stripped of life; yet, shortly, fungi send out strands, binding together the particles, holding them in place while seeds of colonizing plants gain a foothold. It is the same story, with infinite variations, of all the triumphs and tragedies that have occurred since the seas first receded and left a forlorn patch of dry ground.

• *The Dark World*

This solid earth is not solid at all; in fact, many soils are more than half empty, filled only with air, water, and a multitude of living things between the particles. The incalculable numbers of the soil population do not live *in* the soil but rather *between* the soil grains.

The grains make up a skeleton and they vary greatly in size. Clay soil, the finest, has particles that are smaller than 1/2000ths of an inch in diameter, beyond the reach of many optical microscopes. Particles of sand, the largest, range up to one-twelfth of an inch. Silt is midway between sand and clay; any particles larger than sand are simply gravel. Each of these soil particles has a tremendous area, and collectively they provide a vast surface for living. Only an ounce of soil, sampled at Britain's Rothamsted Experiment Station, was found to have surfaces adding up to 250,000 square feet—about six acres.

The spaces between the soil grains offer a variety of habitats. The smaller pores and channels are filled with water, the larger ones mostly with air. Clay soils have narrow, threadlike channels that twist and taper downward; in sand, as might be imagined from seeing it on the beach, there are air pockets in the tiny spaces between the grains. Draped upon the skeleton of the soil are the sinews and flesh of a teeming life: each particle, even the finest, has a tight-fitting film of oxides, water, bits of organic matter. This skin is what gives life to the soil underfoot.

The soil is a most hospitable environment for life, and in many kinds, the conditions approximate those of an incubator. For one thing, moisture is abundant, and even a bone-dry soil, baked by the desert sun, still contains comparatively large amounts of water, held by tremendous pressure on the surface of the grains. The small animals of the soil differ markedly in their water requirements: the earthworm usually requires some liquid water at all times, but the larvae of many insects can make do with water-saturated air. Adult insects withstand dry air for short periods, but will often do everything possible to avoid it—like some ground beetles which swarm out of the earth only after sundown and when the air is very humid.

The underground world, too, knows mists, monsoons, and cloudbursts. A sudden rain is the undoing of many: some animals are suffocated where they lie, others burrow deeper to escape the onrushing waters. The earthworm can swim quite well, but it is bewildered and rushes toward the surface where it becomes paralyzed by the rays of the sun. The shrew sounds a shrill cry and crowds the furthest reaches of its tunnel. The larva of the crane-fly becomes soaked and uncomfortable, but can resist the flooding. Mole-crickets, good swimmers, are only slightly inconvenienced.

As the rain fills the spaces between the soil particles, oxygen is cut off. Suddenly the whole microbial world undergoes a transformation. Most bacteria demand oxygen, and these forms become inert. But in their places other kinds flourish; these are called anaerobes, similar except that they can multiply in the complete absence of oxygen. The protozoa awaken from their protective cysts and decimate the bacterial hordes, swimming through the new underground lakes and picking off the dying game. But a few of the billions somehow manage to survive the storm; here a lone bacterium sheltered in an air pocket, there a solitary insect clutching its bubble of air, ready to repopulate its bit of earth when the floodwaters recede. The soil life is harsh on the individual, but mindful of the species.

The water-filled tubes and pores between the grains, and the moisture films on the particles, provide homes for soil creatures who make up the "water fauna." The smallness of the cavities in which they spend their entire lives eliminates all larger forms, and biologists have recently come to learn that these tenants are but dwarfed species of those more commonly found living in ponds. Extremely small specimens of some rotifers, protozoa, and nematodes have been collected from between the particles of soil; they correspond very closely with specimens taken in pools of water. One protozoan which normally reaches a size as great as 1/500th of an inch in ponds, measures but a third as much in the soil-water film. Biologists are uncertain whether these are merely undersized individuals which managed to penetrate the soil spaces, or whether they represent hereditary smaller strains.

In adapting their water needs to life in the soil, the animals have had to overcome many obstacles. None have done it more intricately than the woodlice (also called pillbugs). Their ancestors, and even their present-day relations like the crabs and shrimp, lived in the sea. How the woodlice managed to break with their ancient home is not known, but it was obviously an event requiring millions of years. Possibly, the first arthropods to make the migration from sea to land were similar to the woodlice; but out of recollection of things past, or as if not yet committed wholly to life on land, woodlice still wear gills.

Woodlice are common principally in moist forest soils, and they much resemble dark, armor-plated pills with seven pairs of legs. A woodlouse can often be found by poking around in the leaf litter for a few moments; if examined carefully, it is seen to be very ill-equipped to solve the problems of water conservation. For one thing, this is a small animal; smallness means a large surface area in proportion to volume and thus more chance for water to be lost by evaporation. Insects have a similar problem, but many of them have skins containing a waxy coating which resists evaporation. Not only does the woodlouse lack this impermeable coat, but the water loss from its gills is very great.

Nature has provided the woodlice with very few physical modifications for a successful life in the soil. But they do have intricate behavior patterns which virtually insure that if there is any moisture around, the woodlice will locate it. The most notable thing about the behavior of woodlice is that they usually bunch together in moist areas; the advantages are tremendous, for when one body surface is in contact with another, there is less surface exposed to cause water loss. But how do woodlice unerringly manage to find, and remain in, these damp spots? This troubled biologists until they took the animals into the laboratory and performed controlled experiments. The scientists found that a high humidity caused the woodlice to move more slowly and also to change their direction more frequently. Thus, at very high humidity, the woodlice moved in lazy circles, the effect being to keep them in approximately the same spot.

But it is not that simple; few biological problems are. Their responses to light, although very complicated, are also important in survival. When woodlice are in a moist area, an automatic mechanism within them makes the animals avoid light. However, should their damp spot dry up, then their response to light reverses and they become attracted to it, wandering about in the open and seeking another moist area. When they do find moisture, they avoid the light again, decrease their speed, and move in slow circles. A combination of all these mechanisms, built into the woodlice at birth and working with great precision, has placed them among the most successful soil-dwellers.

Microbes demonstrate extreme sensitivity to moisture conditions in the soil. So prodigious are their rates of reproduction when conditions are favorable that their equilibrium is constantly in flux. There is a different response to moisture among the bacteria that live on the outside of a soil crumb and those that live inside. With delicate instruments scientists have measured the variations in populations; they take place within minutes after the wetting of the crumb and continue even while it is drying out. The awakening is rapid, as, in a logarithmic scale, the bacteria multiply and reach astonishing proportions. Then their bursts of creation sputter out and the grand show is repeated by other forms. Whole species are annihilated, new lords ascend to the throne of that speck of earth.

Although the tenants of the soil are limited by moisure conditions, they find underground temperatures considerably more even than those above ground. Soil temperature studies made at Tucson, Arizona showed that the temperature remained constant throughout the day at a depth of twenty inches, while in the air above, the thermometer hovered between 52 and 108 degrees. An equable temperature is one of the reasons why soil microorganisms do not differ so much as might be expected in tropic, temperate, and even Arctic soils. At a depth of perhaps two feet below the soil surface, there is a more or less constant temperature around the globe.

It was only recently that scientists learned about the microorganisms of Arctic soils; in fact, it was not until 1934, when the Russians isolated seven groups of bacteria which were also common to temperate regions of the globe. More recent studies made at the Arctic Research Laboratory in Point Barrow, Alaska, show that some soils there support relatively large numbers of bacteria, as many as ninety million to a teaspoonful. But the Eskimos have obviously known this all along; the summer before they plan to construct their skinboats, they bury the seal pelts in the soil, allowing them to rot to the point where the hair can be easily removed. Were it not for bacteria being present in the soil, the rotting could not be explained.

Great ingenuity has been shown by the soil inhabitants in altering the temperature conditions. One Australian termite builds its mound in the shape of a wedge, a dozen feet high and as many long. This long, thin mound always points directly north-south, like a compass needle. The orientation of the nest protects the termites from overheating, since each side of the mound receives sunlight for only half a day, and the noonday sun strikes only its thin edge.

The large black ants of the woods, *Formica,* common throughout much of the world, are expert at making living in the soil as comfortable as possible. Nests made by different colonies of the same species often vary greatly in design, depending upon the local living conditions. Many even build a summer residence, a solarium practically on the surface, but their home nest is usually deep in the soil. Here they lie all winter, several thousands of them clustered together in a tight ball. In fact, the ball is made up of sleep-walking ants: the mass is constantly churning as those on the outside move towards the center; that way, all get an equal chance at the interior warmth. But always remaining at the warm center of the churning mass is the queen, most necessary for survival of the underground city.

With the rodents, a rock lying on the surface of the soil becomes a solar heater that conducts and stores warmth. It is the hub of an underground world. About a foot or two from the rock, there may be an average of eight animal burrows and runways per foot. Nearer to the rock, the tunnels come closer together, until under the stone they practically merge. A diagram of their underground passageways would reveal a crooked wheel with the tunnels radiating like warped spokes from the hub-cap rock.

The soil tenants have little difficulty in obtaining air, since it seeps through the pores and channels. Although carbon dioxide is produced in great amounts by the heartbeat of soil life, it does not accumulate there. The renewal rate of air is very rapid: in some soils, a complete turnover of all the air in the top six inches takes place about every hour. Air easily enters and leaves by the tiny passageways between the grains because the air molecules are extremely minute, perhaps only a thousandth the size of a typical pore in the soil.

The soil is a friendly place for life to be carried on in all its variety. There are abundant raw materials to provide energy, an equable climate, sufficient water supplies, no air pollution. In fact, the physical environment of the soil is hospitable, save in a single respect: it is a land where sunlight never penetrates, of darkness that knows no relief.

Here is a world in which many animals live without sight, as the common mole whose eyelids are permanently sealed, or the tarantula who may carry vestigial seeing organs of little use. Many of the soil-dwellers never leave the pit of darkness, others divide their lives with time in the light. Some, like the reproductive castes of termites and subterranean ants, have only an hour in the sun to disperse, mate, and found future colonies. As the earth suddenly opens where it was solid before, the last particles of soil removed by the workers, up come the virgin queens and males for their single moment above ground. Hundreds mill around at the exit hole, pushed on by those behind, lacking even lids to blink out the harsh light, burdened with untried wings.

Watching are the birds, toads, salamanders, other ants, centipedes —all come for a banquet of slaughter. The cloud of young virgins never gets off the ground; it is decimated before flight as other creatures of the forest gorge themselves. The toll taken is tremendous, and of those who get aloft to find a mate, perhaps only one out of a thousand ever becomes the founding mother of a successful colony. It is ended as suddenly as it began; the earth is closed over again and those behind remain in their unremitting darkness.

In the depths of the soil live algae which are the exact counterparts in every way, but one, of the sunlight-loving algae—those plants which may commonly be seen as green scum on a pond or giant seaweeds of the ocean. They contain not a bit of chlorophyll. There is good evidence that many of the present-day microbes may have originated from forms of life similar to the colorless algae. For they seem to be moving in two directions: one, toward the familiar green algae and the higher plants; the other, toward the protozoa and minute animals. The dividing line between animals and plants is often a slim and artificial one.

The tiny organisms found in the soil demonstrate a most exquisite organization and complexity. Many are microscopic, but by no means simple. Protozoan means "first animal" and although it is the simplest kind on the planet today, it must have evolved from considerably simpler animals. Protozoa are one-celled, but they represent the highest degree of specialization in the unicellular line.

Even the first faint spark of life on the planet must have had behind it a long history of chemical evolution from the "primordial soup." Although life today does not originate spontaneously from non-living matter in the soil, it probably began that way. Glimpses of what original life may have been like can be seen through the electron microscope. Its tremendous resolving power reveals that the line between living and non-living forms is not so sharp as once supposed.

Viruses, for example, have characteristics of both worlds. They behave much like chemical substances, yet they can also reproduce once they arrive inside the cell of a host. In the world of the soil, the viruses are only one of the borderline forms. Plants that act like animals and animals that resemble plants, matter that is living and at the same time not living—all are inhabitants of the strange environment of the soil.

• *Questions for Study*

1. How effective, in style and in content, is the opening section? Why does Farb tell the story of Dr. Beebe and the soil from Brazil?
2. How does the author enliven a topic which might easily have been dull? Does he include too many details? Explain.
3. Sum up characteristics of the soil and of the ways in which soil-inhabitants adjust to conditions for existence. What does the example concerning the woodlice show?
4. Do you find Carrington's essay "What is Life?" useful in clarifying the meaning of Farb's concluding paragraphs?

NORBERT WIENER

•

PROGRESS AND ENTROPY

We are immersed in a life in which the world as a whole obeys the second law of thermodynamics: confusion increases and order decreases. Yet, as we have seen, the second law of thermodynamics, while it may be a valid statement about the whole of a closed system, is definitely not valid concerning a non-isolated part of it. There are local and temporary islands of decreasing entropy in a world in which the entropy as a whole tends to increase, and the existence of these islands enables some of us to assert the existence of progress. What can we say about the general direction of the battle between progress and increasing entropy in the world immediately about us?

The Enlightenment, as we all know, fostered the idea of progress, even though there were among the men of the eighteenth century some who felt that this progress was subject to a law of diminishing returns, and that the Golden Age of society would not differ very much from what they saw about them. The crack in the fabric of the Enlightenment, marked by the French Revolution, was accompanied by doubts of progress elsewhere. Malthus, for example, sees the culture of his age about to sink into the slough of an uncontrolled increase in population, swallowing up all the gains so far made by humanity.

The line of intellectual descent from Malthus to Darwin is clear. Darwin's great innovation in the theory of evolution was that he conceived of it not as a Lamarckian spontaneous ascent from higher to higher and from better to better, but as a phenomenon in which living beings showed (a) a spontaneous tendency to develop in many directions, and (b) a tendency to follow the pattern of their ancestors. The combination of these two effects was to prune an overlush developing nature and

From *The Human Use of Human Beings*, Boston: Houghton Mifflin Company, 1954.
Reprinted by permission of Houghton Mifflin Company.

to deprive it of those organisms which were ill-adapted to their environment, by a process of "natural selection." The result of this pruning was to leave a residual pattern of forms of life more or less well adapted to their environment. This residual pattern, according to Darwin, assumes the appearance of universal purposiveness.

The concept of a residual pattern has come to the fore again in the work of Dr. W. Ross Ashby. He uses it to explain the concept of machines that learn. He points out that a machine of rather random and haphazard structure will have certain near-equilibrium positions, and certain positions far from equilibrium, and that the near-equilibrium patterns will by their very nature last for a long time, while the others will appear only temporarily. The result is that in Ashby's machine, as in Darwin's nature, we have the appearance of a purposefulness in a system which is not purposefully constructed simply because purposelessness is in its very nature transitory. Of course, in the long run, the great trivial purpose of maximum entropy will appear to be the most enduring of all. But in the intermediate stages an organism or a society of organisms will tend to dally longer in those modes of activity in which the different parts work together, according to a more or less meaningful pattern.

I believe that Ashby's brilliant idea of the unpurposeful random mechanism which seeks for its own purpose through a process of learning is not only one of the great philosophical contributions of the present day, but will lead to highly useful technical developments in the task of automatization. Not only can we build purpose into machines, but in an overwhelming majority of cases a machine designed to avoid certain pitfalls of breakdown will look for purposes which it can fulfill.

Darwin's influence on the idea of progress was not confined to the biological world, even in the nineteenth century. All philosophers and all sociologists draw their scientific ideas from the sources available at their time. Thus it is not surprising to find that Marx and his contemporary socialists accepted a Darwinian point of view in the matter of evolution and progress.

In physics, the idea of progress opposes that of entropy, although there is no absolute contradiction between the two. In the forms of physics directly dependent on the work of Newton, the information which contributes to progress and is directed against the increase of entropy may be carried by extremely small quantities of energy, or perhaps even by no energy at all. This view has been altered in the present century by the innovation in physics known as *quantum theory*.

Quantum theory has led, for our purposes, to a new association of energy and information. A crude form of this association occurs in the theories of line noise in a telephone circuit or an amplifier. Such background noise may be shown to be unavoidable, as it depends on the discrete character of the electrons which carry the current; and yet it has a definite power of destroying information. The circuit therefore demands a certain amount of communication power in order that the message may not be swamped by its own energy. More fundamental than this example is the fact that light itself has an atomic structure, and that light of a given frequency is radiated in lumps which are known as light quanta, which have a determined energy dependent on that frequency. Thus there can be no radiation of less energy than a single light quantum. The transfer of information cannot take place without a certain expenditure of energy, so that there is no sharp boundary between energetic coupling and informational coupling. Nevertheless, for most practical purposes, a light quantum is a very small thing; and the amount of energy transfer which is necessary for an effective informational coupling is quite small. It follows that in considering such a local process as the growth of a tree or of a human being, which depends directly or indirectly on radiation from the sun, an enormous local decrease in entropy may be associated with quite a moderate energy transfer. This is one of the fundamental facts of biology; and in particular of the theory of photosynthesis, or of the chemical process by which a plant is enabled to use the sun's rays to form starch, and other complicated chemicals necessary for life, out of the water and carbon dioxiode of the air.

Thus the question of whether to interpret the second law of thermodynamics pessimistically or not depends on the importance we give to the universe at large, on the one hand, and to the islands of locally decreasing entropy which we find in it, on the other. Remember that we ourselves constitute such an island of decreasing entropy, and that we live among other such islands. The result is that the normal prospective difference between the near and the remote leads us to give far greater importance in the regions of decreasing entropy and increasing order than to the universe at large. For example, it may very well be that life is a rare phenomenon in the universe, confined perhaps to the solar system, or even, if we consider life on any level comparable to that in which we are principally interested, to the earth alone. Nevertheless, we live on this earth, and the possible absence of life elsewhere is of no great concern to us, and certainly of no concern proportionate to the overwhelming size of the remainder of the universe.

Again, it is quite conceivable that life belongs to a limited stretch of time; that before the earliest geological ages it did not exist, and that the time may well come when the earth is again a lifeless, burnt-out, or frozen planet. To those of us who are aware of the extremely limited range of physical conditions under which the chemical reactions necessary to life as we know it can take place, it is a foregone conclusion that the lucky accident which permits the continuation of life in any form on this earth, even without restricting life to something like human life, is bound to come to a complete and disastrous end. Yet we may succeed in framing our values so that this temporary accident of living existence, and this much more temporary accident of human existence, may be taken as all-important positive values, notwithstanding their fugitive character.

In a very real sense we are shipwrecked passengers on a doomed planet. Yet even in a shipwreck, human decencies and human values do not necessarily vanish, and we must make the most of them. We shall go down, but let it be in a manner to which we may look forward as worthy of our dignity.

Up to this point we have been talking of a pessimism which is much more the intellectual pessimism of the professional scientist than an emotional pessimism which touches the layman. We have already seen that the theory of entropy, and the considerations of the ultimate heat-death of the universe, need not have such profoundly depressing moral consequences as they seem to have at first glance. However, even this limited consideration of the future is foreign to the emotional euphoria of the average man, and particularly to that of the average American. The best we can hope for the role of progress in a universe running downhill as a whole is that the vision of our attempts to progress in the face of overwhelming necessity may have the purging terror of Greek tragedy. Yet we live in an age not over-receptive to tragedy.

· *Questions for Study*

1. Characterize Wiener's style. Why do you think that it is necessary for Wiener to use terms such as "entropy," "residual pattern," "quantum theory"?
2. What does the author mean when he says, "In a very real sense, we are shipwrecked passengers on a doomed planet"? In what sense can this view of mankind be called "tragic"?
3. Sum up Wiener's view of progress.
4. Wiener attempts to give a philosophic interpretation of a scientific law (the second law of thermodynamics) without specifically defining the law on the assumption that his readers are familiar with it. Can you infer what the second law of thermodynamics is from the author's philosophic comments?

JOSEPH WOOD KRUTCH

•

THE MEANING OF AWARENESS

Suppose you play the childish game. Suppose you ask yourself which you would rather be—a farmer ant or a robin. Only the perverse would hesitate. "A robin, of course." But why? What it would come to would certainly be something like this: "Because being a robin would be more fun. Because the robin exhibits the joy of life. Because he seems to be glad to be a robin and because it is hard to believe that an ant is glad to be what he is." Of course we can't say positively that he isn't. We cannot understand his language and he may be proclaiming to the world of other ants with what ecstasy he contemplates the fact that he is one of them. But he cannot communicate with us, and, justifiably or not, we find it hard to believe that he is glad.

Privately, biologists often share our prejudice. But few, I am afraid, would agree to classify animals as "higher" or "lower" on any such basis. They would reply, and rightly so far as biology is concerned, that to say a robin is higher than an ant because he has more joy in living is to cease to be scientific. Also, some might think that it smacks of immoral hedonism. Nevertheless a hierarchy ordered on that basis is meaningful in human terms as the scientific one is not.

If the joy of living is the most enviable good any of the lower animals can attain to and at least the second-best available to man himself, that implies in both a more general capacity which can only be called "awareness"—something that is different from intelligence as usually defined and not perfectly equatable with logic, or insight, or adaptability; also something the salamander has more of than the ant has. There is no way of measuring it, and even the psychologist would be for that reason rather loth to take it much into consideration or even to admit that it

From *The Great Chain of Life*, Boston: Houghton Mifflin Company, 1956. Reprinted by permission of Houghton Mifflin Company.

exists as distinguished from reason, insight, and the rest. That it does exist in human beings, any contemplative man knows from his own experience.

The best solver of puzzles is not necessarily the man most aware of living. The animal who most skillfully adapts himself to the conditions for survival is not necessarily the one who has the greatest joy in living. And from the standpoint of one kind of interest in living creatures it is perfectly legitimate to think of them as "high" or "low" in proportion to the degree of awareness they exhibit.

We can freely admit that the ant's technique of making a living is far more advanced than that of the bird or, indeed, of any vertebrate animal except man. We can see that some species of ants have reached what in terms of human history corresponds to an agricultural society, whereas there is no vertebrate who is not still a mere nomad hunter. But living— as some men have got around to telling themselves—can be more important than making a living. And making a living seems to be all the ant does, while the robin and many another vertebrate live abundantly.

Yes, I say to myself, the "higher" animals really are higher. Even the sluggish, dim-witted salamander, cold-blooded but vertebrate and with the beginnings of a vertebrate brain, is "higher" than the industrious ant. But it is not for any of the objective reasons either the biologist or the social anthropologist will consent to give that I call him so.

It is because even the salamander has some sort of awareness the insects have not; because, unlike them, he is on his way to intelligence, on his way to pain and pleasure, on his way to courage, and even to a sense of honor as the bighorn is beginning to feel it; on his way to Love, which the birds, bungling parents though they are, can feel and the wise wasp cannot. On the way to the joy of life, which only one or more of these things can make possible.

Once you admit this fact there is something obviously wrong with the orthodox view of the aims and methods of that evolutionary process through which both the blindly efficient ant and the blunderingly emotional bird arrived at their present state. According to that orthodox view "survival value" is the key to everything. But though intelligence does have an obvious survival value, it is by no means obvious that it works any better than the instinct of the insect. As for the emotions, their survival value is not always obvious at all. And if you want to include man in the scheme of evolution, it is so far from obvious that the complexities of civilized emotional and intellectual life have any survival value at all that many recent philosophers have suspected them of being fatal handicaps instead.

This is a fact that raises a question for the evolutionist. If the survival value of intelligence is real enough though no greater than that of instinct, if many of our emotions and the kind of awareness upon which they depend have no obvious survival value at all, then why have certain animals developed both to such a high degree? Why, for that matter, have either they or we developed them at all? Doubtless an intelligent *individual* has a better chance of individual survival than a merely instinctive one. But if nature is careful of the type, careless of the individual, then why should that weigh anything in the scales?

Darwin himself formulated a "law." No organism, he said, ever develops a characteristic beyond the point where it is useful for survival. But, as we have been asking, how useful in that sense is intelligence or even consciousness? Doesn't instinct have an even higher survival value?

It is pretty generally recognized that the insects are the most successful organisms on earth. It is also generally recognized that they get along either with the dimmest consciousness and intelligence, or perhaps without any at all. It is even believed by many that they lost a good deal of what they once had because instinct proved to have a higher survival value. If all this is true does it not suggest that orthodox evolutionism may be in one respect wrong? Does it not suggest that nature (or whatever you want to call it) puts a value on things which do not have any simple survival value? Is it not possible that mammals look after their young with bumbling consciousness rather than with the expertness of instinct because nature has, in some way, been interested not merely in the survival of the fittest, but in "the fittest" for something more than mere survival?

This last question, in a somewhat different form, was actually asked and then left unanswered in the earliest days of Darwinism. Alfred Russel Wallace, generously acknowledged by Darwin as the co-propounder of the theory of natural selection, steadily and from the beginning maintained one difference with his more famous co-worker. It was not and could not be demonstrated, he said, that natural selection could account for "the higher qualities of man." Most notable among these "higher qualities" was, he maintained, the moral sense.

No doubt some manifestations of it had a survival value in society. But not all of them. Man's willingness, sometimes at least, not only to sacrifice himself but to sacrifice himself and others for an ideal, his human conviction that "survival value" is not the only value, did not in themselves have any "survival value." How then could they have arisen if it was, as Darwin said, the inviolable rule of nature that no organism can develop what is not biologically useful to it? An all-inclusive explanation of the phenomenon of life in terms of natural selection would have to account somehow for the very conception of "values which have no survival value." And no such inclusive explanation is forthcoming.

For the most part this question has been simply brushed aside by orthodox evolutionists. Along with other related questions it has been kept alive chiefly by "mere men of letters"—by Samuel Butler, Bergson, Bernard Shaw, and the rest. But it will not down. And there are even signs that some scientists, perhaps especially the neurologists, are less sure than they once were that the mechanistic explanations of all the phenomena of living matter is complete. But if nature has been working toward something besides survival, what is it?

Julian Huxley, one of the most enlightened of present-day evolutionists, has tangled with the question. Evolution, he says, implies progress. But in what does "progress" consist? Certainly, as he admits, it includes something more than a mere progressive increase in the amount of living matter on the earth. That could be achieved by the simplest forms. Nature "wants" not merely more organisms but more complex organisms. But how can it want them if they do not survive more abundantly? Greater complexity implies, he says, "improvement." But what constitutes an "improved" organism? Not, he says, mere complexity itself but a complexity which opens the way to further "improvement." That, it seems, simply closes the circle. The question of what constitutes "improvement" and what sort of values other than mere survival value nature does recognize is still unanswered.

Perhaps the only way to escape from the dilemma that a Huxley recognizes is to make an assumption bolder than he would probably be willing to accept. But the difficulties do vanish if we are willing to accept the possibility that what nature has been working toward is not merely survival; that, ultimately, it is not survival itself but Consciousness and Intelligence *themselves*—partly at least for their own sake.

If Nature has advanced from the inanimate to the animate; if she "prefers" the living to the lifeless and the forms of life which survive rather to those that perish; then there is nothing which forbids the assumption that she also "prefers" conscious intelligence to blind instinct; that just as complex organization was developed even though it had no obvious survival value for the species, so also the awareness of itself which complex organization made possible is also one of her goals.

Whenever man's thinking starts with himself rather than with his possible origins in lower forms of life he usually comes to the conclusion that consciousness is the primary fact. "I think therefore I am" seems to be the most inescapably self-evident of propositions. Only when he starts as far away from himself as possible can he get into the contrary habit of assuming what the nineteenth century did assume: namely, that his own mind is so far from being the most significant thing in the universe that it has no substantial significance at all, being a mere illusion, some sort of insubstantial by-product of those ultimate realities which are unconscious, automatic, and mechanical.

Ever since the seventeenth century, science actually has tended to begin as far away from man himself as possible, while metaphysics has continued to start with man's own mind. Hence the undoubted fact that for a long time, at least, science and metaphysics either grew farther and farther apart, or, as with the positivists, metaphysics simply surrendered to science and tended to become no more than an abstractly stated theory of the validity of science. Yet, as we have just seen, science and positivism leave certain stubborn questions unanswered. Perhaps these questions will ultimately have to be attacked again and from the older point of view.

Aristotle is the acknowledged father of natural history. But because Aristotle lived in an age when it still seemed natural to start with the human mind itself, he reached the conclusion that at least so far as man himself is concerned Contemplation is what he is "for." And if Aristotle had had any clear idea of evolution he would certainly have supposed that a more and more complete awareness, not mere survival, was what nature was aiming at.

Most present-day biologists, following the lead of the nineteenth century, have no patience with any such metaphysical notions. When you come right down to it man is, they say, an animal; and there is only one thing that any animal is "for"—namely, survival and reproduction. Some animals accomplish this purpose in one way and some in another. Man's way happens to involve some consciousness of what he is doing and of why he does it. But that is a mere accident. If what we call intelligence had not had a high survival value it would never have developed. And one of the consequences of this fact is that man is most successful when he uses his intelligence to facilitate his survival. Thinking, or even awareness, for its own sake is a biological mistake. What he is "for" is *doing*, certainly not mooning over what he has done— unless of course that mooning has survival value, as under certain circumstances it may.

What we have been asking is, then, simply this: How good is the evidence—even their own kind of evidence—which those who take this position can offer in its support? If they are right, then man ought biologically to be the most successful of all animals. No other ought to flourish so exuberantly or have a future which, biologically, looks so bright. But what grounds do we really have for believing anything like that to be the real state of affairs? Does conscious intelligence really work any better than instinct?

No doubt you and I are the most successful of the mammals. When we take possession of any part of this earth the others go into a decline. No bear or wolf, no whale or buffalo, can successfully compete with us. But that doesn't really mean much, because all the mammals are creatures who have already started down the road we have followed so much farther than they. To some considerable extent they too are conscious, intelligent, capable of learning much from experience. Like us they are born with mental slates which, if not entirely blank, have much less written on them than is indelibly inscribed before birth on the nervous systems of many a "lower" animal.

Obviously if you are going to have to depend upon conscious intelligence, then it is an advantage to have that conscious intelligence highly developed. The other mammals over whom we triumph so easily have to fight us chiefly with inferior versions of our own weapons and it is no wonder that they lose. But what of the creatures who learn little or nothing, who can hardly be said to be capable of thought, who are conscious only dimly if at all? Are they really, from the biological standpoint, any less "successful" than we or the other mammals? Can they be said to "succeed" any less well? Are they deprived of anything except consciousness itself?

It is certainly not evident that they are. As a matter of fact the insects are the only conspicuous creatures indubitably holding their own against man. When he matches wits with any of the lower mammals they always lose. But when he matches his wit against the instinct and vitality of the insects he merely holds his own, at best. An individual insect is no match for an individual man. But most species of insects have done very well at holding their own as a species against him. And if you believe the biologists it is only with the prosperity of the species that Nature, or evolution, has ever, or could ever, concern herself.

Who is the more likely to be here on what evolution calls tomorrow —i.e., ten million years hence? Certainly the chance that man will have destroyed himself before then seems greater than the chance that the insects will have done so. Their instincts seem not to have created for them the difficulties and the dangers man's intelligence and emotion have created for him. They have been here much longer than he and it certainly seems not improbable that they will remain here much longer also. As a matter of fact the bacteria are even more "successful" than the insects. There are far more of them alive at this moment than there are of even insects, and it is even more difficult to imagine them ever extinct. If survival is the only thing that counts in nature then why or how did any life higher than that of a bacterium ever come into being?

No answer to that question seems possible unless we are willing to assume that for Nature herself, as well as for us, the instinct of the insect is "better" than the vegetative life of the bacterium, and the conscious concern of the bird for its offspring better than the unconscious efficiency of the wasp. Yet vegetation is not better than instinct and consciousness is not better than instinct if the only criterion is survival value. And if man's mind does not help him to survive more successfully than creatures having no mind at all, then what on earth can it be for? Can it be for anything except itself? Can its value be other than absolute rather than instrumental?

The bird and the man are more successful than the wasp only if you count their consciousness as, itself, some kind of success. The "purpose" of parental concern cannot be merely the successful rearing of offspring, because that can be accomplished quite as successfully without any consciousness at all.

Is it not possible, then, that Aristotle was right, that contemplation is not only the true end of man but the end that has been pursued ever since vertebrates took the road leading to a keener and keener consciousness? Have we been trying to understand the meaning of evolution by beginning at the wrong end? Is it possible that, for instance, the real, the only true "purpose" served by conscious concern over the young is the fact that out of it comes parental love itself? Has what evolution worked toward been not "survival" but "awareness"? Is the ultimate answer to the question "Why is a bungling mammal higher than an efficient wasp" simply that it is higher because it can experience parental love? Was it this, rather than mere survival, that nature was after all along?

• Questions for Study

1. What is Krutch's central point about the nature of man? He is primarily a humanist rather than a scientist. Is this orientation obvious from his treatment of the scientific subject? Explain.
2. If you are familiar with other approaches to evolution which the author mentions (Charles Darwin, Samuel Butler, Henri Bergson, George Bernard Shaw), discuss them.
3. In what special ways does Krutch use the words "survival," "awareness," and "consciousness"? Sum up the meanings that Krutch gives to these words.
4. Can you think of any arguments which might be made against the author's insistence on parental love as a triumph of nature in the evolution of man?
5. Write a theme on the subject: "How Animal is Man?"

IV

THE LIFE WITHIN

MARTIN BUBER

•

I AND THOU

To MAN THE WORLD IS TWOFOLD, in accordance with his twofold attitude.

The attitude of man is twofold, in accordance with the twofold nature of the primary words which he speaks.

The primary words are not isolated words, but combined words.

The one primary word is the combination *I–Thou*.

The other primary word is the combination *I–It*; wherein, without a change in the primary word, one of the words *He* and *She* can replace *It*.

Hence the *I* of man is also twofold.

For the *I* of the primary word *I–Thou* is a different *I* from that of primary word *I–It*.

PRIMARY WORDS DO NOT SIGNIFY THINGS, but they intimate relations.

Primary words do not describe something that might exist independently of them, but being spoken they bring about existence.

Primary words are spoken from the being.

If *Thou* is said, the *I* of the combination *I–Thou* is said along with it.

If *It* is said, the *I* of the combination *I–It* is said along with it.

The primary word *I–Thou* can only be spoken with the whole being.

The primary word *I–It* can never be spoken with the whole being.

THERE IS NO *I* TAKEN IN ITSELF, but only the *I* of the primary word *I–Thou* and the *I* of the primary word *I–It*.

When a man says *I* he refers to one or other of these. The *I* to which he refers is present when he says *I*. Further, when he says *Thou* or *It*, the *I* of one of the two primary words is present.

The existence of *I* and the speaking of *I* are one and the same thing.

When a primary word is spoken the speaker enters the word and takes his stand in it.

THE LIFE OF HUMAN BEINGS is not passed in the sphere of transitive verbs alone. It does not exist in virtue of activities alone which have some *thing* for their object.

I perceive something. I am sensible of something. I imagine something. I will something. I feel something. I think something. The life of human beings does not consist of all this and the like alone.

This and the like together establish the realm of *It*.

But the realm of *Thou* has a different basis.

When *Thou* is spoken, the speaker has no thing for his object. For where there is a thing there is another thing. Every *It* is bounded by others; *It* exists only through being bounded by others. But when *Thou* is spoken, there is no thing. *Thou* has no bounds.

When *Thou* is spoken, the speaker has no *thing*; he has indeed nothing. But he takes his stand in relation.

IT IS SAID THAT MAN EXPERIENCES HIS WORLD. What does that mean?

Man travels over the surface of things and experiences them. He extracts knowledge about their constitution from them: he wins an experience from them. He experiences what belongs to the things.

But the world is not presented to man by experiences alone. These present him only with a world composed of *It* and *He* and *She* and *It* again.

I experience something.—If we add "inner" to "outer" experiences, nothing in the situation is changed. We are merely following the uneternal division that springs from the lust of the human race to whittle away the secret of death. Inner things or outer things, what are they but things and things!

I experience something.—If we add "secret" to "open" experiences, nothing in the situation is changed. How self-confident is that wisdom which perceives a closed compartment in things, reserved for the initiate and manipulated only with the key. O secrecy without a secret! O accumulation of information! It, always It!

THE MAN WHO EXPERIENCES has not part in the world. For it is "in him" and not between him and the world that the experience arises.

The world has no part in the experience. It permits itself to be experienced, but has no concern in the matter. For it does nothing to the experience, and the experience does nothing to it.

As EXPERIENCE, the world belongs to the primary word *I–It*.

The primary word *I–Thou* establishes the world of relation.

THE SPHERES IN WHICH THE WORLD OF RELATION ARISES are three.

First, our life with nature. There the relation sways in gloom, beneath the level of speech. Creatures live and move over against us, but cannot come to us, and when we address them as *Thou*, our words cling to the threshold of speech.

Second, our life with men. There the relation is open and in the form of speech. We can give and accept the *Thou*.

Third, our life with spiritual beings. There the relation is clouded, yet it discloses itself; it does not use speech, yet begets it. We perceive no *Thou*, but none the less we feel we are addressed and we answer—forming, thinking, acting. We speak the primary word with our being, though we cannot utter *Thou* with our lips.

But with what right do we draw what lies outside speech into relation with the world of the primary word?

In every sphere in its own way, through each process of becoming that is present to us we look out toward the fringe of the eternal *Thou;* in each we are aware of a breath from the eternal *Thou;* in each *Thou* we address the eternal *Thou.*

I CONSIDER A TREE.

I can look on it as a picture: stiff column in a shock of light, or splash of green shot with the delicate blue and silver of the background.

I can perceive it as movement: flowing veins on clinging, pressing pith, suck of the roots, breathing of the leaves, ceaseless commerce with earth and air—and the obscure growth itself.

I can classify it in a species and study it as a type in its structure and mode of life.

I can subdue its actual presence and form so sternly that I recognise it only as an expression of law—of the laws in accordance with which a constant opposition of forces is continually adjusted, or of those in accordance with which the component substances mingle and separate.

I can dissipate it and perpetuate it in number, in pure numerical relation.

In all this the tree remains my object, occupies space and time, and has its nature and constitution.

It can, however, also come about, if I have both will and grace, that in considering the tree I become bound up in relation to it. The tree is now no longer *It.* I have been seized by the power of exclusiveness.

To effect this it is not necessary for me to give up any of the ways in which I consider the tree. There is nothing from which I would have to turn my eyes away in order to see, and no knowledge that I would have to forget. Rather is everything, picture and movement, species and type, law and number, indivisibly united in this event.

Everything belonging to the tree is in this: its form and structure, its colours and chemical composition, its intercourse with the elements and with the stars, are all present in a single whole.

The tree is no impression, no play of my imagination, no value depending on my mood; but it is bodied over against me and has to do with me, as I with it—only in a different way.

Let no attempt be made to sap the strength from the meaning of the relation: relation is mutual.

The tree will have a consciousness, then, similar to our own? Of that I have no experience. But do you wish, through seeming to succeed in it with yourself, once again to disintegrate that which cannot be disintegrated? I encounter no soul or dryad of the tree, but the tree itself.

I F I FACE A HUMAN BEING AS MY *Thou,* and say the primary word *I–Thou* to him, he is not a thing among things, and does not consist of things.

Thus human being is not *He* or *She,* bounded from every other *He* and *She,* a specific point in space and time within the net of the world; nor is he a nature able to be experienced and described, a loose bundle of named qualities. But with no neighbour, and whole in himself, he is *Thou* and fills the heavens. This does not mean that nothing exists except himself. But all else lives in *his* light.

Just as the melody is not made up of notes nor the verse of words nor the statue of lines, but they must be tugged and dragged till their unity has been scattered into these many pieces, so with the man to whom I say *Thou.* I can take out from him the colour of his hair, or of his speech, or of his goodness. I must continually do this. But each time I do it he ceases to be *Thou.*

And just as prayer is not in time but time in prayer, sacrifice not in space but space in sacrifice, and to reverse the relation is to abolish the reality, so with the man to whom I say *Thou.* I do not meet with him at some time and place or other. I can set him in a particular time and place; I must continually do it: but I set only a *He* or a *She,* that is an *It,* no longer my *Thou.*

So long as the heaven of *Thou* is spread out over me the winds of causality cower at my heels, and the whirlpool of fate stays its course.

I do not experience the man to whom I say *Thou.* But I take my stand in relation to him, in the sanctity of the primary word. Only when I step out of it do I experience him once more. In the act of experience *Thou* is far away.

Even if the man to whom I say *Thou* is not aware of it in the midst of his experience, yet relation may exist. For *Thou* is more than *It* realises. No deception penetrates here; here is the cradle of the Real Life.

THIS IS THE ETERNAL SOURCE OF ART: a man is faced by a form which desires to be made through him into a work. This form is no offspring of his soul, but is an appearance which steps up to it and demands of it the effective power. The man is concerned with an act of his being. If he carries it through, if he speaks the primary word out of his being to the form which appears, then the effective power streams out, and the work arises.

The act includes a sacrifice and a risk. This is the sacrifice: the endless possibility that is offered up on the altar of the form. For everything which just this moment in play ran through the perspective must be obliterated; nothing of that may penetrate the work. The exclusiveness of what is facing it demands that it be so. This is the risk: the primary word can only be spoken with the whole being. He who gives himself to it may withhold nothing of himself. The work does not suffer me, as do the tree and the man, to turn aside and relax in the world of *It;* but it commands. If I do not serve it aright it is broken, or it breaks me.

I can neither experience nor describe the form which meets me, but only body it forth. And yet I behold it, splendid in the radiance of what confronts me, clearer than all the clearness of the world which is experienced. I do not behold it as a thing among the "inner" things nor as an image of my "fancy," but as that which exists in the present. If test is made of its objectivity the form is certainly not "there." Yet what is actually so much present as it is? And the relation in which I stand to it is real, for it affects me, as I affect it.

To produce is to draw forth, to invent is to find, to shape is to discover. In bodying forth I disclose. I lead the form across—into the world of *It*. The work produced is a thing among things, able to be experienced and described as a sum of qualities. But from time to time it can face the receptive beholder in its whole embodied form.

• Questions for Study

1. Comment on the aphoristic method which Buber employs to present his ideas. In what ways is it especially effective in expressing his ideas?
2. In your own words explain the nature of the three spheres of the world of

relation. Why, for Buber, is an understanding of the relation an understanding of "Real Life"? Consider especially the illustration of the Tree and
the Man.
3. Why does Buber consider the act of true art an excellent example of the
the I-Thou relation?

PAUL TILLICH

•

MAN AND GOD

———————————

• *The Divine-Human Relationship and*
the Search for Ultimate Reality

God speaks to man in biblical religion. The *word*, literally taken, is a
spoken sound or a written sign, pointing to a meaning with which it is
conventionally connected. But it is obvious that the God of the Bible
does not speak or hear in this way. His Word is an event created by the
divine Spirit in the human spirit. It is both driving power and infinite
meaning. The Word of God is God's creative self-manifestation and not
a conversation between two beings. Therefore, the Word is one of the
aspects of God himself; it is God manifesting himself to himself. It is an
expression of God as living and, as trinitarian thinking has always
realized, an element in the power of being itself. It is ontological in its
implications, although it is a genuinely religious symbol. This makes the
doctrines of creation and salvation through the Logos possible and
necessary, and it should make it impossible to confuse a theology of
the Word with a theology of talk. The Word is an element in ultimate
reality; it is the power of being, expressing itself in many forms, in nature
and history, in symbols and sacraments, in silent and in spoken words.

Reprinted from *Biblical Religion and the Search for Ultimate Reality* by Paul Tillich
by permission of the University of Chicago Press, 1955.

But it is not bound to spoken words. The nature of the word is a problem as old as ontology, and the divine Word is a symbol as old as religion. Without knowing something about the nature of the word, without an ontology of the Logos, theology cannot interpret the speaking of God, the divine Word. But, if theology uses this insight into the ontological nature of the word, it can teach meaningfully about the nature of the divine Word, the Logos who is with God.

The most devastating conflict between biblical religion and ontology appears to be the conflict between reciprocity and participation in the divine-human relationship. Ontology seems to remove the living interdependence between God and man, and it seems to remove the meaning of prayer, especially of the prayer of supplication.

The problem is present within biblical religion itself in the tensions between the unconditional emphasis on God's working in everything, even evil, sin, and death, and human responsibility for good and evil. A divine determinism often seems to conquer biblical personalism, and in men like Augustine, Thomas, Luther, and Calvin this determinism reaches sharpest expression. But at no point do these men and the biblical writers allow their emphasis on the divine activity to destroy the divine-human reciprocity. This can be understood only through the ontological polarity of freedom and destiny and through a distinction between the levels of being, namely, between the ground of being, which transcends all polarities, and finite being, which is subjected to them.

The divine determinism of biblical thought does not make the prayer of supplication impossible. No religious act expresses more obviously the reciprocity between God and man. Without the presupposition that the prayer changes the will of God in some respect, whether he hears or rejects the prayer, no prayer of supplication seems to be meaningful. But the early theologians, whose prayers underlie most of the Christian liturgies, emphasized the unchangeability of God against all paganism. God, the immovable, the transcendent One, was the first object of their theology. They were thoroughly ontological, and their relation to God was thoroughly reciprocal and full of prayer, including the prayer of supplication. This was and is possible because every serious prayer includes surrender to the will of God. It is aware of the ultimate inadequacy of words, the literal meaning of which is the attempt to move the divine will into the direction of one's own will. In every true prayer God is both he to whom we pray and and he who prays through us. For it is the divine Spirit who creates the right prayer. At this point the ontological structure which makes God an object of us as subjects is infinitely transcended. God stands in the divine-human reciprocity, but only as he who transcends it and comprises both sides of the reciprocity. He reacts, but he reacts to that which is his own act working through our finite freedom. He never can become a mere object. This is the limit of the symbols of reciprocity. This makes the ontological question necessary.

• God as the Ground of Being in
Ontology and Biblical Religion

Our confrontation of biblical religion and the search for ultimate reality started with the doctrine of God. And our attempts to show the ultimate unity of ontology and biblical personalism must return to the doctrine of God. It is the beginning and the end of all theological thought. There is an element in the biblical and ecclesiastical idea of God which makes the ontological question necessary. It is the assertion that God *is*. Of course not everyone asks what this word "is" in relation to God means. Most people, including the biblical writers, take the word in its popular sense: something "is" if it can be found in the whole of potential experience. That which can be encountered within the whole of reality is real. Even the more sophisticated discussions about the existence or nonexistence of God often have this popular tinge. But, if God can be found within the whole of reality, then the whole of reality is the basic and dominant concept. God, then, is subject to the structure of reality. As in Greek religion, fate was above Zeus, determining him and his decisions, so God would be subject to the polarities and categories of reality as constituting his fate. The fight against this dangerous consequence of biblical personalism started in the Bible itself and continued in all periods of church history. The God who is *a* being is transcended by the God who is Being itself, the ground and abyss of every being. And the God who is *a* person is transcended by the God who is the Personal-Itself, the ground and abyss of every person. In statements like these, religion and ontology meet. Without philosophies in which the ontological question we have raised appears, Christian theology would have been unable to interpret the nature of the being of God to those who wanted to know in what sense one can say that God *is*. And the question is asked in prephilosophical, as well as in philosophical, terms by very primitive and very sophisticated people.

This means that *being* and *person* are not contradictory concepts. Being includes personal being; it does not deny it. The ground of being is the ground of personal being, not its negation. The ontological question of being creates not a conflict but a necessary basis for any theoretical dealing with the biblical concept of the personal God. If one starts to think about the meaning of biblical symbols, one is already in the midst of ontological problems.

Religiously speaking, this means that our encounter with the God who is a person includes the encounter with the God who is the ground of everything personal and as such not *a* person. Religious experience, particularly as expressed in the great religions, exhibits a deep feeling for the tension between the personal and the nonpersonal element in the encounter between God and man. The Old as well as the New Testament has the astonishing power to speak of the presence of the divine in such a way that the I-thou character of the relation never darkens the transpersonal power and mystery of the divine, and vice versa. Examples of this can be found in the seemingly simple words of Jesus about the hairs on our head, all of which are counted, and the birds which do not fall without the will of God. These words imply that no single event among the infinite number of events that happen in every infinitely small moment of time happens without the participation of God. If anything transcends primitive personalism, it is such a saying. And it is only a continuation of this line of biblical religion when Luther, who was very suspicious of philosophy, speaks of God as being nearer to all creatures than they are to themselves, or of God being totally present in a grain of sand and at the same time not being comprehended by the totality of all things, or of God giving the power to the arm of the murderer to drive home the murderous knife. Here Luther's sometimes unreflective biblical personalism is transcended, and God as the power of Being in everything is ontologically affirmed.

The correlation of ontology and biblical religion is an infinite task. There is no special ontology which we have to accept in the name of the biblical message, neither that of Plato nor that of Aristotle, neither that of Cusanus nor that of Spinoza, neither that of Kant nor that of Hegel, neither that of Laotze nor that of Whitehead. There is no saving ontology, but the ontological question is implied in the question of salvation. To ask the ontological question is a necessary task. *Against* Pascal I say: The God of Abraham, Isaac, and Jacob and the God of the philosophers is the same God. He is a person and the negation of himself as a person.

Faith comprises both itself and the doubt of itself. The Christ is Jesus and the negation of Jesus. Biblical religion is the negation and the affirmation of ontology. To live serenely and courageously in these tensions and to discover finally their ultimate unity in the depths of our own souls and in the depth of the divine life is the task and the dignity of human thought.

• *Questions for Study*

1. Like Buber in "I and Thou," Tillich emphasizes the importance of what he calls the "divine-human relationship." Compare the differences in their way of approaching this relationship.

2. From Tillich's remarks, can you define the word "ontology"? Does he explain clearly for the lay reader what he means by the "correlation of ontology and biblical religion"? Discuss.
3. How does the author defend "prayer of supplication"? What does he mean by the cryptic sentence, "God is both He to whom we pray and He who prays through us"?
4. In his concluding statements, Tillich offers a series of tensions or paradoxes of significance in his view of religious thought. Does his essay lead clearly to these paradoxes? In what ways do you think that it is possible to resolve the paradoxes?

CHRISTOPHER DAWSON

•

WHAT IS A CHRISTIAN CIVILIZATION?

The question which I have taken as the title for the present chapter is one of the vital questions of our times. It is very necessary that we should ask it, yet the fact that we are doing so is a symptom of the state of doubt and uncertainty in which modern man exists. For in the past it was no problem to the ordinary man. Everyone thought—however mistakenly—that he knew what Christian civilization was; no one doubted that it was possible; and most people would have said that it was the only form of civilization possible for Western man.

This was true of the whole Christian world down to the eighteenth century, and the fact that I can use this expression—the Christian world —and assume that the reader will know what I mean is sufficient in itself to prove the point. No doubt after the eighteenth century this was no longer the case on the European continent, and there the concept of Christian civilization had already become a controversial one. But this change did not occur to anything like the same degree in England and America. The Anglo-Saxon missionary movement of the nineteenth century, for example, as represented by men like David Livingstone, seems to have taken for granted that the expansion of Christianity was inseparable from the expansion of Western civilization. In the eyes of such men Western civilization was still a Christian civilization as compared with pagan barbarism and the non-Christian civilizations of the ancient peoples.

It is easy enough for us today to realize their mistake and to see its tragic consequences. But the danger today is that we should go to the opposite extreme by denying the social or cultural significance of Christianity. A man like Livingstone could not have done his work without the Christian background in which he had been bred. He was the offspring of a Christian society and a Christian society involves a Christian culture. For however widely one separates the Word and the World, Christian faith and secular activity, Church and State, religion and business, one cannot separate faith from life or the life of the individual believer from the life of the community of which the individual is a member. Wherever there are Christians, there must be a Christian society, and if a Christian society endures long enough to develop social traditions and institutions, there will be a Christian culture and ultimately a Christian civilization.

But perhaps I have gone too far in assuming general agreement in the use of terms which are by no means so clear as they appear at first sight. For words like "civilization," "culture," and "Christian" are all of them likely to become highly charged with emotional and moral associations. I mean that the word "Christian" is used or was used in the recent past in the sense of morally excellent; "civilization" usually involved a judgment of value and implies a very high type of social and intellectual development; while "culture" is used in two quite different senses but usually implies a rather sophisticated type of higher education.

But for the purposes of the present discussion I shall attempt to use these words in a purely descriptive way, without implying moral judgments—that is to say, judgments of value. I use the word "culture" as the social anthropologists do, to describe any social way of life which possesses a permanent institutional or organized form, so that one can speak of the culture of a tribe of illiterate cannibals. And I use the word "civilization," of any culture that is sufficiently complex to have developed cities and states. Similarly, when I speak of individuals or societies as Christian, I mean that they profess the Christian faith or some form of Christian faith, and not that they are men or peoples who behave as we believe Christians ought to behave.

Let us start at the beginning and inquire what culture—any culture, even the lowest—involves. No culture is so low as to be devoid of some principle of moral order. Indeed, I think we may go further than that and say that a culture is essentially a moral order and this is just what makes it a culture. Even those sociologists who are most inclined to minimize or deny the spiritual element in culture and to view it in a purely behavioristic fashion, like the late Professor W. G. Sumner, are ready to admit that a culture is essentially a system or pattern of "folkways" or "mores" and their use of this Latin term points to a fundamental agreement in the conception of culture. For the word "mores" means morals as well as manners, and though we today make a sharp distinction between ethics and customs, the distinction is a very recent one. The Romans themselves, who were exceptionally aware of ethical problems and possessed a genuine moral philosophy, still had only one word for the two concepts, so that while to the Roman *"boni mores"* had come to mean what we call "good morals," it was also used indifferently to describe good manners. Even today we cannot ignore the close relationship and parallelism between moral education and training in good manners, so that children do not distinguish very clearly between the guilt of a moral offense and the shame of a breach of good manners.

Now when we come to primitive societies, we cannot expect to find any clear distinction such as we take for granted between ethics and customs. But this does not mean that ethics are less important; on the contrary, they cover a much wider field and extend further in both directions, inward to religion as well as outward to society. For in all primitive cultures, ethics are related to a whole series of concepts which are now distinguished from one another, but which formerly constituted different provinces of one moral kingdom, and embraced law and religious rites as well as morals and social customs. Take the case of law: the distinction between the moral and the legal codes is relatively modern, not only in simple cultures but even in the great historic civilizations of the ancient world. For the great legal codes were all-inclusive and possessed a sacred character which conferred the same ultimate sanctions on the precepts which we should regard as secular, public or political as on those which seem to us moral or religious or ceremonial.

This unification of standards is familiar to us historically in the case of the Hebrew Torah: here the unity of religion, ethics, law, rites and ceremonies is peculiarly clear and we see how this sacred law is also regarded as the foundation of the national culture and the very essence of the people's being. But there is a similar relation between religion, law, morals and rites, in the great world cultures of China and India and Islam no less than in the more primitive cultures.

In China, for example, we see how the Confucian ethics have been the moral foundations of Chinese culture for more than two thousand years, so that it is impossible to understand any aspect of Chinese history without them. They were linked on the one hand with Chinese religion and ritual, and on the other with the Chinese political and social order. And they were also inseparably connected with Chinese education and the Chinese tradition of learning. Seen in this light, Chinese culture is an indivisible whole—a web of social and moral relations woven without seam from top to bottom.

We are now in a better position to understand what Christian civilization means. For in the past Christianity has played the same part in Western civilization as Confucianism did in China or Islam in the Middle East. It was the principle of moral unity which gave the Western peoples their spiritual values, their moral standards, and their conception of a divine law from which all human laws ultimately derive their validity and their sanction. Without Christianity there would no doubt have been some kind of civilization in the West, but it would have been quite a different civilization from that which we know: for it was only as Christendom—the society of Christian peoples—that the tribes and peoples and nations of the West acquired a common consciousness and a sense of cultural and spiritual unity. This is not just the theory of a Christian apologist. It is admitted just as much by historians who have no sympathy with Christianity. Edward Gibbon, for example, was notoriously hostile to the whole Christian tradition. Yet he never denied that the Church was the maker of Europe and he concludes his highly critical survey of Christian origins by showing how religious influences and "the growing authority of the Popes cemented the union of the Christian republic; and gradually produced the similar manners and the common jurisprudence which has distinguished from the rest of mankind the independent and even hostile nations of modern Europe."

But when Gibbon speaks of "manners" we must understand it in the extended sense which I have been discussing. For what distinguished the new Christian peoples of Europe from their pagan ancestors was their acceptance of a new set of moral standards and ideals. No doubt their adhesion to these new standards was very imperfect in practice, but the same thing was probably true of their old standards, for there is always a considerable gap between the moral standards of a society and the moral practice of individuals, and the higher the standards, the wider the gap; so that we should naturally expect the contrast between moral principles and social behavior to be much wider in the case of Christianity than in a pagan society. Nevertheless, this does not mean that moral and spiritual values are socially negligible. They influence culture in all sorts of ways

—through institutions and symbols and literature and art, as well as through personal behavior. Take for example the case of the transformation of the barbarian king or war leader by the sacramental rite of consecration as practiced throughout Europe in the Middle Ages. This obviously did not convert the ordinary feudal monarch into a St. Louis or a King Alfred, but it did establish an ideal norm by which rulers were judged and which moralized the institution itself. And the same is true of the institution of knighthood, and still more true of essentially Christian institutions, like priesthood and episcopacy and monasticism. A Christian civilization is certainly not a perfect civilization, but it is a civilization that accepts the Christian way of life as normal and frames its institutions as the organs of a Christian order. Such a civilization actually existed for a thousand years more or less. It was a living and growing organism—a great *tree of culture* which bore rich fruit in its season. As I say, it was by no means a perfect civilization. In its origins, it was a civilization of converted barbarians and it retained certain barbaric elements which reasserted themselves again and again in the course of its history.

Now our modern Western civilization in Europe and America is the direct successor and heir of this Christian civilization. Without the latter, it would never have existed. Nevertheless, our modern civilization is not a Christian one. It is the result of two hundred years of progressive secularization during which the distinctively Christian institutions and social standards have been gradually eliminated. This process was a complex one. On the continent of Europe, especially in France, it was a violent and catastrophic change, which involved political revolutions and religious persecutions. In England on the other hand it was extremely gradual and piecemeal and even today some of the typical institutions of the old Christian order, like the State establishment of the national Church and the solemn religious consecration of the monarch, still survive. The case of America, or rather of the United States, differs from each of these types. It was the first country in the Christian world to inaugurate the complete separation of the State from the Church. But this did not at first involve the secularization of culture. Throughout the greater part of the nineteenth century it was the churches rather than the State that were responsible for education and culture, especially in the newly settled territories of the Middle and Far West. The complete secularization of public education is a relatively recent factor; so that its impact on American culture has only recently been fully realized.

Thus in all Western lands the outcome of the last two hundred years' development has led to similar results. The traditional Christian civilization has now become a part of history and can only be understood by a considerable effort of study and imagination, while the whole Western world is coming to share a common secular technological civilization which it has transmitted and is in the course of transmitting to the rest of the world—to the old civilizations of Asia and to the new peoples of Africa and Oceania. Yet this secularized civilization both in Europe and America still bears marks of its Christian origins and contains living Christian traditions and institutions, though these are, so to speak, scattered and no longer integrated into the organic structure of the civilization.

Opinions differ as to the relative importance of these elements, according to the personal experience of the individual. As far back as the end of the eighteenth century there were localities and social strata in which the Christian religion was no longer practiced, while there are other regions where it is still accepted today as the basis of social life and education. And it is this broken pattern of Christian culture which is the source of most of our practical difficulties in finding clear answers and satisfactory solutions to the problem that we are discussing. On the one hand we have the point of view presented by Mr. T. S. Eliot in his thoughtful and provocative studies in Christian culture.

In the first of them, *The Idea of a Christian Society,* he writes:

A society has not ceased to be Christian until it has become positively something else. It is my contention that we have today a culture which is mainly negative, but which in so far as it is positive, is still Christian. I do not think that it can remain negative, because a negative culture has ceased to be efficient in a world where economic as well as spiritual forces are proving the efficiency of cultures which, even when pagan, are positive; and I believe the choice before us is between the formation of a new Christian culture and the acceptance of a pagan one. Both involve radical changes; but I believe that the majority of us, if we could be faced immediately with all the changes which will only be accomplished in several generations, would prefer Christianity.

Now though I naturally agree with Mr. Eliot about the choice we should make, I think he underestimates the degree to which modern civilization has acquired a positively secularized character and I am doubtful whether the majority of modern men are unwilling to accept this state of things. Christian civilization was inaugurated by the acceptance of the Cross as the Standard—*In hoc signo, vinces.* But modern civilization has adopted a different standard and it is the sign of the dollar rather than the cross that now marshals the forces of western civilization. I do not think that the majority of men are unwilling to accept this new standard. The dollar is a very good thing in its way and there are many good Christians who are quite ready to make it the standard of our civilization. It is true that they do not fully realize what the total secularization of our civilization would mean. They are ready to accept a secular state and

secular education, but they still hope to maintain Christian ethical standards and they do not understand how deeply and in how many ways the
spirit of a civilization influences the moral values of its individual
members.

No doubt in the past it has proved possible for churches and other
minority groups to maintain their ethical standards against those of the
dominant culture. But they paid a high price for this. In the case of the
early Christians it meant a fight to the death between the Church and
the pagan world, in which Christianity triumphed only after long centuries of persecution. In the case of the Jews in Europe, it has meant the
life of the ghetto and the cramping and impoverishment of their culture;
and in the case of the minority groups in the modern Christian world,
like the Mennonites and the Quakers, it produced a somewhat parallel
phenomenon in the form of sectarianism which sets the group apart from
the wider national culture.

Now if it were possible to preserve the Christian standards in the
life of the family and the religious group, it might well be worth paying
the price, even if it meant a certain loss of social advantages. But in the
highly organized life of the modern secular state it is becoming increasingly difficult for such separate groups to exist and to maintain their own
way of life in a sort of religious underworld or subculture. For the modern
state, whether it is democratic as in the United States, or communistic
as in the U.S.S.R., or Fascist as in pre-war Italy and Germany, or nationalistic as in the new states of Asia and Africa, is no longer content
to confine itself to certain limited functions like the liberal state of the
nineteenth century. In fact all modern states are totalitarian in so far as
they seek to embrace the spheres of economics and culture, as well as
politics in the strict sense of the word. They are concerned not merely
with the maintenance of public order and the defense of the people
against its external enemies. They have taken on responsibility for all the
different forms of communal activity which were formerly left to the individual or to independent social organizations such as the churches, and
they watch over the welfare of their citizens from the cradle to the grave.

Thus the modern democratic state even in America is something
quite different from the form of state envisaged by the men who formed
the American Constitution. Generally speaking one can say that they
were the enemies of state intervention and aimed at creating a system
which would leave the community and the individual free to lead their
own lives and frame their own cultural institutions. But the modern democratic state partakes of the nature of the Church. It is the educator and
spiritual guide of its citizens and any influence which withdraws the

citizen and especially the citizen's children from this universal guidance is felt to be undesirable, if not positively disloyal.

It is clear that such a situation is full of dangers for a Christian society. In the United States, at least, the danger is not acute at present. So long as an overwhelming majority of members of the American Congress are at least nominal church members, there is little possibility of the State adopting an actively anti-Christian policy. But the prospect for the future is more disquieting. For the more completely secularized public education becomes, and the more the State acquires an educational monopoly, as it is bound to do, considering the growing cost of education, the more the Christian element in our culture will diminish and the more complete will be the victory of secularization as the working religion, or rather counter-religion, of the American people. Even today the public school is widely regarded not as a purely educational institution in the nineteeenth century sense—that is, as an elementary introduction to the literary and scientific traditions of culture—but as a moral training in citizenship, an initiation and indoctrination in the American way of life; and since the public school is essentially secular this means that only the secular aspects of American culture are recognized as valid. It is only a short step from here to the point at which the Christian way of life is condemned and outlawed as a deviation from the standard patterns of social behavior.

The Christians, like the Jews before them, have held that the fear of God is the beginning of wisdom, so that without the knowledge of God there can be no true education. Our modern secular civilization has decided otherwise. As the former head of UNESCO, Dr. Julian Huxley, has recently said, "Today God is becoming the erroneous hypothesis in all aspects of reality, including man's spiritual life." Hence it seems clear that the present state of the post-Christian world, a world which is no longer Christian but which retains a vague sympathy for or sentimental attachment to Christian moral ideals, is essentially a temporary one. Unless there is a revival or restoration of Christian culture—of the social life of the Christian community—modern civilization will become secularist in a more positive and aggressive way than it is today. And in a Godless civilization of this kind, it will be far more difficult for the individual Christian to exist and practice his religion than it has ever been before, even in ages of persecution. In the past, as for instance under the Roman Empire, the family formed an independent society which was almost immune from the state, so that it could become the primary cell of an unrecognized Christian society or culture. But today the very existence of the family as a social unit is threatened by the all-persuasive influence of the state and the secular mass culture. Yet without the Christian family there can be no Christian community life and indeed no church in the traditional sense of the word: only a few scattered individuals who maintain an isolated prophetic witness, like Elias in the wilderness.

But, it will be asked, is not the idea of a return to Christian civilization irreconcilable with the conditions of the modern world which are accepted today by Christians as well as secularists? Certainly there can be no question of a return to the old regime of the alliance of Church and State or the ecclesiastical domination of society. But this does not mean that we can afford to reject the ideal of a Christian civilization or the need for a return to spiritual unity. The kingdom of God is a universal kingdom: there is no aspect of human life that stands outside it or which is not in some way tributary to it. It is the nature of Christianity to be a world-transforming movement. It transforms humanity itself and in the course of this process it changes societies and civilizations. At St. Pius X wrote half a century ago, "To restore all things in Christ has always been the Church's motto, to restore in Christ not only what directly depends on the divine mission of the Church to lead souls to God but also, as we have explained, that which flows naturally from this divine mission, i.e.: Christian civilization in each and all the elements that compose it."

This same doctrine runs through the whole series of the social Encyclicals from the time of Leo XIII to the present time and I do not suppose that anyone will question that this is the normal accepted teaching of the Catholic Church. But, of course, it may be objected that this does not hold good for Protestants and that this is one of the main points on which Catholics and Protestants differ. This is certainly true of some Protestants and in our days the rejection of the idea of Christian civilization has become one of the hallmarks of the school of existentialist neo-Kierkegaardian Christianity which has had such an influence on the religious intelligentsia, if one may use the expression. But so far as my reading goes, it has never been characteristic of Protestantism in general. One of the most influential of the English Protestant thinkers of the last century, F. D. Maurice, made the positive affirmation of the universal kingship of Christ over every aspect of human culture and every form of human life the center of his whole teaching; and one of his modern disciples, Canon Alec Vidler, in his Hale lectures here in the United States some years ago, maintained that though Maurice may seem an isolated and almost fugitive thinker, his views are being endorsed by many of the most representative Biblical and dogmatic theologians of our day.

No doubt it is equally possible to find names on the opposite side;

and in the United States especially there is an old established tradition of religious individualism and minority movements which is naturally uninterested in the problem of civilization in its religious aspects. This tradition, if I understand it right, is due to the meeting of two different influences—the Calvinist doctrine of the elect minority on the one hand, and the revivalist insistence on a particular type of intense religious experience on the other. But it certainly does not hold good of the Calvinist tradition in its pure form. For no Protestant was more insistent than Calvin on the importance of Christian standards in the life of the community and on the religious duties of the Christian State, and the same is true of the Puritans in New England. Indeed the reaction against the Puritans alike in seventeenth century England and in modern America was due to a resistance to the Puritan attempt to impose too rigid a standard of Calvinist ethics and culture on society. But here the attack came not from theologians who disbelieved in the possibility of a Christian civilization, but from humanists, or secularists who wished to emancipate culture from ecclesiastical control.

And the objections are still strong today. The average man's objection to Christian civilization is not an objection to medieval culture, which incorporated every act of social life in a sacred order of sacramental symbols and liturgical observances—such a culture is too remote from our experience to stir our emotions one way or the other: it is the dread of moral rigorism, of alcoholic prohibition or the censorship of books and films or of the fundamentalist banning of the teaching of biological evolution.

But what the advocates of a Christian civilization wish is not this narrowing of the cultural horizons, but just the reverse: the recovery of that spiritual dimension of social life the lack of which has cramped and darkened the culture of the modern world. We have acquired new resources of power and knowledge of which the old Christian civilization had hardly dreamed. Yet at the same time, we have lost that spiritual vision man formerly possessed—the sense of an eternal world on which the transitory temporal world of human affairs was dependent. This vision is not only a Christian insight: for it is intrinsic to the great civilizations of the ancient East and to the pagan world as well, so that it is not Christian civilization alone that is at stake. Here I think John Baillie, in his little book on *What is Christian Civilization?*, makes a useful and necessary distinction when he objects to the use of the word "pagan" to describe the dominant spirit of a secularist society.

The word pagan [he says] is often unthinkingly used as if it meant a man who was devoid of all religious sentiment and worshipped no gods. But all real pagans are full of religious sentiment and their fundamental error rather lies in worshipping too many gods. The alternative today is not between being Christian or being pagan, but between being Christian and being nothing in particular, not between belonging to the Church and belonging to some social spiritual community that claims an equally wholehearted allegiance, but between belonging to the Church and belonging nowhere, giving no wholehearted allegiance to anything. Such is the tragedy that has overtaken so much of our common life that it belongs nowhere, has no spiritual home, no ultimate standards of reference and little definite conception of the direction in which it desires to move.

I think this is surely true as a diagnosis of our present civilization. But society cannot remain stationary in this kind of spiritual no man's land. It will inevitably become a prey to the unclean spirits that seek to make their dwelling in the empty human soul. For a secular civilization that has no end beyond its own satisfaction is a monstrosity—a cancerous growth which will ultimately destroy itself. The only power that can liberate man from this kingdom of darkness is the Christian faith. For in the modern Western world there are no alternative solutions, no choice of possible other religions. It is a choice between Christianity or nothing. And Christianity is still a live option. The scattered elements of Christian tradition and Christian culture still exist in the modern world, though they may be temporarily forgotten or neglected. Thus the revival of Christian civilization does not involve the creation of a totally new civilization, but rather the cultural reawakening or reactivization of the Christian minority. Our civilization has become secularized largely because the Christian element has adopted a passive attitude and allowed the leadership of culture to pass to the non-Christian minority. And this cultural passivity has not been due to any profound existentialist concern with the human predicament and divine judgment, but on the contrary to a tendency toward social conformity and too ready an acceptance of the values of a secularized society. It is the intellectual and social inertia of Christians that is the real obstacle to a restoration of Christian culture. For if it is true that more than half the population of this country are church members, Christians can hardly say that they are powerless to influence society. It is the will, not the power, that is lacking.

• Questions for Study

1. Is Dawson wise in defining early in his essay such terms as "Christian," "culture," and "civilization"? In what ways would his argument be weak if he omitted these definitions? Do these definitions strike you as accurate? Can you qualify them in any way?

2. Dawson claims that "a culture is essentially a moral order." Do you think that he is justified in making this claim? How is he using the word "moral"?
3. Dawson opposes a Christian civilization to a "secularized" one. What does he mean by "secularized"? Do you see any advantages to a secularized society? Explain.
4. Does the author advocate a return to Christianity as medieval man knew it? What characteristics does he think a modern Christian civilization would have?

JAMES W. JOHNSON

·

LOGICAL THINKING

Thoughts, Ideas, Conceptions—we do not know why the brain functions as it does to produce these; but we know, largely from the word of experts who have observed and tested their way into knowledge, that our verbal thoughts form in three discernible ways. Of course, there are other ways that non-verbal ideas develop: association of sensation, memory, reverie, and so on. However, if we want to build upon something more solid than whim or mood, we must abandon castles in the air and take to the hard-rock base of logic. The intellectual processes which underpin logical thought are Inductive Thinking, Deductive Thinking, and what we can call Reductive Thinking (or Simplification).

· Inductive Thought

"Induction" comes from the Latin words *in* and *duco*, which mean "lead into" or "lead up to." As a form of thinking or reasoning, it is *the process of weighing observed evidence in order to arrive at a proposition governing that evidence.* When we observe through our physical senses some situation, set of circumstances, objects, or other *data,* we try to understand these by conjecturing a proposition that either *explains* the data or *applies* the data to other, similar data. In the first case, we construct a probable cause or *hypothesis;* in the second, we are universalizing about the category to which the data belongs and therefore making a *generalization.* We are already somewhat familiar with the ways these forms of induction are used in causation and classification.

You will remember that in forming a hypothesis, we first observe certain evidence or phenomena; we then assume these facts were *caused* by something; and finally, using our previous experience and the laws of probability, we surmise the nature of the unknown cause. In arriving at the hypothesis, we are reasoning *inductively* and passing from the known into the unknown. Any time we use the observable to conjecture about the unobservable or use the factual as the basis of the possible or probable, we jump from facts to assumptions. Sometimes this necessary step is "guessing;" sometimes, if it follows the established tests of valid induction, it becomes the somewhat more dignified but still risky *inductive leap.*

In the other form of inductive thinking, *generalizing,* we know that limited data about members of the same category are expanded to be applied to *all* the members of that category. The characteristics present in a few instances are postulated to be present in all instances; thus a categorical principle is extended to cover unknown members of the category. It is in the going from the few to the totality that a generalization takes the inductive leap. T. H. Huxley's famous example of the man who bites successively into three hard, green apples, only to discover that each is sour, and then concludes that *all* hard, green apples are sour is an instance of generalization in daily usage.

Though much of human knowledge is a store of inductively developed generalizations—all men must die, and so on—the inductive leap necessary in making a generalization sometimes causes us to slip and fall into mistakes. Just as a hypothesis can be a false one, so a generalization can be false, too. Erroneous generalizations are usually called *Hasty Generalizations;* they are caused by universalizing from two few examples or attributing the characteristic of a few objects to other like objects which differ in that particular respect. The man who buys a Powhatan automobile only to find that it has a malfunctioning carburetor, and thereupon declares that all Powhatans are junk, is guilty of hasty generalization. Or the woman who hires a Mexican cook, also a thief by trade, is generalizing wrongly if she then decides that *all* Mexicans are thieves. The human tendency to exaggerate often takes the form of a hasty generalization.

What constitutes sufficient evidence to serve as the basis for a valid generalization? If one Powhatan is not enough, then are ten? Fifty? A thousand? How many green apples must a man eat before he can decide whether or not every green apple is sour? Obviously, the more examples you have to illustrate the truth of your generalization, the better the generalization is. But even if you have six million hard, green apples that are sour and only one this is not, you cannot properly generalize about *all* hard green apples. You must generalize that "most," "many," or "some" green apples are sour. As long as you generalize about every member of a class, unknown as well as known, you can never be positive that your generalization is true in *all* instances.

Since generalizations are by nature *assertions* rather than *facts*, it is wise when you read someone else's generalizations or when you write your own to establish upon how large a sampling of members of a category each generalization is based. The famous study of *Sexual Behavior in the Human Male* made many assertions and painstakingly charted percentages to prove certain "facts" about human males as a total category, but the study actually was based on the cases of slightly over 5,000 men, many of them college students from Ohio, Indiana, and Illinois. Perhaps this sampling is large enough to be accurate; it certainly is larger than the samplings which appear in newspapers as Public Opinion Polls or Television Rating Surveys. Many a high sounding generalization—"With medical experts, Goddard's Drops are the favorites, two to one"—sounds absurd when reduced to actual figures—"Ten doctors we talked to liked Goddard's Drops, but five didn't." Never accept, or use, the flimsy phrase "Statistics tell us . . ." as a substitute for the data supporting a generalization.

If you feel that generalizations are rather suspect, you are right. At the same time, it is true that facts are generalizations for which there is a large amount of supporting and no contradictory evidence. All men must die. Tomatoes are edible. Dodos are extinct. Any of these facts could be made into erroneous generalizations with the appearance of one immortal man, one poisonous tomato, or one live dodo. To keep our generalizations extensive and yet accurate is one of the difficulties of using our inductive powers to advantage.

Perhaps one of the most direct ways to understand types of generalizations is to see how they derive from classification. Do you recall the classification we made of duck-billed platypuses? It ran in part like this:

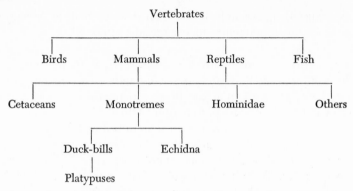

Now, if you look carefully at the categories and sub-categories on this classification chart, you can see at once that certain generalizations can be made, such as:

> All monotremes are mammals
> All platypuses are vertebrates
> No birds are reptiles
> No cetaceans are monotremes
> Some vertebrates are fish
> Some mammals are platypuses
> Some vertebrates are not mammals
> Some mammals are not hominidae

Clearly, when we generalize about objects in their categorical relationships, there are four types of statement we can make:

> All .... are ...... (Categorical Affirmative)
> No .... are ...... (Categorical Negative)
> Some .. are ...... (Limited Affirmative)
> Some .. are not ... (Limited Negative)

Even such statements as "Bears hibernate in the winter" or "A few moles are brown" can but put in the form of one of these types, as: "All bears are creatures that hibernate" or "Some moles are brown objects."

All generalizations deal with a whole group of objects or a part of a group (even if the group is "things"). If the statement declares that something is true or not true of a group as a whole, it is a *categorical statement*. The statement applies to every member of the group; thus the group is said to be *distributed*. In a Categorical Affirmative such as

X
All snarks are boojums

we are dealing with the category of snarks as a whole, but we are *not* dealing with the category of boojums as a whole, since there may be boojums which are not snarks. We indicate distribution of categories by placing an (x) over the distributed category.

In a Categorical Negative statement, both of the categories are distributed:

X   X
No snarks are boojums
X   X
Boojums are not snarks

In these statements the total categories (snarks and boojums) completely exclude each other; thus we are dealing with both categories as wholes.

In the Case of limited statements, the term preceded by "some" shows us at once that the category is only partially dealt with, and we can see that in a Limited Affirmative statement, the second category is not treated as a whole either.

Some snarks are boojums

This is the equivalent of saying

Some boojums are snarks

and though the categories overlap, neither is distributed.

So to the Limited Negative statement, which is perplexing unless you think carefully. In a Limited Negative statement such as

X
Some snarks are not boojums

it is obvious that we are not treating the entire category of snarks since we specify only "some." But we *are* dealing with the category of boojums as a whole because the statement says that this category *excludes* a specific portion of the category of snarks. If we reverse the statement, it would read

X
No boojums are some snarks

Thus in a Limited Negative statement, the first (or subject) category is not distributed, but the second (or predicate) category *is* distributed.

If you find the matter of distribution confusing, then simply memorize this chart of generalizations and distribution. Distributed terms are marked with an (x). For those who want to speculate a bit more on why each of the four kinds of generalization deals with whole or partial categories, each generalization is reversed in parentheses, showing equivalent statements that illustrate why predicate categories are or are not treated as a whole (distributed).

   X

All boys are human beings.	(Some human beings are boys)	Cat. Aff.
X X		
No boys are girls.	(No girls are boys)	Cat. Neg.
Some boys are athletes.	(Some athletes are boys)	Lim. Aff.
X		
Some boys are not athletes.	(No athletes are some boys)	Lim. Neg.

When we accept certain generalizations as *facts*, we must be positive that the generalization is accurately formulated and precisely stated. Otherwise when we try to apply them to actual situations, we will make grievous mistakes. If we think that *all* Italians are musical or *all* dogs are friendly, we may find ourselves suffering through a concert by a tone deaf Roman or taking anti-rabies shots. If you know *several* non-musical Italians or you consider most dogs friendly, state your conviction as a limited generalization. Whether you say "a few," "many," "almost all," or "99 44/100 percent," phrase the generalization as a Limited Affirmative or Limited Negative statement. You will then be using generalizations in their only effective way.

• Deductive Thought

If human beings simply observed data, hypothesized or generalized about them, and tucked the resulting inductive thought away in the back of their heads, never to be used again, we would not have to worry about whether the induction is valid or not. But each of us constantly uses inductive "truths" as the starting point of another thought process. This process is *deduction*, from the Latin *de* and *duco*, "lead down from." Deduction is *the application of a generalization to a specific instance, thereby reaching a conclusion.*

We employ deduction any time we confront a situation slightly different from, yet resembling, situations we have faced before. When you approach a strange door, you automatically look for a knob to turn because your previous experience has left you with a generalization: doors are opened by turning knobs. Your "first impression" of a new acquaintance is determined in part by deduction. You try to place him in a category of familiar personalities; thus you categorize him and impute qualities of the category to him. You meet an insurance salesman; all insurance salesmen are brash, so this fellow is probably brash, too. Deduction is the essence of most argumentation, and it is virtually impossible to read a topical essay in which deduction does not play a major part.

The most formal and complete type of deduction is the *syllogism*, which is a three-step thought process. These steps are the Major Premise, which predicates a generalization about members of a category; the Minor Premise, which identifies a specific object as a member of that category; and the Conclusion, which applies the categorical principle to the specific object. Here is an example:

All human beings must die	(Major Premise)
The King of Ethiopia is human	(Minor Premise)
The King will die	(Conclusion)

Obviously, in these three steps a specific object (the King) is connected with a category (human beings) which has a common characteristic (mortality). Whether our deduction is worth anything depends on: 1. the truth of each of the statements, and 2. the way these statements are treated in relationship to each other. To test the validity of our syllogism, we should rephrase it so that the categories are clear, thus:

X	
All human beings are mortal creatures	(Major Premise)
X	
The King of Ethiopia is a human being	(Minor Premise)
X	
The King of Ethiopia is a mortal creature	(Conclusion)

The x's indicate distributed categories in each statement. Notice that the first (subject) term in the minor premise is a categorical affirmative one. The King is an individual who makes up the total category—there is only *one* King of Ethiopia—so he is *sui generis,* in a class by himself. Any statement about a *sui generis* category necessarily is a categorical one.

These are the tests of a valid syllogistic relationship:

1. The syllogism must consist of three statements, each relating two categories.

2. One category, and only one, must appear in *both* the major and minor premises. It must be distributed at least once.

3. In the entire syllogism a total of only three categories must be used. Each category appears twice, once in each of any two of the three statements.

4. There must be no category distributed in the conclusion which has not been distributed in one of the premises.

5. There must not be two negative premises. If there are, no conclusion can be made. Two negatives cannot be logically related.

Applying these tests, we find that our syllogism about the mortality of the King of Ethiopia is logically valid; it has not violated any basic principles of deduction. There are only three terms in all; both premises are positive (or affirmative); the category common to the two premises is distributed in the major premise; and the only term distributed in the conclusion (King of Ethiopia) was distributed in the minor premise. The syllogism is *valid* as a logical process; if each of the premises is true, then our conclusion must be true too.

If your taste for the mediaeval practice of solving syllogisms has been whetted, you will find some to occupy you in the Exercises at the end of the chapter. Before you sample the syllogistic fare, however, you must be warned about the *disjunctive syllogism*. You know the disjunction is a type of antithetical statement containing two ideas in an "either. . . . or. . . ." relationship. In the disjunction, a choice of alternatives is given. If a disjunctive statement is used as the major premise of a syllogism, one of the alternatives *denied* in the minor premise and the remaining statement taken as a conclusion, the result is deduction in syllogistic form, as in:

> Either Rudolph Valentino is dead or else he has retired from films
> He has not retired
> _____
> He must be dead

Or we could have denied the first alternative and concluded that the second was true. Our disjunctive syllogism would have been just as *valid* logically, though it might not have been *true*.

On the other hand, if two alternatives are established in a disjunctive major premise and then one is affirmed in the minor premise, as

> Either the Grettla-saga was Icelandic or else it was Finnish
> It was Icelandic
> _____
> It was not Finnish

then the syllogism is guilty of a *false disjunction*. The minor premise must always *deny* one of the alternatives, never affirm. The reasons for this are subtle ones, and your best course is to take this principle on faith—or sign up for a course in Logic. Either you will sign up for the course or accept the rule on faith; but you probably will not sign up for Logic; therefore . . . what?

Unfortunately, deductive thinking does not always take the easily examinable form of the syllogism. More often, one of the three logical steps in deduction is omitted, with the result of a partial syllogism or *enthymeme*. The following are enthymemes:

> She's bound to be sophisticated; she lives in New York.
> Students who don't study fail exams, and you didn't study.
> Ectomorphs are highly nervous, so of course Wilbur is nervous.
> Certainly Nehru is a pacifist. He's an Indian, isn't he?

Each of these two-part deductions leaves out an essential statement:

All people who live in New York are sophisticated.   (Major Premise)
You failed.   (Conclusion)
Wilbur is an ectomorph.   (Minor Premise)
All Indians are pacifists.   (Major Premise)

Because the enthymeme assumes an essential statement, it can appear to be a reasonable piece of deduction when it actually is fusty thinking. The logical errors called *non-sequiturs* are really enthymemes which rest upon an assumed and erroneous major premise. At first glance, a *non-sequitur* may look like the error we met long ago: the *post hoc* fallacy. But a *post hoc fallacy* correlates two events in sequence and a *non-sequitur* applies an unspoken generalization to a specific object. It is such apparent "causal" words as "because," "since," and so on, that blur our perception of the *non-sequitur* and make us think it something else.

In statements using such causal terms, a substitution of "therefore" in the proper place will mark it clearly as a piece of deduction. For instance:

"Joe will never marry because he's so homely" becomes "Joe is homely; therefore he'll never marry."

"Gertrude ought to get a job with the State Department; she reads Sanskrit" becomes "Gertrude reads Sanksrit; therefore she ought to get a job with the State Department."

"Naturally, Vermeer was a great painter. He lived in 17th century Holland" becomes "Vermeer lived in 17th century Holland; therefore he was a great painter."

Each of these pairs of statements is an enthymeme composed of a minor premise (a specific object) and a conclusion (the application of a categorical principle to it). The reconstruction of the assumed major premise in each enthymeme shows what nonsense the deduction is made upon:

Homely people never marry.
People who read Sanskrit ought to get jobs with the State Department.
All people living in 17th century Holland were great painters.

Of course, not all enthymemes are false. These are valid and true:

Being human, Aristotle made mistakes at times.
Lotus Flower is a Siamese cat, so she has blue eyes.
Obviously canaries lay eggs; they're birds.
Abelard wrote in Latin because he was a scholastic.

When you think or write, using deduction—whether in syllogistic, en-
thymemic, or disjunctive form—remember that not only must your deductions be valid (logically accurate in method) but your individual generalizations must be true (or facts). Unless deductive thought is both true
and valid, it does not amount to much.

• Reductive Thought

Although "reductive" is not an established term like "inductive" or
"deductive," it is a helpful word to indicate the third major way by which
we form our verbal thoughts. As we use it, *reductive thinking* is *simplification for the sake of initial understanding*. It is the method of comprehension which Thomas Mann has urged us to adopt as the first step
toward mastery of the unknown, and we have already encountered the
chief forms of it.

Obviously, the simplification of data or relationships may be made in
two ways: 1. Only the outstanding pieces of information about a topic are
dealt with, the lesser known or understood being relegated to a position
of unimportance, or 2. the data or relationship is understood in terms of
some other, more tangible data or relationship. With these kinds of
simplification in view, we have no trouble in identifying *outlines, disjunc-
tions,* and *generalizations* as variations of the first sort and *analogies* and
figures of speech as examples of the second. The technique of simplification is used to an extent in all of these types of logical arrangement, and
we already have investigated the proper ways of developing and applying
these in thinking and writing.

The main trouble with reductive thinking is that it often tends to
oversimplify, reducing something to the point at which the essential nature of the data or relationship is distorted or ignored. This is a type of
reductio ad absurdum, which is a logical term applied to disproving a
proposition by showing the logical consequences of an assumption. As
we use the term, however, it means what it literally says, "reduce (or
simplify) to an absurdity:" thinkers and writers who oversimplify ideas,
whether to convey "information" or "argue a point," may not be aware of
the logical ridiculousness of their assertions, but they are in fact refuting
their own arguments by reducing them to restricted and narrow interpretations. The oversimplification chooses to ignore certain data in order to
make a point, or it refuses to admit that an exact equation cannot exist
between two separate sets of conditions. Forms of oversimplification
which we have looked at include the *hasty generalization, argument by
analogy, false analogy, false dilemma,* and *post hoc fallacy*. Even the
forced hypothesis may be counted as a form of oversimplification if it
ignores some of the data it purports to account for.

Simplification is quite an acceptable way of *beginning* to master a subject, but many areas of knowledge in life are by nature complex and unsusceptible to much simplification. Theoretical physics or mathematics, philosophy, history—none is a "simple" subject; when you try to understand or explain human emotions and actions, the causes and effects of subjectivity, it is downright dangerous to assume that *any* data are irrelevant or any relationship easily simplified. Yet, most of us cling tenaciously to the simplified explanations we learned as children when we think our thoughts or speak our opinions. In written rhetoric, too, ideas often come forth in the form of simplified assertions which are highly suspect.

Whether an assertion is one of causation, obligation, evaluation, or generalization, it is liable to oversimplification. Take these declarative sentences, for instance:

"Stop juvenile delinquency? It's easy. All we have to do is throw every one of those young hoodlums in jail until they see the light."

"Alcoholism is simple self-indulgence. Alcoholics are people who just don't exercise any self-control."

"Why all this jabbering over a conference table with foreigners? We should go ahead and drop a bomb on Moscow and all the rest of those Communist countries. After all, it's them or us, isn't it?"

"Once artificial class structures are eliminated, everyone will live together in peace and harmony with sufficient goods for all."

Each of these sentences can be classified as a type of assertion posing as a fact. Each ignores a complex relationship or ignores vital data. All are oversimplification to a dangerous degree. The speaker of each statement is assuming that the very intricate fields of sociology, psychology, international politics, and economics can be reduced to so-called "common sense." As a form of simplified thinking, common sense is all right; but as a basis for comprehending anything but the most uninvolved, obvious facts, common sense is too common to be trusted.

Like induction and deduction, reductive thought is a fundamental method of developing and applying ideas. Actually, in our minds all three processes are so intertwined as to be inseparable; the rhetorical presentation of ideas is likely to reflect this intertwining with a combination of ways of developing its central themes. In our artificial separation of the elementary kinds of thinking into such logical and rhetorical forms as the process, causation, organic structures, classification, and comparison and contrast, we have been isolating (and thus simplifying) aspects of logical relationships. The specimens of prose illustrating these different aspects have been dominantly indicative of one approach, though elements of more than one sort of logical order can be found in all of them. The thing to keep in mind is that any attempt to isolate a "pure" example of logic or a "clearcut" rhetorical example is largely academic. In our minds and our writing, we combine various ways of thinking to arrive at our view of truth.

• *Questions for Study*

1. Discuss in your own terms and with your own illustrations the crucial distinctions between inductive thought and deductive thought.
2. What considerations are involved in making generalizations? Why is a knowledge of the categorical and the limited generalization important in logical thinking?
3. Define "hasty generalization," the "four types of categorical relationships," "syllogism," "enthymeme," "false disjunction," and "reductive thinking."
4. Considering Johnson's discussion of logic, make observations about the following statements: (1) Women are less intellectual than men; (2) Some artists are neurotic; (3) All our truths are half-truths; (4) The shortest distance between two points is a straight line; (5) He's bound to be intelligent; he's a Democrat.

GORDON E. BIGELOW

•

A PRIMER OF EXISTENTIALISM

For some years I fought the word by irritably looking the other way whenever I stumbled across it, hoping that like dadaism and some of the other "isms" of the French *avant garde* it would go away if I ignored it. But existentialism was apparently more than the picture it evoked of uncombed beards, smoky basement cafes, and French beatniks regaling one another between sips of absinthe with brilliant variations on the

From *College English*, December 1961. Reprinted with the permission of the National Council of Teachers of English and Gordon E. Bigelow.

theme of despair. It turned out to be of major importance to literature and the arts, to philosophy and theology, and of increasing importance to the social sciences. To learn more about it, I read several of the self-styled introductions to the subject, with the baffled sensation of a man who reads a critical introduction to a novel only to find that he must read the novel before he can understand the introduction. Therefore, I should like to provide here something most discussions of existentialism take for granted, a simple statement of its basic characteristics. This is a reckless thing to do because there are several kinds of existentialism and what one says of one kind may not be true of another, but there is an area of agreement, and it is this common ground that I should like to set forth here. We should not run into trouble so long as we understand from the outset that the six major themes outlined below will apply in varying degrees to particular existentialists. A reader should be able to go from here to the existentialists themselves, to the more specialized critiques of them, or be able to recognize an existentialist theme or coloration in literature when he sees it.

A word first about the kinds of existentialism. Like transcendentalism of the last century, there are almost as many varieties of this *ism* as there are individual writers to whom the word is applied (not all of them claim it). But without being facetious we might group them into two main kinds, the *ungodly* and the *godly*. To take the ungodly or atheistic first, we would list as the chief spokesmen among many others Jean-Paul Sartre, Albert Camus, and Simone de Beauvoir. Several of this important group of French writers had rigorous and significant experience in the Resistance during the Nazi occupation of France in World War II. Out of the despair which came with the collapse of their nation during those terrible years they found unexpected strength in the single indomitable human spirit, which even under severe torture could maintain the spirit of resistance, the unextinguishable ability to say "No." From this irreducible core in the human spirit, they erected after the war a philosophy which was a twentieth-century variation of the philosophy of Descartes. But instead of saying "I think, therefore I am," they said "I can say No, therefore I exist." As we shall presently see, the use of the word "exist" is of prime significance. This group is chiefly responsible for giving existentialism its status in the popular mind as a literary-philosophical cult.

Of the godly or theistic existentialists we should mention first a mid-nineteenth-century Danish writer, Søren Kierkegaard; two contemporary French Roman Catholics, Gabriel Marcel and Jacques Maritain; two Protestant theologians, Paul Tillich and Nicholas Berdyaev; and Martin Buber, an important contemporary Jewish theologian. Taken together, their writings constitute one of the most significant developments in modern theology. Behind both groups of existentialists stand other important figures, chiefly philosophers, who exert powerful influence upon the movement—Blaise Pascal, Friedrich Nietzsche, Henri Bergson, Martin Heidegger, Karl Jaspers, among others. Several literary figures, notably Tolstoy and Dostoievsky, are frequently cited because existentialist attitudes and themes are prominent in their writings. The eclectic nature of this movement should already be sufficiently clear and the danger of applying too rigidly to any particular figure the general characteristics of the movement which I now make bold to describe:

• 1. *Existence before Essence*

Existentialism gets its name from an insistence that human life is understandable only in terms of an individual man's existence, his particular experience of life. It says that a man *lives* (has existence) rather than *is* (has being or essence), and that every man's experience of life is unique, radically different from everyone else's and can be understood truly only in terms of his involvement in life or commitment to it. It strenuously shuns that view which assumes an ideal of Man or Mankind, a universal of human nature of which each man is only one example. It eschews the question of Greek philosophy, *"What is mankind?"* which suggests that man can be defined if he is ranged in his proper place in the order of nature; it asks instead the question of Job and St. Augustine, *"Who am I?"* with its suggestion of the uniqueness and mystery of each human life and its emphasis upon the subjective or personal rather than the objective or impersonal. From the outside a man appears to be just another natural creature; from the inside he is an entire universe, the center of infinity. The existentialist insists upon this latter radically subjective view, and from this grows much of the rest of existentialism.

• 2. *Reason Is Impotent to Deal with the Depths of Human Life*

There are two parts to this proposition—first, that human reason is relatively weak and imperfect, and second, that there are dark places in human life which are "non-reason" and to which reason scarcely penetrates. Since Plato, Western civilization has usually assumed a separation of reason from the rest of the human psyche, and has glorified reason as suited to command the nonrational part. The classic statement of this separation appears in the *Phaedrus,* where Plato describes the psyche in the myth of the chariot which is drawn by the white steeds of the emotions and the black unruly steeds of the appetites. The driver of the chariot is Reason who holds the reins which control the horses and the whip to subdue the surging black steeds of passion. Only the driver, the rational nature, is given human form; the rest of the psyche, the non-rational part, is given a lower, animal form. This separation and exalta-tion of reason is carried further in the allegory of the cave in the *Republic.* You recall the sombre picture of human life with which the story begins: men are chained in the dark in a cave, with their backs to a flickering firelight, able to see only uncertain shadows moving on the wall before them, able to hear only confused echoes of sounds. One of the men, breaking free from his chains, is able to turn and look upon the objects themselves and the light which casts the shadows; even, at last, he is able to work his way entirely out of the cave into the sunlight beyond. All this he is able to do through his reason; he escapes from the bondage of error, from time and change, from death itself, into the realm of changeless eternal ideas or Truth, and the lower nature which had chained him in darkness is left behind.

Existentialism in our time, and this is one of its most important characteristics, insists upon reuniting the "lower" or irrational parts of the psyche with the "higher." It insists that man must be taken in his wholeness and not in some divided state, that whole man contains not only intellect but also anxiety, guilt, and the will to power—which modify and sometimes overwhelm the reason. A man seen in this light is funda-mentally ambiguous, if not mysterious, full of contradictions and tensions which cannot be dissolved simply by taking thought. "Human life," said Berdyaev, "is permeated by underground streams." One is reminded of D. H. Lawrence's outburst against Franklin and his rational attempt to achieve moral perfection: "The Perfectability of Man! . . . The perfectabil-ity of which man? I am many men. Which of them are you going to perfect? I am not a mechanical contrivance. . . . It's a queer thing is a man's soul. It is the whole of him. Which means it is the unknown as well as the known. . . . The soul of man is a dark vast forest, with wild life in it." The emphasis in existentialism is not on idea but upon the thinker who has the idea. It accepts not only his power of thought, but his con-tingency and fallibility, his frailty, his body, blood, and bones, and above all his death. Kierkegaard emphasized the distinction between *subjective* truth (what a person *is*) and *objective* truth (what the person *knows*), and said that we encounter the true self not in the detachment of thought but in the involvement and agony of choice and in the pathos of com-mitment to our choice. This distrust of rational systems helps to explain why many existential writers in their own expression are paradoxical or prophetic or gnomic, why their works often belong more to literature than to philosophy.

• 3. *Alienation or Estrangement*

One major result of the dissociation of reason from the rest of the psyche has been the growth of science, which has become one of the hallmarks of Western civilization, and an ever-increasing rational ordering of men in society. As the existentialists view them, the main forces of history since the Renaissance have progressively separated man from concrete earthly existence, have forced him to live at ever higher levels of abstraction, have collectivized individual man out of existence, have driven God from the heavens, or what is the same thing, from the hearts of men. They are convinced that modern man lives in a fourfold condition of alienation: from God, from nature, from other men, from his own true self.

The estrangement from God is most shockingly expressed by Nietzsche's anguished cry, "God is dead," a cry which has continuously echoed through the writings of the existentialists, particularly the French. This theme of spiritual barrenness is a commonplace in literature of this century, from Eliot's "Hollow Man" to the novels of Dos Passos, Hemingway, and Faulkner. It often appears in writers not commonly associated with the existentialists as in this remarkable passage from *A Story-Teller's Story*, where Sherwood Anderson describes his own awakening to his spiritual emptiness. He tells of walking alone late at night along a moonlit road when,

I had suddenly an odd, and to my own seeming, a ridiculous desire to abase myself before something not human and so stepping into the moonlit road, I knelt in the dust. Having no God, the gods having been taken from me by the life about me, as a personal God has been taken from all modern men by a force within that man himself does not understand but that is called the intellect, I kept smiling at the figure I cut in my own eyes as I knelt in the road. . . .

There was no God in the sky, no God in myself, no conviction in myself that I had the power to believe in a God, and so I merely knelt in the dust in silence and no words came to my lips.

In another passage Anderson wondered if the giving of itself by an entire generation to mechanical things was not really making all men impotent, if the desire for a greater navy, a greater army, taller public buildings, was not a sign of growing impotence. He felt that Puritanism and the industrialism which was its offspring had sterilized modern life, and proposed that man return to a healthful animal vigor by renewed contact with simple things of the earth, among them untrammeled sexual expression. One is reminded of the unkempt and delectable raffishness of Steinbeck's *Cannery Row* or of D. H. Lawrence's quasi-religious doctrine of sex, "blood-consciousness" and the "divine otherness" of animal existence.

Man's estrangement from nature has been a major theme in literature at least since Rousseau and the Romantic movement, and can hardly be said to be the property of existentialists. But this group nevertheless adds its own insistence that one of modern man's most urgent dangers is that he builds ever higher the brick and steel walls of technology which shut him away from a health-giving life according to "nature." Their treatment of this theme is most commonly expressed as part of a broader insistence that modern man needs to shun abstraction and return to "concreteness" or "wholeness."

A third estrangement has occured at the social level and its sign is a growing dismay at man's helplessness before the great machine-like colossus of industrialized society. This is another major theme of Western literature, and here again, though they hardly discovered the danger or began the protest, the existentialists in our time renew the protest against any pattern or force which would stifle the unique and spontaneous in individual life. The crowding of men into cities, the subdivision of labor which submerges the man in his economic function, the burgeoning of centralized government, the growth of advertising, propaganda, and mass media of entertainment and communication—all the things which force men into Riesman's "Lonely Crowd"—these same things drive men asunder by destroying their individuality and making them live on the surface of life, content to deal with things rather than people. "Exteriorization," says Berdyaev, "is the source of slavery, whereas freedom is interiorization. Slavery always indicates alienation, the ejection of human nature into the external." This kind of alienation is exemplified by Zero, in Elmer Rice's play "The Adding Machine." Zero's twenty-five years as a bookkeeper in a department store have dried up his humanity, making him incapable of love, of friendship, of any deeply felt, freely expressed emotion. Such estrangement is often given as the reason for man's inhumanity to man, the explanation for injustice in modern society. In Camus' short novel, aptly called *The Stranger*, a young man is convicted by a court of murder. This is a homicide which he has actually committed under extenuating circumstances. But the court never listens to any of the relevant evidence, seems never to hear anything that pertains to the crime itself; it convicts the young man on wholly irrelevant grounds —because he had behaved in an unconventional way at his mother's funeral the day before the homicide. In this book one feels the same dream-like distortion of reality as in the trial scene in *Alice in Wonderland*, a suffocating sense of being enclosed by events which are irrational or absurd but also inexorable. Most disturbing of all is the young man's aloneness, the impermeable membrane of estrangement which surrounds him and prevents anyone else from penetrating to his experience of life or sympathizing with it.

The fourth kind of alienation, man's estrangement from his own true self, especially as his nature is distorted by an exaltation of reason, is another theme having an extensive history as a major part of the Romantic revolt. Of the many writers who treat the theme, Hawthorne comes particularly close to the emphasis of contemporary existentialists. His Ethan Brand, Dr. Rappaccini, and Roger Chillingworth are a recurrent figure who represents the dislocation in human nature which results when an overdeveloped or misapplied intellect serves "the magnetic chain of human sympathy." Hawthorne is thoroughly existential in his concern for the sanctity of the individual human soul, as well as in his preoccupation with sin and the dark side of human nature, which must be seen in part as his attempt to build back some fullness to the flattened image of man bequeathed to him by the Enlightenment. Whitman was trying to do this when he added flesh and bone and a sexual nature to the spiritualized image of man he inherited from Emerson, though his image remains diffused and attenuated by the same cosmic optimism. Many of the nineteenth-century depictions of man represent him as a figure of power or of potential power, sometimes as daimonic, like Melville's Ahab, but after World War I the power is gone; man is not merely distorted or truncated, he is hollow, powerless, faceless. At the time when his command over natural forces seems to be unlimited, man is pictured as weak, ridden with nameless dread. And this brings us to another of the major themes of existentialism.

• 4. *"Fear and Trembling," Anxiety*

At Stockholm when he accepted the Nobel Prize, William Faulkner said that "Our tragedy today is a general and universal physical fear so long sustained by now that we can even bear it. There are no longer problems of the spirit. There is only one question: When will I be blown up?" The optimistic vision of the Enlightenment which saw man, through reason and its extensions in science, conquering all nature and solving all social and political problems in a continuous upward spiral of Progress, cracked open like a melon on the rock of World War I. The theories which held such high hopes died in that sickening and unimaginable butchery. Here was a concrete fact of human nature and society which the theories could not contain. The Great Depression and World War II deepened the sense of dismay which the loss of these ideals brought, but only with the atomic bomb did this become an unbearable terror, a threat of instant annihilation which confronted all men, even those most insulated by the thick crust of material goods and services. Now the most unthinking person could sense that each advance in mechanical technique carried not only a chromium and plush promise of comfort but a threat as well.

Sartre, following Kierkegaard, speaks of another kind of anxiety which oppresses modern man—"the anguish of Abraham"—the necessity which is laid upon him to make moral choices on his own responsibility. A military officer in wartime knows the agony of choice which forces him to sacrifice part of his army to preserve the rest, as does a man in high political office, who must make decisions affecting the lives of millions. The existentialists claim that each of us must make moral decisions in our own lives which involve the same anguish. Kierkegaard finds that this necessity is one thing which makes each life unique, which makes it impossible to speculate or generalize about human life, because each man's case is irretrievably his own, something in which he is personally and passionately involved. His book *Fear and Trembling* is an elaborate and fascinating commentary on the Old Testament story of Abraham, who was commanded by God to sacrifice his beloved son Isaac. Abraham thus becomes the emblem of man who must make a harrowing choice, in this case between love for his son and love for God, between the universal moral law which says categorically, "thou shalt not kill," and the unique inner demand of his religious faith. Abraham's decision, which is to violate the abstract and collective moral law, has to be made not in arrogance but in fear and trembling, one of the inferences being that sometimes one must make an exception to the general law because he is (existentially) an exception, a concrete being whose existence can never be completely subsumed under any universal.

• 5. *The Encounter with Nothingness*

For the man alienated from God, from nature, from his fellow man and from himself, what is left at last but Nothingness? The testimony of the existentialists is that this is where modern man now finds himself, not on the highway of upward Progress toward a radiant Utopia but on the brink of a catastrophic precipice, below which yawns the absolute void, an uncompromised black Nothingness. In one sense this is Eliot's Wasteland inhabited by his Hollow Man, who is

> *Shape without form, shade without color*
> *Paralyzed force, gesture without motion.*[1]

---

[1] T. S. Eliot's "The Hollow Men" from *Collected Poems of T. S. Eliot*, New York: Harcourt, Brace & World, Inc., 1963. Reprinted by permission of Harcourt, Brace & World, Inc.

This is what moves E. A. Robinson's Richard Cory, the man who is everything that might make us wish that we were in his place, to go home one calm summer night and put a bullet through his head.

One of the most convincing statements of the encounter with Nothingness is made by Leo Tolstoy in "My Confession." He tells how in good health, in the prime of life, when he had everything that a man could desire—wealth, fame, aristocratic social position, a beautiful wife and children, a brilliant mind and great artistic talent in the height of their powers, he nevertheless was seized with a growing uneasiness, a nameless discontent which he could not shake or alleviate. His experience was like that of a man who falls sick, with symptoms which he disregards as insignificant; but the symptoms return again and again until they merge into a continuous suffering. And the patient suddenly is confronted with the overwhelming fact that what he took for mere indisposition is more important to him than anything else on earth, that it is death! "I felt the ground on which I stood was crumbling, that there was nothing for me to stand on, that what I had been living for was nothing, that I had no reason for living. . . . To stop was impossible, to go back was impossible; and it was impossible to shut my eyes so as to see that there was nothing before me but suffering and actual death, absolute annihilation." This is the "Sickness Unto Death" of Kierkegaard, the despair in which one wishes to die but cannot. Hemingway's short story, "A Clean, Well-Lighted Place," gives an unforgettable expression of this theme. At the end of the story, the old waiter climbs into bed late at night saying to himself, "What did he fear? It was not fear or dread. It was a nothing which he knew too well. It was all a nothing and a man was nothing too. . . . Nada y pues nada, y nada y pues nada." And then because he has experienced the death of God he goes on to recite the Lord's Prayer in blasphemous despair: "Our Nothing who art in Nothing, nothing be thy nothing. . . ." And then the Ave Maria, "Hail nothing, full of nothing. . . ." This is stark, even for Hemingway, but the old waiter does no more than name the void felt by most people in the early Hemingway novels, a hunger they seek to assuage with alcohol, sex, and violence in an aimless progress from bar to bed to bull-ring. It goes without saying that much of the despair and pessimism in other contemporary authors springs from a similar sense of the void in modern life.

• 6. *Freedom*

Sooner or later, as a theme that includes all the others, the existentialist writings bear upon freedom. The themes we have outlined above describe either some loss of man's freedom or some threat to it, and all existentialists of whatever sort are concerned to enlarge the range of human freedom.

For the avowed atheists like Sartre freedom means human autonomy. In a purposeless universe man is *condemned* to freedom because he is the only creature who is "self-surpassing," who can become something other than he is. Precisely because there is no God to give purpose to the universe, each man must accept individual responsibility for his own becoming, a burden made heavier by the fact that in choosing for himself he chooses for all men "the image of man as he ought to be." A man *is* the sum total of the acts that make up his life—no more, no less—and though the coward has made himself cowardly, it is always possible for him to change and make himself heroic. In Sartre's novel, *The Age of Reason,* one of the least likable of the characters, almost overwhelmed by despair and self-disgust at his homosexual tendencies, is on the point of solving his problem by mutilating himself with a razor, when in an effort of will he throws the instrument down, and we are given to understand that from this moment he will have mastery over his aberrant drive. Thus in the daily course of ordinary life must men shape their becoming in Sartre's world.

The religious existentialists interpret man's freedom differently. They use much the same language as Sartre, develop the same themes concerning the predicament of man, but always include God as a radical factor. They stress the man of faith rather than the man of will. They interpret man's existential condition as a state of alienation from his essential nature which is God-like, the problem of his life being to heal the chasm between the two, that is, to find salvation. The mystery and ambiguity of man's existence they attribute to his being the intersection of two realms. "Man bears within himself," writes Berdyaev, "the image which is both the image of man and the image of God, and is the image of man as far as the image of God is actualized." Tillich describes salvation as "the act in which the cleavage between the essential being and the existential situation is overcome." Freedom here, as for Sartre, involves an acceptance of responsibility for choice and a *commitment* to one's choice. This is the meaning of faith, a faith like Abraham's, the commitment which is an agonizing sacrifice of one's own desire and will and dearest treasure to God's will.

A final word. Just as one should not expect to find in a particular writer all of the characteristics of existentialism as we have described them, he should also be aware that some of the most striking expressions of existentialism in literature and the arts come to us by indirection, often through symbols or through innovations in conventional form. Take the preoccupation of contemporary writers with time. In *The Sound and the*

Fury, Faulkner both collapses and expands normal clock time, or by juxtapositions of past and present blurs time into a single amorphous pool. He does this by using various forms of "stream of consciousness" or other techniques which see life in terms of unique, subjective experience —that is, existentially. The conventional view of externalized life, a rational orderly progression cut into uniform segments by the hands of a clock, he rejects in favor of a view which sees life as opaque, ambiguous, and irrational—that is, as the existentialist sees it. Graham Greene does something like this in *The Power and the Glory.* He creates a scene isolated in time and cut off from the rest of the world, steamy and suffocating as if a bell jar had been placed over it. Through this atmosphere fetid with impending death and human suffering, stumbles the whiskey priest, lonely and confused, pursued by a police lieutenant who has experienced the void and the death of God.

Such expressions in literature do not mean necessarily that the authors are conscious existentialist theorizers, or even that they know the writings of such theorizers. Faulkner may never have read Heidegger—or St. Augustine—both of whom attempt to demonstrate that time is more within a man and subject to his unique experience of it than it is outside him. But it is legitimate to call Faulkner's views of time and life "existential" in this novel because in recent years existentialist theorizers have given such views a local habitation and a name. One of the attractions, and one of the dangers, of existential themes is that they become like Sir Thomas Browne's quincunx: once one begins to look for them, he sees them everywhere. But if one applies restraint and discrimination, he will find that they illuminate much of contemporary literature and sometimes the literature of the past as well.

• Questions for Study

1. Bigelow bases his essay upon the definition of a term. What methods does he use to develop the definition of existentialism?
2. At the heart of existentialism is the idea that "each man must accept individual responsibility for his own becoming." Do you think that this idea makes existentialism too subjective an approach to life? Explain. What would happen if, for example, a man chose to become a thief or a murderer?
3. Can you recognize any of Bigelow's existential themes in such writers as Buber, Tillich, Dawson, or Maritain, or in other writers who are not formally existentialists?
4. How wide has the influence of existential ideas been on modern authors with which you are familiar?

WILLIAM BARRETT

•

INTRODUCTION TO *ZEN BUDDHISM*

I

What we call the Western tradition is formed by two major influences, Hebraic and Greek, and both these influences are profoundly dualistic in spirit. That is, they divide reality into two parts and set one part off against the other. The Hebrew makes his division on religious and moral grounds: God absolutely transcends the world, is absolutely separate from it; hence there follow the dualisms of God and creature, the Law and the erring members, spirit and flesh. The Greek, on the other hand, divides reality along intellectual lines. Plato, who virtually founded Western philosophy single-handed—Whitehead has remarked that 2500 years of Western philosophy is but a series of footnotes to Plato—absolutely cleaves reality into the world of the intellect and the world of the senses. The great achievement of the Greeks was to define the ideal of rationality for man; but in doing so, Plato and Aristotle not only made reason the highest and most valued function, they also went so far as to make it the very center of our personal identity. The Orientals never succumbed to this latter error; favoring intuition over reason, they grasped intuitively a center of the personality which held in unity the warring opposites of reason and unreason, intellect and senses, morality and nature. So far as we are Westerners, we inherit these dualisms, they are part of us: an irrationally nagging conscience from the Hebrews, an excessively dividing rational mind from the Greeks. Yet the experience of modern culture, in the most diverse fields, makes them less and less acceptable.

Medieval Christianity still lives in the rational world of the Greeks.

The universe of St. Thomas Aquinas is the same bandbox universe of Aristotle, a tight tiny tidy rational whole, where all is in apple-pie order, and everything occupies it logical and meaningful place in the absolute hierarchy of Being. When we turn from such humanized universes to Indian thought, we are at first staggered by the vision of vast spaces, endless aeons of time, universe upon universe, against which man looks very small and meaningless; then we realize these are the spaces and times of modern astronomy, and the Indian idea is therefore closer to us. The distinguished Protestant theologian Paul Tillich has described the essential experience of modern man as an encounter with "meaninglessness": lost in the vastness of the universe, man begins to think that his own existence and that of the universe are "meaningless." The God of Theism, says Tillich echoing Nietzsche, is dead, and Western man must find a God beyond the God of Theism: the God offered us by rational theology is no longer acceptable. From the point of view of the medieval Catholic (and many still survive) the very premises of Buddhist thinking would look "meaningless"; they are also more difficult and grim, but they look much closer to what we moderns may have to swallow.

In science itself, modern developments have combined to make our inherited rationalism more shaky. Physics and mathematics, the two most advanced of Western sciences, have in our time become paradoxical: that is, arrived at the state where they breed paradoxes for reason itself. One hundred fifty years ago the philosopher Kant attempted to show that there were ineluctable limits to reason, but the Western mind, positivistic to the core, could be expected to take such a conclusion seriously only when it showed up in science itself. Well, science in this century has at last caught up with Kant: almost simultaneously Heisenberg in physics, and Godel in mathematics, have shown ineluctable limits to human reason. Heisenberg's Principle of Indeterminacy shows essential limits to our ability to know and predict physical states of affairs, and opens up to us the glimpse of a nature irrational and chaotic at bottom. Godel's results would seem to have even more far-reaching consequences when one reflects that in the Western tradition, from the Pythagoreans and Plato onward, mathematics has inspired the most absolute claims of rationalism. Now it turns out that even in his most precise science—in the province where his reason had seemed omnipotent—man cannot escape his essential finitude: every system of mathematics that he constructs is doomed to incompleteness. Mathematics is like a ship in mid-ocean that has sprung leaks (paradoxes) which have been temporarily plugged, but our reason can never guarantee that the ship will not spring other leaks. That this human insecurity should manifest itself in what had hitherto been the very citadel of reason, mathematics, marks a new turn in Western thinking. The next step would be to recognize the essentially paradoxical nature of reason itself.

This step has been taken by some modern philosophers. The most original and influential philosopher now alive on the European continent is the German Existentialist Martin Heidegger. A German friend of Heidegger told me that one day when he visited Heidegger he found him reading one of Suzuki's books; "If I understand this man correctly," Heidegger remarked, "this is what I have been trying to say in all my writings." This remark may be the slightly exaggerated enthusiasm of a man under the impact of a book in which he recognizes some of his own thoughts; certainly Heidegger's philosophy in its tone and temper and sources is Western to its core, and there is much in him that is not in Zen, but also very much more in Zen that is not in Heidegger; and yet the points of correspondence between the two, despite their disparate sources, are startling enough. For what, after all, is Heidegger's final message but that Western philosophy is a great error, the result of the dichotomizing intellect that has cut man off from unity with Being itself and from his own Being. This error begins (in Plato) with locating truth in the intellect; the world of nature thereby becomes a realm of objects set over against the mind, eventually objects to be manipulated by scientific and practical calculation. Twenty-five hundred years of Western metaphysics move from Plato's intellectualism to Nietzsche's Will to Power, and concurrently man does become in fact the technological master of the whole planet; but the conquest of nature merely estranges him from Being itself and from his own Being and delivers him over to an ever ascending, ever more frantic will to power. "Divide and conquer" might thus be said to be the motto which Western man has adopted toward Being itself; but this of course is the counsel of power not of wisdom. Heidegger repeatedly tells us that this tradition of the West has come to the end of its cycle; and as he says this, one can only gather that he himself has already stepped beyond that tradition. Into the tradition of the Orient? I should say at least that he has come pretty close to Zen.

If these happenings in science and philosophy indicate changed ways of thinking in the West, our modern art would seem to indicate very new ways of feeling. Whatever may be said on the thorny subject of modern art, the one fact that is clear is that to the artistic conservative it represents a scandal and a break with the tradition. Our modern art presents a surface so irrational, bizarre, and shocking that it must be considered a break with the older more rational canons of Western art. That Western painters and sculptors in this century have gone outside their tradition to nourish themselves with the art of the rest of the world

—Oriental, African, Melanesian—signifies that what we knew as *the* tradition is no longer able to nourish its most creative members; its confining mould has broken, under pressures from within. Our painting has detached itself from three-dimensional space, the arena of Western man's power and mobility; detached itself from the object, the supreme fixation of Western man's extroversion; and it has become subjective, contrary to the whole tenor of our Western life. Is all this merely malaise and revolt, or prophecy of a different spirit to come? In the past, new styles of painting have often been thus prophetic. In the art of literature, of course, the writer can be vocal about the new and revolutionary thing, and we find a novelist like D. H. Lawrence preaching against the bloodless rationalism of his culture. Lawrence urged the necessity of something he called "mindlessness," of becoming "mindless," if the meddlesome and self-conscious intellect were not in the end to cut off Western man irreparably from nature and even the possibility of real sexual union. Oddly enough, this "mindlessness" of Lawrence is a groping intuition after the doctrine of "no-mind" which Zen Buddhism had elaborated a thousand years before. Unlike Lawrence, however, the Zen masters developed this doctrine without falling into primitivism and the worship of the blood. In Lawrence's behalf it must be remembered that his culture gave him no help at all on these matters, and he had to grope in the dark pretty much on his own. And to change to one final literary example that involves no preaching or thesis whatsoever: the most considerable work of prose in English in this century is probably James Joyce's *Ulysses,* and this is so profoundly Oriental a book that the psychologist C. G. Jung recommended it as a long-needed bible for the white-skinned peoples. Joyce shattered the aesthetic of the Georgians that would divide reality into a compartment of the Beautiful forever separate from the opposite compartments of the Ugly or Sordid. *Ulysses,* like the Oriental mind, succeeds in holding the opposites together: light and dark, beautiful and ugly, sublime and banal. The spiritual premise of this work is an acceptance of life that no dualism—whether puritanical or aesthetic—could ever possibly embrace.

Admittedly, all these happenings I have cited—from science, philosophy, art—make up a very selective list; this list could be expanded greatly; nevertheless even as it stands, these instances make up a body of "coincidence" so formidable that they must make us pause. When events run parallel this way, when they occur so densely together in time and in such diverse fields, they can no longer be considered as mere meaningless "coincidence" but as very meaningful symptoms; in this case symptoms that the West in its own depths begins to experience new things, begins in fact to experience its own opposite. In this new climate a concern with something like Zen Buddhism can no longer be taxed as idle exoticism, for it has to do with the practical daily bread of the spirit.

The really somber paradox about all these changes is that they have happened in the deep and high parts of our culture, while in the areas in between everything goes on as usual. Despite the discoveries of its artists, philosophers, theoretical scientists, the West, in its public and external life at any rate, is just as Western as ever, if not more so. Gadgets and traffic accumulate, the American way of life (or else the Russian) spreads all over the globe, the techniques for externalizing life become year by year more slick and clever. All of which may only show what a creature of contradictions Western man has become. And now that at last his technology has put in his hands the hydrogen bomb, this fragmented creature has the power to blow himself and his planet to bits. Plain common sense would seem to advise that he turn to look inward a little.

II

None of the above considerations has to do with Zen itself. Or rather —to put it abruptly as Zen likes to do—Zen has nothing at all to do with them. They deal with the complicated abstractions of the intellect —philosophy, culture, science, and the rest—and what Zen seeks above all is the concrete and the simple that lie beyond the snarled tangles of intellectualization. Zen *is* the concrete itself. Zen eschews abstractions, or uses them only to get beyond them. Even when Zen declares against abstractions, it has to put the matter concretely: thus when the great Master Tokusan has his enlightenment, he does not merely say in pallid fashion that concepts are not enough; no, he burns all his philosophic texts, declaring, "All our understanding of the abstractions of philosophy is like a single hair in the vastness of space." Let the Western reader fasten upon this image and he will find it harder to miss the point. Or when another Master remarks on the difficulty of solving one of the Zen questions—which is equivalent to answering the riddle of existence itself—he does not merely say that it is difficult or so very very difficult that it is well-nigh impossible, but this: "It is like a mosquito trying to bite into an iron bull." The image lives because the image suggests the meaning beyond conceptualization.

Now it is just this concreteness of expression, this extraordinary profusion of images and examples, that can make Zen most helpful to the Westerner, who in fact derives from a more highly abstract culture. But

it would be a mistake for the Western reader to imagine that these are
merely so many literary devices or adornments adopted by the Zen
masters. On the contrary, the language of Zen is of the essence, the
manner of expression is one with the matter. Zen expresses itself concretely because Zen is above all interested in facts not theories, in realities
and not those pallid counters for reality which we know as concepts.
"Fact" may suggest to the Western mind something merely quantitative
or statistical—therefore also a lifeless and abstract thing. Zen wants,
rather, the facts as living and concrete. In this sense, Zen might be
described as Radical Intuitionism—if the Westerner wishes a handle by
which to lay hold of it. This does not mean that it is merely a philosophy
of intuition like Bergson's, though it agrees with Bergson that the con-
ceptualizing intellect does not reach reality; rather, it is radical intuition
in the act itself. Radical Intuitionism means that Zen holds that thinking
and sensing live, move, and have their being within the vital medium of
intuition. We see with the two eyes only insofar as we are also seeing
(though we may not know it) with the third eye—the eye of intuition.
Hence, any sensory facts will do for Zen provided they serve to awaken
the third eye, and we encounter in the Zen writings the most extraordinary incidents of illumination in connection with the most humble
objects. In the end all language is pointing: we use language to point
beyond language, beyond concepts to the concrete. The monk asks the
Master, "How may I enter in the Way?", and the Master, pointing to the
mountain spring, responds, "Do you hear the sound of that torrent?
There you may enter." Another time Master and monk are walking upon
the mountain, and the master asks, "Do you smell the mountain laurel?"
"Yes." "There, I have held nothing back from you."

In its emphasis upon the living fact over the mere idea, Zen is true
to the essential teaching of Buddha. Buddha cared very little for the
philosophers; there were said to be already some 63 schools in existence
in his time, and he had occasion to observe from their wrangling how
imprisoned in the labyrinths of the intellect the human spirit can become.
Thus Zen itself is not a philosophy (the Western reader must be warned
here), though there lie behind it some of the great philosophies of
Mahayana Buddhism. Though Buddha began by opposing the philosophers, nevertheless in the course of its history Buddhism evolved one of
the greatest and most profound philosophies ever created. Is this a contradiction of the original spirit of the founder? No; for Buddhist philosophy is activated by an altogether different purpose from that of Western
philosophy: Buddhism takes up philosophy only as a device to save the
philosopher from his conceptual prison; its philosophy is, as it were, a
non-philosophy, a philosophy to undo philosophy. A comparison of the

mind of Buddha and Plato—probably the greatest intellects of East and West—may make us understand how sharply East and West diverge on this crucial point. For Plato philosophy is a discipline that leads us from the lower to the higher world, from the world of the senses to the world of ideas, to leave us abiding in this latter world as much as is humanly possible; for the Buddhist, philosophy should lead us beyond the intellect back into the one real world that was always there in its undivided wholeness. Zen presupposes this view of philosophy, but goes beyond the mere restatement of it to make actual use of it in its practical and concrete Chinese fashion.

This passion for the living fact accounts for that quality in the Zen masters which must seem most amazing to the Westerner: their supreme matter-of-factness. "What is the Tao (the way, the truth)?" asks the disciple. "Your everyday mind," replies the Master; and he goes on to amplify: "When I am hungry, I eat; when tired, I sleep." The disciple is puzzled, and asks whether this is not what everybody else does too. No, the Master replies; most people are never wholly in what they are doing; when eating, they may be absent-mindedly preoccupied with a thousand different fantasies; when sleeping, they are not sleeping. The supreme mark of the thoroughly integrated man is to be without a divided mind. This matter-of-fact spirit of Zen is expressed in another paradoxical statement: "Before you have studied Zen, mountains are mountains and rivers are rivers; while you are studying it, mountains are no longer mountains and rivers no longer rivers; but once you have had Enlightenment, mountains are once again mountains and rivers are rivers." The stories of their arduous struggles for Enlightenment teach us that this matter-of-fact spirit of the Zen masters is not a thing easily come by: they are indeed awesome figures who have crossed the mountains and rivers, floods and fires of the spirit in order to come back sole and whole to the most banal things of daily life. The nearest thing to this, so far as I know, that the West has produced is Kierkegaard's wonderful comparison of the Knight of Resignation and the Knight of Faith: the former all fidgets and romanticism, aspiring after the infinite but never at home with the finite, while the Knight of Faith sits so solidly in his existence that from without he looks as prosaic and matter-of-fact as a tax-collector. But this ideal of being in direct and unmediated relation to ordinary reality was somethting that poor Kierkegaard, who waged a feverish lifelong struggle against the mediating and devouring power of his intelligence, could only aspire after but never realize.

In this striving for an unmediated relation to reality, as well as in its doctrine of an enlightenment (satori) that goes beyond reason, Zen would seem to be a form of Mysticism. But Zen is not mysticism as the

West understands mysticism. The mystic, as defined by William James in *Varieties of Religious Experience* (James did not know about Zen), is one who pierces the veil of the natural or sensuous world in order to experience direct union with the higher reality. This formula holds for most of the great Western mystics from Plotinus onward, but it would not hold of Zen, which would reject this kind of mysticism as dualistic through and through, since it divides reality into lower and higher worlds. For Zen, higher and lower are one world; and in the records of Zen enlightenment which Suzuki sets before us there does not seem to occur anywhere the blurring of consciousness, the trancelike or semi-hallucinated state, which you will find among Western mystics. Even where it seems to move closest to mysticism, Zen remains supremely matter-of-fact. Nor is Zen to be confused with anything like pantheism, even though the Zen writings abound in statements that the Buddha-nature is to be found everywhere, in the dried up dirt-scraper, the cypress tree in the courtyard, etc., etc. Pantheism involves a division between the God who penetrates nature and nature itself as the phenomenal garment of God. But this too is a dualism that Zen leaves behind.

Neither a philosophy, then, in the Western sense, nor a mysticism, not Pantheism and not Theism, Zen might seem to the reader at this point so much a matter of subtlety and nuance as to be devoid of all practical value. On the contrary; for the greatest contemporary tribute to the practicality of Zen comes not from philosophers or artists, but from two prominent *practicing* psychiatrists, C. C. Jung and Karen Horney, who became passionately interested in Zen for its therapeutic possibilities. Jung has written about Zen, and before her death Karen Horney visited Japan to observe the life of a Zen monastery at first hand. What attracted Jung to Zen was its remarkable pursuit of psychological wholeness. Horney saw something similar, but in terms of her own psychology: namely, the search for self-realization without either the false image of an idealized self ("We are saved such as we are," says the Zen master), or without the resigned and dependent clinging to eternal props like family, social group, or church (after his enlightenment the disciple slaps the Master Obaku's face, remarking "There is not, after all, very much in the Buddhism of Obaku", and the master is pleased, for the disciple shows he can now stand on his own two feet). Certainly the Zen masters, as we read of them in Suzuki's pages give us the powerful impression of fully individuated individuals, carved out of one whole and solid block. What is most incredible to the Westerner is that this demand for the individuation of the disciple should be made by a *religion!* Western religions have always been willing to settle for less, very much less, from the believer—his filial obedience or docility, let him be a miserable psychological fragment otherwise. The reason is that Western religion has always placed the weight of emphasis upon the religious object outside the individual—God beyond the world, the Mosaic Law, the Church, the divine personality of Jesus. One can hardly imagine a Western religion producing a saying like the Zen Master's to his monks, "When you utter the name of Buddha, wash your mouth out". Zen is individualistic, and so iconoclastic and antinomian in its individualism that it will seem irreverent to many Westerners; but this is only because Zen wishes to strip the individual naked in order to return him to himself: in the end he cannot lean even upon the image of Buddha. Here precisely is the aspect of Zen Buddhism which is the greatest challenge to Western religions, and which needs to be studied most by us Westerners; for the march of our own history, as the great world of medieval religious images recedes ever further from our grasp and an inceasingly secularized society engulfs us, has stripped Western man naked and left no rocklike security anywhere to lean upon. Here there looms before the frightened eyes of the Westerner what Buddhism calls the Great Emptiness; but if he does not run away in fear, this great void may bloom with all manner of miracles, and heaven and earth, in consort once again, engender effortlessly all their ancient marvels.

As to what Zen is, I leave the reader to discover in Suzuki's own pages that follow; what I have provided have been but a few negative warnings, signposts not to stray off the road, which come out of my own earlier failures of understanding. But there is one final misgiving I imagine taking shape in the reader's mind, because it has been taking shape in mine as I write, which needs to be faced before we are done; and it is this: Must not Buddhism forever remain an alien form to the Westerner? something he cannot appropriate and make his own? Are not the conditions that make ourselves and our lives what they are such that something like Zen could never be lived here? The question cannot be shirked; Zen itself would insist upon it, since Zen holds that it is not the abstract or bookish truth but the lived truth that counts. Indeed, the question looms so intensely before my mind that it seems almost to take on the imaginary body of some Zen master shaking his stick, threatening thirty blows and crying, "Speak quick, quick!" Well then, quickly: I would agree with Suzuki when he holds that Zen is the living fact in all religions East or West; or, a little more modestly, that Zen touches what is the living fact in all religions. For the readers of this book the question will hardly arise of becoming a Buddhist, but that does not lessen the importance of Zen to them: for however small the fragment of Zen that makes live contact with the Westerner, its influence is bound to work through, and he will never be quite the same again. In the beautiful words of the Master Hoyen: *When water is scooped up in the hands, the moon is reflected in them; when flowers are handled, the scent soaks into the robe.*

• Questions for Study

1. What is essentially the tradition of Western philosophy, according to Barrett? How does Barrett show, in his examples from science, philosophy, art, and psychiatry, that this tradition "has come to the end of its cycle"?
2. What does the Zen Master mean when he says, "All our understanding of the abstractions of philosophy is like a single hair in the vastness of space"? Why might Zen be called Radical Intuitionism? Give some examples of negative definition.
3. Both Barrett and Buber, in his essay "I and Thou," are presenting subjects that are somewhat similar. In what ways do their treatments differ? Which presentation makes the subject easier to understand? Explain.
4. Write a theme in which you suggest your own definition of what Zen is from the hints which you have received from Barrett's essay. How would the last sentence (italicized) help you in defining Zen?

SIGMUND FREUD

•

MISTAKES IN SPEECH

In the psychotherapeutic procedure which I employ in the solution and removal of neurotic symptoms, I am often confronted with the task of discovering from the accidental utterances and fancies of the patient the thought contents, which, though striving for concealment, nevertheless unintentionally betray themselves. In doing this the mistakes often per-

From *Psychopathology of Everyday Life,* New York: The Macmillan Company, 1925. Separate division of the Crowell Collier Publishing Co. Reprinted by permission of Ernest Benn Limited.

form the most valuable service, as I can show through most convincing and still most singular examples.

For example, patients speak of an aunt and later, without noting the mistake, call her "my mother," or designate a husband as a "brother." In this way they attract my attention to the fact that they have "identified" these persons with each other, that they have placed them in the same category, which for their emotional life signifies the recurrence of the same type. Or, a young man of twenty years presents himself during my office hours with these words: "I am the father of N. N., whom you have treated—pardon me, I mean the brother; why, he is four years older than I." I understand through this mistake that he wishes to express that, like the brother, he too, is ill through the fault of the father; like his brother, he wishes to be cured, but that the father is the one most in need of treatment. At other times an unusual arrangement of words, or a forced expression, is sufficient to disclose in the speech of the patient the participation of a repressed thought having a different motive.

Hence, in coarse as well as in finer speech disturbances, which may, nevertheless, be subsumed as "speech-blunders," I find that it is not the contact effects of the sound, but the thoughts outside the intended speech, which determine the origin of the speech-blunder, and also suffice to explain the newly formed mistakes in speech. I do not doubt the laws whereby the sounds produce changes upon one another; but they alone do not appear to me sufficiently forcible to mar the correct execution of speech. In those cases which I have studied and investigated more closely they merely represent the preformed mechanism, which is conveniently utilized by a more remote psychic motive. The latter does not, however, form a part of the sphere of influence of these sound relations. *In a large number of substitutions caused by mistakes in talking there is an entire absence of such phonetic laws.* In this respect I am in full accord with Wundt, who likewise assumes that the conditions underlying speech-blunders are complex and go far beyond the contact effect of the sounds.

If I accept as certain "these more remote psychic influences," following Wundt's expression, there is still nothing to detain me from conceding also that in accelerated speech, with a certain amount of diverted attention the causes of speech-blunder may be easily limited to the definite law of Meringer and Mayer. However, in a number of examples gathered by these authors a more complicated solution is quite apparent.

In some forms of speech-blunders we may assume that the disturbing factor is the result of striking against obscene words and meanings. The purposive disfigurement and distortion of words and phrases, which is so popular with vulgar persons, aims at nothing else but the employing of a harmless motive as a reminder of the obscene, and this sport is so frequent that it would not be at all remarkable if it appeared unintentionally and contrary to the will.

I trust that the readers will not depreciate the value of these interpretations, for which there is no proof, and of these examples which I have myself collected and explained by means of analysis. But if secretly I still cherish the expectation that even the apparently simple cases of speech-blunder will be traced to a disturbance caused by a half-repressed idea outside of the intended context, I am tempted to it by a noteworthy observation of Meringer. This author asserts that it is remarkable that nobody wishes to admit having made a mistake in speaking. There are many intelligent and honest people who are offended if we tell them that they made a mistake in speaking. I would not risk making this assertion as general as does Meringer, using the term "nobody." But the emotional trace which clings to the demonstration of the mistake, which manifestly belongs to the nature of shame, has its significance. It may be classed with the anger displayed at the inability to recall a forgotten name, and with the surprise at the tenaciousness of an apparently indifferent memory, and it invariably points to the participation of a motive in the formation of the disturbance.

The distorting of names amounts to an insult when done intentionally, and could have the same significance in a whole series of cases where it appears as unintentional speech-blunders. The person who, according to Mayer's report, once said "Freuder" instead of "Freud," because shortly before he pronounced the name "Breuer", and who at another time spoke of the "Freuer-Breudian" method, was certainly not particularly enthusiastic over this method. . . .

As a disturbing element in these cases there is an intermingling of a criticism which must be omitted, because at the time it does not correspond to the intention of the speaker.

Or it may be just the reverse; the substituted name, or the adoption of the strange name, signifies an appreciation of the same. The identification which is brought about by the mistake is equivalent to a recognition which for the moment must remain in the background. An experience of this kind from his school days is related by Dr. Sandor Ferenczi:

"While in my first year at college I was obliged to recite a poem before the whole class. It was the first experience of the kind in my life, but I was well prepared. As soon as I began my recitation I was dismayed at being disturbed by an outburst of laughter. The professor later explained to me this strange reception. I started by giving the title, 'From the Distance,' which was correct, but instead of giving the name of the real author, I mentioned—my own. The name of the poet is Alexander Petofi. The identity of the first name with my own favored the interchange of names, but the real reason was surely the fact that I identified myself at that time with the celebrated poet-hero. Even consciously I entertained for him a love and respect which verged on adoration. The whole ambition-complex hides itself under this faulty action."

A similar identification was reported to me concerning a young physician who timidly and reverently introduced himself to the celebrated Virchow with the following words: "I am Dr. Virchow." The surprised professor turned to him and asked, "Is your name also Virchow?" I do not know how the ambitious young man justified his speech-blunder, whether he thought of the charming excuse that he imagined himself so insignificant next to this big man that his own name slipped from him, or whether he had the courage to admit that he hoped that he, too, would some day be as great a man as Virchow, and that the professor should therefore not treat him in too disparaging a manner. One or both of these thoughts may have put this young man in an embarrassing position during the introduction.

Owing to very personal motives I must leave it undecided whether a similar interpretation may also apply in the case to be cited. At the International Congress in Amsterdam, in 1907, my theories of hysteria were the subject of a lively discussion. One of my most violent opponents, in his diatribe against me, repeatedly made mistakes in speech in such a manner that he put himself in my place and spoke in my name. He said, for example, "Breuer and I, as is well known, have demonstrated," etc., when he wished to say "Breuer and Freud." The name of this opponent does not show the slightest sound similarity to my own. From this example, as well as from other cases of interchanging names in speech-blunders, we are reminded of the fact that the speech-blunder can fully forego the facility afforded to it through similar sounds, and can achieve its purpose if only supported in content by concealed relations.

In other and more significant cases it is a self-criticism, an internal contradiction against one's own utterance, which causes the speech-blunder, and even forces a contrasting substitution for the one intended. We then observe with surprise how the wording of an assertion removes the purpose of the same, and how the error in speech lays bare the inner dishonesty. Here the *lapsus linguae* becomes a mimicking form of expression, often, indeed, for the expression of what one does not wish to say. It is thus a means of self-betrayal.

Brill relates: "I had recently been consulted by a woman who showed many paranoid trends, and as she had no relatives who could co-operate with me, I urged her to enter a state hospital as a voluntary patient. She was quite willing to do so, but on the following day she told me that her friends with whom she leased an apartment objected to her going to a hospital, as it would interfere with their plans, and so on. I lost patience and said: 'There is no use listening to your friends who know nothing about your mental condition; you are quite *incompetent* to take care of your own affairs.' I meant to say 'competent.' Here the *lapsus linguae* expressed my true opinion."

Favored by chance the speech material often gives origin to examples of speech-blunders which serve to bring about an overwhelming revelation or a full comic effect, as shown by the following examples reported by Brill:

"A wealthy but not very generous host invited his friends for an evening dance. Everything went well until about 11.30 P.M., when there was an intermission, presumably for supper. To the great disappointment of most of the guests there was no supper; instead, they were regaled with thin sandwiches and lemonade. As it was close to Election Day the conversation centered on the different candidates; and as the discussion grew warmer, one of the guests, an ardent admirer of the Progressive Party candidate, remarked to the host: 'You may say what you please about Teddy, but there is one thing—he can always be relied upon; he always gives you a *square meal*,' wishing to say *square deal.* The assembled guests burst into a roar of laughter, to the great embarrassment of the speaker and the host, who fully understood each other."

"While writing a prescription for a woman who was especially weighed down by the financial burden of the treatment, I was interested to hear her say suddenly: 'Please do not give me *big bills*, because I cannot swallow them.' Of course she meant to say *pills.*"

•

WHY WAR?

I can now proceed to add a gloss to another of your remarks. You express astonishment at the fact that it is so easy to make men enthusiastic about a war and add your suspicion that there is something at work in them—an instinct for hatred and destruction—which goes halfway to meet the efforts of the warmongers. Once again, I can only express my entire agreement. We believe in the existence of an instinct of that kind and have in fact been occupied during the last few years in studying its manifestations. Will you allow me to take this opportunity of putting before you a portion of the theory of the instincts which, after much tentative groping and many fluctuations of opinion, has been reached by workers in the field of psycho-analysis?

According to our hypothesis human instincts are of only two kinds: those which seek to preserve and unite—which we call "erotic," exactly in the sense in which Plato uses the word 'Eros' in his *Symposium*, or "sexual," with a deliberate extension of the popular conception of "sexuality"—and those which seek to destroy and kill and which we class together as the aggressive or destructive instinct. As you see, this is in fact no more than a theoretical clarification of the univerally familiar opposition between Love and Hate which may perhaps have some fundamental relation to the polarity of attraction and repulsion that plays a part in your own field of knowledge. We must not be too hasty in introducing ethical judgements of good and evil. Neither of these instincts is any less essential than the other; the phenomena of life arise from the operation of both together, whether acting in concert or in opposition. It seems as though an instinct of the one sort can scarcely ever operate in isolation; it is always accompanied—or, as we say, alloyed—with an element from the other side, which modifies its aim or is, in some cases, what enables it to achieve that aim. Thus, for instance, the instinct of self-preservation is certainly of an erotic kind, but it must nevertheless

From a letter to Albert Einstein in *The Collected Papers of Sigmund Freud*, Volume V, New York: Basic Books, Inc., 1959. Reprinted by permission of Basic Books, Inc.

have aggressiveness at its disposal if it is to fulfil its purpose. So, too, the instinct of love, when it is directed towards an object, stands in need of some contribution from the instinct of mastery if it is in any way to possess that object. The difficulty of isolating the two classes of instinct in their actual manifestations is indeed what has so long prevented us from recognizing them.

If you will follow me a little further, you will see that human actions are subject to another complication of a different kind. It is very rarely that an action is the work of a *single* instinctual impulse (which must in itself be compounded of Eros and destructiveness). In order to make an action possible there must be as a rule a *combination* of such compounded motives. This was perceived long ago by a specialist in your own subject, a Professor G. C. Lichtenberg who taught physics at Göttingen during our classical age—though perhaps he was even more remarkable as a psychologist than as a physicist. He invented a Compass of Motives, for he wrote: "The motives that lead us to do anything might be arranged like the thirty-two winds and might be given names on the same pattern: for instance, 'food-food-fame' or 'fame-fame-food'." So that when human beings are incited to war they may have a whole number of motives for assenting—some noble and some base, some of which they speak openly and others on which they are silent. There is no need to enumerate them all. A lust for aggression and destruction is certainly among them: the countless cruelties in history and in our everyday lives vouch for its existence and its strength. The gratification of these destructive impulses is of course facilitated by their admixture with others of an erotic and idealistic kind. When we read of the atrocities of the past, it sometimes seems as though the idealistic motives served only as an excuse for the destructive appetites; and sometimes—in the case, for instance, of the cruelties of the Inquisition—it seems as though the idealistic motives had pushed themselves forward in consciousness, while the destructive ones lent them an unconscious reinforcement. Both may be true.

I fear I may be abusing your interest, which is after all concerned with the prevention of war and not with our theories. Nevertheless I should like to linger for a moment over our destructive instinct, whose popularity is by no means equal to its importance. As a result of a little speculation, we have come to suppose that this instinct is at work in every living being and is striving to bring it to ruin and to reduce life to its original condition of inanimate matter. Thus it quite seriously deserves to be called a death instinct, while the erotic instincts represent the effort to live. The death instinct turns into the the destructive instinct if, with the help of special organs, it is directed outwards, on to objects.

The living creature preserves its own life, so to say, by destroying an extraneous one. Some portion of the death instinct, however, remains operative *within* the living being, and we have sought to trace quite a number of normal and pathological phenomena to this internalization of the destructive instinct. We have even been guilty of the heresy of attributing the origin of conscience to this diversion inwards of aggressiveness. You will notice that it is by no means a trivial matter if this process is carried too far: it is positively unhealthy. On the other hand if these forces are turned to destruction in the external world, the living creature will be relieved and the effect must be beneficial. This would serve as a biological justification for all the ugly and dangerous impulses against which we are struggling. It must be admitted that they stand nearer to Nature than does our resistance to them, for which an explanation also needs to be found. It may perhaps seem to you as though our theories are a kind of mythology and, in the present case, not even an agreeable one. But does not every science come in the end to a kind of mythology like this? Cannot the same be said to-day of your own Physics?

For our immediate purpose then, this much follows from what has been said: there is no use in trying to get rid of men's aggressive inclinations. We are told that in certain happy regions of the earth, where nature provides in abundance everything that man requires, there are races whose life is passed in tranquillity and who know neither compulsion nor aggressiveness. I can scarcely believe it and I should be glad to hear more of these fortunate beings. The Russian Communists, too, hope to be able to cause human aggressiveness to disappear by guaranteeing the satisfaction of all material needs and by establishing equality in other respects among all the members of the community. That, in my opinion, is an illusion. They themselves are armed to-day with the most scrupulous care and not the least important of the methods by which they keep their supporters together is hatred of everyone beyond their frontiers. In any case, as you yourself have remarked, there is no question of getting rid entirely of human aggressive impulses; it is enough to try to divert them to such an extent that they need not find expression in war.

Our mythological theory of instincts makes it easy for us to find a formula for *indirect* methods of combating war. If willingness to engage in war is an effect of the destructive instinct, the most obvious plan will be to bring Eros, its antagonist, into play against it. Anything that encourages the growth of emotional ties between men must operate against war. These ties may be of two kinds. In the first place they may be relations resembling those towards a loved object, though without having a sexual aim. There is no need for psychoanalysis to be ashamed to speak of love in this connection, for religion itself uses the same words: "Thou shalt love thy neighbour as thyself." This, however, is more easily said than done. The second kind of emotional tie is by means of identification. Whatever leads men to share important interests produces this community of feeling, these identifications. And the structure of human society is to a large extent based on them.

A complaint which you make about the abuse of authority brings me to another suggestion for the indirect combating of the propensity to war. One instance of the innate and ineradicable inequality of men is their tendency to fall into the two classes of leaders and followers. The latter constitute the vast majority; they stand in need of an authority which will make decisions for them and to which they for the most part offer an unqualified submission. This suggests that more care should be taken than hitherto to educate an upper stratum of men with independent minds, not open to intimidation and eager in the pursuit of truth, whose business it would be to give direction to the dependent masses. It goes without saying that the encroachments made by the executive power of the State and the prohibition laid by the Church upon freedom of thought are far from propitious for the production of a class of this kind. The ideal condition of things would of course be a community of men who had subordinated their instinctual life to the dictatorship of reason. Nothing else could unite men so completely and so tenaciously, even if there were no emotional ties between them. But in all probability that is a Utopian expectation. No doubt the other indirect methods of preventing war are more practicable, though they promise no rapid success. An unpleasant picture comes to one's mind of mills that grind so slowly that people may starve before they get their flour.

The result, as you see, is not very fruitful when an unworldly theoretician is called in to advise on an urgent practical problem. It is a better plan to devote oneself in every particular case to meeting the danger with whatever weapons lie to hand. I should like, however, to discuss one more question, which you do not mention in your letter but which specially interests me. Why do you and I and so many other people rebel so violently against war? Why do we not accept it as another of the many painful calamities of life? After all, it seems quite a natural thing, no doubt it has a good biological basis and in practice it is scarcely avoidable. There is no need to be shocked at my raising this question. For the purpose of an investigation such as this, one may perhaps be allowed to wear a mask of assumed detachment. The answer to my question will be that we react to war in this way because everyone has a right to his own life, because war puts an end to human lives that are full of hope, because it brings individual men into humiliating situations, because it compels them against their will to murder other men, and because it destroys precious material objects which have been produced by the labours of humanity. Other reasons besides might be given, such as that in its present-day form war is no longer an opportunity for achieving the old ideals of heroism and that owing to the perfection of instruments of destruction a future war might involve the extermination of one or perhaps both of the antagonists. All this is true, and so incontestably true that one can only feel astonished that the waging of war has not yet been unanimously repudiated. No doubt debate is possible upon one or two of these points. It may be questioned whether a community ought not to have a right to dispose of individual lives; every war is not open to condemnation to an equal degree; so long as there exist countries and nations that are prepared for the ruthless destruction of others, those others must be armed for war. But I will not linger over any of these issues; they are not what you want to discuss with me, and I have something different in mind. It is my opinion that the main reason why we rebel against war is that we cannot help doing so. We are pacifists because we are obliged to be for organic reasons. And we then find no difficulty in producing arguments to justify our attitude.

No doubt this requires some explanation. My belief is this. For incalculable ages mankind has been passing through a process of evolution of culture. (Some people, I know, prefer to use the term "civilization.") We owe to that process the best of what we have become, as well as a good part of what we suffer from. Though its causes and beginnings are obscure and its outcome uncertain, some of its characteristics are easy to perceive. It may perhaps be leading to the extinction of the human race, for in more than one way it impairs the sexual function; uncultivated races and backward strata of the population are already multiplying more rapidly than highly cultivated ones. The process is perhaps comparable to the domestication of certain species of animals and it is undoubtedly accompanied by physical alterations; but we are still unfamiliar with the notion that the evolution of culture is an organic process of this kind. The psychical modifications that go along with the cultural process are striking and unambiguous. They consist in a progressive displacement of instinctual aims and a restriction of instinctual impulses. Sensations which were pleasurable to our ancestors have become indifferent or even intolerable to ourselves; there are organic grounds for the changes in our ethical and aesthetic ideals. Of the psychological characteristics of culture two appear to be the most important: a strengthening of the intellect, which is beginning to govern instinctual life, and an internalization of the aggressive impulses, with all its consequent advantages and perils. Now war is in the crassest opposition to the psychical attitude imposed on us by the cultural process, and for that reason we are bound to rebel against it; we simply cannot any longer put up with it. This is not merely an intellectual and emotional repudiation; we pacifists have a constitutional intolerance of war, an idiosyncracy magnified, as it were, to the highest degree. It seems, indeed, as though the lowering of aesthetic standards in war plays a scarcely smaller part in our rebellion than do its cruelties.

And how long shall we have to wait before the rest of mankind become pacifists too? There is no telling. But it may not be Utopian to hope that these two factors, the cultural attitude and the justified dread of the consequences of a future war, may result within a measurable time in putting an end to the waging of war. By what paths or by what side-tracks this will come about we cannot guess. But one thing we *can* say: whatever fosters the growth of culture works at the same time against war.

I trust you will forgive me if what I have said has disappointed you, and I remain, with kindest regards,

Yours sincerely,
SIGM. FREUD

• Questions for Study

1. In "Mistakes in Speech," Freud skillfully utilizes anecdotes or illustrations to emphasize a central idea. Examine closely two or three of these and point out characteristics which they have in common.
2. What two opposing causes of word-slips does Freud give? Can you suggest any other reasons for word-slips which Freud does not consider in his essay?
3. It is important to remember that Freud's essays are translated from the German. What special problems did the translator probably face?
4. In "Why War?" Freud recognizes two principles, the Love and Death instincts, which govern human action and which serve as the basis for his views on pacificism and war. How does he define the Love and Death instincts and how does he apply them to his central thesis?
5. Do you agree with his statement in "Why War?" that "there is no use trying to get rid of man's aggressive inclinations"? Might wars be caused by protective instincts, by man's desire to defend his country, rather than by aggressive instincts?

CARL G. JUNG

•

GOD, THE DEVIL,

AND THE HUMAN SOUL

For more than fifty years we have known, or could have known, that there is an unconscious as a counterbalance to consciousness. Medical psychology has furnished all the necessary empirical and experimental proofs of this. There is an unconscious psychic reality which demonstrably influences consciousness and its contents. All this is known, but no practical conclusions have been drawn from it. We still go on thinking and acting as before, as if we were *simplex* and not *duplex*. Accordingly we imagine ourselves to be innocuous, reasonable, and humane. We do not think of distrusting our motives or of asking ourselves how the inner man feels about the things we do in the outside world. But actually it is frivolous, superficial, and unreasonable of us, as well as psychically unhygienic, to overlook the reaction and viewpoint of the unconscious.

One can regard one's stomach or heart as unimportant and worthy of contempt, but that does not prevent overeating or overexertion from having consequences that affect the whole man. Yet we think that psychic mistakes and their consequences can be got rid of with mere words, for "psychic" means less than air to most people. All the same, nobody can deny that without the psyche there would be no world at all and still less a human world. Virtually everything depends on the human soul and its functions. It should be worthy of all the attention we can give it, especially today, when everyone admits that the weal or woe of the future will be decided neither by the attacks of wild animals nor by natural catastrophes nor by the danger of world-wide epidemics but simply by the psychic changes in man.

It needs only an almost imperceptible disturbance of equilibrium in a few of our rulers' heads to plunge the world into blood, fire, and radioactivity. The technical means necessary for this are present on both sides. And certain conscious deliberations, uncontrolled by any inner opponent, can be indulged in all too easily, as we have seen already from the example of one "leader." The consciousness of modern man still clings so much to outward objects that he makes them exclusively responsible, as if it were on them that the decision depended. That the psychic state of certain individuals could emancipate itself for once from the behavior of objects is something that is considered far too little, although irrationalities of this sort are observed every day and can happen to everyone.

The forlornness of consciousness in our world is due primarily to the loss of instinct, and the reason for this lies in the development of the human mind over the past aeon. The more power man had over nature the more his knowledge and skill went to his head and the deeper became his contempt for the merely natural and accidental, for that which is irrationally given—including the objective psyche, which is all that consciousness is not.

In contrast to the subjectivism of the conscious mind, the unconscious is objective, manifesting itself mainly in the form of contrary feelings, fantasies, emotions, impulses, and dreams, none of which one makes oneself but which come upon one objectively. Even today psychology is still for the most part the science of conscious contents, measured as far as possible by collective standards. The individual psyche became a mere accident, a "random" phenomenon, while the unconscious, which can only manifest itself in the real, "irrationally given" human being, was ignored altogether. This was not the result of carelessness or of lack of knowledge, but of downright resistance to the mere possibility of there being a second psychic authority besides the ego. It seems a positive menace to the ego that its monarchy could be doubted. The religious person, on the other hand, is accustomed to the thought of not being sole master in his own house. He believes that God, and not he himself, decides in the end. But how many of us would dare to let the will of God decide, and which of us would not feel embarrassed if he had to say how far the decision came from God himself?

The religious person, so far as one can judge, stands directly under the influence of the reaction from the unconscious. As a rule he calls this the operation of *conscience*. But since the same psychic background produces reactions other than moral ones, the believer is measuring his conscience by the traditional ethical standard and thus by a collective value, in which endeavor he is assiduously supported by his Church. So long as the individual can hold fast to his traditional beliefs, and the circumstances of his time do not demand stronger emphasis on individual autonomy, he can rest content with the situation. But the situation is radically altered when the worldly-minded man who is oriented to external factors and has lost his religious beliefs appears en masse, as is the case today. The believer is then forced into the defensive and must catechize himself on the foundation of his beliefs. He is no longer sustained by the tremendous suggestive power of the *consensus omnium*, and is keenly aware of the weakening of the Church and the precariousness of its dogmatic assumptions.

To counter this the Church recommends more faith, as if this gift of grace depended on man's good will and pleasure. The seat of faith, however, is not consciousness but spontaneous religious experience, which brings man's faith into immediate relation with God.

Here we must ask: Have I any religious experience and immediate relation to God, and hence that certainty which will keep me, as an individual, from dissolving in the crowd?

To this question there is a positive answer only when the individual is willing to fulfill the demands of rigorous self-examination and self-knowledge. If he follows through his intention, he will not only discover some important truths about himself, but will also have gained a psychological advantage: he will have succeeded in deeming himself worthy of serious attention and sympathetic interest. He will have set his hand to a declaration of his own human dignity and taken the first step toward the foundations of his consciousness—that is, toward the unconscious, the only accessible source of religious experience.

This is certainly not to say that what we call the unconscious is identical with God or is set up in his place. It is the medium from which the religious experience seems to flow. As to what the further cause of such an experience may be, the answer to this lies beyond the range of human knowledge. Knowledge of God is a transcendental problem.

The religious person enjoys a great advantage when it comes to answering the crucial question that hangs over our time like a threat: he has a clear idea of the way his subjective existence is grounded in his relation to "God." I put the word "God" in quotes in order to indicate that we are dealing with an anthropomorphic idea whose dynamism and symbolism are filtered through the medium of the unconscious psyche. Anyone who wants to can at least draw near the source of such experiences, no matter whether he believes in God or not. Without this approach it is only in rare cases that we witness those miraculous conversions of which Paul's Damascus experience is the prototype.

That religious experiences exist no longer needs proof. But it will always remain doubtful whether what metaphysics and theology call God and the gods is the real ground of these experiences. The question is idle, actually, and answers itself by reason of the subjectively overwhelm-

ing numinosity of the experience. Anyone who has had it is *seized* by it
and therefore not in a position to indulge in fruitless metaphysical or
epistemological speculations. Absolute certainty brings its own evidence
and has no need of anthropomorphic proofs.

In view of the general ignorance of and bias against psychology it
must be accounted a misfortune that the one experience which makes
sense of individual existence should seem to have its origin in a medium
that is certain to catch everybody's prejudices. Once more the doubt is
heard: "What good can come out of Nazareth?" The unconscious, if not
regarded outright as a sort of refuse bin underneath the conscious mind,
is at any rate supposed to be of "merely animal nature." In reality, however, and by definition it is of uncertain extent and constitution, so that
over- or under-valuation of it is groundless and can be dismissed as mere
prejudice. At all events such judgments sound very queer in the mouths
of Christians whose Lord was himself born on the straw of a stable, among
the domestic animals. It would have been more to the taste of the multitude if he had got himself born in a temple. In the same way, the worldly-
minded mass man looks for the numinous experience in the mass meeting,
which provides an infinitely more imposing background than the individual soul. Even Church Christians share this pernicious delusion.

Psychology's insistence on the importance of unconscious processes
for religious experience is extremely unpopular, no less with the Right
than with the Left. For the former the deciding factor is the historical
revelation that came to man from outside; to the latter this is sheer nonsense, and man has no religious function at all, except belief in the party
doctrine, when suddenly the most intense faith is called for. On top of
this, the various creeds assert quite different things, and each of them
claims to possess the absolute truth. Yet today we live in a unitary world
where distances are reckoned by hours and no longer by weeks and
months. Exotic races have ceased to be peep shows in ethnological museums. They have become our neighbors, and what was yesterday the
prerogative of the ethnologist is today a political, social, and psychological
problem. Already the ideological spheres begin to touch, to interpene-
trate, and the time may not be so far off when the question of mutual
understanding in this field will become acute.

To make oneself understood is certainly impossible without far-
reaching comprehension of the other's viewpoint. The insight needed for
this will have repercussions on both sides. History will undoubtedly pass
over those who feel it is their vocation to resist this inevitable development, however desirable and psychologically necessary it may be to cling
to what is essential and good in our own tradition. Despite all the differences, the unity of mankind will assert itself irresistibly. On this card

Marxist doctrine has staked its life, while the West hopes to get through with technology and economic aid. Communism has not overlooked the enormous importance of the ideological element and the universality of basic principles. The nations of the Far East share this ideological weakness with us and are just as vulnerable as we are.

The underestimation of the psychological factor is likely to take bitter revenge. It is therefore high time we caught up with ourselves in this matter. For the present this must remain a pious wish, because self-knowledge, in addition to being highly unpopular, seems to be unpleasantly idealistic, reeks of morality, and is preoccupied with the psychological shadow, which is denied whenever possible or at least not spoken of. The task that faces our age is indeed almost insuperably difficult. It makes the highest demands on our responsibility if we are not to be guilty of another *trahison des clercs*. It addresses itself to those guiding and influential personalities who have the necessary intelligence to understand the situation our world is in.

One might expect them to consult their consciences. But since it is not only a matter of intellectual understanding but of moral conclusions, there is unfortunately no cause for optimism. Nature, as we know, is not so lavish with her boons that she joins to a high intelligence the gifts of the heart also. As a rule, where one is present the other is lacking, and where one capacity is present to perfection it is generally at the cost of all the others. The discrepancy between intellect and feeling, which get in each other's way at the best of times, is a particularly painful chapter in the history of the human psyche.

There is no sense in formulating the task that our age has forced upon us as a moral demand. We can, at best, merely make the psychological world situation so clear that it can be seen even by the myopic, and give utterance to words and ideas which even the hard of hearing can hear. We may hope for men of understanding and men of good will, and must therefore not grow weary of reiterating those thoughts and insights which are needed. Finally, even the truth can spread and not only the popular lie.

With these words I should like to draw the reader's attention to the main difficulty he has to face. The horror which the dictator states have of late brought upon mankind is nothing less than the culmination of all those atrocities of which our ancestors made themselves guilty in the not so distant past. Quite apart from the barbarities and blood baths perpetrated by the Christian nations among themselves throughout European history, the European has also to answer for all the crimes he has committed against the dark-skinned peoples during the process of colonization. In this respect the white man carries a very heavy burden indeed.

It shows us a picture of the common human shadow that could hardly be painted in blacker colors. The evil that comes to light in man and which undoubtedly dwells within him is of gigantic proportions, so that for the Church to talk of original sin and to trace it back to Adam's relatively innocent slip-up with Eve is almost a euphemism. The case is far graver and is grossly underestimated.

Since it is universally believed that man *is* merely what his consciousness knows of itself, he regards himself as harmless and so adds stupidity to iniquity. He does not deny that terrible things have happened and still go on happening, but it is always the others who do them. And when such deeds belong to the recent or remote past, they quickly and conveniently sink into the sea of forgetfulness, and that state of chronic woolly-mindedness returns which we describe as "normality."

In shocking contrast to this is the fact that nothing has finally disappeared and nothing has been made good. The evil, the guilt, the profound unease of conscience, the obscure misgiving, are there before our eyes, if only we would see. Man has done these things; I am a man who has his share of human nature; therefore I am guilty with the rest and bear unaltered and indelibly within me the capacity and the inclination to do them again at any time. Even if, juristically speaking, we were not accessories to the crime, we are always, thanks to our human nature, potential criminals. In reality we merely lacked a suitable opportunity to be drawn into the infernal melee. None of us stands outside humanity's black collective shadow. Whether the crime lies many generations back or happens today, it remains the symptom of a disposition that is always and everywhere present—and one would therefore do well to possess some "imagination in evil," for only the fool can permanently neglect the conditions of his own nature. In fact, this negligence is the best means of making him an instrument of evil. Harmlessness and naïveté are as little helpful as it would be for a cholera patient and those in his vicinity to remain unconscious of the contagiousness of the disease. On the contrary, they lead to projection of the unrecognized evil into the "other." This strengthens the opponent's position in the most effective way, because the projection carries the *fear* which we involuntarily and secretly feel for our own evil over to the other side and considerably increases the formidableness of his threat.

What is even worse, our lack of insight deprives us of the *capacity to deal with evil*. Here, of course, we come up against one of the main prejudices of the Christian tradition, and one that is a great stumbling block to our policies. We should, so we are told, eschew evil and if possible neither touch nor mention it. For evil is also the thing of ill omen, that which is tabooed and feared. This apotropaic attitude toward evil, and the apparent circumventing of it, flatter the primitive tendency in us to shut our eyes to evil and drive it over some frontier or other, like the Old Testament scapegoat, which was supposed to carry the evil into the wilderness.

But if one can no longer avoid the realization that evil, without man's ever having chosen it, is lodged in human nature itself, then it bestrides the psychological stage as the equal and opposite partner of good. This realization leads straight to a psychological dualism, already unconsciously prefigured in the political world-schism and in the even more unconscious dissociation in modern man himself. The dualism does not come from this realization; rather, we are in a split condition to begin with. It would be an insufferable thought that we had to take personal responsibility for so much guiltiness. We therefore prefer to localize the evil with individual criminals or groups of criminals, while washing our hands in innocence and ignoring the general proclivity to evil.

This sanctimoniousness cannot be kept up in the long run, because the evil, as experience shows, lies in man—unless, in accordance with the Christian view, one is willing to postulate a metaphysical principle of evil. The great advantage of this view is that it exonerates man's conscience of too heavy a responsibility and fobs it off on the Devil, in correct psychological appreciation of the fact that man is much more the victim of his psychic constitution than its inventor. Considering that the evil of our day puts everything that has ever agonized mankind in the deepest shade, one must ask oneself how it is that, for all our progress in the administration of justice, in medicine, and in technics, for all our concern for life and health, monstrous engines of destruction have been invented which could easily exterminate the human race.

No one will maintain that the atomic physicists are a pack of criminals because it is to their efforts that we owe that peculiar flower of human ingenuity, the hydrogen bomb. The vast amount of intellectual work that went into the development of nuclear physics was put forth by men who devoted themselves to their task with the greatest exertions and self-sacrifice and whose moral achievement could just as easily have earned them the merit of inventing something useful and beneficial to humanity. But even though the first step along the road to a momentous invention may be the outcome of a conscious decision, here as everywhere the spontaneous idea—the hunch or intuition—plays an important part. In other words, the unconscious collaborates too and often makes decisive contributions.

So it is not the conscious effort alone that is responsible for the result; somewhere or other the unconscious, with its barely discernible goals and intentions, has its finger in the pie. If it puts a weapon in your hand, it is aiming at some kind of violence. Knowledge of the truth is the foremost goal of science, and if in pursuit of the longing for light we stumble upon an immense danger, then one has the impression more of fatality than of premeditation. It is not that present-day man is capable of greater evil than the man of antiquity or the primitive. He merely has incomparably more effective means with which to realize his proclivity to evil. As his consciousness has broadened and differentiated, so his normal nature has lagged behind. That is the great problem before us today. *Reason alone does not suffice.*

In theory, it lies within the power of reason to desist from experiments of such hellish scope as nuclear fission if only because of their dangerousness. But fear of the evil which one does not see in one's own bosom, but always expects in somebody else's, checks reason every time, although one knows that the use of this weapon means the certain end of our present human world. The fear of universal destruction may spare us the worst, yet the possibility of it will nevertheless hang over us like a dark cloud so long as no bridge is found across the world-wide psychic and political split—a bridge as certain as the existence of the hydrogen bomb. If a world-wide consciousness could arise that all division and all fission is due to the splitting of opposites in the psyche, then one would really know where to attack. But if even the smallest and most personal stirrings of the individual soul—so insignificant in themselves—remain as unconscious and unrecognized as they have done hitherto, they will go on accumulating and produce mass groupings and mass movements which cannot be subjected to reasonable control or manipulated to a good end. All direct efforts to do so are no more than shadow boxing, the most infatuated by illusion being the gladiators themselves.

The deciding factor lies with the individual man, who knows no answer to his dualism. This abyss has suddenly yawned open before him with the latest events in world history, after mankind had lived for many centuries in the comfortable belief that a unitary God had created man in his own image, as a little unity. Even today people are largely unconscious of the fact that every individual is a cell in the structure of various international organisms and is therefore causally implicated in their conflicts. He knows that as an individual being he is more or less meaningless and feels himself the victim of uncontrollable forces, but on the other hand he harbors within himself a dangerous shadow and opponent who is involved as an invisible helper in the dark machinations of the political monster.

• *Questions for Study*

1. Compare and contrast Jung's ideas with those of Freud in "Why War?" Compare also the style of both writers. Defend or attack the proposition that Jung's style is difficult. To what extent can we say that Jung's subject demands a difficult style?
2. How does Jung view the relationship between the unconscous and the conscious? In what new ways does he use such familiar concepts as "God," the "Devil," and "Human Soul"?
3. Why, according to the author, is it important to recognize that evil is "lodged in human nature" and how does he suggest that our capacity to deal with evil be developed?
4. What does the author mean when he says that "Reason alone does not suffice"?

STANLEY E. HYMAN

•

A CRITICAL LOOK
AT PSYCHOLOGY

A considerable presumption is involved when a man criticizes a field not his own, particularly when that field is as multiverse as psychology. The presumption increases when the criticism is based on a reading acquaintance with only the tiniest fraction of the literature in one small area, and a few friends in the field who must be thoroughly unrepresentative, in that they exhibit none of its defects or failings. All I can say in extenuation

Reprinted from *The American Scholar*, Volume 29, Number 1, Winter 1959–1960. Copyright © 1959 by the United Chapters of Phi Beta Kappa. By permission of the publishers and the author. Selections of Yeats' poetry from *Collected Poems of William Butler Yeats*, 2d ed., New York: The Macmillan Company. Separate division of the Crowell Collier Publishing Co., 1950.

is that it is the engagingly old-fashioned habit of literary criticism to insist that it still takes all knowledge to be its province, and that the impulse is friendly, based on an enormous respect for the field of psychology and a sharing of its aspirations. Sometimes an amateur can see things that the professional misses, or at the very least his insolence can annoy the professional into considering matters usually outside his specialized sphere. Still, perhaps "look" in my title is overambitious. Call it "glance" or "squint."

Psychology arose historically as a branch of philosophy (where it is still ensconced in some booksellers' catalogues, if no longer in academic departments). The earliest development of its insights, however, came from writers, Sigmund Freud repeatedly credited the poets with anticipating his discoveries (by delving into their own psyches, he said), and how could he have acknowledged the debt more prettily than by naming the complex he considered nuclear after the protagonist in two plays by Sophocles? Thomas Hardy knew psychoanalysis, Freud once told C. P. Oberndorf, meaning it in the sense in which we rediscover the mechanisms of depth psychology each time we open Shakespeare.

In noting these anticipations and intuitions, however, we must not minimize the difference between writers and psychologists. Athenian tragedies are, in fact, oddly unpsychological (someone remarked that there was more psychology in a page of Proust than in the whole extant corpus of Greek drama), in that in them character always arises out of action, never the reverse. King Oedipus, we must remember, has no explicit Oedipus complex in Sophocles' play of that name: he killed his father and married his mother in all innocence, although he *is* oddly short-tempered with gentlemen of his father's generation, and he seems to have shown no reluctance about marrying a widow well along in years. Oedipus' daughter Antigone has something that looks much more like a traditional complex, although even here it is not very explicit. Sophocles' predecessor Aeschylus is fuller and clearer about motivation in such characters as Clytemnestra in the *Agamemnon,* but only by the time we get to Euripides do we begin to rival case history: the marvelous comic agon between anal-character father and anal-character son in the *Alcetis;* the classic disintegration of the repressed homosexual personality of King Pentheus in *The Bacchae.*

Even in the adventure stories of that busy syndicate we call Homer there are touches that stagger us by their psychological truth: the boy Astyanax' terror of his father's great erect helmet crest in *Iliad* 6; Penelope's dream of the eagle and geese in *Odyssey* 19, with its eloquent wish-fulfillment and elaborate condensation and displacement. Nor did the ancient Greeks have a monopoly on psychological insight. The other major progenitor of Western culture, the Hebrew Bible, is fully as knowledgeable, and it should be a chastening experience for the modern psychologist to reread (or read) the history of Saul and his "bloody house" in the books of Samuel, and see the complexities of emotional relationship in the odd triangle of mad, hostile Saul, smitten Jonathan and ambivalent David.

All this is perhaps a long running start for some strictures against current American psychology, except insofar as the literary critic, with his tiny capital invested in Homer and the Bible, Greek drama and Shakespeare, Proust and Thomas Hardy, can fairly ask what the new management thinks it is doing to the old firm. Perhaps, to paraphrase a cynical saying, every country gets the psychologists it deserves; but I am not sure that justice is that poetic. In any case, I should like to suggest five limitations in current American psychology as I have encountered them. The examples are drawn almost entirely from the human-adjustment psychology we outsiders get to read about—psychoanalysis, psychiatry, clinical psychology—but no evidence suggests that these things are less true of the manipulators of earthworms and golden hamsters.

The first is an inadequate history and culture, ranging from simple, provincial ignorance to a self-righteous hostility, strongly Calvinist in nature. Many psychologists seem to be ignorant even of the history of their own field, or to despise their founding fathers as obsolete, unscientific old fuddy-duddies. "We *know* so much more than they did," T. S. Eliot says, phrasing a similar attitude in regard to the poets of the past, and answers it, "Precisely, and they are that which we know." I have heard a young psychologist dismiss as ludicrous the most enthralling case history I have read, Morton Prince's *The Dissociation of a Personality*, because Prince had the misfortune to write it in 1905 rather than in 1959, to know less depth psychology in 1905 than my young acquaintance does in 1959, and not to be equally aware that the successive personalities Miss Beauchamp developed might be artifacts of Prince's own creation. Yet the imaginative power and breadth of Prince's picture of the human personality still make the case a revelation to read, and Prince was improvising his theory as he went along, like Charcot, Janet or Freud. When Drs. Corbett H. Thigpen and Hervey M. Cleckley published the record of a similar case as *The Three Faces of Eve* in 1957, with far less excuse than Prince for being unaware that the successive personalities might be artifacts of the therapists', their book, written as sensationally and badly as Prince's book was written with dignity and style, was introduced rapturously by a past president of the American Psychological Association and apparently was taken seriously in the field.

If many American psychologists know little about the history of their own discipline, they seem to know less about the history and values of anything else. When they are concerned with literature or the arts at all, it is as simple projective tests for revealing the warp of the individual or the culture, and they are far more apt to take their examples exclusively from films, soap operas and comic strips than from Cervantes, Pushkin or Montaigne. This seems much less true of the European-born among American psychologists, perhaps because their education was broader, perhaps because they have been encouraged to see themselves as heirs of the culture, rather than new settlers building on its ruins. How far we have come from the ideal of a man like William James, at home in half a dozen disciplines, or Freud, reading eight languages and their literatures, studying archaeology and anthropology, collecting antiquities and Yiddish jokes.

The second weakness I see in American psychology is a philosophical shallowness and superficial optimism. I have already stated my views along these lines in an essay, "Psychoanalysis and the Climate of Tragedy," in *Partisan Review* for Spring, 1956, and I do not here propose to repeat those chilling blithe quotations about human nature and destiny from such neo-Freudians as Karen Horney, Erich Fromm and Clara Thompson. I have since, however, encountered a book that seems to me a representative specimen of inspirational psychology, *Why You Do What You Do: A Guide to Self-Understanding*, edited by two laymen, Robert N. Linscott and Jess Stein. Here, along with some excellent contributions by serious therapists, one can learn from "a leading American psychiatrist" that adolescent hostility and aggression can be cured by "a well-organized social program," or see "one of New York's leading psychiatrists" solve the problems of impotence and frigidity with such vulgar wisdom as "Encouragement by a wife, even a well-placed bit af flattery after a successful contact, may pay enormous dividends." I hope there is no need to quote further. A similar philosophic shallowness and optimism, it seems to me, distinguishes those psychologists at the other end of the tonal spectrum from these cheery oracles, the cynical whores of motivation research who are so contemptuous of mankind that they believe we are "easier to be played on than a pipe" (a quotation, incidentally, from the creator of one of the earliest motivation analysts in literature, Dr. Iago).

Third, I should like to note the tendency of American psychology toward oversimplification, its apparent preference for the reductive and the mechanistic rather than the complex tangled bank of life. This, among the experimental psychologists, results in a passion for quantification and results that are expressible in statistical tables. These rigors are always defended as the only way in which psychology can become a true em-

pirical science, yet in reality they are the only way psychology can eliminate so many factors not susceptible of quantification as to become as
shapely and remote from life as classical economics. Where the experimental psychologists want quantification, many clinical psychologists
appear to want a similarly reductive empirical success: tests that will
have a high diagnostic efficiency even if the actual relationship of manifestations to meanings remains as mysterious as augury; short-cut treatments that will calm or cure as magically as exorcism. And so many
psychoanalysts and psychiatrists seem principally to want a showy new
term or theory they can call their own, an "Orestes" complex or a "gambling" neurosis. The latter term, by the way, I get from a book, Edmund
Bergler's *The Psychology of Gambling*, which has one of the funniest
unconscious puns I know—the author's boast that a patient he treated
for impotence "is today one of the pillars of the bar association." Perhaps
all of these—tables and statistics, tests and short cuts, terms and theories
—similarly can be pillars of the impotent.

My fourth criticism is the related matter of narrowness and overspecialization. I would regard its characteristic myopic preoccupation
with a facet of a segment of an approach to one aspect of a problem as
primarily responsible (cultural inadequacy is certainly a factor too) for
the awful prose in which most current psychology seems to be written.
Early in the twenties, I learn from Frederick J. Hoffman's *Freudianism
and the Literary Mind*, a girl named Mercy Rogers read through 102
books on psychoanalysis and allied subjects and then killed herself.
Today she could not have gotten through the curdled and clotted prose
of half that number anywhere in the field of psychology before turning
on the gas.

We have for so long been told of the gains (and they are impressive
gains) obtained through specialization, teamwork and interdisciplinary
co-operation, that it is about time we began to notice the losses. As long
ago as 1950, in *Childhood and Society*, Erik H. Erikson warned that interdisciplinary teamwork was "a kind of halt-and-blind cooperation, in
which a social scientist with little psychological vision carries in a piggy-
back fashion a psychologist who has not learned to move with ease in
the larger events of this world, so that together they may grope their way
through contemporary history." In the Summer, 1958, issue of the *North-
west Review*, a political scientist, Lucian C. Marquis, delivered a full-
scale attack on interdisciplinary teamwork. "It is time," he suggested,
"that we call for a cease-fire, in order to assess the price of our victory
and to count the casualities," which include, in his view, initiative, independence, creativity, invention, "thwarted individuality and the leveling
of tastes and interests." Specialization seems inevitably forced on the

modern social scientist, and some co-operation of specialists must follow
as a consequence, but none of the by-products is inevitable, least of all the
new "team man," with his extraordinary efficiency in a narrow groove, his
unconcerned and routine respect for all fellow specialists, and his nervous
resentment of anything intuitive, imaginative, sweeping and uncate-
gorizable, or anything that might menace the easy money for projects in
which everyone is a neatly-fitting cog.

My final stricture, and the only one perhaps less valid now than in
the past, is the amazing tolerance of psychology for superstition and
occultism. I am aware that my own hero, Freud, was an incorrigible
sucker for telepathy (as he was for the curious delusion that the Earl
of Oxford was William Shakespeare), but at least he had the good sense
to make it extracanonical. He wrote to Ernest Jones: "When anyone
adduces my fall into sin, just answer him calmly that conversion to telepathy is my private affair like my Jewishness, my passion for smoking and
many other things, and that the theme of telepathy is in essence alien to
psychoanalysis." Carl Jung, on the other hand, has made an impressive
range of occultisms part of his dogmatic system, of which the possibility
of flying saucers is only the latest and funniest.

I am not, however, primarily referring to such famous aberrations
as these, but to the tolerance and even respect accorded by American
psychology to a wide variety of charlatans and necromancers. I would
instance Wilhelm Reich and the "orgone" box as an example of the
former, and J. B. Rhine and "parapsychology" as an example of the
latter. Before he died Reich was put out of business, not by any organization of psychologists, but by the Food and Drug Administration. Rhine
continues to prosper in an academic institution, while his experiments
are respectfully repeated in a number of places, as if one were to reproduce the experiments of the Fox sisters in table rapping. When a pol-
tergeist recently manifested itself on Long Island in a household containing two adolescent children, the representatives of psychological science
who investigated it were not the child psychologists we might expect, but
a team of parapsychologists from Duke University, and their learned
report concluded that "psychokinesis" (the manipulation of matter by
mental powers) seemed the likeliest explanation. It is a disturbing experience to look up "Psychologists" in the New York classified telephone
directory and see the listings for "metaphysician," "psychometaphysical
healing," "auto-suggestion," "mental healing," "Yoga" and "astrological
interpretation of human nature."

I should not like, in this foolhardy endeavor, to create either of two
false impressions: that I undervalue the enormous wealth of knowledge
and benefit psychology has produced in its brief history; or that I believe

the field of literature to be free of comparable failings. Even where the two disciplines come together, literature has often been more sinning than sinned against. For the work of every I. A. Richards, creating something like experimental conditions in which to study the reading of poems, or Lionel Trilling, bringing the full range of Freud's tragic vision to bear on literature, or Kenneth Burke, synthesizing a complex and rewarding eclectic psychology for the uses of literary criticism, there are surely a hundred critics for whom psychology is a narrowly reductive positivism, a chance to become a pundit of parlor psychoanalysis and play Peeping Tom with impunity, or a weapon with which to mutilate the corpses of the illustrious dead. After all, it was a literary critic, not a wild-eyed psychologist, who indicted the California orange as "an extraverted thing."

Nevertheless, the imaginative insights of the literary arts can broaden and enrich the field of psychology. Psychologists must approach them, however, with humility and even a touch of awe, not with the arrogance and self-assurance that seem to go with an M.D. in the field. I have in mind Edmund Bergler, pontificating in *The Writer and Psychoanalysis* about the mysteries of "the creative process" after analytic experience with a handful of neurotic hacks, or A. Bronson Feldman, in his contribution to *Explorations in Psychoanalysis,* exploring Dante, Goethe and Shakespeare primarily as repressed homosexuals with castration complexes, paranoia and masochistic cyclothymia.

Let us be clear, for example, about just what that masochistic cyclothymic William Butler Yeats is saying when he writes in "A Prayer for My Daughter":

> *It's certain that fine women eat*
> *A crazy salad with their meat*

or in "Two Songs from a Play":

> *Whatever flames upon the night*
> *Man's own resinous heart has fed.*

or in "The Circus Animals' Desertion":

> *Now that my ladder's gone,*
> *I must lie down where all the ladders start,*
> *In the foul rag-and-bone shop of the heart.*

He is not, for one thing, parading his neurotic symptoms for us, although they were plentiful enough, certainly. He is not making a series of denotative statements or pseudo statements about reality, ranging from the truism (that ladies eat tossed salads), through the mistaken (that the heart is a pine knot rather than the large muscle we know it to be), to the meaningless (that unspecified lost ladders can be retrieved in an unattractive junk shop somehow associated with the circulatory system, or, perhaps, the emotions). Nor is he projecting his hopes and fears as they are triggered by phantasms, nor pouring out his free associations, nor even producing a kind of entertaining nonsense patterned by meter and rhyme. What he is doing is telling us the profoundest truths he knows about the human condition, in a metaphoric language not paraphrasable in any other words, and he is giving us these truths in as controlled and impersonal a fashion (although the manner of discourse differs) as any experimental scientist reporting his conclusions.

Characteristically, Yeat's insights are neither optimistic nor cheering. They suggest that man is a wounded animal condemned to die, his impulses nasty and destructive, his hopes largely confined to enduring his condition and controlling his nature. These are the traditional conclusions of the gloomier philosophers and poets, and we call them the tragic vision if we choose to emphasize the brightness of the flame as the resinous heart burns, or stoicism if we focus on the charred tissue itself. There is less difference than twenty-two centuries might suggest between Freud's remarks in *The Future of an Illusion* on "the painful riddle of death, for which no remedy at all has yet been found, nor probably ever will be," and Callimachus' epigram on Charidas of Cyrene in the Greek Anthology:

> *"What is it like below, Charidas?"*
> *"Very dark."*
> *"And what about the resurrection?"*
> *"All lies."*
> *"And Pluto?"*
> *"A fable."*
> *"Then I am done for."*

What are traditionally called the humanities can furnish psychology, or, more properly, psychologists, with this bitter yet ultimately most rewarding vision of human nature and destiny. Actually, the relationship is wholly symbiotic, since literature in turn needs and must increasingly lean on this sort of deeper and truer psychology (along with a comparably enriched sociology and anthropology, and perhaps eventually a great unified science of man, clearing *all* the jungles). Beyond the parochial concerns of the literary critic, the whole world needs a better, more profound, and more influential psychology. It was easy enough to get into our present predicaments in innocent ignorance, like the younger son in a fairy tale, but only that combination of knowledge and virtue we call wisdom seems likely to get us even part-way out.

• *Questions for Study*

1. How seriously may we take a literary critic's comments on activities in a field where, as Hyman himself states, he is not a specialist? Why, on the other hand, is his province of study especially pertinent in his criticism? Discuss what you think the relationship is between literature and psychology.
2. What is the basic principle of organization in this essay? Which of Hyman's five objections do you consider most significant? Which least significant? Explain the reasons for your answers.
3. Are Hyman's numerous references to writers and to books useful in his discussion or do they tend to obscure his main points? Defend your answer.

V

CREATIVE MAN

WALTER PATER

•

STUDIES FROM *THE RENAISSANCE*

Preface

Many attempts have been made by writers on art and poetry to define beauty in the abstract, to express it in the most general terms, to find some universal formula for it. The value of these attempts has most often been in the suggestive and penetrating things said by the way. Such discussions help us very little to enjoy what has been well done in art or poetry, to discriminate between what is more and what is less excellent in them, or to use words like beauty, excellence, art, poetry, with a more precise meaning than they would otherwise have. Beauty, like all other qualities presented to human experience, is relative; and the definition of it becomes unmeaning and useless in proportion to its abstractness. To define beauty, not in the most abstract but in the most concrete terms possible, to find not its universal formula, but the formula which expresses most adequately this or that special manifestation of it, is the aim of the true student of aesthetics.

"To see the object as in itself it really is," has been justly said to be the aim of all true criticism whatever; and in aesthetic criticism the first step towards seeing one's object as it really is, is to know one's own impression as it really is, to discriminate it, to realize it distinctly. The objects with which aesthetic criticism deals—music, poetry, artistic and accomplished forms of human life—are indeed receptacles of so many powers or forces: they possess, like the products of nature, so many virtues or qualities. What is this song or picture, this engaging personality presented in life or in a book, to *me?* What effect does it really produce on me? Does it give me pleasure? and if so, what sort or degree of pleasure? How is my

---

From *Studies in the History of the Renaissance*, 1873.

nature modified by its presence, and under its influence? The answers to
these questions are the original facts with which the aesthetic critic has to
do; and, as in the study of light, of morals, of number, one must realize
such primary data for one's self, or not at all. And he who experiences
these impressions strongly, and drives directly at the discrimination and
analysis of them, has no need to trouble himself with the abstract question
what beauty is in itself, or what its exact relation to truth or experience—
metaphysical questions, as unprofitable as metaphysical questions elsewhere. He may pass them all by as being, answerable or not, of no interest to him.

The aesthetic critic, then, regards all the objects with which he has
to do, all works of art, and the fairer forms of nature and human life, as
powers or forces producing pleasurable sensations, each of a more or less
peculiar or unique kind. This influence he feels, and wishes to explain, by
analyzing and reducing it to its elements. To him, the picture, the landscape, the engaging personality in life or in a book, "La Gioconda," the
hills of Carrara, Pico of Mirandola, are valuable for their virtues, as we
say, in speaking of a herb, a wine, a gem; for the property each has of
affecting one with a special, a unique, impression of pleasure. Our education becomes complete in proportion as our susceptibility to these impressions increases in depth and variety. And the function of the aesthetic
critic is to distinguish, to analyze, and separate from its adjuncts, the
virtue by which a picture, a landscape, a fair personality in life or in
a book, produces this special impression of beauty or pleasure, to indicate
what the source of that impression is, and under what conditions it is
experienced. His end is reached when he has disengaged that virtue, and
noted it, as a chemist notes some natural element, for himself and others;
and the rule for those who would reach this end is stated with great
exactness in the words of a recent critic of Sainte-Beuve: *De se borner à
connaître de près les belles choses, et à s'en nourrir en exquis amateurs,
en humanistes accomplis.*[1]

What is important, then, is not that the critic should possess a correct
abstract definition of beauty for the intellect, but a certain kind of temperament, the power of being deeply moved by the presence of beautiful
objects. He will remember always that beauty exists in many forms. To
him all periods, types, schools of taste, are in themselves equal. In all
ages there have been some excellent workmen, and some excellent work
done. The question he asks is always: In whom did the stir, the genius,
the sentiment of the period find itself? where was the receptacle of its

---

[1] "To confine themselves to knowing beautiful things intimately, and to sustain themselves by these, as sensitive amateurs and accomplished humanists do."

refinement, its elevation, its taste? "The ages are all equal," says William Blake, "but genius is always above its age."

Often it will require great nicety to disengage this virtue from the commoner elements with which it may be found in combination. Few artists, not Goethe or Byron even, work quite cleanly, casting off all debris, and leaving us only what the heat of their imagination has wholly fused and transformed. Take, for instance, the writings of Wordsworth. The heat of his genius, entering into the substance of his work, has crystallized a part, but only a part, of it; and in that great mass of verse there is much which might well be forgotten. But scattered up and down it, sometimes fusing and transforming entire compositions, like the stanzas on *Resolution and Independence,* or the *Ode on the Recollections of Childhood,* sometimes, as if at random, depositing a fine crystal here or there, in a matter it does not wholly search through and transmute, we trace the action of his unique, incommunicable faculty, that strange, mystical sense of a life in natural things, and of man's life as a part of nature, drawing strength and color and character from local influences, from the hills and streams, and from natural sights and sounds. Well! that is the *virtue,* the active principle in Wordsworth's poetry; and then the function of the critic of Wordsworth is to follow up that active principle, to disengage it, to mark the degree in which it penetrates his verse.

The subjects of the following studies are taken from the history of the *Renaissance,* and touch what I think the chief points in that complex, many-sided movement. I have explained in the first of them what I understand by the word, giving it a much wider scope than was intended by those who originally used it to denote that revival of classical antiquity in the fifteenth century which was only one of many results of a general excitement and enlightening of the human mind, but of which the great aim and achievements of what, as Christian art, is often falsely opposed to the Renaissance, were another result. This outbreak of the human spirit may be traced far into the Middle Age itself, with its motives already clearly pronounced, the care for physical beauty, the worship of the body, the breaking down of those limits which the religious system of the Middle Age imposed on the heart and the imagination. I have taken as an example of this movement, this earlier Renaissance within the Middle Age itself, and as an expression of its qualities, two little compositions in early French; not because they constitute the best possible expression of them, but because they help the unity of my series, inasmuch as the Renaissance ends also in France, in French poetry, in a phase of which the writings of Joachim du Bellay are in many ways the most perfect illustration. The Renaissance, in truth, put forth in France an aftermath, a wonderful later growth, the products of which have to the full that subtle and delicate sweetness which belongs to a refined and comely decadence, just as its earliest phases have the freshness which belongs to all periods of growth in art, the charm of *ascêsis*[2] of the austere and serious girding of the loins in youth.

But it is in Italy, in the fifteenth century, that the interest of the Renaissance mainly lies—in that solemn fifteenth century which can hardly be studied too much, not merely for its positive results in the things of the intellect and the imagination, its concrete works of art, its special and prominent personalities, with their profound aesthetic charm, but for its general spirit and character, for the ethical qualities of which it is a consummate type.

The various forms of intellectual activity which together make up the culture of an age, move for the most part from different starting points, and by unconnected roads. As products of the same generation they partake indeed of a common character, and unconsciously illustrate each other; but of the producers themselves, each group is solitary, gaining what advantage or disadvantage there may be in intellectual isolation. Art and poetry, philosophy and the religious life, and that other life of refined pleasure and action in the conspicuous places of the world, are each of them confined to its own circle of ideas, and those who prosecute either of them are generally little curious of the thoughts of others. There come, however, from time to time, eras of more favorable conditions, in which the thoughts of men draw nearer together than is their wont, and the many interests of the intellectual world combine in one complete type of general culture. The fifteenth century in Italy is one of these happier eras, and what is sometimes said of the age of Pericles is true of that of Lorenzo: it is an age productive in personalities, many-sided, centralized, completed. Here, artists and philosophers and those whom the action of the world has elevated and made keen, do not live in isolation, but breathe a common air, and catch light and heat from each other's thoughts. There is a spirit of general elevation and enlightenment in which all alike communicate. The unity of this spirit gives unity to all the various products of the Renaissance; and it is to this intimate alliance with mind, this participation in the best thoughts which that age produced, that the art of Italy in the fifteenth century owes much of its grave dignity and influence.

I have added an essay on Winckelmann, as not incongruous with the studies which precede it, because Winckelmann, coming in the eighteenth century, really belongs in spirit to an earlier age. By his enthusiasm for the things of the intellect and the imagination for their

---

[2] Asceticism.

own sake, by his Hellenism, his lifelong struggle to attain to the Greek spirit, he is in sympathy with the humanists of a previous century. He is the last fruit of the Renaissance, and explains in a striking way its motive and tendencies.

La Gioconda

"La Gioconda"[3] is, in the truest sense, Leonardo's masterpiece, the revealing instance of his mode of thought and work. In suggestiveness, only the "Melancholia" of Dürer is comparable to it; and no crude symbolism disturbs the effect of its subdued and graceful mystery. We all know the face and hands of the figure, set in its marble chair, in that circle of fantastic rocks, as in some faint light under sea. Perhaps of all ancient pictures time has chilled it least. As often happens with works in which invention seems to reach its limit, there is an element in it given to, not invented by, the master. In that inestimable folio of drawings, once in the possession of Vasari, were certain designs by Verrocchio, faces of such impressive beauty that Leonardo in his boyhood copied them many times. It is hard not to connect with these designs of the elder, by-past master, as with its germinal principle, the unfathomable smile, always with a touch of something sinister in it, which plays over all Leonardo's work. Besides, the picture is a portrait. From childhood we see this image defining itself on the fabric of his dreams, and but for express historical testimony, we might fancy that this was but his ideal lady, embodied and beheld at last. What was the relationship of a living Florentine to this creature of his thought? By what strange affinities had the dream and the person grown up thus apart, and yet so closely together? Present from the first incorporeally in Leonardo's brain, dimly traced in the designs of Verrocchio, she is found present at last in Il Giocondo's house. That there is much of mere portraiture in the picture is attested by the legend that by artificial means, the presence of mimes and flute-players, that subtle expression was protracted on the face. Again, was it in four years and by renewed labor never really completed, or in four months and as by stroke of magic, that the image was projected?

The presence that rose thus so strangely beside the waters, is expressive of what in the ways of a thousand years men had come to desire. Hers is the head upon which all "the ends of the world are come," and the eyelids are a little weary. It is a beauty wrought out from within

---

[3] This painting is also called the *Mona Lisa*.

upon the flesh, the deposit, little cell by cell, of strange thoughts and fantastic reveries and exquisite passions. Set it for a moment beside one of those white Greek goddesses or beautiful women of antiquity, and how would they be troubled by this beauty, into which the soul with all its maladies has passed! All the thoughts and experience of the world have etched and molded there, in that which they have of power to refine and make expressive the outward form, the animalism of Greece, the lust of Rome, the mysticism of the Middle Age with its spiritual ambition and imaginative loves, the return of the Pagan world, the sins of the Borgias. She is older than the rocks among which she sits; like the vampire, she has been dead many times, and learned the secrets of the grave; and has been a diver in deep seas, and keeps their fallen day about her; and trafficked for strange webs with Eastern merchants, and, as Leda, was the mother of Helen of Troy, and, as Saint Anne, the mother of Mary; and all this has been to her but as the sound of lyres and flutes, and lives only in the delicacy with which it has molded the changing lineaments, and tinged the eyelids and the hands. The fancy of a perpetual life, sweeping together ten thousand experiences, is an old one; and modern philosophy has conceived the idea of humanity as wrought upon by, and summing up in itself, all modes of thought and life. Certainly Lady Lisa might stand as the embodiment of the old fancy, the symbol of the modern idea.

Conclusion

To regard all things and principles of things as inconstant modes or fashions has more and more become the tendency of modern thought. Let us begin with that which is without—our physical life. Fix upon it in one of its more exquisite intervals, the moment, for instance, of delicious recoil from the flood of water in summer heat. What is the whole physical life in that moment but a combination of natural elements to which science gives their names? But those elements, phosphorus and lime and delicate fibers, are present not in the human body alone: we detect them in places most remote from it. Our physical life is a perpetual motion of them—the passage of the blood, the waste and repairing of the lenses of the eye, the modification of the tissues of the brain under every ray of light and sound—processes which science reduces to simpler and more elementary forces. Like the elements of which we are composed, the action of these forces extends beyond us: it rusts iron and ripens corn. Far out on every side of us those elements are broadcast, driven in many currents; and birth and gesture and death and the springing of violets from the grave are but a few out of ten thousand resultant combinations. That clear, perpetual outline of face and limb is but an image of ours, under which we group them—a design in a web, the actual threads of which pass out beyond it. This at least of flamelike our life has, that it is but the concurrence, renewed from moment to moment, of forces parting sooner or later on their ways.

Or, if we begin with the inward world of thought and feeling, the whirlpool is still more rapid, the flame more eager and devouring. There it is no longer the gradual darkening of the eye, the gradual fading of color from the wall—movements of the shore-side, where the water flows down indeed, though in apparent rest—but the race of the midstream, a drift of momentary acts of sight and passion and thought. At first sight experience seems to bury us under a flood of external objects, pressing upon us with a sharp and importunate reality, calling us out of ourselves in a thousand forms of action. But when reflection begins to play upon those objects they are dissipated under its influence; the cohesive force seems suspended like some trick of magic; each object is loosed into a group of impressions—color, odor, texture—in the mind of the observer. And if we continue to dwell in thought on this world, not of objects in the solidity with which language invests them, but of impressions, unstable, flickering, inconsistent, which burn and are extinguished with our consciousness of them, it contracts still further: the whole scope of observation is dwarfed into the narrow chamber of the individual mind. Experience, already reduced to a group of impressions, is ringed round for each one of us by that thick wall of personality through which no real voice has ever pierced on its way to us, or from us to that which we can only conjecture to be without. Every one of those impressions is the impression of the individual in his isolation, each mind keeping as a solitary prisoner its own dream of a world. Analysis goes a step farther still, and assures us that those impressions of the individual mind to which, for each one of us, experience dwindles down, are in perpetual flight; that each of them is limited by time, and that as time is infinitely divisible, each of them is infinitely divisible also; all that is actual in it being a single moment, gone while we try to apprehend it, of which it may ever be more truly said that it has ceased to be than that it is. To such a tremulous wisp constantly reforming itself on the stream, to a single sharp impression, with a sense in it, a relic more or less fleeting, of such moments gone by, what is real in our life fines itself down. It is with this movement, with the passage and dissolution of impressions, images, sensations, that analysis leaves off—that continual vanishing away, that strange, perpetual weaving and unweaving of ourselves.

Philosophiren, says Novalis, *ist dephlegmatisiren, vivificiren.*[4] The service of philosophy, of speculative culture, towards the human spirit is to rouse, to startle it to a life of constant and eager observation. Every moment some form grows perfect in hand or face; some tone on the hills or the sea is choicer than the rest; some mood of passion or insight or intellectual excitement is irresistibly real and attractive to us—for that moment only. Not the fruit of experience, but experience itself, is the end. A counted number of pulses only is given to us of a variegated, dramatic life. How may we see in them all that is to be seen in them by the finest senses? How shall we pass most swiftly from point to point, and be present always at the focus where the greatest number of vital forces unite in their purest energy?

To burn always with this hard, gemlike flame, to maintain this ecstasy, is success in life. In a sense it might even be said that our failure is to form habits: for, after all, habit is relative to a stereotyped world, and meantime it is only the roughness of the eye that makes any two persons, things, situations, seem alike. While all melts under our feet, we may well grasp at any exquisite passion, or any contribution to knowledge that seems by a lifted horizon to set the spirit free for a moment, or any stirring of the senses, strange dyes, strange colors, and curious odors, or work of the artist's hands, or the face of one's friend. Not to discriminate every moment some passionate attitude in those about us, and in the very brilliancy of their gifts some tragic dividing of forces on their ways, is, on this short day of frost and sun, to sleep before evening. With this sense of the splendor of our experience and of its awful brevity, gathering all we are into one desperate effort to see and touch, we shall hardly have time to make theories about the things we see and touch. What we have to do is to be forever curiously testing new opinions and courting new impressions, never acquiescing in a facile orthodoxy of Comte, or of Hegel, or of our own. Philosophical theories or ideas, as points of view, instruments of criticism, may help us to gather up what might otherwise pass unregarded by us. "Philosophy is the microscope of thought." The theory or idea or system which requires of us the sacrifice of any part of this experience, in consideration of some interest into which we cannot enter, or some abstract theory we have not identified with ourselves, or of what is only conventional, has no real claim upon us.

One of the most beautiful passages of Rousseau is that in the sixth book of the *Confessions,* where he describes the awakening in him of

---

4 "To philosophize is to cast off inertia, to make oneself alive."

the literary sense. An undefinable taint of death had clung always about him, and now in early manhood he believed himself smitten by mortal disease. He asked himself how he might make as much as possible of the interval that remained; and he was not biased by anything in his previous life when he decided that it must be by intellectual excitement, which he found just then in the clear, fresh writings of Voltaire. Well! we are all *condamnés* as Victor Hugo says: we are all under sentence of death but with a sort of indefinite reprieve—*les hommes sont tous condamnés à mort avec des sursis indéfinis:* we have an interval, and then our place knows us no more. Some spend this interval in listlessness, some in high passions, the wisest, at least among "the children of this world," in art and song. For our one chance lies in expanding that interval, in getting as many pulsations as possible into the given time. Great passions may give us this quickened sense of life, ecstasy and sorrow of love, the various forms of enthusiastic activity, disinterested or otherwise, which come naturally to many of us. Only be sure it is passion—that it does yield you this fruit of a quickened, multiplied consciousness. Of such wisdom, the poetic passion, the desire of beauty, the love of art for its own sake, has most. For art comes to you proposing frankly to give nothing but the highest quality to your moments as they pass, and simply for those moments' sake.

• *Questions for Study*

1. What, generally speaking, are the purposes of an author's preface? In what ways can you say that Pater's "Preface" carries out these purposes?
2. What, according to Pater, are the functions of an aesthetic critic? Can you think of any aspects of a critic's role that he has neglected?
3. Compare Pater's view of the critical function, especially in the matters of taste and subjective impressionism, with that of Reynolds in "On Taste."
4. Why has Pater chosen to write about works of the Italian Renaissance?
5. Does it seem to you that his comments in "La Gioconda" adequately illustrate the critical principles he enunciates in the "Preface"?
6. Does Pater's style in the "Conclusion" differ appreciably from his style in the other sections? Describe the analogies, submerged and overt, that characterize the "Conclusion."
7. Pater is often attacked for advocating "art for art's sake" and neglecting the duty of the artist toward society. Do you agree that this criticism of Pater is accurate? In your opinion, does the artist have an obligation to society?

W A S S I L Y   K A N D I N S K Y

•

THE SPIRITUAL IN ART

I

Every work of art is the child of its time; often it is the mother of our emotions. It follows that each period of culture produces an art of its own, which cannot be repeated. Efforts to revive the art principles of the past at best produce works of art that resemble a stillborn child. For example, it is impossible for us to live and feel as did the ancient Greeks. For this reason those who follow Greek principles in sculpture reach only a similarity of form, while the work remains for all time without a soul. Such imitation resembles the antics of apes: externally a monkey resembles a human being; he will sit holding a book in front of his nose, turning over the pages with a thoughtful air, but his actions have no real significance.

But among the forms of art there is another kind of external similarity, which is founded on a fundamental necessity. When there is, as sometimes happens, a similarity of inner direction in an entire moral and spiritual milieu, a similarity of ideals, at first closely pursued but later lost to sight, a similarity of "inner mood" between one period and another, the logical consequence will be a revival of the external forms which served to express those insights in the earlier age. This may account partially for our sympathy and affinity with and our comprehension of the work of primitives. Like ourselves, these pure artists sought to express only inner and essential feelings in their works; in this process they ignored as a matter of course the fortuitous.

This great point of inner contact is, in spite of its considerable importance, only one point. Only just now awakening after years of ma-

From *Concerning the Spiritual In Art and Painting in Particular*, Volume 5, Documents of Modern Art Series. New York: George Wittenborn, Inc., 1955. Reprinted by permission of George Wittenborn, Inc.

terialism, our soul is infected with the despair born of unbelief, of lack of purpose and aim. The nightmare of materialism, which turned life into an evil, senseless game, is not yet passed; it still darkens the awakening soul. Only a feeble light glimmers, a tiny point in an immense circle of darkness. This light is but a presentiment; and the mind, seeing it, trembles in doubt over whether the light is a dream and the surrounding darkness indeed reality. This doubt and the oppression of materialism separate us sharply from primitives. Our soul rings cracked when we sound it, like a precious vase, dug out of the earth, which has a flaw. For this reason, the primitive phase through which we are now passing, in its present derivative form, must be short-lived.

The two kinds of resemblance between the forms of art of today and of the past can be easily recognized as diametrically opposed. The first, since it is external, has no future. The second, being internal, contains the seed of the future. After a period of materialist temptation, to which the soul almost succumbed, and which it was able to shake off, the soul is emerging, refined by struggle and suffering. Cruder emotions, like fear, joy and grief, which belonged to this time of trial, will no longer attract the artist. He will attempt to arouse more refined emotions, as yet unnamed. Just as he will live a complicated and subtle life, so his work will give to those observers capable of feeling them emotions subtle beyond words.

The observer of today is seldom capable of feeling such vibrations. He seeks instead an imitation of nature with a practical function (for example, a portrait, in the ordinary sense) or an intuition of nature involving a certain interpretation (e.g., "impressionist" painting) or an inner feeling expressed by nature's forms (as we say, a picture of "mood"). When they are true works of art, such forms fulfil their purposes and nourish the spirit. Though this remark applies to the first case, it applies more strongly to the third, in which the spectator hears an answering chord in himself. Such emotional chords cannot be superficial or without value; the feeling of such a picture can indeed deepen and purify the feeling of the spectator. The spirit at least is preserved from coarseness: such pictures tune it up, as a tuning fork does the strings of a musical instrument. But the subtilization and extension of this chord in time and space remained limited, and the potential power of art is not exhausted by it.

Imagine a building, large or small, divided into rooms; each room is covered with canvases of various sizes, perhaps thousands of them. They represent bits of nature in color—animals in sunlight or shadow, or drinking, standing in water, or lying on grass; close by, a "Crucifixion," by a painter who does not believe in Christ; then flowers, and human figures, sitting, standing, or walking, and often naked; there are many naked women foreshortened from behind; apples and silver dishes; a portrait of Mister So-and-So; sunsets; a lady in pink; a flying duck; a portrait of Lady X; flying geese; a lady in white; some cattle in shadow, flecked by brilliant sunlight; a portrait of Ambassador Y; a lady in green. All this is carefully reproduced in a book with the name of the artist and the name of the picture. Book in hand, people go from wall to wall, turning pages, reading names. Then they depart, neither richer nor poorer, again absorbed by their affairs, which have nothing to do with art. Why did they come? In every painting a whole life is mysteriously enclosed, a whole life of tortures, doubts, of hours of enthusiasm and inspiration.

What is the direction of that life? What is the cry of the artist's soul, if the soul was involved in the creation? "To send light into the darkness of men's hearts—such is the obligation of the artist," said Schumann. "A painter is a man who can draw and paint everything," said Tolstoi.

Of these two definitions we must choose the second, if we think of the exhibition just described. With more or less skill, virtuosity and vigor, objects are created on a canvas, "painted" either roughly or smoothly. To bring the whole into harmony on the canvas is what leads to a work of art. With cold eye and indifferent mind the public regards the work. Connoisseurs admire "technique," as one might admire a tight-rope walker, or enjoy the "painting quality," as one might enjoy a cake. But hungry souls go hungry away.

The public ambles through the rooms, saying "nice" or "interesting." Those who could speak have said nothing; those who could hear have heard nothing. This condition is called "art for art's sake." This annihilation of internal vibrations that constitute the life of the colors, this dwindling away of artistic force, is called "art for art's sake."

The artist seeks material rewards for his facility, inventiveness and sensitivity. His purpose becomes the satisfaction of ambition and greediness. In place of an intensive cooperation among artists, there is a battle for goods. There is excessive competition, over-production. Hatred, partisanship, cliques, jealousy, intrigues are the natural consequences of an aimless, materialist art.

The public turns away from artists who have higher ideals, who find purpose in an art without purpose.

"Comprehension" is educating the spectator to the point of view of the artist. It has been said that art is the child of its time. But such an art can only repeat artistically what is already clearly realized by the contemporary. Since it is not germinative, but only a child of the age, and unable to become a mother of the future, it is a castrated art. It is transitory; it dies morally the moment the atmosphere that nourished it alters.

There is another art capable of further developments, which also springs from contemporary feeling. Not only is it simultaneously its echo and mirror but it possesses also an awakening prophetic power which can have far-reaching and profound effect.

The spiritual life to which art belongs, and of which it is one of the mightiest agents, is a complex but definite movement above and beyond, which can be translated into simplicity. This movement is that of cognition. Although it may take different forms, it holds basically to the same internal meaning and purpose.

The causes of the necessity to move forward and upward—through sweat, suffering, evil and torments—are obscure. When a stage has been reached at which obstacles have been cleared from the way, a hidden, malevolent hand scatters new obstacles. The path often seems blocked or destroyed. But someone always comes to the rescue—someone like ourselves in everything, but with a secretly implanted power of "vision."

He sees and points out. This high gift (often a heavy burden) at times he would gladly relinquish. But he cannot. Scorned and disliked, he drags the heavy weight of resisting humanity forward and upward.

Sometimes, after his body has vanished from the earth, men try by every means to recreate it in marble, iron, bronze, or stone, and on an enormous scale. As though there were any intrinsic value in the bodily existence of such divine martyrs and servants of humanity, who despised the flesh but wanted only to serve the spirit. But raising marble is evidence that a number of men have reached the point where the one they would now honor formerly stood alone.

II

The life of the spirit may be graphically represented as a large acute-angled triangle, divided horizontally into unequal parts, with the narrowest segment uppermost. The lower the segment, the greater it is in breadth, depth and area.

The whole triangle moves slowly, almost invisibly forward and upward. Where the apex was today, the second segment will be tomorrow; what today can be understood only by the apex, is tomorrow the thought and feeling of the second segment.

At the apex of the highest segment often stands one man. His joyful vision is the measure of his inner sorrow. Even those who are nearest to him in sympathy do not understand. Angrily they abuse him as a charlatan or madman. So in his lifetime Beethoven stood, solitary and insulted. How long will it be before a larger segment of the triangle reaches the spot where he once stood? Despite memorials, are there really many who have risen to his level?

There are artists in each segment of the triangle. He who can see beyond the limits of his own segment is a prophet and helps the advance. But those who are near-sighted, or who retard the movement for base reasons, are fully understood and acclaimed. The larger the segment (i.e., the lower it lies in the triangle), the greater the number of people capable of understanding the artist. Every segment hungers, consciously or unconsciously, for adequate spiritual satisfactions. These are offered by artists, and for such satisfactions the segment below will tomorrow stretch out eager hands.

This schematical presentation, however, does not exploit the entire picture of spiritual life. Among other things it does not show the dark side, a great, dead black spot. It happens too often that the spiritual "bread" becomes nourishment for many who live already in a higher segment. This bread becomes poisonous for such eaters: in smaller quantities it has the effect that the soul gradually sinks from a high segment to a lower one. When used in greater quantity, this poison casts the soul into ever lower divisions. In one of his novels, Sienkiewicz compares the spiritual life to swimming; the man who does not strive tirelessly against sinking will go under. In this strait a man's talent (again in the biblical sense) becomes a curse—not only for the artist, but also for those who partake of his poison. The artist uses his strength to flatter base needs; in an ostensibly artistic form he presents what is impure, what draws weaker elements to him, betrays them and helps them to betray themselves, while they convince themselves and others that they are spiritually thirsty, that they can quench their thirst at this spring. Such art does not help the forward movement, but hinders it, dragging back those who are striving to press onward, and spreading pestilence abroad.

During periods when art has no champion, when true spiritual food is wanting, there is retrogression in the spiritual world. Souls fall ceaselessly from the higher to the lower segments of the triangle, and the whole seems motionless, or even to move down and backwards. During these mute and blind times men attribute a special and exclusive value to external success, for they judge them by outward results, thinking of material well-being. They hail some technical advance, which can help nothing but the body. Real spiritual gains are undervalued or ignored.

The love visionaries, the hungry of soul, are ridiculed or considered mentally abnormal. But the rare souls, who cannot be lulled into lethargy and who feel dark longings for spiritual life, knowledge and advancement, sound, amid the vulgar materialistic chorus, lamentful and disconsolate. The spiritual night falls deeper and deeper around such frightened souls; and their bearers, tortured and weakened by doubt and fear, often prefer complete obliteration to this gradual darkening.

In such periods art ministers to lower needs and is used for material ends. It seeks its content in crude substance, because it knows nothing fine. Objects remaining the same, their reproduction is thought to be the aim of art. The question "what?" disappears; only the question "how?" remains. By what method are these material objects reproduced? The method becomes a rationale. Art loses its soul.

The search for the "how" continues. Art becomes specialized, comprehensible only to artists, and they complain of public indifference to their work. For, since the artist in such times has no need to *say* much, but only to be notorious for some small originality among a small group of patrons and connoisseurs (which incidentally is also profitable), many externally gifted and skilful people come forward, so easy does the conquest of art appear. In each "art center" there are thousands of such artists, of whom the majority seek only some new mannerism, producing millions of works of art, without enthusiasm, with cold hearts and souls asleep.

Meanwhile competition grows. The savage battle for success becomes more and more material. Small groups who have fought their way to the top entrench themselves in the territory they have won. The public, left behind, looks on bewildered, loses interest and turns away.

Despite this confusion, this chaos, this wild hunt for notoriety, the spiritual triangle moves ahead, slowly but surely, with irresistible strength moving ever forward and upward.

An invisible Moses descends from the mountain and sees the dancing around the golden calf. But he brings to man fresh stores of wisdom.

His voice, inaudible to the crowd, is first heard by the artist. Almost unwittingly artists follow the voice. In the very question "how" lies a hidden seed of renascence. Sterile though this "how" may be on the whole, there is always a possibility that the "difference" which we still call personal distinction may be able to see, in the objects about it, not only what is purely material, but also something less corporeal than was seen in the period of realism, when the universal aim was to reproduce things "as they really are," without indulging in fancies.

If the emotional power of the artist can overwhelm the "how" and give free scope to his feelings, then art has started on the path by which she will not fail to find the "what" she lost, the "what" which forms the spiritual necessity of the nascent awakening. This "what" will no longer be the material, objective "what" of a stagnant period, but an artistic substance, the soul of art, without which the body (i.e., the "how") can never be healthy, whether an individual or a whole people.

This "what" is the substance which only art can comprise, which only art can clearly express by those means of expression that are proper to it.

• Questions for Study

1. This essay represents an attempt by an artist to explain the artistic experience. In your opinion, is an artist more qualified than a critic, such as Pater, to talk about art? In what ways is Kandinsky successful? In what ways does he fail?
2. Compare and contrast the views of Kandinsky and Pater. Compare also Kandinsky's view of the creative act with Buber's in "I and Thou."
3. How, according to Kandinsky, is art the product of its times? How can it be said to reflect the past?
4. Kandinsky is at his most concrete when he describes the catalogue of pictures and the spiritual triangle. Do these attempts at concreteness succeed in clarifying his points?

JACQUES MARITAIN

•

ART FOR ART'S SAKE

I

I have tried to make clear the state of tension, or even of conflict, which naturally exists between Art and Morality, and which proceeds from the basic fact that Art is intent on the good of the work, not on the good of man, whereas Morality is intent on the good of man, not on the good of the work.

Of this opposition between the good or perfection of the work and the good of man or the perfection of his life the artists are clearly aware. They even overemphasize the opposition, as Yeats did in *The Choice:*

> The intellect of man is forced to choose
> Perfection of the life, or of the work,
> And if it take the second must refuse
> A heavenly mansion, raging in the dark.
> When all that story's finished, what's the news?
> In luck or out the toil has left its mark:
> That old perplexity an empty purse,
> Or the day's vanity, the night's remorse.

Now it is of a vicious conception, a misuse and misinterpretation of the truths I emphasized concerning Art, or the fact that Art, of itself, tends only to the good of the work, that I should like to speak. In other words, I shall discuss the motto *Art for Art's sake,* a motto which in the last analysis originates in a *hypostasierung,* a substantification or hypostatization of Art, or a confusion between Art taken in itself and separately, which exists only in our mind, and Art as it really exists, that is, as a virtue of man—in other words a confusion between the artist abstractly cut off from man, and man the artist.

The motto *Art for Art's sake* simply disregards the world of morality, and the values and rights of human life. *Art for Art's sake* does not mean Art for the work, which is the right formula. It means an absurdity, that is, a supposed necessity for the artist to be only an artist, not a man, and for art to cut itself off from its own supplies, and from all the food, fuel and energy it receives from human life.

To tell the truth, art took to enclosing itself in its famous ivory tower, in the XIXth century, only because of the disheartening degradation of its environment—positivist, sociologist or materialist attitudes. But the normal condition of art is altogether different. Aeschylus, Dante, Cervantes, Shakespeare or Dostoievsky did not write in a vacuum bell. They had large human purposes. They did not write assuming that it did not matter what they wrote. Did not Dante believe he was giving only a higher course in catechism and turning his readers toward the business of their eternal salvation? Did not Lucretius intend to spread the Epicurean system, Virgil, when he composed the *Georgics,* to bring man-power back to the land and Wagner to glorify the Teutonic religion? For all that, they did not go in for propaganda art—even Wagner, though with Wagner I am not so sure. But the fact that Frenchmen of my generation consider Wagner a great corrupter of music, an abortive magician is beside the point. What I mean is that with all the genuine artists and poets, the richer the human stuff, the more strongly was everything mastered for the good of the work and subordinated to the inner self-sufficiency of this self-subsisting cosmos.

For, as I have said, Art is not an abstract entity without flesh and bones, a separate Platonic Idea supposedly come down on earth and acting among us as the Angel of Making or a metaphysical Dragon let loose; Art is a virtue of the practical intellect, and the intellect itself does not stand alone, but is a power of Man. When the intellect thinks, it is not the intellect which thinks: it is man, a particular man, who thinks through his intellect. When Art operates, it is man, a particular man, who operates through his Art.

In the very line of the artistic production or creation, that which exists and requires our consideration, that which is the agent, is man the artist.

It is nonsense to believe that the genuineness or the purity of a work of art depends upon a rupture with, a moving away from the living forces which animate and move the human being—it is nonsense to believe that this purity of the work depends on a wall of separation built up between art and desire or love. The purity of the work depends upon the strength of the inner dynamism which generates the work, that is, the strength of the virtue of art.

No wall of separation isolates the virtue of art from the inner universe of man's desire and love.

There exists, to be sure, a special desire and love which is simply one with the activity of the artist, consubstantial with this activity. That is the desire and love to create a work. Discussing Henri Bremond's book on pure poetry T. S. Eliot said: "My first qualm is over the assertion that 'the more of a poet any particular poet is, the more he is tormented by the need of communicating his experience.' This is a downright sort of statement which is very easy to accept without examination; but the matter is not so simple as all that. I should say that *the poet is tormented primarily by the need to write a poem.*" Yet Eliot's accurate remark must not mislead us: in the very urge toward the work and toward creation the desire is involved, not precisely to communicate our experience to another, but to express it: for what is creation if not an expression of the creator? Man's substance is unknown to himself. It is when he grasps things through emotion that for the poet things and the self are awakened together, in a particular kind of knowledge, obscure, ineffable in itself, which can be expressed only in a work, and which is poetic knowledge.

At this point we are confronted with the essential part played by subjectivity, by the self, in poetic knowledge and poetic activity.

An oriental critic, Mr. Lionel de Fonseka, in his book *On the Truth of Decorative Art, A Dialogue between an Oriental and an Occidental,* has written that vulgarity always says *I.* Well, vulgarity says *one* also, and this is the same thing, for vulgarity's *I* is nothing but a neuter subject of predicates or of phenomena, a subject as matter, marked with the opacity and voracity of matter, like the *I* of the egoist.

But in an entirely different manner poetry likewise always says *I.* Listen to the Psalms: "*My* heart hath uttered a good word," "Vivify *me* and *I* will keep thy commandment . . ." Poetry's *I* is the substantial depth of the living and loving subjectivity, it is a subject as act, marked with the diaphaneity and expansiveness proper to the operations of the spirit. Poetry's *I* resembles in this regard the *I* of the Saint, and likewise, although in other fashions, it is a subject which gives. The art of China and of India, like that of the Middle Ages, may well shelter itself behind the rite or the simple duty of ornamenting life; it is as personal as that of the individualistic Occident. The more or less rigorous canonicity of art is here a secondary condition; in the days of old it was a condition favorable for hiding art from itself. But the consciousness of itself, and at the same time its newly acquired taste for freedom are fine dangers which mobilized poetry.

Well, my contention is that, by necessity, as a corollary of the preceding observations on the nature of poetic knowledge, which is at the core of poetic activity, poetic activity is, of itself, essentially disinterested. It engages the human self in its deepest recesses—but in no way for the sake of the human Ego. The very engagement of the artist's Self in poetic activity, the very revelation of the artist's Self in his work, together with the revelation of the particular secret he has obscurely grasped in things, are for the sake of the work. The self is both revealing itself and sacrificing itself, because it is given, it is drawn out of itself in that sort of ec-stasy which is creation, it dies to itself in order to live in the work, and how humbly and defenselessly!

What does this essential disinterestedness of the poetic activity mean? It means that egoism is the natural enemy of poetic activity.

The artist as a man can be busy only with his desire and love for creation. He can say like Baudelaire "I don't give a damn for the human race," he can be concerned only with his work, like Proust, he can be an out-and-out egoist, as Goethe was: in his process of creation, insofar as he is an artist, he is not an egoist, he is freed from the greed of the Ego.

And obviously the artist can also have his desire and love for creation involved in the movement of expansion and generosity of a soul whose passions and ambitions are not of an egoist. And such internal abundance and magnanimity are even the normal and connatural climate of the virtue of the poet; narrowness and avarice in human desires make it live in cold and hail. After all, Shelley was right in writing that the "state of mind" naturally linked with poetic inspiration *"is at war with every base desire"*; though he went perhaps a little too far when he added: "A poet, as he is the author to others of the highest wisdom, pleasure, virtue and glory, so he ought personally to be the happiest, the best, the wisest and the most illustrious of men." The artists of the Renaissance were not, as men, models of wisdom, disinterestedness and benevolence. But at least they were interested in great causes and ideals, they had great human aspirations, and even their pride and their vices throve on a generous blood.

Let us observe in addition that many elements in the work itself can convey the resentment or the maliciousness of its author. A rhythm, a musical motif, a brush stroke, a color can be malicious. But the melody in a work, sonata, picture or poem cannot be malicious. The melody, as Arthur Lourié put it, is always good, *la mélodie est toujours bonne,* because the melody is the most immediate vehicle of the poetic sense. And he went on to say: "It is perhaps because we have become wicked that we have lost or claim to have lost melody."

It is, I think, by reason of the essential disinterestedness, which I just pointed out, of the poet in the very act of poetry, and by reason of his natural orientation toward creation, that the poets and artists of the past have given us such poor indications of their own inner creative experience. They spoke in the most conventional and shallow rhetoric and in the most commonplace stock phrases—*nascentur poetae,* the Muses, the genius, the poetic faculty, the divine spark, later on the Goddess of Imagination—of this experience which at least the greatest among them lived in fact, no doubt, but which their conscious intellect did not seek to grasp. They were not interested in reflective self-awareness. The age of reflection, the age of *prise de conscience,* which roughly speaking started for Mysticism at the time of St. Theresa of Avila and St. John of the Cross, came later for Poetry. When it did come for Poetry, at the time of Romanticism, it brought to completion the slow process of revelation of the Self which had progressively developed in the course of modern centuries. This revelation of the creative Self is a blessing to the extent to which it takes place in the genuine line of Poetry. But it becomes a curse when it shifts from the line of Poetry, and of the Self in the fire of spiritual communication, to the line of man's material individuality, and of the Self as jealous proprietor and center of insatiable lusts. Then the egoism of man enters the very sphere of the poetic act, not only to spoil it, but to feed on it. On the one hand such growth of the human egoism, being unnatural, becomes boundless; on the other hand, as regards the creative art, the artist no longer manifests himself and the world in his work—he unloads himself in it, pours his own complexes and poisons into it, and into the reader, thus achieving a psychological cure at the expense of both.

The accident came about, sad to say, simultaneously with the most glorious discoveries achieved by the self-awareness of Poetry as Poetry. And nevertheless—this is the point I should like to make—the essential disinterestedness of the poetic act is so ineradicable that the final result of this invasion of the human Ego in the universe of art was not, in actual fact, to make the artist into a creative usurer (that is a contradiction in terms) but to make him into a hero, a priest, or a savior, offering himself in sacrifice no longer to his work but both to mankind and to his own glory.

II

Let us come back now to the discussion of *Art for Art's sake*. The previous considerations help us to realize that, from the point of view of ends, or of final causality, it is only normal that the desires and loves with which human life is filled should be at play in the soul of the artist. They tend toward ends which are not the proper ends of art. But they feed and nourish art and poetry, and they will not warp the work, they will enrich it, if only art and poetry themselves tend purely and unyieldingly to their own ends in the making of the work. No doubt, I know that when it comes to a particular human purpose for which the work is done —propaganda plays, patriotic poems and moralizing literature do not add up to much as a rule. But this is so because, as a rule, the artist has allowed his moral idea to enter the very sphere of the making and to act as a way of making, which it is not. I also know that the cathedral builders had no sort of thesis in mind, nor did they want to suggest a Christian emotion. But they had Faith, and it was enough. The human ends with which I am concerned here are not particular purposes, but rather the things in which the artist believes, and which he loves. In this sense it is only normal that a poet or a writer, a man who works with words should have a message, not only his proper artistic message (which is the essential) but also a human message of his own, silly, foolish or momentous, to deliver to men. Otherwise there would be a serious possibility that his work would have nothing to say. Such was, I dare say, the fate of Mallarmé's narcissism. Earlier I mentioned Dante, Virgil and Lucretius;

to these I might add Tolstoy, Walt Whitman, William Blake, Léon Bloy, Nietzsche. There is nothing to stop Gide from saying: it does not matter what one writes. But in reality he himself was constantly prodded by a kind of apostolic zeal—rather particular in nature, to be sure, but that's another question—the chief intent of which was to justify himself in the eyes of men.

The workman works for his wages, and the most disincarnate artist has a concern, concealed or repressed as it may be, to act upon human souls and to serve an idea. What is required is the perfect practical discrimination between the aim of the workman (*finis operantis*, as the Schoolmen put it) and the aim of the work (*finis operis*): so that the workman should work for his wages, but the work should be ruled and shaped and brought into being only with regard to its own good and in nowise with regard to the wages. Thus the artist may work for any and every human intention he likes, but the work taken in itself must be made and constructed only with regard to the creative intuition in which it originates and to the rules of making which it calls for.

Similar considerations may be put forward from the point of view of the agent who operates or of efficient causality. Plato said that a philosopher must philosophize with his whole soul (though the intellect alone is the proper organ of philosophy). The same may be said of the artist.

The virtue of art does not allow the work to be interfered with or immediately ruled by anything other than itself. It insists that it alone shall touch the work in order to bring it into being. In short, art requires that nothing shall attain the work except through art itself. It is through His word and His art that God attains, rules and brings into being everything He makes. In the same way it is through art that the human artist must attain, rule and bring into being all his work.

But this in no way implies that the work depends on art alone, and not on the entire soul of the artist; that it is made by the art alone, separate, cut off from all the rest in man, and not by man the artist with all the human purposes, desires, and longings, all the human thoughts and beliefs he has in his heart. Theologians tell us that everything was made *per Verbum*, through the Divine Word, yet it is also true that everything was made by the whole undivided Trinity: in a manner totally free from the least interested intention, but to an end nevertheless, an end which is not simply the perfection of the work to be achieved, and which is of an order superior to art—the communication of divine goodness.

Finally, our issue has also to do with the perspective of material causality.

It would simplify many questions to make a distinction between art itself and its material or subjective conditions. Art being of man, how could it not depend on the pre-existing structures and inclinations of the subject in which it dwells? They remain extrinsic to art, but they influence it.

Art as such, for instance, transcends, like the spirit, every frontier of space or time, every historical or national boundary. Like science and philosophy, it is universal of itself.

But art does not reside in an angelic mind: it resides in a soul which animates a living body, and which, by the natural necessity in which it finds itself of learning, and progressing little by little and with the assistance of others, makes the rational animal a naturally social animal. Art is therefore basically dependent upon everything which the human community, spiritual tradition and history transmit to the body and mind of man. By its human subject and its human roots, art belongs to a time and a country.

• *Questions for Study*

1. Pater, Kandinsky, and Maritain all use the phrase "art for art's sake"—or a version of it. How do their attitudes toward what the phrase means differ?
2. Maritain uses such abstruse words as "*hypostasierung*," "*substantification*," "*diaphaneity*." Does he need to use these words in order to make his meaning clear, or might he have chosen less formal ones? Explain.
3. What does he mean when he says that "egoism is the natural enemy of poetic activity"? That "a rhythm, a musical motif, a brush stroke, a color can be malicious"?
4. Discuss the variety of ways in which this essay employs comparison and contrast.
5. Write a theme in which you discuss *either* the function of the artist *or* the purpose of art.

CLEMENS E. BENDA

•

ILLNESS AND ARTISTIC CREATIVITY

Over the centuries, no doubt many great artists have fallen ill, but no record is at hand to indicate whether their illnesses had a significant influence on their creativity. It was only in the nineteenth century that the illnesses of two contemporaries, Friedrich Nietzsche and Vincent van Gogh, both of whom spent considerable time in mental hospitals, gave rise to the question of how their illnesses were related to their work.

"The more I become decomposed," wrote Van Gogh in one of his letters, "the more sick and fragile I am, the more I become an artist." Few painters have been so articulate in their expression, and few men have so much insight into their own conditions.

Characteristic of his "mental attacks" was an intensification of his imagery. This intensification of perception occasionally came over Van Gogh in the midst of his work and brought about his representation of inner visions, which assumed a new reality. He found it surprising that he, a modern man who admired Zola, the Goncourts, and modern naturalism, was subject to spells wherein religious ideas assumed a reality previously recorded only by the great religious mystics. He observed the landscape with an emotional depth in which the objects of his perception and his own experience fused together into a new reality, but the experienced bliss was often interrupted by anxiety and fear.

The greatest intensity of Van Gogh's work fell in the year 1888; 46 of 108 major paintings were done in that year, whereas before 1887 there were only 12. His work decreased after the acute onset of his illness, and somewhat fewer pictures are recorded for 1889 and 1890 than for 1888. Through his letters, we have an accurate account of the change in attitude which took place in the transition from impressionism to his new expressionistic style. In one letter he remarks, "Instead of reproduc-

From *The Atlantic Monthly*, July 1961. Reprinted by permission of *The Atlantic Monthly* and of the author.

ing exactly what I see, I use the colors arbitrarily in order to express myself more vigorously. I exaggerate the blonde of the hair. I arrive at orange colors, chrome, and light lemon yellow. Behind the head, in place of the ordinary wall of a common room, I paint the infinite. I achieve a background of purest blue, the strongest that I can express, and in this way the blonde radiant head achieves a mystical effect on the background of rich blue like a star in the deep azure. I am groping to find simpler and simpler techniques which may be not impressionistic. I would like to paint so that everyone who has eyes can see with complete clearness. Alas, I call this 'simplicity of technique.'"

With Van Gogh's case, the problem of the artist and psychiatry suddenly moved into the public eye. Van Gogh's rather intimate contact with his psychiatrist, Dr. Gachet, testifies to the possibility of a warm and understanding relationship between the artist and science and raises a number of interesting questions. Is illness a factor in modern art? Does sickness support or suppress the creative process? Can Van Gogh's painting be explained in any way by his illness? Do diagnosis and treatment of mental illness contribute to the understanding of the arts?

Since Van Gogh's time, a number of great artists, among them the Norwegian painter Edvard Munch, have been known to suffer from mental disturbances. In our age of neurosis, when it is almost a prerequisite to be neurotic if one is to share in the cultural achievement of our times, the relationship between creative art and psychiatry has become even closer.

Munch's history in many points resembles that of Van Gogh. Born in 1863 as the son of an army surgeon, he spent his childhood in Oslo. His mother died of tuberculosis when he was only five, and his oldest sister, who had been very close to him, also died of tuberculosis, when he was fourteen years old. Munch's haunting paintings of deathbeds and illness reproduced time and again the impact of these early experiences. Moreover, after the death of his mother, his father turned to religion in a way which was frightening to the children. As an old man, Munch recalled that his father "had a difficult temper, exhibited nervousness with periods of religious anxiety which could reach the borders of insanity as he paced back and forth in his room praying to God. . . . Disease and insanity were the black angels on guard at my cradle. . . . In my childhood I felt always that I was treated in an unjust way, without a mother, sick, and with threatened punishment in Hell hanging over my head."

Munch was frequently ill during childhood, and poor health often interrupted his attendance at school. At the age of twenty-seven, he was for the first time in a hospital, in France, for several months. From 1892 until 1908 he spent most of his time in voluntary exile abroad, mostly in

Berlin, where he gained great success and recognition. In 1908 he had a "complete nervous collapse," culminating in excessive drinking, which led him into a sanitarium. The crisis which obsessed Munch found its most vivid expression in his painting called *Marat's Death*, in which the theme of Samson and Delilah is taken up and interpreted in the massive dead body of a man lying perpendicular with the head toward the left lower edge, while the woman stands "erect and rigid, pressing her arms against her sides, excluding every feeling but that of her own self-justification expressed by the frozen and obsessive determination of her face."

Munch lived his last thirty years in solitude on the outskirts of Oslo, restricting his contacts to a few close friends.

The cases of Van Gogh and Munch, as well as those of their respective literary contemporaries Nietzsche and Strindberg, prove beyond doubt that illness as such does not necessarily produce creativity, but often destroys the creative process. Moreover, the various forms of mental disturbance have very different effects upon different artists. Illness can give man a detachment and a courage which the average person does not command. Many artists have broken through the narrow bars of conventionality because of illness and have reached new frontiers which could never have been attained without it. An advancing illness often intensifies anxiety and dread, with a resultant increase in creative output. In Van Gogh, the intensification of perceptual experience gave his vision a depth and color of unheard-of power. In Munch, on the other hand, illness caused suspicious withdrawal from friends, with a progressive narrowing of his experience.

When psychiatry became a biological science, scientists, as well as the public, confused the sick artist's work with his illness and denounced his paintings as fever-sick hallucinations, the output of a morbid mind. Many rather embarrassing studies of a pseudoscientific character are on record. But, in general, this period of psychiatric adventures has now come to an end. With the dawn of psychoanalytical investigations, a new approach to the artist was made. Interest was centered on the unconscious.

Since unconscious dynamics play a very important role in all creative achievements, it is not surprising that works of art attracted psychoanalytical attention. Freud himself did not expect too much from the study of mental illness, but thought that psychoanalysis would unearth significant themes in the work of great painters and writers. His controversial studies of Leonardo da Vinci, of Michelangelo's *Moses,* and of Dostoevsky have been equally acclaimed and rejected. Some of his minor disciples could not resist applying the analytical knife to the works and personalities of great artists, and many slipped into the pitfall of identifying creativity with neurosis, concluding that creativity stems from only partially successful sublimation of an unresolved Oedipus complex.

A number of psychoanalytical studies of artists are based on the theory that visual curiosity and the infantile urge to ask questions persist in the artist and philosophical thinker, that the artist continues in an infantile fixation, instead of living like ordinary human beings and taking for granted what life has to offer. One famous analyst wrote that creative people "stop at those early problems of life which give the child cause to ponder: the problems of birth and death, good and evil, aim and purpose of one's own existence." The creative artist and philosopher "ponders life instead of living it," thus failing to achieve a successful "sublimation of his infantile interests and inquisitiveness. [He] reveals by his endless doubting, searching, struggling that he is never done with the primary problems and suffers from them all his life."

Although the artist is credited with an ability to express his unconscious wealth of fantasy in a manner that "gives pleasure to himself and others," such achievement is said to be due to narcissism, interpreted as a kind of self-love concentrated on one's own personality, such as can best be observed in children. On this basis, the creative person lives only for self and concentrates on his ego and his work.

In evaluating the creative process as narcissism, inhibition, and failure to adjust to reality, psychoanalysts have made a serious mistake. Many an artist has feared that psychoanalysis might rob him of his creativity and produce a well-adjusted haberdashery salesman. The confusion between creativity and neurotic inhibition of creative expression unfortunately still exists in artistic circles and in psychiatric literature.

In an industrialized society, adjustment to reality is the main theme of mental health programs, and the best adjustment is often identified with sexual and financial successes. In the light of such ideas, many artists appear as victims of their own mother and father complexes. Not only does the world look down on artists as outsiders who are incapable of social adjustment, but the artists themselves are guilt-ridden and full of anxiety. It is regrettable that psychoanalysis has often reinforced their guilt feelings by overemphasizing the neurotic aspects of their conflicts. Jung and his school have generally avoided these pitfalls and have centered their attention on different aspects of the creative unconscious, achieving considerable understanding of mystic and primitive art.

To understand the relationship between illness and creativity, one must analyze the essence of creativity and study the effect of pathogenic influences on it. Fortunately, some scientific data are now available. Dr. Charles Hersch and Dr. Leslie Phillips, psychological researchers at Worcester State Hospital, in Massachusetts, have used the conceptual framework of Professor Heinz Werner of Clark University and some of Dr. Anne Roe's earlier material on artists in an investigation comparing the creative mind with the average mind and with that of the schizophrenic patient. For the creative group they used a sample of eminent painters who have achieved national recognition.

In interpreting the Rorschach ink-blot test, the answers are scored in various categories according to whether movements, forms, colors, or other aspects determine the created image. This enables the psychologist to gain insight into the relative strength of various pressures within the individual and thus understand how he perceives the world and reacts to it. Certain types of answers are considered mature and indicate a high degree of integration, while others suggest emotionality and primitive diffuse emotionalism. Traditional interpretation of the Rorschach test did not permit discovery of creative aspects in the personality, and the misinterpretation of certain types of answers as primitive or regressive added to the confusion. The new study assumes that the creative personality does not operate at a fixed level of function but, rather, varies in its level of performance.

Creativity requires a constant reorganization which cannot be achieved without constant fluctuation or mobility between progressive integration and regressive starting anew. Thus, creativity is a bi-phasic process. The creative artist has to command a flexibility which enables him to differentiate fixed configurations and reorganize the elements in nonexisting new patterns of imagery. And the creative person needs a greater ability to integrate those processes which we identify with maturity, as well as the more primitive personality patterns which enable him to regress and identify with objects on a rather primitive level. These primitive aspects of artistic personalities have often been confused in psychology with primitivity, infantilism, or schizophrenic lack of ego boundaries.

In an era when the unconscious and primitive patterns were the sole object of interest, artists were confused with neurotics and psychotics, who have only this aspect of creativity but lack the formative integration and real creative power. What especially distinguishes the great artist from the average person, and, even more, from neurotic inefficiency and schizophrenic decomposition? Artists give more mature, form-dominant responses than average people do, and both give significantly more integrative responses than the schizophrenics do. On the other hand, artists have more primitive responses than the average on what have been called "primitive" scores, but the artist's is a different type of primitive response from the schizophrenic's. Artists excel in the physiognomic responses of both groups.

The investigation showed that artists have a high percentage of mature responses of a specific nature, including movement conceptions, form-dominant responses, and primitive thought responses. The nature of their responses indicates that a creative personality is able to shift back and forth between self and environment. First, the boundaries between self and environment can be readily relaxed in a mode of identification. On the other hand, the boundaries are readily reinstated, with self and environment maintaining discrete and polar differentiation.

This research gives new insight into artistic creativity. Creative personalities have greater abilities than ordinary people for both progression and regression in their dealings with the world around them, but the regression in artistic creativity has no connection with the infantile regression of neurosis or mental illness. . . .

The great artist represents the rare combination of strong unconscious drives with a strange power of controlled and mature integration of experience and the ability to express such order in symbolic forms of painted imagery or poetry. Studies of the unconscious alone will often find the painter near the neurotic, and even schizophrenic, with whom he may share tendencies to daydreaming and increased imagery formation; but in contrast to the ineffectiveness of the neurotic, the artist has strong forces of integration, control, and creativity at his disposal. It is this ability to transform the imagery into symbolic forms that distinguishes the artist from his less favored contemporaries.

With the new developments in psychodynamic psychiatry, based on social science, psychology, and existential psychiatric thinking, modern psychiatry is much better prepared to deal with the artist and the creative personality in general. Psychiatry now realizes that man's unconscious forms only one aspect, while his interpersonal, cultural, and spiritual experiences are the formative forces which pattern the whole personality. But beyond stands man's power of self-expression and realization of his aspirations, and the great artist is the rare personality who is able to transform his shifting experiences into lasting works of art.

Modern psychiatry recognizes the cognitive conscious and creative forces in man as that human attribute which enables him to transcend his emotional impressions and to be the creator of an inner world. Psychiatry can help reinforce and integrate the creative abilities and eliminate those fixations which inhibit the free shift between primitive and mature integrative functions. The painter needs identification in empathy and intuition, but at the same time needs the ability to withdraw and fall back on his own self-differentiation. In the neurotic we often find the anxious defense of one aspect of being. Some people never achieve a strong personality structure because the ego boundaries are too fluctuant. In others, the structure is rigid and compulsively petrified, and these people are never able to reorganize themselves and start anew with unprejudiced attitudes.

Man does not live in a reality common to all; each person lives in his own world, reflected in his imagery. To create this imagery in visual and literary forms, sharable by the creator and beholder alike, is the problem of all great art. In this way the artist and thinker moves again into the center of a civilization. If psychiatry succeeds in making the "outsider" again the true "insider," the representative of the best in humanity, it will serve the contemporary world in a manner previously denied to medicine.

• Questions for Study

1. What use does Benda make of the case histories of Van Gogh and Munch as organizational devices?
2. Can you relate Maritain's idea of the ego in art in "Art for Art's Sake" to the problem of illness and artistic creativity as discussed by Benda?
3. What does Benda mean by the statement "it is almost a prerequisite to be neurotic if one is to share in the cultural achievement of our times"? To what artists do you think he is referring? Do you agree?
4. Does Benda consider the relationship of the artist to his audience in any way? What is the function of art implied in his discussion?
5. How do you think the great artist differs from the neurotic or psychotic person? Are there some artists, like Edgar Allan Poe and Dostoevsky, whose whole creation stems from their morbidity? Does Benda's distinction between the artist and the neurotic sufficiently take into consideration these people? Is Benda guilty of oversimplification? Explain.

LEO STEIN

•

ON SEEING PICTURES

What you don't know won't hurt you, says the proverb. But it often makes you talk nonsense, and what one man sees and another does not, makes intercourse difficult when it has to do with the kinds of things that are not really capable of explanation. The qualities of art are perceived, as it were, by a multitude of senses, and he who hasn't them operative, is not in communication with him who has. The difference between these psychic senses and the physical ones is that the former are not simple but composed, and the compositions are very variable. So it happens that a little juggling and shocking can produce a capacity for seeing, even when rational explanation cannot.

A chapter on reading poetry and seeing pictures must deal with this essential question of *seeing*, for that is the heart of the matter. People commonly assume that they can see, and need only learn what they should look at. My experience contradicts this, and insists on the all-importance of learning to see. The *what* will take care of itself if the *how* has been acquired. I don't mean to say that then one will see everything, as the authorities say you should. But if you remember that the authorities are for the most part commonplace persons who, with no extraordinary qualifications, make criticism their business, there is no reason why you should *so* see things. If you learn to *see*, you will be able to see for yourself, and will be content to skip much of what is offered but does not really concern you. I shall now tell how I went about the business of learning to see.

I was interested in esthetics even in childhood, though I did not know it by that name. When we were children, we used often to go for picnics to Dimond's Canon, which was a few miles from our home in

East Oakland. Scrub oak was a common tree in those hills, but I was again and again struck by a little bunch of these that stood at the turning of a road and seemed singularly beautiful. The trees themselves were not exceptional, and it was only after a time that I understood this to be a matter of composition, their somewhat unusual placement at this spot.

Once aware of composition, I noticed it elsewhere and often. When I was fourteen, my brother, who had been at college in the East, brought home some etchings—among them one of apple trees. There were plenty of apple trees all about, and to see why this etching pleased me so I took it into the orchard and compared it with the trees. Then I saw that the artist had simplified and made more evident certain characteristics of the trees themselves—once more a matter of composition—and I improvised a definition of art: that it is nature seen in the light of its significance. Then, recognizing that this significance was one of forms, I added "formal" to "significance." Significant Form was then born for me.

Gradually I came on to realize that art and composition are one. Not that in poetry and painting there is nothing else. Shakespeare goes beyond Milton as much in intellect, in varied knowledge, in penetration, as he does in power of composition. He was great enough to be an immoralist, and to make and sympathize with such a rascal as Falstaff. But insight into human nature and ability to appreciate are not a speciality to artists. They are shared by men and women of the world—politicians, detectives, executives—many of whom see much more deeply and wisely than artists in general do. But they are not artists, and when they give some sort of form to their appreciations, that form is not essential. They do not compose what they have to say in any significant manner, and do not make literature.

Long ago, forty-five years ago, I tried to get to the bottom of this matter. Up to then I had taken composition as I found it. I had discovered in myself no aptitude for any of the arts, and thought of myself as essentially a scientist—one who tried to find out why and how things were, rather than to create or re-create them. But one day it occurred to me to ask the definite question: how does a painter see when he paints? What he produces is a translation into another medium. The thing seen exists outside, and yet it is presumably not what everyone sees. There must be a possibility of seeing things in such a way that they are related to the picture without being it. The problem was to see, and then to learn what was particular about this way of seeing. There is no use speculating when one can experiment; so I began to experiment.

I put on the table a plate of the kind common in Italy, an earthenware plate with a simple pattern in color, and this I looked at every day for minutes or for hours. I had in mind to see it as a picture, and waited for it to become one. In time it did. The change came suddenly when the plate as an inventorial object, one made up of parts that could be separately listed, a certain shape, certain colors applied to it, and so on, went over into a composition to which all these elements were merely contributory. The painted composition on the plate ceased to be *on* it but became a part of a larger composition which was the plate as a whole. I had made a beginning to seeing pictorially.

What had been begun was carried out in all directions. I wanted to be able to see anything *as* a composition, and found that it was possible to do this. I tried it on everything from a scrap of paper torn from the corner of a sheet, to a line of trees extending half a mile into the distance; and I found that with practice seeing pictures was possible everywhere. I soon found that things could be seen in two ways, pictorially and sculpturally, as though one saw with reference to a plane in front of the object, or with reference to a plane behind the object. In one case the thing was seen as flat, but in deep space, which is the paradox of pictorial composition. In the other, it was seen as round, but in shallow space.

This habit of mine of seeing pictorial composition in nature, of seeing it anywhere and whenever I am so inclined, in little or on the grandest scale, makes me difficult in the acceptance of pictures. Such landscape as Claude's and Turner's is for me picturesque only, not really pictorial. It is landscape as anyone sees it, composed, that is, within the limits of a naturalistic vision. In many cases Cézanne does not get beyond that in his composition as a whole. Only in China and Japan was this higher grade of landscape common, and its greatest master in Europe is Poussin.

The difference between the pictorial and the sculpturesque vision is interesting. In the pictorial one sees as though the pictured thing were seen within the limits of a frame, which marks the plane to which the focus is referred. What lies beyond is in a way brought to this plane, or at least adjusted to it. The recession of planes is rhythmic, and never goes off into a meaningless infinity of distance. The infinities of art are inward and not outward. Every good work of art is a self-contained whole, and that which is not, however many good things it may contain, is fragmentary.

The same is true of the sculptural, though this is applicable only to things rather near. I used often, when sitting opposite persons in a tram, to look at them now as pictures, then as sculpture, simply by changing the focus. The same thing can be done for architecture, and is specially interesting for interiors. In fact, I first noticed this when I saw what a change there was in the space of a corridor beyond an open door. The space grew deep or shallow as I changed the focus from the door to the wall beyond. Further trials led to developments. In the interior of churches with columns, the different effects are striking.

It often happened to me in my earlier experiment that I was not able to complete my nature compositions; and sometimes what might have been, but did not come off, was very beautiful. Then the tension was agonizing; then I used to find myself humming or whistling a certain theme, which would bring the needed relief as though on another plane completion had come. It was always the same theme, which I had not chosen and which I couldn't place. A musical friend with whom I was discussing rhythm, played, for purposes of illustration, what he said was the most intense expression of rhythmic emotion in all music, something from the Ninth Symphony of Beethoven, and that was my theme. I was not aware till then that I remembered anything from the Ninth Symphony, which I had rarely heard. It is many years since I have used it for this purpose, as with practice I came to be able to fill the composition without recourse to any outer aid. But this incident will show how intense may be the demand for total compositional realization.

People have commonly to wait upon the artist to show them pictures, except when there is something obviously picturesque before them; but if they have become educated to pictorial seeing, this is not at all necessary. The beauty of the world is immensely increased; it becomes all, potentially, beautiful. Every man, woman and child is beautiful, and any group of them. The superabundant beauty becomes at times exasperating; one feels a need of doing something about it; one is almost forced to try being an artist, not only in seeing but in doing; one tries to paint. One soon learns that there is no mystery in the fact that things not beautiful to ordinary vision can be made beautiful in pictures. It is nothing more or less than a question of composition—not, of course, arrangement, which is the ordinary photographer's notion of composition; but the artist's, which I have spoken of at such length.

• Questions for Study

1. How does Stein vitalize the stages of his recognition of "Significant Form"? Do you think his description of form is an adequate one?
2. How successful is he in using examples to clarify what he has to say? How could he have made the one concerning the apple trees clearer than it is?
3. What does Stein mean by "seeing"? Why does he distinguish between "picture" and "picturesque"?
4. Which of the artists mentioned in this essay are you familiar with? What sources would you consult for further information concerning them?

FRANK LLOYD WRIGHT

•

THE USONIAN HOUSE

The house of moderate cost is not only America's major architectural problem but the problem most difficult for her major architects. As for me, I would rather solve it with satisfaction to myself and Usonia, than build anything I can think of at the moment except the modern theater now needed by the legitimate drama unless the stage is to be done to death by "the movies." In our country the chief obstacle to any real solution of the moderate-cost house problem is the fact that our people do not really know how to live. They imagine their idiosyncrasies to be their "tastes," their prejudices to be their predilections, and their ignorance to be virtue—where any beauty of living is concerned.

To be more specific, a small house on the side street might have charm if it didn't ape the big house on the Avenue, just as the Usonian village itself might have a great charm if it didn't ape the big town. Likewise, Marybud on the old farm, a jewel hanging from the tip of her pretty nose on a cold, cold day, might be charming in clothes befitting her state and her work, but is only silly in the Sears-Roebuck finery that imitates the clothes of her city sisters who imitate Hollywood stars: lipstick, rouge, high heels, silk stockings, bell skirt, cock-eyed hat, and all. Exactly that kind of "monkey-fied" business is the obstacle to architectural achievement in our U.S.A. This provincial "culture-lag" in favor of the leg which does not allow the person, thing, or thought to be simple and naturally itself. It is the real obstacle to a genuine Usonian culture.

I am certain that any approach to the new house needed by indigenous culture—why worry about the house wanted by provincial "tasteful" ignorance!—is fundamentally different. That house must be a pattern for more simplified and, at the same time, more gracious living:

From *Autobiography* by Frank Lloyd Wright, by permission of Duell, Sloan & Pearce, an affiliate of Meredith Press.

necessarily new, but suitable to living conditions as they might so well be in this country we live in today.

This need of a house of moderate cost must sometime face not only expedients but Reality. Why not face it now? The expedient houses built by the million, which journals propagate, and government builds, do no such thing.

To me such houses are stupid makeshifts, putting on some style or other, really having no integrity. Style *is* important. A style is not. There is all the difference when we work *with* style and not for *a* style.

I have insisted on that point for forty-five years.

Notwithstanding all efforts to improve the product, the American "small house" problem is still a pressing, needy, hungry, confused issue. But where is a better thing to come from while Authority has pitched into perpetuating the old stupidities? I do not believe the needed house can come from current education, or from big business. It isn't coming by way of smart advertising experts either. Or professional streamliners. It is only super-common-sense that can take us along the road to the better thing in building.

What would be really sensible in this matter of the modest dwelling for our time and place? Let's see how far the Herbert Jacobs house at Madison, Wisconsin, is a sensible house. This house for a young journalist, his wife, and small daughter, is now under roof. Cost: Fifty-five hundred dollars, including architect's fee of four hundred and fifty. Contract let to P. B. Grove.

To give the small Jacobs family the benefit of the advantages of the era in which they live, many simplifications must take place. Mr. and Mrs. Jacobs must themselves see life in somewhat simplified terms. What are essentials in their case, a typical case? It is not only necessary to get rid of all unnecessary complications in construction, necessary to use work in the mill to good advantage, necessary to eliminate so far as possible, field labor which is always expensive: it is necessary to consolidate and simplify the three appurtenance systems—heating, lighting, and sanitation. At least this must be our economy if we are to achieve the sense of spaciousness and vista we desire in order to liberate the people living in the house. And it would be ideal to complete the building in one operation as it goes along. Inside and outside should be complete in one operation. The house finished inside as it is completed outside. There should be no complicated roofs.

Every time a hip or a valley or a dormer window is allowed to ruffle a roof the life of the building is threatened.

The way the windows are used is naturally a most useful resource to achieve the new characteristic sense of space. All this fenestration can be made ready at the factory and set up as the walls. But there is no longer sense of speaking of doors and windows. These walls are largely a system of fenestration having its own part in the building scheme— the system being as much a part of the design as eyes are part of the face.

Now what can be eliminated? These:

1. Visible roofs are expensive and unnecessary.
2. A garage is no longer necessary as cars are made. A carport will do, with liberal overhead shelter and walls on two sides. Detroit still has the livery-stable mind. It believes that the car is a horse and must be stabled.
3. The old-fashioned basement, except for a fuel and heater space, was always a plague spot. A steam-warmed concrete mat four inches thick laid directly on the ground over gravel filling, the walls set upon that, is better.
4. Interior "trim" is no longer necessary.
5. We need no radiators, no light fixtures. We will heat the house the "hypocaust" way—in or between the floors. We can make the wiring system itself be the light fixture, throwing light upon and down the ceiling. Light will thus be indirect, except for a few outlets for floor lamps.
6. Furniture, pictures and bric-a-brac are unnecessary because the walls can be made to include them or *be* them.
7. No painting at all. Wood best preserves itself. A coating of clear resinous oil would be enough. Only the floor mat of concrete squares needs waxing.
8. No plastering in the building.
9. No gutters, no downspouts.

To assist in general planning, what must or may we use in our new construction? In this case five materials: wood, brick, cement, paper, glass. To simplify fabrication we must use our horizontal-unit system in construction. We must also use a vertical-unit system which will be the widths of the boards and batten-bands themselves, interlocking with the brick courses. Although it is getting to be a luxury material, the walls will be wood board-walls the same inside as outside—three thicknesses of boards with paper placed between them, the boards fastened together with screws. These slab-walls of boards—a kind of plywood construction on a large scale can be high in insulating value, vermin-proof, and practically fireproof. These walls like the fenestration may be prefabricated on the floor, with any degree of insulation we can afford, and raised into place, or they may be made at the mill and shipped to the site in sections.

The roof can be built first on props and these walls shoved into place under them.

The appurtenance systems, to avoid cutting and complications, must be an organic part of construction but independent of the walls. Yes, we must have polished plate glass. It is one of the things we have at hand to gratify the designer of the truly modern house and bless its occupants.

The roof framing in this instance is laminated of three 2 x 4's in depth easily making the three offsets seen outside in the eaves of the roof, and enabling the roof span of 2 x 12" to be sufficiently pitched without the expense of "building up" the pitches. The middle offset may be left open at the eaves and fitted with flaps used to ventilate the roof spaces in summer. These 2 x 4's sheathed and insulated, then covered with a good asphalt roof, are the top of the house, shelter gratifying to the sense of shelter because of the generous eaves.

All this is in hand—no, it is in mind, as we plan the disposition of the rooms.

What must we consider essential now? We have a corner lot—say, an acre or two—with a south and west exposure? We will have a good garden. The house is planned to wrap around two sides of this garden.

1. We must have as big a living room with as much vista and garden coming in as we can afford, with a fireplace in it, and open bookshelves, a dining table in the alcove, benches, and living-room tables built in; a quiet rug on the floor.

2. Convenient cooking and dining space adjacent to if not a part of the living room. This space may be set away from the outside walls within the living area to make work easy. This is the new thought concerning a kitchen—to take it away from outside walls and let it turn up into overhead space within the chimney, thus connection to dining space is made immediate without unpleasant features and no outside wall space lost to the principal rooms. A natural current of air is thus set up toward the kitchen as toward a chimney, no cooking odors escaping back into the house. There are steps leading down from this space to a small cellar below for heater, fuel, and laundry, although no basement at all is necessary if the plan should be so made. The bathroom is usually next so that plumbing features of heating kitchen and bath may be economically combined.

3. In this case (two bedrooms and a workship which may become a future bedroom) the single bathroom for the sake of privacy is not immediately connected to any single bedroom. Bathrooms

opening directly into a bedroom occupied by more than one person or two bedrooms opening into a single bathroom have been badly overdone. We will have as much garden and space in all these space appropriations as our money allows after we have simplified construction by way of the technique we have tried out.

A modest house, this Usonian house, a dwelling place that has no feeling at all for the "grand" except as the house extends itself in the flat parallel to the ground. It will be a companion to the horizon. With floor-heating that kind of extension on the ground can hardly go too far for comfort or beauty of proportion, provided it does not cost too much in upkeep. As a matter of course a home like this is an architect's creation. It is not a builder's nor an amateur's effort. There is considerable risk in exposing the scheme to imitation or emulation.

This is true because a house of this type could not be well built and achieve its design except as an architect oversees the building.

And the building would fail of proper effect unless the furnishing and planting were all done by advice of the architect.

Thus briefly these few descriptive paragraphs instead of a floor plan may help to indicate how stuffy and stifling the little colonial hot-boxes, hallowed by government or not, really are where Usonian family life is concerned. You might easily put two of them, each costing more, into the living space of this one and not go much outside the walls. Here is a moderate-cost brick-and-wood house that by our own new technology has been greatly extended both in scale and comfort: a single house suited to prefabrication because the factory can go to the house.

Imagine how the costs would come down were the technique a familiar matter or if many houses were to be executed at one time— probably down to forty-five hundred dollars, according to number built and location.

There is a freedom of movement, and a privacy too, afforded by the general arrangement here that is unknown to the current "boxment." Let us say nothing about beauty. Beauty is an ambiguous term concerning an affair of taste in the provinces of which our big cities are the largest.

But I think a cultured American, we say Usonian, housewife will look well in it. The now inevitable car will seem a part of it.

Where does the garden leave off and the house begin? Where the garden begins and the house leaves off.

Withal, this Usonian dwelling seems a thing loving the ground with the new sense of space, light, and freedom—to which our U.S.A. is entitled.

• Questions for Study

1. Discuss Wright's methods of paragraph organization. What transitional devices does he employ to get from one paragraph to the next?
2. Do you have trouble with any of the architectural terms? Do you believe that Wright has to be technical in his usage? Does the author's personality come through in his use of such words as "stupid," "stupidity," and "super-common-sense"? Do you get any hints through the essay as to what "Usonian" means?
3. What does Wright consider the fundamentals of good living? How does he incorporate them into his theory of architecture?
4. Can you think of any advantages to the "little colonial hot-boxes" he dislikes?

ROBIN BOYD

•

THE COUNTER-REVOLUTION

IN ARCHITECTURE

The saddest thing about architecture today is that "Modern Architecture"—the movement which came to light in Chicago and Central Europe about the turn of the century and held such brilliant promise—was too pure to live. Its principles were too innocent to survive any civilized age to date—least of all this excitable twentieth century. Now it has reached a possible turning point and the principles are in the balance.

Originally, long before it found expression in buildings, modern architecture was not a style and had little enough to do with practical design. It was just an idea, and one which escaped the few attempts made to build it into bricks and mortar. It was one of the revolutionary architectural theories which heaved occasionally under the ornate sur-

From *Harper's Magazine*, September 1959. Reprinted by permission of *Harper's Magazine* and of the author.

face of nineteenth-century building. At first, it was necessarily a destructive theory, denouncing all smug imitations of the past, calling for freedom from ancient habits of building and the irrelevant rules of historic styles. Then it was constructive, substituting for symbolism and decoration the idea of realism: buildings which are what they are, and look it; architecture for living, pure and simple, architecture spared the indignity of any sort of applied art and uncontaminated even by the desire for beauty.

In practical application the idea had to split into two—as is always necessary in architecture, where form and surface are almost independent elements. Thus the new rule of form was to be "the unflinching adaptation of a building to its position and use," as Horatio Greenough, the American sculptor, expressed it in the middle of the nineteenth century. As for ornament, the new rule was to banish it entirely, since it was, Greenough said, no more than "the instinctive effort of infant civilization to disguise its incompetence." To many nineteenth-century progressives the spirit of democracy and the nature of technology sent up an irresistible call for a new, rational approach to building.

Yet the revolt resisted translation from words into structure for half a century. Then rapidly in a few years of the 1890s and 1900s the theories began to bear strange fruit: buildings which were unique in history not only because they allowed themselves to be shaped by new materials like reinforced concrete, but also because they were deliberately unornamented. While being far removed from the utilitarian, they delighted in the look of utility.

But utility is not the best word; the *avant-garde* architects sought suitability on the highest plane. They wanted realism in the interpretation of the needs of the people they were sheltering. They abhorred fake. They did their utmost to be rational.

Now imagine the mood of architects carrying these new rules from the plushy Victorian age into a clean new century—free at last, they imagined, of the suffocating dictatorship of historic styles. Naturally they reacted violently against the grotesque forms and surface confusion of the past fifty years. The concept of rational simplicity led to the placing of bricks and sticks in the simplest geometrical forms. The anti-ornament ethics led to the absolute plainness of unbroken white slabs and sheets of glass on rectilinear, roofless boxes. The principle of allowing the structure freely to suggest the shape led to minor acrobatic feats like cantilevers and corner windows. And sheer cussedness in distaste for the old order led to various gestures of independence from the Greeks, such as deliberate effects of unbalance: weight poised over void, gashes for windows where you least expected them.

All this was done in the name of the principles of rationalism, realism, and functionalism, and while the results were often genuine and
sensitive, they were still no more than artistic expressions of those principles, and it was art performed in a heady mood of rebellion. . . .

The architecture just described was seen briefly in Chicago in the
'eighties and then was more consistently developed in Europe before
the first world war. After the war it established itself, with the inspired
encouragement of Walter Gropius in his Bauhaus school, teaching artistic
teamwork for a technological era. Gradually it leaked across to England,
the U.S.A., South America, and elsewhere. In 1932 Henry-Russell Hitch-
cock and Philip Johnson introduced it formally at the Museum of Modern
Art as "The International Style." Gropius himself has always resented
this term as an insult to the rationalism which the movement stands for.
If the principles are followed, he says, regional variations are automatic.
But the name stuck, and slowly through the 1930s the International Style
won over numbers of architects. All the time it was growing more mature
and sophisticated. In the postwar building boom it ripened rapidly, and
in 1951 Mr. Johnson was able to say: "With the mid-century, modern
architecture has come of age."

Its coming of age was celebrated, you might say, by the United
Nations Secretariat building, a big slice of plain fiftieth-birthday cake.
With its team of architects from member countries, this building exemplified the international approach and teamwork, as opposed to introverted
genius. In its size and elegant slimness it represented the full bloom of
the box. It was a direct descendant of structures like the Fagus factory,
built by Gropius in 1911. The UN building had the same approach, the
same principles, the same aesthetic. All the earlier boxes suddenly looked
tentative. This plain slab was, excepting a few minor imperfections, the
ultimate rectilinear form—one image, unornamented, windowless (while
being all glass). It was a monument to technology and impersonal technique, and stated in a language which the everyday architect could easily
adopt. This was surely near the end of the search. Modern architecture
had arrived at the goal dimly outlined fifty years earlier.

Very soon after Lever House, long before the Seagram Building
began, architects were growing dissatisfied with the cube, the right angle,
the glass wall, and the plain surface. The glass wall had passed from the
mind of the architectural artist over to the hands of the technologist; now
the restless creators of the profession set out in various directions to find
something more interesting, something more exciting hidden behind
the curtain.

Which way to go? There was one obvious way: to follow Frank
Lloyd Wright, who had always disparaged the soulless box. But this did

not suit the searching spirit of the architectural adventurers. The abundant decade of the 1950s unquestionably called for a new approach, a new affluence in architecture. The austerity of the International Style may have been meaningful and refreshing after a surfeit of ornamentation, but now it seemed only a restrictive bore.

Again the quest split into the two parts of architecture: a search for new richness on the surface and a search for new excitement in form. The simplest and most convenient way to study the vigorous development of these two quests is to follow the two men whose work seems to express the spirit of the mid-century more vividly than others': Edward D. Stone—for the surface quest—and Eero Saarinen—for the excitement. These are two of the most distinguished members of modern architecture's second generation, two who helped substantially in their time to promote the perfection and public acceptance of the glass box (and two incidentally who have received the accolade of a *Time* cover story).

Mr. Stone's stylistic swing was gentle and took him through several gradual steps. The first was the U.S. Embassy at New Delhi, classically square and disciplined behind its frankly Taj Mahal atmospherics. Then came a pill factory in Pasadena, which, with rather less reason to be Eastern, had even more pools and many more grilles. These buildings, despite their romanticism and surface frills, were members of the modern movement. They were International Style gift-wrapped. But the very presence of contrived decorative effects, however sophisticated, broke the spell of the modern pioneers' fundamental law that every element must be useful. Once started down the byroad from New Delhi, there seemed to be a fatal fascination to reach the end as soon as possible. The ornamentation was not in itself the chief affront to the principles of the old modern architecture. It represented a general drift away from the realities of the function to literary associations and symbolism, to prettiness for its own sake. The end of this little byroad may not yet be reached, but it cannot be far beyond the Huntington Hartford Museum, with its Venetian arcade and verd-antique marble medallions promising to be as exquisite as a superbly packaged chocolate box.

Mr. Stone's adventures impressed a number of architects, and many who, unlike him, had never been really at home with modern architecture, were relieved to see the discipline broken by one of the old hands. Grilles of various sorts appeared all over the world and in many architectural circles decoration was again considered respectable. But not, by any means, in all circles. Most ordinary architects were not yet ready to dismiss so lightly the accumulated principles of a century of attacks against applied ornament. Edward Stone's supporters might argue that his work retained the essential simple imagery of the modern movement, but to most architects simplicity meant more than lack of clutter. It meant the indivisible quality of "nakedness," as Greenough saw it in 1852, "the majesty of the essential instead of the trappings of pretension." Perhaps Adolf Loos, the great Viennese pioneer of rational design, went a little too far fifty years later when he equated ornament with crime; but many still would accept his treatise that "Evolution of human culture implies the disappearance of ornament from the object of use."

The simplest way to study the galloping development of the excitement—the new search for form—is, as I have said, to follow the second of the two leaders of second-generation modern: Eero Saarinen, forty-eight, son of the famous Finnish-born architect Eliel Saarinen who came to live in the U. S. in 1923. Eero first achieved world fame as a brilliant exponent of Mies van der Rohe's principles in the General Motors' showplace laboratory at Detroit—elegant glass boxes in a supremely regular, rectilinear, and reasonable model of the last phase of the International Style. But "there are many ways of being influenced by Mies," says Saarinen. "I would say that I have been most influenced by him in the MIT [Kresge] auditorium—not by his form but by his . . . principle of making structure the dominant element in architecture and letting the functional ones fit in."

The tri-cornered dome of the Kresge auditorium, designed in 1953, was Saarinen's first important essay in exciting shape, but it was not a structural concept. A dome does not stand naturally and comfortably on three tiny pointed shoes. It had to be cramped into them and it suffered accordingly. And it was not a functional idea. Saarinen let the functional elements fit in, as he says, and finally the lid was shut. But the success was not inevitable; the container was neither a soft-sided zipper bag nor a violin case; it was an inflexible piece of geometry. In order to give privacy to the back-stage space, about a quarter of the "glass" area in the open segments where the slices were removed from the dome had to be opaque. And it is not a visual, expressive, or emotional idea. It does not convey music or meetings and it could have been made much prettier with more feet, or more projections above the bulging glass—if prettiness had been the aim.

The MIT auditorium in Cambridge was entirely an intellectual concept, as pure and cold as an International Style cube but suggesting a break free from the cube, a tentative side-step round the curtain wall.

In Eero Saarinen's next notable essay in excitement, the Yale Hockey Rink designed in 1956, the shape is not so pure and rigid. It is more relaxed and much more convincing as a form derived from functional and structural requirements. An upright arch of a central spine is matched on each side by a reclining arch of a beam running around the back of the raised seating. Thus the basis of two roof saddles is framed from structural requirements. Whether it was absolutely necessary to extend the central arch at each end, curving upwards to shape the whole like a cupid's bow, is another matter; at least the body of the building has an authentic and imperative air. But if it does "express" any idea, or activity, this would seem to be accidental; at the most it might appear that the hunch-backed curves express the movements of Ivy Leaguers on skates.

For his next, third, exciting shape, Saarinen changed his starting point again. His design for the TWA terminal building at Idlewild is one of the most fluid designs in the movement. In forming it Saarinen retreated from the box about as far as anyone could go. He shaped it as freely as a sculptor would, with the only qualification that he retained the traditional architectural quality of symmetry. He actually designed it against a mirror which represented the center line of the building. The mirror balanced every move he made. Thus the roof springs out like graceful wings from the central axis giving it something of the look of "a giant bird in flight" as one ecstatic journalist described the model. Inside the giant bird the functions of an airport terminal were fitted easily and loosely, like a weekend's luggage in an ample trunk, with no sign of the squeezing apparent in the MIT auditorium. And the structure was again well considered and convincing, as in the Yale rink.

But the initial stimulus was not functional or structural; nor was it intellectual as at MIT. It was emotional. The *Architectural Forum* decribed at the time (January 1958) the way "Saarinen and co-designer Kevin Roche set the key to the planning in their design discussions: the sense of movement, which is an intrinsic part of a terminal should show in the design." The design team was described at work sculpturing the cardboard model of the terminal, cutting, trying, altering, and discussing. In the end they satisfied themselves in shaping the interior to give a visual effect of flow coinciding with the passengers' bodily movement through the building.

Thus Saarinen, under the gaze of a lost, impressionable generation of younger architects, developed in a few years from reasoned rectangles to felt space. But while many hearts warmed to the giant bird, the question still plagued some heads; is it reasonable? The problem of fitting modern services, lavatories, and elevators into a bird brought problems that were only partially, only visually, solved. The plans showed some awkward pockets where rectilinear equipment was caught in organic intestines, and the main pedestrian bridge across the voluptuous space had a peculiar kink in the middle which could hardly be called "functional." But to dwell on these points would be fatuous. This is a key building which marks a transition from one architectural approach to

another; if it has practical imperfections, we can rest assured that
Saarinen will overcome them later, assuming he continues on the same
road. Very few rectilinear buildings are without practical sin. Any irregular building is victim to much more searching and spiteful scrutiny, but
there is no inherent reason why a flowing shape should be less functional
than a square one. On the contrary—consider the human shape.

The question facing Saarinen and all who would follow him is not
the comparatively simple matter of mastering the technique of bending
functional and structural requirements with acceptable logic. After the
technique—the language of curves—is mastered, what have architects to
say? The Saarinen trail leads to the fundamental question of the nature
of architectural expression.

Much of the new architecture of excitement is so strong and confident that it may delude us for a moment that it is leading to new realms
of architectural beauty. But birds and curves can pall at least as quickly
as boxes. All the shapes of architecture are of equal importance or insignificance in the cosmic pattern. Only associations of familiar shapes
and surprise in unfamiliar shapes affect the immediate reaction of the
eye. Ultimate satisfaction is achieved only when the long-term visual
reaction is appropriate to the human activities involved—and when the
architectural environment engenders a quicker sense of the realities of
the situation, a sharpening of each experience.

Appropriateness of expression has been the aim in most of the "exciting shape" buildings. Stubbins' Berlin Congress Hall, with its jaunty
saddle roof, clearly sought to express the concept of freedom in the
speech which it was built to house. Utzon's opera house caught up the
sails of Sydney Harbor. A restaurant by the sea in Puerto Rico by Toro-
Ferrer shaped its concrete roof after a magnified sea shell. At TWA Saarinen and Roche let the movement of the crowd lead them.

But all this is symbolism, or somewhat shallow emotionalism, or
plain high-class advertising. It has nothing to do with the appropriateness of an enclosure as *experienced by an occupant*. If curves and swirls
really do convey a feeling of movement, what has this to do with the
emotional state of the average passenger waiting for his flight signal?
Must he be swept up in a feeling of movement? The mutual adjustment
of the spatial expression and the psychological state of a sensitive occupant is more valuable than any ordained symbolism or poetic abstraction.
Excitement, in short, should be pertinent.

Architecture is, as most architects will frequently remind you, an
expressive art. Frank Lloyd Wright used to insist that no building had a
right to exist unless it had poetry. Yet there never have been and never
will be enough artists or poets to go round, and the world-wide architec-

tural mess which is the disgrace of the twentieth century is largely caused because we expect plodding, conscientious architectural technicians to act like artists.

Attempts to solve this anomaly sometimes lead to a concept—which has some support—of a frank division in architectural practice: a separation of the technology from the artistry. Thus the repetitive, reasonable curtain-wall grid—the boxlike building—might become a universal backdrop silhouetting a foreground of special individual gems. The most likely impediments to this scheme are the commercial need to advertise the importance of unimportant buildings and the egotistical urge of some builders and architects to raise monuments on their own inadequate ability. The only counter to this, and ultimately the only cure for architecture's ills, is a better educated public taste.

At present it must be admitted that few people outside the higher ranks of the architectural and engineering professions take their architectural excitement with any discrimination. To many a somnambulant eye there is no essential difference between a Saarinen shape on the brink of greatness and some convulsive curve bent only to attract attention—Googie Style, as it is sometimes called, after the remarkable California restaurant chain.

The International Style's plainness was accepted as a fashion and has now run the brief course of any fashionable style. Irresponsible new sorts of enrichment and excitement threaten from all sides. Infant civilization still demands the paint and feathers. At this critical stage the unexpected structural shapes of an imaginative engineer might well hold the greatest promise for the sensible revitalization of architecture. But they are not appropriate, or even possible, for *all* buildings and the architectural profession will have another nervous breakdown if it tries to find the common denominator, for universal application, of the box and the bird. Architectural poetry is not practically possible for every building and automatically is limited to the poetic potential of the community. You can't spread it thin; somehow no one would contemplate mass-producing giant birds.

The main problem is how to control irrelevant enrichment and irresponsible structural gymnastics and to restrict the foreground gems to genuine poetry. This is a task which involves everyone. The better architects should practice relevance in their excitement. Less gifted architects should be encouraged to keep to the anonymous, unexciting, but lucrative backdrop. The audience should learn to see the line which divides any sincere expression from the displays and advertisements, and to keep raising the line another peg. This is not altogether an unrealistic cry for a knowledgeable and sophisticated public eye. Calls for better public taste have always been forlorn, we know; but increasing discretion may not be out of the question. It requires only that people grow more aware of the possibilities of architectural expression, and awareness is undoubtedly being stimulated even now by the experiments in enrichment and excitement. Later, if this awareness can develop into a public demand for genuine and appropriate character, architecture will be on the way back to its former status at the head of the family of arts.

Will that happy day mark the end of the International Style? Not at all, for technology will continue to work on the problem of universal shelter. Beyond the latest curtain wall there will be more boxes or bubbles offering perfection of press-button control of light, privacy, and climate. These buildings will be direct descendants of the early Moderns: rational, realistic, as scientific as can be. Must we assume that the rationalism and realism will have to be forsaken by those other buildings which seek appropriate character? This appears to be the general assumption today and it holds all the seeds of another breakdown for architecture on parallel lines to that of the late nineteenth century. The principles of early Modern Architecture were no more than a restatement, in the tightest, almost legalistic, terms, of timeless architectural virtues. They are still as valid this year as ever they were. They do not necessarily lead always to a glass or to a box. They need not be applied in a mood of revolt against tradition. They do not by any means debar excitement or genuine poetry. They exert serious restriction only on those who would use architecture as a kind of monumental advertisement.

• Questions for Study

1. In what ways did "The International Style" break away from older styles?
2. Do you think that Frank Lloyd Wright would have agreed with Boyd's comments concerning the UN building? Explain.
3. Summarize the contributions of Stone and Saarinen to architecture.
4. In your opinion should ornament be a legitimate part of architecture or should the functional alone be emphasized?
5. According to Boyd, what are some of the main problems facing both architects and the general public with regard to taste?
6. To what extent is it possible to talk about sincerity in art? Does Boyd's discussion of "sincere" as opposed to "insincere" architectural expression clarify your thinking on the issue? Explain.

H. L. MENCKEN

•

THE LIBIDO FOR THE UGLY

On a Winter day some years ago, coming out of Pittsburgh on one of the expresses of the Pennsylvania Railroad, I rolled eastward for an hour through the coal and steel towns of Westmoreland county. It was familiar ground; boy and man, I had been through it often before. But somehow I had never quite sensed its appalling desolation. Here was the very heart of industrial America, the center of its most lucrative and characteristic activity, the boast and pride of the richest and grandest nation ever seen on earth—and here was a scene so dreadfully hideous, so intolerably bleak and forlorn that it reduced the whole aspiration of man to a macabre and depressing joke. Here was wealth beyond computation, almost beyond imagination—and here were human habitations so abominable that they would have disgraced a race of alley cats.

I am not speaking of mere filth. One expects steel towns to be dirty. What I allude to is the unbroken and agonizing ugliness, the sheer revolting monstrousness, of every house in sight. From East Liberty to Greensburg, a distance of twenty-five miles, there was not one in sight from the train that did not insult and lacerate the eye. Some were so bad, and they were among the most pretentious—churches, stores, warehouses, and the like—that they were downright startling; one blinked before them as one blinks before a man with his face shot away. A few linger in memory, horrible even there: a crazy little church just west of Jeannette, set like a dormer-window on the side of a bare, leprous hill; the headquarters of the Veterans of Foreign Wars at another forlorn town, a steel stadium like a huge rat-trap somewhere further down the line. But most of all I recall the general effect—of hideousness without a break. There was not a single decent house within eye-range from the

Pittsburgh suburbs to the Greensburg yards. There was not one that was not misshapen, and there was not one that was not shabby.

The country itself is not uncomely, despite the grime of the endless mills. It is, in form, a narrow river valley, with deep gullies running up into the hills. It is thickly settled, but not noticeably overcrowded. There is still plenty of room for building, even in the larger towns, and there are very few solid blocks. Nearly every house, big and little, has space on all four sides. Obviously, if there were architects of any professional sense or dignity in the region, they would have perfected a chalet to hug the hillsides—a chalet with a high-pitched roof, to throw off the heavy Winter snows, but still essentially a low and clinging building, wider than it was tall. But what have they done? They have taken as their model a brick set on end. This they have converted into a thing of dingy clapboards, with a narrow, low-pitched roof. And the whole they have set upon thin, preposterous brick piers. By the hundreds and thousands these abominable houses cover the bare hillsides, like gravestones in some gigantic and decaying cemetery. On their deep sides they are three, four and even five stories high; on their low sides they bury themselves swinishly in the mud. Not a fifth of them are perpendicular. They lean this way and that, hanging on to their bases precariously. And one and all they are streaked in grime, with dead and eczematous patches of paint peeping through the streaks.

Now and then there is a house of brick. But what brick! When it is new it is the color of a fried egg. When it has taken on the patina of the mills it is the color of an egg long past all hope or caring. Was it necessary to adopt that shocking color? No more than it was necessary to set all of the houses on end. Red brick, even in a steel town, ages with some dignity. Let it become downright black, and it is still sightly, especially if its trimmings are of white stone, with soot in the depths and the high spots washed by the rain. But in Westmoreland they prefer that uremic yellow, and so they have the most loathsome towns and villages ever seen by mortal eye.

I award this championship only after laborious research and incessant prayer. I have seen, I believe, all of the most unlovely towns of the world; they are all to be found in the United States. I have seen the mill towns of decomposing New England and the desert towns of Utah, Arizona and Texas. I am familiar with the back streets of Newark, Brooklyn and Chicago, and have made scientific explorations to Camden, N.J. and Newport News, Va. Safe in a Pullman, I have whirled through the gloomy, God-forsaken villages of Iowa and Kansas, and the malarious tide-water hamlets of Georgia. I have been to Bridgeport, Conn., and to Los Angeles. But nowhere on this earth, at home or abroad, have I seen anything to compare to the villages that huddle along the line of the Pennsylvania from the Pittsburgh yards to Greensburg. They are incomparable in color, and they are incomparable in design. It is as if some titanic and aberrant genius, uncompromisingly inimical to man, had devoted all the ingenuity of Hell to the making of them. They show grotesqueries of ugliness that, in retrospect, become almost diabolical. One cannot imagine mere human beings concocting such dreadful things, and one can scarcely imagine human beings bearing life in them.

Are they so frightful because the valley is full of foreigners—dull, insensate brutes, with no love of beauty in them? Then why didn't these foreigners set up similar abominations in the countries that they came from? You will, in fact, find nothing of the sort in Europe—save perhaps in the more putrid parts of England. There is scarcely an ugly village on the whole Continent. The peasants, however poor, somehow manage to make themselves graceful and charming habitations, even in Spain. But in the American village and small town the pull is always toward ugliness, and in that Westmoreland valley it has been yielded to with an eagerness bordering upon passion. It is incredible that mere ignorance should have achieved such masterpieces of horror.

On certain levels of the American race, indeed, there seems to be a positive libido for the ugly, as on other and less Christian levels there is a libido for the beautiful. It is impossible to put down the wallpaper that defaces the average American home of the lower middle class to mere inadvertence, or to the obscene humor of the manufacturers. Such ghastly designs, it must be obvious, give a genuine delight to a certain type of mind. They meet, in some unfathomable way, its obscure and unintelligible demands. They caress it as "The Palms" caresses it, or the art of the movie, or jazz. The taste for them is as enigmatical and yet as common as the taste for dogmatic theology and the poetry of Edgar A. Guest.

Thus I suspect (though confessedly without knowing) that the vast majority of the honest folk of Westmoreland county, and especially the 100% Americans among them, actually admire the houses they live in, and are proud of them. For the same money they could get vastly better ones, but they prefer what they have got. Certainly there was no pressure upon the Veterans of Foreign Wars to choose the dreadful edifice that bears their banner, for there are plenty of vacant buildings along the track-side, and some of them are appreciably better. They might, indeed, have built a better one of their own. But they chose that clapboarded horror with their eyes open, and having chosen it, they let it mellow into its present shocking depravity. They like it as it is: beside it, the Parthenon would no doubt offend them. In precisely the same way the authors of the rat-trap stadium that I have mentioned made a deliberate choice. After painfully designing and erecting it, they made it perfect in their own sight by putting a completely impossible pent-house, painted a staring yellow, on top of it. The effect is that of a fat woman with a black eye. It is that of a Presbyterian grinning. But they like it.

Here is something that the psychologists have so far neglected: the love of ugliness for its own sake, the lust to make the world intolerable. Its habitat is the United States. Out of the melting pot emerges a race which hates beauty as it hates truth. The etiology of this madness deserves a great deal more study than it has got. There must be causes behind it; it arises and flourishes in obedience to biological laws, and not as a mere act of God. What, precisely, are the terms of those laws? And why do they run stronger in America than elsewhere? Let some honest *Privat Dozent* in pathological sociology apply himself to the problem.

• *Questions for Study*

1. The style of this essay illustrates one of Mencken's main characteristics. He was a "disturber of the peace." How do such phrases as "lacerate the eye," "decomposing New England," and "even in Spain" show his emotional attitudes toward his subjects? What precisely does he mean by the title of the essay?
2. Compare and contrast the views on architecture of Mencken and Wright.
3. Why is the beginning effective?
4. Point out elements of autobiography, description, narration, persuasion, and show how these are unified by tone and content.

ERNEST VAN DEN HAAG

·

CREATING CITIES FOR HUMAN BEINGS

The drawbacks of the city have been stressed by social philosophers such
as Nietzsche, Simmel and Scheler, and their followers and popularizers
(including Spengler, Mumford and others).

There is first of all de-individualization and anonymity. People tend
to live externally crowded but internally lonely, morally isolated lives.
We each know more people and fewer persons. The city fosters rootlessness. Traditional bonds, beliefs, institutions and norms are weakened,
and relationships become discontinuous, impersonal, functional and,
above all, less intimate. Ultimately people, disaffected and disengaged,
float freely, like specks of dust. It is not an enjoyable freedom. Political
mass movements, like dust storms, may sweep the loosened soil hither
and thither—in the end the bleak shelter of totalitarianism beckons to
the uprooted and homeless. Thirty years ago, Ortega y Gasset already
heard the "formidable cry rising like the howling of innumerable dogs
to the stars, asking for someone or something to impose an occupation, a
duty." For normally we are secured to reality and life by social bonds that
tie us to persons, positions, ambitions, norms and things. Life is real to
us and meaningful only if it has continuity and gives us parts to play
that let us partake in more than social boredom and in more than being
"distracted from distraction by distraction." When we each feel but tenu-
ously and casually linked to what we do and are, and to those that do
and are with us, social ties easily come undone and personalities un-
strung.

Scope for spontaneous gestures also is necessarily narrowed. The
bigger the city, the more impersonal regulation is required, until we become accustomed to being told when to cross the street and where, when

Reprinted from *The American Scholar*, Volume 28, Number 4, Autumn 1959. Copyright © 1959 by the United Chapters of Phi Beta Kappa. By permission of the publishers and of the author.

to stop and go. At the same time, the great variety of the urban environment, the many kinds and classes of people we meet and work with, the constant din and the infinite diversions offered may overstimulate us to the point of nervous exhaustion. In defense, city dwellers develop a blasé attitude—a tendency to reject indiscriminately all stimulation, a denial that anything can be really new and interesting. We are all aware of the glazed, unseeing gaze we offer fellow passengers on public conveyances—a gaze meant to deny the very contact into which our bodies may have been obscenely thrown.

Whereas the countryside may be dull because it lacks novelty, because nothing happens, the city generates boredom by offering or imposing stimulation so relentlessly that people are numbed. Both absolute stillness or constant din tire our minds and spirits. Further, city dwellers become altogether accustomed to being entertained and diverted from the outside. Thus inner resources atrophy; cumulative and meaningful relations are discarded for the merely exciting and thrilling. Nothing, in the end, can be more monotonous. So many bells toll so deafeningly all the time that it is hard to participate in any of the services they are meant to announce. Typically, the city produces restless or agitated boredom, displayed in activity as meaningless as it is unceasing; less frequently it produces listless boredom, an apathetic withdrawal. In either case, there is an insatiable craving for excitement as well as an inability actually to get excited—to respond to anything.

The city permits and encourages a high degree of specialization. Rational calculation and efficient routines often must take the place of personal or customary relations. In short, the city dweller must routinize and stereotype the world and himself in it, or else he would be constantly perplexed and stunned by the unlimited possibilities that rush at him.

Among the physical drawbacks of city living are noise; air pollution, which causes lung cancer to be twice as frequent in cities as in the countryside; unsafeness; traffic accidents; and many other familiar nuisances—if that is not too weak a word.

That much will have to do as a rough sketch of the main criticisms leveled against the city. How valid are they? Some merely point to the defects of the virtues of urban living—there can be too much of a good thing; however, others suggest the erosion of these very virtues, an erosion that might well leave cities barren alike of urbanity and interest.

It is true that overstimulation may lead to withdrawal or excessive tension. But cities may stimulate without overstimulating. It seems unreasonable to inveigh against alcohol simply because some people drink too much. After all, it is not alcohol that makes one drunk—it is drinking too much that does it. As for the impersonality of the city, it may give one a wider choice in personal relations than the countryside does. Specialization can, but need not, go so far as to reduce the specialist to his specialty; and without the population density of the city, we could not support such specialists as coloratura singers, ballet dancers, psychoanalysts, and countless others—not to speak of such institutions as theaters, museums, specialized shops, et cetera.

If the virtues of cities as centers of civilization remain, occasional discomfort may be a price well worth paying. The real trouble is that cities are losing their social and cultural *raison d'être* as living communities. This is not an unavoidable process. On the contrary, it is happening entirely because of our own foolishness, which, perhaps, is unavoidable.

Of course, American cities cannot boast the ancient traditions that are embodied in the monuments and fountains, the castles, the piazzas and the palazzi—the grandeur, the nobility and fascination of Europe. They are comparatively formless, therefore. But need this go as far as it does?

Is it really necessary for us to build houses that are not expected to stand more than fifty years and usually are torn down before? Must we always sacrifice tradition to efficiency? How can we hope thus to inspire architects? And, indeed, the effects of our attitude are obvious if one looks around. Particularly in monumental building we are quite unable to develop any style of our own. We either imitate or resort to the "international modern," "functional" style about which the best that can be said is that it is fairly inoffensive.

If the first mistake of builders and planners is their disregard for tradition, their sacrifice of the established and living to the mechanically more efficient, a second frequent mistake is excessive *social* functionalism. Business and residential quarters often are entirely divorced. The effect is that *both* become monotonous and uninteresting. Much of downtown New York is a desolate ghost city after dark. This imposes uneconomic burdens on transportation systems and high overhead per unit on, for instance, restaurants crowded at lunch time and deserted at dinner time. More important, it deprives both the residential and business districts of the diversity and the continuous life that are the glory of cities.

I am aware of the high cost of real estate that makes it impossible to maintain residences in downtown districts. But this is not unavoidable. We could make laws prescribing that no more than a certain proportion of each block can be devoted to business purposes. This would solve the economic problem that private interests, left to their own devices, cannot possibly solve.

The entirely planned Australian capital of Canberra is a warning, although unheeded. The residential part—essentially a sprawling garden city—is quite separated from the government offices in which the inhabitants work and from the shopping centers. The result is that in this small city of less than 20,000 inhabitants, where no transportation should be needed, everybody has to ride to and from the office, to and from the shopping centers, and nobody can go home for lunch. Worse, each part of the town is only half alive most of the time.

In a big city, it is not possible, of course, for everybody to live near their places of work. Nor do all people want to, although many more would like such an arrangement than are now able to have it. I believe we should do everything we can to minimize functional separation— particularly separation of residential and business districts. They can enrich each other, and the separation impoverishes both and creates more problems than it solves. Unfortunately, the trend, unchecked by legislation and favored by city planners—it makes things neater—is toward utmost spatial separation of functions.

Functionalism takes other forms, too. For instance, in New York a new center of the arts is to be built to combine in a few blocks concert halls, the Metropolitan Opera house, dance recital stages, theaters and whatever else smacks of art. Apparently the planners are under the impression that people, after taking in a concert, go to the opera, then to the theater, and on to finish up the evening at a dance recital. It will be hard to persuade people to do this. One may go from one bar, or night club, to another; but surely not from the opera to a concert. Without actually enriching the center of the arts, the rest of the city, from which these cultural institutions must migrate, will suffer. And in practical terms, quite a traffic problem will be created.

Speaking of night clubs and bars, here too functionalism denatures the city. What makes city streets exciting are spontaneously located restaurants, bars, night clubs, specialty shops, candy stores, groceries— all the things that are usually excluded from planned developments. But these places not only lend interest to city streets, they are neighborhood social centers. To be sure, there is usually an official restaurant with a liquor license and an antiseptic supermarket; but I cannot imagine anyone feeling at home there.

Housing developments may be a necessary evil—although I doubt it. People too poor for reasons beyond their control to afford the rent required might just as well be subsidized with money rather than being given subsidized apartments. If there is demand, builders will build. The people then could spend their subsidy either on better housing—or on anything else they choose. It is this last prospect that scares social workers and politicians who are convinced that they know what is good for other people—and that other people do not. Hence they are willing to offer people subsidized apartments, but not the money with which they could decide whether to rent them. Further, the middle classes have been taught that slums breed crime, disease and what not. They do, in the same way in which one may say that hospitals breed death, by attracting sick people. Shall we abolish hospitals? Slums may be the *locus*, but not the *cause* of crimes, which have to do not with lack of bathrooms but with poverty and many other conditions. Slums will exist as long as there are people poorer than others; the poorest part of town will be the slum. Slums will indeed spread because people try to crowd into cities faster than lodgings can be built. The prospect, therefore, is for more slums in the next one hundred years.

To raze slums and rebuild in such a way as to house fewer people is pointless. Those who have lost their lodgings are compelled to crowd in elsewhere. The slum thus is displaced but not eliminated. As much as possible, we should add rather than raze buildings.

Incidentally, there is more life, and perhaps more communal feeling, in a slum than in many a suburb, although it be less well-scrubbed. I am not even convinced that an empty lot is not a better place for children to play than an institutional playground. It surely fosters independence, imagination and spontaneity far more than most playgrounds.

Must developments be as unpleasantly institutional as they are? Would it not be possible to build some big, towering structures together with some small ones with gardens and patios, one near to the other so as to offer sunlight to all and variety to the eye? This would not require additional space, only additional imagination. In most developments the high, rising towers are surrounded by well-shaved lawns (off which you must keep). The lawns are needed to give sunlight to the towers, and they please the architect. They set off his creations. But gardens owned or used by some tenants, and which at the same time could give delight to those who only can see and feel them, would be far more rewarding. Public things that are owned by everybody often turn out not to be possessed by anybody. They do not receive the individual care given to private plots. Public parks are needed, of course, and more of them. But small plots near residences should be owned by the residents. We must allow for spontaneous growth, variety and initiative. People should be allowed to arrange their environment and not be arranged by it.

Housing development tenants often are selected according to economic and family status. This, too, makes for tiresome monotony and is quite unnecessary. Why not include in the development some houses with large apartments and some with small ones, renting the big apartments at high rents to people who can pay and the small ones at lower rents? We should foster variety and surprise, not monotony.

The difficulties just listed have contributed to the rush to the suburbs, which adds some problems and solves none. Many reasons pull or push people to the suburbs. Some wish to own their own house; some wish to live in the country. (Alas, the countryside they seek vanishes as they reach it.) Some hope for lower taxes and better schools, or believe that children are better off in suburbs. One reason that I think is important, although seldom mentioned, is that when you buy a house in the suburbs, you get your future friends thrown in—you do not have to make friends: your neighbors automatically (and interchangeably) become your friends. Some think this is an advantage.

On the whole, the young middle-class set migrates to the suburbs, leaving the city largely to the very rich and the very poor, as well as to the old. Mostly, but not always, the suburbanites commute to work in the city. This effectively cuts them off from both city and country life.

There are now many sociological and fictional studies of suburbs. The high degree of conformity required, the de-individualization and the absence of spontaneity are well known, as is the monotony produced by having people of about the same age and income group, with about the same family and occupational problems, all getting up in about the same houses, feeding, catching trains, returning, drinking cocktails, sleeping, and starting all over again—all on the same schedule. Attempts to relieve the deadly boredom that oozes through suburbs—by drinking, adultery and nervous breakdowns—are usually unsuccessful.

Most suburbs do not provide either the privacy or the semirural life that lured their inhabitants. Because utilities would be too costly otherwise, houses are often built so near to each other that neighbors interfere more than they do in the city. (Sometimes I also have a sneaking suspicion that people like to look into each other's windows.) One cannot avoid seeing and hearing the neighbors and their television sets. And there is no escape, no point in going out—the suburban street, although clean, is totally, desolately uninteresting. There is not life on it; only cars.

As more people move to the suburbs, transportation to and from the city becomes a more and more unpleasant ordeal, while the suburb loses its remaining bucolic charms without acquiring any of the attractions of the city. They are still nice to visit—although I wouldn't want to live there. Soon they won't be nice to visit either.

• *Questions for Study*

1. According to the author, what are some disadvantages to living in the city? Do you agree with him? Explain.
2. What does the planning of Canberra show? Do you think the planners of

that city had a reason for separating the business section from the residential?

3. According to the author, how does the new arts center in New York illustrate some disadvantages of functionalism?

4. Are there any advantages to living in a slum? Defend the idea that poorer sections have a color and character of their own that cannot be transferred to the projects that replace them.

E . M . F O R S T E R

•

NOT LISTENING TO MUSIC

Listening to music is such a muddle that one scarcely knows how to start describing it. The first point to get clear in my own case is that during the greater part of every performance I do not attend. The nice sounds make me think of something else. I wool-gather most of the time, and am surprised that others don't. Professional critics can listen to a piece as consistently and as steadily as if they were reading a chapter in a novel. This seems to me an amazing feat, and probably they only achieve it through intellectual training; that is to say, they find in the music the equivalent of a plot; they are following the ground bass or expecting the theme to re-enter in the dominant, and so on, and this keeps them on the rails. But I fly off every minute: after a bar or two I think how musical I am, or of something smart I might have said in conversation; or I wonder what the composer—dead a couple of centuries—can be feeling as the flames on the altar still flicker up; or how soon an H.E. bomb would extinguish them. Not to mention more obvious distractions: the tilt of the soprano's chin or chins; the antics of the conductor, that impassioned beetle, especially when it is night time and he waves his shards; the affectation of the pianist when he takes a top note with difficulty, as if he too were a soprano; the backs of the chairs; the bumps on the ceiling; the extreme physical ugliness of the audience. A classical audience is surely the plainest collection of people anywhere assembled for any common purpose; contributing my quota, I have the right to point this out. Compare us with a gang of navvies or with an office staff, and you will be appalled. This, too, distracts me.

What do I hear during the intervals when I do attend? Two sorts of music. They melt into each other all the time, and are not easy to christen, but I will call one of them "music that reminds me of something," and the other "music itself." I used to be very fond of music that reminded me of something, and especially fond of Wagner. With Wagner I always knew where I was; he never let the fancy roam; he ordained that one phrase should recall the ring, another the sword, another the blameless fool and so on; he was as precise in his indications as an oriental dancer. Since he is a great poet, that did not matter, but I accepted his leitmotiv system much too reverently and forced it on to other composers whom it did not suit, such as Beethoven and Franck. I thought that music must be the better for having a meaning. I think so still, but am less clear as to what "a meaning" is. In those days it was either a non-musical object, such as a sword or a blameless fool, or a non-musical emotion, such as fear, lust, or resignation. When music reminded me of something which was not music, I supposed it was getting me somewhere. "How like Monet!" I thought when listening to Debussy, and "How like Debussy!" when looking at Monet. I translated sounds into colours, saw the piccolo as apple-green, and the trumpets as scarlet. The arts were to be enriched by taking in one another's washing.

I still listen to some music this way. For instance, the slow start of Beethoven's Seventh Symphony invokes a grey-green tapestry of hunting scenes, and the slow movement of his Fourth Piano Concerto (the dialogue between piano and orchestra) reminds me of the dialogue between Orpheus and the Furies in Gluck. The climax of the first movement of the Appassionata (the "più allegro") seems to me sexual, although I can detect no sex in the Kreutzer, nor have I come across anyone who could, except Tolstoy. That disappointing work, Brahms' Violin Concerto, promises me clear skies at the opening, and only when the violin has squealed up in the air for page after page is the promise falsified. Wolf's "Ganymed" does give me sky—stratosphere beyond stratosphere. In these cases and in many others music reminds me of something non-musical, and I fancy that to do so is part of its job. Only a purist would condemn all visual parallels, all emotional labellings, all programmes.

Yet there is a danger. Music that reminds does open the door to that imp of the concert hall, inattention. To think of a grey-green tapestry is not very different from thinking of the backs of the chairs. We gather a superior wool from it, still we do wool-gather, and the sounds slip by blurred. The sounds! It is for them that we come, and the closer we can get up against them the better. So I do prefer "music itself" and listen to it and for it as far as possible. In this connection, I will try to analyse a mishap that has recently overtaken the Coriolanus Overture. I used to listen to the Coriolanus for "itself," conscious when it passed of something important and agitating, but not defining further. Now I learn that Wagner, endorsed by Sir Donald Tovey, has provided it with a Programme: the opening bars indicate the hero's decision to destroy the Volscii, then a sweet tune for female influence, then the dotted-quaver-restlessness of indecision. This seems indisputable, and there is no doubt that this was, or was almost, Beethoven's intention. All the same, I have lost my Coriolanus. Its largeness and freedom have gone. The exquisite sounds have been hardened like a road that has been tarred for traffic. One has to go somewhere down them, and to pass through the same domestic crisis to the same military impasse, each time the overture is played.

Music is so very queer that an amateur is bound to get muddled when writing about it. It seems to be more "real" than anything, and to survive when the rest of civilisation decays. In these days I am always thinking of it with relief. It can never be ruined or nationalised. So that the music which is untrammelled and untainted by reference is obviously the best sort of music to listen to; we get nearer the centre of reality. Yet though it is untainted, it is never abstract; it is not like mathematics, even when it uses them. The Goldberg Variations, the last Beethoven Sonata, the Franck Quartet, the Schumann Piano Quintet and the Fourth Symphonies of Tchaikovsky and of Brahms certainly have a message. Though what on earth is it? I shall get tied up trying to say. There's an insistence in music —expressed largely through rhythm; there's a sense that it is trying to push across at us something which is neither an esthetic pattern nor a sermon. That's what I listen for specially.

So music that is itself seems on the whole better than music that reminds. And now to end with an important point: my own performances upon the piano. These grow worse yearly, but never will I give them up. For one thing, they compel me to attend—no wool-gathering or thinking myself clever here—and they drain off all non-musical matter. For another thing, they teach me a little about construction. I see what becomes of a phrase, how it is transformed or returned, sometimes bottom upward, and get some notion of the relation of keys. Playing Beethoven, as I generally do, I grow familiar with his tricks, his impatience, his sudden softnesses, his dropping of a tragic theme one semitone, his love, when tragic, for the

key of C minor, and his aversion to the key of B major. This gives me a
physical approach to Beethoven which cannot be gained through the
slough of "appreciation." Even when people play as badly as I do, they
should continue: it will help them to listen.

• Questions for Study

1. Essays are often grouped into two types: the formal that describes a process
   or appeals to the intellect, and the informal that reveals much concerning
   the author's personality. To which type does this essay belong? Give your
   reasons.
2. What three types of listening does Forster describe? Which does he consider the highest type? Why?
3. Is it necessary for the reader to be familiar with the compositions that Forster
   uses to illustrate his ideas in order to understand the points he is making?
   Consider this question with regard to those pieces mentioned in the essay
   with which you are familiar and those with which you are unfamiliar.
4. Discuss the appropriateness of Forster's title.
5. Explain how the last paragraph contributes to Forster's tone and to his
   meaning.

LEONARD BERNSTEIN

•

SPEAKING OF MUSIC

Ever since I can remember I have talked about music, with friends,
colleagues, teachers, students, and just plain simple citizens. But in the
last few years I have found myself talking about it publicly, thus joining
the long line of well-meaning but generally doomed folk who have tried
to explain the unique phenomenon of human reaction to organized sound.

From *The Atlantic Monthly*, December 1957. Reprinted by permission of *The Atlantic
Monthly* and The Leonard Bernstein Foundation, Inc.

It is almost like trying to explain a freak of nature (whatever that may be); ultimately one must simply accept the loving fact that people enjoy listening to organized sound (certain organized sounds, anyway); that this enjoyment can take the form of all kinds of responses from animal excitement to spiritual exaltation; and that people who can organize sounds so as to evoke the most exalted responses are commonly called geniuses. These axioms can be neither denied nor explained. But, in the great tradition of man burrowing through the darkness with his mind, hitting his head on cave walls, and sometimes perceiving a pin point of light, we can at least try to explain; in fact, there's no stopping us.

There have been many more words written about the *Eroica* Symphony than there are notes in it; in fact, I should imagine that the proportion of words to notes, if anyone could get an accurate count, would be flabbergasting. And yet has anyone ever successfully "explained" the *Eroica?* Can anyone explain in mere prose the wonder of one note following or coinciding with another so that we feel that it is exactly how those notes had to be? Of course not. No matter what rationalists we may profess to be, we are stopped cold at the border of this mystic area. It is not too much to say *mystic* or even *magic:* no art lover can be an agnostic when the chips are down. If you love music, you are a believer, however dialectically you try to wriggle out of it.

The most rational minds in history have always yielded to a slight mystic haze when the subject of music has been broached, recognizing the beautiful and utterly satisfying combination of mathematics and magic that music is. Plato and Socrates knew that the study of music is one of the finest disciplines for the adolescent mind, and insisted on it as a *sine qua non* of education; and just for those reasons of its combined scientific and "spiritual" qualities.

Yet when Plato speaks of music—scientific as he is about almost everything else—he wanders into vague generalizations about harmony, love, rhythm, and those deities who could presumably carry a tune. But he knew that there was nothing like piped music to carry soldiers inspired into battle—and everyone else knows it too. And that certain Greek modes were better than others for love or war or wine festivals or crowning an athlete. Just as the Hindus, with their most mathematically complicated scales, rhythms, and ragas, knew that certain ones had to be for morning hours, or sunset, or Siva festivals, or marching, or windy days. And no amount of mathematics could or can explain that.

We are still, in our own day, faced with this magical block. We try to be scientific about it, in our bumbling way—to employ principles of physics, acoustics, mathematics, and formal logic. We employ philosophical devices like empiricism and teleological method. But what does it accomplish for us? The magic questions are still unanswered. For example, we can try to explain the "shape" of a theme from a Beethoven quartet by saying that it follows the formal principle of synthesis: that there is a short statement (thesis), followed by a questioning answer (antithesis), followed by a development arising out of the conflict of the two (synthesis).

The Germans calls this form *Stollen*. Others say "syllogistic." Words, words, words. Why is the theme beautiful? There's the rub. We can find a hundred themes shaped in this way, or based on variants of this principle; but only one or two will be beautiful.

When I was at Harvard, Professor Birkhoff was working hard on a system of aesthetic measure—actually trying to evolve a mathematical system whereby any object of art could be awarded a beauty rating on a given continuum of aesthetic worth. It was a noble effort; but when all is said and done, it comes to a dead end. The five human senses are capable of measuring objects up to a certain point (the eye can decide that x is twice as long as y; the ear can guess that one trombone is playing twice as loud as the other), but can the senses be measured? Or can their aesthetic responses be measured? How far is the smell of pork from the smell of beans? What beans? Cooked how? Raw? In what climate? If the *Eroica* earns a grade of 3.2, what mark do you give *Tristan?* Or a one-page Bach prelude?

We bumble. We imitate scientific method in our attempts to explain magic phenomena by fact, forces, mass, energy. But we simply can't explain human reaction to these phenomena. Science can explain thunderstorms, but can it explain the fear with which people react to them? And even if it can, somehow, how does science explain the sense of glory we feel in a thunderstorm, break down this sense of glory into its parts? Three parts electrical stimulation, one part aural excitement, one part visual excitment, four parts identification-feelings with the beyond, two parts adoration of almighty forces—an impossible cocktail.

But some people *have* explained the glory of a thunderstorm, and such people are called poets. Only artists can explain magic; only art can substitute for nature. By the same token, only art can substitute for art. And so the only way one can really say anything about music is to write music.

Still we go on trying to shed some light on the mystery. There is a human urge to clarify, rationalize, justify, analyze, limit, describe. There is also a great urge to sell music, arising out of the transformation of music in the last two hundred years into an industry. Suddenly there is a mass market, a tremendous recording industry, professional careerists, civic competitiveness, musical chambers of commerce. And out of this has come something called "music appreciation"—once felicitously called by Virgil Thomson the "music-appreciation racket."

It is, in the main, a racket, because it is in the main specious and commercial. It uses every device to sell music—cajoling, coyness, flattery, oversimplification, irrelevant entertainment, tall tales—all in order to keep the music business humming. And in so doing it has itself become a business. The next step is obviously a new parasitic development: music-appreciation appreciation.

The racket operates in two styles, depending on the audience involved, and one is duller than the other. Type A is the birds-bees-and-rivulets variety, which invokes anything at all under the sun as long as it is extramusical. It turns every note or phrase or chord into a cloud or crag or Cossack. It tells homey tales about the great composers, either spurious or irrelevant. It abounds in anecdotes, quotes from famous performers, indulges itself in bad jokes and unutterable puns, teases the hearer, and tells us nothing about music.

Type B is concerned with analysis—a laudably serious endeavor—but is as dull as Type A is coy. It is the "now comes the theme upside down in the second oboe" variety. A guaranteed soporific. What it does, ultimately, is to supply you with a road map of themes, a kind of Baedeker to the bare geography of a composition; but again, it tells us nothing about music except those superficial geographical facts.

Luckily all talk about music is not restricted to the level of music appreciation. There are writers in the learned journals who make sense, but only to other musicians, or to the cultivated amateur. The musical layman is harder put to find intelligent talk about music. But every once in a while someone appears who strikes an illuminating spark, who can give the layman some insight into music, if only into a cadence, or a melodic contour, or a single harmonic progression.

Such people are rare, and invaluable. Plato had some moments, as did Shakespeare. Certain critics can be perceptive and at the same time intelligible to the layman—men like Sullivan and Newman and Thomson. Certain novelists, like Mann and Huxley, have turned out memorable paragraphs, or even chapters, on musical matters. But most novelists, and writers in general, tend to put their feet in their mouths whenever they part lips to speak of music. And they do it often. For some reason literary minds seem magnetized by musical terminology—probably because they are awe-struck by the abstractness of it all. Nothing can be more different from the representational literary mind, with its literal conceptuality, than the nonobjective musical mind, with its concentration on shapes, lines, and sonorous intensities. And this fascinates the writer—

makes him even a little envious, I have found—so that he longs for some participation in that strange, foreign medium.

As a result, when he reaches for the elusive *mot juste* he often winds up with *glissando* or *crescendo* to express (usually wrongly) what he means—precisely because the musical word seems so elusive. Besides, it's so pretty; what chic and grace those Italian words carry with them! *Scherzo. Vivace. Andantino. Crescendo.* We are constantly running across the word *crescendo* in literature, almost always used synonymously with *climax.* "The storm rose to a great crescendo." "As they kissed, their hearts reached a crescendo of pounding passion." Nonsense. Obviously *crescendo* can mean only "growing," "increasing,"—specifically, getting louder. So a crescendo can mean growing to a climax of storm or passion or anything you wish; but it can't be what you grow to.

This digression is only by way of pointing up the rarity of intelligent musical talk, even among first-class writers. The Huxleys and the Manns of this world are few and far between. Huxley's description of part of Beethoven's Op. 132 in *Point Counter Point* is unforgettable. Mann has some thrilling passages on music in *The Magic Mountain* and in *Dr. Faustus.* And because of people like these—who can sometimes evoke with words the quality of a piece of music or some sense of its essential weight or thrust—because of them we musicians are encouraged to go on trying to elucidate, in the hope that, even if only here and there, we can shed a little light on that terrible bugaboo, musical meaning.

Meaning in music has preoccupied aestheticians, musicians, and philosophers for centuries. The treatises pile up and usually succeed only in adding more words to an already obscure business. In all this mass of material we can discern four levels of meaning in music: 1) Narrative-literary meanings as in *Till Eulenspiegel* and *The Sorcerer's Apprentice;* 2) Atmospheric-pictorial meanings as in *La Mer* and *Pictures at an Exhibition;* 3) Affective-reactive meanings such as triumph, pain, wistfulness, regret, cheerfulness, melancholy, apprehension—most typical of nineteenth-century romanticism; 4) Purely musical meanings.

Of these, the last is the only really important one, the one worthy of analysis. The first three don't actually involve analysis, but rather arbitrary justification, or prettifying for the commercial reasons mentioned before. If we are to try to explain music, we must explain the *music,* not the whole array of extramusical notions which have grown like parasites around it.

Which makes musical analysis for the layman extremely difficult. Obviously we can't use musical terminology exclusively, or we will simply drive the victim away. We must have intermittent recourse to certain extramusical ideas, like religion, or social factors, or historical forces, which may have influenced music. We don't ever want to talk down; but how *up* can we talk without losing contact? There is a happy medium somewhere between the music-appreciation racket and purely technical discussion; it is hard to find, but it can be found.

It is with this certainty that it can be found that I have made so bold as to discuss music on television, on records, and in public lectures. Whenever I feel that I have done it successfully, it is because I may have found that happy medium. And finding it is impossible without the conviction that the public is not a great beast but an intelligent organism, more often than not longing for insight and knowledge. Wherever possible, therefore, I try to talk about music—the *notes* of music; and whereever extramusical concepts are needed for referential or clarifying purposes, I try to choose concepts that are musically relevant, such as nationalistic tendencies or spirtual development, which may even have been part of the composer's own thinking.

For example, in explaining jazz I have avoided the usual pseudohistorical discussions (up the river from New Orleans) and concentrated on those aspects of melody, harmony, rhythm, which make jazz different from all other music. In talking of Bach I have had to make references to his religious and spiritual convictions, but always in terms of the notes he produced. In analyzing Dvořák's *New World* Symphony for a lay audience listening to a recording, I have displayed all the thematic material, as music appreciation would demand, but in terms of Dvořák's attempt at nationalistic results.

In other words, music appreciation doesn't have to be a racket. The extramusical kind of reference can be useful if it is put in the service of explaining the *notes;* and the road-map variety can also be serviceable if it functions along with some central idea that can engage the intelligence of the listener. Therein lies the happy medium.

But, in the end, we can never really interpret music through words, or give even a shadowy equivalent. If it were possible for words to "tell" a Chopin mazurka—its sad-gay quality, the abundance of its brevity, the polish of its detail—why, then, would Chopin have had to write it in the first place?

• Questions for Study

1. E. M. Forster is a novelist. Leonard Bernstein is a professional musician. Does this difference make itself apparent in their approaches to the discussion of music? Explain.
2. Bernstein says that "most novelists, and writers in general, tend to put their feet in their mouth whenever they part lips to speak of music." Do you

think this criticism can be applied to Forster? Is there anything in the tone of Forster's essay to show that he is aware of this type of criticism?
3. Why does Bernstein reject the first three levels of music as not "really important"? Do you agree with him?
4. In the last analysis what does he say is wrong with all attempts to "interpret music through words"? Is it possible, in your opinion, to explain verbally the essence of any masterpiece in art, music, or literature?

IGOR STRAVINSKY

•

APROPOS

"LE SACRE DU PRINTEMPS"

The idea of "Le Sacre du Printemps" came to me while I was still composing "The Firebird." I had dreamed a scene of pagan ritual in which a chosen sacrificial virgin dances herself to death. This vision was not accompanied by concrete musical ideas, however, and as I was soon impregnated with another and purely musical conception that began quickly to develop into, as I thought, a *Konzertstück* for piano and orchestra, the latter piece was the one I started to compose. I had already told Diaghilev about "Le Sacre" before a visit of his to me in Lausanne at the end of September 1910, but he did not know about "Petroushka" —which is what I called the *Konzertstück*, thinking the style of the piano part suggested the Russian puppet. Though Diaghilev may have been disappointed not to hear music for "pagan rites," in his delight with "Petroushka," which he encouraged me to develop into a ballet before undertaking "Le Sacre du Printemps," he did not show it.

    I first became conscious of thematic ideas for "Le Sacre" in the summer of 1911. ("Petroushka" had been performed in June, 1911, in

Oustiloug, our summer home in Volhynia.) The themes were those of "Les Augures Printanières," the first dance I was to compose. Reaching Switzerland in the fall, I rented a house in Clarens for my family and began to work. The entire "Sacre du Printemps" was written in a tiny room of this house, an eight-feet-by-eight closet, rather, whose only furniture was a small upright piano which I kept muted, a table, and two chairs. I began with the "Augures Printanières," as I said, and composed from there to the end of the first part; the Prelude was written afterward. The dances of the second part were composed in the order in which they now appear, and composed very quickly, too, until the "Danse Sacrale," which I could play but did not, at first, know how to write. The composition of "Le Sacre" was completed by the beginning of 1912 and the instrumentation—a mechanical job, largely, since I always compose the instrumentation when I compose the music—took me four more months in the late Spring.

I had pushed myself to finish "Le Sacre," as I wanted Diaghilev to produce it in the 1912 season. At the end of January I went to Berlin, where the Ballet then was, to discuss the performance with him. I found him in a state of upset about Nijinsky's health. He would talk about Nijinsky by the hour, but all he ever said about "Le Sacre" was that he could not mount it in 1912. He saw my disappointment and tried to console me by inviting me to accompany the Ballet to Budapest, London, and Venice, its next stops. I did journey with him to those cities—all three were new to me then, and all three I have loved ever since—but the real reason I accepted the postponement of "Le Sacre" so easily was that I was already beginning to think about "Les Noces." Incidentally, at this Berlin meeting Diaghilev encouraged me to use a huge orchestra for "Le Sacre," promising that the size of our orchestra would be greatly increased in the following season.

I am not sure my orchestra would have been as large otherwise.

That the first performance of "Le Sacre du Printemps" was attended by a scandal must be known to everybody. I was unprepared for the explosion myself. The reactions of the musicans who came to the orchestra rehearsals betrayed no intimation of it. (Dubussy, who might well have been upset by "Le Sacre," was, in fact, much more upset by the success of it a year later.) Nor did the stage spectacle seem likely to precipitate a riot. The dancers had been rehearsing for months; they knew what they were doing at least, even though what they were doing often had nothing to do with the music. "I will count to forty while you play," Nijinsky would say to me, "and we will see where we come out." He could not understand that though we might at some point "come out" together, this did not mean we had been together on the way. The dancers followed

Nijinsky's count, too, rather than the musical count; he spoke Russian of course, and as Russian numbers above ten are polysyllabic—eighteen, for example, is *vosemnadsat*—in the fast tempo movements neither he nor they could keep up.

At the performance mild protests against the music could be heard from the beginning. Then, when the curtain opened on a group of knock-kneed and long-braided Lolitas jumping up and down ("Danses des Adolescents"), the storm broke. Cries of *"ta geule"* came from behind me. I left the hall in a rage (I was sitting on the right near the orchestra, and I remember slamming the door). I have never again been that angry. The music was so familiar to me; I loved it, and I could not understand why people who had not yet heard it wanted to protest in advance. I arrived backstage in a fury. There I saw Diaghilev switching the house lights on and off in the hope that this might quiet the hall. For the rest of the performance I stood in the wings behind Nijinsky and holding the tails of his *frac*, while he stood on a chair shouting numbers to the dancers, like a coxswain.

I remember with more pleasure the first concert performance of "Le Sacre" the following year, a triumph such as few *composers* can have known the like of. Whether the acclaim of the young people who filled the Casino de Paris was more than a mere reversal of the verdict of bad manners a year before is not for me to say, but it seemed to me much more. (Incidentally, Saint-Saëns, a sharp little man—I had a good view of him—was present at *this* performance; I do not know who invented the story that he was present at, but soon walked out of, the première.) Monteux again conducted, and the musical realization was ideal. He had been doubtful about programming "Le Sacre," in view of the original scandal, but he had had a great success with a concert performance of "Petroushka," and was proud of his prestige with avant-garde musicians; I argued that "Le Sacre" was more symphonic, more of a concert piece, than "Petroushka." Let me say here that Monteux never cheapened "Le Sacre," or looked for his own glory in it, and he was always scrupulously faithful to the music. At the end of the "Danse Sacrale" the entire audience stood up and cheered. I came on stage and hugged Monteux, who was a river of perspiration—it was the saltiest hug of my life. A crowd swept backstage. I was hoisted to anonymous shoulders, carried out into the street this way, and up to the Place de la Trinité. A policeman pushed his way to my side, in an effort to protect me. It was this policeman Diaghilev later fixed upon in his accounts of the story: "Our little Igor now needs police escorts out of his concerts, like a prize fighter." (Diaghilev was verdantly envious of any success of mine outside of his Ballet.)

I have seen only one stage version of "Le Sacre" since 1913, and that was Diaghilev's 1921 revival. Music and dancing were better coordinated this time than in 1913—they could hardly have been otherwise—but the choreography (by Massine) was still too gymnastic and Dalcrozian to please me. I decided then that I prefer "Le Sacre" as a concert piece.

I conducted "Le Sacre" myself for the first time in 1928, in a recording by English Columbia. My concert debut with it came the following year, in Amsterdam, with the Concertgebouw, and thereafter I conducted it frequently throughout Europe. One of the most memorable (to me) performances of these years was in the Salle Pleyel, an official occasion, with official speeches to me pronounced by the President of the Republic, M. Poincaré, and by his First Minister, M. Herriot. I have conducted "Le Sacre" only once in the United States, however, and that was twenty years ago, in April, 1940.

In 1937 or 1938 I received a request from the Disney office in America for permission to use "Le Sacre" in a cartoon film. The request was accompanied by a gentle warning that if permission were withheld the music would be used anyway ("Le Sacre," being "Russian," was not copyrighted in the United States), but as the owners of the film wished to show it abroad (i.e., in Berne Copyright countries) they offered me $5,000, a sum I was obliged to accept (though, in fact, the "percentages" of a dozen crapulous intermediaries reduced it to $1,200). I saw the film with George Balanchine in a Hollywood studio at Christmas time, 1939. I remember someone offering me a score, and, when I said I had my own, the someone saying "But it is all changed." It was indeed. The order of the pieces had been shuffled and the most difficult of them eliminated— though this didn't help the musical performance, which was execrable. I will say nothing about the visual complement (for I do not wish to criticize an unresisting imbecility), but the musical point of view of the film involved a dangerous misunderstanding.

I have twice revised portions of "Le Sacre," first in 1921 for the Diaghilev performances, and again in 1943 (the "Danse Sacrale" only) for a performance (unrealized) by the Boston Symphony Orchestra. The differences between these revisions have been much discussed, though I think they are not well known or even often perceived. In at least two of the dances the bar lengths were longer in the 1913 original. At that time I tried to bar according to the phrasing, but my 1921 experience had led me to prefer smaller divisions (a comparison of the "Evocation des Ancêtres" in the two versions, although I think I possess the only copy of the original, should show the principle of subdivision applied in the later one). The smaller bars did prove more manageable for the conductor and clearer for the orchestra. I also felt that they clarified the scansion of the music. (I was thinking about a similar question yesterday while reading a quatrain from one of the "Sonnets of Orpheus"; did the poet write the lines at this length or, as I think, did he cut them in half?) My main purpose in revising the "Danse Sacrale" was to facilitate performance by means of an easier-to-read unit of beat. But the instrumentation has been changed, too—improved, I think—in many ways. For example, the music of the second group of four horns has been considerably amended in the later version; I was never satisfied with the horn parts. The muted horn note following the five-note trombone solo has been given to the much stronger bass trumpet in this version, too, and the string parts have been to a great extent rewritten. Amateurs of the older versions have been disturbed by the fact that the last chord has been changed. I was never content with this chord, however; it was a noise before and is now an aggregation of distinct pitches. But I would go on revising my music forever, were I not too busy composing more of it, and I am still not content with everything in "Le Sacre." (The first violin part in the "Cortège du Sage," for example, is badly overbalanced.)

I was guided by no system whatever in "Le Sacre du Printemps." When I think of the music of the other composers of that time who interest me—Berg's music, which is synthetic (in the best sense), and Webern's, which is analytic—how much more *theoretical* it seems than "Le Sacre." And these composers belonged to and were supported by a great tradition. Very little immediate tradition lies behind "Le Sacre du Printemps," however, and no theory. I had only my ear to help me; I heard and I wrote what I heard. I am the vessel through which "Le Sacre" passed.

• Questions for Study

1. Stravinsky has been acclaimed a musical genius. What insight into the actual process of artistic creation does this essay give? Is the purport of the last sentence fully illustrated in the essay itself? Explain.
2. Describe the composer's personality as it emerges in this essay. Show that there is some ambiguity in Stravinsky's attitude toward Diaghilev.
3. Note the language he uses in criticizing the film by Disney. Does it effectively express his attitude?
4. To what extent is it necessary for the reader to be familiar with "Le Sacre" in order to understand Stravinsky's remarks?

BARRY ULANOV

•

WHAT IS JAZZ?

In *The American Scene,* Henry James said of American cities, "So there it all is; arrange it as you can. Poor dear bad bold beauty; there must indeed be something about her . . . !" The same thing can be said of American jazz.

On the surface there is disorder and conflict in jazz. No common definition of this music has been reached. It resists dictionary definition, and its musicians splutter nervously and take refuge in the colorful ambiguities of its argot. Nonetheless, its beauty can be probed; its badness can be separated from its boldness. The process is a difficult one, as it is in any art, and in jazz two arts, the composing and the performing arts, are joined together. But if one goes beneath the surface and does not allow the contradictions and the confusions of appearances to put one off, much becomes clear, and the mystery at the center is seen to be the central mystery of all the arts.

The cortex of jazz consists of several layers, alternately hard and soft, complex in structure, and hard to take apart. It is compounded of the history of the music and of the many styles of jazz. At first the history seems disjointed and the styles contradictory. One marks a confounding series of shifts in place and person and style. One finds a music dominated by Negroes in New Orleans, by white musicians in Chicago, by important but apparently unrelated figures in New York. One discovers a disastrous split in jazz inaugurated by the swing era and intensified during the days of bebop and so-called progressive jazz. But then one looks and listens more closely, and order and continuity appear.

Americans have long been wedded to the boom-and-bust cycle, and their culture reflects that dizzying course. Jazz is not like that; it has no cycles; it doesn't spiral. Whether you adopt the approach of the economic historian, the cultural anthropologist, or the aesthetic philosopher, you will not find an easy reflection of a theory in jazz. While much of America—crises and ecstasies and even a moment or two of exaltation—has found its way into jazz, the history of jazz is a curiously even one, chaotic at any instant, but always moving ahead in what is for an art form almost a straight line.

For most of its history, jazz, rejected in its homeland, has had consciously to seek survival, conscientiously to explain and defend its existence. From its early homes, the Ozark hills, the Louisiana bayous, the Carolina cotton fields, the Virginia plantations, through the New Orleans bordellos and barrelhouses to its latter-day efflorescence it has been alternately condemned and misunderstood. Variously banned and bullied and sometimes cheered beyond its merits, jazz has led a lonely life but a full one. It is still with us and looks to be around for quite a while.

No matter what the fortunes of jazz, its nucleus has remained constant, little touched by extravagances of opinion, sympathetic or unsympathetic. The nucleus of jazz—as differentiated from its cortex—contains its nerve center, its source of life, and here are its mystery and meaning. The nucleus of jazz is made up of melody, harmony, and rhythm, the triune qualities of the art of music which, as everybody knows, can be fairly simply defined. In bare definition, melody is any succession of notes, harmony any simultaneity of tones, rhythm the arithmetic measure of notes or tones. In closer examination, melody appears as a vast variety of things, ranging from so simple a tune as "Yankee Doodle" to the complexity of one of Arnold Schoenberg's constructions. In more detailed analysis, harmony shows up as a vertical ordering of a Bach fugue, or a tight structuring based entirely on whole tones in the impressionism of Debussy. But bewildering as the complications of melody and harmony can be, they are easier to analyze and verbalize than rhythm or any of its parts, and rhythm is the most important of the three in jazz.

Before attempting a synoptic definition of jazz as a noun (or discussing the misuse of "jazz" as a verb and "jazzy" as an adjective), and of the various corollary terms that explain the meaning of this music, it might be instructive to examine definitions by musicians themselves. The following definitions were made by jazz musicians in 1935, when their music was undergoing a revival as a result of the then current vogue for the jazz that went by the new name of swing. Benny Goodman was a great success, and jam sessions had become public again. Musicians themselves found it difficult to define "swing," by which of course they merely meant the 1935 version of jazz, which wasn't very different from the 1930 or 1925 music. Let us examine the definitions.

WINGY MANONE: "Feeling an increase in tempo though you're still playing at the same tempo."

MARSHALL STEARNS and JOHN HAMMOND (jazz authorities) and BENNY GOODMAN: "A band swings when its collective improvisation is rhythmically integrated."

GENE KRUPA: "Complete and inspired freedom of rhythmic interpretation."

JESS STACY: "Syncopated syncopation."

MORTON KARN and PAYSON RE: "Feeling a multitude of subdivisions in each beat and playing or implying the accents that you feel; that is, if the tune is played at the proper tempo, so that when you're playing it, you'll feel it inside."

GLENN MILLER: "Something that you have to feel; a sensation that can be conveyed to others."

FRANKIE FROEBA: "A steady tempo, causing lightness and relaxation and a feeling of floating."

TERRY SHAND: "A synthetic cooperation of two or more instruments helping along or giving feeling to the soloist performing."

OZZIE NELSON: "A vague something that you seem to feel pulsating from a danceable orchestra. To me it is a solidity and compactness of attack by which the rhythm instruments combine with the others to create within the listeners the desire to dance."

CHICK WEBB: "It's like lovin' a gal, and havin' a fight, and then seein' her again."

LOUIS ARMSTRONG: "My idea how a tune should go."

ELLA FITZGERALD: "Why, er—swing is—well, you sort of feel—uh—uh—I don't know—you just swing!"

These musicians were looking for a new set of terms that would catch the beat so basic to jazz; they were stumped for the words to describe the kind of improvisation necessary to jazz.

In the simple, compressed, sometimes too elliptic vocabulary of the jazz musician, one learns a great deal about the music he plays. One learns that "jazz" is a noun, that it is not American popular music (as it has often been thought to be), that the jazz musician is most interested in the rhythmic connotation of the word and in little else. If you tell him that some say the term comes from the phonetic spelling of the abbreviation of a jazz musician named Charles (Charles, Chas., Jass, Jazz), he is not in the least interested. If you tell him that there is a great deal of

substance to the claim that the word comes from the French word *jaser*
—to pep up, to exhilarate—he may nod his head with a degree of interest
but ask you, "What about the beat?" You will learn from the jazz
musician that "swing" is no longer a noun, in spite of the fact that it was
first so used in the title of a Duke Ellington recording in 1931, "It Don't
Mean a Thing if It Ain't Got that Swing," which gives it a kind of ex
cathedra endorsement. You will learn that "swing" is a verb, a way of describing the beat, even as Ellington's title for another tune, "Bouncing
Buoyancy," is a description of the same beat, even as the term "jump" is,
even as "leaps" is, even as the description of jazz as "music that goes"
is, even as in the thirties the compliment of "solid" to performer or performance was like "gone," "crazy," "craziest," "the end," and "cool"
today. They are descriptions of the beat.

From an examination of jazz musicians' own words, it is possible to
glean the subtle, unruly, and almost mystical concept of the jazz spirit,
or feeling, or thinking—it is all these things and is so understood by the
jazz musician himself. The jazzman has his own way of getting at the
center of his music, and thus he formulates his own musical language.
Also he converts the musical language into a verbal dialect of his own.
In his own set of terms, musical and verbal, he thinks, he feels; he re-
hearses, he performs; he scores, he improvises; he gets a beat.

To get that elusive beat a jazzman will do anything. Without it, he
cannot do anything. With it, he is playing jazz, and that is a large and
satisfying enough accomplishment. When a jazzman picks up a familiar
tune, banal or too well-known through much repetition, and alters its
rhythmic pattern in favor of a steady if sometimes monotonous beat, and
varies its melodies and maybe even changes its chords, he is working
freely, easily, and with as much spontaneity as he can bring to his music.
That freedom, ease, and spontaneity brought him to jazz; within those
determining limits he will find a place for himself or get out, or join
one of the bands whose frightening parodies of jazz are so often more
popular than the real thing. It is by his formal understanding of certain
definite values that the jazz musician has conceived, organized, and developed his art. It has been hot; it has become cool. It has jumped and
swung; it has sauntered. It has borrowed; it has originated. It has affected
a change, a literal transformation; inherited conventions have gradually
been restated, reorganized, and ultimately restructured as a new expression. It may be that jazz musicians have simply rediscovered a controlling
factor in music, the improvising performer. Without any awareness of
what he has done, the jazzman may have gone back to some of the
beginnings of music, tapping once more the creative roots which nourished ancient Greek music, the plain chant, the musical baroque and its

immediate successors and predecessors. We know that seventeenth- and eighteenth-century composers were improvisers and that when they brought their scores to other musicians they left the interpretation of parts to the discretion of the performers, even as an arranger for a jazz band does today.

But the jazz musician has bought more than procedures, composing conceptions, and improvisation to his music. Techniques have been developed that have broadened the resources and intensified the disciplines of certain instruments far beyond their use in other music. Colors have been added to solo instruments and to various combinations and numbers of instruments that are utterly unlike any others in music. New textures have emerged from a conception of tonality and of pitch that is not original but is entirely fresh in its application. The improvising jazz musician has a different and more responsible and rewarding position from that of his counterparts in earlier art and folk music. The rhythmic base of music has been reinterpreted, making the central pulse at once more primitive than it has been before in Western music, and more sophisticated in its variety.

This, then, is how one might define jazz: it is a new music of a certain distinct rhythmic and melodic character, one that constantly involves improvisation—of a minor sort in adjusting accents and phrases of the tune at hand, of a major sort in creating music extemporaneously, on the spot. In the course of creating jazz, a melody or its underlying chords may be altered. The rhythmic valuations of notes may be lengthened or shortened according to a regular scheme, syncopated or not, or there may be no consistent pattern of rhythmic variations so long as a steady beat remains implicit or explicit. The beat is usually four quarter-notes to the bar, serving as a solid rhythmic base for the improvisation of soloists or groups playing eight or twelve measures, or some multiple or dividend thereof.

These things are the means. The ends are the ends of all art, the expression of the universal and the particular, the specific and the indirect and the intangible. In its short history, jazz has generally been restricted to short forms and it has often been directed toward the ephemeral and the trivial, but so too has it looked toward the lasting perception and the meaningful conclusion. Much of the time jazz musicians have sought and obtained an unashamed aphrodisiac effect; they have also worshiped in their music, variously devout before the one God and the unnamed gods. Like poets and painters, they are of all faiths, their doctrines are many; but they are united in one conviction, that they have found a creative form for themselves, for their time, for their place.

At the opening of the *Gradus ad Parnassum*, the dialogue offered as a study of counterpoint by Johann Josef Fux in 1725, the music master Aloysius warns the student Josef: "You must try to remember whether or not you felt a strong natural inclination to this art even in childhood." The student answers: "Yes, most deeply. Even before I could reason, I was overcome by the force of this strange enthusiasm and I turned all my thoughts and feelings to music. And now the burning desire to understand it possesses me, drives me almost against my will, and day and night lovely melodies seem to sound around me. Therefore I think I no longer have reason to doubt my inclination. Nor do the difficulties of the work discourage me, and I hope that with the help of good health I shall be able to master it." Several jazz musicians have read Fux, even as Haydn and Beethoven did, though perhaps with less immediate application. They have, however, echoed the pupil's "strange enthusiasm"; that, these jazzmen said, was their experience, their "burning desire." Following the "inclination," jazz musicians have not had much of the help of good health; some of them have flaunted their doggedly unreasonable living habits and suffered the personal and public consequences of the habits and of the flaunting. All this their music has reflected, and sometimes it is noisy and grotesque as a result. More often it has a fullness and richness of expression. Slowly, clearly, the music is maturing, and, for it and with it and by it, so are the musicians.

• Questions for Study

1. It is generally considered a weakness to begin an essay with a quotation. Do you consider Ulanov's use of a quotation by Henry James at the beginning of this essay a poor way to start?
2. What does Ulanov mean when he says that jazz "resists dictionary definition"? In what respects does his catalogue of definitions fail to define jazz lucidly? Consider the tone, language, and style of each definition. Do you think that Ulanov's definition is an improvement over these?
3. What is the purpose behind Ulanov's discussions of the origins of jazz and swing?
4. Many people consider jazz uncivilized and in some cases immoral. Can music be judged from a moral point of view? You may wish to consider Maritain's essay in this connection.

VI
CIVILIZATION IN PERSPECTIVE

HERODOTUS

•

MARATHON

The Persians, having thus brought Eretria into subjection after waiting a few days, made sail for Attica, greatly straitening the Athenians as they approached, and thinking to deal with them as they had dealt with the people of Eretria. And, because there was no place in all Attica so convenient for their horse as Marathon, and it lay moreover quite close to Eretria, therefore Hippias, the son of Pisistratus, conducted them thither.

When intelligence of this reached the Athenians, they likewise marched their troops to Marathon, and there stood on the defensive, having at their head ten generals, of whom one was Miltiades.

Now this man's father, Cimon, the son of Stesagoras, was banished from Athens by Pisistratus, the son of Hippocrates. In his banishment it was his fortune to win the four-horse chariot-race at Olympia, whereby he gained the very same honor which had before been carried off by Miltiades, his half-brother on the mother's side. At the next Olympiad he won the prize again with the same mares; upon which he caused Pisistratus to be proclaimed the winner, having made an agreement with him that on yielding him this honor he should be allowed to come back to his country. Afterwards, still with the same mares, he won the prize a third time; whereupon he was put to death by the sons of Pisistratus, whose father was no longer living. They set men to lie in wait for him secretly; and these men slew him near the government-house in the nighttime. He was buried outside the city, beyond what is called the Valley Road; and right opposite his tomb were buried the mares which had won the three prizes. The same success had likewise been achieved

From *The Persian Wars*, Fifth Century, B.C.

once previously, to wit, by the mares of Evagoras the Lacedæmonian, but never except by them. At the time of Cimon's death Stesagoras, the elder of his two sons, was in the Chersonese, where he lived with Miltiades his uncle; the younger, who was called Miltiades after the founder of the Chersonesite colony, was with his father in Athens.

It was this Miltiades who now commanded the Athenians, after escaping from the Chersonese, and twice nearly losing his life. First he was chased as far as Imbrus by the Phœnicians, who had a great desire to take him and carry him up to the king; and when he had avoided this danger, and, having reached his own country, thought himself to be altogether in safety, he found his enemies waiting for him, and was cited by them before a court and impeached for his tyranny in the Chersonese. But he came off victorious here likewise, and was thereupon made general of the Athenians by the free choice of the people.

And first, before they left the city, the generals sent off to Sparta a herald, one Pheidippides, who was by birth an Athenian, and by profession and practice a trained runner. This man, according to the account which he gave to the Athenians on his return, when he was near Mount Parthenium, above Tegea, fell in with the god Pan, who called him by his name, and bade him ask the Athenians "wherefore they neglected him so entirely, when he was kindly disposed toward them, and had often helped them in times past, and would do so again in time to come?" The Athenians, entirely believing in the truth of this report, as soon as their affairs were once more in good order, set up a temple to Pan under the Acropolis, and, in return for the message which I have recorded, established in his honor yearly sacrifices and a torch-race.

On the occasion of which we speak, when Pheidippides was sent by the Athenian generals, and, according to his own account, saw Pan on his journey, he reached Sparta on the very next day after quitting the city of Athens. Upon his arrival he went before the rulers, and said to them—

"Men of Lacedæmon, the Athenians beseech you to hasten to their aid, and not allow that state, which is the most ancient in all Greece, to be enslaved by the barbarians. Eretria, look you, is already carried away captive; and Greece weakened by the loss of no mean city."

Thus did Pheidippides deliver the message committed to him. And the Spartans wished to help the Athenians, but were unable to give them any present succor, as they did not like to break their established law. It was then the ninth day of the first decade; and they could not march out of Sparta on the ninth, when the moon had not reached the full. So they waited for the full of the moon.

The barbarians were conducted to Marathon by Hippias, the son of

Pisistratus, who the night before had seen a strange vision in his sleep. He dreamt of lying in his mother's arms, and conjectured the dream to mean that he would be restored to Athens, recover the power which he had lost, and afterwards live to a good old age in his native country. Such was the sense in which he interpreted the vision. He now proceeded to act as guide to the Persians; and, in the first place, he landed the prisoners taken from Eretria upon the island that is called Ægileia, a tract belonging to the Styreans, after which he brought the fleet to anchor off Marathon, and marshalled the bands of the barbarians as they disembarked. As he was thus employed it chanced that he sneezed and at the same time coughed with more violence than was his wont. Now, as he was a man advanced in years, and the greater number of his teeth were loose, it so happened that one of them was driven out with the force of the cough, and fell down into the sand. Hippias took all the pains he could to find it; but the tooth was nowhere to be seen: whereupon he fetched a deep sigh, and said to the bystanders—

"After all, the land is not ours; and we shall never be able to bring it under. All my share in it is the portion of which my tooth has possession."

So Hippias believed that in this way his dream was out.

The Athenians were drawn up in order of battle in a sacred close belonging to Hercules, when they were joined by the Platæans, who came in full force to their aid. Some time before, the Platæans had put themselves under the rule of the Athenians; and these last had already undertaken many labors on their behalf. The occasion of the surrender was the following. The Platæans suffered grievous things at the hands of the men of Thebes; so, as it chanced that Cleomenes, the son of Anaxandridas, and the Lacedæmonians were in their neighborhood, they first of all offered to surrender themselves to them. But the Lacedœmonians refused to receive them, and said—

"We dwell too far off from you, and ours would be but chill succor. Ye might oftentimes be carried into slavery before one of us heard of it. We counsel you rather to give yourselves up to the Athenians, who are your next neighbors, and well able to shelter you."

This they said, not so much out of good will toward the Platæans as because they wished to involve the Athenians in trouble by engaging them in wars with the Bœotians. The Platæans, however, when the Lacedæmonians gave them this counsel, complied at once; and when the sacrifice to the Twelve Gods was being offered at Athens, they came and sat as suppliants about the altar, and gave themselves up to the Athenians. The Thebans no sooner learnt what the Platæans had done than instantly they marched out against them, while the Athenians sent troops to their aid. As the two armies were about to join battle, the Corinthians, who chanced to be at hand, would not allow them to engage; both sides consented to take them for arbitrators, whereupon they made up the quarrel, and fixed the boundary-line between the two states upon this condition: to wit, that if any of the Bœotians wished no longer to belong to Bœotia, the Thebans should allow them to follow their own inclinations. The Corinthians, when they had thus decreed, forthwith departed to their homes: the Athenians likewise set off on their return; but the Bœotians fell upon them during the march, and a battle was fought wherein they were worsted by the Athenians. Hereupon these last would not be bound by the line which the Corinthians had fixed, but advanced beyond those limits, and made the Asôpus the boundary-line between the country of the Thebans and that of the Platæans and Hysians. Under such circumstances did the Platæans give themselves up to Athens; and now they were come to Marathon to bear the Athenians aid.

The Athenian generals were divided in their opinions; and some advised not to risk a battle, because they were too few to engage such a host as that of the Medes, while others were for fighting at once; and among these last was Miltiades. He therefore, seeing that opinions were thus divided, and that the less worthy counsel appeared likely to prevail, resolved to go to the polemarch, and have a conference with him. For the man on whom the lot fell to be polemarch at Athens was entitled to give his vote with the ten generals, since anciently the Athenians allowed him an equal right of voting with them. The polemarch at this juncture was Callimachus of Aphidnæ; to him therefore Miltiades went, and said:—

"With thee it rests, Callimachus, either to bring Athens to slavery, or, by securing her freedom, to leave behind thee to all future generations a memory beyond even Harmodius and Aristogeiton. For never since the time that the Athenians became a people were they in so great a danger as now. If they bow their necks beneath the yoke of the Medes, the woes which they will have to suffer when given into the power of Hippias are already determined on; if, on the other hand, they fight and overcome, Athens may rise to be the very first city in Greece. How it comes to pass that these things are likely to happen, and how the determining of them in some sort rests with thee, I will now proceed to make clear. We generals are ten in number, and our votes are divided; half of us wish to engage, half to avoid a combat. Now, if we do not fight, I look to see a great disturbance at Athens which will shake men's resolutions, and then I fear they will submit themselves; but if we fight the battle before any unsoundness show itself among our citizens, let the gods but give us fair play, and we are well able to overcome the enemy.

On thee therefore we depend in this matter, which lies wholly in thine own power. Thou hast only to add thy vote to my side and thy country will be free, and not free only, but the first state in Greece. Or, if thou preferrest to give thy vote to them who would decline the combat, then the reverse will follow."

Miltiades by these words gained Callimachus; and the addition of the polemarch's vote caused the decision to be in favour of fighting. Hereupon all those generals who had been desirous of hazarding a battle, when their turn came to command the army, gave up their right to Miltiades. He however, though he accepted their offers, nevertheless waited, and would not fight, until his own day of command arrived in due course.

Then at length, when his own turn was come, the Athenian battle was set in array, and this was the order of it. Callimachus the polemarch led the right wing; for it was at that time a rule with the Athenians to give the right wing to the polemarch. After this followed the tribes, according as they were numbered, in an unbroken line; while last of all came the Platæans, forming the left wing. And ever since that day it has been a custom with the Athenians, in the sacrifices and assemblies held each fifth year at Athens, for the Athenian herald to implore the blessing of the gods on the Platæans conjointly with the Athenians. Now, as they marshalled the host upon the field of Marathon, in order that the Athenian front might be of equal length with the Median, the ranks of the center were diminished, and it became the weakest part of the line, while the wings were both made strong with a depth of many ranks.

So when the battle was set in array, and the victims showed themselves favorable, instantly the Athenians, so soon as they were let go, charged the barbarians at a run. Now the distance between the two armies was little short of eight furlongs. The Persians, therefore, when they saw the Greeks coming on at speed, made ready to receive them, although it seemed to them that the Athenians were bereft of their senses, and bent upon their own destruction; for they saw a mere handful of men coming on at a run without either horsemen or archers. Such was the opinion of the barbarians; but the Athenians in close array fell upon them, and fought in a manner worthy of being recorded. They were the first of the Greeks, so far as I know, who introduced the custom of charging the enemy at a run, and they were likewise the first who dared to look upon the Median garb, and to face men clad in that fashion. Until this time the very name of the Medes had been a terror to the Greeks to hear.

The two armies fought together on the plain of Marathon for a length of time; and in the mid battle, where the Persians themselves and the Sacæ had their place, the barbarians were victorious, and broke and pursued the Greeks into the inner country; but on the two wings the Athenians and the Platæans defeated the enemy. Having so done, they suffered the routed barbarians to fly at their ease, and joining the two wings in one, fell upon those who had broken their own center, and fought and conquered them. These likewise fled, and now the Athenians hung upon the runaways and cut them down, chasing them all the way to the shore, on reaching which they laid hold of the ships and called aloud for fire.

It was in the struggle here that Callimachus the polemarch, after greatly distinguishing himself, lost his life; Stesilaüs too, the son of Thrasilaüs, one of the generals, was slain; and Cynægirus, the son of Euphorion, having seized on a vessel of the enemy's by the ornament at the stern, had his hand cut off by the blow of an axe, and so perished; as likewise did many other Athenians of note and name.

Nevertheless the Athenians secured in this way seven of the vessels; while with the remainder the barbarians pushed off, and taking aboard their Eretrian prisoners from the island where they had left them, doubled Cape Sunium, hoping to reach Athens before the return of the Athenians. The Alcmæonidæ were accused by their countrymen of suggesting this course to them; they had, it was said, an understanding with the Persians, and made a signal to them, by raising a shield, after they were embarked in their ships.

The Persians accordingly sailed round Sunium. But the Athenians with all possible speed marched away to the defence of their city, and succeeded in reaching Athens before the appearance of the barbarians: and as their camp at Marathon had been pitched in a precinct of Hercules, so now they encamped in another precinct of the same god as Cynosarges. The barbarian fleet arrived, and lay to off Phalerum, which was at that time the haven of Athens; but after resting awhile upon their oars, they departed and sailed away to Asia.

There fell in this battle of Marathon, on the side of the barbarians, about six thousand and four hundred men; on that of the Athenians, one hundred and ninety-two. Such was the number of the slain on the one side and the other. A strange prodigy likewise happened at this fight. Epizêlus, the son of Cuphagoras, an Athenian, was in the thick of the fray, and behaving himself as a brave man should, when suddenly he was stricken with blindness, without blow of sword or dart; and this blindness continued thenceforth during the whole of his after life. The following is the account which he himself, as I have heard, gave of the matter: he said that a gigantic warrior, with a huge beard, which shaded all his shield, stood over against him; but the ghostly semblance passed him by, and slew the man at his side. Such, as I understand, was the tale which Epizêlus told.

• Questions for Study

1. Herodotus is called the "Father of History." He saw himself as a chronicler whose duty it was to report historical events objectively. In this selection he is recounting one of the most decisive battles of Western history. Does he reproduce in the reader a sense of the battle's excitement? Explain. To what extent is the author's use of detail and of dialogue effective in creating a dramatic sense of the event? How might a novelist or popular historian have treated the material?
2. What tactic won the battle for the Greeks?
3. Can Freud's concepts, in "Why War?", be applied to the attitude of the Greeks before and during the battle of Marathon?

TACITUS

•

THE BURNING OF ROME

A disaster followed, whether accidental or treacherously contrived by the emperor, is uncertain, as authors have given both accounts, worse, however, and more dreadful than any which have ever happened to this city by the violence of fire. It had its beginning in that part of the circus which adjoins the Palatine and Cælian hills, where, amid the shops containing inflammable wares, the conflagration both broke out and instantly became so fierce and so rapid from the wind that it seized in its grasp the entire length of the circus. For here there were no houses fenced in by solid masonry, or temples surrounded by walls, or any other obstacle to interpose delay. The blaze in its fury ran first through the level portions

From *The Annals of Imperial Rome*, First Century, A.D.

of the city, then rising to the hills, while it again devastated every
place below them, it outstripped all preventive measures; so rapid was
the mischief and so completely at its mercy the city, with those narrow
winding passages and irregular streets, which characterised old Rome.
Added to this were the wailings of terror-stricken women, the feebleness
of age, the helpless inexperience of childhood, the crowds who sought to
save themselves or others, dragging out the infirm or waiting for them,
and by their hurry in the one case, by their delay in the other, aggravat-
ing the confusion. Often, while they looked behind them, they were
intercepted by flames on their side or in their face. Or if they reached
a refuge close at hand, when this too was seized by the fire, they found
that, even places, which they had imagined to be remote, were involved
in the same calamity. At last, doubting what they should avoid or
whither betake themselves, they crowded the streets or flung themselves
down in the fields, while some who had lost their all, even their very
daily bread, and others out of love for their kinsfolk, whom they had been
unable to rescue, perished, though escape was open to them. And no
one dared to stop the mischief, because of incessant menaces from a
number of persons who forbade the extinguishing of the flames, because
again others openly hurled brands, and kept shouting that there was one
who gave them authority, either seeking to plunder more freely, or obeying orders.

Nero at this time was at Antium, and did not return to Rome until
the fire approached his house, which he had built to connect the palace
with the gardens of Mæcenas. It could not, however, be stopped from
devouring the palace, the house, and everything around it. However, to
relieve the people, driven out homeless as they were, he threw open to
them the Campus Martius and the public buildings of Agrippa, and even
his own gardens, and raised temporary structures to receive the destitute
multitude. Supplies of food were brought up from Ostia and the neigh-
bouring towns, and the price of corn was reduced to three sesterces a
peck. These acts, though popular, produced no effect, since a rumor had
gone forth everywhere that, at the very time when the city was in flames,
the emperor appeared on a private stage and sang of the destruction of
Troy, comparing present misfortunes with the calamities of antiquity.

At last, after five days, an end was put to the conflagration at the foot
of the Esquiline hill, by the destruction of all buildings on a vast space,
so that the violence of the fire was met by clear ground and an open sky.
But before people had laid aside their fears, the flames returned, with
no less fury this second time, and especially in the spacious districts of
the city. Consequently, though there was less loss of life, the temples of
the gods, and the porticoes which were devoted to enjoyment, fell in a

yet more widespread ruin. And to this conflagration there attached the greater infamy because it broke out on the Æmilian property of Tigellinus, and it seemed that Nero was aiming at the glory of founding a new city and calling it by his name. Rome, indeed, is divided into fourteen districts, four of which remained uninjured, three were levelled to the ground, while in the other seven were left only a few shattered, half-burnt relics of houses.

It would not be easy to enter into a computation of the private mansions, the blocks of tenements, and of the temples, which were lost. Those with the oldest ceremonial, as that dedicated by Servius Tullius to Luna, the great altar and shrine raised by the Arcadian Evander to the visibly appearing Hercules, the temple of Jupiter the Stayer, which was vowed by Romulus, Numa's royal palace, and the sanctuary of Vesta, with the tutelary deities of the Roman people, were burnt. So too were the riches acquired by our many victories, various beauties of Greek art, then again the ancient and genuine historical monuments of men of genius, and, notwithstanding the striking splendor of the restored city, old men will remember many things which could not be replaced. Some persons observed that the beginning of this conflagration was on the 19th of July, the day on which the Senones captured and fired Rome. Others have pushed a curious inquiry so far as to reduce the interval between these two conflagrations into equal numbers of years, months, and days.

Nero meanwhile availed himself of his country's desolation, and erected a mansion in which the jewels and gold, long familiar objects, quite vulgarised by our extravagance, were not so marvellous as the fields and lakes, with woods on one side to resemble a wilderness, and, on the other, open spaces and extensive views. The directors and contrivers of the work were Severus and Celer, who had the genius and the audacity to attempt by art even what nature had refused, and to fool away an emperor's resources. They had actually undertaken to sink a navigable canal from the lake Avernus to the mouths of the Tiber along a barren shore or through the face of hills, where one meets with no moisture which could supply water, except the Pomptine marshes. The rest of the country is broken rock and perfectly dry. Even if it could be cut through, the labour would be intolerable, and there would be no adequate result. Nero, however, with his love of the impossible, endeavored to dig through the nearest hills to Avernus, and there still remain the traces of his disappointed hope.

Of Rome meanwhile, so much as was left unoccupied by his mansion, was not built up, as it had been after its burning by the Gauls, without any regularity or in any fashion, but with rows of streets according to measurement, with broad thoroughfares, with a restriction on the height of houses, with open spaces, and the further addition of colonnades, as a protection to the frontage of the blocks of tenements. These colonnades Nero promised to erect at his own expense, and to hand over the open spaces, when cleared of the débris, to the ground landlords. He also offered rewards proportioned to each person's position and property, and prescribed a period within which they were to obtain them on the completion of so many houses or blocks of building. He fixed on the marshes of Ostia for the reception of the rubbish, and arranged that the ships which had brought up corn by the Tiber, should sail down the river with cargoes of this rubbish. The buildings themselves, to a certain height, were to be solidly constructed, without wooden beams, of stone from Gabii or Alba, that material being impervious to fire. And to provide that the water which individual license had illegally appropriated, might flow in greater abundance in several places for the public use, officers were appointed, and everyone was to have in the open court the means of stopping a fire. Every building, too, was to be enclosed by its own proper wall, not by one common to others. These changes which were liked for their utility, also added beauty to the new city. Some, however, thought that its old arrangement had been more conducive to health, inasmuch as the narrow streets with the elevation of the roofs were not equally penetrated by the sun's heat, while now the open space, unsheltered by any shade, was scorched by a fiercer glow.

Such indeed were the precautions of human wisdom. The next thing was to seek means of propitiating the gods, and recourse was had to the Sibylline books, by the direction of which prayers were offered to Vulcanus, Ceres, and Proserpina. Juno, too, was entreated by the matrons, first, in the Capitol, then on the nearest part of the coast, whence water was procured to sprinkle the fane and image of the goddess. And there were sacred banquets and nightly vigils celebrated by married women. But all human efforts, all the lavish gifts of the emperor, and the propitiations of the gods, did not banish the sinister belief that the conflagration was the result of an order. Consequently, to get rid of the report, Nero fastened the guilt and inflicted the most exquisite tortures on a class hated for their abominations, called Christians by the populace. Christus, from whom the name had its origin, suffered the extreme penalty during the reign of Tiberius at the hands of one of our procurators, Pontius Pilatus, and a most mischievous superstition, thus checked for the moment, again broke out not only in Judæa, the first source of the evil, but even in Rome, where all things hideous and shameful from every part of the world find their center and become popular. Accordingly, an arrest was first made of all who pleaded guilty; then, upon their information, an immense multitude was convicted, not so much of the crime of firing the city, as of hatred against mankind. Mockery of every sort was added to their deaths. Covered with the skins of beasts, they were torn by dogs and perished, or were nailed to crosses, or were doomed to the flames and burnt, to serve as a nightly illumination, when daylight had expired.

Nero offered his gardens for the spectacle, and was exhibiting a show in the circus, while he mingled with the people in the dress of a charioteer or stood aloft on a car. Hence, even for criminals who deserved extreme and exemplary punishment, there arose a feeling of compassion; for it was not, as it seemed, for the public good, but to glut one man's cruelty, that they were being destroyed.

• *Questions for Study*

1. Is the incident of the burning of Rome more inherently dramatic than the battle of Marathon recounted by Herodotus? Explain.
2. What details does Tacitus use to sharpen his historical narrative? Tacitus obviously dislikes Nero. What emotionally charged words and phrases particularly reveal his dislike?
3. To what extent does Tacitus support the generally held belief that Nero fiddled while Rome burned? Can you form some idea of how apocryphal stories originate from this instance? Explain.
4. Take a brief factual account of an incident printed in a recent newspaper and develop it as though you were writing it as part of a dramatic historical narrative?

NICCOLÒ MACHIAVELLI

•

THE CONDUCT OF A PRINCE

• *Concerning Things for which Men, and Especially Princes, Are Praised or Blamed*

It remains now to see what ought to be the rules of conduct for a prince towards subject and friends. As I know that many have written on this point, I expect I shall be considered presumptuous in mentioning it again, especially as in discussing it I shall depart from the methods of other people. But, it being my intention to write a thing which shall be useful to him who apprehends it, it appears to me more appropriate to follow up the real truth of a matter than the imagination of it; for many have pictured republics and principalities which in fact have never been known or seen, because how one lives is so far distant from how one ought to live, that he who neglects what is done for what ought to be done, sooner effects his ruin than his preservation; for a man who wishes to act entirely up to his professions of virtue soon meets with what destroys him among so much that is evil.

Hence it is necessary for a prince wishing to hold his own to know how to do wrong, and to make use of it or not according to necessity. Therefore, putting on one side imaginary things concerning a prince, and discussing those which are real, I say that all men when they are spoken of, and chiefly princes for being more highly placed, are remarkable for some of those qualities which bring them either blame or praise; and thus it is that one is reputed liberal, another miserly, using a Tuscan term (because an avaricious person in our language is still he who desires to possess by robbery, whilst we call one miserly who deprives himself too much of the use of his own); one is reputed generous, one rapacious; one cruel, one compassionate; one faithless, another faithful; one effeminate and cowardly, another bold and brave; one affable, an-

---

From *The Prince*, 1532.

other haughty; one lascivious, another chaste; one sincere, another cunning; one hard, another easy; one grave, another frivolous; one religious, another unbelieving, and the like. And I know that every one will confess that it would be most praiseworthy in a prince to exhibit all the above qualities that are considered good; but because they can neither be entirely possessed nor observed, for human conditions do not permit it, it is necessary for him to be sufficiently prudent that he may know how to avoid the reproach of those vices which would lose him his state; and also to keep himself, if it be possible, from those which would not lose him it; but this not being possible, he may with less hesitation abandon himself to them. And again, he need not make himself uneasy at incurring a reproach for those vices without which the state can only be saved with difficulty, for if everything is considered carefully, it will be found that something which looks like virtue, if followed, would be his ruin; whilst something else, which looks like vice, yet followed brings him security and prosperity.

• *Concerning Liberality and Meanness*

Commencing then with the first of the above-named characteristics, I say that it would be well to be reputed liberal. Nevertheless, liberality exercised in a way that does not bring you the reputation for it, injures you; for if one exercises it honestly and as it should be exercised, it may not become known, and you will not avoid the reproach of its opposite. Therefore, any one wishing to maintain among men the name of liberal is obliged to avoid no attribute of magnificence; so that a prince thus inclined will consume in such acts all his property, and will be compelled in the end, if he wish to maintain the name of liberal, to unduly weigh down his people, and tax them, and do everything he can to get money. This will soon make him odious to his subjects, and becoming poor he will be little valued by any one; thus, with his liberality, having offended many and rewarded few, he is affected by the very first trouble and imperilled by whatever may be the first danger; recognising this himself, and wishing to draw back from it, he runs at once into the reproach of being miserly.

Therefore, a prince, not being able to exercise this virtue of liberality in such a way that it is recognised, except to his cost, if he is wise he ought not to fear the reputation of being mean, for in time he will come to be more considered than if liberal, seeing that with his economy his revenues are enough, that he can defend himself against all attacks, and is able to engage in enterprises without burdening his people; thus it comes to pass that he exercises liberality towards all from whom he does not take, who are numberless, and meanness towards those to whom he does not give, who are few.

We have not seen great things done in our time except by those who have been considered mean; the rest have failed. Pope Julius the Second was assisted in reaching the papacy by a reputation for liberality, yet he did not strive afterwards to keep it up, when he made war on the King of France; and he made many wars without imposing any extraordinary tax on his subjects, for he supplied his additional expenses out of his long thriftiness. The present King of Spain would not have undertaken or conquered in so many enterprises if he had been reputed liberal. A prince, therefore, provided that he has not to rob his subjects, that he can defend himself, that he does not become poor and abject, that he is not forced to become rapacious, ought to hold of little account a reputation for being mean, for it is one of those vices which will enable him to govern.

And if any one should say: Cæsar obtained empire by liberality, and many others have reached the highest positions by having been liberal, and by being considered so, I answer: Either you are a prince in fact, or in a way to become one. In the first case this liberality is dangerous, in the second it is very necessary to be considered liberal; and Cæsar was one of those who wished to become pre-eminent in Rome; but if he had survived after becoming so, and had not moderated his expenses, he would have destroyed his government. And if any one should reply: Many have been princes, and have done great things with armies, who have been considered very liberal, I reply: Either a prince spends that which is his own or his subjects' or else that of others. In the first case he ought to be sparing, in the second he ought not to neglect any opportunity for liberality. And to the prince who goes forth with his army, supporting it by pillage, sack, and extortion, handling that which belongs to others, this liberality is necessary, otherwise he would not be followed by soldiers. And of that which is neither yours nor your subjects' you can be a ready giver, as were Cyrus, Cæsar, and Alexander; because it does not take away your reputation if you squander that of others, but adds to it; it is only squandering your own that injures you.

And there is nothing wastes so rapidly as liberality, for even whilst you exercise it you lose the power to do so, and so become either poor or despised, or else, in avoiding poverty, rapacious and hated. And a prince should guard himself, above all things, against being despised and hated; and liberality leads you to both. Therefore it is wiser to have a reputation for meanness which brings reproach without hatred, than to be compelled through seeking a reputation for liberality to incur a name for rapacity which begets reproach with hatred.

• *Concerning Cruelty and Clemency, and*
  Whether It Is Better to be Loved
  Than Feared

Coming now to the other qualities mentioned above, I say that every prince ought to desire to be considered clement and not cruel. Nevertheless he ought to take care not to misuse this clemency. Cesare Borgia was considered cruel; notwithstanding, his cruelty reconciled the Romagna, unified it, and restored it to peace and loyalty. And if this be rightly considered, he will be seen to have been much more merciful than the Florentine people, who, to avoid a reputation for cruelty, permitted Pistoia to be destroyed. Therefore a prince, so long as he keeps his subjects united and loyal, ought not to mind the reproach of cruelty; because with a few examples he will be more merciful than those who, through too much mercy, allow disorders to arise, from which follow murder or robbery; for these are wont to injure the whole people, whilst those executions which originate with a prince offend the individual only.

And of all princes, it is impossible for the new prince to avoid the imputation of cruelty, owing to new states being full of dangers. Hence Virgil, through the mouth of Dido, excuses the inhumanity of her reign owing to its being new, saying:—

> "Res dura, et regni novitas me talia cogunt
> Moliri, et late fines custode tueri."[1]

Nevertheless he ought to be slow to believe and to act, nor should he himself show fear, but proceed in a temperate manner with prudence and humanity, so that too much confidence may not make him incautious and too much distrust render him intolerable.

Upon this a question arises: whether it be better to be loved than feared or feared than loved? It may be answered that one should wish to be both, but, because it is difficult to unite them in one person, it is much safer to be feared than loved, when, of the two, either must be dispensed with. Because this is to be asserted in general of men, that they are ungrateful, fickle, false, cowards, covetous, and as long as you succeed they are yours entirely; they will offer you their blood, property, life, and children, as is said above, when the need is far distant; but when it approaches they turn against you. And that prince who, relying entirely on their promises, has neglected other precautions, is ruined; because friendships that are obtained by payments, and not by greatness

---

[1] "The harshness of the situation and the newness of my kingdom compel me to construct such safeguards and to cast a far flung guard around my realm."

or nobility of mind, may indeed be earned, but they are not secured, and in time of need cannot be relied upon; and men have less scruple in offending one who is beloved than one who is feared, for love is preserved by the link of obligation which, owing to the baseness of men, is broken at every opportunity for their advantage; but fear preserves you by a dread of punishment which never fails.

Nevertheless a prince ought to inspire fear in such a way that, if he does not win love, he avoids hatred; because he can endure very well being feared whilst he is not hated, which will always be as long as he abstains from the property of his citizens and subjects and from their women. But when it is necessary for him to proceed against the life of some one, he must do it on proper justification and for manifest cause, but above all things he must keep his hands off the property of others, because men more quickly forget the death of their father than the loss of their patrimony. Besides, pretexts for taking away the property are never wanting; for he who has once begun to live by robbery will always find pretexts for seizing what belongs to others; but reasons for taking life, on the contrary, are more difficult to find and sooner lapse. But when a prince is with his army, and has under control a multitude of soldiers, then it is quite necessary for him to disregard the reputation of cruelty, for without it he would never hold his army united or disposed to its duties.

Among the wonderful deeds of Hannibal this one is enumerated: that having led an enormous army, composed of many various races of men, to fight in foreign lands, no dissensions arose either among them or against the prince, whether in his bad or in his good fortune. This arose from nothing else than his inhuman cruelty, which, with his boundless valour, made him revered and terrible in the sight of his soldiers, but without that cruelty, his other virtues were not sufficient to produce this effect. And short-sighted writers admire his deeds from one point of view and from another condemn the principal cause of them. That it is true his other virtues would not have been sufficient for him may be proved by the case of Scipio, that most excellent man, not only of his own times but within the memory of man, against whom, nevertheless, his army rebelled in Spain; this arose from nothing but his too great forbearance, which gave his soldiers more licence than is consistent with military discipline. For this he was upbraided in the Senate by Fabius Maximus, and called the corrupter of the Roman soldiery. The Locrians were laid waste by a legate of Scipio, yet they were not avenged by him, nor was the insolence of the legate punished, owing entirely to his easy nature. Insomuch that some one in the Senate, wishing to excuse him, said there were many men who knew much better how not to err than to correct the errors of others. This disposition, if he had been continued in the command, would have destroyed in time the fame and glory of Scipio; but, he being under the control of the Senate, this injurious characteristic not only concealed itself, but contributed to his glory.

Returning to the question of being feared or loved, I come to the conclusion that, men loving according to their own will and fearing according to that of the prince, a wise prince should establish himself on that which is in his own control and not in that of others; he must endeavour only to avoid hatred, as is noted.

• *Concerning the Way in Which Princes Should Keep Faith*

Every one admits how praiseworthy it is in a prince to keep faith, and to live with integrity and not with craft. Nevertheless our experience has been that those princes who have done great things have held good faith of little account, and have known how to circumvent the intellect of men by craft, and in the end have overcome those who have relied on their word. You must know there are two ways of contesting, the one by the law, the other by force; the first method is proper to men, the second to beasts; but because the first is frequently not sufficient, it is necessary to have recourse to the second. Therefore it is necessary for a prince to understand how to avail himself of the beast and the man. This has been figuratively taught to princes by ancient writers, who describe how Achilles and many other princes of old were given to the Centaur Chiron to nurse, who brought them up in his discipline; which means solely that, as they had for a teacher one who was half beast and half man, so it is necessary for a prince to know how to make use of both natures, and that one without the other is not durable. A prince, therefore, being compelled knowingly to adopt the beast, ought to choose the fox and the lion; because the lion cannot defend himself against snares and the fox cannot defend himself against wolves. Therefore, it is necessary to be a fox to discover the snares and a lion to terrify the wolves. Those who rely simply on the lion do not understand what they are about. Therefore a wise lord cannot, nor ought he to, keep faith when such observance may be turned against him, and when the reasons that caused him to pledge it exist no longer. If men were entirely good this precept would not hold, but because they are bad, and will not keep faith with you, you too are not bound to observe it with them. Nor will there ever be wanting to a prince legitimate reasons to excuse this non-observance. Of this endless modern examples could be given, showing how many treaties and engagements have been made void and of no effect through the faithlessness of princes; and he who has known best how to employ the fox has succeeded best.

But it is necessary to know well how to disguise this characteristic, and to be a great pretender and dissembler; and men are so simple, and so subject to present necessities, that he who seeks to deceive will always find some one who will allow himself to be deceived. One recent example I cannot pass over in silence. Alexander the Sixth did nothing else but deceive men, nor ever thought of doing otherwise, and he always found victims; for there never was a man who had greater power in asserting, or who with greater oaths would affirm a thing, yet would observe it less; nevertheless his deceits always succeeded according to his wishes, because he well understood this side of mankind.

Therefore it is unnecessary for a prince to have all the good qualities I have enumerated, but it is very necessary to appear to have them. And I shall dare to say this also, that to have them and always to observe them is injurious, and that to appear to have them is useful; to appear merciful, faithful, humane, religious, upright, and to be so, but with a mind so framed that should you require not to be so, you may be able and know how to change to the opposite.

And you have to understand this, that a prince, especially a new one, cannot observe all those things for which men are esteemed, being often forced, in order to maintain the state, to act contrary to fidelity, friendship, humanity, and religion. Therefore it is necessary for him to have a mind ready to turn itself accordingly as the winds and variations of fortune force it, yet, as I have said above, not to diverge from the good if he can avoid doing so, but, if compelled, then to know how to set about it.

For this reason a prince ought to take care that he never lets anything slip from his lips that is not replete with the above-named five qualities, that he may appear to him who sees and hears him altogether merciful, faithful, humane, upright, and religious. There is nothing more necessary to appear to have than this last quality, inasmuch as men judge generally more by the eye than by the hand, because it belongs to everybody to see you, to few to come in touch with you. Every one sees what you appear to be, few really know what you are, and those few dare not oppose themselves to the opinion of the many, who have the majesty of the state to defend them; and in the actions of all men, and especially of princes, which it is not prudent to challenge, one judges by the result.

For that reason, let a prince have the credit of conquering and holding his state, the means will always be considered honest, and he will be praised by everybody; because the vulgar are always taken by what a thing seems to be and by what comes of it; and in the world there are only the vulgar, for the few find a place there only when the many have no ground to rest on.

One prince of the present time, whom it is not well to name, never preaches anything else but peace and good faith, and to both he is most hostile, and either, if he had kept it, would have deprived him of reputation and kingdom many a time.

• *Questions for Study*

1. Machiavelli's advice to a prince on the governing of his realm has shocked many people ever since it was first given in the sixteenth century. The word "Machiavellian" has become a term of abuse. Do these selections indicate the reasons for the author's name becoming a word of disapproval?
2. It has been said that Machiavelli believes that "the end justifies the means." Do you see any indication of this belief in these selections?
3. Does a political leader need to apply devious methods in his conduct of affairs? Explain, giving if you can specific examples of leaders who have not compromised their morality in high office.
4. Do his ideas apply only to the conduct of heads of state or may they be applied more widely to the conduct of ordinary people in their day to day living?

EDWARD GIBBON

•

ON CHRISTIANITY

It has been remarked with more ingenuity than truth that the virgin purity of the church was never violated by schism or heresy before the reign of Trajan or Hadrian, about one hundred years after the death of Christ. We may observe with much more propriety that, during that period, the disciples of the Messiah were indulged in a freer latitude both of faith and practice than has ever been allowed in succeeding ages. As

From *The History of the Decline and Fall of the Roman Empire,* Six volumes, 1776–1788.

the terms of communion were insensibly narrowed, and the spiritual authority of the prevailing party was exercised with increasing severity, many of its most respectable adherents, who were called upon to renounce, were provoked to assert their private opinions, to pursue the consequences of their mistaken principles, and openly to erect the standard of rebellion against the unity of the church. The Gnostics were distinguished as the most polite, the most learned, and the most wealthy of the Christian name; and that general appellation, which expressed a superiority of knowledge, was either assumed by their own pride, or ironically bestowed by the envy of their adversaries. They were almost without exception of the race of the Gentiles, and their principal founders seem to have been natives of Syria or Egypt, where the warmth of the climate disposes both the mind and the body to indolent and contemplative devotion. The Gnostics blended with the faith of Christ many sublime but obscure tenets, which they derived from oriental philosophy, and even from the religion of Zoroaster, concerning the eternity of matter, the existence of two principles, and the mysterious hierarchy of the invisible world. As soon as they launched out into that vast abyss, they delivered themselves to the guidance of a disordered imagination; and as the paths of error are various and infinite, the Gnostics were imperceptibly divided into more than fifty particular sects, of whom the most celebrated appear to have been the Basilidians, the Valentinians, the Marcionites, and, in a still later period, the Manichæans. Each of these sects could boast of its bishops and congregations, of its doctors and martyrs; and, instead of the Four Gospels adopted by the church, the heretics produced a multitude of histories, in which the actions and discourses of Christ and of his apostles were adapted to their respective tenets. The success of the Gnostics was rapid and extensive. They covered Asia and Egypt, established themselves in Rome, and sometimes penetrated into the provinces of the West. For the most part they arose in the second century, flourished during the third, and were suppressed in the fourth or fifth, by the prevalence of more fashionable controversies, and by the superior ascendant of the reigning power. Though they constantly disturbed the peace, and frequently disgraced the name of religion, they contributed to assist rather than to retard the progress of Christianity. The Gentile converts, whose strongest objections and prejudices were directed against the law of Moses, could find admission into many Christian societies, which required not from their untutored mind any belief of an antecedent revelation. Their faith was insensibly fortified and enlarged, and the church was ultimately benefited by the conquests of its most inveterate enemies.

But whatever difference of opinion might subsist between the Orthodox, the Ebionites, and the Gnostics, concerning the divinity or the obligation of the Mosaic law, they were all equally animated by the same exclusive zeal, and by the same abhorrence for idolatry, which had distinguished the Jews from the other nations of the ancient world. The philosopher, who considered the system of polytheism as a composition of human fraud and error, could disguise a smile of contempt under the mask of devotion, without apprehending that either the mockery or the compliance would expose him to the resentment of any invisible, or, as he conceived them, imaginary powers. But the established religions of Paganism were seen by the primitive Christians in a much more odious and formidable light. It was the universal sentiment both of the church and of heretics, that the dæmons were the authors, the patrons, and the objects of idolatry. Those rebellious spirits who had been degraded from the rank of angels, and cast down into the infernal pit, were still permitted to roam upon earth, to torment the bodies and to seduce the minds of sinful men. The dæmons soon discovered and abused the natural propensity of the human heart towards devotion, and, artfully withdrawing the adoration of mankind from their Creator, they usurped the place and honours of the Supreme Deity. By the success of their malicious contrivances, they at once gratified their own vanity and revenge, and obtained the only comfort of which they were yet susceptible, the hope of involving the human species in the participation of their guilt and misery. It was confessed, or at least it was imagined, that they had distributed among themselves the most important characters of polytheism, one dæmon assuming the name and attributes of Jupiter, another of Æsculapius, a third of Venus, and a fourth perhaps of Apollo; and that, by the advantage of their long experience and aërial nature, they were enabled to execute, with sufficient skill and dignity, the parts which they had undertaken. They lurked in the temples, instituted festivals and sacrifices, invented fables, pronounced oracles, and were frequently allowed to perform miracles. The Christians, who, by the interposition of evil spirits, could so readily explain every præternatural appearance, were disposed and even desirous to admit the most extravagant fictions of the Pagan mythology. But the belief of the Christian was accompanied with horror. The most trifling mark of respect to the national worship he considered as a direct homage yielded to the dæmon, and as an act of rebellion against the majesty of God.

In consequence of this opinion, it was the first but arduous duty of a Christian to preserve himself pure and undefiled by the practice of idolatry. The religion of the nations was not merely a speculative doctrine professed in the schools or preached in the temples. The innumerable deities and rites of polytheism were closely interwoven with every circumstance of business or pleasure, of public or of private life; and it seemed impossible to escape the observance of them, without, at the same time, renouncing the commerce of mankind, and all the offices and amusements of society. The important transactions of peace and war were prepared or concluded by solemn sacrifices, in which the magistrate, the senator, and the soldier were obliged to preside or to participate. The public spectacles were an essential part of the cheerful devotion of the Pagans, and the gods were supposed to accept, as the most grateful offering, the games that the prince and people celebrated in honor of their peculiar festivals. The Christian, who with pious horror avoided the abomination of the circus or the theatre, found himself encompassed with infernal snares in every convivial entertainment, as often as his friends, invoking the hospitable deities, poured out libations to each other's happiness. When the bride, struggling with well-affected reluctance, was forced in hymenæal pomp over the threshold of her new habitation, or when the sad procession of the dead slowly moved towards the funeral pile, the Christian, on these interesting occasions, was compelled to desert the persons who were the dearest to him, rather than contract the guilt inherent to those impious ceremonies. Every art and every trade that was in the least concerned in the framing or adoring of idols was polluted by the stain of idolatry; a severe sentence, since it devoted to eternal misery the far greater part of the community which is employed in the exercise of liberal or mechanic professions. If we cast our eyes over the numerous remains of antiquity, we shall perceive that, besides the immediate representations of the gods and the holy instruments of their worship, the elegant forms and agreeable fictions consecrated by the imagination of the Greeks were introduced as the richest ornaments of the houses, the dress, and the furniture of the Pagans. Even the arts of music and painting, of eloquence and poetry, flowed from the same impure origin. In the style of the fathers, Apollo and the Muses were the organs of the infernal spirit; Homer and Virgil were the most eminent of his servants; and the beautiful mythology which pervades and animates the compositions of their genius is destined to celebrate the glory of the dæmons. Even the common language of Greece and Rome abounded with familiar but impious expressions, which the imprudent Christian might too carelessly utter, or too patiently hear.

The dangerous temptations which on every side lurked in ambush to surprise the unguarded believer assailed him with redoubled violence on the days of solemn festivals. So artfully were they framed and disposed throughout the year, that supersition always wore the appearance of pleasure, and often of virtue. Some of the most sacred festivals in the Roman ritual were destined to salute the new calends of January with vows of public and private felicity; to indulge the pious remembrance of the dead and living; to ascertain the inviolable bounds of property; to hail, on the return of spring, the genial powers of fecundity; to perpetuate the two memorable eras of Rome, the foundation of the city, and that of the republic; and to restore, during the humane licence of the Saturnalia, the primitive equality of mankind. Some idea may be conceived of the abhorrence of the Christians for such impious ceremonies, by the scrupulous delicacy which they displayed on a much less alarming occasion. On days of general festivity it was the custom of the ancients to adorn their doors with lamps and with branches of laurel, and to crown their heads with a garland of flowers. This innocent and elegant practice might perhaps have been tolerated as a mere civil insitution. But it most unluckily happened that the doors were under the protection of the household gods, that the laurel was sacred to the lover of Daphne, and that garlands of flowers, though frequently worn as a symbol either of joy or mourning, had been dedicated in their first origin to the service of supersition. The trembling Christians, who were persuaded in this instance to comply with the fashion of their country and the commands of the magistrate, labored under the most gloomy apprehensions, from the reproaches of their own conscience, the censures of the church, and the denunciations of divine vengeance.

Such was the anxious diligence which was required to guard the chastity of the Gospel from the infectious breath of idolatry. The superstitious observances of public or private rites were carelessly practised, from education and habit, by the followers of the established religion. But as often as they occurred, they afforded the Christians an opportunity of declaring and confirming their zealous opposition. By these frequent protestations their attachment to the faith was continually fortified; and in proportion to the increase of zeal, they combated with the more ardor and success in the holy war which they had undertaken against the empire of the dæmons.

The writings of Cicero represent in the most lively colors the ignorance, the errors, and the uncertainty of the ancient philosophers with regard to the immortality of the soul. When they are desirous of arming their disciples against the fear of death, they inculcate, as an obvious though melancholy position, that the fatal stroke of our dissolution releases us from the calamities of life; and that those can no longer suffer who no longer exist. Yet there were a few sages of Greece and Rome who had conceived a more exalted, and, in some respects, a juster idea of human nature, though it must be confessed that, in the sublime inquiry, their reason had been often guided by their imagination, and that their imagination had been prompted by their vanity. When they viewed with complacency the extent of their own mental powers, when they exercised the various faculties of memory, of fancy, and of judgment, in the most profound speculations or the most important labors, and when they reflected on the desire of fame, which transported them into future ages, far beyond the bounds of death and of the grave, they were unwilling to confound themselves with the beasts of the field, or to suppose that a being, for whose dignity they entertained the most sincere admiration, could be limited to a spot of earth, and to a few years of duration. With this favourable prepossession they summoned to their aid the science, or rather the language, of Metaphysics. They soon discovered that, as none of the properties of matter will apply to the operations of the mind, the human soul must consequently be a substance distinct from the body, pure, simple, and spiritual, incapable of dissolution, and susceptible of a much higher degree of virtue and happiness after the release from its corporeal prison. From these specious and noble principles the philosophers who trod in the footsteps of Plato deduced a very unjustifiable conclusion, since they asserted, not only the future immortality, but the past eternity of the human soul, which they were too apt to consider as a portion of the infinite and self-existing spirit which pervades and sustains the universe. A doctrine thus removed beyond the senses and the experience of mankind might serve to amuse the leisure of a philosophic mind; or, in the silence of solitude, it might sometimes impart a ray of comfort to desponding virtue; but the faint impression which had been received in the schools was soon obliterated by the commerce and business of active life. We are sufficiently acquainted with the eminent persons who flourished in the age of Cicero and of the first Cæsars, with their actions, their characters, and their motives, to be assured that their conduct in this life was never regulated by any serious conviction of the rewards or punishments of a future state. At the bar and in the senate of Rome the ablest orators were not apprehensive of giving offence to their hearers by exposing that doctrine as an idle and extravagant opinion, which was rejected with contempt by every man of a liberal education and understanding.

Since therefore the most sublime efforts of philosophy can extend no farther than feebly to point out the desire, the hope, or, at most, the probability of a future state, there is nothing, except a divine revelation than can ascertain the existence and describe the condition of the invisible country which is destined to receive the souls of men after their separation from the body. But we may perceive several defects inherent to the popular religions of Greece and Rome which rendered them very unequal to so arduous a task. 1. The general system of their mythology was unsupported by any solid proofs; and the wisest among the Pagans had already disclaimed its usurped authority. 2. The description of the infernal regions had been abandoned to the fancy of painters and of poets, who peopled them with so many phantoms and monsters who dispensed their rewards and punishments with so little equity, that a solemn truth, the most congenial to the human heart, was oppressed and disgraced by the absurd mixture of the wildest fictions. 3. The doctrine of a future state was scarcely considered among the devout polytheists of Greece and Rome as a fundamental article of faith. The providence of the gods, as it related to public communities rather than to private individuals, was principally displayed on the visible theatre of the present world. The petitions which were offered on the altars of Jupiter or Apollo expressed the anxiety of their worshippers for temporal happiness, and their ignorance or indifference concerning a future life. The important truth of the immortality of the soul was inculcated with more diligence as well as success in India, in Assyria, in Egypt, and in Gaul; and since we cannot attribute such a difference to the superior knowledge of the barbarians, we must ascribe it to the influence of an established priesthood, which employed the motives of virture as the instrument of ambition.

We might naturally expect that a principle so essential to religion would have been revealed in the clearest terms to the chosen people of Palestine, and that it might safely have been intrusted to the hereditary priesthood of Aaron. It is incumbent on us to adore the mysterious dispensations of Providence, when we discover that the doctrine of the immortality of the soul is omitted in the law of Moses; it is darkly insinuated by the prophets; and during the long period which elapsed between the Egyptian and the Babylonian servitudes, the hopes as well as fears of the Jews appear to have been confined within the narrow compass of the present life. After Cyrus had permitted the exiled nation to return into the promised land, and after Ezra had restored the ancient records of their religion, two celebrated sects, the Sadducees and the Pharisees, insensibly arose at Jerusalem. The former, selected from the more opulent and distinguished ranks of society, were strictly attached to the literal sense of the Mosaic law, and they piously rejected the immortality of the soul as an opinion that received no countenance from the divine book, which they revered as the only rule of their faith. To the authority of Scripture the Pharisees added that of tradition, and they accepted, under the name of traditions, several speculative tenets from the philosophy or religion of the eastern nations. The doctrines of fate or predestination, of angels and spirits, and of a future state of rewards and punishments, were in the number of these new articles of belief; and as the Pharisees, by the austerity of their manners, had drawn into their party the body of the Jewish people, the immortality of the soul became the prevailing sentiment of the synagogue under the reign of the Asmonæan princes and pontiffs. The temper of the Jews was incapable of contenting itself with such a cold and languid assent as might satisfy the mind of a Polytheist; and as soon as they admitted the idea of a future state, they embraced it with the zeal which has always formed the characteristic of the nation. Their zeal, however, added nothing to its evidence, or even probability; and it was still necessary that the doctrine of life and immortality, which had been dictated by nature, approved by reason, and received by superstition, should obtain the sanction of divine truth from the authority and example of Christ.

When the promise of eternal happiness was proposed to mankind on condition of adopting the faith, and of observing the precepts, of the Gospel, it is no wonder that so advantageous an offer should have been accepted by great numbers of every religion, of every rank, and of every province in the Roman empire. The ancient Christians were animated by a contempt for their present existence, and by a just confidence of immortality, of which the doubtful and imperfect faith of modern ages cannot give us any adequate notion. In the primitive church the influence of truth was very powerfully strengthened by an opinion which, however it may deserve respect for its usefulness and antiquity, has not been found agreeable to experience. It was universally believed that the end of the world, and the kingdom of heaven, were at hand. The near approach of this wonderful event had been predicted by the apostles; the tradition of it was preserved by their earliest disciples, and those who understood in their literal sense the discourses of Christ himself were obliged to expect the second and glorious coming of the Son of Man in the clouds, before that generation was totally extinguished which had beheld his humble condition upon earth, and which might still be witness of the calamities of the Jews under Vespasian or Hadrian. The revolution of seventeen centuries has instructed us not to press too closely the mysterious language of prophecy and revelation; but as long as, for wise purposes, this error was permitted to subsist in the church, it was productive of the most salutary effects on the faith and practice of Christians, who lived in the awful expectation of that moment when the globe itself, and all the various race of mankind, should tremble at the appearance of their divine Judge.

· *Questions for Study*

1. The eighteenth century is often called "The Age of Reason." It stressed moderation and decorum. Gibbon was a man of his age. Does the tone of the essay reveal a "reasonable" approach to his materials?

2. Take a paragraph and analyze closely Gibbon's tone, style, and sentence structure.
3. What is Gibbon's attitude toward the zeal of the Christians in preserving the purity of their religion? In what phrases is this attitude best shown?
4. What does he try to show by tracing the history of the doctrine of the immortality of the soul? For what primary purpose does he think the Christians used the doctrine?

THOMAS JEFFERSON

•

THE DANGER OF TRADITION

Some men look at constitutions with sanctimonious reverence, and deem them like the ark of the covenant, too sacred to be touched. They ascribe to the men of the preceding age a wisdom more than human, and suppose what they did to be beyond amendment. I knew that age well; I belonged to it, and labored with it. It deserved well of its country. It was very like the present, but without the experience of the present; and forty years of experience in government is worth a century of book-reading; and this they would say themselves, were they to rise from the dead. I am certainly not an advocate for frequent and untried changes in laws and constitutions. I think moderate imperfections had better be borne with; because, when once known, we accommodate ourselves to them, and find practical means of correcting their ill effects. But I know also, that laws and institutions must go hand in hand with the progress of the human mind. As that becomes more developed, more enlightened, as new discoveries are made, new truths disclosed, and manners and opinions change with the change of circumstances, institutions must advance also, and keep pace with the times. We might as well require a man to wear still the coat which fitted him when a boy, as civilized society to remain

From a letter to Samuel Kercheval, July 12, 1816.

ever under the regimen of their barbarous ancestors. It is this preposterous idea which has lately deluged Europe in blood. Their monarchs,
instead of wisely yielding to the gradual change of circumstances, of
favoring progressive accommodation to progressive improvement, have
clung to old abuses, entrenched themselves behind steady habits, and
obliged their subjects to seek through blood and violence rash and
ruinous innovations, which, had they been referred to the peaceful deliberations and collected wisdom of the nation, would have been put
into acceptable and salutary forms. Let us follow no such examples, nor
weakly believe that one generation is not as capable as another of taking
care of itself, and of ordering its own affairs. Let us, as our sister States
have done, avail ourselves of our reason and experience, to correct the
crude essays of our first and unexperienced, although wise, virtuous, and
well-meaning councils. And lastly, let us provide in our constitution for
its revision at stated periods. What these periods should be, nature herself
indicates. By the European tables of mortality, of the adults living at any
one moment of time, a majority will be dead in about nineteen years. At
the end of that period then, a new majority is come into place; or, in
other words, a new generation. Each generation is as independent of the
one preceding, as that was of all which had gone before. It has then, like
them, a right to choose for itself the form of government it believes most
promotive of its own happiness; consequently, to accommodate to the
circumstances in which it finds itself, that received from its predecessors;
and it is for the peace and good of mankind, that a solemn opportunity of
doing this every nineteen or twenty years, should be provided by the
constitution; so that it may be handed on, with periodical repairs, from
generation to generation, to the end of time, if anything human can so
long endure. It is now forty years since the constitution of Virginia was
formed. The same tables inform us, that, within that period, two-thirds of
the adults then living are now dead. Have then the remaining third, even
if they had the wish, the right to hold in obedience to their will, and to
laws heretofore made by them, the other two-thirds, who, with themselves, compose the present mass of adults? If they have not, who has?
The dead? But the dead have no rights. They are nothing; and nothing
cannot own something. Where there is no substance, there can be no
accident. This corporeal globe, and everything upon it, belong to its
present corporeal inhabitants, during their generation. They alone have a
right to direct what is the concern of themselves alone, and to declare
the law of that direction; and this declaration can only be made by their
majority. That majority, then, has a right to depute representatives to a
convention, and to make the constitution what they think will be the
best for themselves. But how collect their voice? This is the real diffi-

culty. If invited by private authority, or country or district meetings, these divisions are so large that few will attend; and their voice will be imperfectly, or falsely pronounced. Here, then, would be one of the advantages of the ward divisions I have proposed. The mayor of every ward, on a question like the present, would call his ward together, take the simple yea or nay of its members, convey these to the county court, who would hand on those of all its wards to the proper general authority; and the voice of the whole people would be thus fairly, full, and peaceably expressed, discussed, and decided by the common reason of the society. If this avenue be shut to the call of sufferance, it will make itself heard through that of force, and we shall go on, as other nations are doing, in the endless circle of oppression, rebellion, reformation; and oppression, rebellion, reformation, again; and so on forever.

• *Questions for Study*

1. This selection is part of a letter Jefferson wrote to a friend. Consider the tone and style. Evaluate the quality of it as a letter from your own experience with writing and receiving letters.
2. Today we tend to idealize the founding fathers. What was Jefferson's attitude toward them? In what ways do the two views differ? Why do they differ?
3. What does Jefferson say concerning the rights of each generation?
4. What words and phrases of emotional force does Jefferson use to persuade his reader of the importance of progress and change in government?
5. Write a theme in which you evaluate the place of tradition in modern political life.

THOMAS B. MACAULAY

•

THE WRITING OF HISTORY

The effect of historical reading is analogous, in many respects, to that produced by foreign travel. The student, like the tourist, is transported into a new state of society. He sees new fashions. He hears new modes of expression. His mind is enlarged by contemplating the wide diversities of laws, of morals, and of manners. But men may travel far, and return with minds as contracted as if they had never stirred from their own market-town. In the same manner, men may know the dates of many battles and the genealogies of many royal houses, and yet be no wiser. Most people look at past times as princes look at foreign countries. More than one illustrious stranger has landed on our island amidst the shouts of a mob, has dined with the King, has hunted with the master of the stag-hounds, has seen the guards reviewed, and a knight of the garter installed, has cantered along Regent Street, has visited Saint Paul's, and noted down its dimensions; and has then departed, thinking that he has seen England. He has, in fact, seen a few public buildings, public men, and public ceremonies. But of the vast and complex system of society, of the fine shades of national character, of the practical operation of government and laws, he knows nothing. He who would understand these things rightly must not confine his observations to palaces and solemn days. He must see ordinary men as they appear in their ordinary business and in their ordinary pleasures. He must mingle in the crowds of the exchange and the coffee-house. He must obtain admittance to the convivial table and the domestic hearth. He must bear with vulgar expression. He must not shrink from exploring even the retreats of misery. He who wishes to understand the condition of mankind in former ages must proceed on the same principle. If he attends only to public transactions, to wars, congresses, and debates, his studies will be as unprofitable as the travels of

From "History," *Edinburgh Review*, May 1828.

those imperial, royal, and serene sovereigns who form their judgment of our island from having gone in state to a few fine sights, and from having held formal conferences with a few great officers.

The perfect historian is he in whose work the character and spirit of an age is exhibited in miniature. He relates no fact, he attributes no expression to his characters, which is not authenticated by sufficient testimony. But, by judicious selection, rejection, and arrangement, he gives to truth those attractions which have been usurped by fiction. In his narrative a due subordination is observed: some transactions are prominent; others retire. But the scale on which he represents them is increased or diminished, not according to the dignity of the person concerned in them, but according to the degree in which they elucidate the condition of society and the nature of man. He shows us the court, the camp, and the senate. But he shows us also the nation. He considers no anecdote, no peculiarity of manner, no familiar saying, as too insignificant for his notice which is not too insignificant to illustrate the operation of laws, of religion, and of education, and to mark the progress of the human mind. Men will not merely be described, but will be made intimately known to us. The changes of manners will be indicated, not merely by a few general phrases or a few extracts from statistical documents, but by appropriate images presented in every line.

If a man, such as we are supposing, should write the history of England, he would assuredly not omit the battles, the sieges, the negotiations, the seditions, the ministerial changes. But with these he would intersperse the details which are the charm of historical romances. At Lincoln Cathedral there is a beautiful painted window, which was made by an apprentice out of the pieces of glass which had been rejected by his master. It is so far superior to every other in the church, that, according to the tradition, the vanquished artist killed himself from mortification. Sir Walter Scott, in the same manner, has used those fragments of truth which historians have scornfully thrown behind them in a manner which may well excite their envy. He has constructed out of their gleanings works which, even considered as histories, are scarcely less valuable than theirs. But a truly great historian would reclaim those materials which the novelist has appropriated. The history of the government, and the history of the people, would be exhibited in that mode in which alone they can be exhibited justly, in inseparable conjunction and intermixture. We should not then have to look for the wars and votes of the Puritans in Clarendon, and for their phraseology in *Old Mortality*; for one half of *King James* in Hume, and for the other half in *The Fortunes of Nigel*.

The early part of our imaginary history would be rich with coloring from romance, ballad, and chronicle. We should find ourselves in the company of knights, such as those of Froissart, and of pilgrims, such as those who rode with Chaucer from the Tabard. Society would be shown from the highest to the lowest—from the royal cloth of state to the den of the outlaw; from the throne of the Legate to the chimney-corner where the begging friar regaled himself. Palmers, ministrels, crusaders—the stately monastery, with the good cheer in its refectory and the high-mass in its chapel—the manor-house, with its hunting and hawking—the tournament, with the heralds and ladies, the trumpets and the cloth of gold—would give truth and life to the representation. We should perceive, in a thousand slight touches, the importance of the privileged burgher, and the fierce and haughty spirit which swelled under the collar of the degraded villein. The revival of letters would not merely be described in a few magnificent periods. We should discern, in innumerable particulars, the fermentation of mind, the eager appetite for knowledge, which distinguished the sixteenth from the fifteenth century. In the Reformation we should see, not merely a schism which changed the ecclesiastical constitution of England and the mutual relations of the European powers, but a moral war which raged in every family, which set the father against the son, and the son against the father, the mother against the daughter, and the daughter against the mother. Henry would be painted with the skill of Tacitus. We should have the change of his character from his profuse and joyous youth to his savage and imperious old age. We should perceive the gradual progress of selfish and tyrannical passions in a mind not naturally insensible or ungenerous; and to the last we should detect some remains of that open and noble temper which endeared him to a people whom he oppressed, struggling with the hardness of despotism and the irritability of disease. We should see Elizabeth in all her weakness and in all her strength, surrounded by the handsome favorites whom she never trusted, and the wise old statesman whom she never dismissed, uniting in herself the most contradictory qualities of both her parents—the coquetry, the caprice, the petty malice of Anne— the haughty and resolute spirit of Henry. We have no hesitation in saying that a great artist might produce a portrait of this remarkable woman at least as striking as that in the novel of *Kenilworth*, without employing a single trait not authenticated by ample testimony. In the meantime, we should see arts cultivated, wealth accumulated, the conveniences of life improved. We should see the keeps, where nobles, insecure themselves, spread insecurity around them, gradually giving place to the halls of peaceful opulence, to the oriels of Longleat, and the stately pinnacles of Burleigh. We should see towns extended, deserts cultivated, the hamlets of fishermen turned into wealthy havens, the meal of the peasant improved, and his hut more commodiously furnished. We should see those opinions and feelings which produced the great struggle against the House of Stuart slowly growing up in the bosom of private families, before they manifested themselves in parliamentary debates. Then would come the Civil War. Those skirmishes on which Clarendon dwells so minutely would be told, as Thucydides would have told them, with perspicuous conciseness. They are merely connecting links. But the great characteristics of the age, the loyal enthusiasm of the brave English gentry, the fierce licentiousness of the swearing, dicing, drunken reprobates whose excesses disgraced the royal cause—the austerity of the Presbyterian Sabbaths in the city, the extravagance of the independent preachers in the camp, the precise garb, the severe countenance, the petty scruples, the affected accent, the absurd names and phrases which marked the Puritans—the valor, the policy, the public spirit, which lurked beneath these ungraceful disguises—the dreams of the raving Fifth-monarchy-man, the dreams, scarcely less wild, of the philosophic republican—all these would enter into the representation, and render it at once more exact and more striking.

The instruction derived from history thus written would be of a vivid and practical character. It would be received by the imagination as well as by the reason. It would be not merely traced on the mind, but branded into it. Many truths, too, would be learned, which can be learned in no other manner. As the history of states is generally written, the greatest and most momentous revolutions seem to come upon them like supernatural inflictions, without warning or cause. But the fact is, that such revolutions are almost always the consequences of moral changes, which have gradually passed on the mass of the community, and which ordinarily proceed far, before their progress is indicated by any public measure. An intimate knowledge of the domestic history of nations is therefore absolutely necessary to the prognosis of political events. A narrative, defective in this respect, is as useless as a medical treatise which should pass by all the symptoms attendant on the early stage of a disease and mention only what occurs when the patient is beyond the reach of remedies.

A historian such as we have been attempting to describe would indeed be an intellectual prodigy. In his mind, powers scarcely compatible with each other must be tempered into an exquisite harmony. We shall sooner see another Shakespeare or another Homer. The highest excellence to which any single faculty can be brought would be less surprising than such a happy and delicate combination of qualities. Yet the contemplation of imaginary models is not an unpleasant or useless employment of the mind. It cannot indeed produce perfection; but it produces improvement, and nourishes that generous and liberal fastidiousness which is not inconsistent with the strongest sensibility to merit, and which, while it exalts our conceptions of the art, does not render us unjust to the artist.

• Questions for Study

1. What specific analogies, contrasts, comparisons and examples enliven the opening section of the essay?
2. What, according to Macaulay, makes a historian perfect? Can we say that Herodotus, Tacitus, and Gibbon qualify as perfect historians from the point of view expressed in this essay?
3. It may be interesting to note that Macaulay's own histories are not regarded too highly by modern historians. Is there a danger in Macaulay's emphasis on the necessity for the historian to use small detail? In what ways do his references to Sir Walter Scott suggest the danger? Does the essay state any views that might be considered unsound? Explain.

THOMAS CARLYLE

•

THE HERO AS KING

The Commander over men; he to whose will our wills are to be subordinated, and loyally surrender themselves, and find their welfare in doing so, may be reckoned the most important of Great Men. He is practically the summary for us of *all* the various figures of Heroism; Priest, Teacher, whatsoever of earthly or of spiritual dignity we can fancy to reside in a man, embodies itself here, to *command* over us, to furnish us with constant practical teaching, to tell us for the day and hour what we are to *do*. He is called *Rex*, Regulator, *Roi*: our own name is still better; King, *Könning*, which means *Can*-ning, Ableman.

From *On Heroes, Hero-Worship, and the Heroic in History*, 1841.

Numerous considerations, pointing towards deep, questionable, and indeed unfathomable regions, present themselves here: on the most of which we must resolutely for the present forbear to speak at all. As Burke said that perhaps fair *Trial by Jury* was the Soul of Government, and that all legislation, administration, parliamentary debating, and the rest of it, went on, in "order to bring twelve impartial men into a jury-box,"—so, by much stronger reason, may I say here, that the finding of your *Able-man* and getting him invested with the *symbols of ability*, with dignity, worship (*worth*ship), royalty, kinghood, or whatever we call it, so that *he* may actually have room to guide according to his faculty of doing it, —is the business, well or ill accomplished, of all social procedure what-soever in this world! Hustings-speeches, Parliamentary motions, Reform Bills, French Revolutions, all mean at heart this; or else nothing. Find in any country the Ablest Man that exists there; raise *him* to the supreme place, and loyally reverence him: you have a perfect government for that country; no ballot-box, parliamentary eloquence, voting, constitu-tion-building, or other machinery whatsoever can improve it a whit. It is in the perfect state: an ideal country. The Ablest Man; he means also the truest-hearted, justest, the Noblest Man: what he *tells us to do* must be precisely the wisest, fittest, that we could anywhere or anyhow learn; —the thing which it will in all ways behove us, with right loyal thankful-ness, and nothing doubting, to do! Our *doing* and life were then, so far as government could regulate it, well regulated; that were the ideal of constitutions.

Alas, we know very well that Ideals can never be completely em-bodied in practice. Ideals must ever lie a very great way off; and we will right thankfully content ourselves with any not intolerable approximation thereto! Let no man, as Schiller says, too querulously "measure by a scale of perfection the meager product of reality" in this poor world of ours. We will esteem him no wise man; we will esteem him a sickly, discon-tented, foolish man. And yet, on the other hand, it is never to be forgotten that Ideals do exist; that if they be not approximated to at all, the whole matter goes to wreck! Infallibly. No bricklayer builds a wall *perfectly* perpendicular, mathematically this is not possible; a certain degree of perpendicularity suffices him; and he, like a good bricklayer, who must have done with his job, leaves it so. And yet if he sway *too much* from the perpendicular; above all, if he throw plummet and level quite away from him, and pile brick on brick heedless, just as it comes to hand—! Such bricklayer, I think, is in a bad way. *He* has forgotten himself: but the Law of Gravitation does not forget to act on him; he and his wall rush-down into confused welter of ruin!—

This is the history of all rebellions, French Revolutions, social explosions in ancient or modern times. You have put the too *Un*able man at the head of affairs! The too ignoble, unvaliant, fatuous man. You have forgotten that there is any rule, or natural necessity whatever, of putting the Able Man there. Brick must lie on brick as it may and can. Unable Simulacrum of Ability, *quack,* in a word, must adjust himself with quack, in all manner of administration of human things;—which accordingly lie unadministered, fermenting into unmeasured masses of failure, of indigent misery: in the outward, and in the inward or spiritual, miserable millions stretch-out the hand for their due supply, and it is not there. The "law of gravitation" acts; Nature's laws do none of them forget to act. The miserable millions burst-forth into Sansculottism, or some other sort of madness; bricks and bricklayers lie as a fatal chaos!—

Much sorry stuff, written some hundred years ago or more, about the "Divine right of Kings," moulders unread now in the Public Libraries of this country. Far be it from us to disturb the calm process by which it is disappearing harmlessly from the earth, in those repositories! At the same time, not to let the immense rubbish go without leaving us, as it ought, some soul of it behind—I will say that it did mean something; something true, which it is important for us and all men to keep in mind. To assert that in whatever man you chose to lay hold of (by this or the other plan of clutching at him); and clapt a round piece of metal on the head of, and called King,—there straightway came to reside a divine virtue, so that *he* became a kind of God, and a Divinity inspired him with faculty and right to rule over you to all lengths: this,—what can we do with this but leave it to rot silently in the Public Libraries? But I will say withal, and that is what these Divine-right men meant, That in Kings, and in all human Authorities, and relations that men god-created can form among each other, there is verily either a Divine Right or else a Diabolic Wrong; one or the other of these two! For it is false altogether, what the last Sceptical Century taught us, that this world is a steamengine. There is a God in this world; and a God's-sanction, or else the violation of such, does look-out from all ruling and obedience, from all moral acts of men. There is no act more moral between men than that of rule and obedience. Woe to him that claims obedience when it is not due; woe to him that refuses it when it is! God's law is in that, I say, however the Parchment-laws may run: there is a Divine Right or else a Diabolic Wrong at the heart of every claim that one man makes upon another.

It can do none of us harm to reflect on this: in all the relations of life it will concern us; in Loyalty and Royalty, the highest of these. I esteem the modern error, That all goes by self-interest and the checking and balancing of greedy knaveries, and that, in short, there is nothing divine whatever in the association of men, a still more despicable error, natural as it is to an unbelieving century, than that of a "divine right" in people *called* Kings. I say, Find me the true *Kōnning*, King, or Able-man, and he *has* a divine right over me. That we knew in some tolerable measure how to find him, and that all men were ready to acknowledge his divine right when found: this is precisely the healing which a sick world is every-where, in these ages, seeking after! The true King, as guide of the practical, has ever something of the Pontiff in him,—guide of the spiritual, from which all practice has its rise. This too is a true saying, That the *King* is head of the *Church*.—But we will leave the Polemic stuff of a dead century to lie quiet on its bookshelves.

• *Questions for Study*

1. What are some of the peculiarities of sentence structure, diction, and tone in this selection? Consider the means by which Carlyle develops the analogy of the bricklayer in the third paragraph. Can we say that this analogy is skillfully developed? Why? Does he make any effort to sustain it in the rest of the essay? Why does he capitalize so many of his nouns?
2. Carlyle believed that all history is comprised essentially of the biographies of great men. What dangers do you think are inherent in such a view? Do men make events or do events call forth great qualities in men?
3. In a later section of his essay, Carlyle uses Napoleon and Cromwell as examples of his "Able-man." From your knowledge of history, can you surmise the reasons for his adulation of these men?
4. Compare and contrast Carlyle's views of the leader with those of Machiavelli in "The Conduct of a Prince."
5. Write a theme on some living person, either famous or obscure, who embodies qualities which you consider heroic. You may wish to consider some of Carlyle's views of the heroic in your theme.

JOHN F. KENNEDY

•

EDMUND G. ROSS

In a lonely grave, forgotten and unknown, lies "the man who saved a President," and who as a result may well have preserved for ourselves and posterity constitutional government in the United States—the man who performed in 1868 what one historian has called "the most heroic act in American history, incomparably more difficult than any deed of valor upon the field of battle"—but a United States Senator whose name no one recalls: Edmund G. Ross of Kansas.

The impeachment of President Andrew Johnson, the event in which the obscure Ross was to play such a dramatic role, was the sensational climax to the bitter struggle between the President, determined to carry out Abraham Lincoln's policies of reconciliation with the defeated South, and the more radical Republican leaders in Congress, who sought to administer the downtrodden Southern states as conquered provinces which had forfeited their rights under the Constitution. It was, moreover, a struggle between Executive and Legislative authority. Andrew Johnson, the courageous if untactful Tennessean who had been the only Southern Member of Congress to refuse to secede with his state, had committed himself to the policies of the Great Emancipator to whose high station he had succeeded only by the course of an assassin's bullet. He knew that Lincoln prior to his death had already clashed with the extremists in Congress, who had opposed his approach to reconstruction in a constitutional and charitable manner and sought to make the Legislative Branch of the government supreme. And his own belligerent temperament soon destroyed any hope that Congress might now join hands in carrying out Lincoln's policies of permitting the South to resume its place in the Union with as little delay and controversy as possible.

By 1866, when Edmund Ross first came to the Senate, the two branches of the government were already at each other's throats, snarling and bristling with anger. Bill after bill was vetoed by the President on the grounds that they were unconstitutional, too harsh in their treatment of the South, an unnecessary prolongation of military rule in peacetime or undue interference with the authority of the Executive Branch. And for the first time in our nation's history, important public measures were passed over a President's veto and became law without his support.

But not all of Andrew Johnson's vetoes were overturned; and the "Radical" Republicans of the Congress promptly realized that one final step was necessary before they could crush their despised foe (and in the heat of political battle their vengeance was turned upon their President far more than their former military enemies of the South). That one remaining step was the assurance of a two-thirds majority in the Senate —for under the Constitution, such a majority was necessary to override a Presidential veto. And more important, such a majority was constitutionally required to accomplish their major ambition, now an ill-kept secret, conviction of the President under an impeachment and his dismissal from office!

The temporary and unstable two-thirds majority which had enabled the Senate Radical Republicans on several occasions to enact legislation over the President's veto was, they knew, insufficiently reliable for an impeachment conviction. To solidify this bloc became the paramount goal of Congress, expressly or impliedly governing its decisions on other issues—particularly the admission of new states, the readmission of Southern states and the determination of senatorial credentials. By extremely dubious methods a pro-Johnson Senator was denied his seat. Over the President's veto Nebraska was admitted to the Union, seating two more anti-administration Senators. Although last minute maneuvers failed to admit Colorado over the President's veto (sparsely populated Colorado had rejected statehood in a referendum), an unexpected tragedy brought false tears and fresh hopes for a new vote, in Kansas.

Senator Jim Lane of Kansas had been a "conservative" Republican sympathetic to Johnson's plans to carry out Lincoln's reconstruction policies. But his frontier state was one of the most "radical" in the Union. When Lane voted to uphold Johnson's veto of the Civil Rights Bill of 1866 and introduced the administration's bill for recognition of the new state government of Arkansas, Kansas had arisen in outraged heat. A mass meeting at Lawrence had vilified the Senator and speedily reported resolutions sharply condemning his position. Humiliated, mentally ailing, broken in health and laboring under charges of financial irregularities, Jim Lane took his own life on July 1, 1866.

With this thorn in their side removed, the Radical Republicans in Washington looked anxiously toward Kansas and the selection of Lane's successor. Their fondest hopes were realized, for the new Senator from Kansas turned out to be Edmund G. Ross, the very man who had introduced the resolutions attacking Lane at Lawrence.

There could be no doubt as to where Ross's sympathies lay, for his entire career was one of determined opposition to the slave states of the South, their practices and their friends. In 1854, when only twenty-eight, he had taken part in the mob rescue of a fugitive slave in Milwaukee. In 1856, he had joined that flood of antislavery immigrants to "bleeding" Kansas who intended to keep it a free territory. Disgusted with the Democratic party of his youth, he had left that party, and volunteered in the Kansas Free State Army to drive back a force of proslavery men invading the territory. In 1862, he had given up his newspaper work to enlist in the Union Army, from which he emerged a Major. His leading role in the condemnation of Lane at Lawrence convinced the Radical Republican leaders in Congress that in Edmund G. Ross they had a solid member of that vital two-thirds.

The stage was now set for the final scene—the removal of Johnson. Early in 1867, Congress enacted over the President's veto the Tenure-of-Office Bill which prevented the President from removing without the consent of the Senate all new officeholders whose appointment required confirmation by that body. At the time nothing more than the cry for more patronage was involved, Cabinet Members having originally been specifically exempt.

On August 5, 1867, President Johnson—convinced that the Secretary of War, whom he had inherited from Lincoln, Edwin M. Stanton, was the surreptitious tool of the Radical Republicans and was seeking to become the almighty dictator of the conquered South—asked for his immediate resignation; and Stanton arrogantly fired back the reply that he declined to resign before the next meeting of Congress. Not one to cower before this kind of effrontery, the President one week later suspended Stanton, and appointed in his place the one man whom Stanton did not dare resist, General Grant. On January 13, 1868, an angry Senate notified the President and Grant that it did not concur in the suspension of Stanton, and Grant vacated the office upon Stanton's return. But the situation was intolerable. The Secretary of War was unable to attend Cabinet meetings or associate with his colleagues in the administration; and on February 21, President Johnson, anxious to obtain a court test of the act he believed obviously unconstitutional, again notified Stanton that he had been summarily removed from the office of Secretary of War.

While Stanton, refusing to yield possession, barricaded himself in his office, public opinion in the nation ran heavily against the President. He had intentionally broken the law and dictatorially thwarted the will of Congress! Although previous resolutions of impeachment had been defeated in the House, both in committee and on the floor, a new resolution was swiftly reported and adopted on February 24 by a tremendous vote. Every single Republican voted in the affirmative, and Thaddeus Stevens of Pennsylvania—the crippled, fanatical personification of the extremes of the Radical Republican movement, master of the House of Representatives, with a mouth like the thin edge of an ax—warned both Houses of the Congress coldly: "Let me see the recreant who would vote to let such a criminal escape. Point me to one who will dare do it and I will show you one who will dare the infamy of posterity."

With the President impeached—in effect, indicted—by the House, the frenzied trial for his conviction or acquittal under the Articles of Impeachment began on March 5 in the Senate, presided over by the Chief Justice. It was a trial to rank with all the great trials in history— Charles I before the High Court of Justice, Louis XVI before the French Convention, and Warren Hastings before the House of Lords. Two great elements of drama were missing: the actual cause for which the President was being tried was not fundamental to the welfare of the nation; and the defendant himself was at all times absent.

But every other element of the highest courtroom drama was present. To each Senator the Chief Justice administered an oath "to do impartial justice" (including even the hot-headed Radical Senator from Ohio, Benjamin Wade, who as President Pro Tempore of the Senate was next in line for the Presidency). The chief prosecutor for the House was General Benjamin F. Butler, the "butcher of New Orleans," a talented but coarse and demagogic Congressman from Massachusetts. (When he lost his seat in 1874, he was so hated by his own party as well as his opponents that one Republican wired concerning the Democratic sweep, "Butler defeated, everything else lost.") Some one thousand tickets were printed for admission to the Senate galleries during the trial, and every conceivable device was used to obtain one of the four tickets allotted each Senator.

From the fifth of March to the sixteenth of May, the drama continued. Of the eleven Articles of Impeachment adopted by the House, the first eight were based upon the removal of Stanton and the appointment of a new Secretary of War in violation of the Tenure-of-Office Act; the ninth related to Johnson's conversation with a general which was said to induce violations of the Army Appropriations Act; the tenth recited that Johnson had delivered "intemperate, inflammatory and scandalous harangues . . . as well against Congress as the laws of the United

States"; and the eleventh was a deliberately obscure conglomeration of all the charges in the preceding articles, which had been designed by Thaddeus Stevens to furnish a common ground for those who favored conviction but were unwilling to identify themselves on basic issues. In opposition to Butler's inflammatory arguments in support of this hastily drawn indictment, Johnson's able and learned counsel replied with considerable effectiveness. They insisted that the Tenure-of-Office Act was null and void as a clear violation of the Constitution; that even if it were valid, it would not apply to Stanton, for the reasons previously mentioned; and that the only way that a judicial test of the law could be obtained was for Stanton to be dismissed and sue for his rights in the courts.

But as the trial progressed, it became increasingly apparent that the impatient Republicans did not intend to give the President a fair trial on the formal issues upon which the impeachment was drawn, but intended instead to depose him from the White House on any grounds, real or imagined, for refusing to accept their policies. Telling evidence in the President's favor was arbitrarily excluded. Prejudgment on the part of most Senators was brazenly announced. Attempted bribery and other forms of pressure were rampant. The chief interest was not in the trial or the evidence, but in the tallying of votes necessary for conviction.

Twenty-seven states (excluding the unrecognized Southern states) in the Union meant fifty-four members of the Senate, and thirty-six votes were required to constitute the two-thirds majority necessary for conviction. All twelve Democratic votes were obviously lost, and the forty-two Republicans knew that they could afford to lose only six of their own members if Johnson were to be ousted. To their dismay, at a preliminary Republican caucus, six courageous Republicans indicated that the evidence so far introduced was not in their opinion sufficient to convict Johnson under the Articles of Impeachment. "Infamy!" cried the Philadelphia *Press*. The Republic has "been betrayed in the house of its friends!"

But if the remaining thirty-six Republicans would hold, there would be no doubt as to the outcome. All must stand together! But one Republican Senator would not announce his verdict in the preliminary poll— Edmund G. Ross of Kansas. The Radicals were outraged that a Senator from such an anti-Johnson stronghold as Kansas could be doubtful. "It was a very clear case," Senator Sumner of Massachusetts fumed, "especially for a Kansas man. I did not think that a Kansas man could quibble against his country."

From the very time Ross had taken his seat, the Radical leaders had been confident of his vote. His entire background, as already indicated, was one of firm support of their cause. One of his first acts in the Senate had been to read a declaration of his adherence to Radical Republican policy, and he had silently voted for all of their measures. He had made it clear that he was not in sympathy with Andrew Johnson personally or politically; and after the removal of Stanton, he had voted with the majority in adopting a resolution declaring such removal unlawful. His colleague from Kansas, Senator Pomeroy, was one of the most Radical leaders of the anti-Johnson group. The Republicans insisted that Ross's crucial vote was rightfully theirs, and they were determined to get it by whatever means available. As stated by DeWitt in his memorable *Impeachment of Andrew Johnson,* "The full brunt of the struggle turned at last on the one remaining doubtful Senator, Edmund G. Ross."

When the impeachment resolution had passed the House, Senator Ross had casually remarked to Senator Sprague of Rhode Island, "Well, Sprague, the thing is here; and, so far as I am concerned, though a Republican and opposed to Mr. Johnson and his policy, he shall have as fair a trial as an accused man ever had on this earth." Immediately the word spread that "Ross was shaky." "From that hour," he later wrote, "not a day passed that did not bring me, by mail and telegraph and in personal intercourse, appeals to stand fast for impeachment, and not a few were the admonitions of condign visitations upon any indication even of lukewarmness."

Throughout the country, and in all walks of life, as indicated by the correspondence of Members of the Senate, the condition of the public mind was not unlike that preceding a great battle. The dominant party of the nation seemed to occupy the position of public prosecutor, and it was scarcely in the mood to brook delay for trial or to hear defense. Washington had become during the trial the central point of the politically dissatisfied and swarmed with representatives of every state of the Union, demanding in a practically united voice the deposition of the President. The footsteps of the anti-impeaching Republicans were dogged from the day's beginning to its end and far into the night, with entreaties, considerations, and threats. The newspapers came daily filled with not a few threats of violence upon their return to their constituents.

Ross and his fellow doubtful Republicans were daily pestered, spied upon and subjected to every form of pressure. Their residences were carefully watched, their social circles suspiciously scrutinized, and their every move and companions secretly marked in special notebooks. They were warned in the party press, harangued by their constituents, and sent dire warnings threatening political ostracism and even assassination. Stanton himself, from his barricaded headquarters in the War Department, worked day and night to bring to bear upon the doubtful Senators all the weight of his impressive military associations. The Philadelphia *Press* reported "a fearful avalanche of telegrams from every section of the country," a great surge of public opinion from the "common people" who had given their money and lives to the country and would not "willingly or unavenged see their great sacrifice made naught."

The New York *Tribune* reported that Edmund Ross in particular was "mercilessly dragged this way and that by both sides, hunted like a fox night and day and badgered by his own colleagues, like the bridge at Arcola now trod upon by one Army and now trampled by the other." His background and life were investigated from top to bottom, and his constituents and colleagues pursued him throughout Washington to gain some inkling of his opinion. He was the target of every eye, his name was on every mouth and his intentions were discussed in every newspaper. Although there is evidence that he gave some hint of agreement to each side, and each attempted to claim him publicly, he actually kept both sides in a state of complete suspense by his judicial silence.

But with no experience in political turmoil, no reputation in the Senate, no independent income and the most radical state in the Union to deal with, Ross was judged to be the most sensitive to criticism and the most certain to be swayed by expert tactics. A committee of Congressmen and Senators sent to Kansas, and to the states of other doubtful Republicans, this telegram: "Great danger to the peace of the country and the Republican cause if impeachment fails. Send to your Senators public opinion by resolutions, letters, and delegations." A member of the Kansas legislature called upon Ross at the Capitol. A general urged on by Stanton remained at his lodge until four o'clock in the morning determined to see him. His brother received a letter offering $20,000 for revelation of the Senator's intentions. Gruff Ben Butler exclaimed of Ross, "There is a bushel of money! How much does the damned scoundrel want?" The night before the Senate was to take its first vote for the conviction or acquittal of Johnson, Ross received this telegram from home:

Kansas has heard the evidence and demands the conviction of the President.
(*signed*) D. R. ANTHONY AND 1,000 OTHERS

And on that fateful morning of May 16 Ross replied:

To D. R. Anthony and 1,000 Others: I do not recognize your right to demand that I vote either for or against conviction. I have taken an oath to do impartial justice according to the Constitution and laws, and trust that I shall have the courage to vote according to the dictates of my judgment and for the highest good of the country.
[signed]—E. G. Ross

That morning spies traced Ross to his breakfast; and ten minutes before the vote was taken his Kansas colleague warned him in the presence of Thaddeus Stevens that a vote for acquittal would mean trumped up charges and his political death.

But now the fateful hour was at hand. Neither escape, delay or indecision was possible. As Ross himself later described it: "The galleries were packed. Tickets of admission were at an enormous premium. The House had adjourned and all of its members were in the Senate chamber. Every chair on the Senate floor was filled with a Senator, a Cabinet Officer, a member of the President's counsel or a member of the House." Every Senator was in his seat, the desperately ill Grimes of Iowa being literally carried in.

It had been decided to take the first vote under that broad Eleventh Article of Impeachment, believed to command the widest support. As the Chief Justice announced the voting would begin, he reminded "the citizens and strangers in the galleries that absolute silence and perfect order are required." But already a deathlike stillness enveloped the Senate chamber. A Congressman later recalled that "Some of the members of the House near me grew pale and sick under the burden of suspense"; and Ross noted that there was even "a subsidence of the shuffling of feet, the rustling of silks, the fluttering of fans, and of conversation."

The voting tensely commenced. By the time the Chief Justice reached the name of Edmund Ross twenty-four "guilties" had been pronounced. Ten more were certain and one other practically certain. Only Ross's vote was needed to obtain the thirty-six votes necessary to convict the President. But not a single person in the room knew how this young Kansan would vote. Unable to conceal the suspense and emotion in his voice, the Chief Justice put the question to him: "Mr. Senator Ross, how say you? Is the respondent Andrew Johnson guilty or not guilty of a high misdemeanor as charged in this Article?" Every voice was still; every eye was upon the freshman Senator from Kansas. The hopes and fears, the hatred and bitterness of past decades were centered upon this one man.

As Ross himself later described it, his "powers of hearing and seeing seemed developed in an abnormal degree."

Every individual in that great audience seemed distinctly visible, some with lips apart and bending forward in anxious expectancy, others with hand uplifted as if to ward off an apprehended blow . . . and each peering with an intensity that was almost tragic upon the face of him who was about to cast the fateful vote. . . . Every fan was folded, not a foot moved, not the rustle of a garment, nor a whisper was heard. . . . Hope and fear seemed blended in every face, instantaneously alternating, some with revengeful hate . . . others lighted with hope. . . . The Senators in their seats leaned over their desks, many with hand to ear. . . . It was a tremendous responsibility, and it was not strange that he upon whom it had been imposed by a fateful combination of conditions should have sought to avoid it, to put it away from him as one shuns, or tries to fight off, a nightmare. . . . I almost literally looked down into my open grave. Friendships, position, fortune, everything that makes life desirable to an ambitious man were about to be swept away by the breath of my mouth, perhaps forever. It is not strange that my answer was carried waveringly over the air and failed to reach the limits of the audience, or that repetition was called for by distant Senators on the opposite side of the Chamber.

Then came the answer again in a voice that could not be misunderstood—full, final, definite, unhesitating and unmistakable: "Not guilty." The deed was done, the President saved, the trial as good as over and the conviction lost. The remainder of the roll call was unimportant, conviction had failed by the margin of a single vote and a general rumbling filled the chamber until the Chief Justice proclaimed that "on this Article thirty-five Senators having voted guilty and nineteen not guilty, a two-thirds majority not having voted for conviction, the President is, therefore, acquitted under this Article."

A ten-day recess followed, ten turbulent days to change votes on the remaining Articles. An attempt was made to rush through bills to readmit six Southern states, whose twelve Senators were guaranteed to vote for conviction. But this could not be accomplished in time. Again Ross was the only one uncommitted on the other Articles, the only one whose vote could not be predicted in advance. And again he was subjected to terrible pressure. From "D. R. Anthony and others," he received a wire informing him that "Kansas repudiates you as she does all perjurers and skunks." Every incident in his life was examined and distorted. Professional witnesses were found by Senator Pomeroy to testify before a special House committee that Ross had indicated a willingness to change his vote for a consideration. (Unfortunately this witness was so delighted in his exciting role that he also swore that Senator Pomeroy had made an offer to produce three votes for acquittal for $40,000.) When Ross, in his capacity as a Committee Chairman, took several bills to the President, James G. Blaine remarked: "There goes the rascal to get his pay." (Long afterward Blaine was to admit: "In the exaggerated denunciation caused by the anger and chagrin of the moment, great injustice was done to statesmen of spotless character.")

Again the wild rumors spread that Ross had been won over on the remaining Articles of Impeachment. As the Senate reassembled, he was the only one of the seven "renegade" Republicans to vote with the majority on preliminary procedural matters. But when the second and third Articles of Impeachment were read, and the name of Ross was reached again with the same intense suspense of ten days earlier, again came the calm answer "Not guilty."

Why did Ross, whose dislike for Johnson continued, vote "Not guilty"? His motives appear clearly from his own writings on the subject years later in articles contributed to *Scribner's* and *Forum* magazines:

In a large sense, the independence of the executive office as a coordinate branch of the government was on trial. . . . If . . . the President must step down . . . a disgraced man and a political outcast . . . upon insufficient proofs and from partisan considerations, the office of President would be degraded, cease to be a coordinate branch of the government, and ever after subordinated to the legislative will. It would practically have revolutionized our splendid political fabric into a partisan Congressional autocracy. . . . This government had never faced so insidious a danger . . . control by the worst element of American politics. . . . If Andrew Johnson were acquitted by a nonpartisan vote . . . America would pass the danger point of partisan rule and that intolerance which so often characterizes the sway of great majorities and makes them dangerous.

The "open grave" which Edmund Ross had foreseen was hardly an exaggeration. A Justice of the Kansas Supreme Court telegraphed him that "the rope with which Judas Iscariot hanged himself is lost, but Jim Lane's pistol is at your service." An editorial in a Kansas newspaper screamed:

On Saturday last Edmund G. Ross, United States Senator from Kansas, sold himself, and betrayed his constituents; stultified his own record, basely lied to his friends, shamefully violated his solemn pledge . . . and to the utmost of his poor ability signed the death warrant of his country's liberty. This act was done deliberately, because the traitor, like Benedict Arnold, loved money better than he did principle, friends, honor and his country, all combined. Poor, pitiful, shriveled wretch, with a soul so small that a little pelf would outweigh all things else that dignify or ennoble manhood.

Ross's political career was ended. To the New York *Tribune,* he was nothing but "a miserable poltroon and traitor." The Philadelphia *Press* said that in Ross "littleness" had "simply borne its legitimate fruit," and that he and his fellow recalcitrant Republicans had "plunged from a precipice of fame into the groveling depths of infamy and death." The Philadelphia *Inquirer* said that "They had tried, convicted and sentenced themselves." For them there could be "no allowance, no clemency."

Comparative peace returned to Washington as Stanton relinquished his office and Johnson served out the rest of his term, later—unlike his Republican defenders—to return triumphantly to the Senate as Senator from Tennessee. But no one paid attention when Ross tried unsuccessfully

to explain his vote, and denounced the falsehoods of Ben Butler's investigating committee, recalling that the General's "well known grovelling
instincts and proneness to slime and uncleanness" had led "the public to
insult the brute creation by dubbing him 'the beast.' " He clung unhappily
to his seat in the Senate until the expiration of his term, frequently referred to as "the traitor Ross," and complaining that his fellow Congressmen, as well as citizens on the street, considered association with him
"disreputable and scandalous," and passed him by as if he were "a leper,
with averted face and every indication of hatred and disgust."

Neither Ross nor any other Republican who had voted for the
acquittal of Johnson was ever re-elected to the Senate, not a one of them
retaining the support of their party's organization. When he returned to
Kansas in 1871, he and his family suffered social ostracism, physical
attack, and near poverty.

Who was Edmund G. Ross? Practically nobody. Not a single public
law bears his name, not a single history book includes his picture, not a
single list of Senate "greats" mentions his service. His one heroic deed
has been all but forgotten. But who might Edmund G. Ross have been?
That is the question—for Ross, a man with an excellent command of
words, an excellent background for politics and an excellent future in
the Senate might well have outstripped his colleagues in prestige and
power throughout a long Senate career. Instead, he chose to throw all of
this away for one act of conscience.

But the twisting course of human events eventually upheld the faith
he expressed to his wife shortly after the trial: "Millions of men cursing
me today will bless me tomorrow for having saved the country from the
greatest peril through which it has ever passed, though none but God can
ever know the struggle it has cost me." For twenty years later Congress
repealed the Tenure-of-Office Act, to which every President after Johnson, regardless of party, had objected; and still later the Supreme Court,
referring to "the extremes of that episode in our government," held it to
be unconstitutional. Ross moved to New Mexico, where in his later years
he was to be appointed Territorial Governor. Just prior to his death when
he was awarded a special pension by Congress for his service in the Civil
War, the press and the country took the opportunity to pay tribute to his
fidelity to principle in a trying hour and his courage in saving his government from a devastating reign of terror. They now agreed with Ross's
earlier judgment that his vote had "saved the country from . . . a strain
that would have wrecked any other form of government." Those Kansas
newspapers and political leaders who had bitterly denounced him in
earlier years praised Ross for his stand against legislative mob rule: "By
the firmness and courage of Senator Ross," it was said, "the country was

saved from calamity greater than war, while it consigned him to a political martyrdom, the most cruel in our history. . . . Ross was the victim of a wild flame of intolerance which swept everything before it. He did his duty knowing that it meant his political death. . . . It was a brave thing for Ross to do, but Ross did it. He acted for his conscience and with a lofty patriotism, regardless of what he knew must be the ruinous consequences to himself. He acted right."

• *Questions for Study*

1. Kennedy wrote this selection as part of *Profiles in Courage* when he was a senator. What interesting implications are there now concerning the author and his choice of subject?
2. By means of what specific devices does Kennedy make the events of the impeachment dramatic and interesting? What devices are the most effective? The least effective? Why does he prolong suspense after the Chief Justice has asked the fatal question? Does he overdo the suspense?
3. Consider the character of Ross in connection with Carlyle's observations on the hero in "The Hero as King" and with Machiavelli's concept of the dissimulating leader in "The Conduct of a Prince." Would Carlyle have admired a man like Ross? Would Machiavelli have considered him an able leader?
4. If the great majority of Ross's Kansan constitutents were for impeachment, can we say that Ross failed in his moral obligation to reflect their will since he was their appointed spokesman? Defend or criticize Ross's action.
5. Do you think that "legislative mob rule" is possible today? Explain.

LEARNED HAND

•

FREEDOM OF DISSENT

What do we mean by "principles of civil liberties and human rights"? We cannot go far in that inquiry until we have achieved some notion of what we mean by Liberty; and that has always proved a hard concept to define. The natural, though naïve, opinion is that it means no more than that each individual shall be allowed to pursue his own desires without let or hindrance; and that, although it is true that this is practically impossible, still it does remain the goal, approach to which measures our success. Why, then, is not a beehive or an anthill a perfect example of a free society? Surely you have been a curious and amused watcher beside one of these.

In and out of their crowded pueblo the denizens pass in great number, each bent upon his own urgent mission, quite oblivious of all the rest except as he must bend his path to avoid them. It is a scene of strenuous, purposeful endeavor in which each appears to be, and no doubt in fact is, accomplishing his own purpose; and yet he is at the same time accomplishing the purpose of the group as a whole. As I have gazed at it, the sentence from the Collect of the Episcopal prayer-book has come to me: "Whose service is perfect freedom."

Why is it, then, that we so positively rebel against the hive and the hill as a specimen of a free society? Why is it that such prototypes of totalitarianisms arouse our deepest hostility? Unhappily it is not because they cannot be realized, or at least because they cannot be approached, for a substantial period. Who can be sure that such appalling forecasts as Aldous Huxley's *Brave New World* or Orwell's *1984* are not prophetic? Indeed, there have often been near approaches to such an order.

Germany at the end of 1940 was probably not far removed from one, and who of us knows that there are not countless persons today living within the boundaries of Russia and perhaps of China who are not willing partners, accepting as their personal aspirations the official definitions of the good, the true and the beautiful? Indeed, there have been, and still are, in our own United States large and powerful groups who, if we are to judge their purposes by their conduct, see treason in all dissidence and would welcome an era in which all of us should think, feel and live in consonance with duly prescribed patterns.

Human nature is malleable, especially if you can indoctrinate the disciple with indefectible principles before anyone else reaches him. (I fancy that the Janissaries were as fervent Mohammedans as the authentic Turks.) Indeed, we hear from those who are entitled to an opinion that at times the abject confessions made in Russia by victims who know that they are already marked for slaughter are not wrung from them by torture or threats against their families. Rather, they come from partisans, so obsessed with the faith that when they are told that the occasion calls for scapegoats and that they have been selected, recognize and assent to the propriety of the demand and cooperate in its satisfaction. It is as though when the right time comes, the drones agreed to their extinction in the interest of the hive.

Nor need we be surprised that men so often embrace almost any doctrines, if they are proclaimed with a voice of absolute assurance. In a universe that we do not understand, but with which we must in one way or another somehow manage to deal, and aware of the conflicting desires that clamorously beset us, between which we must choose and which we must therefore manage to weigh, we turn in our bewilderment to those who tell us that they have found a path out of the thickets and possess the scales by which to appraise our needs.

Over and over again such prophets succeed in converting us to unquestioning acceptance; there is scarcely a monstrous belief that has not had its day and its passionate adherents, so eager are we for safe footholds in our dubious course. How certain is any one of us that he, too, might not be content to follow any fantastic creed, if he was satisfied that nothing would ever wake him from the dream? And, indeed, if there were nothing to wake him, how should he distinguish its articles from the authentic dictates of verity?

Remember, too, that it is by no means clear that we are happier in the faith we do profess than we should be under the spell of an orthodoxy that was safe against all heresy. Cruel and savage as orthodoxies have always proved to be, the faithful seem able to convince themselves that the heretics, as they continue to crop up, get nothing worse than their due, and to rest with an easy conscience.

In any event, my thesis is that the best answer to such systems is not so much in their immoral quality—immoral though they be—as in the fact that they are inherently unstable, because they are at war with our only trustworthy way of living in accord with the facts. For I submit that it is only by trial and error, by insistent scrutiny and by readiness to re-examine presently accredited conclusions that we have risen, so far as in fact we have risen, from our brutish ancestors, and I believe that in our loyalty to these habits lies our only chance, not merely of progress, but even of survival.

They were not indeed a part of our aboriginal endowment: Man, as he emerged, was not prodigally equipped to master the infinite diversity of his environment. Obviously, enough of us did manage to get through; but it has been a statistical survival, for the individual's native powers of adjustment are by no means enough for his personal safety any more than are those of other creatures. The precipitate of our experience is far from absolute verity, and our exasperated resentment at all dissent is a sure index of our doubts. Take, for instance, our constant recourse to the word, "subversive," as a touchstone of impermissible deviation from accepted canons.

All discussions, all debate, all dissidence tends to question and in consequence to upset existing convictions: that is precisely its purpose and its justification. He is, indeed, a "subversive" who disputes those precepts that I most treasure and seeks to persuade me to substitute his own. He may have no shadow of desire to resort to anything but persuasion; he may be of those to whom any forcible sanction of conformity is anathema; yet it remains true that he is trying to bring about my apostasy, and I hate him just in proportion as I fear his success.

Contrast this protective resentment with the assumption that lies at the base of our whole system that the best chance for truth to emerge is a fair field for all ideas. Nothing, I submit, more completely betrays our latent disloyalty to this premise to all that we pretend to believe than the increasingly common resort to this and other question-begging words. Their imprecision comforts us by enabling us to suppress arguments that disturb our complacency and yet to continue to congratulate ourselves on keeping the faith as we have received it from the Founding Fathers.

Heretics have been hateful from the beginning of recorded time; they have been ostracized, exiled, tortured, maimed and butchered;

but it has generally proved impossible to smother them, and when it has not, the society that has succeeded has always declined. Facades of authority, however imposing, do not survive after it has appeared that they rest upon the sands of human conjecture and compromise.

And so, if I am to say what are "the principles of civil liberties and human rights," I answer that they lie in habits, customs—conventions, if you will—that tolerate dissent and can live without irrefragable certainties; that are already to overhaul existing assumptions; that recognize that we never see save through a glass, darkly, and that at long last we shall succeed only so far as we continue to undertake "the intolerable labor of thought"—that most distasteful of all our activities.

If such a habit and such a temper pervade a society, it will not need institutions to protect its "civil liberties and human rights"; so far as they do not, I venture to doubt how far anything else can protect them: whether it be Bills of Rights, or courts that must in the name of interpretations read their meaning into them.

This may seem to you a bleak and cheerless conclusion, too alien to our nature to be practical. "We must live from day to day"—you will say—"to live is to act, and to act is to choose and decide. How can we carry on at all without some principles, some patterns to meet the conflicts in which each day involves us?" Indeed, we cannot, nor am I suggesting that we should try; and I *am* suggesting that it makes a vital difference—*the* vital difference—whether we deem our principles and our patterns to be eternal verities, rather than the best postulates so far attainable.

Was it not Holmes who said: "The highest courage is to stake everything on a premise that you know tomorrow's evidence may disprove"? "Ah"—you will reply—"there's the rub. That may be the highest courage, but how many have it? You are hopelessly wrong if you assume the general prevalence of such a virtue; ordinary men must be given more than conjectures if they are to face grave dangers."

But do you really believe that? Do you not see about you every day and everywhere the precise opposite? Not alone on the battlefield but in the forest, the desert and the plain; in the mountains, at sea, on the playing field, even in the laboratory and the factory—yes (do not laugh), at the card table and the racetrack—men are forever putting it "upon the touch to win or lose it all." Without some smack of uncertainty and danger, to most of us the world would be a tepid, pallid show.

Surely, like me, you have all felt something of this when you have looked on those pathetic attempts to depict in paint or stone the delights of Paradise. I own that the torments of hell never fail to horrify me; not even the glee of the demons in charge is an adequate relief, though the artist has generally been successful in giving a veracious impression of the gusto with which they discharge their duties.

But when I turn to the Congregation of the Blessed, I cannot avoid a sense of anti-climax; strive as I may, the social atmosphere seems a bit forced; and I recall those very irreverent verses of Lowes Dickinson:

> Burning at first no doubt would be worse,
> But time the impression would soften,
> While those who are bored with praising the Lord,
> Would be more bored with praising him often.

By some happy fortuity man is a projector, a designer, a builder, a craftsman; it is among his most dependable joys to impose upon the flux that passes before him some mark of himself, aware though he always must be of the odds against him. His reward is not so much in the work as in its making; not so much in the prize as in the race. We may win when we lose, if we have done what we can; for by so doing we have made real at least some part of that finished product in whose fabrication we are most concerned—ourselves.

And if at the end some friendly critic shall pass by and say, "My friend, how good a job do you really think you have made of it all?" we can answer, "I know as well as you that it is not of high quality, but I did put into it whatever I had, and that was the game I started out to play."

It is still in the lap of the gods whether a society can succeed, based on "civil liberties and human rights," conceived as I have tried to describe them; but of one thing at least we may be sure: the alternatives that have so far appeared have been immeasurably worse, and so, whatever the outcome, I submit to you that we must press along. Borrowing from Epictetus, let us say to ourselves: "Since we are men we will play the part of a Man," and how can I better end than by recalling to you the concluding passage of "Prometheus Unbound"?

> To suffer woes which Hope thinks infinite;
> To forgive wrongs darker than death or night;
> To defy Power, which seems omnipotent
> To love, and bear; to hope till Hope creates
> From its own wreck the thing it contemplates;
> Neither to change, nor falter, nor repent;
> This, like thy glory, Titan, is to be
> Good, great and joyous, beautiful and free;
> This is alone Life, Joy, Empire and Victory.

• *Questions for Study*

1. Sum up Learned Hand's view of the importance of liberty. How does liberty depend for its vitality upon dissent?
2. Hand uses insect hives as an analogy to clarify his concept of an enslaved society. For what reasons is this analogy effective?
3. Do you find any examples that fail to illustrate clearly the author's meaning?
4. How do the poems illustrate what the author is trying to say? In what ways does ending the essay with Shelley's lines make the conclusion effective?
5. Write a theme in which you explore the extent to which individual liberty conflicts with the good of society as a whole. You may wish to focus upon one or two of the following specific situations in your discussion: the liberty of an individual to get drunk; the refusal of an individual to take a loyalty oath; the right of a driver to pass a red light.

CLINTON ROSSITER

•

THE CONSERVATIVE VIEW

OF MAN AND SOCIETY

The Conservative holds rather strong opinions about man's nature, his capacity for self-government, his relations with other men, the kind of life he should lead, and the rights he may properly claim. On these opinions, which taken together represent a stiff questioning of the bright promises of Liberalism, rests the whole Conservative tradition.

Man, says the Conservative (who conceals only poorly his distaste for such an abstraction), is a fabulous composite of some good and much evil, a blend of several ennobling excellencies and several more degrading imperfections. "Man is not entirely corrupt and depraved," William McGovern and David Collier have written, "but to state that he is, is to come closer to the truth than to state that he is essentially good." As no man is perfect, so no man is perfectible. If educated properly, placed in a favorable environment, and held in restraint by tradition and authority, he may display innate qualities of rationality, sociability, industry, and decency. Never, no matter how he is educated or situated or restrained, will he throw off completely his other innate qualities of irrationality, selfishness, laziness, depravity, corruptibility, and cruelty. Man's nature is essentially immutable, and the immutable strain is one of deep-seated wickedness. Although some Conservatives find support for their skeptical view of man in recent experiments in psychology, most continue to rely on religious teaching and the study of history. Those who are Christians, and most Conservatives are, prefer to call the motivation for iniquitous and irrational behavior by its proper name: Original Sin.

The Conservative is often accused of putting too much stress on man's wickedness and irrationality and of overlooking his many good qualities, especially his capacity for reason. The Conservative's answer is candid enough. While he is well aware of man's potentialities, he must counter the optimism of the Liberal with certain cheerless reminders that are no less true for telling not quite all the truth: that evil exists independently of social or economic maladjustments; that we must search for the source of our discontents in defective human nature rather than in a defective social order; and that man, far from being malleable, is subject to cultural alteration only slowly and to a limited degree. The Conservative therefore considers it his stern duty to call attention, as did John Adams, to the "general frailty and depravity of human nature" and to the weakness of reason as a guide to personal conduct or collective endeavor. He is, in his most candid moments, an admirer of instinct, the "innate feeling for the good and the bad," and at least an apologist for prejudice, "the poor man's wisdom."

This view of human nature is saved from churlish cynicism by two beliefs. First, man is touched with eternity. He has a precious soul; he is a religious entity. His urges toward sin are matched, and with God's grace can be overmatched if never finally beaten down, by his aspiration for good. For this reason, the Conservative asserts man is an object of reverence, and a recognition of man's heaven-ordained shortcomings serves only to deepen this reverence. Second, to quote from Burke, the father of all Conservatives, "The nature of man is intricate." The confession of an eminent psychologist, Gardner Murphy, "Not much, I believe, is known about man," is applauded by the Conservative, who then adds, "Not much, I believe, will ever be known about him." Man is a mysterious and complex being, and no amount of psychological research will ever solve the mystery or unravel the complexity.

No truth about human nature and capabilities, the Conservative says, is more important than this: man can govern himself, but there is no certainty that he will; free government is possible but far from inevitable. Man will need all the help he can get from education, religion, tradition, and institutions if he is to enjoy even a limited success in his experiments in self-government. He must be counseled, encouraged, informed, and checked. Above all, he must realize that the collective wisdom of the community, itself the union of countless partial and imperfect wisdoms like his own, is alone equal to this mightiest of social tasks. A clear recognition of man's conditional capacity for ruling himself and others is the first requisite of constitution-making.

The Conservatism that celebrates Burke holds out obstinately against two popular beliefs about human relations in modern society: individualism and equality. Putting off a discussion of individualism for a few pages, let us hear what the Conservative has to say about the explosive question of equality.

Each man is equal to every other man in only one meaningful sense: he is a man, a physical and spiritual entity, and is thus entitled by God and nature to be treated as end rather than means. From the basic fact of moral equality come several secondary equalities that the modern Conservative recognizes, more eloquently in public than in private: equality of opportunity, the right of each individual to exploit his own talents up to their natural limits; equality before the law, the right to justice on the same terms as other men; and political equality, which takes the form—and a rather distressing form it often seems —of universal suffrage. Beyond this the Conservative is unwilling to go. Recognizing the infinite variety among men in talent, taste, appearance, intelligence, and virtue, he is candid enough to assert that this variety extends vertically as well as horizontally. Men are grossly unequal— and, what is more, can never be made equal—in most qualities of mind, body, and spirit.

The good society of Conservatism rests solidly on this great truth. The social order is organized in such a way as to take advantage of ineradicable natural distinctions among men. It exhibits a class struc-ture in which there are several quite distinct levels, most men find their level early and stay in it without rancor, and equality of opportunity keeps the way at least partially open to ascent and decline. At the same time, the social order aims to temper those distinctions that are not natural. While it recognizes the inevitability and indeed the necessity of orders and classes, it insists that all privileges, ranks, and other visible signs of inequality be as natural and functional as possible. The Conservative, of course—and this point is of decisive importance—is much more inclined than other men to consider artificial distinctions as natural. Equity rather than equality is the mark of his society; the reconciliation rather than the abolition of classes is his constant aim. When he is forced to choose between liberty and equality, he throws his support unhesitatingly to liberty. Indeed, the preference for liberty over equality lies at the root of the Conservative tradition, and men who subscribe to this tradition never tire of warning against the "rage for equality."

While Conservatism has retreated some distance from Burke and Adams under the pressures of modern democracy, it has refused to yield one salient: the belief in a ruling, serving, taste-making aristocracy. "If there is any one point," Gertrude Himmelfarb writes, "any single empirical test, by which conservatism can be distinguished from liberalism, it is a respect for aristocracy and aristocratic institutions. Every tenet of liberalism repudiates the idea of a fixed aristocracy; every tenet of conservatism affirms it." If it is no longer good form to use the word "aristocracy" in political debate, nor good sense to expect that an aristocracy can be "fixed" to the extent that it was one hundred and fifty years ago, the Conservative is still moved powerfully by the urge to seek out the "best men" and place them in positions of authority. Remembering Burke's warning that without the aristocracy "there is no nation," he continues to assert the beneficence of a gentry of talent and virtue, one that is trained for special service and thus entitled to special consideration. He continues to believe that it takes more than one generation to make a genuine aristocrat. His best men are "best" in manners as well as in morals, in birth as well as in talents.

The world being what it is today, the Conservative spends a good deal of his time in the pulpit exhorting his fellow men to live godly, righteous, and sober lives. He does not do this gladly, for he is not by nature a Puritan, but the times seem to have made him our leading "moral athlete."

Man, the Conservative asserts, is stamped with sin and carnality, but he is also blessed with higher aspirations. If human nature in general can never be much improved, each individual may nevertheless bring his own savage and selfish impulses under control. It is his duty to himself, his fellows, and God to do just this—to shun vice, cultivate virtue, and submit to the guidance of what Lincoln called "the better angels of our nature." Only thus, through the moral striving of many men, can free government be secured and society be made stable.

What virtues must the individual cultivate? The Conservative of the tower, the Conservative of the field, the Conservative of the market place, and the Conservative of the assembly each give a somewhat different answer to this question, yet all seem to agree to this catalogue of primary virtues: wisdom, justice, temperance, and courage; industry, frugality, piety, and honesty; contentment, obedience, compassion, and manners. The good man is peaceful but not resigned and is conservative through habit and choice rather than sloth and cowardice. He assumes that duty comes before pleasure, self-sacrifice before self-indulgence. Believing that the test of life is accomplishment rather than enjoyment, he takes pride in doing a good job in the station to which he has been called. He is alert to the identity and malignity of the vices he must shun: ignorance, injustice, intemperance, and cowardice; laziness, luxury, selfishness, and dishonesty; envy, disobedience, violence, and bad manners. And he is aware, too, of the larger implications of his own life of virtue: self-government is for moral men; those who would be free must be virtuous.

At the center of that constellation of virtues which make up the good man (who is also, needless to say, the good Conservative) is prudence. "Prudence," Burke wrote, "is not only first in rank of the virtues political and moral, but she is the director" of all the others. The literature of Conservatism spends a good deal more time celebrating this quality than defining it, yet there is no doubt that it represents a cluster of urges—toward caution, deliberation, and discretion, toward moderation and calculation, toward old ways and good form—which gives every other standard virtue a special look when displayed by a true Conservative.

Education looms importantly in the literature of Conservatism, for it is the road that leads through virtue to freedom. Only through education—in family, church, and school—can children be shaped into civilized men. Only through education can man's vices, which are tough, be brought under control and his virtues, which are frail, be nourished into robust health. The instruments of education should teach a man to think, survive, ply a trade, and enjoy his leisure. Their great mission, however, it to act as a conserving, civilizing force: to convey to each man his share of the inherited wisdom of the race, to train him to lead a moral, self-disciplined life, and to foster a love of order and respect for authority.

The Conservative's understanding of the mission of education explains his profound mistrust of modern theories, most of which, he feels, are grounded in a clear misreading of the nature and needs of children. The school has always been a conservative force in society, and the Conservative means to keep it that way. He admits that there is a stage in the education of some individuals—those who are to go on to leadership—when self-development and self-expression should get prime consideration. First things must come first, however, and before this stage is reached, the individual must be taught his community's values and be integrated into its structure.

Before we can describe the Conservative consensus on freedom and responsibility, we must learn more of the circumstances in which men can enjoy the one because they accept the other.

Some of the Conservative's best thoughts are directed to society and the social process. The key points of his social theory appear to be these:

Society is a living organism with roots deep in the past. The true community, the Conservative likes to say, is a tree, not a machine. It rose to its present strength and glory through centuries of growth, and men must forbear to think of it as a mechanical contrivance that can be dismantled and reassembled in one generation. Not fiat but prescription, not the open hand of experiment but the hidden hand of custom, is the chief creative force in the social process.

Society is cellular. It is not an agglomeration of lonely individuals, but a grand union of functional groups. Man is a social animal whose best interests are served by cooperating with other men. Indeed, he has no real meaning except as contributing member of his family, church, local community, and, at certain stages of historical development, occupational association. The group is important not only because it gives life, work, comfort, and spiritual support to the individual, but because it joins with thousands of other groups to form the one really stubborn roadblock against the march of the all-powerful state. The Conservative is careful not to ride the cellular analogy too hard, for he is aware that it can lead to a social theory in which man loses all dignity and personality.

In addition to intrinsic groups like the family and church, a healthy society will display a balanced combination of "institutions": constitution, common law, monarchy or presidency, legislature, courts, civil service, armed services and subdivisions, colleges, schools, forms of property, corporations, trade unions, guilds, fraternal orders, and dozens of other instrumentalities and understandings that mold the lives of men. Such symbols of tradition, of national unity and continuity, as anthems, flags, rituals, battlefields, monuments, and pantheons of heroes are equally dear to the Conservative heart. All men are staunch defenders of the institutions that meet their practical and spiritual needs, but the Conservative places special trust in them. "Individuals may form communities," Disraeli warned, "but it is institutions alone that can create a nation."

Society is structured. The Conservative, as we have learned already, recognizes the existence of classes and orders as a positive good. By no means wedded to the habit of making rigid distinctions, he sees the social structure not as a series of neat strata laid one on top of another, but, in Coleridge's phrase, as "an indissoluble blending and interfusion of persons from top to bottom." There must, in any case, be a top, visible and reasonably durable; and it is not surprising that the self-conscious Conservative is usually to be found in or around it.

Society is a unity. In the healthy community all these groups and institutions and classes fit together into a harmonious whole, and attempts to reshape one part of society must inevitably disturb other parts. The Conservative, though something of a pluralist, never loses sight of the ultimate unity into which all the parts of society must finally merge.

Society cannot be static. Change is the rule of life, for societies as for men. A community cannot stand still; it must develop or decay. And the Conservative must not be afraid to abandon patently outworn institutions and ideals. In the words of Tennyson's *Hands All Round:*

> *May Freedom's oak forever live*
> *With stronger life from day to day;*
> *That man's the true Conservative,*
> *Who lops the moulder'd branch away.*

"Society must alter," Russell Kirk acknowledges, "for slow change is the means of its conservation, like the human body's perpetual renewal." In recognizing, however grudgingly, this great social truth, the Conservative shows himself to be neither a reactionary nor a standpatter. Yet he is just as emphatically not a liberal or radical, and he therefore sets servere conditions upon social change, especially if it is to be worked by active reform. Change, he insists, must never be taken for its own sake; must have preservation, if possible even restoration, as its central object; must be severely limited in scope and purpose; must be a response to an undoubted social need—for example, the renovation or elimination of an institution that is plainly obsolete; must be worked out by slow and careful stages; must be brought off under Conservative auspices, or with Conservatives intervening at the decisive moment (this is known as "stealing the Whigs' clothes"); and finally, in Disraeli's words, must "be carried out in deference to the manners, the customs, the laws, the traditions of the people." The essence of Conservatism is the feeling for the possibilities and limits of natural, organic change, and the kindred feeling that, in the words of McGovern and Collier, "while change is constant and inevitable, progress is neither constant nor inevitable." In the eloquent phrases of R. J. White of Cambridge:

To discover the order which inheres in things rather than to impose an order upon them; to strengthen and perpetuate that order rather than to dispose things anew according to some formula which may be nothing more than a fashion; to legislate along the grain of human nature rather than against it; to pursue limited objectives with a watchful eye; to amend here, to prune there; in short, to preserve the method of nature in the conduct of the state . . . this is Conservatism.

Society must be stable. Although men can never hope to see their community completely stable, they can create an endurable condition of peace and order. To achieve this great end of order—without which, as Richard Hooker wrote long ago, "there is no living in public society"—they must work unceasingly for a community that has this ideal appearance:

Common agreement on fundamentals exists among men of all ranks and stations. Loyalty, good will, fraternal sympathy, and a feeling for compromise pervade the political and social scene.

Institutions and groups are in functional adjustment; the social order is the outward expression of an inner, largely uncoerced harmony. Political, economic, social, and cultural power is widely diffused among persons, groups, and other instruments; these are held by law, custom, and constitution in a state of operating equilibrium. For every show of power there is corresponding responsibility. A minimum of friction and maximum of accommodation exist between government and group, government and individual, group and individual.

The authority of each group and instrument, and especially of the government, is legitimate. The laws honor the traditions of the nation, are adjusted to the capacities of the citizenry, meet the requirements of natural justice, and satisfy the needs of society. Men obey the laws cheerfully and readily, and they know why they obey them. They know, too, the difference between authority and authoritarianism, and are thankful that the former helps to govern their lives.

Men are secure; they have a sense of being, belonging, and creating. Their labors are rewarded, their sorrows comforted, their needs satisfied. They have the deep feeling of serenity that arises not merely from material well-being, but from confidence in the future, from daily contact with decent and trustworthy men, and from participation in an even-handed system of justice. Predicatibilty, morality, and equity are important ingredients of this condition of security. Most important, however, is ordered liberty, which makes it possible for men to pursue their talents and tastes within a sheltering framework of rights and duties.

Change and reform are sure-footed, discriminating, and respectful of the past. "Men breathe freely," as F. E. Dessauer puts it, "because change is limited. . . . The changes which are taking place do not frighten the affected."

Unity, harmony, authority, security, continuity—these are the key elements of social stability. In longing for a society in which peace and order reign, the Conservative comes closest to the utopianism that he ridicules in others. . . .

It unsettles the Conservative to see the Liberal flirt with radicalism: it frightens the Liberal to hear the Conservative talk like a reactionary. But both are coming more and more to realize that they are brothers in the struggle against those who would hurry ahead to Utopia or back to Eden. This leaves them more than a hundred years behind Ralph Waldo Emerson, who said of Liberalism and Conservatism that "each is a good half, but an impossible whole. . . . In a true society, in a true man, both must combine."

Having said all these kind words about his friend, the Sensible Liberal, the Conservative, who doesn't think many Liberals are sensible anyway, takes most of them back and reaffirms his faith in Conservatism as a unique, superior way of life. When pressed for a final reckoning of the differences between Conservatism and Liberalism, he finds at least three worth serious consideration:

First, there is what we have already noted as the difference of temper, of "mood and bias." The Conservative's stated preferences for stability over change, experience over experiment, intuition over reason, tradition over curiosity, and self-control over self-expression are enough in themselves to set him apart from the Liberal. His urges are toward aristocracy, the Liberal's toward democracy. He makes peace, the Liberal disturbs it. He likes to look back, the Liberal to look ahead. He rallies to Burke, the Liberal to Tom Paine. Perhaps it is too simple to say that these differences in temper boil down to the contrast between pessimism and optimism, but it cannot be denied that the Conservative's confidence in man, democracy, and progress is far weaker than the Liberal's, even the Sensible Liberal's. The Conservative finds this the best of all possible worlds and is generally content to leave well enough alone. The Liberal thinks the world can stand a lot of improving and cannot wait to get on the job. (Or, as Ambrose Bierce put it, the

Conservative is "a statesman enamored of existing evils," the Liberal one "who wishes to replace them with others.")

Next, the Conservative cannot understand how anyone could mistake his political principles for those of Liberalism. If the Liberal wants to draw on his stockpile for such ideas as the diffusion of power and the balancing of rights and duties, the Conservative will enter no strong objection; but he wants it clearly understood that some of his ideas are private property. If the Liberal wants to share them, he will first have to abandon Liberalism, for the hard core of Conservatism is an austere distrust of the hopes of Jefferson and the promises of Bentham. Certainly the Liberal cannot challenge the Conservative's peculiar claim to the preference for liberty over equality, emphasis on constitutionalism rather than democracy, fear of majority rule, admiration for aristocracy, and devotion to the rights of property. Certainly the Conservative's mission, so different from the Liberal's, gives his political faith a quality all its own.

In the end, the difference between Conservatism and Liberalism seems to be this: both are devoted to liberty as we have known it in the West, but the Conservative thinks of liberty as something to be preserved, the Liberal thinks of it as something to be enlarged. The Conservative suspects that a country like the United States or Britain has got just about as much liberty as it will ever have, that the liberty we enjoy cannot be increased but only redistributed among ourselves, and that persistent efforts either to increase or redistribute it may bring the whole structure of freedom down in ruins. The Liberal, on the other hand, is confident that no country has yet approached the upper limits of liberty, that giving new freedoms to some men does not necessitate taking away old liberties from others, and that the structure of freedom will fall slowly into decay if it is not enlarged by the men of each generation.

• Questions for Study

1. According to Rossiter, what is the conservative's attitude toward (a) man's nature, (b) religion, (c) equality, (d) class distinctions, (e) education, (f) man's role in society, (g) change.
2. Discuss the organization and the purpose of Rossiter's essay. Analyze closely his methods of paragraph development in the section concerning society.
3. Does Rossiter show whether he himself is a liberal or a conservative? Has he maintained objectivity in his discussion? To what extent does he attempt to evaluate the conservative view and to persuade the reader of its validity?
4. What is the main point of disagreement between liberals and conservatives according to the author?

5. Such terms as "conservative" and "liberal" are relative terms. Who in Soviet society would be termed "conservative"? Apply the labels to the two major political parties in the United States and consider the extent to which Rossiter's considerations of these terms are useful in distinguishing the parties.

LOUIS J. HALLE

•

DOES HISTORY HAVE A FUTURE?

As the nineteenth century passed, men became increasingly conscious of the fact that they were moving through time; conscious of it as they had hardly been at all before. Geological studies, undertaken for the first time, showed how much time the world had already moved through. The history of human societies, and even of mankind as a whole, became a new academic subject. Darwinism gave dramatic evidence that we men had always been on a sort of production line, that we had always been in the making and presumably still were in the making.

The new idea of evolution, which did not remain confined to the natural sciences, gave cause for optimism. Opposed to the nostalgia one felt as the old scenes fell behind, opposed to the insecurity that came from having constantly to face new and unfamiliar situations, was the belief that we were moving through time in the direction of a progessive betterment. We were going up from the ape, up toward the omnipotent superman (in the scientific eschatology) who was all brain and master of his environment. We were rising out of the jungle toward some eventually perfected civilization in which we would all push buttons for a living. The spectacular development of the physical sciences, just at this time, suggested to our forebears in the late nineteenth and early twentieth centuries that we were, in fact, approaching the point of

From the *Saturday Review*, April 23, 1960. Reprinted by permission of the *Saturday Review* and of the author.

arrival at last. The station was just around the next bend. My generation, therefore, was raised in the confidence of a linear progress from primitive beginnings to a scientific Utopia that we thought we might live to see. (Our parents used to tell us, in fact, that though they would not live to see it, we would.)

Already, however, the reaction to the concept of a linear progress was building up in the minds of the *fin de siècle* intellectuals—men like Henry and Brooks Adams, like Oswald Spengler. Concerned with the life of the mind and the spirit, they saw the increasing vulgarization of our age, an expression of mass democracy with its materialism, its sordid or trivial preoccupations, its spiritual rootlessness, its lack of any cultivated inner discipline, and its consequent instability. The imminent passing of the *Pax Britannica*, under which order had been kept throughout the world; the rise of undomesticated new empires in Germany and Japan; the rise of a still uncouth America; and the decreasing power of the cultivated "governing classes" everywhere—all these tendencies gave rise to the plausible notion that our civilization, like the classical Greco-Roman civilization before it, was in the decline that would lead to its fall. A renewal of the Dark Ages was freely predicted and, with Spengler and Toynbee, the cyclical concept of history, the concept that it repeated itself in cycles, came to replace the concept of a linear progress in the common mind.

Now the cyclical concept of history, too, has had its day in fashion and has fallen into the disdain that always awaits yesterday's fashions. It has moved from the realm of "what we now know" into the realm of "what people used to believe."

What has replaced it? What is it that we now know? Where have we at last arrived in our thinking?

The clearest answer may be found, I think, in the view advanced by E. H. Carr in the first of the lectures he delivered in 1951 (and which were later published as "The New Society"). What has replaced the cyclical concept is the concept of cultural relativism. There is no objective pattern in history. The pattern that the historian thinks he sees in it is the product of his own mind, which has been conditioned by the circumstances of his time and place. The sky isn't really blue, blue being a color that exists only in the eye of the observer.

It is hard to escape the conclusion that this represents, not a new concept of history but the discarding of history as something that has meaning and reality. Mr. Carr is too intelligent to escape this conclusion altogether, although almost clever enough to do it. "Needless to say," he writes, "I should reject absolutely the conception once put forward by H. A. L. Fisher (and tacitly held, I suspect, by some other modern historians) of a 'patternless' history, that is to say of history as an inconsequential narration having no coherence and therefore no meaning for the present. . . . For me the pattern in history is what is put there by the historian." The reader has to be alert here, if he is to see what Mr. Carr does with the rabbit in his hat. He appears to save himself from nihilism or futility by denying (with a "needless to say" and an "absolutely") that he is among those who view history as being without meaning. History, he says, does have meaning. It has one meaning for Edward Gibbon, another meaning for J. B. Bury, and a third for Oswald Spengler. Needless to say, it would be ridiculous to maintain that it did not have a meaning for Mr. Spengler. It did have a meaning for him—only the meaning that it had for him was without any validity. (Now, where's the rabbit?)

A few pages later Mr. Carr writes: "To admit that our judgments are wholly and irrevocably conditioned is to plead moral and intellectual bankruptcy. But to recognize the conditioned element in them is the best way to put us on our guard against too readily yielding to intellectual fashions—of which the nineteenth-century belief in progress and the twentieth-century belief in decadence are excellent examples." The second sentence, it should be noted, does not cancel out the conditional first sentence, in spite of the "but" with which it begins. What I understand Mr. Carr to be saying is that, by holding no belief, we can avoid holding a wrong belief.

Spengler would have felt that this vindicated him, for he asserted that his theory of history was the last of the great creative concepts of the West, its swan song. After it, the nullity of an extinguished civilization would prevail. It is true that what until recently seemed a fruitful field for human thought, the philosophy of history, is generally discredited by Western historians today, who have come to regard it as a desert. This is the result of a combination of factors: cultural relativism, the rejection of value-judgments, and the unconscious assumption of scientific positivism that what cannot be proved does not exist. It has also been promoted by the increasing pressure on historians (as on all other scholars) to specialize, to eschew any attempt at a large view of history. The historian who knows nothing outside the War of the Roses denies that there is any pattern in history. (When he reads Spengler or Toynbee he finds mistakes about the War of the Roses, which confirms his opinion.) If this is truly where we have at last arrived, at the conclusion that history has no valid meaning, then we may as well abandon the study of history altogether.

To suggest such an extreme, however, is immediately to raise doubts in the mind and to provoke a reaction. For the fact is that we don't really believe history to be without meaning, any more than we really believe that the alternation of day and night is an illusion (though we cannot prove it to be otherwise). We have simply gone to such reactionary lengths in demolishing the theories of yesterday that, for the moment at least, the scene has been swept clean of intellectual content. But the theories of yesterday are like the grass we cut down this morning. They will be back again tomorrow.

I recall a conversation with a natural scientist, ten or fifteen years ago, in which he told me that no respectable natural scientist would be caught dead "today" advancing the theories of Darwinism. This puzzled me because, being an outsider to natural science, I fall behind in the march of fashion, and I tried to find out why Darwinism was considered wrong. But the question for the scientist was not really whether it was right or wrong. All I could find out from him was that it was rejected by all thinkers considered sound "today." A few years later, by the time the centenary of the publication of "The Origin of Species" had come around, it was once more back in fashion, and I daresay my natural scientist was giving lectures in which he extolled it. (The debate, by this time, is not over the validity of Darwinism but, rather, over the question whether a rather stuffy Victorian gentleman, not at all a popular type, wasn't being given too much credit by having his name attached to it.)

One of these days we may recognize that there are some things in Spengler that have not borne the passage of time altogether badly, that still illuminate within limits the meaning of history. Publishers will bring out new editions of "The Decline of the West," with scholarly introductions that warn against what has become obsolete and point to what is still valid in it (as Bury did for Gibbon when *fin de siècle* thinking began to interest itself in the decline of Rome). We shall have Spengler corrected in terms of what people believed then and what we know today.

But how about the earlier theory, the theory of linear progress for which Bury himself stood and which was most vividly popularized, at the end of its career, by H. G. Wells? The cyclical theory, in its heyday, demolished it in its short-term predictions. It foretold that we were declining rather than ascending. But the cyclical theory said nothing about eschatological matters; it was without the concept of a point of final arrival. The picture it presented was that of civilizations succeeding one another indefinitely, and if this process was leading somewhere in the fullness of time it had no observations to offer on this eventuality. The theory of linear progression, on the other hand, was strongly eschatological, since it is impossible to imagine an upward progress which goes on forever, which does not finally come to an end in some great glory. The glory that Marxism looked forward to was that of the voluntarily ordered beehive-society. The glory that H. G. Wells looked forward to was presided over by scientists in white coats.

Except in the short term, there is no essential conflict between Bury's idea of progress and Spengler's idea of civilizations rising and dying. No believer in progress has ever denied that its path is littered with the bones of dead men, and there is no reason why it should not be littered with the bones of dead civilizations (which is the way Macauley saw it). The straight upward line of the nineteenth-century optimists could be reconciled with Spengler's rise and fall by supposing that it is rather longer than they thought and that, looked at closely, it proves to be wavy. We may be on a down-cycle now and on an up-cycle again 1,000 years from now. The curve we describe over the centuries is like that of a pedal on a bicycle going uphill.

It seems to me conceivable, then, that we shall discover, one of these days that man's evolution from the ape has so far shown a certain upward tendency on the whole (if we allow ourselves to accept, quite consciously, and knowing them to be arbitrary, certain standards on which to base value-judgments). While we shall recognize how naïve the earlier proponents of the idea of progress were, in the light of what we now know, we shall acknowledge that a long view shows that there has been a rise in the human standard of living, or in man's capacity for abstract imagery, or in man's knowledge of distant stellar galaxies, or in man's command of nature, or in man's capacity for intellectual analysis—or in whatever generally acceptable criteria of judgment we think fit to adopt. On that basis we may now predict what we may again, one of these days, be predicting.

• *Questions for Study*

1. How does the author answer the question posed by the title of the selection? Why is the title a particularly interesting one?
2. What does Halle mean by each of these terms: "linear progress," "cyclical concept," "cultural relativism"? Discuss the ways in which the implications of each of these permits us to examine history from a different point of view.
3. What use does Halle make of Carr's argument? In what ways does he criticize it?

ROBERT L. HEILBRONER

•

THE IMPASSE OF AMERICAN OPTIMISM

We Americans are by temperament of a sanguine turn of mind. We are naturally sympathetic to ideas that stress the plasticity and promise, the openness of the future, and impatient with ideas that emphasize the "fated" aspect of human affairs. We strive to see in the challenges that beset us not obstacles but opportunities. In a word, we are an optimistic people.

When it is called to our attention in this fashion, we tend to conceive of our traditional optimism as a *personal* philosophy—as a character trait that sets our aspirations above the horizon of private circumstance. Thus we often overlook something that is much more fundamental. This is the fact that optimism, for all its emphasis on personal striving, does not ultimately rest on a judgment about our private capacities. It rests on a judgment about our *historic* capacities. At bottom, a philosophy of optimism is a historic attitude about the future—an attitude based on the tacit premise that the future will accommodate the striving which we bring to it.

Needless to say, we have never consciously based our outlook on a calculated estimate of the prospects for historic change. On the contrary, we have always been convinced that the future would be propitious because we would *make* it so. Yet it must be clear that for all the naturalness and spontaneity of our self-assurance, behind it lies a tacit estimate of the forces of historic change. If we have little doubt as to our ability to create a better world, it is because we have never questioned the kind of a world which is being created by the mass effects of scientific technology, by popular political aspiration, and by the dynamic inherent

---

in our prevailing economic institutions. Thus when we say we are optimists, what we mean in fact is that we see no conflict between our chosen goals and the flow of history's currents. Indeed, we see each furthering the other.

To compare our continued trust in the future with the European distrust in it is not merely to contrast differences of psychologies or of national characteristics. We need only reflect on the course of the European disillusion to recognize that our different expectations toward the future reflect different experiences with the past. For it is apparent that our exposure to history has not been that of Europe. To mention only the most obvious but centrally important fact, we have enjoyed a geographic isolation from history's assaults utterly unknown in Europe. No explanation of our persistent optimism can overlook the inexpressible importance of our ocean boundaries and weak neighbors as a cushion and buffer against history's blows. The ever-present threat of military conquest, the frictions of international coexistence at close quarters— these paramount realities of European history have played, until the very recent past, only a negligible role in our national consciousness.

Then, too, the equally unique advantage of our material independence must not be forgotten. It has often been remarked that the American character was shaped by the presence of a huge and virtually uncontested continent, an enormous wealth of soil and ore and timber, a rugged but not impenetrable wilderness. Because the influence is well known does not mean that we can afford to lose sight of it. The abundance of nature has also been a circumstance of history that has markedly differentiated our expectations from those born in the more cramped environment of Europe.

A further cause of the optimistic mood that has always enthralled America must be sought in this nation's lack of an onerous past. If we have never displayed Europe's characteristic penchant for tragic thought, it is partly because we have never shared Europe's acquaintance with tragedy as an inseparable aspect of history. Unlike our mother nations, America has never known the enervating memories of long and inconclusive dynastic struggles, has never experienced the dragging weight of a changeless past, has never had to cope with the peasant tradition or with its resistance to change. In America we have no chastening ruins of past glories, no crumbling monuments to forgotten vanities. Of all these pointed and poignant traces of the past, these counsels of futility, we have been as unencumbered as a people could be.

As a consequence, the direction and the impact of the same historic forces were very different in Europe and in America. In Europe, for example, the democratic movement brought with it an inheritance of social bitterness. On the one hand, it grated on the sensibilities and the privileges of an entrenched aristocracy; on the other hand, it was from the beginning a movement with an inexpungeable animus toward the past. In America there was no such social inheritance. From the outset American democracy was the *only* political movement of consequence, and therefore it developed in a mood of uncontested self-assurance. Hence, when democracy in America, as in Europe, displayed its cultural and political shortcomings, it did not develop them in an atmosphere of tension, or with the possible consequences of total political upheaval or collapse. The historic force of democracy in America never displayed the face of *revolution* with which it was always uneasily associated abroad.

Again, in Europe the thrust of the new technology came upon a world already built, parceled out, stratified and orderly. From the beginning, the disruption caused by its mass industry was resisted or acquiesced in only fearfully—not alone by the old aristocracy but also by the newly arising laboring classes. In America, on the contrary, where patterns of society had not yet crystallized, the social disturbance brought about by the new industry was minimized. This is not to say that it did not exist or that the growth of industry did not blight American cities and stunt American lives. It was rather that these side-effects of technology did not impinge upon a community which was rooted with the tenacity of centuries in a division of labor and status inherited from the past. If technology upset American society, at least it upset a society which believed in mobility and which trusted in change.

As a result, the forces of technology and democracy were able to develop here with a minimum of fears and resistances from the past. In an atmosphere of general enthusiasm, their electrifying influences combined with our natural abundance to impart to American capitalism an élan very different from that of Europe. The only thought that accurately reflected the social and economic openness of America was *expansion;* the corresponding thought which matched the closed realities of Europe was that of *restraint.* While European capitalism was from the beginning socially defensive and economically constricted, capitalism in America was free of both the rigidities of social structure and the boundaries of economic horizons. Hence, America planned and built on a gargantuan scale, and its pace of advance was prodigious. Within fifty years of the death of Daniel Webster, our national wealth increased from less than a third that of Great Britain's to surpass it by more than a quarter. Our share of the world's total industrial production grew from insignificance in the beginning of the nineteenth century to over 20 per cent by 1860, and then to over 40 per cent by 1913.

Against this background of spectacular expansion, the fact that growth was uneven, attended by outrageous differentials between rich and poor, often wasteful and socially ruthless, simply did not matter—at least so far as our expectations were concerned. The accumulation of wealth on an unprecedented scale was the overriding reality of American history that carried all dissents and discontents before it.

Therefore, whereas we may have begun as optimists out of conviction, we remained so out of conditioning. For looking back over the special circumstances that favored our national career and that shaped our national character, we can see that we were spared the one exposure fatal for a philosophy of optimism. This was the experience that Europe suffered, first by small degrees, and then in overwhelming assault: an exposure to the forces of history not as the proponents but as the opponents of our volitions. Not only were we saved, by virtue of our geographic quarantine, from the impact of national wills other than our own, but by virtue of our clean historic slate, we were spared the drag and friction of an encumbering past. Thus circumstances conspired to give full rein to the historic forces at work in our midst, rather than, as in Europe, presenting them at every turn with obstacles and barriers. Democracy, technology and capitalism all enjoyed an unobstructed course within the American environment, and all displayed a corresponding vitality of development.

Only once in our history, until the very recent past, did we find ourselves confronted with a situation in which these aspects of our national development seemed to run perversely and unaccountably counter to our expectations and efforts. This was the Great Depression. But the dazed perplexity which that experience aroused in us, the sense of incredulity that the Depression would not "cure itself," the extreme reluctance to believe that its cause might be rooted deep in the historic force of capitalist expansion—all this was testimony to the degree with which our experience with a benign past resulted in a fixity of expectations concerning the future.

H. G. Wells, writing on *The Future in America* in 1906, characterized the national temper as "a sort of optimistic fatalism." It was an apt observation. For as we strove to move in the very direction in which our social, political and economic drives propelled us, and for which our geographic advantages fitted and protected us, we were never aware that our movement was due to any source other than the power of our wills, or that it might have any limitation other than our own aspirations. Still less did we entertain the idea that the forces of history might go against our volitions. The knowledge that history was replete with instances in which nations had been defeated, rebuffed or denied their aims, not through errors of their own making, but by the opposition of sheer adverse circumstance, was a fact without relevance for our national experience. As have been few peoples on earth, we were permitted the belief that we were the sole masters of our destiny; and as have been few peoples on earth, we were.

It is precisely this sense of mastery of the past that contrasts so sharply with the present. For the common attribute of contemporary events is not their responsiveness to our designs, but their indifference to them. Try as we will to steer our national course as we wish, we find our course being steered by events over which we seem to exert little if any control: the threat of nuclear war, the chronic disorders of the newly aroused nations of the East and South, the relentless pressure of communism, or simply the internal changes of our own society. History less and less presents itself as something we *make,* and more and more as something we find made for us. The mastery over our destiny, which has always been an unthinking assumption of our voyage into the hopeful future, now seems in danger of being wrested away by forces that neither precedent nor intuitive understanding illumine for us.

Yet when we look more closely at the disturbing trends of current events, we find to our surprise that they are all familiar to us. One of them, which presents itself in the guise of the frightening technology of war, is of course the outgrowth of the scientific and technological development of the past. A second, which manifests itself as the revolutionary turbulence of the newly risen areas of the world, reflects nothing so much as the ideas of political aspiration that burst upon the world in 1789. A third, the global movement toward communism and socialism, can be seen also in the grand line of economic development whose early stages produced the capitalism of Adam Smith.

And so it is that when we seek to identify the currents of world history that now assail and defy us, we find ourselves ironically enough considering the very forces that some three centuries ago infused the future with hope and gave rise to the optimistic philosophy. Now, however, these forces have assumed a direction and dimension utterly unlike that of their appearance in our own history. It is obvious that the scientific and technological revolution has attained a momentum compared with which even our own past pace of technical progress appears as only a first stage of crude tooling-up. Certainly the ideas of political aspiration, planted among the billion and a half human beings who have until now existed in unspeakable poverty and neglect, will have a different outcome from the cultivation of those same ideas among the peoples of eighteenth-century Europe or our own nation. And equally clearly, the economic development of capitalism takes on a wholly new guise when it is viewed in the context of a world which is now largely organized into non- or even anti-capitalist societies.

Thus if the origins of today's forces of historic change are familiar to us, their contemporary portents are very different from the era in which they gave rise to our optimistic expectations of history. Cast in a wholly new setting, these forces are bringing about changes so vast, in a time span so compressed, and with adjustments so convulsive, that it is as if huge seismic slippages were occurring in the deepest substratum of history. As this ponderous shifting of historic masses takes place, it is not surprising that the globe shakes and that fissures open up beneath the strongest fortress walls.

Before these ominous developments of history, we react with the natural attitudes of our optimistic conditioning. If there are "forces" in history, we prefer not to think about them; and if we must think about them, we assume that they will be, as they always have been, on our side. As a result, while history has made mock of our plans, it has not weakened our confidence in our ability to shape our destiny as we wish. We are certain that the blame for the untoward drift of things can be laid at the doorstep of this President or that Congress. We continue to tell ourselves, in the face of successive rebuffs, that what we need above all is a fresh sense of purpose, a fresh idea of what to do. The one thought that does not enter our minds is that what we may more urgently need is a fresh sense of what to expect.

Yet it must be apparent that our philosophy of expectations is a parochial and sheltered one. The idea that there may be challenges in history that are irresistible, pitiless, unyielding; the thought that a people may often be not the masters but the prisoners of their time with no alternative but to bow before its demands; the intimation that there may sometimes be very little that a nation can do to bring about a state of world affairs or of domestic society that would approximate its desires— these are all conceptions about history which our optimism makes it extremely difficult for us to consider, much less accept.

Whether we shall have to accept these ideas only the future will tell. But what is already beyond peradventure of doubt is that the essential nature of the American encounter with history is changing, and that our optimism is a handicap in appreciating that change and in assessing its implications. For our optimism blinds us to a central reality of our historic situation: that after a long voyage in which the favoring currents of history bore us in the direction in which we sought to navigate, we have emerged into an open sea where powerful contrary winds come directly into conflict with our passage. To America—if not to Europe or to most of the rest of the world—this is an utterly new experience. It is as if history of a kind we had never known before were closing in upon us. We must try to understand what its portents for the future may be.

• *Questions for Study*

1. Heilbroner's essay is based upon a number of contrasts. What are they?
2. According to the author, how and why have we confused our personal philosophies with the momentum of history? Why was democracy in Europe forced to emphasize "restraint" while democracy in the United States was able to emphasize "expansion"?
3. Why does Heilbroner use the word "impasse" in connection with our optimism? What reality does he say that we must face at the present time?
4. Do you think that Heilbroner's concept of the dangers of American optimism is accurate or inaccurate? Write a theme evaluating the author's opinions.

VII

MAN IN THE MARKETPLACE

ADAM SMITH

•

ECONOMICS AND THE
CLASS STRUCTURE

The second duty of the sovereign, that of protecting, as far as possible every member of the society from the injustice or oppression of every other member of it, or the duty of establishing an exact administration of justice requires two very different degrees of expence in the different periods of society.

Among nations of hunters, as there is scarce any property, or at least none that exceeds the value of two or three days labor; so there is seldom any established magistrate or any regular administration of justice. Men who have no property can injure one another only in their persons or reputations. But when one man kills, wounds, beats, or defames another, though he to whom the injury is done suffers, he who does it receives no benefit. It is otherwise with the injuries to property. The benefit of the person who does the injury is often equal to the loss of him who suffers it. Envy, malice, or resentment, are the only passions which can prompt one man to injure another in his person or reputation. But the greater part of men are not very frequently under the influence of those passions; and the very worst men are so only occasionally. As their gratification too, how agreeable soever it may be to certain characters, is not attended with any real or permanent advantage, it is in the greater part of men commonly restrained by prudential considerations. Men may live together in society with some tolerable degree of security, though there is no civil magistrate to protect them from the injustice of those passions. But avarice and ambition in the rich, in the poor the hatred of labor and the love of present ease and enjoyment, are the passions which

From *An Inquiry into the Nature and Causes of the Wealth of Nations*, 1776.

prompt to invade property, passions much more steady in their operation, and much more universal in their influence. Wherever there is great property, there is great inequality. For one very rich man, there must be at least five hundred poor, and the affluence of the few supposes the indigence of the many. The affluence of the rich excites the indignation of the poor, who are often both driven by want, and prompted by envy, to invade his possessions. It is only under the shelter of the civil magistrate that the owner of that valuable property, which is acquired by the labor of many years, or perhaps of many successive generations, can sleep a single night in security. He is at all times surrounded by unknown enemies, whom, though he never provoked, he can never appease, and from whose injustice he can be protected only by the powerful arm of the civil magistrate continually held up to chastise it. The acquisition of valuable and extensive property, therefore, necessarily requires the establishment of civil government. Where there is no property, or at least none that exceeds the value of two or three days labor, civil government is not so necessary.

Civil government supposed a certain subordination. But as the necessity of civil government gradually grows up with the acquisition of valuable property, so the principal causes which naturally introduce subordination gradually grow up with the growth of that valuable property.

The causes or circumstances which naturally introduce subordination, or which naturally, and antecedent to any civil institution, give some men some superiority over the greater part of their brethren, seem to be four in number.

The first of those causes or circumstances is the superiority of personal qualifications, of strength, beauty, and agility of body; of wisdom, and virtue, of prudence, justice, fortitude, and moderation of mind. The qualifications of the body, unless supported by those of the mind, can give little authority in any period of society. He is a very strong man, who, by mere strength of body, can force two weak ones to obey him. The qualifications of the mind can alone give very great authority. They are, however, invisible qualities; always disputable, and generally disputed. No society, whether barbarous or civilized, has ever found it convenient to settle the rules or precedency of rank and subordination, according to those invisible qualities; but according to something that is more plain and palpable.

The second of those causes or circumstances is the superiority of age. An old man, provided his age is not so far advanced as to give suspicion of dotage, is every where more respected than a young man of equal rank, fortune, and abilities. Among nations of hunters, such as the native tribes of North America, age is the sole foundation of rank and precedency. Among them, father is the appellation of a superior; brother, of an equal; and son, of an inferior. In the most opulent and civilized nations, age regulates rank among those who are in every other respect equal, and among whom, therefore, there is nothing else to regulate it. Among brothers and among sisters, the eldest always take place; and in the succession of the paternal estate everything which cannot be divided, but must go entire to one person, such as a title of honor, is in most cases given to the eldest. Age is a plain and palpable quality which admits of no dispute.

The third of those causes or circumstances is the superiority of fortune. The authority of riches, however, though great in every age of society, is perhaps greatest in the rudest age of society which admits of any considerable inequality of fortune. A Tartar chief, the increase of whose herds and flocks is sufficient to maintain a thousand men, cannot well employ that increase in any other way than in maintaining a thousand men. The rude state of his society does not afford him any manufactured produce, any trinkets or baubles of any kind, for which he can exchange that part of his rude produce which is over and above his own consumption. The thousand men whom he thus maintains, depending entirely upon him for their subsistence, must both obey his orders in war, and submit to this jurisdiction in peace. He is necessarily both their general and their judge, and his chieftainship is the necessary effect of the superiority of his fortune. In an opulent and civilized society a man may possess a much greater fortune, and yet not be able to command a dozen of people. Though the produce of his estate may be sufficient to maintain, and may perhaps actually maintain more than a thousand people, yet as those people pay for everything which they get from him, as he gives scarce any thing to any body but in exchange for an equivalent, there is scarce any body who considers himself as entirely dependent upon him, and his authority extends only over a few menial servants. The authority of fortune, however, is very great even in an opulent and civilized society. That it is much greater than that, either of age, or of personal qualities, has been the constant complaint of every period of society which admitted of any considerable inequality of fortune. The first period of society, that of hunters, admits of no such inequality. Universal poverty establishes there universal equality, and the superiority, either of age, or of personal qualities, are the feeble, but the sole foundations of authority and subordination. There is therefore little or no authority or subordination in this period of society. The second period of society, that of shepherds, admits of very great inequalities of fortune, and there is no period in which the superiority of fortune gives so great authority to those who possess it. There is no period accordingly in which authority and subordination are more perfectly established. The authority of an Arabian scherif is very great; that of a Tartar khan altogether despotical.

The fourth of those causes or circumstances is the superiority of birth. Superiority of birth supposes an ancient superiority of fortune in the family of the person who claims it. All families are equally ancient; and the ancestors of the prince, though they may be better known, cannot well be more numerous than those of the beggar. Antiquity of family means every where the antiquity either of wealth, or of that greatness which is commonly either founded upon wealth, or accompanied with it. Upstart greatness is every where less respected than ancient greatness. The hatred of usurpers, the love of the family of an ancient monarch, are, in a great measure, founded upon the contempt which men naturally have for the former, and upon their veneration for the latter. As a military officer submits without reluctance to the authority of a superior by whom he has always been commanded, but cannot bear that his inferior should be set over his head; so men easily submit to a family to whom they and their ancestors have always submitted; but are fired with indignation when another family, in whom they had never acknowledged any such superiority, assumes a dominion over them.

• Questions for Study

1. This selection, taken from *The Wealth of Nations*, is a classic statement of the capitalistic philosophy of economics. What views of Smith are still characteristic of modern capitalism? What views are not?
2. What is Smith's attitude toward poverty? Toward the role of government?
3. Do you believe that his explanations of the superiority of some people are still valid? Explain your own opinions concerning the factors that seem to make some people superior to others.
4. Does Smith's method of classification make his meaning emphatic or is it merely labored in its obviousness? Comment generally on Smith's style.

KARL MARX
AND
FRIEDRICH ENGELS

•

THE CLASS STRUGGLE

The history of all hitherto existing society is the history of class struggles.

Freeman and slave, patrician and plebeian, lord and serf, guildmaster and journeyman, in a word, oppressor and oppressed, stood in constant opposition to one another, carried on an uninterrupted, now hidden, now open fight, a fight that each time ended, either in a revolutionary reconstitution of society at large, or in the common ruin of the contending classes.

In the earlier epochs of history we find almost everywhere a complicated arrangement of society into various orders, a manifold gradation of social rank. In ancient Rome we have patricians, knights, plebeians, slaves; in the Middle Ages, feudal lords, vassals, guildmasters, journeymen, apprentices, serfs; in almost all of these classes, again, subordinate gradations.

The modern bourgeois society that has sprouted from the ruins of feudal society has not done away with class antagonisms. It has but established new classes, new conditions of oppression, new forms of struggle in place of the old ones.

Our epoch, the epoch of the bourgeoisie, possesses, however, this distinctive feature; it has simplified the class antagonisms. Society as a whole is more and more splitting up into two great hostile camps, into two great classes directly facing each other: Bourgeoisie and Proletariat.

From the serfs of the Middle Ages sprang the chartered burghers of the earliest towns. From these burgesses the first elements of the bourgeoisie were developed.

The discovery of America, the rounding of the Cape, opened up

---

From the *Communist Manifesto*, 1848.

fresh ground for the rising bourgeoisie. The East Indian and Chinese markets, the colonization of America, trade with the colonies, the increase in the means of exchange and in commodities generally, gave to commerce, to navigation, to industry, an impulse never before known, and thereby, to the revolutionary element in the tottering feudal society, a rapid development.

The feudal system of industry, under which industrial production was monopolized by close guilds, now no longer sufficed for the growing wants of the new market. The manufacturing system took its place. The guildmasters were pushed on one side by the manufacturing middle class; division of labor between the different corporate guilds vanished in the face of division of labor in each single workshop.

Meantime the markets kept ever growing, the demand ever rising. Even manufacture no longer sufficed. Thereupon, steam and machinery revolutionized industrial production. The place of manufacture was taken by the giant Modern Industry, the place of the industrial middle class, by industrial millionaires, the leaders of whole industrial armies, the modern bourgeois.

Modern industry has established the world market, for which the discovery of America paved the way. This market has given an immense development to commerce, to navigation, to communication by land. This development has, in its turn, reacted on the extension of industry; and in proportion as industry, commerce, navigation, railways extended, in the same proportion the bourgeoisie developed, increased its capital, and pushed into the background every class handed down from the Middle Ages.

We see, therefore, how the modern bourgeosie is itself the product of a long course of development, of a series of revolutions in the modes of production and of exchange.

Each step in the development of the bourgeoisie was accompanied by a corresponding political advance of that class. An oppressed class under the sway of the feudal nobility; an armed and self-governing association in the medieval commune (here independent urban republic, as in Italy and Germany, there taxable "third estate" of the monarchy, as in France); afterwards, in the period of manufacture proper, serving either the semi-feudal or the absolute monarchy as a counterpoise against the nobility, and, in fact, cornerstone of the great monarchies in general—the bourgeoisie has at last, since the establishment of modern industry and of the world market, conquered for itself, in the modern representative State, exclusive political sway. The executive of the modern State is but a committee for managing the common affairs of the whole bourgeoisie.

The bourgeoisie, historically, has played a most revolutionary part.

The bourgeoisie, wherever it has got the upper hand, has put an end to all feudal, patriarchal, idyllic relations. It has pitilessly torn asunder the motley feudal ties that bound man to his "natural superiors," and has left no other nexus between man and man than naked self-interest, than callous "cash payment." It has drowned the most heavenly ecstasies of religious fervor, of chivalrous enthusiasm, of philistine sentimentalism, in the icy water of egotistical calculation. It has resolved personal worth into exchange value, and in place of the numberless indefeasible chartered freedoms, has set up that single, unconscionable freedom—Free Trade. In one word, for exploitation, veiled by religious and political illusions, it has substituted naked, shameless, direct, brutal exploitation.

The bourgeoisie has stripped of its halo every occupation hitherto honored and looked up to with reverent awe. It has converted the physician, the lawyer, the priest, the poet, the man of science, into its paid wage laborers.

The bourgeoisie has torn away from the family its sentimental veil, and has reduced the family relation to a mere money relation.

The bourgeoisie has disclosed how it came to pass that the brutal display of vigor in the Middle Ages, which reactionists so much admire, found its fitting complement in the most slothful indolence. It has been the first to show what man's activity can bring about. It has accomplished wonders far surpassing Egyptian pyramids, Roman aqueducts, and Gothic cathedrals; it has conducted expeditions that put in the shade all former Exoduses of nations and crusades.

The bourgeoisie cannot exist without constantly revolutionizing the instruments of production, and thereby the relations of production, and with them the whole relations of society. Conservation of the old modes of production in unaltered form was, on the contrary, the first condition of existence for all earlier industrial classes. Constant revolutionizing of production, uninterrupted disturbance of all social conditions, everlasting uncertainty and agitation distinguished the bourgeois epoch from all earlier ones. All fixed, fast-frozen relations, with their train of ancient and venerable prejudices and opinions, are swept away, all new-formed ones become antiquated before they can ossify. All that is solid melts into the air, all that is holy is profaned, and man is at last compelled to face with sober senses his real conditions of life, and his relations with his kind.

The need of a constantly expanding market for its products drives the bourgeoisie over the whole surface of the globe. It must elbow-in everywhere, settle everywhere, establish connections everywhere.

The bourgeoisie has through its exploitation of the world market given a cosmopolitan character to production and consumption in every country. To the great chagrin of reactionists, it has drawn from under the feet of industry the national ground on which it stood. All old-established national industries have been destroyed or are daily being destroyed. They are dislodged by new industries, whose introduction becomes a life and death question for all civilized nations, by industries that no longer work up indigenous raw material, but raw material drawn from the remotest zones; industries whose products are consumed, not only at home, but in every quarter of the globe. In place of the old wants, satisfied by the productions of the country, we find new wants, requiring for their satisfaction the products of distant lands and climes. In place of the old local and national seclusion and self-sufficiency, we have intercourse in every direction, universal interdependence of nations. And as in material, so also in intellectual production. The intellectual creations of individual nations become common property. National one-sidedness and narrow-mindedness become more and more impossible, and from the numerous national and local literatures there arises a world literature.

The bourgeoisie, by the rapid improvement of all instruments of production, by the immensely facilitated means of communication, draws all, even the most barbarian nations, into civilization. The cheap prices of its commodities are the heavy artillery with which it batters down all Chinese walls, with which it forces the barbarians' intensely obstinate hatred of foreigners to capitulate. It compels all nations, on pain of extinction, to adopt the bourgeois mode of production; it compels them to introduce what it calls civilization into their midst, i.e., to become bourgeois themselves. In a word, it creates a world after its own image.

The bourgeoisie has subjected the country to the rule of the towns. It has created enormous cities, has greatly increased the urban population as compared with the rural, and has thus rescued a considerable part of the population from the idiocy of rural life. Just as it has made the country dependent on the towns, so it has made barbarian and semi-barbarian countries dependent on civilized ones, nations of peasants on nations of bourgeois, the East on the West.

The bourgeoisie keeps more and more doing away with the scattered state of the population, of the means of production, and of property. It has agglomerated population, centralized means of production, and has concentrated property in a few hands. The necessary consequence of this was political centralization. Independent, or but loosely connected provinces, with separate interests, laws, governments, and systems of taxation, became lumped together in one nation, with one government, one code of laws, one national class interest, one frontier and one customs' tariff.

The bourgeoisie, during its rule of scarce one hundred years, has created more massive and more colossal productive forces than have all preceding generations together. Subjection of nature's forces to man, machinery, application of chemistry to industry and agriculture, steam navigation, railways, electric telegraphs, clearing of whole continents for cultivation, canalization of rivers, whole populations conjured out of the ground—what earlier century had even a presentiment that such productive forces slumbered in the lap of social labor?

We see then: the means of production and of exchange on whose foundation the bourgeoisie built itself up were generated in feudal society. At a certain stage in the development of these means of production and of exchange, the conditions under which feudal society produced and exchanged, the feudal organization of agriculture and manufacturing industry—in one word, the feudal relations of property—became no longer compatible with the already developed productive forces; they became so many fetters. They had to burst asunder; they were burst asunder.

Into their places stepped free competition, accompanied by a social and political constitution adapted to it, and by the economical and political sway of the bourgeois class.

A similar movement is going on before our own eyes. Modern bourgeois society with its relations of production, of exchange, and of property, a society that has conjured up such gigantic means of production and of exchange, is like the sorcerer, who is no longer able to control the powers of the nether world whom he has called up by his spells. For many a decade past, the history of industry and commerce is but the history of the revolt of modern productive forces against modern conditions of production, against the property relations that are the conditions for the existence of the bourgeoisie and of its rule. It is enough to mention the commercial crises that by their periodical return put on its trial, each time more threateningly, the existence of the entire bourgeois society. In these crises a great part not only of the existing products, but also of the previously created productive forces, are periodically destroyed. In these crises there breaks out an epidemic that, in all earlier epochs, would have seemed an absurdity—the epidemic of overproduction. Society suddenly finds itself put back into a state of momentary barbarism; it appears as if a famine, a universal war of devastation, had cut off the supply of every means of subsistence; industry and commerce seem to be destroyed; and why? Because there is too much civilization, too much means of subsistence, too much industry, too much commerce. The productive forces at the disposal of society no longer tend to further the development of the conditions of bourgeois property; on the contrary, they have become too powerful for these conditions by which they are confined, and as soon as they overcome these limitations they bring disorder into the whole bourgeois society, endanger the existence of bourgeois property. The conditions of bourgeois society are too narrow to comprise the wealth created by them. And how does the bourgeoisie get over these crises? On the one hand by enforced destruction of a mass of productive forces; on the other, by the conquest of new markets, and by the more thorough exploitation of the old ones. That is to say, by paving the way for more extensive and more destructive crises, and by diminishing the means whereby crises are prevented.

The weapons with which the bourgeoisie felled feudalism to the ground are now turned against the bourgeoisie itself.

But not only has the bourgeoisie forged the weapons that bring death to itself; it has also called into existence the men who are to wield those weapons—the modern working class—the proletarians.

In proportion as the bourgeoisie, that is, capital, is developed, in the same proportion is the proletariat, the modern working class, developed, a class of laborers who live only so long as they find work, and who find work only so long as their labor increases capital. These laborers, who must sell themselves piecemeal, are a commodity, like every other article of commerce, and are consequently exposed to all the vicissitudes of competition, to all the fluctuations of the market.

Owing to the extensive use of machinery and to division of labor, the work of the proletarians has lost all individual character, and, consequently, all charm for the workman. He becomes an appendage of the machine, and it is only the most simple, most monotonous, and most easily acquired knack that is required of him. Hence, the cost of production of a workman is restricted almost entirely to the means of subsistence that he requires for his maintenance, and for the propagation of his race. But the price of a commodity and also of labor is equal to its cost of production. In proportion, therefore, as the repulsiveness of the work increases, the wage decreases. Nay more, in proportion as the use of machinery and division of labor increase, in the same proportion of burden of toil increases, whether by prolongation of the working hours, by increase of the work enacted in a given time, or by increased speed of the machinery, and so forth.

Modern industry has converted the little workshop of the patriarchal master into the great factory of the industrial capitalist. Masses of laborers, crowded into factories, are organized like soldiers. As privates of the industrial army they are placed under the command of a perfect hierarchy of officers and sergeants. Not only are they the slaves of the bourgeois class and of the bourgeois state, they are daily and hourly enslaved by the machine, by the foreman, and, above all, by the individual bourgeois manufacturer himself. The more openly this despotism proclaims gain to be its end and aim, the more petty, the more hateful and the more embittering it is.

The less the skill and exertion or strength implied in manual labor, in other words, the more modern industry becomes developed, the more is the labor of men superseded by that of women. Differences of age and sex have no longer any distinctive social validity for the working class. All are instruments of labor, more or less expensive to use, according to their age and sex.

No sooner is the exploitation of the laborer by the manufacturer so far at an end that he receives his wages in cash, then he is set upon by the other portions of the bourgeoisie, the landlord, the shopkeeper, the pawnbroker, and so forth.

The lower strata of the middle class—the small tradespeople, shop-keepers and retired tradesmen generally, the handicraftsmen and peasants—all these sink gradually into the proletariat, partly because their diminutive capital does not suffice for the scale on which modern industry is carried on, and is swamped in the competition with the large capitals, partly because their specialized skill is rendered worthless by new methods of production. Thus the proletariat is recruited from all classes of the population.

The proletariat goes through various stages of development. With its birth begins its struggle with the bourgeoisie. At first the contest is carried on by individual laborers, then by the workpeople of a factory, then by the operatives of one trade, in one locality, against the individual bourgeois who directly exploits them. They direct their attacks not against the bourgeois conditions of production, but against the instruments of production themselves; they destroy imported wares that compete with their labor, they smash machinery, they set factories ablaze, they seek to restore by force the vanished status of the workman of the Middle Ages.

At this stage the laborers still form an incoherent mass scattered over the whole country, and broken up by their mutual competition. If anywhere they unite to form more compact bodies, this is not yet the consequence of their own active union, but of the union of the bourgeoisie, which class, in order to attain its own political ends, is compelled to set the whole proletariat in motion, and is moreover, for a time, still able to do so. At this stage, therefore, the proletarians do not fight their enemies, but the enemies of their enemies, the remnants of absolute monarchy, the landowners, the nonindustrial bourgeois, the petty bourgeoisie. Thus the whole historical movement is concentrated in the hands of the bourgeoisie, every victory so obtained is a victory for the bourgeoisie.

But with the development of industry the proletariat not only increases in number; it becomes concentrated in greater masses, its strength grows and it feels that strength more. The various interests and conditions of life within the ranks of the proletariat are more and more equalized, in proportion as machinery obliterates all distinctions of labor, and nearly everywhere reduces wages to the same low level. The growing competition among the bourgeois, and the resulting commercial crises make the wages of the workers ever more fluctuating; the unceasing improvement of machinery, ever more rapidly developing, makes their livelihood more and more precarious; the collisions between individual workmen and individual bourgeois take more and more the character of collisions between two classes. Thereupon the workers begin to form combinations (trade unions) against the bourgeois; they club together in order to keep up the rate of wages; they found permanent associations in order to make provision beforehand for these occasional revolts. Here and there the contest breaks out into riots.

Now and then the workers are victorious, but only for a time. The real fruit of their battle lies not in the immediate result, but in the ever expanding union of workers. This union is helped on by the improved means of communication that are created by modern industry, and that places the workers of different localities in contact with one another. It was just this contact that was needed to centralize the numerous local struggles, all of the same character, into one national struggle between classes. But every class struggle is a political struggle. And that union, to attain which the burghers of the Middle Ages with their miserable highways, required centuries, the modern proletarians, thanks to railways, achieve in a few years.

This organization of the proletarians into a class, and consequently into a political party, is continually being upset again by the competition between the workers themselves. But it ever rises up again, stronger, firmer, mightier. It compels legislative recognition of particular interests of the workers by taking advantage of the divisions among the bourgeoisie itself. Thus the Ten Hours Bill in England was carried.

Altogether collisions between the classes of the old society further, in many ways, the development of the proletariat. The bourgeoisie finds itself involved in a constant battle—at first with the aristocracy; later on, with those portions of the bourgeoisie itself whose interests have become antagonistic to the progress of industry; at all times, with the bourgeoisie of foreign countries. In all these battles it sees itself compelled to appeal to the proletariat, to ask for its help, and thus to drag it into the political arena. The bourgeoisie itself, therefore, supplies the proletariat with its own elements of political and general education; in other words, it furnishes the proletariat with weapons for fighting the bourgeoisie.

Further, as we have already seen, entire sections of the ruling classes are, by the advance of industry, precipitated into the proletariat, or are at least threatened in their conditions of existence. These also supply the proletariat with fresh elements of enlightenment and progress.

Finally, in times when the class struggle nears the decisive hour, the process of dissolution going on within the ruling class, in fact within the whole range of an old society, assumes such a violent, glaring character that a small section of the ruling class cuts itself adrift and joins the revolutionary class, the class that holds the future in its hands. Just as, therefore, at an earlier period, a section of the nobility went over to the bourgeoisie, so now a portion of the bourgeoisie goes over to the proletariat, and in particular, a portion of the bourgeois ideologists, who have raised themselves to the level of comprehending theoretically the historical movements as a whole.

Of all the classes that stand face to face with the bourgeoisie today the proletariat alone is a really revolutionary class. The other classes decay and finally disappear in the face of modern industry; the proletariat is its special and essential product.

The lower middle class, the small manufacturer, the shopkeeper, the artisan, the peasant, all these fight against the bourgeoisie, to save from extinction their existence as fractions of the middle class. They are therefore not revolutionary, but conservative. Nay, more; they are reactionary, for they try to roll back the wheel of history. If by chance they are revolutionary, they are so only in view of their impending transfer into the proletariat; they thus defend not their present, but their future interests; they desert their own standpoint to place themselves at that of the proletariat.

The "dangerous class," the social scum, that passively rotting mass thrown off by the lowest layers of the old society, may here and there be swept into the movement by a proletarian revolution; its conditions of life, however, prepare it far more for the part of a bribed tool of reactionary intrigue.

In the conditions of the proletariat, those of old society at large are already virtually swamped. The proletarian is without property; his relation to his wife and children has no longer anything in common with the bourgeois family relations; modern industrial labor, modern subjection to capital, the same in England as in France, in America as in Germany, has stripped him of every trace of national character. Law, morality, religion are to him so many bourgeois prejudices, behind which lurk in ambush just as many bourgeois interests.

All the preceding classes that got the upper hand sought to fortify their already acquired status by subjecting society at large to their conditions of appropriation. The proletarians cannot become masters of the productive forces of society, except by abolishing their own previous mode of appropriation, and thereby also every other previous mode of appropriation. They have nothing of their own to secure and to fortify; their mission is to destroy all previous securities for and insurances of individual property.

All previous historical movements were movements of minorities, or in the interest of minorities. The proletarian movement is the self-conscious, independent movement of the immense majority. The proletariat, the lowest stratum of our present society, cannot stir, cannot raise itself up without the whole superincumbent strata of official society being sprung into the air.

Though not in substance, yet in form, the struggle of the proletariat with the bourgeoisie is at first a national struggle. The proletariat of each country must, of course, first of all settle matters with its own bourgeoisie.

In depicting the most general phases of the development of the proletariat, we have traced the more or less veiled civil war, raging within existing society, up to the point where that war breaks out into open revolution, and where the violent overthrow of the bourgeoisie, lays the foundation for the sway of the proletariat.

Hitherto every form of society has been based, as we have already seen, on the antagonism of oppressing and oppressed classes. But in order to oppress a class, certain conditions must be assured to it under which it can at least continue its slavish existence. The serf in the period of serfdom raised himself to membership in the commune, just as the petty bourgeois, under the yoke of feudal absolutism, managed to develop into a bourgeois. The modern laborer, on the contrary, instead of rising with the progress of industry, sinks deeper and deeper below the conditions of existence of his own class. He becomes a pauper, and pauperism develops more rapidly than population and wealth. And here it becomes evident that the bourgeoisie is unfit any longer to be the ruling class in society, and to impose its conditions of existence upon society as an overriding law. It is unfit to rule, because it is incompetent to assure an existence to its slave within his slavery, because it cannot help letting him sink into such a state that it has to feed him, instead of being fed by him. Society can no longer live under this bourgeoisie; in other words, its existence is no longer compatible with society.

The essential condition for the existence, and for the sway of the bourgeois class, is the formation and augmentation of capital; the condition for capital is wage labor. Wage labor rests exclusively on competition between the laborers. The advance of industry, whose involuntary promoter is the bourgeoisie, replaces the isolation of the laborers, due to competition, by their revolutionary combination, due to association. The development of modern industry, therefore, cuts from under its feet the very foundation on which the bourgeoisie produces and appropriates products. What the bourgeoisie therefore produces, above all, are its own gravediggers. Its fall and the victory of the proletariat are equally inevitable.

• *Questions for Study*

1. *The Communist Manifesto* is central to an understanding of world Communism; it was first written in 1848. The fundamental assumption is stated in the first sentence. What validity does the statement have? Can history be so easily summed up? Is an economic view of history the only one that has validity? What noneconomic interpretations of the meaning of history might be given?
2. Why are the following the key words and phrases in the essay: "proletariat," "feudalism," "bourgeoisie," "revolution," "Free Trade," "universal interdependence of nations," and "conservative"? Can you define their meanings as Marx and Engels use them?
3. What is the tone of the essay? Rational? Emotional?
4. How have changes that have occurred between 1848 and the present in the United States invalidated some of the basic assumptions of Marx and Engels?

THORSTEIN VEBLEN

•

DRESS AS AN EXPRESSION
OF PECUNIARY CULTURE

No one finds difficulty in assenting to the commonplace that the greater part of the expenditure incurred by all classes for apparel is incurred for the sake of a respectable appearance rather than for the protection of the person. And probably at no other point is the sense of shabbiness so keenly felt as it is if we fall short of the standard set by social usage in this matter of dress. It is true of dress in even a higher degree than of most other items of consumption, that people will undergo a very considerable degree of privation in the comforts or the necessaries of life in order to afford what is considered a decent amount of wasteful consumption; so that it is by no means an uncommon occurrence, in an inclement climate, for people to go ill clad in order to appear well dressed. And the commercial value of the goods used for clothing in any modern community is made up to a much larger extent of the fashionableness, the reputability of the goods than of the mechanical service which they render in clothing the person of the wearer. The need of dress is eminently a "higher" or spiritual need.

This spiritual need of dress is not wholly, nor even chiefly, a naïve propensity for display of expenditure. The law of conspicuous waste guides consumption in apparel, as in other things, chiefly at the second remove, by shaping the canons of taste and decency. In the common run of cases the conscious motive of the wearer or purchaser of conspicuously wasteful apparel is the need of conforming to established usage, and of living up to the accredited standard of taste and reputability. It is not only that one must be guided by the code of proprieties in dress in order to avoid the mortification that comes of unfavorable notice and comment, though that motive in itself counts for a great deal; but besides that, the requirement of expensiveness is so ingrained into our habits of thought in matters of dress that any other than expensive apparel is instinctively odious to us. Without reflection or analysis, we feel that what is inexpensive is unworthy. "A cheap coat makes a cheap man." "Cheap and nasty" is recognised to hold true in dress with even less mitigation than in other lines of consumption. On the ground both of taste and of serviceability, an inexpensive article of apparel is held to be inferior, under the maxim "cheap and nasty." We find things beautiful, as well as serviceable, somewhat in proportion as they are costly. With few and inconsequential exceptions, we all find a costly hand-wrought article of apparel much preferable, in point of beauty and of serviceability, to a less expensive imitation of it, however cleverly the spurious article may imitate the costly original; and what offends our sensibilities in the spurious article is not that it falls short in form or color, or, indeed, in visual effect in any way. The offensive object may be so close an imitation as to defy any but the closest scrutiny; and yet so soon as the counterfeit is detected, its æsthetic value, and its commercial value as well, declines precipitately. Not only that, but it may be asserted with but small risk of contradiction that the æsthetic value of a detected counterfeit in dress declines somewhat in the same proportion as the counterfeit is cheaper than its original. It loses caste æsthetically because it falls to a lower pecuniary grade.

But the function of dress as an evidence of ability to pay does not end with simply showing that the wearer consumes valuable goods in excess of what is required for physical comfort. Simple conspicuous waste of goods is effective and gratifying as far as it goes; it is good *prima facie* evidence of pecuniary success, and consequently *prima facie* evidence of social worth. But dress has subtler and more far-reaching possibilities than this crude, first-hand evidence of wasteful consumption only. If, in addition to showing that the wearer can afford to consume freely and uneconomically, it can also be shown in the same stroke that he or she is not under the necessity of earning a livelihood, the evidence of social worth is enhanced in a very considerable degree. Our dress, therefore, in order to serve its purpose effectually, should not only be expensive, but it should also make plain to all observers that the wearer is not engaged in any kind of productive labor. In the evolutionary process by which our system of dress has been elaborated into its present admirably perfect adaptation to its purpose, this subsidiary line of evidence has received due attention. A detailed examination of what passes in popular apprehension for elegant apparel will show that it is contrived at every point to convey the impression that the wearer does not habitually put forth any useful effort. It goes without saying that no apparel can be considered elegant, or even decent, if it shows the effect of manual labor on the part of the wearer, in the way of soil or wear. The pleasing effect of neat and spotless garments is chiefly, if not altogether, due to their carrying the suggestion of leisure—exemption from personal contact with industrial processes of any kind. Much of the charm that invests the patent-leather shoe, the stainless linen, the lustrous cylindrical hat, and the walking-stick, which so greatly enhance the native dignity of a gentleman, comes of their pointedly suggesting that the wearer cannot when so attired bear a hand in any employment that is directly and immediately of any human use. Elegant dress serves its purpose of elegance not only in that it is expensive, but also because it is the insignia of leisure. It not only shows that the wearer is able to consume a relatively large value, but it argues at the same time that he consumes without producing.

The dress of women goes even farther than that of men in the way of demonstrating the wearer's abstinence from productive employment. It needs no argument to enforce the generalisation that the more elegant styles of feminine bonnets go even farther towards making work impossible than does the man's high hat. The woman's shoe adds the so-called French heel to the evidence of enforced leisure afforded by its polish; because this high heel obviously makes any, even the simplest and most necessary manual work extremely difficult. The like is true even in a higher degree of the skirt and the rest of the drapery which characterizes woman's dress. The substantial reason for our tenacious attachment to the skirt is just this: it is expensive and it hampers the wearer at every turn and incapacitates her for all useful exertion. The like is true of the feminine custom of wearing the hair excessively long.

But the woman's apparel not only goes beyond that of the modern man in the degree in which it argues exemption from labor; it also adds a peculiar and highly characteristic feature which differs in kind from anything habitually practised by the men. This feature is the class of contrivances of which the corset is the typical example. The corset is, in economic theory, substantially a mutilation, undergone for the purpose of lowering the subject's vitality and rendering her permanently and obviously unfit for work. It is true, the corset impairs the personal attractions of the wearer, but the loss suffered on that score is offset by the gain in reputability which comes of her visibly increased expensiveness and infirmity. It may broadly be set down that the womanliness of woman's apparel resolves itself, in point of substantial fact, into the more effective hindrance to useful exertion offered by the garments peculiar to women. This difference between masculine and feminine apparel is here simply pointed out as a characteristic feature. The ground of its occurrence will be discussed presently.

So far, then, we have, as the great and dominant norm of dress, the broad principle of conspicuous waste. Subsidiary to this principle, and as a corollary under it, we get as a second norm the principle of conspicuous leisure. In dress construction this norm works out in the shape of divers contrivances going to show that the wearer does not and, as far as it may conveniently be shown, can not engage in productive labor. Beyond these two principles there is a third of scarcely less constraining force, which will occur to any one who reflects at all on the subject. Dress must not only be conspicuously expensive and inconvenient; it must at the same time be up to date. No explanation at all satisfactory has hitherto been offered of the phenomenon of changing fashions. The imperative require-ment of dressing in the latest accredited manner, as well as the fact that this accredited fashion constantly changes from season to season, is suf-ficiently familiar to every one, but the theory of this flux and change has not been worked out. We may of course say, with perfect consistency and truthfulness, that this principle of novelty is another corollary under the law of conspicuous waste. Obviously, if each garment is permitted to serve for but a brief term, and if none of last season's apparel is carried over and made further use of during the present season, the wasteful expenditure on dress is greatly increased. This is good as far as it goes, but it is negative only. Pretty much all that this consideration warrants us in saying is that the norm of conspicuous waste exercises a controlling surveillance in all matters of dress, so that any change in the fashions must conform to the requirement of wastefulness; it leaves unanswered the question as to the motive for making and accepting a change in the prevailing styles, and it also fails to explain why conformity to a given style at a given time is so imperatively necessary as we know it to be.

For a creative principle, capable of serving as motive to invention and innovation in fashions, we shall have to go back to the primitive, noneconomic motive with which apparel originated,—the motive of adornment. Without going into an extended discussion of how and why this motive asserts itself under the guidance of the law of expensiveness, it may be stated broadly that each successive innovation in the fashions is an effort to reach some form of display which shall be more acceptable to our sense of form and color or of effectiveness, than that which it displaces. The changing styles are the expression of a restless search for something which shall commend itself to our æsthetic sense; but as each innovation is subject to the selective action of the norm of conspicuous waste, the range within which innovation can take place is somewhat restricted. The innovation must not only be more beautiful, or perhaps oftener less offensive, than that which it displaces, but it must also come up to the accepted standard of expensiveness.

It would seem at first sight that the result of such an unremitting

430

THORSTEIN VEBLEN

struggle to attain the beautiful in dress should be a gradual approach to artistic perfection. We might naturally expect that the fashions should show a well-marked trend in the direction of some one or more types of apparel eminently becoming to the human form; and we might even feel that we have substantial ground for the hope that today, after all the ingenuity and effort which have been spent on dress these many years, the fashions should have achieved a relative perfection and a relative stability, closely approximating to a permanently tenable artistic ideal. But such is not the case. It would be very hazardous indeed to assert that the styles of today are intrinsically more becoming than those of ten years ago, or than those of twenty, or fifty, or one hundred years ago. On the other hand, the assertion freely goes uncontradicted that styles in vogue two thousand years ago are more becoming than the most elaborate and painstaking constructions of today.

The explanation of the fashions just offered, then, does not fully explain, and we shall have to look farther. It is well known that certain relatively stable styles and types of costume have been worked out in various parts of the world; as, for instance, among the Japanese, Chinese, and other Oriental nations; likewise among the Greeks, Romans, and other Eastern peoples of antiquity; so also, in later times, among the peasants of nearly every country of Europe. These national or popular costumes are in most cases adjudged by competent critics to be more becoming, more artistic, than the fluctuating styles of modern civilised apparel. At the same time they are also, at least usually, less obviously wasteful; that is to say, other elements than that of a display of expense are more readily detected in their structure.

These relatively stable costumes are, commonly, pretty strictly and narrowly localised, and they vary by slight and systematic gradations from place to place. They have in every case been worked out by peoples or classes which are poorer than we, and especially they belong in countries and localities and times where the population, or at least the class to which the costume in question belongs, is relatively homogeneous, stable, and immobile. That is to say, stable costumes which will bear the test of time and perspective are worked out under circumstances where the norm of conspicuous waste asserts itself less imperatively than it does in the large modern civilised cities, whose relatively mobile, wealthy population today sets the pace in matters of fashion. The countries and classes which have in this way worked out stable and artistic costumes have been so placed that the pecuniary emulation among them has taken the direction of a competition in conspicuous leisure rather than in conspicuous consumption of goods. So that it will hold true in a general way that fashions are least stable and least becoming in those communities where the principle of a conspicuous waste of goods asserts itself most imperatively, as among ourselves. All this points to an antagonism between expensiveness and artistic apparel. In point of practical fact, the norm of conspicuous waste is incompatible with the requirement that dress should be beautiful or becoming. And this antagonism offers an explanation of that restless change in fashion which neither the canon of expensiveness nor that of beauty alone can account for.

The standard of reputability requires that dress should show wasteful expenditure; but all wastefulness is offensive to native taste. The psychological law has already been pointed out that all men—and women perhaps even in a higher degree—abhor futility, whether of effort or of expenditure,—much as Nature was once said to abhor a vacuum. But the principle of conspicuous waste requires an obviously futile expenditure; and the resulting conspicuous expensiveness of dress is therefore intrinsically ugly. Hence we find that in all innovations in dress, each added or altered detail strives to avoid instant condemnation by showing some ostensible purpose, at the same time that the requirement of conspicuous waste prevents the purposefulness of these innovations from becoming anything more than a somewhat transparent pretense. Even in its freest flights, fashion rarely if ever gets away from a simulation of some ostensible use. The ostensible usefulness of the fashionable details of dress, however, is always so transparent a make-believe, and their substantial futility presently forces itself so baldly upon our attention as to become unbearable, and then we take refuge in a new style. But the new style must conform to the requirement of reputable wastefulness and futility. Its futility presently becomes as odious as that of its predecessor; and the only remedy which the law of waste allows us is to seek relief in some new construction, equally futile and equally untenable. Hence the essential ugliness and the unceasing change of fashionable attire.

Having so explained the phenomenon of shifting fashions, the next thing is to make the explanation tally with everyday facts. Among these everyday facts is the well-known liking which all men have for the styles that are in vogue at any given time. A new style comes into vogue and remains in favour for a season, and, at least so long as it is a novelty, people very generally find the new style attractive. The prevailing fashion is felt to be beautiful. This is due partly to the relief it affords in being different from what went before it, partly to its being reputable. As indicated previously, the canon of reputability to some extent shapes our tastes, so that under its guidance anything will be accepted as becoming until its novelty wears off, or until the warrant of reputability is transferred to a new and novel structure serving the same general purpose.

That the alleged beauty, or "loveliness," of the styles in vogue at any given time is transient and spurious only is attested by the fact that none of the many shifting fashions will bear the test of time. When seen in the perspective of half-a-dozen years or more, the best of our fashions strike us as grotesque, if not unsightly. Our transient attachment to whatever happens to be the latest rests on other than æsthetic grounds, and lasts only until our abiding æsthetic sense has had time to assert itself and reject this latest indigestible contrivance.

The process of developing an æsthetic nausea takes more or less time; the length of time required in any given case being inversely as the degree of intrinsic odiousness of the style in question. This time relation between odiousness and instability in fashions affords ground for the inference that the more rapidly the styles succeed and displace one another, the more offensive they are to sound taste. The presumption, therefore, is that the farther the community, especially the wealthy classes of the community, develop in wealth and mobility and in the range of their human contact, the more imperatively will the law of conspicuous waste assert itself in matters of dress, the more will the sense of beauty tend to fall into abeyance or be overborne by the canon of pecuniary reputability, the more rapidly will fashions shift and change, and the more grotesque and intolerable will be the varying styles that successively come into vogue.

• Questions for Study

1. According to Veblen, why is dress more than other items a commodity through which the concept of "conspicuous consumption" can be shown? Do you believe that Veblen's ideas are applicable to all levels of society in present-day America? Explain.
2. Describe the tone of the essay. Do you detect any elements of humor? How does Veblen make economic concepts interesting and clear to the general reader? Compare and contrast Veblen's approach to economic problems with that of Marx and Engels. In what ways is Veblen's tone and style different from theirs? Do you think that Marx and Engels would have agreed with Veblen's ideas?
3. What is meant by the term "fashion"? Why are people interested in fashions? Write a theme in which you defend or attack this interest.

CARL BECKER

•

THE MARXIAN

PHILOSOPHY OF HISTORY

I sometimes find myself discussing communism with those who profess that faith; and not infrequently I note an implicit assumption on their part that I, as an intelligent person with some knowledge of history, ought either, (1) to refute the Marxian philosophy of history, or (2) in all honesty to support the communist cause. In such discussions I have maintained, (1) that an intelligent person may regard the Marxian philosophy of history as an illuminating interpretation of the past without subscribing to it as a law of history, and, (2) that even if convinced that the Marxian doctrine is a valid law of history, one might still with excellent reasons refuse to support the communist cause. Such discussions, developed more fully and presented more formally, may for convenience be put in the form of a discussion between a communist and a liberal.

Communist: Don't you think, Professor, that history proves that social progress, or change if you prefer, is the result of an inevitable class-conflict?

Liberal: Put in that precise way, no. I can't see that history proves anything except that what happened did happen, or that anything is inevitable except what happened; but what happened is precisely the question at issue. In using the words "prove" and "inevitable" you are, as the logicians say, begging the question.

Communist: I don't insist on those precise words.

Liberal: Very well. I agree then that history does support, or can easily be made to support, the Marxian doctrine in a general way. For example, in the middle ages the chief source of wealth was certainly land; and it is obvious that at that time the landowning aristocracy was the ruling class. No great ingenuity is required to show that political,

social, and religious customs and ideas of that time were suited to maintaining the political and economic ascendancy of the aristocracy. Likewise, it is obvious that during the last three centuries land has gradually
been replaced by capital as the chief source of wealth; and the history of
this time may easily be regarded as a conflict between the middle-class
capitalist and the landowning aristocracy, as a result of which the former
have replaced the latter as the ruling class and have substituted, in their
interest, a new set of institutions and ideas (representative government,
individual liberty, popular sovereignty, free competition) for the old.
Yes, as an interpretation of the last thousand years of European history,
the Marxian theory is most illuminating.

Communist: Isn't it a bit more than merely illuminating? Can you
deny that it is a more convincing and realistic interpretation than any
other?

Liberal: I could very easily deny it, but I have no wish to do so. Let
us admit that it is the most convincing interpretation. I will go farther.
For purposes of argument I will admit that it is the only valid interpretation.

Communist: Very well then. If you admit that Marx has correctly
interpreted the past, why not admit that he has correctly interpreted the
future? Why not admit that just as the bourgeois-capitalist class displaced
the landowning aristocracy as the ruling class, so the proletariat will in
its turn replace the bourgeois-capitalist class? And if they do so, isn't it
reasonable to suppose that the characteristic ideas of the present society
(representative government, freedom of speech, *laissez-faire*) will in
turn give way to others suited to the interests of the proletariat?

Liberal: If I accept Marx's interpretation of the past it is because
I know what it is, and can test it. If I hesitate to accept his interpretation
of the future it is partly because I do not know precisely what it is, and
partly because, even if I know what it is, I cannot test it. I willingly
admit that the future will, in some way that can after the event be
rationalized, resemble the past. Certainly change is the law of life, and
it is obvious that the institutions and ideas of the nineteenth century,
which were so well suited to the interests of the capitalist class, will not
suffice without modification for the needs of the complex mechanized
society of the twentieth. I willingly admit also that the ideas and institutions of today will be changed in such a way as to conform more closely
with the economic interests of the workers, the mass of the people, the
proletariat. But that is not to say that the change will come about in the
way predicted by Marx, or that the result will be the sort of utopia
predicted by him.

Communist: Utopia! I am not aware that Marx predicted any utopia.

Liberal: Well, let us say that he didn't. What then did he predict?

Communist: He predicted that the capitalist régime would by its own nature destroy itself. Its nature is to be ruthlessly competitive, so that in any industrial society the tendency is for wealth to be more highly concentrated in the hands of a few, while the mass of the people tend to fall to the condition of wage slaves. When this process reaches a certain point, the system breaks down, as it is now breaking down because it has deprived the people of the means of buying the commodities which it is the sole aim of the capitalist class to make and sell for a profit. When the system ceases to work the people will necessarily take control, and, since it is their interest to do so, they will establish a classless society based upon the common ownership of instruments of production, and a more equitable distribution of the product. This is the social revolution that Marx predicted, and it has already begun—in Russia.

Liberal: In Russia, yes. In Russia, that is to say not the most highly industrialized society but the least highly industrialized society. That is surely not according to Marx.

Communist: No, it is not. But you cannot maintain that because Marx's prediction is not verified in every detail it is not therefore valid in its general outline. The Great War created a special set of circumstances which were peculiarly favorable to the social revolution in Russia.

Liberal: Very true. The social revolution clearly occurred before its time in Russia. Providence, or Dialectic Materialism, or whatever it is that regulates social changes, certainly did a very curious thing in bringing the social revolution to Russia before it brought it to more highly industrialized countries, such as England. For my part I don't think the Russian revolution does anything to verify the predictions of Marx; to me it indicates only that in a country in which the people were accustomed to being ruled by a dictatorship, a country moreover in which the prevailing form of dictatorship was especially corrupt and incompetent, it was very easy to establish a dictatorship of a different sort. But let that pass. My reluctance to accept the Marxian doctrine arises from something far more fundamental than the Russian accident. There are two difficulties which have always troubled me. Perhaps you can solve them. One is that it is extremely difficult to predict the future on the basis of past experience; or rather it is extremely easy to find in the past support for diverse predictions of the future. The other difficulty is to understand why a persistent economic class conflict in the past justifies us in predicting a classless society in the future.

As to the first difficulty. What little I know of history makes me chary of any prediction as to the form which social institutions will take in the future. Especially so when such predictions, based upon a realistic view of the past, take an idealistic view of the future. During the last two thousand years all the saints and sages of the world, deploring greed and strife, poverty and injustice, have looked forward to the time when a more just society would be established. They have many times predicted the coming of a classless society in which everyone would have enough; but the course of events has never yet verified their hopes. This generalization is as solidly based on historical fact as any that Marx has made, and it is more widely based; and if I am to judge the future by the past, I see no reason for discarding this generalization for that which Marx offers me. The less so, since Marx's interpretation of the past, if projected into the future, seems to refute his own prediction.

Communist: I don't understand that.

Liberal: Perhaps it will become clear if I elaborate the second difficulty I just mentioned. Marx's interpretation of the past is explicit and realistic; his forecast of the future seems to me vague and idealistic. I have called it utopian, but you object to that word. I do not insist on it. I will even surrender the word "idealistic." But the point is this. Marx finds that in the past the effective force that has determined social change is the economic class conflict. He points out that this economic class conflict explains the rise of the present capitalistic society. He shows, or at least his disciples show, how this economic class conflict is working to undermine our capitalistic society. Very well. If then I project this explanation of social changes into the future, what does it tell me? It seems to tell me that there will be in the future what there has been in the past —an endless economic class conflict, an endless replacement of one dominant class by another, an endless transformation of institutions and ideas in accordance with the changes effected by the class conflict. But this is not what Marx predicts. What he predicts is the end of the economic class conflict, the establishment of a classless society. What you and he are asking me to accept is an explanation of history that will explain it only up to a certain point. Marx criticised Hegel for that very weakness. Hegel explained past history as a transformation effected by the Transcendent Idea realizing itself in the actual events of history; according to him the great objective of history was the complete realization of the Idea in the form of Freedom, and this great objective had already been in some sense attained in the Prussian state. Marx wanted to know what the Transcendent Idea would find to do in the future, now that it was entirely realized. That is a sound criticism. Now, my difficulty is to know how Marx has improved on Hegel. To be sure Marx does not say that the great objective of history has already been attained. He says the economic class conflict will bring about another social revolution.

But after the social revolution, what then? What becomes of the economic class conflict after the revolution has established a classless society? I can't find that it will have anything more to do than Hegel's Transcendent Idea. A law of history which, at some determinate moment, ceases to explain history, a law of history which is required, at the appropriate moment, to commit hari-kari on the doorstep of the ideal, surely leaves something to be desired.

Communist: Well, that's a point. But really, Professor, you know very well that this objection has been noted before, and that there is a good answer to it. Marx was not so blind as to overlook it. How could he have done so, since he pointed out that very weakness in Hegel's philosophy of history?

Liberal: I should be glad to learn how Marx avoids that difficulty.

Communist: I am not sure that Marx himself does altogether avoid it. But you must allow Marxian philosophy to be elaborated and interpreted by his followers in the light of later experience. You have no objection to that?

Liberal: None at all. We must by all means discuss Marxianism at its best, as it is now interpreted by the most expert exegesis available.

Communist: Very well. According to a recent interpreter of Marxianism, history is explainable in terms of a dialectic of transformation, in which conflicts appear only to be resolved in a higher synthesis. This conflict is not necessarily always an economic class conflict. After the classless society is established the conflict will continue, but on a different level. According to Professor Sidney Hook, a recent interpreter of Marx, the dialectic in a communist, classless society, will not be "historically conditioned in the same sense" as in earlier times. "It finds expression . . . on a more elevated plane. Although in advance no one can describe the detailed forms it will take, it is clear that its general locus is individual and personal." In other words, having solved the economic problem by establishing a classless society, men will be occupied with the higher, spiritual problems of human development.

Liberal: Well, I must confess that this greatly surprises me. A while back you would not allow me to apply the term "utopian" to the future society predicted by Marx; and yet this sounds to me very similar to all the utopian societies I ever heard of. Throughout the past men have engaged in brutal conflict for material gain; but this brutal conflict is somehow to bring about a classless society in which men will suddenly change their natures and devote themselves to the nobler things of life. A dialectic materialism will be replaced by what we may call a dialectic spiritualism; or to put it in simple English, conflict will cease on the economic plane, and continue only on the moral plane.

Well, it may be so: and if it should turn out so, it would be grand. I point out merely that this is what all the idealistic prophets of the world have always hoped would happen. It is what the early prophets of democracy predicted. It is what all humane liberals may hope for. But what I don't understand is how the Marxian philosophy permits us to hope for it. I suppose it to be a fundamental tenet of Marxian philosophy that the conduct of men is strictly conditioned; and if their conduct in the past has been strictly conditioned by the economic class conflict, how can it cease to be so conditioned in the future?

Communist: Your difficulty arises from a false assumption—an assumption that is made by many of the hostile critics of Marx. The assumption is that Marx accepted the nineteenth-century doctrine of mechanistic determinism. That is not so. Marx always insisted that "man makes his own history." He contributes something novel to the conditions that determine his own conduct. Marx says explicitly: "By acting on the external world man changes his own nature." This means that man can, by acquiring knowledge, modify his environment, and so modify also his own ways of submitting to the environment. Therefore it is quite possible that men might for a very long time submit blindly to the influence of the economic class conflict; for a long time, but not necessarily forever; since, having become aware that they had been in the past submitting to the economic class conflict, they would, in the future, even if they submitted to it, not be submitting to it blindly. This awareness that their conduct has been determined by the economic class conflict becomes a new element in the conditions, and so changes the conditions that will determine men's conduct in the future. One might say that the great object of Marx was just this: to make men aware of the conditions that made social revolutions in the past, so that in the coming social revolution, being aware of what was happening, they could consciously direct it. To quote once more from Professor Sidney Hook: "Once man acquires control of the conditions of social life, he can consciously make over his own nature in accordance with a morally free will, in contradistinction to men in the past, whose nature has been unconsciously made over by the economically determined will of economic classes."

Liberal: I see; at least I think so, in spite of Professor Hook's somewhat obscure academic phraseology. But what it comes to, I suppose, is this. In the physical world a law operates forever in the same way because the physical object is not aware of, and is indifferent to, what happens. A billiard ball (to use the classic example) has no desire to make over its nature. But man is aware of, and is not indifferent to, what happens. His acts are indeed strictly conditioned, but as soon as he becomes aware of what it is that conditions them, his awareness enables him to react differently; his acts are then not less strictly conditioned than formerly, but his own awareness becomes a new element that changes and complicates the conditions. For a long time men may worship the sun; when they become aware of the influences that make them worship the sun, this awareness may become an influence that will make them cease to worship the sun. Freedom of the will, as Engels said, is no more than man's knowledge that his acts are conditioned.

Very well, Marx then (or perhaps his disciples) applies this principle of freedom to the social changes or revolutions that occur in history. In the past, social revolutions have been conditioned by the economic class conflict. As long as men are not aware of this fact, social revolutions will continue to be conditioned by the economic class conflict. But when men become fully aware, through the great discovery of Marx, that social revolutions in the past have been conditioned by the class conflict, this knowledge will enable them to react differently—to react in such a way as to abolish the class conflict. This, I take it, is how you interpret Marx.

Communist: Yes, that is right.

Liberal: Well, I agree with this idea of free will. It seems to me obvious that as men acquire knowledge of the influences that determine their acts, this knowledge becomes a new influence that enables them to act differently. But if we accept this principle it seems odd to me that men shouldn't have acquired, before the time of Marx, some knowledge of the fact that their conduct was determined by the economic class conflict. I should have supposed that this element of awareness would have been steadily modifying the conditions that determine social changes from the time of the Neanderthal man down to the present. How does it happen that this element of awareness has had no appreciable influence up to the time of Marx? Marx must have been a much greater man than I have always thought—a veritable Messiah, who at a single stroke has given mankind this epoch-making revelation that is to transform so radically the conditions that determine human history. I find it difficult to believe that. It seems more reasonable to believe that knowledge has been steadily modifying the economic influences that have determined social changes in the past, and that in the future further knowledge, knowledge unknown to Marx, will continue to modify those influences in ways not dreamed of by Marx.

But that is a minor point. Let us assume that up to the time of Marx men have been submitting blindly to the economic class conflict, and that now, thanks to Marx, they are in the way of becoming aware of that fact, and that being aware of it they are in a position to modify profoundly the conditions that will determine social changes. What then? Well, it seems to me that this great revelation made by Marx is precisely what makes it impossible for him to predict the character of the coming social revolution. If we did not know that social changes had been conditioned by the economic class conflict, the coming social revolution would presumably follow the course of previous ones, in which case no classless society would emerge from it. But since we do know that social revolutions in the past were conditioned by the class conflict, this very knowledge, according to Marx, will make the coming social revolution follow some different course, in which case we may hope, but cannot be sure, that a classless society will emerge from it. In short, in so far as Marx has made men aware of the influence of the economic class conflict in the past, he has destroyed the very conditions that would have enabled him to predict the nature of the social revolution in the future. If Marx wished to predict correctly the nature of the coming social revolution, he should not have told us what it is that makes social revolutions: since he has told us, the secret is out, and hence no one can predict it. The great secret is out, thanks to Marx, and this knowledge will enable us to make of the coming social revolution something different than it otherwise would have been. Marxian philosophy presents his disciples with a dilemma which they either do not see or refuse to meet. It is this. Either social changes are always determined by the same conditions, in which case we may be sure that the coming social revolution will be similar to those in the past—it will transform the present class conflict only to create the conditions that will issue in a new one. Or else knowledge of the conditions that have determined social revolutions in the past introduces a novel influence in the conditions that will determine social revolutions in the future, in which case we cannot predict with any certainty the nature of those revolutions. The profound conviction of Communists that the proletariat is destined to establish a classless society on the ruins of the present capitalist régime is not justified by Marxian philosophy: if you interpret Marx in terms of mechanistic determinism, this profound communist conviction is a pure delusion; on the other hand, if you interpret Marx in terms of free will, this conviction is no more than a splendid hope. That is why I cannot accept the Marxian philosophy as a law of history.

Communist: Very well. Suppose, for purposes of argument, that the communist conviction is only a splendid hope. You yourself have said that the present capitalist régime must be changed in such a way as to harmonize better with the interests of the mass of the people, the proletariat. That is just what the Communists want. Since you sympathize with their object, and believe that it will in some measure be realized, why not join the Communists and help to realize this splendid hope?

Liberal: I refuse to join the Communists because, while I sympathize with their desire to make a better world for the mass of the people, I have no faith in the methods which they propose for obtaining this object. If I understand them, they claim that nothing really worth while can be done until conditions are ripe for the application of the revolutionary technique. When that time comes, they propose, following the example of the Bolsheviks in Russia, to seize control of the government, forcibly expropriate the bourgeois class, and ruthlessly suppress the expression of all opinion that a dictatorial government judges to be hostile to the welfare of the community of workers.

Now I have no faith in force and repression as the *primary* means of achieving the good life. I am not as yet a non-resistance pacifist. Any government is probably better than none, and all government rests at last on force. But I believe that the essential test of civilized society is the extent to which law and public authority rest on free discussion and voluntary consent. A resort to force as a means of obtaining consent may be sometimes necessary to prevent a society from falling into virtual anarchy; but the resort to force in place of persuasion is so far a confession of failure. I have no faith in the possibility of abolishing oppression by oppressing oppressors. I have no faith in the infallibility of any man, or of any group of men, or of the doctrines or dogmas of any man or group of men, except in so far as they can stand the test of free criticism and analysis. I agree with Pascal that "thought makes the dignity of man"; and I believe therefore that all the great and permanently valuable achievements of civilization have been won by the free play of intelligence in opposition to, or in spite of, the pressure of mass emotion and the effort of organized authority to enforce conformity in conduct and opinion. I do not believe that there has been, or that there will be, a high civilization in any country in which the mind of man is limited to the expression of ideas authorized by public authority. Dictatorship is as old as European society; and whether it be the dictatorship of a Stalin, a Mussolini, or a Hitler, it does not become something new and admirable by being dressed up in a new and mystical ideology. I recognize it as a possibility that our modern, complex, machine civilization may so far fall into confusion that a dictatorship will in fact replace the present régime; but I refuse to recognize this outcome as inherently desirable, and I refuse to join in any effort to make it inevitable.

This is why I do not join the Communists. I believe that profound changes in our economic and industrial system are necessary; but I believe that they can and I hope that they will be made, in this country, without resorting to violent revolution, without resorting to dictatorship, without abandoning our traditional reliance on free discussion and criticism of public authority and of the measures it proposes for the solution of social ills. And there is nothing in the Marxian philosophy, as you expound it, that makes it illogical for me to take this position. According to you, now that Marx has made us aware of the influence of the economic class conflict in the past, this very awareness will enable us to master and modify the class conflict in the future. I agree. But why is it necessary to assume that this knowledge which Marx has revealed to us is the exclusive possession of the proletariat? After all the bourgeoisie have a certain amount of intelligence. They can read Marx, or at least Sidney Hook. They can observe what has occurred in Russia, in Italy, in Germany. It is possible for them, too, to understand that the capitalist competitive system is in a fair way of destroying itself. Marxian doctrine tells me that capitalists, like proletarians, are motivated by their economic class interest; it does not tell me that they, any more than the proletarians, must forever be motivated by a blind illusion as to what that interest is. At the present moment it obviously is not to the interest of the capitalist class that the mass of the people should be without the means of buying the goods which the capitalist class produces in order to sell. It is still possible that the capitalist system in this country, subjected to the pressure of economic necessity and the force of public discontent, may by reasonably peaceful procedure be sufficiently transformed into a coördinated and planned economic system to make it, not a utopia indeed, but at least a decently workable system. And a decently workable system which preserves our traditional liberty of discussion and criticism will, in my opinion, be superior in the long run to any system that can be established by the repressive measures now employed by the Communists of Russia, the Fascists of Italy, or the Nazis of Germany.

Communist: A decently workable system. That's certainly vague enough—as vague as Marx's idealistic society of the future which you derided. No doubt a decently workable system is one which you would prefer to something which you don't like, such as the Russian communist state.

Liberal: It is. But you must permit me to prefer a decently workable system which I like to a decently workable system which I don't like. You can hardly expect me to become a Communist until I am convinced that communism would be preferable to the system under which I live.

Communist: No. But you have already admitted that the "decently workable system" which you hope will be established may fail to be established—that the present system may end in a dictatorship. That I think is the more probable outcome. It is likely that in the long run the capitalist class, confronted by the rising power of the proletariat, will resort to force, as it has done in Italy and Germany. If then you are faced with the alternative of supporting a dictatorship of the proletariat or a dictatorship of the bourgeoisie, what will you do? What then will become of freedom of speech and the appeal to persuasion? Since you sympathize with the objectives of the Communists, will you not then be forced to join them? Why wait till then? Why not join now the side which is bound to win in the long run because it is in harmony with the dominant trend of social forces?

Liberal: I do not admit that communism is necessarily in harmony with the dominant trend of social forces. I see that when it suits your argument you, like most Communists, fall back on the doctrine of a fatalistic determinism which makes the communist revolution inevitable whatever men do about it; but when your argument requires another doctrine you admit that the social revolution may be mastered and directed by the conscious purposes of men. You ought really to accept one doctrine or the other, and stick to it. But no matter. Accept one doctrine or both, as you like. In either case I see no good reason for joining the Communists. If the communist revolution is inevitable, whatever men do about it, why do anything? Why join either side, if you know before hand that one side is bound to win anyway? But if the communist revolution is not inevitable, then the proletariat can indeed do something to hasten it, and by the same token the bourgeoisie can do something to retard it. And in that case why should I join the Communists? I am a professor; and the Communists are never weary of telling me that professors as a class support the capitalist régime because it is their economic interest to do so. Very well, I will be a sufficiently good Marxian to accept the doctrine that men's actions are motivated by their economic class interest. If then my economic interests are bound up with the capitalist régime, and I can do something to retard the communist revolution, I should be, according to Marx himself, a poor humanitarian fool to desert my class and work for a revolution which, if successful, would ruthlessly suppress me. As a liberal humanitarian, or a Christian mystic, I might logically sacrifice myself and my class for the welfare of the masses; but as a Marxian that would be to adopt the very "utopian" attitude which Marx never ceased to ridicule. You really ask too much. The Marxian philosophy teaches me either that the communist revolution is inevitable, in which case I merely resign myself to it: or else it teaches me that the communist revolution can be hastened or retarded by the conscious efforts of men, in which case I stick to my class and do what I can to retard it. In either case I have the profound consolation of knowing that my conduct is based on the solid foundation of the Marxian philosophy of history.

These, you are to understand, are choices logically open to me on the assumption that I accept the Marxian philosophy of history. But life is less simple than logic. In logic you can present me with clear-cut alternatives. You can ask me whether I will "choose" to support the dictator-

ship of the proletariat or the dictatorship of the bourgeoisie, quite as if
some day, the two contending parties being lined up in battle array on a
champs de mars, I should be asked to step out and join one side or the
other. In actual life it does not seem to me that I am ever confronted
with choices as simple or as dramatically staged as that. When I voted
for Mr. Roosevelt (if I *did* vote for him—I can't be sure now) I made
a choice, without being certain (any more than Mr. Roosevelt himself
was) what would come of it. I am now "supporting" (so far as I am supporting anything) the Roosevelt administration, and it is possible that in
1936 I shall vote for the reëlection of Mr. Roosevelt. Does this mean
that I am "choosing" to support a fascist rather than a communist régime?
Thoroughgoing Communists appear to know what I am: the New Deal,
they say, is obviously an American species of fascist technique. But I am
sufficiently naïve not to be aware of having made any choice between
communism and fascism. And very glad I am that it is so. I should dislike
very much to be confronted with a clear-cut choice between a dictatorship of the proletariat and a dictatorship of the bourgeoisie. I should be
inclined to say, "A plague on both your houses!" I find Mussolini as offensive as Stalin, and Hitler more offensive than either.

Communist: That is all very well, but a real revolution is not impossible. There are plenty of Russians who could assure you that the alternative you so much dislike has been presented to them in a quite sufficiently
clear-cut and dramatic manner. If it should be similarly presented in this
country, it seems to me that you would, however much you might dislike it, have to choose one side or the other.

Liberal: Not necessarily. There would still be another possibility.

Communist: What would that be?

Liberal: I might still refuse to join either side. I might persist in the
futility of expressing my faith in the superior virtues of persuasion.

Communist: That would have serious consequences for you. You
would be suppressed.

Liberal: True enough. But I might accept the consequences. I might
choose to be suppressed rather than to support what I object to. In short,
I might, as a last refuge from imbecility, become a Christian and practise
the precept that it is better to suffer evil than to do it.

Communist: That would be to fall back upon a far more mystical
type of idealism than Marx ever contemplated, and I fail to see that it
would get you anywhere.

Liberal: I dare say it wouldn't. But, as I said before, I am a professor,
and a professor, as the German proverb has it, is "a man who thinks otherwise": if he is not permitted to talk freely he cannot get anywhere anyway.

• *Questions for Study*

1. What is the form of the essay? Why does Becker choose to present his ideas in this manner? What might have been lost if he presented his points in ordinary expository form? Compare this selection with Plato's "On Poets and Poetry."
2. What devices of logical thinking discussed in Johnson's essay appear in this selection? What fallacies are in evidence?
3. Sum up the arguments presented by the Communist speaker. How does the Liberal refute each? What reasons does the Liberal give for his unwillingness to accept predictions concerning future history?
4. Compare and contrast the tones and modes of presentation used by Marx and Engels, Veblen, and Becker.

JOHN K. GALBRAITH

•

LABOR, LEISURE, AND

THE NEW CLASS

———————

I

In a society of high and increasing affluence there are three plausible tendencies as regards toil. As the production of goods comes to seem less urgent, and as individuals are less urgently in need of income for the purchase of goods, they will work fewer hours or days in the week. Or they will work less hard. Or, as a final possibility, it may be that fewer people will work all the time.

In the last century a drastic decline has occurred in the work week. In 1850 it is estimated to have averaged just under seventy hours, the equivalent of seven ten-hour days a week or roughly six at from six in the

From *The Affluent Society* by John K. Galbraith, Boston: Houghton Mifflin Company, 1958. Reprinted by permission of Houghton Mifflin Company.

morning to six at night. A hundred years later the average was 40.0 hours or five eight-hour days.

This decline reflects a tacit but unmistakable acceptance of the declining marginal urgency of goods. There is no other explanation. However, such is the hold of production on our minds that this explanation is rarely offered. The importance and rewards of leisure are urged, almost never the unimportance of goods. Or, since production per hour has been increasing as the work week has declined, it is said that we are able to reduce the work because more is produced in less time. No mention is made of the fact that even more would be produced in more time. Or, finally, the decline is related to the feeling that steps must be taken to share the available work as productivity per worker rises. This also implies that the marginal urgency of production is low or negligible, but again the point remains unmade.

A reduction in the work week is an exceedingly plausible reaction to the declining marginal urgency of product. Over the span of man's history, although a phenomenal amount of education, persuasion, indoctrination, and incantation have been devoted to the effort, ordinary people have never been quite persuaded that toil is as agreeable as its alternatives. Thus to take increased well-being partly in the form of more goods and partly in the form of more leisure is unquestionably rational. In addition, the institution of overtime enables the worker to go far to adjust work and income to his own taste and requirements. It breaks with the barbarous uniformity of the weekly wage with its assumption that all families have the same tastes, needs, and requirements. Few things enlarge the liberty of the individual more substantially than to grant him a measure of control over the amount of his income.

Unfortunately in the conventional wisdom the reduction in hours has emerged as the only legitimate response to increasing affluence. This is at least partly because the issue has never been faced in terms of the increasing unimportance of goods. Accordingly, though we have attributed value to leisure, a ban still lies on other courses which seem to be more directly in conflict with established attitudes on productive efficiency. In a society rationally concerned with its own happiness these alternatives have a strong claim to consideration.

II

The first of these is that work can be made easier and more pleasant.

The present-day industrial establishment is a great distance removed from that of the last century or even of twenty-five years ago. This improvement has been the result of a variety of forces—government standards and factory inspection; general technological and architectural advance; the fact that productivity could be often increased by substituting machine power for heavy or repetitive manual labor; the need to compete for a labor force; and union intervention to improve working conditions in addition to wages and hours.

However, except where the improvement contributed to increased productivity, the effort to make work more pleasant has had to support a large burden of proof. It was permissible to seek the elimination of hazardous, unsanitary, unhealthful, or otherwise objectionable conditions of work. The speed-up might be resisted—to a point. But the test was not what was agreeable but what was unhealthful or, at a minimum, excessively fatiguing. The trend toward increased leisure is not reprehensible, but we resist vigorously the notion that a man should work less hard while on the job. Here older attitudes are involved. We are gravely suspicious of any tendency to expend less than the maximum effort, for this has long been a prime economic virtue.

In strict logic there is as much to be said for making work pleasant and agreeable as for shortening hours. On the whole it is probably as important for a wage earner to have pleasant working conditions as a pleasant home. To a degree, he can escape the latter but not the former— though no doubt the line between an agreeable tempo and what is flagrant featherbedding is difficult to draw. Moreover, it is a commonplace of the industrial scene that the dreariest and most burdensome tasks, requiring as they do a minimum of thought and skill, frequently have the largest numbers of takers. The solution to this problem lies, as we shall see presently, in drying up the supply of crude manpower at the bottom of the ladder. Nonetheless the basic point remains: the case for more leisure is not stronger on purely *prima facie* grounds than the case for making labor-time itself more agreeable. The test, it is worth repeating, is not the effect on productivity. It is not seriously argued that the shorter work week increases productivity—that men produce more in fewer hours than they would in more. Rather it is whether fewer hours are always to be preferred to more but more pleasant ones.

III

The third of the obvious possibilities with increasing affluence is for fewer people to work. This tendency has also been operating for many years although in a remarkably diverse form. Since 1890, when one boy in four and one girl in ten between the ages of ten and fifteen were gainfully employed, large numbers of juveniles have been retired from the labor force and their number now is negligible. At the same time a large number of women have been added. In 1890 19.5 per cent of the female population ten years and over was in the labor force and by 1953 this proportion had risen to 29.7 per cent. However, this change reflects in considerable measure the shift of tasks—food preparation, clothing manufacture, even child-rearing—out of the home. Women who previously performed them have gone along to other work. The woman who takes charge of a day nursery has joined the labor force, as have the women whose children she cares for.

For seventy-five years the proportion of the male population in the labor force has been constant at around seventy-five per cent of those over ten years of age. There are a smaller percentage of the very young and of those over sixty-five, but this has been offset by the increase in population in the ages between twenty and sixty-five where the proportion of workers to the total is very high.

With diminishing marginal urgency of goods it is logical that the first to be spared should be old and young. We have yet, however, to view this tendency consistently and comprehensively. We are able to dispense with the labor of those who have reached retiring age because the goods they add are a low order of urgency, whereas a poor society must extract the last ounce of labor effort from all. But we have ordinarily subjected those who retire to a drastic reduction in income and living standards. Obviously, if the retirement can be afforded because the product is no longer urgent, a satisfactory—meaning for most purposes the customary—living standard can be accorded to the retired employee for the same reason. Similarly we have excluded youngsters from the labor market, partly on the ground that labor at too early an age is unduly painful and injurious to health, and partly to make way for educational opportunity. But while we have felt it possible to dispense with the goods that the youngsters produce, we have yet to provide them, at least in full and satisfactory measure, with the education that their exemption from labor was designed to make possible. If we are affluent enough to dispense with the product of juvenile labor, it again follows that we are affluent enough to provide the education that takes its place.

In addition to releasing the old and young, it may be that we need not use all of the labor force at all times. This possibility was explored. . . . If the marginal urgency of goods is low, then so is the urgency of employing the last man or the last million men in the labor force. By allowing ourselves such slack, in turn, we reduce the standards of economic performance to a level more nearly consonant with the controls available for its management. And in so widening the band of what is deemed tolerable performance lies our best hope of minimizing the threat of inflation with its further and persistent threat to social balance.

Such a step requires much more adequate provision than now for those who are temporarily unemployed. We have seen, however, that such measures are possible and, indeed, have a vital stabilizing effect. And again such compensation accords with the logic of the situation. If our need for production is of such a low order of urgency that we can afford some unemployment in the interest of stability—a proposition, incidentally, of impeccably conservative antecedents—then we can afford to give those who are unemployed the goods that enable them to sustain their accustomed standard of living. If we don't need what the unemployed do not make, we can obviously afford them what they customarily eat and wear.

IV

However, the greatest prospect that we face—indeed what must now be counted one of the central economic goals of our society—is to eliminate toil as a required economic institution. This is not a utopian vision. We are already well on the way. Only an extraordinarily elaborate exercise in social camouflage has kept us from seeing what has been happening.

Nearly all societies at nearly all times have had a leisure class—a class of persons who were exempt from toil. In modern times and especially in the United States the leisure class, at least in any identifiable phenomenon, has disappeared. To be idle is no longer considered rewarding or even entirely respectable.

But we have barely noticed that the leisure class has been replaced by another and much larger class to which work has none of the older connotation of pain, fatigue, or other mental or physical discomfort. We have failed to appreciate the emergence of this New Class, as it may be simply called, largely as the result of one of the oldest and most effective obfuscations in the field of social science. This is the effort to assert that all work—physical, mental, artistic, or managerial—is essentially the same.

This effort to proclaim the grand homogeneity of work has commanded, for different reasons, the support of remarkably numerous and diverse groups. To economists it has seemed a harmless and, indeed, an indispensable simplification. It has enabled them to deal homogeneously with all of the different kinds of productive effort and to elaborate a general theory of wages applying to all who receive an income for services. Doubts have arisen from time to time, but they have been suppressed or considered to concern special cases. The identity of all classes of labor is one thing on which capitalist and communist doctrine wholly agree. The president of the corporation is pleased to think that his handsomely appointed office is the scene of the same kind of toil as the assembly line and that only the greater demands in talent and intensity justify his wage differential. The Communist officeholder cannot afford to have it supposed that his labor differs in any significant respect from that of the comrade at the lathe or on the collective farm with whom he is ideologically one. In both societies it serves the democratic conscience of the more favored groups to identify themselves with those who do hard physical labor. A lurking sense of guilt over a more pleasant, agreeable, and remunerative life can often be assuaged by the observation "I am a worker too" or, more audaciously, by the statement that "mental labor is far more taxing than physical labor." Since the man who does physical labor is intellectually disqualified from comparing his toil with that of the brainworker, the proposition is uniquely unassailable.

In fact the differences in what labor means to different people could not be greater. For some, and probably a majority, it remains a stint to be performed. It may be preferable, especially in the context of social attitudes toward production, to doing nothing. Nevertheless it is fatiguing or monotonous or, at a minimum, a source of no particular pleasure. The reward rests not in the task but in the pay.

For others work, as it continues to be called, is an entirely different matter. It is taken for granted that it will be enjoyable. If it is not, this is a source of deep dissatisfaction or frustration. No one regards it as remarkable that the advertising man, tycoon, poet, or professor who suddenly finds his work unrewarding should seek the counsel of a psychiatrist. One insults the business executive or the scientist by suggesting that his principal motivation in life is the pay he receives. Pay is not unimportant. Among other things it is a prime index of prestige. Prestige—the respect, regard, and esteem of others—is in turn one of the more important sources of satisfaction associated with this kind of work. But, in general, those who do this kind of work expect to contribute their best regardless of compensation. They would be disturbed by any suggestion to the contrary.

Such is the labor of the New Class. No aristocrat ever contemplated the loss of feudal privileges with more sorrow than a member of this class would regard his descent into ordinary labor where the reward was only the pay. In the years following World War II a certain number of grade school teachers left their posts for substantially higher paid factory work. The action made headlines because it represented an unprecedented desertion of an occupation which was assumed to confer the dignity of the New Class. The college professor, who is more securely a member of the New Class than the schoolteacher, would never contemplate such a change even as an exercise in eccentricity and no matter how inadequate he might consider his income.

In keeping with all past class behavior, the New Class seeks energetically to perpetuate itself. Offspring are not expected to plan their lives in order to make a large amount of money. (Those who go into business are something of an exception at least partly because income, in business, is uniquely an index of prestige.) But from their earliest years the children are carefully indoctrinated in the importance of finding an occupation from which they will derive satisfaction—one which will involve not toil but enjoyment. One of the principal sources of sorrow and frustration in the New Class is the son who fails to make the grade—who drops down into some tedious and unrewarding occupation. The individual who meets with this misfortune—the son of the surgeon who becomes a garage hand—is regarded by the community with pity not unmixed with horror. But the New Class has considerable protective powers. The son of the surgeon rarely does become a garage hand. However inadequate, he can usually manage to survive, perhaps somewhat exiguously, on the edge of his caste. And even if, as a salesman or an investment counselor, he finds little pleasure in his work, he will be expected to assert the contrary in order to affirm his membership in the New Class.

• *Questions for Study*

1. Compare this essay with Adam Smith's "Economics and the Class Structure," written approximately two hundred years earlier. In what ways is it clear that the society for which each man is writing is fundamentally different?
2. What contrast is implicit throughout Galbraith's essay? How does the author define the "New Class"? Is there anything in your own personal experience that might make you wish to modify the definition?
3. Explain the meaning of the key phrase "the increasing unimportance of goods."
4. How do Galbraith's views tend to refute the Marxian concept of class conflict?
5. Compare and contrast the attitudes toward work of Smith, Marx and Engels, Veblen, and Galbraith.

REYNOLDS GIRDLER

•

THE BUSINESSMAN:

HERO OR SCAPEGOAT?

Throughout the ages the businessman has helped build civilization's great cities, provide people with luxuries and artists with patronage, and lift his fellow-citizens to undreamed-of standards of living. In the last few centuries the businessman has seeded the Industrial Revolution around the world.

Yet he has seldom been able to win friends or influence people.

While the businessman has managed to collect sparse kudos for his pains, it has not been unusual for whole countries to worship at the feet of men like Napoleon or Genghis Khan, the slaughterers and egoists of history, or, in the words of Miss Miriam Beard's "The History of the Businessman" (Macmillan, 1938), the "perverts and maniacs who might succeed as monarchs but who never, even in the Renaissance, could manage a cloth factory." But the economic adventurers and engineers who through their imagination, audacity, and persistence have actually made life better for the common man have most often cut comic figures in the eyes of that same common man.

This general misunderstanding and unpopularity harass the spirit of the average American businessman. He yearns to lay claim to a defined, respected, and secure position in the social order, consonant with his intentions and his achievements; and, in these modern days, he has set out to promote his own image of himself by means of substantial public-relations programs. And don't think that a present-day public-relations program doesn't run into plenty of heavy weather. The modern businessman changes a price, either up or down, and there is always at least one politician who wants to hale him to Washington for a Congressional investigation, a Justice Department suit, or both. The executive

From the *Saturday Review*, April 19, 1958. Reprinted by permission of the *Saturday Review* and of the author.

goes out to the theatre, or tries to watch TV, and finds an ugly caricature of himself betraying his wife, friend, or brother in a drive for power. Press and pulpit attack his sales and advertising managers for their efforts to probe the consumer's subconscious and cater to it.

Surrounded by these unremitting, widespread evidences of hostility and rancor (for so they seem to the businessman), the modern corporation executive vaguely and plaintively ascribes their origin to Marx or the second Roosevelt. Not so, says Miss Beard, looking back over 3,000 years of recorded history. Such antagonisms have been endemic in all societies, whether headed by a king, the nobility, the landed gentry, a dictator, by warriors or by priests. In every form of society known to man, the businessman has had to contend with the recurring animus of the ruling political class, endure the barbs and strictures of writers, artists, comedians, and teachers, and suffer consequent unpopularity with the general public. Nor is it a comfort to the businessman to know that other occupational groups feel just as maligned and unappreciated.

The writer and moral philosopher, Seneca, observing the palatial homes being built by the rich Roman bourgeois, "tells how the rising parvenus bought books in sets to fill the shelves in their new abodes, even though they never peeped inside one of the volumes." This, then, is a hallowed charge of the literati against the businessman, skilfully revived by Scott Fitzgerald in his memorable scene in Gatsby's library.

Precedents for today's popular sport of lampooning businessmen on television screen and in books go back a long way, we learn from Miss Beard. "The forerunner of the business suit of today," she says, "made its earliest dramatic appearance in the Italian *commedia dell'arte* in the closing part of the sixteenth century. It was worn by the comic stock figure of the Venetian merchant *Pantalone,* who gave his name to pantaloons. . . . He is a doddering, meddling, suspicious old fellow who does well enough in matters of finance, but remains unlucky in love," losing *Columbine* to *Harlequin.* Harlequin's family has left trade, and he is therefore home free as far as the dramatists are concerned. In the hands of Molière, the comic merchant Pantalone became M. Jourdain "The Bourgeois Gentilhomme." To seventeenth-century society, of course, the bite in that title was sharper than to us today. The idea that a businessman, a *bourgeois,* could also be a gentleman was good for a belly-laugh any place in Europe at that time.

Nor has the businessman ever fared too well with the clergy. There was, for instance, "Savonarola, the dark-browed depression phenomenon, the prophet of doom, who attacked business at a time of economic crisis, when even Florentines were discouraged and ready to renounce the world." Even the "charming, gentle, charitable, and laborious Archbishop

Antoninus [a fifteenth-century archbishop of Florence, and in his day a famous theologian], who finally made business respectable within the Roman Church, by personal example and through his epochal work, 'The Summa Theologica,' was full of medieval doctrinaire notions," says Miss Beard. "Advertising which explains the real merits of the article is useful," Antoninus decided, "but that consisting only of *verba adulatoria*, words that flatter the consumer, is theologically reprehensible."

In other words, the appeal to the ego, to the reader's desire to think well of himself, was not considered cricket even then.

From Plato, who insisted that "the merchant must be degraded . . . never to share in the pure, ideal life of the ruling state," to Prussia, "where burghers and their wives were separated from personages of rank at palace receptions by a cord stretched across the ballroom," the business-man historically has been at odds with the ruling class.

But his real torture began, we learn, "with the creation of that magnificent seventeenth-century fiction—the State." "In varying degrees," says Miss Beard, "the States of Europe had become laboratories in which all sorts of curious and edifying experiments in controlling economic development were being performed . . . under the full pressure of autocracy, businesses were stunted or fostered by arbitrary decrees; industries were transplanted or uprooted; working habits and consumption habits were altered; immense shifts and dislocations were undertaken light-heartedly."

In England, the Government monopolized Bible printing, produced the howler "the *un*righteous shall inherit the earth" . . . in Prussia, the king's agent sniffed for the illicit coffee-bean in every street . . . in Bavaria, the dukes destroyed the native linen manufacture, wasted fortunes trying to hot-house a printed cotton industry . . . in France, a state campaign to crush the cotton industry cost the lives of 16,000 men in riots and hangings. Finally, Louis XIV stamped out capitalistic enterprise, decimated ports, impoverished centers of trade, and drove capital from the country."

Miss Beard finds two reasons for the businessman's continuing difficulties: 1) the businessman has no history, "and a man who lacks one nowadays may be said to go unarmed"; 2) "he has had no *wohir*, no whither, no discoverable, ultimate purpose." In other words, the businessman has never developed a creed historically or of the present that would explain him to the public and protect him against the recurring attacks of the other institutions comprising society.

Not that he hasn't sought a creed, an ideology to match those of the individuals and institutions bent on his annihilation. He has tried, according to Miss Beard, reliance on Fortuna, the guileful symbol and reminder of the uncertainty of things temporal. He has relied upon natural law, the inevitability of progress, and seen his shining new financial empires crash in ruins. Again and again he has returned to that noble concept of the Renaissance, the freedom of the individual, only to see the masses prefer security to liberty.

More than other businessmen, the American wants a creed, for "a vague unrest has filled him for a long time, which no professors and counselors have so far been able to allay. . . . No precedent can be found for his situation, amid a democratic multitude, still fond of the successful man, but ready to jeer at his slightest mistaken antic, and with revolution for its only tradition."

With this observation, Historian Beard approaches a recommendation that brings her within the pages of this issue of *The Saturday Review*. The shoemaker Filene, she notes, developed the formula of "Service" to society, and Miss Beard, rightly and from the vantage point of historical observation, terms it "one of the most potent ever devised."

It is, for incalculable service to society is inherent in the daily operations of almost every corporation. In the identification of the private corporate interest with a public need, in the extension of a private interest into a public service, lies one of the surest means by which the privately owned and managed company can dramatize its value and unique contribution to society. Herein lies the opportunity for the corporation to project itself as a "good" corporate personality, easily recognizable as such, and serving a recognizable public need.

This is scarcely an original observation. Others have seen it, but have said it in other words. This is the concept Denny Griswold, publisher of *Public Relations News*, is seeking to limn in her definition of public relations:

"Public Relations is the management function which evaluates public attitudes, *identifies the policies and procedures of an individual or an organization with the public interest,* and executes a program of action to earn public understanding and acceptance." (Italics ours.)

It is the concept around which John Hill, of Hill and Knowlton, steps from time to time in his recent book, "Corporate Public Relations" (Harpers, 1958). And public-relations practitioners by the hundreds, and corporation executives by the hundreds, have skirted the edges of the idea with that neat, crisp definition of public relations: "Being good and getting credit for it."

If there then exists a formula, known to businessmen and their counselors alike, which could help to win for business a *defined, respected, and secure* niche in organized society, the question obviously follows: Why hasn't business achieved the goal it so very much desires, and upon which it lavishes millions yearly in the name of public relations?

Like the answer to any other obvious question, the answer to this one needs some spelling out.

In the first place, if there is any point to the study of history, it is to learn basic lessons from the past, and apply them correctly to the present. The Founding Fathers of this Republic, historians generally acknowledge, did just that, and did it well. Miss Beard is right when she accuses businessmen of not knowing business history, and of having memories that scarcely run back to the last Depression.

Nor does the businessman realize the legitimacy of the modern corporation's claim to a rightful place in society. No king ever had a more legitimate, honorable, and unquestioned right to a throne than the modern corporation has to a respected and secure place in the body politic. Its lineage is distinguished, its pedigree honorable and established. But of these historical facts and their pertinence to modern public debate the business executive seems to know little. Or if he is aware of the honorable antecedents of the type of organization he directs, and their potential value in establishing for him a secure, respected, and publicly accepted place in society, he gives little sign of it.

Yet these facts were all set out for him by Dr. W. R. Scott, lecturer in political economy at Cambridge, in 1912. In his towering, three-volume work, "The Constitution and Finance of English, Scottish and Irish Joint-Stock Companies to 1720," Dr. Scott traces the growth of the concept of "perpetual succession," of the idea of a corporate body's having a life of its own, independent of the lives of the human beings operating it. This concept was rooted in custom and sanctioned by law through the guilds hundreds of years before Sebastian Cabot co-founded *"the Mysterie and Companie of Marchants Adventurers for the discoverie of regions, dominions, islands and places unknown,"* which Scott says was one of the two first joint-stock bodies we would now call "a corporation."

The rights of shareholders, the negotiability of pieces of the common stock, the necessary divisions of rights and responsibilities of the various elements of a corporation all derive from custom, tradition, and law long established and recognized. Many of the challenges to corporate action and corporate management today are challenges against thousands of years of experience, tradition, custom, and law.

Scott also clearly portrays the services the corporate firm first performed for England, enabling that people to launch and nourish voyages of discovery, engage in foreign trade, develop new inventions and finance governments with an efficiency no other form of economic organization could equal then or can equal now. Now and then a William McChesney

Martin, Jr., will arise to show his familiarity with Scott in the effective policies by which he restores the New York Stock Exchange to respectability and dignity, or controls the nation's credit with rare understanding and sagacity. But such deep, historical understanding, and its practical value today, seem lacking in most modern business leaders when they seek to engage in public debate on politics and economics. They are overlooking a powerful arsenal.

Being little acquainted with history, the modern executive has incorrectly looked upon his public relations problems as born of the New Deal, and destined someday to die with it. It is Miss Beard's special contribution that she has demonstrated that these antagonisms, hostilities, misunderstandings, call them what you will, which the businessman regards as of fairly recent and dubious origin, are built into every society of which we have had any knowledge, and will rise and fall with the standard economic indices.

The businessman, therefore, must reckon as permanent his differences of opinion with the ruling political power. He must accept as permanent the skepticism and hostility of the dramatist, the artist, the poet, the teacher, and often the clergy. He must face the fact that he must take these inherent antagonisms into daily account, even as he does the resistance of the consumer, the bargaining power of his labor, and the economics of transportation as they affect him and his competitors. These manifestations of other institutions are not just bothersome flies that will disappear with a kindly, killing frost—they are permanent forces which figure into his consolidated income account and, curiously, when properly used, can figure *profitably* in that all-important final summation.

If he succeeds in making this mental adjustment, what then, is his next step?

He can then follow the advice given so many times by his associates, and by John Hill, Mrs. Griswold, and SR's William Patterson and Elmo Roper, and hundreds of others interested in public relations. He must "Do good, and get credit for it." To do this, he can, for instance, follow the example of The Metropolitan Life Insurance Company. He can identify a private corporate interest with a public need. He can extend a private interest into a public service. To his astonishment, he may then find himself with a potent public-relations formula.

The Metropolitan Life Insurance Company is the largest agglomeration of capital in the world. As such, it strides about in awesome dimensions that could, in another aspect, frighten the people into destructive panic. Such has been the fate of many lesser capital aggregations. But the Metropolitan presents quite another face to the American people. To the American public it is a warm-hearted, human institution vitally interested in keeping the average citizen healthy. For thirty-six years, through its public-health advertising, the Metropolitan has ministered tenderly to the average American's heart, his bowels, spleen and other organs in words and pictures of genuine helpfulness and exemplary clarity. It has successfully identified its private corporate interest in having people outlive the actuarial tables with the individual's foremost concern—his health.

The Metropolitan Life has executed this program primarily in the form of paid advertising. And this has misled the johnny-come-latelys to the field of public relations. It never occurs to some of them, simply because it is executed through the form of paid advertising, that here is one of the most effective public relations programs ever devised.

Assuming then, that the modern corporation executive admits that public relations will always be with him, and that a potent formula for a program can be found according to Hill, Griswold, *et al.*, what is the third essential step?

He must then make the supreme sacrifice: He must give up his corporate self-centeredness and, instead of thinking from his executive suite outward, he must first concern himself with the viewpoint, the preoccupations, the loves, and the laughter of the people whose understanding he is seeking. Until he understands them, he can never hope for reciprocal understanding. It is at this point that we encounter the most obvious reason for the obvious failures of most so-called public-relations programs. The man who pays the piper is under the irresistible temptation to call the tune. By God, he's paying the money, and he's going to tell 'em what he wants 'em told, whether they want to hear it or not, and no matter how scattered, complicated, and disparate his messages and the media carrying them. So he sends his messages out by personal representatives, by mailed copies of speeches, by news releases and by other media at his command, to try to grab 170 million preoccupied people by the lapels and lecture them into loving him and his company. Inevitably, he seeks to cram down 170 million throats a tangled text of facts and figures of no interest to anyone but himself. If it were not so tragic for the basic principles of the Republic, this spectacle, apparent daily in our lives, would be laughable.

There is one other must for American business. This is the necessity for couching its programs in the dramatic simplicity that distinguishes the attacks of its adversaries. "Triple A Plowed Under," "One Third of a Nation," "The 200 Thriftiest Families," "Merchants of Death," "The River." Here are titles and phrases that evoke memories of words and tableaux that raised bleeding welts on the body of private enterprise only a few short years ago. Each was an example of simplified, dramatic presentation of a single idea.

Can the American businessman match the simple, direct weapons of his antagonists? Precedent suggests an affirmative answer. The men who built the first big American companies were masters of simplicity. They organized a company, they selected a trademark, they devised a slogan. And in the limited media then at their command, they launched these simple words and symbols, and repeated them, and repeated them *ad nauseam*, until they became part and parcel of the lives of everyone who lives today.

The rock of Gibraltar, the stag of Hartford, Bull Durham, the Dutch Boy, the Gold Dust Twins, "Hasn't Scratched Yet," "Ask the Man Who Owns One." Does any American over forty have to be told the corporate name or the product associated with these words? Yet how many corporations apply this technique to their public relations programs today?

Somewhere, sometime, during the evolution of Madison Avenue, the genius of business for simplicity, and its instinctive understanding of the public mind, was lost in a maze of account executives, copywriters, and plans boards. Business and its counselors have forgotten the potency of the single idea and the power of repetition. Instead, they try to sell ten chapters of fundamental economics to 170 million people in succeeding instalments.

The moral is obvious: *A public-relations program must not only be founded in genuine public service, but it must be expressed with the great drama of which simplicity alone is capable.* It can never be accomplished by the complicated, self-centered forms and substances which pass for public-relations *programs* today, and on which so many millions of dollars are being wasted.

Never did private enterprise have such an opportunity as it has today to carve out, in organized society the world over, a place for itself that is clearly defined, respected, and secure. In the early Thirties the Socialist blueprint looked beautiful to many. But since then we have had Hitler, Mussolini, Stalin, Korea, and finally Hungary. People are beginning to learn that someone must organize the world's work. Organized by the state, the end result must be a minimum of human liberty. Organized by private individuals, the end result . . . ? In their public-relations programs, let American companies dramatically portray the social and economic contributions each is making as an inherent part of its operations. Then people in the mass may get a better understanding of the virtues of, and interdependence of, capitalism, democracy, well-being, and freedom.

• *Questions for Study*

1. For what purposes does Girdler use source material (for example, Miriam
   Beard's *The History of the Businessman*) in the first half of this essay?
2. According to the author, what essential fact is indicated through history
   concerning the businessman's relationship to society? What two reasons
   does the author quote from Miss Beard's book for this relationship?
3. What three steps must the businessman take to improve his status? What
   does the example of the Metropolitian Life Insurance Company show?
4. Enumerate the arguments showing the importance of a public relations
   program. Do you think there are any dangers to the general public in such
   a program? If so, explain them. Is it possible, in your opinion, to manipulate
   the views of large segments of society? Explain.

ROBERT THEOBALD

•

THE NEEDS OF POOR COUNTRIES

The problem facing us is to decide how much emphasis the poor countries should lay on the need for economic growth, how drastically they
should revise their social system to encourage economic growth. The
most vital difference between the rich and poor countries is that the poor
countries have not attached much importance to economic growth in
the past and are not organized to encourage the changes required if they
are to attain it. Economic growth in the Western countries, in Russia,
and in Japan resulted from the dissolution and destruction of social patterns that limited the rate of change in response to economic forces.
In America, where this process has gone furthest, the individual often
moves his home every two or three years, leaving behind him all but his

From *The Challenge of Abundance,* New York: Clarkson N. Potter, Inc., 1961. Reprinted by permission of Clarkson N. Potter, Inc.

immediate family. This caused a major—if little noticed—revolution that separates the generation born around the turn of the century from those born between the two World Wars. The older generation typically knew every limb of its family tree, and can trace all the great-uncles and second cousins twice removed. To the younger generation this is slightly amusing or downright ridiculous: the family usually consists of husband, wife, and children. Some residual loyalty may remain for one's parents and perhaps for brothers and sisters, but this is the normal limit of interest.

Many people will go where their jobs take them—their work is the controlling factor in their lives. If one line of industry declines, people are increasingly willing to enter another—they feel no emotional bond with their trade or even their profession. The concept of man as a unit of labor is still gaining ground simply because men have subordinated their social interests to their economic—we have made arrangements that allow men to be used "efficiently" and moved from one occupation to another with the minimum of difficulty.

It is obvious that this process of depersonalization is not complete. But the emotional tie between an individual and his profession or trade has declined. We have only to go back one century to see the extent of this change. One of the tragedies of the nineteenth century was the slow death of the profession of the hand-loom weaver in England. They were deprived of their occupation by the invention of power looms, but they did not leave their traditional field. Almost unbelievable suffering resulted from their continuance in a dying occupation. The failure to find new jobs stemmed from two radically different causes. First, the people were emotionally attached to their work and showed reluctance to leave it. Second, the employment "market" hardly existed; there were no efficient methods of moving people from one industry to another.

In most of the poor countries an emotional loyalty to a way of life continues. Unless we realize this difference between the present loyalty patterns of the rich and poor countries, intervention to cause more "efficient" production can lead to widespread misery and hardship. The people in the poor countries of the world are still generally attached to their trades and professions; their satisfaction is greatly decreased if they are forced to change from one type of employment to another. Moreover, in many areas of the poor countries there are no possibilities for change —the removal of one type of employment opportunity for any reason *automatically* deprives some people of work, for there is already considerable unemployment.

The disruptive economic effects of changes in the poor countries are greatly enhanced by the social effects. The prevailing social order in the poor countries is still kin-based or tribal-based. Movement from one

place to another to seek work often destroys the moral and social sup-
ports through which man has lived. We continue to forget that economic
growth is for people and that their lives should not be distorted to serve
economic growth. Indeed, in the West we have so completely accepted
the argument that economic behavior does not involve values that we
have forgotten that it is capable of arousing great emotional reactions.
Karl Polanyi in *Trade and Market in the Early Empires,* calls our attention to this: ". . . only in the presence of a system of price-making markets
will exchange acts of individuals result in fluctuating prices that integrate
the economy. Otherwise such acts of barter will remain ineffective and
therefore tend not to occur. Should they nevertheless happen, in a
random fashion, a violent emotional reaction would set in, as against
acts of indecency or acts of treason, since trading behavior is never
emotionally indifferent behavior and is not, therefore, tolerated by
opinion outside of the approved channels."

The West wants the people of the poor countries to live as we do
ourselves. We pity the nomad who is clearly "poverty-stricken." We fail
to understand that his life can be more richly satisfying than our own.
The Iranian Government has attempted to encourage many of the migratory tribes to settle in recent years. For a complex of economic, social,
and spiritual reasons the result was sometimes the destruction of the
way of life, the health, and even the limited economic wealth of the tribe.

In our desire to improve the material condition of the world we are
forgetting that the standard of living is not an end in itself but a means.
We analyze societies to see whether they are capable of rapid economic
growth, rather than examining them in order to see how the necessary
economic growth can be used to preserve the values of these countries.
We fail to realize that man can understand life only if his values allow
him to comprehend the situation. Our plans often do not take account
of the fact that, although the human mind has great capacities for adjustment, it can easily be overloaded, and overloading it can lead to mental
stress or even mental breakdown. We are only now beginning to understand that the result of such overstrain may be irrational and inexplicable behavior; that people trapped in situations they find too difficult of
solution may become childlike or may return to old forms of behavior
they had previously abandoned. Only if people "understand" situations
in the fullest sense will they be able to make sensible decisions.

One of the major limits to any realistic program for improving conditions in the proper countries must therefore be in terms of the ability
of the society and the individual to accept change. In addition, any program must also recognize that many of the present reactions in the poor
countries are unfavorable to economic growth. These behavior patterns

lead to the "vicious circle" analysis, which is basic to economic development theory. It is correctly argued that unless we can find ways to change certain reactions much of the money contributed by the Western countries cannot be successfully used.

The vicious circle most often examined is the increase in population that usually follows any increase in production and income. None of the poor countries has a really effective birth-control program; population increase has been limited in the past by the death of the majority of children before they reached adulthood. The death of children resulted from two different causes; first, the extremely poor health conditions in most countries and, second, the fact that famines occurred periodically following failures in harvests, and this led to large increases in the death rate.

Both these forces, which kept the rate of population increase low in earlier centuries, are now being limited in their effects. In the years since World War II each country has tried to reduce the toll of disease; the work of the World Health Organization has had dramatic results in reducing the incidence of malaria and other diseases. Also, few famines have developed, emergency exports of grains from those countries with surplus stocks being made whenever a dearth threatened. As a result of these changes death rates have declined throughout the world and the number of people in many poor countries has risen rapidly. In far too many countries the rise in population has taken up *all* the available increase in production; none of it has been available to *raise* standards of living.

A second type of vicious circle results from the increasing importance of consumer goods in almost all countries of the world. It is generally agreed that growth can be attained only if part of the resources of a country is devoted to investment—to the production of dams, factories, machinery, which will increase production in future years. The "revolution of rising expectations" is continually cutting into the resources available for investment and thus the rate of growth.

This vicious circle is inevitable in a world divided into two types of countries—the rich and the poor; the poor countries wish to attain the standards of the rich before it is possible for them to do so. However, the actions of both the rich and the poor countries have greatly increased the force behind the "revolution of rising expectations." The rich countries have done their best to bring their higher standard of living to the attention of the inhabitants of the poor in the years since the war. The result, in all too many cases, has been to build up resentment. In addition, the governments of the poor countries have themselves encouraged the trend toward a desire for greater consumption. Advertising, which must

inevitably increase felt wants, is allowed; some governments have introduced commercial television and some have even permitted time-
payment plans that allow consumers to buy goods before they have
money available. In the poor countries where the overwhelming problem
is a shortage of resources, such steps can only be unfavorable and act to
reduce the rate of economic growth.

The third—and almost certainly least-understood—vicious circle
depends on the relation between the income the individual receives and
the amount he is willing to do. If the price a producer gets for his goods
doubles, he needs to do only about half the amount of work to obtain
the same standard of living. Under these circumstances what should he
do? What would be his rational course of action? This depends on what
his goal in life may be. If he has fixed wants, and has no desire to work
for its own sake, he will decrease the amount of time he spends producing goods. This reaction has plagued those from the Western countries
for many decades; they have tended to call this reaction "laziness." In
many cases wage increases have had to be reversed because they decreased the amount of work people were willing to do.

We have not been much concerned with this problem of laziness in
Western countries in the twentieth century, for those who do not work
are looked upon askance, and a continuing increase in consumption is
generally accepted. Social prestige in the Western countries demands
that one have a job. A humorous plot for a highly successful television
play will illustrate this better than any argument. The story turned on
the fact that the husband liked housework and the wife liked to go out to
work. They therefore resolved to change their roles—the husband would
cease to work in an office while the wife would take a job. This unortho-
dox division of labor was heartily despised by the neighbors. The
resulting problems were solved only when the wife arranged for the
publication of one of *her* manuscripts under her *husband's* name. It was
then accepted that he was respectably employed writing—he was not
"idling." However, we must remember that the evolution of these attitudes is recent. As late as the mid-nineteenth century the complaint was
general that the result of higher wages was not more but less labor, not
a better but an inferior standard of work. The laborer was only too willing to quit his job and get drunk for a portion of the week if his wages
permitted it.

Although work is usually considered necessary in the rich countries,
it is often less acceptable in the poor. One particular facet of this reaction is particularly serious for the possibilities of economic development. Not only do employees tend to quit their work when they have
obtained the amount of money they feel they need; those in charge of

firms react in the same way. The entrepreneur, the person who causes economic growth by making changes that lead to greater efficiency in the economic system, tends to do less work if his income increases. Unlike the employer or director of firms in Western countries, his prestige is not tied up with the economic growth of his firm. Robert Heilbroner, in *The Quest for Wealth*, pointed up the difference between the businessman in North and South America: ". . . what is it which drives the American businessman so relentlessly when his easier-going Latin counterpart has long ago retired? What is it which makes us feel that there is a moral value in work and an inherent indecorum in idleness? These, too, are attitudes not shared in countries which have not undergone the baptism of asceticism. The Calvinist seed is too deeply implanted in our traditions to be extirpated with ease; and while the attitudes it engenders may be useful, we should beware of mistaking them for universal or inevitable." This unwillingness of entrepreneurs to continue working in the poor countries is made particularly serious by the fact that the educational pattern and the value system of the poor countries usually severely limits the number of people who are willing to set up factories and produce goods.

The successful development of the poor countries depends therefore to a large extent on our ability to destroy the forces creating vicious circles and to bring about reactions favorable to economic growth. Until this takes place, growth will not be built into the economy of each of the poor countries. W. W. Rostow, one of the most eminent authorities working in this field, has developed this conclusion. He has shown that economic growth depends upon the pre-existence of particular social attitudes. But we are unable to wait until education has led to this change. Our crucial problem at the present time is that we must find a way to use our available material resources to help the poor countries to develop despite the fact that vicious circles will interfere with their growth.

How can these three vicious circles be overcome and how can the poor countries take steps to help themselves at the present time? First, measures must be taken to limit the rate at which desires for consumption increase, for they will cut into the amount available for investment. The rate of increase in the demand for goods is *already* so great, because of the revolution of rising expectations, that no unnecessary encouragement to consumption should be allowed. This does not mean that consumption can be kept from rising, for the revolution of rising expectations is irreversible. However, promotional expenditure and time-payment plans should be limited and the rich countries prevented from flaunting their wealth. Although wants will still continue to rise—and Hollywood films and slick magazines will add to the pressure—any reductions in the rate would be beneficial.

That this problem is a major one can be seen by the attitude of the Jamaican authorities to tourism. They recognize that it is essential if they are to maintain a sufficient rate of economic growth, but they are deeply concerned lest the high standard of living of the visitors disrupt the pattern of life in the rural areas. They are also disturbed by the severe upward pressures it has caused on the cost of living, particularly for the middle classes.

The present rate of population increase, which leads to the second vicious circle, leaves us with only two choices: either we resort to birth control or we allow a 3 per cent increase in world population. Only the first of these choices is realistic in the long run and will make possible a rising standard of living in the short run. Education should force us to try to understand and control the changes taking place in the world for the good of mankind. We cannot be satisfied until we have examined closely and clearly whether our present attitudes are justified.

Although a willingness to look squarely at this issue would help, it would not solve the problem. None of the existing methods of birth control can be satisfactory in the insufficiently educated and traditionally oriented societies of the world. Two steps must be taken if a useful program of birth control is to be inaugurated. The first is to develop a cheap contraceptive—probably oral—that does not require a strict sense of time and is acceptable in each society. The second and usually more difficult step is to make sure that the resultant contraceptive is actually used by those in the poor countries.

Failure to pay for research on birth-control methods is often justified by the assertion that the people in the poor countries will not practice birth control. Such a belief is largely based on a lack of knowledge of recent surveys. When the attitudes of the populations of the poor countries with heavy population densities and high birth rates have been examined, there is usually a very large proportion of the people in favor of family limitation, even if the religious authorities are opposed. The West cannot evade its obligation on the grounds that birth-control methods would not be used; it must spend the money required to ensure the most rapid possible development of contraceptives.

Unfortunately, money is not the only, or even the most vital, factor needed for this research. The scarcest commodity is time, and this cannot be increased. Many years will be needed to be reasonably certain that new methods of contraception will not have undesirable side effects and to reduce manufacturing costs. Thus even if a revolution in the attitudes of the rich countries could be achieved in the immediate future—a revolution that, it may be said, does not appear to be imminent—there could be no dramatic decrease in births within the next decade. Indeed the continuing fall in the death rate and the change in the age structure of the poor countries must be expected to lead to a further rapid rise in the rate of population increase in coming years.

What can be done to solve the problems raised by the third vicious circle—that people in the poor countries, particularly entrepreneurs, reduce the amount of work they do when their income increases? One proposed solution is to increase the standard of living each individual hopes to attain, for if the amount he wishes to buy rises he will be willing to work longer hours. Such a change will often be unsatisfactory, for the favorable effect of the increased willingness to work would be offset by the increased desire for additional consumer goods. Indeed, because it is not usually possible to satisfy all the existing desires of consumers, a deliberate attempt to increase wants might well raise discontent in the community to a dangerous level.

A second possibility would be to try to encourage workers to lend their money to the government for investment purposes rather than to use it for consumption. The problem with this solution—apart from the ever-present difficulty of changing attitudes—is that the process of growth in many of the poor countries will almost inevitably cause inflation. Those who lend their money may find that the sum they receive when they require it back will buy less than they could originally have bought. This is not only unfortunate from the point of view of equity; it is also a serious block to any attempt to encourage people to save their money rather than to spend it.

A third possibility is for the government to attempt to influence people to work longer hours and more intensively. There are two major ways in which this can be done. The first is by the imposition of taxation. Those who are forced to pay increased taxes may try to make good the decrease in their post-tax income and therefore increase their amount of work. There is, however, always the danger that, if the rate of taxation is too heavy, people will actually cut the amount of work they do or spend a large part of their time working out how to avoid taxes.

An increase in taxes has often been proposed by the Western social scientist as the appropriate solution for the poor countries, and the adoption of tax systems similar to those used in the West has usually been suggested. Our acceptance of present patterns of direct (income) taxes has caused us to forget that our methods of taxation are largely the result of historical accident and inaccurate economic analysis. It may well be that other forms of taxation will be more "efficient" in the poor countries. For example, it might often be better to use indirect (sales) taxes, which are less obvious than direct taxes. Their rates can be adjusted so as to encourage the use of abundant resources and to discourage the use of those in scarce supply.

One of the main reasons why the amount of work is limited is that people do not think the rewards from work worthwhile. They therefore prefer doing nothing to producing goods. It is obvious that this pattern can be changed by encouraging people to consider work for their country as the most important way of spending their time. This is the second method open to the government as it tries to increase the number of hours of work each person is willing to contribute. The result of such exhortation can be a new dynamism among the people, as has occurred in Cuba, China, Guinea, Ghana, and many other areas. But as we have found to our cost, the construction of new patterns of life is usually accompanied by pressure against recalcitrants and by revolutionary fervor directed toward both interior and exterior problems. The world that results is not a comfortable one, particularly for the rich countries. We must realize, however, that the cake of custom will not break easily, and it may only be under the influence of such a revolutionary (charismatic) personality that it will be possible to change attitudes rapidly. Weber, in the celebrated analysis of types of authority mentioned in an earlier chapter, stated that only charismatic power based on personal magnetism could effectively break through precedents and previous logic. Unfortunately, it will appear to those living in other societies that the personality of the individual who achieves this breakthrough is illogical and even fanatic.

We must make the mental effort necessary to allow us to realize that revolutionary attitudes *will* often be essential if the required increase in production is to be achieved. The labor battalions used in China, Cuba, and the African states under different names are not *necessarily* evidence of communism or totalitarianism—they show that the rulers of these countries have seen that their unused labor force is their greatest available resource. We must accept that human capital will be employed to carry out necessary investment work. We must not condemn this practice as always wrong. It seems possible that the payment of some of this available labor with the surplus food available in the rich countries would increase the potential of this method and reduce some of the dangers always inherent in it.

The basic lesson for the West is that the poor countries will be able to benefit from sustained growth only if they change their economic systems and their social and political processes. None of the Western countries was forced to make changes at the rate that will be necessary in the poor countries. If we continue to denigrate their efforts—as we often have in the past—simply because they depart from the pattern that exists in the West, it is certain that the present lack of understanding between the poor and the rich will develop further. It is only if we take the trouble to understand why a state accepts a certain policy—all policies are rational at least from the point of view of those who adopted them—that the rich countries will survive the revolutionary ferment that will shake the whole world during the remainder of the century.

However large the amount of help the West may give, it is far from certain that violence can be avoided as the poor countries leave the "Middle Ages" and try to catapult themselves into the twentieth century. This should be no surprise, for the countries of the West suffered from considerable violence as they tried to change *their* social and political structures. What can the West do to help in this process? Perhaps its greatest contribution would be a minimization of economic strain by an alteration in the conventions that govern economic exchange among countries.

• *Questions for Study*

1. This article tries to acquaint us with problems of poor nations so that we can assist them more effectively than we have in the past. What is the central problem, according to the author, that we face in our attitude toward these countries? Because we are a wealthy nation, does this mean that our attitudes toward production must be the only right ones? Is economic development more important than the maintenance of a particular way of life?
2. What does Theobald mean by "vicious circles"? How does this idea help him to organize his essay?
3. To what extent does he utilize analogy, illustration, and other concrete means of stating his ideas? Characterize his style.
4. How do you think Marx and Engels might have described Theobald's "cures" for the needs of poor countries?

VIII

MAN IN SOCIETY

RUTH BENEDICT

•

THE SCIENCE OF CUSTOM

Anthropology is the study of human beings as creatures of society. It fastens its attention upon those physical characteristics and industrial techniques, those conventions and values, which distinguish one community from all others that belong to a different tradition.

The distinguishing mark of anthropology among the social sciences is that it includes for serious study other societies than our own. For its purposes any social regulation of mating and reproduction is as significant as our own, though it may be that of the Sea Dyaks, and have no possible historical relation to that of our civilization. To the anthropologist, our customs and those of a New Guinea tribe are two possible social schemes for dealing with a common problem, and in so far as he remains an anthropologist he is bound to avoid any weighting of one in favor of the other. He is interested in human behavior, not as it is shaped by one tradition, our own, but as it has been shaped by any tradition whatsoever. He is interested in the great gamut of custom that is found in various cultures, and his object is to understand the way in which these cultures change and differentiate, the different forms through which they express themselves, and the manner in which the customs of any peoples function in the lives of the individuals who compose them.

Now custom has not been commonly regarded as a subject of any great moment. The inner workings of our own brains we feel to be uniquely worthy of investigation, but custom, we have a way of thinking, is behavior at its most commonplace. As a matter of fact, it is the other way around. Traditional custom, taken the world over, is a mass of detailed behavior more astonishing than what any one person can

From *Patterns of Culture*, Boston: Houghton Mifflin Company, 1961. Reprinted by permission of Houghton Mifflin Company.

ever evolve in individual actions no matter how aberrant. Yet that is a rather trivial aspect of the matter. The fact of first-rate importance is the predominant rôle that custom plays in experience and in belief, and the very great varieties it may manifest.

No man ever looks at the world with pristine eyes. He sees it edited by a definite set of customs and institutions and ways of thinking. Even in his philosophical probings he cannot go behind these stereotypes; his very concepts of the true and the false will still have reference to his particular traditional customs. John Dewey has said in all seriousness that the part played by custom in shaping the behavior of the individual as over against any way in which he can affect traditional custom, is as the proportion of the total vocabulary of his mother tongue over against those words of his own baby talk that are taken up into the vernacular of his family. When one seriously studies social orders that have had the opportunity to develop autonomously, the figure becomes no more than an exact and matter-of-fact observation. The life-history of the individual is first and foremost an accommodation to the patterns and standards traditionally handed down in his community. From the moment of his birth the customs into which he is born shape his experience and behavior. By the time he can talk, he is the little creature of his culture, and by the time he is grown and able to take part in its activities, its habits are his habits, its beliefs his beliefs, its impossibilities his impossibilities. Every child that is born into his group will share with him, and no child born into one on the opposite side of the globe can ever achieve the thousandth part. There is no social problem it is more incumbent upon us to understand than this of the rôle of custom. Until we are intelligent as to its laws and varieties, the main complicating facts of human life must remain unintelligible.

The study of custom can be profitable only after certain preliminary propositions have been accepted, and some of these propositions have been violently opposed. In the first place any scientific study requires that there be no preferential weighting of one or another of the items in the series it selects for its consideration. In all the less controversial fields like the study of cacti or termites or the nature of nebulæ, the necessary method of study is to group the relevant material and to take note of all possible variant forms and conditions. In this way we have learned all that we know of the laws of astronomy, or of the habits of the social insects, let us say. It is only in the study of man himself that the major social sciences have substituted the study of one local variation, that of Western civilization.

Anthropology was by definition impossible as long as these distinctions between ourselves and the primitive, ourselves and the barbarian, ourselves and the pagan, held sway over people's minds. It was necessary first to arrive at that degree of sophistication where we no longer set our own belief over against our neighbor's superstition. It was necessary to recognize that those institutions which are based on the same premises, let us say the supernatural, must be considered together, our own among the rest.

In the first half of the nineteenth century this elementary postulate of anthropology could not occur to the most enlightened person of Western civilization. Man, all down his history, has defended his uniqueness like a point of honor. In Copernicus' time this claim to supremacy was so inclusive that it took in even the earth on which we live, and the fourteenth century refused with passion to have this planet subordinated to a place in the solar scheme. By Darwin's time, having granted the solar system to the enemy, man fought with all the weapons at his command for the uniqueness of the soul, an unknowable attribute given by God to man in such a manner that it disproved man's ancestry in the animal kingdom. No lack of continuity in the argument, no doubts of the nature of this "soul," not even the fact that the nineteenth century did not care in the least to defend its brotherhood with any group of aliens —none of these facts counted against the first-rate excitement that raged on account of the indignity evolution proposed against the notion of man's uniqueness.

Both these battles we may fairly count as won—if not yet, then soon; but the fighting has only massed itself upon another front. We are quite willing to admit now that the revolution of the earth about the sun, or the animal ancestry of man, has next to nothing to do with the uniqueness of our human achievements. If we inhabit one chance planet out of a myriad solar systems, so much the greater glory, and if all the ill-assorted human races are linked by evolution with the animal, the provable differences between ourselves and them are the more extreme and the uniqueness of our institutions the more remarkable. But *our* achievements, *our* institutions are unique; they are of a different order from those of lesser races and must be protected at all costs. So that today, whether it is a question of imperialism, or of race prejudice, or of a comparison between Christianity and paganism, we are still preoccupied with the uniqueness, not of the human institutions of the world at large, which no one has ever cared about anyway, but of our own institutions and achievements, our own civilization.

Western civilization, because of fortuitous historical circumstances, has spread itself more widely than any other local group that has so far been known. It has standardized itself over most of the globe, and we have been led, therefore, to accept a belief in the uniformity of human behavior that under other circumstances would not have arisen. Even very primitive peoples are sometimes far more conscious of the rôle of cultural traits than we are, and for good reason. They have had intimate experience of different cultures. They have seen their religion, their economic system, their marriage prohibitions, go down before the white man's. They have laid down the one and accepted the other, often uncomprehendingly enough, but they are quite clear that there are variant arrangements of human life. They will sometimes attribute dominant characteristics of the white man to his commercial competition, or to his institution of warfare, very much in the fashion of the anthropologist.

The white man has had a different experience. He has never seen an outsider, perhaps, unless the outsider has been already Europeanized. If he has travelled, he has very likely been around the world without ever staying outside a cosmopolitan hotel. He knows little of any ways of life but his own. The uniformity of custom, of outlook, that he sees spread about him seems convincing enough, and conceals from him the fact that it is after all an historical accident. He accepts without more ado the equivalence of human nature and his own cultural standards.

Yet the great spread of white civilization is not an isolated historical circumstance. The Polynesian group, in comparatively recent times, has spread itself from Ontong, Java, to Easter Island, from Hawaii to New Zealand, and the Bantu-speaking tribes spread from the Sahara to southern Africa. But in neither case do we regard these peoples as more than an overgrown local variation of the human species. Western civilization has had all its inventions in transportation and all its far-flung commercial arrangements to back up its great dispersion, and it is easy to understand historically how this came about.

The psychological consequences of this spread of white culture have been out of all proportion to the materialistic. This world-wide cultural diffusion has protected us as man had never been protected before from having to take seriously the civilizations of other peoples; it has given to our culture a massive universality that we have long ceased to account for historically, and which we read off rather as necessary and inevitable. We interpret our dependence, in our civilization, upon economic competition, as proof that this is the prime motivation that human nature can rely upon, or we read off the behavior of small children as it is moulded in our civilization and recorded in child clinics, as child psychology or the way in which the young human animal is bound to behave. It is the same whether it is a question of our ethics or of our family organization. It is the inevitability of each familiar motivation that we defend, attempting always to identify our own local ways of behaving with Behavior, or our own socialized habits with Human Nature.

Now modern man has made this thesis one of the living issues in his thought and in his practical behavior, but the sources of it go far back into what appears to be, from its universal distribution among primitive peoples, one of the earliest of human distinctions, the difference in kind between "my own" closed group and the outsider. All primitive tribes agree in recognizing this category of the outsiders, those who are not only outside the provisions of the moral code which holds within the limits of one's own people, but who are summarily denied a place anywhere in the human scheme. A great number of the tribal names in common use, Zuñi, Déné, Kiowa, and the rest, are names by which primitive peoples know themselves, and are only their native terms for "the human beings," that is, themselves. Outside of the closed group there are no human beings. And this is in spite of the fact that from an objective point of view each tribe is surrounded by peoples sharing in its arts and material inventions, in elaborate practices that have grown up by a mutual give-and-take of behavior from one people to another.

Primitive man never looked out over the world and saw "mankind" as a group and felt his common cause with his species. From the beginning he was a provincial who raised the barriers high. Whether it was a question of choosing a wife or of taking a head, the first and important distinction was between his own human group and those beyond the pale. His own group, and all its ways of behaving, was unique.

So modern man, differentiating into Chosen People and dangerous aliens, groups within his own civilization genetically and culturally related to one another as any tribes in the Australian bush are among themselves, has the justification of a vast historical continuity behind his attitude. The Pygmies have made the same claims. We are not likely to clear ourselves easily of so fundamental a human trait, but we can at least learn to recognize its history and its hydra manifestations.

One of these manifestations, and one which is often spoken of as primary and motivated rather by religious emotions than by this more generalized provincialism, is the attitude that has universally held in Western civilizations so long as religion remained a living issue among them. The distinction between any closed group and outside peoples, becomes in terms of religion that between the true believers and the heathen. Between these two categories for thousands of years there were no common meeting-points. No ideas or institutions that held in the one were valid in the other. Rather all institutions were seen in opposing terms according as they belonged to one or the other of the very often slightly differentiated religions: on the one side it was a question of Divine Truth and the true believer, of revelation and of God; on the other it was a matter of mortal error, of fables, of the damned and of devils. There could be no question of equating the attitudes of the opposed groups and hence no question of understanding from objectively studied data the nature of this important human trait, religion.

We feel a justified superiority when we read a description such as this of the standard religious attitude. At least we have thrown off that particular absurdity, and we have accepted the study of comparative religion. But considering the scope a similar attitude has had in our civilization in the form of race prejudices, for example, we are justified in a little scepticism as to whether our sophistication in the matter of religion is due to the fact that we have outgrown naïve childishness, or simply to the fact that religion is no longer the area of life in which the important modern battles are staged. In the really live issues of our civilization we seem to be far from having gained the detachment that we have so largely achieved in the field of religion.

There is another circumstance that has made the serious study of custom a late and often a half-heartedly pursued discipline, and it is a difficulty harder to surmount than those of which we have just spoken. Custom did not challenge the attention of social theorists because it was the very stuff of their own thinking: it was the lens without which they could not see at all. Precisely in proportion as it was fundamental, it had its existence outside the field of conscious attention. There is nothing mystical about this blindness. When a student has assembled the vast data for a study of international credits, or of the process of learning, or of narcissism as a factor in psychoneuroses, it is through and in this body of data that the economist or the psychologist or the psychiatrist operates. He does not reckon with the fact of other social arrangements where all the factors, it may be, are differently arranged. He does not reckon, that is, with cultural conditioning. He sees the trait he is studying as having known and inevitable manifestations, and he projects these as absolute because they are all the materials he has to think with. He identifies local attitudes of the 1930s with Human Nature, the description of them with Economics or Psychology.

Practically, it often does not matter. Our children must be educated in our pedagogical tradition, and the study of the process of learning in our schools is of paramount importance. There is the same kind of justification for the shrug of the shoulders with which we often greet a discussion of other economic systems. After all, we must live within the framework of mine and thine that our own culture institutionalizes.

That is true, and the fact that the varieties of culture can best be discussed as they exist in space gives color to our nonchalance. But it is only limitation of historical material that prevents examples from being drawn rather from the succession of cultures in time. That succession we cannot escape if we would, and when we look back even a generation we realize the extent to which revision has taken place, sometimes in our most intimate behavior. So far these revisions have been blind, the result of circumstances we can chart only in retrospect. Except for our unwillingness to face cultural change in intimate matters until it is forced upon us, it would not be impossible to take a more intelligent and directive attitude. The resistance is in large measure a result of our misunderstanding of cultural conventions, and especially an exaltation of those that happen to belong to our nation and decade. A very little acquaintance with other conventions, and a knowledge of how various these may be, would do much to promote a rational social order.

The study of different cultures has another important bearing upon present-day thought and behavior. Modern existence has thrown many civilizations into close contact, and at the moment the overwhelming response to this situation is nationalism and racial snobbery. There has never been a time when civilization stood more in need of individuals who are genuinely culture-conscious, who can see objectively the socially conditioned behaviour of other peoples without fear and recrimination.

Contempt for the alien is not the only possible solution of our present contact of races and nationalities. It is not even a scientifically founded solution. Traditional Anglo-Saxon intolerance is a local and temporal culture-trait like any other. Even people as nearly of the same blood and culture as the Spanish have not had it, and race prejudice in the Spanish-settled countries is a thoroughly different thing from that in countries dominated by England and the United States. In this country it is obviously not an intolerance directed against the mixture of blood of biologically far-separated races, for upon occasion excitement mounts as high against the Irish Catholic in Boston, or the Italian in New England mill towns, as against the Oriental in California. It is the old distinction of the in-group and the out-group, and if we carry on the primitive tradition in this matter, we have far less excuse than savage tribes. We have travelled, we pride ourselves on our sophistication. But we have failed to understand the relativity of cultural habits, and we remain debarred from much profit and enjoyment in our human relations with peoples of different standards, and untrustworthy in our dealings with them.

The recognition of the cultural basis of race prejudice is a desperate need in present Western civilization. We have come to the point where we entertain race prejudice against our blood brothers, the Irish, and where Norway and Sweden speak of their enmity as if they too represented different blood. The so-called race line, during a war in which France and Germany fight on opposite sides, is held to divide the people

of Baden from those of Alsace, though in bodily form they alike belong
to the Alpine sub-race. In a day of footloose movements of people and of
mixed marriages in the ancestry of the most desirable elements of the
community, we preach unabashed the gospel of the pure race.

To this anthropology makes two answers. The first is as to the nature
of culture and the second is as to the nature of inheritance. The answer as
to the nature of culture takes us back to prehuman societies. There are
societies where Nature perpetuates the slightest mode of behavior by
biological mechanisms, but these are societies not of men but of the
social insects. The queen ant, removed to a solitary nest, will reproduce
each trait of sex behavior, each detail of the nest. The social insects
represent Nature in a mood when she was taking no chances. The pattern
of the entire social structure she committed to the ant's instinctive behavior. There is no greater chance that the social classes of an ant society,
or its patterns of agriculture, will be lost by an ant's isolation from its
group than that the ant will fail to reproduce the shape of its antennæ or
the structure of its abdomen.

For better or for worse, man's solution lies at the opposite pole. Not
one item of his tribal social organization, of his language, of his local
religion, is carried in his germ-cell. In Europe, in other centuries, when
children were occasionally found who had been abandoned and had
maintained themselves in forests apart from other human beings, they
were all so much alike that Linnæus classified them as a distinct species,
Homo ferus, and supposed that they were a kind of gnome that man
seldom ran across. He could not conceive that these half-witted brutes
were born human, these creatures with no interest in what went on about
them, rocking themselves rhythmically back and forth like some wild
animal in a zoo, with organs of speech and hearing that could hardly be
trained to do service, who withstood freezing weather in rags and plucked
potatoes out of boiling water without discomfort. There is no doubt, of
course, that they were children abandoned in infancy, and what they had
all of them lacked was association with their kind, through which alone
man's faculties are sharpened and given form.

We do not come across wild children in our more humane civilization. But the point is made as clearly in any case of adoption of an infant
into another race and culture. An Oriental child adopted by an Occidental
family learns English, shows towards its foster parents the attitudes current among the children he plays with, and grows up to the same professions that they elect. He learns the entire set of the cultural traits of the
adopted society, and the set of his real parents' group plays no part. The
same process happens on a grand scale when entire peoples in a couple
of generations shake off their traditional culture and put on the customs

of an alien group. The culture of the American Negro in northern cities has come to approximate in detail that of the whites in the same cities. A few years ago, when a cultural survey was made of Harlem, one of the traits peculiar to the Negroes was their fashion of gambling on the last three unit figures of the next day's stock turnover. At least it cost less than the whites' corresponding predilection for gambling in the stocks themselves and was no less uncertain and exciting. It was a variation on the white pattern, though hardly a great departure. And most Harlem traits keep still closer to the forms that are current in white groups.

All over the world, since the beginning of human history, it can be shown that peoples have been able to adopt the culture of peoples of another blood. There is nothing in the biological structure of man that makes it even difficult. Man is not committed in detail by his biological constitution to any particular variety of behavior. The great diversity of social solutions that man has worked out in different cultures in regard to mating, for example, or trade, are all equally possible on the basis of his original endowment. Culture is not a biologically transmitted complex.

What is lost in Nature's guaranty of safety is made up in the advantage of greater plasticity. The human animal does not, like the bear, grow himself a polar coat in order to adapt himself, after many generations, to the Arctic. He learns to sew himself a coat and put up a snow house. From all we can learn of the history of intelligence in prehuman as well as human societies, this plasticity has been the soil in which human progress began and in which it has maintained itself. In the ages of the mammoths, species after species without plasticity arose, overreached itself, and died out, undone by the development of the very traits it had biologically produced in order to cope with its environment. The beasts of prey and finally the higher apes came slowly to rely upon other than biological adaptations, and upon the consequent increased plasticity the foundations were laid, bit by bit, for the development of intelligence. Perhaps, as is often suggested, man will destroy himself by this very development of intelligence. But no one has suggested any means by which we can return to the biological mechanisms of the social insect, and we are left no alternative. The human cultural heritage, for better or for worse, is not biologically transmitted.

The corollary in modern politics is that there is no basis for the argument that we can trust our spiritual and cultural achievements to any selected hereditary germ-plasms. In our Western civilization, leadership has passed successively in different periods to the Semitic-speaking peoples, to the Hamitic, to the Mediterranean sub-group of the white race, and lately to the Nordic. There is no doubt about the cultural continuity of the civilization, no matter who its carriers were at the moment. We must accept all the implications of our human inheritance, one of the most important of which is the small scope of biologically transmitted behavior, and the enormous rôle of the cultural process of the transmission of tradition.

The second answer anthropology makes to the argument of the racial purist concerns the nature of heredity. The racial purist is the victim of a mythology. For what is "racial inheritance"? We know roughly what heredity is from father to son. Within a family line the importance of heredity is tremendous. But heredity is an affair of family lines. Beyond that it is mythology. In small and static communities like an isolated Eskimo village, "racial" heredity and the heredity of child and parent are practically equivalent, and racial heredity therefore has meaning. But as a concept applied to groups distributed over a wide area, let us say, to Nordics, it has no basis in reality. In the first place, in all Nordic nations there are family lines which are represented also in Alpine or Mediterranean communities. Any analysis of the physical make-up of a European population shows overlapping: the dark-eyed, dark-haired Swede represents family lines that are more concentrated farther south, but he is to be understood in relation to what we know of these latter groups. His heredity, so far as it has any physical reality, is a matter of his family line, which is not confined to Sweden. We do not know how far physical types may vary without intermixture. We know that inbreeding brings about a local type. But this is a situation that in our cosmopolitan white civilization hardly exists, and when "racial heredity" is invoked, as it usually is, to rally a group of persons of about the same economic status, graduating from much the same schools, and reading the same weeklies, such a category is merely another version of the in- and the out-group and does not refer to the actual biological homogeneity of the group.

What really binds men together is their culture,—the ideas and the standards they have in common. If instead of selecting a symbol like common blood heredity and making a slogan of it, the nation turned its attention rather to the culture that unites its people, emphasizing its major merits and recognizing the different values which may develop in a different culture, it would substitute realistic thinking for a kind of symbolism which is dangerous because it is misleading.

• Questions for Study

1. Ruth Benedict expresses a view widely held among anthropologists, that culture is relative; she suggests that each culture has to be examined on its own terms, not evaluated by the standards of Western civilization. Do you agree

with the author that all cultures are of equal value? What does the word "value" mean? Are the cultures of cannibalistic societies, for example, as "valuable" as those of societies in Western civilization?

2. Define Benedict's phrase "the science of custom." Can it be argued that she is using the word "science" inaccurately? Using your dictionary as a guide, work out a definition of the word "science."

3. What specific point is she trying to make in her analogy of the Queen Ant? In her illustrations of the wild children of Europe? What other striking analogies, illustrations, or examples does she employ?

THEODORA KROEBER

•

THE HUNTER, ISHI

———————

Ishi was an American Indian, his tribe the Yana. What name his parents gave him is not known. The Yana shared the widespread Indian custom of not revealing given names to outsiders. Kroeber got around this awkwardness by renaming him Ishi, a word meaning *man* in Yana. Ishi accepted the new name and, finding himself in a sociey that used personal names freely, answered to his readily enough, but as a Yana born and bred he refrained so far as possible from using it himself. He was not over fifty years old in 1911, probably a year or two under: a man of middle height, build and skin color, well-formed in limbs, body and head. His straight black hair, worn long, framed a rounded face whose features were on the generous side. He was of gentle countenance. His language was the Yahi dialect of Yana; his skills those of the Stone Age of man.

He had lived by the bow, harpoon and fire drill made from material at hand: juniper, willow, obsidian. He conceptualized, rationalized and

Reprinted from *The American Scholar*, Volume 31, Number 3, Summer 1962. Copyright © 1962 by the United Chapters of Phi Beta Kappa. By permission of the publishers.

accepted truths within the frame of Yana doctrine and values, although he had never lived a day of full, normal Yana life. By the time he was born the Yana people, except for his own small southernmost subgroup, the Yahi, were already dispossessed, dispersed or dead, killed by the immigrants of the gold rush who crossed the mountains by way of Lassen Trail straight through the heartland of the Yahi. As a young child Ishi witnessed single and multiple massacres, and as a child of ten years of age or less he went into hiding with a remnant band of Yahi, the only Yana survivors, probably fifteen or sixteen in all. They remained hidden, their numbers dwindling, until there were only four left in 1908 when they were briefly discovered. Ishi alone survived the discovery and consequent dispersal of the little band; he was totally alone for most—perhaps for all—of the time until he was taken into custody three years later. Such then was Ishi's life experience. When the Sheriff picked him up he knew not a single word of English, and he knew the white man only as plunderer, raper, murderer. His memories were of hunger, of hiding, of death.

The only thing in the world that Ishi truly and wholly feared was the white man. When he found himself in his enemy's power he expected to be scalped, shot, hanged or poisoned: he *knew* the white man's ways. His response was a contained passivity. He could and did remain quiet amidst the babel, crude curiosity and cruder fear that were exhibited around him as an ever-growing crowd gathered in the Oroville jail. Locked into the cell for the insane, he ignored so far as he could the succession of strangers who peered at him through the bars, using an incomprehensible speech, gesturing and pointing as at any caged beast. He could and did, starving though he was, refuse the presumably poisoned food and water that was offered him. The Sheriff then, in very pity, shut out the hysterical mob, allowing only the regular jail attendants to go to him. No violence was done him. He consented at last to eat and drink a little.

Then there came to his cell a different kind of white man. This one sat on the cot beside Ishi, drew a sheet of some sort from his pocket and, peering at the tiny birdfoot markings upon it, began to speak. The speech was odd, to be sure, but it nonetheless had some sounds approaching sense. The stranger even said *siwini*, pronouncing it badly but with knowledge of its meaning, for the wood of the cot was *siwini* and the speaker patted the wooden frame as he said the word. Ishi, too, studied the bird tracks. He could make nothing of them, but their magic was indubitable. If you knew how to use them as did this *Kuwi*, this Doctor who sat beside him, they plainly gave the power of Yana speech; not very good Yana, but understandable. After a fashion the *Kuwi* could answer questions put to him by Ishi so long as the questions were very, very simple. Ishi found himself exchanging words and information with another person. After the long, long moons of silence, he was engaged in conversation; he had found a friend! The friend was Professor T. T. Waterman, and the bird tracks, phonetic transcriptions of words from the northern dialect of Yana, gathered by the linguist Edward Sapir from two Yana or part-Yana Indians who had escaped the holocaust and were living as Wintu among other Wintu Indians.

In 1911 the expectation of most people was that not much good for Ishi or for science and history would come of taking him to the Museum to live; it was thought that Ishi was too childish, too primitive, too wild to learn civilized speech and to master civilized ways at even the simplest, lowest animal level. An informed guess in 1962 as to how Ishi did cope with the city, the jungle of steel and white people, might well be equally pessimistic, although it would adduce other reasons for Ishi's failure, such as early conditioning, the deteriorating effects of fifty years of social starvation, destruction of the personality under traumas of long-continued fear, frustration and life without hope, and the schizophrenia resulting from the great gap between the old known culture and the new.

That Ishi did not fulfill these negative expectations is a matter of history. Dozens of photographs and a respectable shelf of ethnographic and linguistic monographs, the results of the work of several scientists with Ishi, testify to an adjustment not only adequate and happy, but creative—except that he died untimely of one of civilization's gifts to him, tuberculosis.

Ishi learned to speak English, brokenly to be sure, but it was better than his friends' spoken Yana; he traveled alone in San Francisco and back and forth to Berkeley; he bought whatever he wanted, making change correctly; he was a useful paid assistant in the Museum; in short, he learned to conduct himself in the business of life as did other men. There were limits to his learning and to his experience. He did not learn to read, beyond common street signs and numbers. He was without wife and family in civilization as he had been in his own country. He had serious bouts with colds and pneumonias which meant days or weeks spent in bed, his activity curtailed but not the inner variety of his life or its essential social adjustment; for, beyond mastery of ordinary living in a modern city, Ishi made deeply impinging friendships with Waterman, Kroeber and Saxton Pope, the physician who cared for him during his illnesses and who learned from him to hunt with bow and arrow. The wild man was, then, like other men, although more enduring and patient than most and, as it happened, more lovable; he was exotic only in having crossed the time zone into the twentieth century with Stone Age experience and equipment.

For the past three years my commitment has been to tell Ishi's story. This task is done, but today, as I write, Ishi is much in my mind. The month-long annual season for deer hunting opened today here in northern California, and as the familiar hunting pattern commences its noisy repetition I compare it with Ishi's way of hunting. In both, a dead deer is the goal. Otherwise Ishi's objectives and means and our own could scarcely be more unlike.

The white man hunts today where Ishi and other hill Indians hunted in earlier times, in the foothills that rise on either side of the great interior valleys of California and in the coast ranges. These remain areas sparsely peopled, now as then, despite the ever-increasing populations in the valleys below, and along the coast. And today as in Ishi's yesterday the August grass is burned golden brown by months of hot sun unrelieved by summer rains; air and grass crackle with dryness, ready to explode into flame from the spark of a campfire, cigarette or match. For the most part the hills are posted against trespassing, and the only hunters will presumably be neighbors or parties sponsored by neighbors. Even so, here in the Napa valley for the past several days the usually empty road leading back into hill country has had a succession of trucks with trailers carrying camp equipment, food, even horses, saddles and food for the horses. Since midnight today there have been as many passenger cars as one would ordinarily see in a month.

One cannot be sure always that this eruption of men with guns is in fact confined to one's neighbors; upon occasion hunters surprise each other in a dangerous crossfire of shots, exchanged across the two sides of a draw or cañon. Red hats and shirts sometimes do not show up in the thick chaparral, and a nervous or trigger-happy visitor from the city may shoot when he sees brush stirring without waiting to make sure who or what is causing the movement.

Since first dawn the air has been ripped by the explosion of gunfire; baying of deerhounds and excited barking of strange dogs meeting in the brush add to the unsettlement. The owners of cattle and horses pastured in the hills will have chosen before today either to round up their stock and feed it for the season's duration, or to accept some losses when their animals are mistaken for deer. As for householders, adults and children, the usual freedom to wander afield alone and at will must be curtailed; walking up the road or across country will be done only in company and conspicuously enough for sure recognition.

If this season is like others, some hunters will not get their limit, despite the present overpopulation of deer which increase alarmingly year after year. Mountain lions, a deer's only natural enemy here except man, have been almost exterminated, and complicated regulations prevent farmers and vineyardists from protecting their crops against depredations of hungry deer during eleven months of the year. The hunters make a poor showing not because they are poor shots but because the bucks, who alone may be shot, are alerted by opening of cabins and club houses and begin to withdraw days or hours ahead of the hunters, retreating to the high waterless ridges for the duration.

By late afternoon hunting parties will begin to straggle in, some with only a tale of near misses and perhaps a rash of poison oak, others with their kill. The foothill deer is a small animal. (A full-grown buck will be less than half the weight of the mule deer, which is found here only in the Sierra Nevada mountains, and which is about the size of the deer of the eastern United States.) To watch one of our slim foothill bucks being butchered and divided amongst a half-dozen men, to go presumably to as many families, a modest little packet of joint, rump, rib or neck to each, is embarrassing in view of the excited, almost orgiastic quality of the preparations. As butchering is done with us, the dogs get most of a deer in the end, and a coyote or dog in all probability drags away the stiffening hide before anyone gets around to taking it to a tanner. The antlers usually are kept, however, and mounted as a trophy.

I do not mean to imply that the butchering is done unskillfully; but that it is done wastefully by any standards other than our own is the fact. Nor do I mean to say that there is no hunting code. There is, and the more experienced the hunter the stricter the code. And, depending upon the degree of interest, hunting lore, the mystique of the chase and reminiscences of "frontier days" become part of the hunting configuration.

The introduction of noise, confusion and fear is basic to our way of hunting. With the crash and crackling of brush from beaters on foot and hunters on horseback, the echoing hollow bark of hounds and the sharp report and reverberation of gun shots, the normal quiet of the hills is shattered; for the animal denizens, terror and disorganization seem to be all about.[1] It does not matter to us that we disrupt our wild life: we hunt for sport. The primitive hunt was a different matter, pursued for different ends and by other means, as an examination of how and why Ishi hunted will make manifest.

---

[1] Felix Salten in his children's book, *Bambi*, pictures the foolish and aberrant behavior of wild animals under stress of introduced noise and confusion. He, of course, anthropomorphizes what goes on in the minds of the fear-crazed birds and animals, but he is a good observer, noting entirely accurately that it is the partridges who "lose their heads" first, take to the open ground when they should remain hidden, and so bring nearer the total breakdown of the deer's instinctive, cautious behavior.

The Yana, Ishi's people, filled large baskets with dried salmon and charqui (dried venison) against the lean days of winter. As soon as the fall run of salmon had passed its peak, Ishi spent his days and often his nights also until winter drove him indoors, hunting, skinning and butchering deer, curing the hides, peeling off the invaluable long leg tendons, selecting and cleaning bones for chippers, awls and other tools, and drying and smoking the thin-cut slices of venison.

Because deer were the largest and most valuable animal ordinarily available to the Yana (they did not get bears except occasionally) they were of almost sacred importance, and every step in killing a deer and reducing it to food and leather and tools was surrounded with protocol and ritual. Before going out to hunt, Ishi would have purified himself through prayer and song and sweat bath; he would also have taken pains to pass the several nights preceding the hunt in the men's house if there were one; in any case he would have kept himself and his bow, which was highly subject to pollution, from contact with any woman whether a relative or not, a woman's touch or proximity being potentially so inimical as to prevent his getting any deer at all. As an extra precaution he would have refrained from smoking for at least the three previous days, the odor of tobacco being most offensive to deer. He would wear only a breechclout. Over the right shoulder and hanging down behind would be his otterskin quiver with bow and arrows, while tucked under the left armpit would be two or three extra arrows ready for instant use. His only other gear would be a knife thrust between the leather thongs holding his breechclout, and a decoy. Arrow points and knife would be of obsidian and, like bow and arrows, of his own manufacture.

His custom was to leave the sweat house at first dawn without having eaten or drunk since the night before. His last act upon leaving would be to rinse his mouth with clean water that he might be as nearly as possible odorless. He would neither eat nor drink until the day's hunt was over. He would move over the familiar ground toward a meadow or clearing that he knew to be frequented by game, setting a steady but not fast pace. Barefoot, he made no noise on loose rocks, through dry brush or crossing creeks. The direction of his approach depended upon the wind: he invariably posted himself downwind from his prey, for it was his business to be aware of the presence of game before any bird or animal was alerted to him. If he heard, smelled or saw an animal, even a rabbit, he went no further but established himself behind or within a clump of bushes or small trees, or behind a boulder or large tree. His principle was never to look for larger game or for a particular buck or doe but to settle for the first animal that presented itself, since his purpose was to bring the game to himself. Hidden, he might imitate a baby rabbit in distress or he might make the whimpering cry of a fawn looking for its mother, or if he glimpsed a deer he might put on the decoy, a stuffed deer's head, and bob it up and down in imitation of a deer looking around and nibbling leaves. Before long he would have an interested audience. Dr. Pope was reminded of a Pied Piper the first time he watched Ishi charm out of hiding squirrels, rabbits, birds, deer. Frequently his audience would include a fox or two and sometimes a bear, a guest Ishi did not relish if he was hunting alone. Patiently Ishi would lure the animals nearer, keeping at his playacting until they, especially the deer, were far more curious than suspicious. Ishi was accustomed to shoot his short hunting bow from a crouch, a half-crouch or standing; he would in any case shoot without changing position. If he missed, he had a second and, if needed, a third arrow ready in his armpit. A deer will let at least two arrows pass close without becoming suspicious; one may pass between the antlers with no more apparent threat than a bird's flight; even if he saw it whizz by, the feathered quiver would not too much startle an adult buck.

When the arrow hit its mark, it completed the act silently; neither victim nor woodland witness knew "what had hit him." And when Ishi came out of hiding, to deliver the *coup de grâce* by knife thrust if the fallen deer were not already dead, and to retrieve his spent arrows, he appeared as a familiar denizen of brush and trees, and the kill no different from that made by a mountain lion or a bear. The audience withdrew prudently within the cover of the brush, wary but not alarmed as it was when a foreign sound or smell assailed the senses. Nonpredators were accustomed to live and share their territory willy-nilly with predators of which man, Indian man, was one, as expectable as mountain lion and as dangerous, no more no less.

What ever could be learned by devoted and accurate observation Ishi knew about the countryside, its plants and animals; upon this knowledge rested his every move when hunting, harpooning, trapping, snaring or netting. His repertory of imitations was fairly simple but effective. Apparently he used it to arouse interest and curiosity as much as to create illusion. The rabbit and fawn and quail calls and some few others were close to their originals, they were "real"; the deer decoy in all likelihood looked no more real to a live deer than it does to us, but it was familiar enough not to terrify and different enough to intrigue. So it was with most of Ishi's bird calls and other disguises: they pretended to no more than imitation and invention within a frame of expectability. Hunters with camera instead of gun in Africa are surprised to discover how curious animals are in the natural state, how easily their interest is engaged, and how frequently those of different orders cross paths, meet at water holes, in the bush or in the open. It is not that they are participating in a deliberate gregariousness; there is rather a knowledgeable tolerance, a sense of when to mingle and when not. These are the sorts of facts that Ishi knew and utilized, but that a hunter with a gun has little opportunity to observe or to benefit from.

It was precisely in the replacement of the bow with firearms that the old hunting patterns fell apart. We know that in the fifteenth century battles were fought with firearms that first supplemented the longbow and then replaced it, thereby changing the scope, social role and impact of soldiering, fighting and war for the Western world and finally for the whole world. We do not know who was the first hunter to use a blunderbuss or primitive flintlock when hunting. Whoever he was, he exploded a custom of hunting with the bow and arrow that had existed from Paleolithic times, and so destroyed the silence of the forests and the ancient and stable perspective from which man and the other animals saw one another. The Indians of the Americas used the bow until the Caucasian invasions of the sixteenth century, and the Yana and other Indians who were untouched by the Spanish incursion into California continued to use the bow until the 1850's. Life for the Yana was reduced to famine economy within months of the coming of the forty-niners through their land. Game became irretrievably gun-shy and man-shy even though it was many years before white men actually took up permanent residence there.

Culture historians have long known that whereas one trait or complex of traits will "pass" from its culture of origin to a foreign one, be adopted and become naturalized to the new environment without distortion to itself and without being the cause of conflict or displacement in its adoptive home, other traits carry the seeds of revolutionary change. Firearms are obviously of this latter sort: implacable, insistent, terrifying, unadaptive. No people has taken to itself guns and arms without undergoing profound change of face, direction and values. The Chinese who invented gunpowder were shrewd enough for many generations after to confine their use of it to the making of fireworks. It is when gunpowder is put to efficient use in firearms that it becomes so irresistible a culture force.

Recognition that some elements are adaptive and others nonadaptive in transplantation gives the culture historian no sure predictive knowledge concerning the role of any particular element or complex of elements. We say "hunting and fishing" in the same breath, tending to think of them as aspects of a single activity; indeed, streamside fishing is as much a sport with us, and was as serious a pursuit with Ishi, as hunting. Its course through the past into the present nonetheless makes it a perfect example of a totally adaptive culture complex. The hand harpoon with toggles, the weir, the dip net, and the casting line, lure, sinker and float come down to us from our remotest human history unchanged in essential form, purpose and climate of use. Any reasonably patient fisherman—and what fisherman is not patient?—could today substitute Ishi's fishing tackle for his own and bring in a normal day's catch of salmon or trout. It is the solitary man or boy whipping a stream for trout or waiting motionless, harpoon poised, for his salmon to come by, who is truly achieving the regression into his own primitive but living past that eludes the man with a gun. (It should perhaps be remarked here that each year sees an increasing number of bowmen reliving their past during the preseason period, usually of only a few days duration, when they may pursue with bow and arrow, and bring down if their skill suffices deer, quail, pheasants and doves.)

Unlike the fishing tackle, which is seen to move through time and space little modified or modifying, matches would appear to be as potent a force for change as firearms. And so they are in one sense: neither Ishi nor any person having at his disposal only the fire drill for making fire would dream of clinging to the old way if the new became available to him. But flint and steel have replaced the fire drill to be themselves replaced with matches, all without other impingement on new environments. The match changes only the technique of getting the first spark. Time and the labor of drilling are saved, but the same sort of fire is lit to be put to the same uses, to cook on and for warmth and sociability. Also, matches and tinder must be similarly cared for since neither will give a spark when damp.

Ishi delighted to use matches, which he rated amongst the white man's most important inventions along with the wheel, whose versatile applications won his total respect. He took to the tools in a well-stocked carpenter's chest with ease and skill, he learned to use expertly the English longbow, to play a fair game of baseball and to sit a horse. But he hunted only on his own terms—those of his bow and the Yana code. He took no part in "our" hunts; he refused so much as to touch a gun, much less to shoot one.

Ishi died in 1916 during World War One, before the modern world of 1962 was more than a shadow of a cloud on the horizon, its mushroom form yet shrouded.

• Questions for Study

1. Relate the experiences of Ishi to the idea of the "science of custom" as set forth by Ruth Benedict. Do these experiences tend to confirm Benedict's statements?

2. Why is the shift in point of view of paragraphs eight and nine effective? In what stylistic ways does Mrs. Kroeber dramatize her account of Ishi? How would a writer of fiction have developed Ishi as a character in a story or novel?

3. Why does Mrs. Kroeber focus attention upon the activity of hunting? State the essential point of contrast made between Ishi and modern man? What is the terrifying implication of the last sentence in the essay?

MALCOLM COWLEY

•

SOCIOLOGICAL HABIT PATTERNS

IN LINGUISTIC TRANSMOGRIFICATION

I have a friend who started as a poet and then decided to take a post-graduate degree in sociology. For his doctoral dissertation he combined his two interests by writing on the social psychology of poets. He had visited poets by the dozen, asking each of them a graded series of questions, and his conclusions from the interviews were modest and useful, though reported in what seemed to me a barbarous jargon. After reading the dissertation I wrote and scolded him. "You have such a fine sense of the poet's craft," I said, "that you shouldn't have allowed the sociologists to seduce you into writing their professional slang—or at least that's my judgmental response to your role selection."

My friend didn't write to defend himself; he waited until we met again. Then dropping his voice, he said: "I knew my dissertation was badly written, but I had to get my degree. If I had written it in English, Professor Blank"—he mentioned a rather distinguished name—"would have rejected it. He would have said it was merely belletristic."

From that time I began to study the verbal folkways of the sociologists. I read what they call "the literature." A few sociologists write the best English they are capable of writing, and I suspect that they are the best men in the field. There is no mystery about them. If they go wrong, their mistakes can be seen and corrected. Others, however—and a vast majority—write in a language that has to be learned almost like Esperanto. It has a private vocabulary which, in addition to strictly sociological terms, includes new words for the commonest actions, feelings, and circumstances. It has the beginnings of a new grammar and syntax, much inferior to English grammar in force and precision. So far as it has an effect on standard English, the effect is largely pernicious.

Sometimes it misleads the sociologists themselves, by making them think they are profoundly scientific at points where they are merely being verbose. I can illustrate by trying a simple exercise in translation, that is, by expressing an idea first in English and then seeing what it looks like in the language of sociology.

An example that comes to hand is the central idea of an article by Norman E. Green, printed in the February, 1956, issue of the *American Sociological Review*. In English his argument might read as follows:

"Rich people live in big houses set farther apart than those of poor people. By looking at an aerial photograph of any American city, we can distinguish the richer from the poorer neighborhoods."

I won't have to labor over a sociological expression of the same idea, because Mr. Green has saved me the trouble. Here is part of his contribution to comparative linguistics. "In effect, it was hypothesized," he says—a sociologist must never say "I assumed," much less "I guessed"—"that certain physical data categories including housing types and densities, land use characteristics, and ecological location"—not just "location," mind you, but "ecological location," which is almost equivalent to locational location—"constitute a scalable content area. This could be called a continuum of residential desirability. Likewise, it was hypothesized that several social data categories, describing the same census tracts, and referring generally to the social stratification system of the city, would also be scalable. This scale could be called a continuum of socio-economic status. Thirdly, it was hypothesized that there would be a high positive correlation between the scale types on each continuum."

Here, after ninety-four words, Mr. Green is stating, or concealing, an assumption with which most laymen would have started, that rich people live in good neighborhoods. He is now almost ready for his deduction, or snapper:

"This relationship would define certain linkages between the social and physical structure of the city. It would also provide a precise definition of the commonalities among several spatial distributions. By the same token, the correlation between the residential desirability scale and the continuum of socio-economic status would provide an estimate of the predictive value of aerial photographic data relative to the social ecology of the city."

Mr. Green has used 160 words—counting "socio-economic" as only one—to express an idea that a layman would have stated in thirty-three. As a matter of fact, he has used many more than 160 words, since the whole article is an elaboration of this one thesis. Whatever may be the virtues of the sociological style—or Socspeak, as George Orwell might have called it—it is not specifically designed to save ink and paper. Let us briefly examine some of its other characteristics.

A layman's first impression of sociological prose, as compared with English prose, is that it contains a very large proportion of abstract words, most of them built on Greek or Latin roots. Often—as in the example just quoted—they are used to inflate or transmogrify a meaning that could be clearly expressed in shorter words surviving from King Alfred's time.

These Old English or Anglo-Saxon words are in number less than one-tenth of the entries in the largest dictionaries. But they are the names of everyday objects, attributes, and actions, and they are also the pronouns, the auxiliary verbs, and most of the prepositions and conjunctions, so that they form the grammatical structure of the language. The result is that most novelists use six Anglo-Saxon words for every one derived from French, Latin, or Greek, and that is probably close to the percentage that would be found in spoken English.

For comparison or contrast, I counted derivations in the passage quoted from the *American Sociological Review*, which is a typical example of "the literature." No less than forty-nine per cent of Mr. Green's prose consists of words from foreign or classical languages. By this standard of measurement, his article is more abstruse than most textbooks of advanced chemistry and higher mathematics, which are said to contain only forty per cent of such words.

In addition to being abstruse, the language of the sociologists is also rich in neologisms. Apparently they like nothing better than inventing a word, deforming a word, or using a technical word in a strange context. Among their favorite nouns are "ambit," "extensity" (for "extent"), "scapegoating," "socializee," "ethnicity," "directionality," "cathexis," "affect" (for "feeling"), "maturation" (for both "maturing" and "maturity"), and "commonalities" (for "points in common"). Among their favorite adjectives are "processual," "prestigeful," and "insightful"—which last is insightful to murder—and perhaps their favorite adverb is "minimally," which seems to mean "in some measure." Their maximal pleasure seems to lie in making new combinations of nouns and adjectives and nouns used as adjectives, until the reader feels that he is picking his way through a field of huge boulders, lost among "universalistic-specific achievement patterns" and "complementary role-expectation-sanction systems," as he struggles vainly toward "ego-integrative action orientation," guided only by "orientation to improvement of the gratification-deprivation balance of the actor"—which last is Professor Talcott Parsons's rather involved way of saying "the pleasure principle."

But Professor Parsons, head of the Sociology Department at Harvard, is not the only delinquent recidivist, convicted time and again of corrupting the language. Among sociologists in general there is a criminal fondness for using complicated terms when there are simple ones available. A child says "Do it again," a teacher says "Repeat the exercise," but the sociologist says "It was determined to replicate the investigation." Instead of saying two things are alike or similar, as a layman would do, the sociologist describes them in being either isomorphic or homologous. Instead of saying that they are different, he calls them allotropic. Every form of leadership or influence is called a hegemony.

A sociologist never cuts anything in half or divides it in two like a layman. Instead he dichotomizes it, bifurcates it, subjects it to a process of binary fission, or restructures it in a dyadic conformation—around polar foci.

So far I have been dealing with the vocabulary of sociologists, but their private language has a grammar too, and one that should be the subject of intensive research by the staff of a very well-endowed foundation. I have space to mention only a few of its more striking features.

The first of these is the preponderance of nouns over all the other parts of speech. Nouns are used in hyphenated pairs or dyads, and sometimes in triads, tetrads, and pentads. Nouns are used as adjectives without change of form, and they are often used as verbs, with or without the suffix "ize." The sociological language is gritty with nouns, like sanded sugar.

On the other hand, it is poor in pronouns. The singular pronoun of the first person has entirely disappeared, except in case histories, for the sociologist never comes forward as "I." Sometimes he refers to himself as "the author" or "the investigator," or as "many sociologists," or even as "the best sociologists," when he is advancing a debatable opinion. On rare occasions he calls himself "we," like Queen Elizabeth speaking from the throne, but he usually avoids any personal form and writes as if he were a force of nature.

The second-personal pronoun has also disappeared, for the sociologist pretends to be speaking not to living persons but merely for the record. Masculine and feminine pronouns of the third person are used with parsimony, and most sociologists prefer to say "the subject," or "X——," or "the interviewee," where a layman would use the simple "he" or "she." As for the neuter pronoun of the third person, it survives chiefly as the impersonal subject of a passive verb. "It was hypothesized," we read, or "It was found to be the case." Found by *whom?*

The neglect and debasement of the verb is another striking feature of "the literature." The sociologist likes to reduce a transitive verb to an intransitive, so that he speaks of people's adapting, adjusting, transferring, relating, and identifying, with no more of a grammatical object than if they were coming or going. He seldom uses transitive verbs of action, like "break," "injure," "help," and "adore." Instead he uses verbs of relation, verbs which imply that one series of nouns and adjectives, used as the compound subject of a sentence, is larger or smaller than, dominant over, subordinate to, causative of, or resultant from another series of nouns and adjectives.

Considering this degradation of the verb, I have wondered how one of Julius Caesar's boasts could be translated into Socspeak. What Caesar wrote was "*Veni, vidi, vici*"—only three words, all of them verbs. The English translation is in six words: "I came, I saw, I conquered," and three of the words are first-personal pronouns, which the sociologist is taught to avoid. I suspect that he would have to write: "Upon the advent of the investigator, his hegemony became minimally coextensive with the areal unit rendered visible by his successive displacements in space."

The whole sad situation leads me to dream of a vast allegorical painting called "The Triumph of the Nouns." It would depict a chariot of victory drawn by the other conquered parts of speech—the adverbs and adjectives still robust, if yoked and harnessed; the prepositions bloated and pale; the conjunctions tortured; the pronouns reduced to sexless skeletons; the verbs dichotomized and feebly tottering—while behind them, arrogant, overfed, roseate, spilling over the triumphal car, would be the company of nouns in Roman togas and Greek chitons, adorned with laurel branches and flowering hegemonies.

• Questions for Study

1. Compare Cowley's comments about style with those of Hazlitt in "On Familiar Style" and Ferguson in "A Sane Approach to Style." How would these writers have classified the jargon of the sociologists? What characteristics of a good style are implied by Cowley in his attack? Are there any ways in which a sociologist who is guilty of the verbal crimes which Cowley cites can defend his usage? Examine closely the language of one paragraph

by Benedict and one by Kroeber. Are these authors guilty of the linguistic crimes discussed by Cowley?

2. Do you consider his concluding paragraph effective or ineffective? Why? What does he mean by *allegory?*

3. Why is Cowley, who has written several books of literary criticism, particularly concerned with the problem he is discussing?

DANIEL BELL

•

AMERICA AS A MASS SOCIETY

The conception of the "mass society" can be summarized as follows: The revolutions in transport and communications have brought men into closer contact with each other and bound them in new ways; the division of labor has made them more interdependent; tremors in one part of society affect all others. Despite this greater interdependence, however, individuals have grown more estranged from one another. The old primary group ties of family and local community have been shattered; ancient parochial faiths are questioned; few unifying values have taken their place. Most important, the critical standards of an educated elite no longer shape opinion or taste. As a result, mores and morals are in constant flux, relations between individuals are tangential or compartmentalized, rather than organic. At the same time, greater mobility, spatial and social, intensifies concern over status. Instead of a fixed or known status, symbolized by dress or title, each person assumes a multiplicity of roles and constantly has to prove himself in a succession of new situations. Because of all this, the individual loses a coherent sense of

From *The End of Ideology*, New York: The Free Press of Glencoe. A division of Crowell-Collier Publishing Co. Formerly Free Press, Glencoe, Ill., 1959. Reprinted by permission of the author.

self. His anxieties increase. There ensues a search for new faiths. The stage is thus set for the charismatic leader, the secular messiah, who, by bestowing upon each person the semblance of necessary grace and of fullness of personality, supplies a substitute for the older unifying belief that the mass society has destroyed.

In a world of lonely crowds seeking individual distinction, where values are constantly translated into economic calculabilities, where in extreme situations shame and conscience can no longer restrain the most dreadful excesses of terror, the theory of the mass society seems a forceful, realistic description of contemporary society, an accurate reflection of the *quality* and *feeling* of modern life. But when one seeks to apply the theory of mass society, analytically, it becomes very slippery. Ideal types, like the shadows in Plato's cave, generally never give us more than a silhouette. So, too, with the theory of "mass society." Each of the statements making up the theory, as set forth in the second paragraph above, might be true, but they do not follow necessarily from one another. Nor can we say that all the conditions described are present at any one time or place. More than that, there is no organizing principle—other than the general concept of a "breakdown of values"—that puts the individual elements of theory together in a logical, meaningful—let alone historical—manner. And when we examine the way the "theory" is used by those who employ it, we find ourselves even more at a loss.

In trying to sort out the ambiguities in the use of the phrase, we can distinguish perhaps five different, and sometimes contradictory, usages:

1. *Mass as undifferentiated number.* As commonly used in the term "mass media," "mass" implies that standardized material is transmitted to "all groups of the population uniformly."[1] As understood generally by sociologists, a *mass* is a heterogeneous and undifferentiated audience, as opposed to a *class,* or any parochial and relatively homogeneous segment. Some sociologists have been tempted to go further and make "mass" a rather pejorative term. Because the mass media subject a diverse audience to a common set of cultural materials, it is argued that these experiences must necessarily lie outside the personal—and therefore meaningful—experiences to which the individual responds directly. A movie audience, for example, is a "mass" because the individuals looking at the screen are, in the words of the American sociologist Herbert Blumer, "separate, detached, and anonymous." The mass "has no social organization, no body of custom and tradition, no established set of rules

[1]For a neutral discussion of the idea of "mass" in "mass media," see, e.g., Paul F. Lazarsfeld and Patricia Kendall, "The Communication Behavior of the Average American," in *Mass Communication,* ed. Wilbur Schramm (Urbana, Ill., 1949).

or rituals, no organized group of sentiments, no structure of status roles and no established leadership."[2]

To become part of the mass is to be divorced—or "alienated"—from oneself. And the instruments which project the dominant social values that men (and women and children) choose as their *imago*, or ideal image and desire—television, radio, and the movies—impose a mass response on their audience.

2. *Mass as the judgment by the incompetent.* As first introduced by the late Ortega y Gasset in 1931, in his famous *Revolt of the Masses*, the terms "masses" and "mass" had a far different meaning than the usage implied by the term "mass media" and its invidious connotations. For Ortega, the word "mass" did not designate a group of persons—the masses were not the workers, even though the revolutionary movements of the time had equated the two—but the low *quality* of modern civilization, resulting from the loss of a commanding position by the "gentlemen" who once made up the educated elite. Modern taste, for Ortega, represents the judgment of the unqualified. Modern life "makes a *tabula rasa* of all classicism." Nothing that is in the past can be "any possible model or standard." Even "the famous Renaissance reveals itself as a period of narrow provincialism—why not use the word?—ordinary." Modern culture, since it disowns the past, seeks a "free expression of its vital desires"; it becomes, therefore, an unrestrained "spoiled child" with no controlling standards, "no limit to its caprice."[3] In Ortega, one finds the most sweeping attack against all "modernity." His is the disdain of the humanist for the vulgar.

3. *Mass as the mechanized society.* In German romanticism, in its idealization of nature and the pastoral, one finds the source of much of the protest against modern life. For these writers—and the poets and critics Ernst and Friedrich George Juenger can be taken as typical—the dehumanizing element is technology.[4] The mass society is a mechanical society. Society has become an "apparatus." The machine impresses its style on man, makes life mathematical and precise; existence takes on a masklike character: the steel helmet and the welder's face-guard symbolize the individual's disappearance into his technical function. The regulated, functional man emerges as a new type, hard and ruthless, a cog in the technological press.

4. *The mass as the bureaucratized society.* Less romantic, but

---

[2] Herbert Blumer, "Collective Behavior," in *New Outlines of the Principles of Sociology*, ed. A. M. Lee (New York, 1936). For a further discussion, see Eliot Friedsen, "Research and the Concept of the Mass," *American Sociological Review*, June 1953.
[3] José Ortega y Gasset, *The Revolt of the Masses* (New York, 1932), pp. 18–19, 39.
[4] Friedrich George Juenger, *The Failure of Technology* (Chicago, 1948).

equally critical, are those theorists who see extreme rationalization and extreme bureaucratization—the *over-organization* of life—as the salient features of the mass society. The idea of "rationalization" goes back to Hegel and Marx, and along with it the notions of "estrangement" or "alienation," "reification," and the "fetishism of commodities"—all of which express the thought that in modern society man has become a "thing," an object manipulated by society, rather than a subject who can remake life in accordance with his own desires. In our time, Georg Simmel, Max Weber, and Karl Mannheim have developed and elaborated these concepts. In Mannheim's work—notably in his *Man and Society in an Age of Reconstruction*—the diverse strands are all brought together.

Mannheim's argument, put schematically, runs as follows: modern large-scale organization, oriented exclusively to efficiency, creates hierarchies that concentrate all decisions at the top. Even technical decisions are removed from the shop floor and centered in specialized bodies that have no direct contact with work. Since the concern is solely with efficiency, rather than human satisfactions, all solutions to problems are defined in relation to this single value. Mannheim calls this "functional rationality," or direct means-ends relationships, in contrast to "substantial rationality," which is the application of Reason to human affairs.[5]

This concentration of decision-making not only creates conformity but stunts the initiative of subordinates and leaves them unsatisfied in their personal needs for gratification and esteem. (In effect, the demand for submission to extreme rationality deprives the individual of the power to act rationally; i.e., in accordance with reason. This frustration seeks release in irrational ways.) Normally, the routinization of one's job dulls the edge of frustration and provides some security. But when unemployment looms, the helplessness becomes sharpened, and self-esteem is threatened. Since individuals cannot rationally locate the source of their frustration (i.e., the impersonal bureaucratic system itself), they will, under these circumstances, seek scapegoats and turn to fascism.

5. *The mass as mob.* While for Mannheim, and the neo-Marxists, mass society is equated with monolithic bureaucratization, for Emil Lederer and Hannah Arendt it is defined by the elimination of difference, by uniformity, aimlessness, alienation, and the failure of integration.

In Lederer's view, society is made up of many social groups united

---

[5] Karl Mannheim, *Man and Society in an Age of Reconstruction* (London, 1940), pp. 53–67. Mannheim uses several other terms to round out his analysis. Modern society, he says, is based on "fundamental democratization," a term that is fuzzy, but close to Ortega's idea of "massification." Because of "fundamental democratization," i.e., the idea that culture should belong to all and that each man's opinion is as good as the next man's, the "creative elites," through whom culture is sustained, have no means of functioning.

by function or self-interest, some rational in purpose, some irrational. So long as society is stratified, these groups can impose only partial control and irrational emotions are restricted. But when the lines dividing social groups break down, the people become volatile and febrile "masses," ready to be manipulated by a leader.[6]

Hannah Arendt, perhaps because she writes a decade later, sees the masses as already overspilling the bounds. The masses are those who, because of indifference or simply sheer number, do not belong to "political parties or municipal governments or professional organizations or trade unions"—in short, organizations that exist to satisfy a common interest—and they "form the majority of those large numbers of neutral, politically indifferent people who never join a party or hardly ever go to the polls."

Such people already stand "outside" of society. The revolt of the masses is a revolt against the "loss of social status along with which [is] lost the whole sector of communal relationships in whose framework common sense makes sense. . . . The masses [become] obsessed by a desire to escape from reality because in their essential homelessness they can no longer bear its accidental incomprehensible aspects."[7]

And so, because modern life sunders all social bonds, and because the techniques of modern communication have perfected the means whereby propaganda can manipulate the masses, the "age of the masses" is now upon us.

What strikes one first about these varied uses of the concept of mass society is how little they reflect or relate to the complex, richly striated social relations of the real world. Take Blumer's example of the movie audience as "separate, detached, and anonymous." Presumably, a large number of individuals, because they have been subjected to similar experiences, now share some common psychological reality in which the differences between individual and individual become blurred; accordingly we get the sociological assumption that each person is now of "equal weight," and therefore a sampling of what such disparate individuals say they think constitutes "*mass* opinion." But is this so? Individuals are not *tabulae rasae*. They bring varying social conceptions to the same experience and go away with dissimilar responses. They may be silent, separate, detached, and anonymous while watching the movie, but afterward they talk about it with friends and exchange opinions and judgments. They are once again members of particular social groups.

[6] Emil Lederer, *The State of the Masses* (New York, 1940), pp. 23–40.
[7] Hannah Arendt, *The Origins of Totalitarianism* (New York, 1951), pp. 305, 341–42.

Would one say that several hundred or a thousand individuals home alone at night, but all reading the same book, constitute a "mass"?

Because romantic feeling colors critical judgment, the attacks on modern life often have an unduly strong emotional charge. The image of "facelessness," for example, is given a metaphysical twist by Gabriel Marcel: "The individual, in order to belong to the mass . . . has had to . . . divest himself of that substantial reality which was linked to his initial individuality. . . . The incredibly sinister role of the press, the cinema, the radio has consisted in passing that original reality through a pair of flattening rollers to substitute it for a superimposed pattern of ideas, an image with no real roots in the deep being of the subject of this experiment."[8] Perhaps terms like "original reality" and "real roots in the deep being" have a meaning that escapes an empiricist temper, but without the press, the radio, etc., etc.—and they are not monolithic—in what way, short of being everywhere at once, can one learn of events that take place elsewhere? Or should one go back to the happy ignorance of earlier days?

Some of the images of life in the mass society, as presented by its critics, border on caricature. According to Ernst Juenger, traffic demands traffic regulations, and so the public becomes conditioned to automatism. Karl Jaspers has written that in the "technical mass order" the home is transformed "into a lair or sleeping place." Even more puzzling is the complaint against modern medicine. "In medical practice . . . patients are now dealt with in the mass according to the principle of rationalization, being sent to institutes for technical treatment, the sick being classified in groups and referred to this or that specialized department. . . . The supposition is that, like everything else, medical treatment has become a sort of manufactured article."[9]

The attack on the mass society sometimes widens into an attack on science itself. For Ortega, "the scientific man is the prototype of the mass-man," because science, by encouraging specialization, has made the scientist "hermetic and self-satisfied within his limitations." Ortega draws from this the sweeping conclusion that "the most immediate result of this unbalanced specialization has been that today, when there are more 'scientists' than ever, there are much less 'cultured' men than, for example, about 1750."[10] But how is one to verify such a comparison between 1750 and the present? Even if we could establish comparable categories, surely Ortega would have been the first to shy away from statistical comparisons. Moreover, can we assume that because a man specializes in his

---

[8] Gabriel Marcel, *Man Against Mass Society* (Chicago, 1952), pp. 101–3.
[9] Karl Jaspers, *Man in the Modern Age* (London, 1951), p. 65.
[10] Ortega, *op. cit.*, p. 124.

work, he is unable, in his leisure and in reflection, to appreciate culture? And what is "culture"? Would not Ortega admit that we have more knowledge of the world than in 1750—knowledge not only of nature but of the inner life of man? Is knowledge to be divorced from culture, or is "true culture" a narrow area of classical learning in which eternal truths reside?

One could argue, of course, that reading a book, to cite my previous example, is a qualitatively different experience from going to a movie. But this leads precisely to the first damaging ambiguity in the theory of the mass society. Two things are mixed up in that theory: a judgment regarding the *quality* of modern experience—with much of which any sensitive individual might agree—and a presumed scientific statement concerning the disorganization of society created by industrialization and by the demand of the masses for equality. It is the second of these statements with which this essay quarrels.

Behind the theory of social disorganization lies a romantic—and somewhat false—notion of the past, which sees society as having once been made up of small, "organic," close-knit communities (called *Gemeinschaften* in the terminology of the sociologists) that were shattered by industrialism and modern life, and replaced by a large, impersonal, "atomistic" society (called *Gesellschaft*) that is unable to provide the basic gratifications, and call forth the loyalties, that the older communities knew.[11] These distinctions are, however, completely riddled by value judgments. Everyone is against atomism and for "organic living." But if we substitute, with good logic, the term "total" for "organic," and "individualistic" for "atomistic," the whole argument looks quite different. In any case, a great weakness in the theory is its lack of history-mindedness. The transition to a mass society, if it be such, was not effected suddenly, explosively, within a single lifetime, but took generations to mature. In its sociological determinism, the hypothesis overlooks the human capacity for adaptiveness and creativeness, for ingenuity in shaping new social forms. Such new forms may be trade unions whose leaders rise from the ranks—there are 50,000 trade-union locals in this country that form little worlds of their own—or the persistence under new conditions of ethnic groups and solidarities.

But more than mere contradictions in usage, ambiguities in terminol-

---

[11] This antithesis, associated with the German sociologist Tonnies, is central to almost every major modern social theory: Weber's traditional–rational behavior, Durkheim's mechanical-organic solidarity, Redfield's folk-urban society, and so on. Sometimes this distinction is presumed to be a historical one, describing societies in some undefined past as against the present; sometime it is used as an ahistorical, analytic distinction, setting up two ideal types in contrast with each other. The result, however, is confusion.

ogy, and a lack of historical sense are involved in the theory of the mass society. It is at heart a defense of an aristocratic cultural tradition—a tradition that does carry with it an important but neglected conception of liberty—and a doubt that the large mass of mankind can ever become truly educated or acquire an appreciation of culture. Thus, the theory often becomes a conservative defense of privilege. This defense is at times so extreme as to pose a conflict between "culture" and "social justice." The argument (reminiscent of the title of Matthew Arnold's book *Culture and Anarchy*) is made that any attempts at social betterment must harm culture. And, while mainly directed against "bourgeois" society, the theory also strikes at radicalism and its egalitarian notions.

The fear of the "mass" has its roots in the dominant conservative tradition of Western political thought, which in large measure still shapes many of the political and sociological categories of social theory—i.e., in authoritarian definitions of leadership and in the image of the "mindless masses." The picture of the "mass" as capable only of violence and excess originates with Aristotle's *Politics*. In his threefold typology, democracy is equated with the rule of *hoi polloi*—who are easily swayed by demagogues—and which must degenerate into tyranny. This notion of the masses, developed in Hellenistic times, was deepened by the struggles between plebes and aristocracy in the Roman republic, and by the efforts of the Caesars to exploit mob support; and the image of the insensate mob fed by "bread and circuses" became deeply imprinted on history. (From Plutarch, for example, came the description of the fickle masses and the wily tribunes that was drawn upon so directly by Shakespeare in his tragedy *Coriolanus*.) Early Christian theory justified its fear of the masses with a theory about human nature. In the religious terms of Augustine— as, later, in the secularized version of Hobbes—the Earthly City bore an ineradicable stain of blood: in Paradise there was neither private property nor government; property and police were the consequence of the Fall of Man; property and police were signs, therefore, not of man's civilization but of his corruption; they were necessary means of keeping man in check.

But it was the French Revolution that transplanted the image of the "mindless masses" into modern consciousness. The destruction of the *ancien régime* and the rallying cry of "equality" sharpened the fear of conservative, and especially Catholic, critics that traditional values (meaning political, social, and religious dogma) would be destroyed.[12]

---

12 For a discussion of the roots of the idea of the "Mindless Masses" in western social theory, see my essay, "Notes on Authoritarian and Democratic Leaders," in *Studies in Leadership*, ed. Alvin Gouldner (New York, 1950).

For a Tocqueville and an Acton, there was an irreducible conflict between liberty and equality; liberty guaranteed each man the right to be different, whereas equality meant a "leveling" of tastes to the lowest common denominator. For a Max Scheler, as well as an Ortega, the mass society meant a "democracy of the emotions," which could unleash only irrational forces. For the Catholic de Maistre, as for the Anglican T. S. Eliot, the equality of men meant the destruction of the harmony and authority so necessary to a healthy, integrated society.[13] From this traditionalist point of view, Nazism has been characterized not as a reaction against, but the inevitable end-product of, democracy. Hitler is seen as a replica of the classical demagogue swaying the mindless masses and leading them in nihilistic revolt against the traditional culture of Europe.

Important as these conceptions are, as reminders of the meaning of liberty, and of excellence, they reflect a narrow conception of human potentialities....

It has been argued that the American mass society imposes an excessive conformity upon its members. But it is hard to discern who is conforming to what. The *New Republic* cries that "hucksters are sugar-coating the culture." The *National Review*, organ of the "radical right," raises the banner of iconoclasm against the domination of opinion-making in our society by "the liberals." *Fortune* decries the growth of "organization man." Each of these tendencies exists, yet in historical perspective there is probably less conformity to an over-all mode of conduct today than at any time within the last half century in America. True, there is less bohemianism than in the twenties (though increased sexual tolerance) and less political radicalism than in the thirties (though the New Deal enacted sweeping reforms). But does the arrival at a political dead center mean the establishment, too, of a dead norm? I do not think so. One would be hard put to find today the "conformity" *Main Street* exacted of Carol Kennicott thirty years ago. With rising educational levels, more individuals are able to indulge a wider variety of interests. ("Twenty years ago you couldn't sell Beethoven out of New York," re-

---

[13] In a brilliant essay, "Daydreams and Nightmares: Reflections on the Criticism of Mass Culture" (*Sewanee Review*, LXV, 1957), Edward Shils points to the curious convergence of both conservative and neo-Marxist critics in their attacks on mass culture. In this respect, the radical has taken over uncritically the aristocratic view that the past was dominated by a high culture that is now being debauched. In fact, as Shils points out, the lives of most people were brutalized by long hours of work at arduous labor, while the entry of the "mass" into society has resulted in the extension of culture—of art, music, and literature—to a degree hitherto undreamed of. This argument is elaborated by Professor Shils in a paper prepared for the Tamiment Conference on Mass Culture, June, 1959, which appears in *Daedalus,* Spring 1960.

ports a record salesman. "Today we sell Palestrina, Monteverdi, Gabrielli, and Renaissance and Baroque music in large quantities.")

The curious fact, perhaps, is that no one in the United States defends conformity. Everyone is against it, and probably everyone always was. Thirty-five years ago, you could easily rattle any middle-class American by charging him with being a "Babbitt." Today you can do so by accusing him of conformity. The problem is to know who is accusing whom. In December, 1958, the *Reader's Digest* (circulation twelve million) reprinted an article from *Woman's Day* (circulation five million) with the title, "The Danger of Being Too Well-Adjusted." The point of the article is that great men were not adjusted, and the article quotes a psychiatrist who says that "we've made conformity into a religion"; we ought to remember, however, that each child is different "and ought to be."

Such citation is no proof that there is not "conformity" in the middle class; but if there is, there is also a great deal of anxiety and finger-pointing about it. Certainly those who live on the margin of society—the Upper Bohemians, whose manners soon become the style for the culture—seek frantically to find different ways of emphasizing their non-conformity. In Hollywood, where Pickfair society in the twenties counterfeited a European monarchy (and whose homes crossed Louis XIV with Barnum & Bailey), "non-conformity," according to *Life* magazine (in its jumbo Entertainment issue of December 22, 1958—readership twenty-five million), "is now the key to social importance and that Angry Middle-Aged man, Frank Sinatra, is its prophet and reigning social monarch." The Sinatra set, *Life* points out, deliberately mocks the old Hollywood taboos and is imitated by a host of other sets that eagerly want to be non-conformist as well. Significantly—a fact *Life* failed to mention—the reigning social set and its leaders, Sinatra, Dean Martin, Sammy Davis, Jr., are all from minority groups and from the wrong side of the tracks. Sinatra and Martin are Italian, Davis a Negro. In earlier times in American life, a minority group, having bulled its way to the top, would usually ape the style and manners of the established status community. In Hollywood, the old status hierarchies have been fragmented, the new sets celebrate their triumph by jeering at the pompous ways of the old.

At the margins of the literary life, and a different social phenomenon, are the Beatniks, a hopped-up, jazzed-up, souped-up, self-proclaimed group of outcasts who are rebelling against the "highly organized academic and literary movement employment agency of the Neoanti-reconstructionist [who form] a dense crust of custom over American cultural life." But the singular fact is, as Delmore Schwartz recently argued, that these Beatniks are imaginary rebels, "since the substance of their work is a violent advocacy of a nonconformism which they already possess . . . since nonconformism of almost every variety had become acceptable and respectable and available to everyone. Unlike the Bohemianism of the past, which had to attack the dominant Puritanism and Victorianism of respectable society in a variety of forms, including the censorship of books, Prohibition and a prudery enforced by the police, the new nonconformism has no genuine enemy . . . hence the new rebel bears a great deal of resemblance to a prize fighter trying to knock out an antagonist who is not in the ring with him."[14] The additional sardonic fact is that the man in the gray flannel suit, the presumed target of the Beatniks, is, as Russell Lynes pointed out, especially if he is in advertising, or the entertainment media, an Upper Bohemian himself. The job is accepted as a means of obtaining an income in order to sport and flaunt his presumed, idiosyncratic tastes in dress, food, travel, and the like.[15] The problem for all these multiple sets is not conformity but added novelty.

To add one more paradox, the early theorists of mass society (e.g., Simmel) condemned it because in the vast metropolitan honeycombs people were isolated, transient, anonymous to each other. Americans, sensitive as they are to the criticism of others, took the charge to heart and, in building the postwar suburbs, sought to create fraternity, communality, togetherness, only to find themselves accused of conformity. In the new, recent trend of people returning to the city, it is clear that, in recoil, people will once again establish barriers and will thus bring on the charge, in the next inspection by European sociology, of anonymity, isolation and soullessness, and *anomie*.

One hears the complaint that divorce, crime, and violence demonstrate a widespread social disorganization in the country. But the rising number of divorces may indicate not the disruption of the family but

---

[14] Delmore Schwartz, "The Present State of Poetry," in American Poetry at Mid-century (The Whittall Lectures, Library of Congress, 1958), p. 26.
[15] "In the richly appointed Lake Shore Drive apartment of Chicago Financier Albert Newman, the guests chatted animatedly, gazed at the original Picasso on the wall, and the Monet, the Jackson Pollock. On tables and shelves stood Peruvian fertility symbols, jade bracelets, sculptures that looked like the superstructure of a Japanese battleship. . . . [The guests] had come to meet 32-year old Allen Ginsberg of Paterson, N.J., author of a celebrated, chock-full catalogue called *Howl* ("I saw the best minds of my generation destroyed by madness, starving hysterical naked."). . . . At length Poet Ginsberg arrived wearing blue jeans and a checked black-and-red lumberjacking shirt with black patches. . . . With the crashing madness of a Marx Brothers scene run in reverse, the Beatniks [Ginsberg and two friends] read their poetry, made their pitch for money for a new Beatnik magazine, *The Big Table*, and then stalked out. . . . The trio was an instant hit with the literary upper crust. . . . [The next evening] at the Sherman Hotel, the Beatniks read more poetry for a curious crowd of 700 (who paid $1 and up) . . ." (*Time*, February 9, 1959).

a freer, more individualistic basis of choice and the emergence of the "companionship" marriage. And as regards crime, I have sought to demonstrate that there is actually much *less* crime and violence (though more vicarious violence through movies and TV, and more "windows" onto crime, through the press) than was the case twenty-five and fifty years ago. Certainly Chicago, San Francisco, and New York were much rougher and tougher cities in those years. But violent crime, which is usually a lower-class phenomenon, was then contained within the ecological boundaries of the slum; hence one can recall quiet, tree-lined, crime-free areas and feel that the tenor of life was more even in the past. But a cursory look at the accounts of those days—the descriptions of the gang wars, bordellos, and street-fighting in San Francisco's Barbary Coast, New York's Five Points, or Chicago's First Ward—would show how much more violent the actual life of those cities was in the past.

At this point, it becomes quite apparent that such large-scale abstractions as "the mass society," with the implicit diagnoses of social disorganization and decay that derive from them, are rather meaningless without standards of comparison. Social and cultural change is probably greater and more rapid today in the United States than in any other country, but the assumption that social disorder and *anomie* inevitably attend such change is not borne out in this case.

This may be due to the singular fact that the United States is probably the first large society in history to have change and innovation "built into" its culture. Almost all human societies, traditionalist and habit-ridden as they have been and still are, tend to resist change. The great efforts to industrialize underdeveloped countries, increase worker mobility in Europe, and broaden markets—so necessary to the raising of productivity and standards of living—are again and again frustrated by ingrained resistance to change. Thus, in the Soviet Union, change has been introduced only by dint of wholesale coercion. In the United States —a culture with no feudal tradition, with a pragmatic ethos, as expressed by Jefferson, that regards God as a "workman"; with a boundless optimism and a restless eagerness for the new that have been bred out of the original conditions of a huge, richly endowed land—change, and the readiness to change, have become the norm. This indeed may be why those consequences of change predicted by theorists basing themselves on European precedent find small confirmation.

The mass society is the product of change—and is itself change. It is the bringing of the "masses" into a society, from which they were once excluded. But the *theory* of the mass society affords us no view of the relations of the parts of the society to each other that would enable us to locate the sources of change. We may not have enough data on which to sketch an alternative theory, but I would argue that certain key factors, in this country at least, deserve to be much more closely examined than they have been: the change from a society once geared to frugal saving and now impelled to spend dizzily; the breakup of family capitalism, with the consequent impact on corporate structure and political power; the centralization of decision-making, politically, in the state and, economically, in a group of large corporate bodies; the rise of status and symbol groups replacing specific interest groups—these indicate that new social forms are in the making and, with them, still greater changes in the complexion of life under mass society. With these may well come new status anxieties—aggravated by the threats of war—changed character structures, and new moral tempers.

The moralist may have his reservations or give approval—as some see in the breakup of the family the loss of a source of essential values, while others see in the new, freer marriages a healthier form of companionship—but the singular fact is that these changes emerge in a society that is now providing one answer to the great challenge posed to Western—and now world—society over the last two hundred years: how, within the framework of freedom, to increase the living standards of the majority of people and at the same time maintain or raise cultural levels. For these reasons, the theory of the mass society no longer serves as a description of Western society but as an ideology of romantic protest against contemporary life.

• *Questions for Study*

1. What is Bell's purpose in examining five different uses of the word *mass?* Explain specifically his criticism of each of the five approaches to the theory of mass society. What false notion of the past does the theory entail? Why is the theory an essentially conservative one?
2. Characterize Bell's view of modern American society. Using illustrations from your own experience, can you supplement Bell's view? Criticize it?
3. Can you think of other words that, like "mass," are loosely used and that have many meanings? Consider, for example, "democracy," "freedom," "equality."
4. Does Bell exhibit the kind of style attacked by Cowley?

MORRIS FREEDMAN

•

THE DANGERS OF NONCONFORMISM

Not long ago I heard one of this country's professional intellectuals—a former university president, a present foundation president—address a university gathering of several hundred persons. The gentleman attacked the blight of conformism in the United States; he deplored the fact that men in gray flannel suits had become "interchangeable"; he lamented the loss of true individualism. I do not mention his name, for I agreed with much of what he said, and what I did not agree with is not quite my point at present. What struck me while listening to his urbane talk was his own "interchangeable" appearance: neat, three-button blue suit, plain tie, precisely coiffured graying hair, erect carriage: the very model of a model executive, not only interchangeable with dozens of men in similar positions and in "gentlemen of distinction" ads, but ready to be played in the movies by a dozen or so actors—Walter Pidgeon, Cary Grant, Gregory Peck, Ray Milland. It struck me as somewhat odd, too, that several hundred persons should applaud in unison a speech urging nonconformity, and that during the question period one of the questions that did not "conform" with the speaker's views should be greeted with derision.

Of course one man's conformism may be another man's heresy. But what seems to have taken place in American intellectual life in recent years is the rising of just about any nonconformity to the status of respectable orthodoxy. It is even more strange that it has become as risky to attack these nonconformist orthodoxies as it ever was to attack a conformist one. These days the best protection is to become a nonconformist. In Mary McCarthy's novel about academic life, *The Groves of Academe*, the central character withstands an attempt by the liberal college administration to fire him for incompetence by falsely claiming to

---

From *The American Scholar*, Winter 1958–1959. Reprinted by permission of *The American Scholar* and of the author.

be a Communist. The nonconformist orthodoxy in that environment clearly required being more than fair with Communists, and the professor changed color accordingly. Indeed, it is probably more comfortable today on many campuses to be politically radical than politically conservative. One sure way of getting a job in an advertising agency, I have been told, is to insist that you are an angry young rebel.

The question of conformity, of course, exercises only those certain portions of the American population that loosely may be called the "intellectual" circles. College communities undoubtedly form the largest of these, although the publishing, advertising and entertainment circles are not insubstantial. The issue of conformity scarcely exists for others, the majority, who conform automatically and happily, without giving the question a second thought. Nonconformists have this majority in mind when they attack conformity. They condemn this majority for deriding individual differences, for responding in herd-fashion to the blandishments of advertising and public relations experts, for being responsible for mass taste and mass opinion. No doubt the nonconformists are right in all of these charges. Yet it may easily be shown that the self-elected nonconformists are culpable on every count on which they attack conformists.

It has been well established that nonconformists, instead of responding to the values of tabloid newspaper, subway car or television advertisements, respond to a no less specific and no less rigid set, particularly those in the advertisements of *The New York Times,* the *New Yorker,* the *Saturday Review* and the like, or of the commercials of FM stations that broadcast classical music all day. Although the nonconformist may refuse, with a shudder, to engage in the barbaric practice of drinking instant coffee, he will no less eagerly sip *espresso.* If you can construct a stereotype of the man in the street, you can build an equally plausible one of the man out of the street. Of course, as I say, this proposition is not new, as was definitively demonstrated by Russell Lynes's wickedly clever classifications some while ago in *Life* of the habits of low-brow, middle-brow and high-brow (classifications which themselves no doubt helped establish new laws of how not to conform).

Were all this merely a matter of an amusing sociological pastime—observing and arranging the eating, drinking, dressing, entertainment, furniture buying, political and general ideological habits of low-, middle- and high-brows, or of conformists and nonconformists—there would not be much point in bringing up the matter again after Lynes, Riesman and others have settled it so exhaustively. Actually, however, much more is involved. It seems to me that the orthodoxy of the nonconformists is especially dangerous since it claims to be the result of free investigation and free thought, the product of the uncontrolled, individual mind. Orthodoxy clearly related to some conformist dogma we can so much more easily accept or reject on its own basis.

Let me cite the subject of education from among a number I might have chosen. The country is engaged in a major debate on the problem: the debate is quite limited, on one side, to the professional educators, referred to as "educationists" by the opposition; and, on the other, to what might be called the humanists, many of whom would also proudly claim the title of nonconformists (for they refuse to accept the majority attitude toward education). Now I like to think of myself as among the humanists; and I am certainly appalled by the more extreme notions of educators who believe in teaching the "whole child" (presumably to the suppression of any talented part of him), who believe in teaching "life adjustment" rather than subject matter, who believe in "social promotion," et cetera, et cetera, ad nauseam. I hold that persons who believe such things without qualification should be opposed vigorously; I believe that they should not have final or exclusive say about the schooling of American children, as they now do in many places. But having said this, I must also say that I do not think that the professional educators are to a man villains or idiots—as many critics of them do say or come close to saying.

I probably would not have come to this last conclusion, mild as it may seem, except for the excess and inconsistency of the professional nonconformist on the subject of education. Like nonconformists elsewhere, the nonconformist here prefers to deal with abstractions rather than with reality. One of the many realities of the problem of American education is surely the immense compulsion for universal schooling. Most states have some kind of law compelling attendance in school of every young person up to a certain age regardless of his willingness to learn. I do not say that such laws offer a blanket excuse to educators for their positions, but these laws, the result of great community pressures in the past, are almost always neglected by extremist critics of the schools who insist on an across-the-board raising of standards. Nor have I seen critics of the schools consider the broader pressures in American life that tend to make American education the very special thing that it is.

Consider *Life* magazine's much-publicized first issue in a series on the "Crisis in Education." It blasts the casual diffuseness of American schools by contrast with the concentrated seriousness of Russian ones. The day of a Russian boy and the day of an American boy of the same age are compared, both in school and after. As one might expect, the American boy is inept at mathematics, which he takes as a joke; he tosses off his homework; he is adept only at rock-and-roll and swimming. In short, the American boy is typical of many American young people, who, among other things, are interested in finding out about the making of a movie, or looking at scantily dressed young actresses changing costumes, or reading about horse racing and the latest trend in cars, or going to church to see their minister perform tricks of magic, or looking at the new fashions in clothes and carpets—or reading the latest *Life*, which, in addition to criticizing American education, devoted that same issue to covering all of these edifying and instructive aspects of the broad American scene for its readers. *Life* magazine itself is certainly one of the main forces in making American life what it is; yet the editors, I am sure, would never think of blaming themselves for emphasizing values possibly inimical to seriousness in education. (Perhaps I ought to mention that I do not belong to the nonconformist faction which criticizes *Life*; all in all, if anyone cares, I think the magazine is all right.)

It was not so long ago that a position taken by a Luce publication would have been instinctively opposed by large numbers of nonconformists; but *Life* in recent years has so well caught the importance of being fashionably nonconformist that it is now a leader in establishing accepted nonconformist thought, which, of course, some while ago spilled over from the high-brow crest onto the extensive middle-brow plateaus. On the matter of education, *Life* and other media shaping mass nonconformist ideology have now laid down the party line, making it intellectually suicidal to suggest that possibly the educators have their own peculiar problems to solve before they can reshape their curricula to respond to the present pressures. On most campuses, I venture, a professor in liberal arts would be read out of the ranks if he said a good word about colleges of education, let alone about educational television, which combines two bogeys. The pressure of nonconformists to force an unmodulated conformity to their present position on education makes it extremely difficult for humanists of good will to conduct that "dialogue" with the educators which the foundation president I spoke of earlier insisted is necessary for understanding and progress. Perhaps it is an exaggeration, even a distortion, to say that nonconformists, like Communists of old, insist on free speech for themselves but not for their opponents; certainly one is tempted to think this when a woman in the audience I mentioned made a remark favorable to the schools and was answered with a quip from the speaker and jeers from the audience.

I have spent this much time on education because the danger of intransigent nonconformism seems to me greatest at this moment in that area; nonconformist opposition may yet do as much damage to American education as the educators themselves have done—although I concede it would probably take nonconformism a long time to establish a record of equal harm. The dangers of nonconformism are to be found wherever opinions, tastes, standards, judgments and beliefs are operative. Let me catalogue from my own recent experience a number of positions, attitudes and habits of behavior and thought no nonconformist in good standing can hold these days. These are, of course, subject to rapid change, like fashions in ladies' dress. Also, I should say, it is not essential to reject *all* to remain a respectable nonconformist—only most of them.

It is impossible, then, for the nonconformist to say a good word about Dulles, Nixon, Lyndon Johnson or (since Dwight MacDonald's critique in *Commentary*) James Gould Cozzens, or a bad one about Henry James, Adlai Stevenson, Lionel Trilling or Freud; to express approval of any television show (except *Omnibus,* Ed Murrow or Sid Caesar) or of any American movie (except the inexpensive and badly lighted ones, or the solemn westerns, like *High Noon*); to dislike any foreign films (except those imitating American ones); to believe that you can buy ready-made a good hi-fi set; to wear a non-Ivy-league suit or long hair if a man, or to wear or not wear a sack dress if a woman (I am not sure what feminine nonconformism calls for at the moment); to prefer American cars, for any reason, to European; to believe that there may be any justice in the official position on Oppenheimer; to defend Western diplomacy on any basis; to invite company to dinner without candles on the table and without chamber music in the background; to criticize Arthur Miller or Tennessee Williams as playwrights or otherwise (of course, the shifting popularity of each is constantly causing nonconformist adjustments); to like Tschaikovsky or Irving Berlin, or to dislike Leonard Bernstein or Mozart; to express admiration for Marilyn Monroe or any other American movie star; to disparage Alec Guiness; and so on and on. Since some of the items I list are clearly considered heinous heresies in some quarters and likely to cost individuals professing them their jobs or at least their reputations, I hasten to add that I know no one guilty of more than one of them; as for myself, I plead the fifth. Nor is this altogether frivolous, for I do know of one college teacher who did not have his contract renewed at least in part for his persistent advocacy of the conformist Southern position on segregation; and I know of one junior executive in advertising who will always remain junior because he occasionally wears a double-breasted, navy-blue Cheviot suit with brown shoes—"like a subway rider reading the *Daily News,*" he was described to me by a disapproving colleague.

There is no more self-righteously, high-mindedly closed mind than that of a nonconformist. It is likely that he will begin every conversation with some such gambit as "I know this isn't a popular position, but. . . ." He will insist that no one since Galileo or Joan of Arc has had as much courage as he. Challenge him, and he will dismiss you as a peasant not worth his attention. "If you don't know what's wrong with American culture," I heard one champion nonconformist say down his nose to someone who mildly demurred on the subject, "then there's no point even talking with you." You can never ask about the emperor's clothes lest you prove at once in the nonconformist's eyes to be a monumental repository of naïveté.

Obviously, neither conformity nor nonconformity is to be accepted or rejected per se. What is to be rejected is the nonconformity that is so sure it is right that it is going to cram itself down your throat. No doubt the heresy of today may well become the orthodoxy of tomorrow, but we should not hurry the process any more than we have to; heresies of worth are quite capable of making their own way. If we have anything to fear from the conformists who wish to change the world in accordance with their ideologies, as we no doubt do, then we have equally much to fear from the phalanxes of the nonconformists—and perhaps more, for I sense an aggressive belligerence among nonconformist sects that seems as zealous as olden W.C.T.U. fanaticism. I am thinking, for example, of the San Francisco howlers for whom anything conventional is to be denigrated for the reason of conventionality alone. There are also those chronic nonconformists who do not have even a principle to guide them; they rebel in every direction at once for the sheer sake of perverseness. College campuses have become populated lately with bearded, anarchic mediocrities who blackmail their fellows and their professors into accepting them for more than their worth by trading on the current high value of nonconformity.

Nonconformism today, whatever particular form it takes, appears to be a legitimate enough descendant of the soft liberalism of the thirties. Like the Stalinist creed with which it was often allied, this liberalism saw the world through glasses that never quite focused on things in themselves. It saw things only as fuzzy abstractions that fitted a variety of inflexible needs of the mind. I recall the argument, for instance, that "decent" people were simply not aware of ethnic differences. An ingredient, too, of this soft liberalism was that puritanism which has always been a part of American intellectual life. It is inclined, a priori, to deny any pleasures or successes in popular culture and to look for its satisfactions in more rarified atmospheres. (American movies are only a recent subject for serious nonconformist discussion.) I suppose, too, that mass production, which was invading every aspect of American life in the twenties and the thirties, had to be resisted by a determined seeking out and idealizing of the unique, the handmade product or thought.

One would have expected, however, or at least hoped, that the impulses that turned "thinking" persons away from the passive acceptance of mass-produced things and ideas would have also brought them to the enlightenment of approaching any thing or idea on its own merits rather than through a conditioned reflex. Certainly something like the Museum of Modern Art's tireless, wholesome independence in considering machine-produced objects as worthy of aesthetic attention should have helped nonconformism to develop more broadly, for the Museum is one of the worshiping places of New York nonconformists (although one should never underestimate the power of a nonconformist to compartmentalize). Certainly, too, one would have liked to think that nonconformism, once it cast off the shackles of Communist dogma, would not harden into similarly thoughtless patterns of response to fixed stimuli.

If nonconformity is to have its rightful say in American life, as it did with Emerson, Thoreau, Whitman and Veblen, it must stop making a fetish of itself. Conformity with its range of established, nonevangelical possibilities may, in the end, prove to have the greater attraction for those genuinely seeking a free and full life. After all, unrestricted amateur nonconformism is one of the honorable paths in American history. In the meanwhile, we must oppose all efforts of the dedicated nonconformists to make us not conform according to their rules.

• Questions for Study

1. Relate the "mass non-conformist ideology" described in this essay to the "theory of the mass society" described by Bell in "America as a Mass Society."
2. Look up the word "nonconformity" in your dictionary. Is the author using this word in any of the senses given? If not, attempt to define his use of it.
3. What does Freedman mean by the "orthodoxy of the nonconformist"?
4. Write a theme in which you discuss the characteristic modern conformity and nonconformity in any specific area—political thinking, the arts, social custom, and so on.

MAX LERNER

•

THE ORDEAL OF
THE AMERICAN WOMAN

During the first quarter of the present century the American woman strove for equal rights with men: having achieved them, she has spent the second quarter wondering about the result. The struggle for the vote, for the right to hold and transfer property in her own name and to have legal control of her income, to go to the same colleges and professional schools as men, engaged the stubborn and persistent energies of a succession of women leaders, from Emma Willard, Mary Lyon, Fanny Wright, Margaret Fuller, Elizabeth Stanton, Catherine Beecher, Lydia Child, Jane Swisshelm, to Jane Addams, Carrie Chapman Catt, and Eleanor Roosevelt. There were career women all through the nineteenth century, but the gap was great; in the twentieth it was narrowed. The boos and cheers that greeted the suffrage parades in the early Twenties seem quaint now, when there have been women mayors and Senators, UN delegates, and even Cabinet officers, along with judges, doctors, scientists, novelists, playwrights, war correspondents.

To be sure, a few of the "equal-rights" militants still resent the protective social legislation for women, on the ground that to single them out for protection is to doom them to a subordinate role. But there can be no question of the glowing victories won in the successive cycles of emancipation. That is her dilemma. What disturbs her most is a doubt that what she wants most is her rights. However important the legal and economic struggle, it has brought no ease to her unquiet spirit and her turmoil of mind, and so her heart is not in it.

I do not mean to underplay her effect in humanizing the rigors of a

---

From *America as a Civilization*, New York: Simon and Schuster, Inc., 1957. Copyright, © 1957, by Max Lerner. Reprinted by permission of Simon and Schuster, Inc.

society bent on power and acquisitiveness. The great achievements in
the history of American reform movements—in civil service, prison reform, labor and social-security legislation, temperance, social case work,
settlement houses, slum clearance and housing, public health and movements for international organization—have owed their patience, passion,
and compassion to women. No small part of the great role Eleanor Roosevelt played in history was to help keep the power aspects of the New Deal
in perspective within the human aspects. Kept out of the full stream of
American power expression, the women often had a capacity few men
develop to insulate themselves against the ruthlessness of an expanding
young nation. Although Hawthorne was contemptuous of the "damned
mob of scribbling women," Henry Adams later said grudgingly, "I suspect that women are the only readers—five to one—and that one's audience must be created among them." It is the view of most American college teachers that the girl students keep alive the flame of the liberal-arts
education. American music and literature depend largely upon women
for an audience.

In a society tending to grow more militarized, American women
blunt the sharpness of the obsession with arms and power. Discussing
the history of the Spartan state, Arnold Toynbee points out that the men
were caught in the rigidity of overspecialization to arms, and only the
women in the end could adapt themselves to changing conditions, win-
ning thus the moral superiority over the men and even the political and
economic control. This was not the last time in history that men's concentration on power stripped them of their flexibility and gave the women
a moral edge on them.

However important the humanizing role of the American woman,
her creative achievements at the top level have not matched those of the
men. There have been good novelists (Edith Wharton, Ellen Glasgow,
Willa Cather), poets, (Emily Dickinson, Edna Millay, Elinor Wylie),
short-story writers (Katherine Anne Porter, Eudora Welty), dramatists
(Lillian Hellman), dancers (Martha Graham). But except perhaps for
Emily Dickinson none have seemed to break through to the furthest
reaches of achievement. But this merely shifts the analysis and poses the
question of whether there may not be certain modes of creating that are
closer to feminine temperament and for which the dominant cultural
drives in America offer little scope. One could, for example, conceive of
an American woman novelist who might be another Henry James, but
not of one who would be another Melville, Dreiser, Hemingway, or
Faulkner. We would have to conclude that the main drives in American
culture are creatively less assessable and congenial to women than to
men, and that the "creative component" in women finds less hospitality

within the American cultural frame. For the dominant energies of American culture are power-saturated, violence-ridden, filled with pursuits and triumphs, so that the creative woman finds herself cut off from them and less expressive within them. Hence she turns to the novel of manners, to the short story, to the dance, in all of which she can either operate as a marginal commentator on the American scene or express her own form of protest against it.

This does not mean that the American woman belongs, as several writers have put it, to the "lost sex." She is no more "lost" than her husband or her brother, except that she finds it harder to perform her variety of social roles without feeling the full weight of the cultural contradictions that bear down on her. Like men, she has suffered a loss of function in losing the productive place she once had in the frontier and farm home; nor has she been able to replace it with a sense of new power over the environment, as the men have largely done. But it is a distortion to think of her as suffering badly from a lack of function.

If anything, she is bedeviled by too many functions. She leads simultaneously a multiplicity of lives, playing at once the role of sexual partner, mother, home manager, hostess, nurse, shopper, figure of glamour, supervisor of the children's schooling and play and trips, culture audience and culture carrier, clubwoman, and often worker or careerist. Of the two sexes, it is the man who is specialized to making a living or money, or working at whatever productive job he is doing; the woman, remaining unspecialized, becomes the converging point for all the pressures of the culture. The usual portrait in the foreign commentaries, picturing the American woman as idle, wasteful, and pampered, is not one she will herself recognize. If she has lost some of the stamina of her slightly mystical pioneer grandmother, she has had to take on jobs and problems that her ancestors never dreamed of. She is prized and bedecked as never before, is freer of a tyrannical husband than ever, is equal to him before the law, and has had opened to her a range of opportunities and activities that no civilization before has ever offered to a woman.

The crux lies neither in the biological nor economic disabilities of women, but in their sense of being caught between a man's world which they have no real will to achieve and a world of their own in which they find it hard to be fulfilled. Thus, Thurber's famous drawings of the "war between the sexes" (where but in America could so savage a conception, so furiously executed, strike so deep a response?) do not reach that most tragic theme, which is the war within women's own hearts. When Walt Whitman exhorted women "to give up toys and fictions and launch forth, as men do, amid real, independent, stormy life," he was thinking—as were many of his contemporaries—of the wrong kind of equalitarianism.

The American woman did it, thinking she was doing it to show she was as good as the man. In the sense that she achieved a new kind of freedom of action for herself and the whole family structure, the movement for equal rights and jobs was a fruitful one. Yet the bobbed hair, the latchkey of her own, the cigarette, the cocktail, the ballet, the pay envelope, proved to be symbols of a quest not so much for equality as for identity. And she has been kept from finding herself mainly because all her cultural conditioning—in the setting of American equalitarianism and the American economy—has been at once to compete with the man and to manipulate him. As she grows up, her preparation is to find the right man for marriage and marry him before her attractiveness and bargaining power have been diminished. What resources she will bring to the marriage is left to the chance of the individual instance. The whole duty of parents is held to be that of teaching their daughters the code of what girls do and don't do, dressing them to the extent of the family means (and sometimes beyond), giving them accomplishments and schooling, and marrying them off well. As to what will happen after marriage, it is assumed that the sum of her wisdom will be to have children (not too many) and look after them, furnish a house or apartment, keep her looks and figure, build a circle of friends, and prevent her husband's attention from wandering too much. The question "Are you happy?" is more often addressed to the woman than to the man and has come to have almost a technical meaning in the American cultural context, as if to say, "Are you content with your domestic arrangements, and are you getting along pretty well with your husband and children?"

What women become is thus largely what they are expected to become by the standards of a culture in which the male is held to be the prized quarry and the female the lucky or luckless hunter. The ultimate disaster for women is to miss out on getting a husband. But the unhappiness of the unmarried woman is less the cultural problem of America than the unhappiness of the married one.

The unhappy wife has become a characteristic American culture type. She may feel that what her husband expects of her is trivial and trivializing. In the low income groups she spends her best energies as the heroic family economist, but not always with a sense that the heroism leads anywhere. In the upper income groups she is often forced back into the erotic dream world of plays, movies, and novels, into psychoanalysis, even into astrology and spiritualism and all the thousand ways by which a discontented woman expresses the autumn of her discontent. Where psychoanalysts are too expensive, there is not less need for help: a recent American study of "where people take their troubles" has revealed the quackeries and charlatanisms that shoot up like weeds out of this psychic need. The classic studies by G. V. Hamilton and Katherine Davis show to what extent women of all income groups feel themselves sexually unsatisfied, and a number of recent studies—including the insights offered by the Kinsey volume on women—evidence the fact that a substantial percentage of American women find fitful sexual adventures in extramarital relations. This sense of being emotionally unfulfilled, along with the sense of being socially unused and functionless, combine to create what Pearl Buck has called the "tinderbox woman" in America.

Nor has it helped the unhappy woman to know that she has become the focus of the system of consumption and adornment, the moon that radiates the shimmering surface of American life. What she wants is not to be treated like a well-dressed toy or called "Baby" but to be a person in her own right, with an emotional and intellectual life that makes her a person. As a brainless charmer, who needs to be protected and who learns to manipulate her protector and provider, or—in recoil from that—as the determined careerist who demands the chance to show she equals the male on every level, the American woman finds herself in a blind alley.

One key to her plight is the freezing of models and roles for the behavior of the sexes in the culture. There is an idealized model for both male and female at which each has been culturally conditioned to aim, as an image of oneself and also as an image of one's desired partner. These cultural models may have little relation to the real life goals of the person. As Margaret Mead has suggested, a woman may have a low level of sexual vitality and a slow life rhythm, and a man may in his own terms be of the same type, yet instead of finding happiness in each other, each is bludgeoned by the demands of the culture into aiming at a model of sexual vitality and aggressiveness which may represent the exactly wrong mate.

A similar freezing of roles applies to the whole life cycle of the woman. In girlhood she is brought up to measure her effectiveness by the standards of popularity and success. In her late teens, on the eve of marriage, she becomes the overvalued darling of the culture on whom concentrated attention is lavished, but what she is valued for is her youth and good looks and not any talent she may have or any function she will fill as wife and mother. Once married and started on her childbearing, she is transferred from one frozen role to another, this time as presiding spirit over the home, where she may feel isolated or crowded; the spotlight is shifted from her, but she takes on a series of tasks for which her education has scarcely prepared her. Where the social role of her husband is that of a man growing to the height of his powers, the ideal of a mature woman is strangely absent in American thinking; from the time she passes the peak of the socially fixed ideal of youth beauty she feels herself on the downward slope, and much of her psychic energy goes into fighting off her anxieties on this score. When her children have grown up and left the home, she tries again to pick up the old threads of her life, but she no longer has the self-assurance of her youth, nor is she likely to have built up a real competence in any field: she marks time until she is frozen again in the role of an elderly lady whose life is filled by grandchildren and good works.

There are signs, however, that these rigid social roles are being relaxed and more fluid ones are taking their place. But if she is to discover her identity, she must start by basing her belief in herself on her womanliness rather than on the movement for feminism. Margaret Mead has pointed out that the biological life cycle of the woman has certain well-marked phases from the menarche through the birth of her children to her menopause; that in these stages of her life cycle, as in her basic bodily rhythms, she can feel secure in her womanhood and does not have to assert her potency as the male does. Similarly, while the multiple roles that she must play in life are bewildering, she can fulfill them without distraction if she knows that her central role is that of a woman.

America has realized better than any other society the vision of Mary Wollstonecraft's "Vindication of the Rights of Women"; yet equal rights do not mean an interchangeable identity with men but scope to lead a diversified life while remaining a woman. In this spirit the American woman is groping for a synthesis of her functions in her home, her community, and her job. Her central function, however, remains that of creating a life style for herself and for the home in which she is life creator and life sustainer. She is learning that she need not lose functions simply because she has talents and because she aims at a productive life which will develop her interests and her inner resources.

• Questions for Study

1. What is the "ordeal" suggested in the title? To what extent is Lerner's picture of the American female dependent upon certain generalized conceptions of the American male?
2. Why does the author say that women have not "seemed to break through to the furthest reaches of achievement"? Do you think that he proves his point? Explain.
3. To what extent are Lerner's numerous generalizations about women "useful"? To what extent may they be "useless" in a consideration of the life of a particular woman?
4. What does Lerner envision as the most satisfactory life for a woman? Write a theme on the woman's role in society.

JOSEPH MARGOLIS

•

JUVENILE DELINQUENTS—
THE LATTER DAY KNIGHTS

No one can hope to discover the cause of juvenile delinquency, just as no one can hope to discover the cause of crime. These are labels applied to large clusters of acts that may have in common nothing more than the breaching of the law by minors or merely the breaching of the law. If we fasten on such fractional uniformities, we are inevitably led to expect simple and adequate causal correlations. We speak, accurately enough, of an upsurge in juvenile delinquency, which, because it is an isolable trend, we expect to be assigned an equally isolable source. But if we asked instead for the cause of crime, we should at once realize that "crime" is an umbrella term held over the heads of some extraordinarily different kinds of things. And even if we invented a term to cover criminal activity committed between the ages of thirty and thirty-nine (say, "trigintennial criminality"), we would still find it odd to inquire into its causes.

This does not mean that it is pointless to search out as many correlations as the traffic will bear between juvenile delinquency and the kinds of lives delinquents actually lead. The trends are clear enough and ugly, and they excite our honest hopes for corrective action. Nothing is lost, for instance, in noticing that delinquency is very highly correlated with the various patterns of the "broken home." But one senses that delinquency is too amorphous a phenomenon to respond to the specific of patching homes. And the causally relevant sequences may even come to minimize the juvenile condition of the delinquents and the delinquent condition of the juveniles. Our concern is, properly, with the fact that it is juveniles, in mounting numbers, who are responsible for our crime records. But this, after all, is an outcome completely detached from any insight into the kinds of careers offending juveniles have come to prefer.

Reprinted from *The American Scholar*, Volume 29, Number 2, Spring 1960. Copyright © 1960 by the United Chapter of Phi Beta Kappa. By permission of the publishers.

I think we are nowadays shocked by delinquency. We are startled and horrified by certain of the most dramatic aspects of much juvenile delinquency. But, above all, we are puzzled by it, failing to find its core of sense and purpose. We notice apparently unmotivated crimes, attacks on total strangers, inordinate punishment for seemingly trivial and imagined slights, bloodthirstiness and excessive violence, the exhilarated state of delinquents during their exploits, their disdain of, and relative independence from, the legal and ethical codes of society. Much of the special bravado that we associate with this kind of delinquency, I admit, collapses when the law uses its teeth; but this is not significant, since the delinquent simply behaves as a hostile captive isolated from the little world in which he finds his former conduct appropriate.

I shall not attempt to isolate the causes of juvenile delinquency. I wish only to make the well-known facts about a certain kind of delinquency fall into place in a coherent pattern whose causal analysis would prove more fruitful than the steady, piecemeal accumulation of statistical data. What we require at the present time is a promising model for interpreting the various patterns of delinquent behavior. Perhaps the model I propose is inadequate; it is, however, at least an attempt at correcting our conception of what the delinquents in question think they are doing in carrying on the way they do. Apparently, we don't understand them, for it is perfectly clear that we regard their behavior as senseless, pointless, unprovoked, inexplicable. But we must be mistaken, from their point of view, since there is among them as much seriousness, devotion to imagined duties, sense of honor and trust and co-operation (however perverse), even heroism and self-sacrifice, industry, incentive and reward, foresight and planning as can be found in any legitimate group endeavor. There is among them, moreover, an impressive enthusiasm, *esprit,* solidarity and even pride that would be genuinely hard to duplicate.

Let me exaggerate somewhat the description of two important features that regularly appear in these delinquency patterns. The first is that "there is a war on." The second is that "there must be witnesses." Although I say these are exaggerations, they would not be unlikely first impressions. The sense of a war stems partly from the quite regular skirmishes ("rumbles") between highly organized, usually well-armed, and even territorially distinct rival gangs. It stems also from the understandable hatred (however unpardonable) of this juvenile underworld toward law-enforcement agencies, a hatred that spills over not infrequently into overt hostilities. And it stems finally from the cruel and usually senseless victimization of random members of the law-abiding community.

But in fact there is no war, there are only patterns that strongly resemble warfare. Even the skirmishes between rival gangs are initiated largely by invitation (although it may not be possible to refuse it): "Do you want a rumble?" is, apparently, a common announcement that sufficient reason has been found for a skirmish to be staged. Nevertheless, there seems to be an understanding between warring companies that a return engagement is always to be expected and that no surrender or compensation could establish peace; moreover, each group seems primarily occupied with the way its own champions conduct themselves. The police are simply a perpetual threat, for the activities of these gangs happen typically to be criminal. That is, I do not believe these delinquents wish merely to be law-breakers; they are fully prepared to break the law and, hence, permanently alienate the police. And again, the victims meaninglessly selected from the law-abiding community are merely victims, the unfortunate innocent bystanders of a gang code that affects them in an altogether contingent way. The code imposes obligations on the membership; compliance leads inevitably to the violence we know so well. But the important matter is compliance and not the breach of law. We, within our adult, law-abiding world, are struck by the frequent horror of these acts; whereas the juveniles themselves have hardly considered the victim's personal plight or the anguish of society at large. They are genuinely thoughtless in this respect, so engrossed are they (apart from their immaturity) in leading lives dictated by their own intimate society and in assessing, by their own standards, the talents and reliability and loyalty of their comrades.

I have said also that there must be witnesses. But in a sense, there always are witnesses, because these delinquents specialize in forays, in group adventures in which more than two boys participate. It is important, apparently, that accredited observers attest the prowess, hardness, strength, courage, cruelty, imagination of any single participant. It would be an absolutely idle waste of energy to commit any of the crimes that are committed and to go unnoticed.

I should like to approach this observation in another way. In my opinion, in the large urban centers in which delinquency is most flagrant (and somewhat less noticeably in smaller cities), juvenile gangs constitute the most coherent, publicly self-conscious, and vigorous communities that can be found. I discount businesses, churches, schools, the police and other similar groups as not, properly, forming neighborhoods. The gangs actually live together as social ensembles, the perfection of their communities marred here and there by the impinging adult world. The city is the locale of disintegrating neighborhoods (in the traditional sense) and, conversely, the locale of a rising, novel and peculiarly mobile neighborhood. In short, increasingly in our cities (as well as in certain of the cities of Europe and Asia) the most effective and powerful neighborhoods that exist are juvenile neighborhoods. They are the ones, ironically, that preserve some measure of face-to-face community living. And they are themselves aware of it, at least in that revealing lapse by which their members boldly attack innocent people without fear of reprisal. The law-abiding adult world is distinctly inert, from their point of view, providing only an endless variety of occasions and targets for the exhibition of the skills that are prized within the gang. Even the unfriendly press provides gratuitous and welcome confirmation of the gang's own chronicles. And, periodically, the forays themselves lead to large-scale rumbles, which, as is well known, are advertised to all except the police and others interested in law enforcement.

So the adult world is abdicating in large part its neighborhood responsibility and authority and, by its increasing inertia, has allowed control to pass into the hands of vigorous and ardent youngsters, whose code, however, does not promise to preserve the law-abiding values of the old neighborhood. It also happens that cities spring up without ever having had the experience of the old neighborhood solidarity; but this hardly is designed to prevent the rise of the new gangs.

I have put forward what I take to be two important clues for any suitable interpretive model of the sort required. I should like to say something now about such a model. The adult world thinks of these delinquents as deviants, outlaws, irresponsibles; and it is baffled by its inability to contain them. But the juveniles themselves actually form a string of genuine and relatively stable neighborhoods, with a day-to-day code of conduct, a system of sanctions and rewards, a calendar of community life, an educational program, and facilities for communications and the provision and distribution of goods and services. It is a simple society in which everyone is known by name and face and accomplishment; it is an aristocratic society—frequently monarchical—but in any case ruled by the most talented persons (discounting the perversity of the talents preferred). It is in fact *the* society to which these juveniles belong. The adult world, from their point of view, is vaguely defined and alien, usually threatening in its intermittent contact with their own; although, of course, the juvenile cannot ever be entirely free of a subordinate participation in that adult world.

The juvenile neighborhood has, I should say, two principal rituals to perform. It is, as a matter of fact, overwhelmingly concerned with ritual forms. But the two I have in mind bear most directly on the terror and violence that have so shocked the adult world. One is the initiation ritual, and the other is what I can only call the ritual sortie. They are essentially indistinguishable as far as overt behavior is concerned; they are different only in their purpose. The initiation ritual has to do with recruitment, the selection of suitable members of an elite society. The ritual sortie has to do with status and prestige within that society, both a requirement of members in good standing and an opportunity for the advancement of the ambitious and the talented. The society is usually, at its most audacious, a society of warriors and "free" souls who accept only those limitations upon conduct that, as a corporation, they themselves impose. But it is also a society of pranksters, gaming companions, exhibitionists, children, concerned as much with extremities of style in dress and speech as with murder and theft. It is always, however, a loyal brotherhood provided with a more or less clear schedule of honors. And it leads what is essentially a public life, protected as far as possible from the eyes of law-enforcement agencies.

If we are to understand this model, we shall find that we must look to some surprising parallels. I should suggest, because of its familiarity, that of the Knights of the Round Table, without at all ignoring the willingness of our own juvenile gangs to give themselves—in all candor and accuracy—sinister and evil and even repugnant names. It is important to notice that there are no ready models (even models that they might pervert) to be found in the law-abiding adult world. And it is important also to isolate that critical feature of their own way of life that is so entirely alien to the more or less official ideology of the adult world.

The feature in question may perhaps most succinctly be described as "climax-technique" (I borrow the term from the accounts of the code of life of the pagan Teutonic knights). I submit that our juvenile gangs implicitly subscribe to this significant principle, however corrupt their particular values may be said to be. Briefly, the routine of ordinary, unadventurous life is quite worthless, boring, idle to our juveniles; it is made supportable only by celebrating previous sorties and by preparation for others. In an odd sense, then, the juvenile does not wish to be idle—idleness is death to him. But, curiously, he considers the life of the adult world (and his submission to it) an idle life and correspondingly, the adult world views his exploits also as a species of idling. The significance of his life lies exclusively in the climactic and perilous mountain peaks of the adventures he enters into so wholeheartedly (an important inversion of the purity of the soul we associate with, say, the devotion of the Round Table Knights). So he proves himself from episode to episode—whether by torture, theft, sexual liberties, murder, fighting, vandalism, drinking— always in accord with the strict code of his own society.

The values of the adult world have to do with docility and safety and, most important, with the merits of prolonged routine work. It is here, therefore, that we have the most dramatic evidence of the break-down in the educational apparatus of the adult world, of the autonomy of the juvenile: we must acknowledge the existence of a subsociety that effectively recruits and instructs novices (willing or not) in a way of life that, in the most fundamental manner possible, is opposed to the values of an otherwise incredibly powerful society. The juvenile world is simply slipping through very strong nets; but, as it does, it is also managing to get control of the vital neighborhood. It repudiates the declared values of the adult world and, finding itself potentially in control of an unorganized neighborhood, simply reinforces the quite naturally intimate and sus-tained society of the young and moves to institutionalize its own values. It is necessarily parasitic, feeding on the wealth and skills and goods of the adult world, relieved therefore of any positive concern with the mainte-nance of the requisite routines; and thus relieved, it is almost entirely free to pursue those special ritual adventures by which it distinguishes itself.

The phenomenon of the delinquent gang is not an altogether new one. Gang and quasi-tribal patterns are quite familiar among adolescents, patterns at once compulsive and inclined toward outlawry. Still, we can-not fail to notice certain distinctive features of the current delinquency: the advanced decline in adult participation in the forming and maintain-ing of neighborhood policy, particularly with respect to the hour-to-hour activities of the adolescent, and the apparently easy accessibility of dangerous weapons. We may also remark the juvenile's interest in the publicized exploits of otherwise unfamiliar criminal "heroes." Delinquency appears to have taken on an epidemic quality, and the criminal achieve-ments of newly discovered offenders invite appraisal and emulation. In fact, the ever-efficient press actually facilitates the standardization of juvenile conduct, hence that of juvenile crime. It has, for example, become altogether common for informal, small and inexperienced groups of juveniles spontaneously to attempt dangerous, violent sorties of the kind formerly reserved for the most desperate criminals: we hear every day of unbelievable crimes motivated by pure whim.

Although it would be madness to refuse to admit the threat posed by juvenile gangs and their responsibility for their own crimes, it would be a serious blunder to imagine that increasing the severity of penalties for juvenile criminals will in any way reduce their activity. Similar measures have not affected senior crime. Given the mentality of the juvenile types I have been trying to describe, such measures can only serve to make their lives more daring and more exciting, without at all disturbing the solidarity of their society. Punishment, then, is a force somewhat misap-plied, since it aims at restraining the juvenile and not at recovering his allegiance. But it is precisely this allegiance that the adult world has lost.

• *Questions for Study*

1. Why can it be said that Margolis is "romanticizing" the problem of juvenile delinquents? What important characteristics of true knighthood are not found in the code of delinquents?
2. Examine the style of the opening paragraph. Comment on such words and phrases as "isolable," "fractional uniformities," "causal correlations," and "trigentennial criminality." What do you think Cowley's attitude toward these phrases would be?
3. How do adults help to create juvenile delinquents, according to Margolis? Why does the city provide the easiest background for the rise of these "latter-day knights"?

THE ENVIRONMENT OF MAN

THOMAS H. HUXLEY

•

THE METHOD OF SCIENCE

The method of scientific investigation is nothing but the expression of the necessary mode of working of the human mind. It is simply the mode at which all phenomena are reasoned about, rendered precise and exact. There is no more difference, but there is just the same kind of difference, between the mental operations of a man of science and those of an ordinary person, as there is between the operations and methods of a baker or of a butcher weighing out his goods in common scales, and the operations of a chemist in performing a difficult and complex analysis by means of his balance and finely-graduated weights. It is not that the action of the scales in the one case, and the balance in the other, differ in the principles of their construction or manner of working; but the beam of one is set on an infinitely finer axis than the other, and of course turns by the addition of a much smaller weight.

You will understand this better, perhaps, if I give you some familiar example. You have all heard it repeated, I dare say, that men of science work by means of induction and deduction, and that by the help of these operations, they, in a sort of sense, wring from Nature certain other things, which are called natural laws, and causes, and that out of these, by some cunning skill of their own, they build up hypotheses and theories. And it is imagined by many, that the operations of the common mind can be by no means compared with these processes, and that they have to be acquired by a sort of special apprenticeship to the craft. To hear all these large words, you would think that the mind of a man of science must be constituted differently from that of his fellow men; but if you will not be frightened by terms, you will discover that you are quite wrong, and that

From *Darwiniana*, 1893.

all these terrible apparatus are being used by yourselves every day and
every hour of your lives.

There is a well-known incident in one of Molière's plays, where the
author makes the hero express unbounded delight on being told that he
had been talking prose during the whole of his life. In the same way, I
trust, that you will take comfort, and be delighted with yourselves, on
the discovery that you have been acting on the principles of inductive and
deductive philosophy during the same period. Probably there is not one
here who has not in the course of the day had occasion to set in motion a
complex train of reasoning, of the very same kind, though differing of
course in degree, as that which a scientific man goes through in tracing
the causes of natural phenomena.

A very trivial circumstance will serve to exemplify this. Suppose you
go into a fruiterer's shop, wanting an apple,—you take up one, and, on
biting it, you find it is sour; you look at it, and see that it is hard and
green. You take up another one, and that too is hard, green, and sour.
The shopman offers you a third; but, before biting it, you examine it, and
find that it is hard and green, and you immediately say that you will
not have it, as it must be sour, like those that you have already tried.

Nothing can be more simple than that, you think; but if you will take
the trouble to analyse and trace out into its logical elements what has been
done by the mind, you will be greatly surprised. In the first place, you
have performed the operation of induction. You found that, in two experiences, hardness and greenness in apples went together with sourness. It
was so in the first case, and it was confirmed by the second. True, it is a
very small basis, but still it is enough to make an induction from; you
generalise the facts, and you expect to find sourness in apples where you
get hardness and greenness. You found upon that a general law, that all
hard and green apples are sour; and that, so far as it goes, is a perfect
induction. Well, having got your natural law in this way, when you are
offered another apple which you find is hard and green, you say, "All
hard and green apples are sour; this apple is hard and green, therefore
this apple is sour." That train of reasoning is what logicians call a syllogism, and has all its various parts and terms,—its major premiss, its
minor premiss, and its conclusion. And, by the help of further reasoning,
which, if drawn out, would have to be exhibited in two or three other
syllogisms, you arrive at your final determination, "I will not have that
apple." So that, you see, you have, in the first place, established a law by
induction, and upon that you have founded a deduction, and reasoned
out the special conclusion of the particular case. Well now, suppose,
having got your law, that at some time afterwards, you are discussing the
qualities of apples with a friend: you will say to him, "It is a very curious

thing,—but I find that all hard and green apples are sour!" Your friend says to you, "But how do you know that?" You at once reply, "Oh, because I have tried them over and over again, and have always found them to be so." Well, if we were talking science instead of common sense, we should call that an experimental verification. And, if still opposed, you go further, and say, "I have heard from the people in Somersetshire and Devonshire, where a large number of apples are grown, that they have observed the same thing. It is also found to be the case in Normandy, and in North America. In short, I find it to be the universal experience of mankind wherever attention has been directed to the subject." Whereupon, your friend, unless he is a very unreasonable man, agrees with you, and is convinced that you are quite right in the conclusion you have drawn. He believes, although perhaps he does not know he believes it, that the more extensive verifications are,—that the more frequently experiments have been made, and results of the same kind arrived at,—that the more varied the conditions under which the same results are attained, the more certain is the ultimate conclusion, and he disputes the question no further. He sees that the experiment has been tried under all sorts of conditions, as to time, place, and people, with the same result; and he says with you, therefore, that the law you have laid down must be a good one, and he must believe it.

In science we do the same thing;—the philosopher exercises precisely the same faculties, though in a much more delicate manner. In scientific inquiry it becomes a matter of duty to expose a supposed law to every possible kind of verification, and to take care, moreover, that this is done intentionally, and not left to a mere accident, as in the case of the apples. And in science, as in common life, our confidence in a law is in exact proportion to the absence of variations in the result of our experimental verifications. For instance, if you let go your grasp of an article you may have in your hand, it will immediately fall to the ground. That is a very common verification of one of the best established laws of nature—that of gravitation. The method by which men of science establish the existence of that law is exactly the same as that by which we have established the trivial proposition about the sourness of hard and green apples. But we believe it in such an extensive, thorough, and unhesitating manner because the universal experience of mankind verifies it, and we can verify it ourselves at any time; and that is the strongest possible foundation on which any natural law can rest.

So much, then, by way of proof that the method of establishing laws in science is exactly the same as that pursued in common life. Let us now turn to another matter (though really it is but another phase of the same question), and that is, the method by which, from the relations of certain phenomena, we prove that some stand in the position of causes towards the others.

I want to put the case clearly before you, and I will therefore show you what I mean by another familiar example. I will suppose that one of you, on coming down in the morning to the parlour of your house, finds that a tea-pot and some spoons which had been left in the room on the previous evening are gone,—the window is open, and you observe the mark of a dirty hand on the window-frame, and, perhaps, in addition to that, you notice the impress of a hob-nailed shoe on the gravel outside. All these phenomena have struck your attention instantly, and before two seconds have passed you say, "Oh, somebody has broken open the window, entered the room, and run off with the spoons and the tea-pot!" That speech is out of your mouth in a moment. And you will probably add, "I know there has; I am quite sure of it!" You mean to say exactly what you know; but in reality you are giving expression to what is, in all essential particulars, an hypothesis. You do not *know* it at all; it is nothing but an hypothesis rapidly framed in your own mind. And it is an hypothesis founded on a long train of inductions and deductions.

What are those inductions and deductions, and how have you got at this hypothesis? You have observed, in the first place, that the window is open; but by a train of reasoning involving many inductions and deductions, you have probably arrived long before at the general law— and a very good one it is—that windows do not open of themselves; and you therefore conclude that something has opened the window. A second general law that you have arrived at in the same way is, that tea-pots and spoons do not go out of a window spontaneously, and you are satisfied that, as they are not now where you left them, they have been removed. In the third place, you look at the marks on the window-sill, and the shoe-marks outside, and you say that in all previous experience the former kind of mark has never been produced by anything else but the hand of a human being; and the same experience shows that no other animal but man at present wears shoes with hob-nails in them such as would produce the marks in the gravel. I do not know, even if we could discover any of those "missing links" that are talked about, that they would help us to any other conclusion! At any rate the law which states our present experience is strong enough for my present purpose. You next reach the conclusion, that as these kinds of marks have not been left by any other animals than men, or are liable to be formed in any other way than by a man's hand and shoe, the marks in question have been formed by a man in that way. You have, further, a general law, founded on observation and experience, and that, too, is, I am sorry to say, a very universal and unimpeachable one,—that some men are thieves; and you assume at once from all these premisses—and that is what constitutes your hypothesis—that the man who made the marks outside and on the window-sill, opened the window, got into the room, and stole your tea-pot and spoons. You have now arrived at a *vera causa;* —you have assumed a cause which, it is plain, is competent to produce all the phenomena you have observed. You can explain all these phenomena only by the hypothesis of a thief. But that is a hypothetical conclusion, of the justice of which you have no absolute proof at all; it is only rendered highly probable by a series of inductive and deductive reasonings.

I suppose your first action, assuming that you are a man of ordinary common sense, and that you have established this hypothesis to your own satisfaction, will very likely be to go off for the police, and set them on the track of the burglar, with the view to the recovery of your property. But just as you are starting with this object, some person comes in, and on learning what you are about, says, "My good friend, you are going on a great deal too fast. How do you know that the man who really made the marks took the spoons? It might have been a monkey that took them, and the man may have merely looked in afterwards." You would probably reply, "Well, that is all very well, but you see it is contrary to all experience of the way tea-pots and spoons are abstracted; so that, at any rate, your hypothesis is less probable than mine." While you are talking the thing over in this way, another friend arrives, one of that good kind of people that I was talking of a little while ago. And he might say, "Oh, my dear sir, you are certainly going on a great deal too fast. You are most presumptuous. You admit that all these occurrences took place when you were fast asleep, at a time when you could not possibly have known anything about what was taking place. How do you know that the laws of Nature are not suspended during the night? It may be that there has been some kind of supernatural interference in this case." In point of fact, he declares that your hypothesis is one of which you cannot at all demonstrate the truth, and that you are by no means sure that the laws of Nature are the same when you are asleep as when you are awake.

Well, now, you cannot at the moment answer that kind of reasoning. You feel that your worthy friend has you somewhat at a disadvantage. You will feel perfectly convinced in your own mind, however, that you are quite right, and you say to him, "My good friend, I can only be guided by the natural probabilities of the case, and if you will be kind enough to stand aside and permit me to pass, I will go and fetch the police." Well, we will suppose that your journey is successful, and that by good luck you meet with a policeman; that eventually the burglar is found with your property on his person, and the marks correspond to his hand and to his boots. Probably any jury would consider those facts a very good experimental verification of your hypothesis, touching the cause of the abnormal phenomena observed in your parlour, and would act accordingly.

Now, in this suppositious case, I have taken phenomena of a very common kind, in order that you might see what are the different steps in an ordinary process of reasoning, if you will only take the trouble to analyse it carefully. All the operations I have described, you will see, are involved in the mind of any man of sense in leading him to a conclusion as to the course he should take in order to make good a robbery and punish the offender. I say that you are led, in that case, to your conclusion by exactly the same train of reasoning as that which a man of science pursues when he is endeavouring to discover the origin and laws of the most occult phenomena. The process is, and always must be, the same; and precisely the same mode of reasoning was employed by Newton and Laplace in their endeavours to discover and define the causes of the movements of the heavenly bodies, as you, with your own common sense, would employ to detect a burglar. The only difference is, that the nature of the inquiry being more abstruse, every step has to be most carefully watched, so that there may not be a single crack or flaw in your hypothesis. A flaw or crack in many of the hypotheses of daily life may be of little or no moment as affecting the general correctness of the conclusions at which we may arrive; but, in a scientific inquiry, a fallacy, great or small, is always of importance, and is sure to be in the long run constantly productive of mischievous, if not fatal results.

Do not allow yourselves to be misled by the common notion that an hypothesis is untrustworthy simply because it is an hypothesis. It is often urged, in respect to some scientific conclusion, that, after all, it is only an hypothesis. But what more have we to guide us in nine-tenths of the most important affairs of daily life than hypotheses, and often very ill-based ones? So that in science, where the evidence of an hypothesis is subjected to the most rigid examination, we may rightly pursue the same course. You may have hypotheses and hypotheses. A man may say, if he likes, that the moon is made of green cheese: that is an hypothesis. But another man, who has devoted a great deal of time and attention to the subject, and availed himself of the most powerful telescopes and the results of the observations of others, declares that in his opinion it is probably composed of materials very similar to those of which our own earth is made up: and that is also only an hypothesis. But I need not tell you that there is an enormous difference in the value of the two hypotheses. That one which is based on sound scientific knowledge is sure to have a corresponding value; and that which is a mere hasty random guess is likely to have but little value. Every great step in our progress in discovering causes has been made in exactly the same way as that which I have detailed to you. A person observing the occurrence of certain facts and phenomena asks, naturally enough, what process, what kind of operation known to occur in Nature applied to the particular case, will unravel and explain the mystery? Hence you have the scientific hypothesis; and its value will be proportionate to the care and completeness with which its basis had been tested and verified. It is in these matters as in the commonest affairs of practical life: the guess of the fool will be folly, while the guess of the wise man will contain wisdom. In all cases, you see that the value of the result depends on the patience and faithfulness with which the investigator applies to his hypothesis every possible kind of verification.

• *Questions for Study*

1. The way men reason is essentially the subject of this essay as well as that of Johnson's "Logical Thinking." Compare and contrast the two treatments of the subject. Which is the more interesting and why?
2. Can you provide illustrations from your own experience in which you used, without realizing it, the scientific method to arrive at a hypothesis?
3. Does Huxley oversimplify when he states that "the method of establishing laws in science is exactly the same as that pursued in common life"? Is "exactly" an accurate word in this context? Explain.
4. Would modern scientists agree with Huxley's claim concerning the final results of discoveries made by the scientific method? What criticism can be made of his strong faith in this method by scientists and by men in other fields? Does Huxley seem aware of criticism of the method?

C. P. SNOW

•

THE AGE OF RUTHERFORD

In 1923, at the meeting of the British Association for the Advancement of Science in Liverpool, Lord Rutherford announced, at the top of his enormous voice: "We are living in the heroic age of physics." He went on saying the same thing, loudly and exuberantly, until he died, fourteen years later.

The curious thing was, all he said was absolutely true. There had never been such a time. The year 1932 was the most spectacular year in the history of science. Living in Cambridge, one could not help picking up the human, as well as the intellectual, excitement in the air. Sir James Chadwick, gray-faced after a fortnight of work with three hours' sleep a night, telling the Kapitza Club how he had discovered the neutron; P. M. S. Blackett, the most handsome of men, not quite so authoritative as usual, because it seemed too good to be true, showing plates which demonstrated the existence of the positive electron; Sir John Cockroft, normally about as given to emotional display as the Duke of Wellington, skimming down King's Parade and saying to anyone whose face he recognized: "We've split the atom! We've split the atom!"

It meant an intellectual climate different in kind from anything else in England at the time. The tone of science was the tone of Rutherford: magniloquently boastful—boastful because the major discoveries were being made—creatively confident, generous, argumentative, lavish, and full of hope. The tone differed from the tone of literary England as much as Rutherford's personality differed from that of T. S. Eliot or F. R. Leavis. During the twenties and thirties, Cambridge was the metropolis of physics for the entire world. Even in the late nineteenth century, during the professorships of Clerk Maxwell and J. J. Thomson, it had never quite been that. "You're always at the crest of the wave," someone said to Rutherford. "Well, after all, I made the wave, didn't I?" Rutherford replied.

I remember seeing him a good many times before I first spoke to him. I was working on the periphery of physics at the time, and so didn't come directly under him. I already knew that I wanted to write novels, and that that was how I should finish, and this gave me a kind of ambivalent attitude to the scientific world; but, even so, I could not avoid feeling some sort of excitement, or enhancement of interest, whenever I saw Rutherford walking down Free School Lane.

He was a big, rather clumsy man, with a substantial bay window that started in the middle of the chest. I should guess that he was less muscular than at first sight he looked. He had large staring blue eyes and a damp and pendulous lower lip. He didn't look in the least like an intellectual. Creative people of his abundant kind never do, of course, but all the talk of Rutherford looking like a farmer was unperceptive nonsense. His was really the kind of face and physique that often goes with great weight of character and gifts. It could easily have been the soma of a great writer. As he talked to his companions in the street, his voice was three times as loud as any of theirs, and his accent was bizarre. In fact, he came from the very poor: his father was an odd-job man in New Zealand and the son of a Scottish emigrant. But there was nothing Antipodean or Scottish about Rutherford's accent; it sounded more like a mixture of West Country and Cockney.

In my first actual meeting with him, perhaps I could be excused for not observing with precision. It was early in 1930; I had not yet been elected a Fellow of my own college, and so had put in for the Stokes studentship at Pembroke. One Saturday afternoon I was summoned to an interview. When I arrived at Pembroke, I found that the short list was only two, Philip Dee and I. Dee was called in first; as he was being interviewed, I was reflecting without pleasure that he was one of the brightest of Rutherford's young men.

Then came my turn. As I went in, the first person I saw, sitting on the right hand of the Master, was Rutherford himself. While the Master was taking me through my career, Rutherford drew at his pipe, not displaying any excessive interest in the proceedings. The Master came to the end of his questions, and said: "Professor Rutherford?"

Rutherford took out his pipe and turned onto me an eye which was blue, cold, and bored. He was the most spontaneous of men; when he felt bored, he showed it. That afternoon he felt distinctly bored. Wasn't his man, and a very good man, in for this job? What was this other fellow doing there? Why were we all wasting our time?

He asked me one or two indifferent questions, in an irritated, impatient voice. What was my present piece of work? What could spectroscopy tell us anyway? Wasn't it just "putting things into boxes"?

I thought that was a bit rough. Perhaps I realized that I had nothing to lose. Anyway, as cheerfully as I could manage, I asked if he couldn't put up with a few of us not doing nuclear physics. I went on, putting a case for my kind of subject.

A note was brought round to my lodgings that evening. Dee had got the job. The electors wished to say that either candidate could properly have been elected. That sounded like a bit of politeness, and I felt depressed. I cheered up a day or two later when I heard that Rutherford was trumpeting that I was a young man of spirit. Within a few months he backed me for another studentship. Incidentally, Dee was a far better scientist than I was or could have been, and neither Rutherford nor anyone else had been unjust.

From that time until he died, I had some opportunities of watching Rutherford at close quarters. Several of my friends knew him intimately, which I never did. It is a great pity that Tizard has not written about him at length. But I belonged to a dining club which he attended, and I think I had serious conversations with him three times, the two of us alone together.

The difficulty is to separate the inner man from the Rutherfordiana, much of which is quite genuine. From behind a screen in a Cambridge tailor's, a friend and I heard a reverberating voice: "That shirt's too tight round the neck. Every day I grow in girth. *And* in mentality." Yet his physical make-up was more nervous than it seemed. In the same way, his temperament, which seemed exuberantly, powerfully, massively simple, rejoicing with childish satisfaction in creation and fame, was not quite so simple as all that. His was a personality of Johnsonian scale. As with Johnson, the façade was overbearing and unbroken. But there were fissures within.

No one could have enjoyed himself more, either in creative work or the honors it brought him. He worked hard, but with immense gusto; he got pleasure not only from the high moments, but also from the hours of what to others would be drudgery, sitting in the dark counting the alpha particle scintillations on the screen. His insight was direct, his intuition, with one curious exception, infallible. No scientist has made less mistakes. In the corpus of his published work, one of the largest in scientific history, there was nothing he had to correct afterwards. By thirty, he had already set going the science of nuclear physics—single-handed, as a professor on five hundred pounds a year, in the isolation of late-Victorian Montreal. By forty, now in Manchester, he had found the structure of the atom on which all modern nuclear physics depends.

It was not done without noise; it was done with anger and storms— but also with an overflow of creative energy, with abundance and generosity, as though research were the easiest and most natural avocation in the world. He had deep sympathy with the creative arts, particularly literature; he read more novels than most literary people manage to do. He had no use for critics of any kind. He felt both suspicion and dislike of the people who invested scientific research or any other branch of creation with an aura of difficulty, who used long, methodological words to explain things which he did perfectly by instinct. "Those fellows," he used to call them. "Those fellows" were the logicians, the critics, the metaphysicians. They were clever; they were usually more lucid than he was; in argument against them he often felt at a disadvantage. Yet somehow they never produced a serious piece of work, whereas he was the greatest experimental scientist of the age.

I have heard greater claims made for him. I remember one discussion in particular, a few years after his death, by half a dozen men, all of whom had international reputations in science. Was Rutherford the greatest experimental scientist since Michael Faraday? Without any doubt. Greater than Faraday? Almost certainly so. And then—it is interesting, as it shows the anonymous Tolstoyan nature of organized science —how many years difference would it have made if he had never lived? How much longer before the nucleus would have been understood as we now understand it? Perhaps ten years. More likely only five.

Rutherford's intellect was so strong that he would, in the long run, have accepted that judgment. But he would not have liked it. His estimate of his own powers was realistic, but if it erred at all, it did not err on the modest side. "There is no room for this particle in the atom as designed by *me*," I once heard him assure a large audience. It was part of his nature that, stupendous as his work was, he should consider it 10 per cent more so. It was also part of his nature that, quite without acting, he should behave constantly as though he were 10 per cent larger than life. Worldly success? He loved every minute of it: flattery, titles, the company of the high official world. He said in a speech: "As I was standing in the drawing room at Trinity, a *clergyman* came in. And I said to him: 'I'm Lord Rutherford.' And he said to me: 'I'm the Archbishop of York.' And I don't suppose either of us believed the other."

He was a great man, a very great man, by any standards which we can apply. He was clever as well as creatively gifted, magnanimous (within the human limits) as well as hearty. He was also superbly and magnificently vain as well as wise—the combination is commoner than we think when we are young. He enjoyed a life of miraculous success. On the whole he enjoyed his own personality. But I am sure that, even quite late in his life, he felt stabs of a sickening insecurity.

Somewhere at the roots of that abundant and creative nature there was a painful, shrinking nerve. One has only to read his letters as a young man to discern it. There are passages of self-doubt which are not to be explained completely by a humble colonial childhood and youth. He was uncertain in secret, abnormally so for a young man of his gifts. He kept the secret as his personality flowered and hid it. But there was a mysterious diffidence behind it all. He hated the faintest suspicion of being patronized, even when he was a world figure. Archbishop Lang was once tactless enough to suggest that he supposed a famous scientist had no time for reading. Rutherford immediately felt that he was being regarded as an ignorant roughneck. He produced a formidable list of his last month's reading. Then, half innocently, half malevolently: "And what do you manage to read, your Grice?" "I am afraid," said the Archbishop, somewhat out of his depth, "that a man in my position really doesn't have the leisure . . ." "Ah, yes, your Grice," said Rutherford in triumph, "it must be a dog's life! It must be a dog's life!"

Once I had an opportunity of seeing that diffidence face to face. In the autumn of 1934 I published my first novel, which was called *The Search* and the background of which was the scientific world. Not long after it came out, Rutherford met me in King's Parade. "What have you been doing to us, young man?" he asked vociferously. I began to describe the novel, but it was not necessary; he announced that he had read it with care. He went on to invite, or rather command, me to take a stroll with him round the Backs. Like most of my scientific friends, he was good-natured about the book, which has some descriptions of the scientific experience which are probably somewhere near the truth. He praised it. I was gratified. It was a sunny October afternoon. Suddenly he said: "I didn't like the erotic bits. I suppose it's because we belong to different generations."

The book, I thought, was reticent enough. I did not know how to reply.

In complete seriousness and simplicity, he made another suggestion. He hoped that I was not going to write all my novels about scientists. I assured him that I was not—certainly not another for a long time.

He nodded. He was looking gentler than usual, and thoughtful. "It's a small world, you know," he said. He meant the world of science. "Keep off us as much as you can. People are bound to think that you are getting at some of us. And I suppose we've all got things that we don't want anyone to see."

I mentioned that his intuitive foresight went wrong just once. As a rule, he was dead right about the practical applications of science just as much as about the nucleus. But his single boss shot sounds ironic now. In 1933 he said, in another address to the British Association, "These transformations of the atom are of extraordinary interest to scientists, but we cannot control atomic energy to an extent which would be of any value commercially, and I believe we are not likely ever to be able to do so. A lot of nonsense has been talked about transmutations. Our interest in the matter is purely scientific."

That statement, which was made only nine years before the first pile worked, was not intended to be either optimistic or pessimistic. It was just a forecast, and it was wrong.

That judgment apart, people outside the scientific world often felt that Rutherford and his kind were optimistic—optimistic right against the current of the twentieth-century literary-intellectual mood, offensively and brazenly optimistic. This feeling was not quite unjustified, but the difference between the scientists and the nonscientists was subtler than that. When the scientists talked of the individual human condition, they did not find it any more hopeful than the rest of us. Does anyone really imagine that Bertrand Russell, G. H. Hardy, Rutherford, Blackett, and the rest were bemused by cheerfulness as they faced their own individual state? Very few of them had any of the consolations of religion: they believed, with the same certainty that they believed in Rutherford's atom, that they were going, after the loneliness of this mortal life, into annihilation. Intellectually they had an unqualified comprehension, without any cushions at all, of the tragic condition of individual man.

Nevertheless it is true that, of the kinds of people I have lived among, the scientists were much the happiest. Somehow scientists were buoyant at a time when other intellectuals could not keep away despair. The reasons for this are complex. Partly, the nature of scientific activity, its complete success on its own terms, is itself a source of happiness; partly, people who are drawn to scientific activity tend to be happier in temperament than other clever men. By the nature of their vocation and also by the nature of their own temperament, the scientists did not think constantly of the individual human predicament. Since they could not alter it, they let it alone. When they thought about people, they thought most of what could be altered, not what couldn't. So they gave their minds not to the individual condition but to the social one.

There, science itself was the greatest single force for change. The scientists were themselves part of the deepest revolution in human affairs since the discovery of agriculture. They could accept what was happening, while other intellectuals shrank away. They not only accepted it, they rejoiced in it. It was difficult to find a scientist who did not believe that the scientific-technical-industrial revolution, accelerating under his eyes, was not doing incomparably more good than harm.

This was the characteristic optimism of scientists in the twenties and thirties. It still is. In some ways it was too easy an optimism, but the counterattitude of the nonscientific intellectuals was too easy a pessimism. Between Rutherford and Blackett on the one hand, and say, Wyndham Lewis and Ezra Pound on the other, who are on the side of their fellow human beings? The only people who would have any doubt about the answer are those who dislike the human race.

So, in Rutherford's scientific world, the liberal decencies were taken for granted. It was a society singularly free from class or national or racial prejudice. Rutherford called himself alternatively conservative or nonpolitical, but the men he wanted to have jobs were those who could do physics. Niels Bohr, Otto Hahn, Georg von Hevesy, Hans Geiger were men and brothers, whether they were Jews, Germans, Hungarians —men and brothers whom he would much rather have near him than the Archbishop of Canterbury or one of "those fellows" or any damned English philosopher. It was Rutherford who, after 1933, took the lead in opening English academic life to Jewish refugees. In fact, scientific society was wide open, as it may not be again for many years. There was coming and going among laboratories all over the world, including Russia. Peter Kapitza, Rutherford's favorite pupil, contrived to be in good grace with the Soviet authorities and at the same time a star of the Cavendish. With a touch of genius and of the inspired Russian clown, he backed both horses for fifteen years until, on one of his holiday trips to Russia, the Soviet bosses blandly told him that they now wanted his services full time.

Kapitza flattered Rutherford outrageously, and Rutherford loved it. Kapitza was as impudent as Peter Lebedev; he had great daring and scientific insight. He once asked a friend of mine whether a foreigner could become an English peer; we strongly suspected that his ideal career would see him established simultaneously in the Soviet Academy of Sciences and as Rutherford's successor in the House of Lords.

Between Leningrad and Cambridge, Kapitza oscillated. Between Copenhagen and Cambridge, there was a stream of travelers, all the nuclear physicists of the world. Copenhagen had become the second scientific metropolis on account of the personal influence of one man, Niels Bohr, who was complementary to Rutherford as a person—patient, reflective, any thought hedged with Proustian qualifications—just as the theoretical quantum physics of which he was the master was comple- mentary to Rutherford's experimental physics. He had been a pupil of

Rutherford's, and they loved and esteemed each other like father and son. (Rutherford was a paterfamilias born, and the death of his only daughter seems to have been the greatest sorrow of his personal life. In his relations with Bohr and Kapitza and others, there was a strong vein of paternal emotion diverted from the son he never had.) But, strong as Rutherford's liking for Bohr was, it was not strong enough to put up with Bohr's idea of a suitable length for a lecture. In the Cavendish lecture room, Bohr went past the hour; Rutherford began to stir. Bohr went past the hour and a half; Rutherford began plucking at his sleeve and muttering in a stage whisper about "another five minutes." Blandly, patiently, determined not to leave a qualification unsaid, Bohr went past the two hours; Rutherford was beginning to trumpet about "bringing the lecture to a close." Soon they were both on their feet at once.

Throughout the twenties and thirties, the quantum physics seemed as exciting as the experiments of the Rutherford school. At times it seemed more so. Looking at young Paul Dirac, in his middle twenties, pale and black-mustached like the bridegroom in an Italian wedding photograph, walking with his arms behind him along the Backs, people wondered if he had not written down the fundamental laws of physics and chemistry forever. Thirty years later, the revolution in theory still seems wonderful, but not quite so final as it did then. At the time, it was part, and in some ways the most dramatic part, of the general air of intellectual triumph which spread, of course, much further than physics —it touched almost all natural science. In physics the triumph was clearest and most dramatic, that was all.

Thus the climate in which English scientists went about their work was crammed full of confidence, socially well-intentioned and, in a serious working sense, international. But coming upon them was the distress of the thirties, the emergence of National Socialism, and the prospect of a war.

People outside the scientific world got the impression that, as soon as the trouble broke, the scientists moved to the Left as one man. That is not true, and yet the impression is not wholly false. More unanimously than any other intellectual group, the scientists were anti-Nazi. There were none of the ambiguous relations with Fascism into which Yeats and T. S. Eliot found themselves entering, none of those uncapitalized references to "the jew." Rutherford and his contemporaries mostly voted Conservative, but they regarded that kind of utterance as intellectually and morally contemptible. In fact, the literary neoclassics, the "men of 1914," made scientists think all the worse of the aesthetic world; in some ways, unfairly so. The social attitudes of Pound, Lewis, and T. E. Hulme are not, of course, representative of all artists. Their importance is symbolic, not statistical. This was a moral debasement the scientists did not know; many of them have not forgotten, and it has widened the gap between the cultures.

In his political attitudes, Rutherford was typical of a large fraction of scientists. He welcomed the Jewish refugees and put himself out for them; he presumably went on voting Conservative but was getting restive and sympathetic to the Churchill wing. He did not dislike Russia nearly as much as a nonscientific Conservative would have done. Like all scientists, conservative or radical, he had, almost without thinking what it meant, the future in his bones. In all those ways the respectable older scientists felt and acted with him. Some of them were already active in preparing for war, such as Tizard, perhaps the ablest scientist who ever devoted himself to military affairs; more than any other man he was responsible for the scientific thinking which lay behind the Battle of Britain.

But an overwhelming majority of the younger scientists had committed themselves to the Left. This was partly due to the social crisis; it was partly that science itself, in its new triumphant phase, was working inside young men's minds. Like their seniors, the young scientists also had the future in their bones. Unlike their seniors, they found it natural to look for a political correlative. By the mid-thirties, it was very rare to find a physicist under forty whose sympathies were not on the Left.

This process of political crystallization had begun years before, when the leaders of the young radical scientists had already emerged: J. D. Bernal, Blackett, J. B. S. Haldane. All three were men of tough character and immense intellectual ability. The two Communists, Bernal and Haldane, suffered from the vagaries of the party line and were as late as 1935 leading a pacifist movement among scientists which they shortly after put into reverse. Nevertheless, Bernal, through charm, courage, and more learning than anyone else in England, became the most powerful intellectual force on the extreme Left; more than anyone else, he made Communism intellectually respectable. It was, however, rare for scientists, even the most radical, to enter the party. For most of them, Blackett—firmly planted on the Left but not a Communist, and a scientist of much greater achievement than Bernal or Haldane—was the chosen symbol. In fact, he spoke for the younger generation of scientists in the thirties very much as Rutherford spoke for the older.

My guess is that if one had taken a poll of the two hundred brightest physicists under the age of forty in 1936, about five would have been Communists, ten fellow travelers, fifty somewhere near the Blackett position, a hundred passively sympathetic to the Left. The rest would have been politically null, with perhaps five (or possibly six) oddities on the Right.

Of those two hundred, a number have since occupied positions of eminence. It is interesting that none of them has drastically altered his political judgment. There has just been a slight stagger, a place and a half to the Right, no more. The scientists who got under the shadow of the Communist Party have come out but have stayed (like Haldane) on the extreme Left. A few who were vaguely Left in the thirties would now be vaguely sympathetic to R. A. Butler. The changes have not been any more dramatic than that. There have not been any renunciations or swings to religious faith, such as a number of writers of the same age, once Left Wing, have gone in for. The scientists' radicalism had deeper roots.

Before Rutherford's death, a number of the younger scientists were already preparing for the war. Blackett, as usual giving them the lead, had been getting himself used to military problems for some years before. He had been put on the Air Defence Council by Tizard, who wanted talent regardless of politics and who was a specially good judge of talent when it came his way. It was for such reasons—and because England had just gone through its greatest age of physics—that the English scientists were by and large more effective than those of any other country throughout the war with Hitler.

That was one of the legacies of the age of Rutherford. The other legacy was that, after the war, some of the same scientists took Britain into the atomic age and got her a standing there which will retain her as a major power, if anything can.

• *Questions for Study*

1. What is Snow's central purpose—exposition or persuasion—in writing this essay? How does the title relate to this purpose?
2. What qualities in Rutherford does Snow emphasize? What methods of characterization does Snow use? What special effect is achieved by the narration of the competition between Dee and Snow?
3. Snow was originally a scientist. He became a novelist. Do you see any touches of the novelist in this essay?
4. According to Snow's account, how does the intellectual climate of scientists differ from that of nonscientists? Why is Snow's consideration of the political views of scientists central to his picture of the intellectual climate of the Age of Rutherford?
5. Snow, like Wiener in his essay "Progress and Entropy," emphasizes the importance of a knowledge of the second law of thermodynamics. Of what crucial importance is this law to both authors?

DAVID BERGAMINI

•

THE LANGUAGE OF SCIENCE

"This is the only place I know where a senator can't ask questions."
The irritation in Senator John Stennis's voice was unmistakable. He was
being prevented from conducting an intelligent cross-examination—and
not by some arbitrary rule of cloture or security which he could do something about, but simply by his own inability to understand what a group
of National Aeronautics and Space Administration scientists were eagerly
trying to explain to him at a recent briefing of a Senate committee.

The senator's exasperation was the kind of baffled feeling—a sense
that one is either obsolete or the butt of intentional double talk—which
grips many intelligent and educated people when they are confronted
with the whirlwind developments of modern science. Of course there *are*
scientists who seem to perplex people on purpose. Smugly inarticulate in
their own jargon, they appear to have come into the world babbling differential equations and to have grown up without troubling to learn the
language of other people. But these scientific snobs are—at least in my
ten years' experience as a science reporter—extremely uncommon (and
usually extremely young). Scientists who are good enough to have done
something worth explaining are invariably eager to explain it, and most
of them are gifted enough to do it lucidly and even eloquently. If they
still remain incomprehensible, it is not their fault but the fault of nature for being complicated.

The truth is that both science and nature *are* difficult. They are as
subtle as the most sophisticated philosophy and a good deal more disciplined. The riddles they pose can make the decisions of a stock-market
analyst or a Secretary of State seem like child's play. Nor is this anything
new. In ancient times the idea that the earth was round—springing as it

From *The Reporter*, March 31, 1960. Copyright 1960 by Reporter Magazine, Inc.
Reprinted by permission of Harold Matson Company, Inc.

surely did from seemingly disconnected observations like "The moon was crossed last night by a shadow" and "That ship out there came *up* over the horizon"—must have seemed impossibly difficult, as well as subversive, to the first Babylonians or Greeks who had it explained to them. Today the roundness of the earth and many of the Newtonian concepts of motions and mechanics that eventually grew out of it seem almost self-evident. They are no longer complicated by the perplexing paths traced on the night sky by the moon and planets. But the process of forgetting the details and assimilating the broad, easy generalizations into the main body of thought and language took centuries.

New truths exposed today in the explosive growth of modern science cannot wait centuries for appreciation. Their immediate practical impact is too great. At a time when laymen like Senator Stennis must wrestle with science as never before, many of the ideas that are important are so new that scientists themselves do not yet appreciate them fully and cannot yet explain them with the kind of perspective which might come with the passage of centuries.

One of the principal reasons for this interpretative lag is that many of the most basic discoveries in science do not come into the world like ordinary ideas, fleshed in words and pictures, but as the gaunt skeletons of formulas. The germs out of which they grew may have been ordinary and commonsensical, but they have been rewrought by the mathematical processes to which they have been subjected.

Mathematics, the language of science, is not like other tongues. Its symbols are atoms of distilled logic, far more compact than words in some ways but uncolored by any of the associations, sights, and feelings that make words immediately meaningful. As a result, mathematics cannot be translated phrase for phrase or symbol by symbol like French or Sanskrit. Most of its content is no more interesting than a housewife's accounts—pure numbers and quantities. The rest, the part that gradually seeps into the core of a culture, is something that it does not really say at all but only implies. In this it is like poetry. And like a poem, a great formula is not so much translated as it is interpreted—rightly or wrongly according to the judgment and taste of each generation.

Perhaps everyone should learn mathematics, so that senators and administrators need not be constantly at the mercy of interpreters. But if everyone did learn to think in equations, would they then understand science and nature? Until fairly recently one might have been sure they would. Confidence in mathematics was part of western man's outlook. As Galileo put it in the seventeenth century: "Nature's great book is written in mathematical symbols." In the eighteenth century the Marquis de Laplace carried the thought further: "All the effects of nature are only the mathematical consequences of a small number of immutable laws." In the nineteenth century the astronomer Sir George Biddell Airy even went so far as to define the entire universe as "a perpetual-motion calculating machine whose gears and ratchets are an infinite system of self-solving differential equations."

Then suddenly, in the twentieth century, Bertrand Russell was calling mathematics "the subject in which we do not know what we are talking about, nor whether what we are saying is true." What had happened? After three centuries of certainty, had the mathematical language suddenly broken down? Not on the surface, anyway. Einstein's theory of relativity, the major scientific event that had intervened in 1905, was an earth-shaking triumph for mathematical abstractness in general, and in particular for one of mathematics' most obscure dialects: non-Euclidean geometry. Yet something *had* happened, not just to mathematics but seemingly to nature herself. Because of relativity and quantum mechanics, because of more acute experimental eyesight, because of introspection into systems of logic, scientists were beginning to suspect that nature did not speak in human accents—that she was what she was and that the most beautiful, workable mathematical expressions of her laws were merely expert translations from a lost original.

To many scientists this new uncertainty was profoundly disheartening. It demoted them from demi-gods to gamblers, and they didn't like it. But a few found it an exhilarating challenge. And today, after unqualified successes with nuclear weapons and electronic gadgetry, scientists generally enjoy their role as successful cardsharps and wouldn't go back to being academic formulators of divine law for anything. They are still wrestling with the limitations and ambiguities of mathematics, but they have been able to pin down with a fair degree of certainty what their uncertainties are.

One of the most basic of the uncertainties was introduced by Einstein's theory of relativity. The very word "relativity" implies a degree of unsureness. According to Einstein's use of it, all scientific measurements are relative to the observer who makes them. Man may be hurtling through space at an alarming speed, but what that speed is he can never know because he has no absolutely fixed point of reference. All the galaxies seem to be in motion, but the motion he measures is partly his own and partly theirs: he cannot separate the two. From this one concrete implication of relativity, many scientists infer a broader relativity that makes any sort of absolute reality a figment of the human mind. Can man, a billion billion billion times bigger than an atom and a billion billion billion times smaller than a star, really discover "laws" governing atoms and stars? Or do his theories reflect only semantics and the workings of his own mind? Do relativity and quantum mechanics contain philosophic truths about the nature of the macro- and microcosmos or do they consist simply of pragmatic rules that allow astrophysicists and atomic engineers to estimate the outcome of natural occurrences with a fair degree of accuracy?

Although philosophers of science are still wrestling with these questions, scientists themselves are mostly willing to admit that their most precise formulations are equivocal and that the only absolute truth is success—making ideas and formulas and machines that work. A good example of the ambiguity that scientists have learned to live with is the concept of curved space introduced into physics and cosmology by Einstein. According to the general theory of relativity, space as a whole is perhaps curved and space locally near any concentration of matter may certainly be considered slightly warped. By "curved" or "warped," Einstein meant that all light rays and other seemingly straight lines would not obey the elementary postulates of Euclid's geometry. Instead they would behave like great circles on a sphere or the curves that represent the shortest routes between points on other kinds of surfaces—doubling back on themselves, failing to satisfy the usual definitions of parallelism, violating the triangulation laws of ordinary surveying. Whether or not space as a whole is curved is still an open cosmological question. But observation has shown that a straight ray of starlight does describe a gentle arc if it passes close to the concentrated mass of the sun. Depending on how the mathematical symbols of relativity are translated, this may mean either that space near the sun is curved or that starlight is subject to the tug of the sun's gravitation. But what is gravitation? Is it a mysterious force like an electrical charge or is it a curve in space? The choice of which concept to apply and which name to call the mathematical symbols seems to be arbitrary and to have nothing to do with nature. Certainly the starlight itself doesn't care whether it is passing through a knothole in the texture of space or is being affected by something called gravity. When and if scientists choose a name for the influence at work on it, they will probably do so only because one concept proves more fruitful than the other and easier to handle mathematically.

But perhaps one concept will not prove more fruitful or simple than the other. In the physics of light, for instance, it is sometimes easier to consider light as continuous waves and sometimes as tiny projectiles of energy, enormous in number but separate. It all depends on the part light is playing during the scientific investigation in question. In the fall of 1957 Niels Bohr, the great Danish physicist who shaped most of our modern concepts about the atom, delivered a speech at M.I.T. that raised this exasperating two-faced trait of nature into a concept of its own, which Bohr called "complementarity." But to most scientists, complementarity seems little more than the same rose by a new name. Mathematicians in particular are inclined to feel a little superior—partly because Bohr is a physicist and partly because they argued out similar ambiguities in mathematics long before relativity and atomic physics were born.

Until early in the nineteenth century, mathematics was based on sets of axioms and postulates that were considered self-evident. But then a succession of innovators began to ask why they were self-evident and to construct new experimental kinds of mathematics—like non-Euclidean geometry—based on axioms that were not self-evident and sometimes seemed to be patent nonsense. Playing with these mental toys, they found that they could construct wonderful edifices of equations on almost any assumptions at all. And though the assumptions might make no sense, the way the assumptions were manipulated did make sense. They found that they could generalize certain kinds of mathematics so that a single framework would hold and handle sensible propositions as one special case among whole sets of comparable nonsense propositions. More important, they found that the nonsense problems often turned out to make sense. An assumption that seemed to be about geometry and seemed to be silly might turn out to be a key truth when interpreted in terms of electricity.

And so mathematicians like Russell became convinced that the symbols in equations need not have verbal meaning. Manipulating the symbols correctly is all that matters. Given x, then y, and the devil take significance. x and y may stand for lines or electrons or explosions in a star or ripples on a pond. All the mathematician does is erect a nonsensical but logical structure on them, and some day a physicist may come along and find that a wonderful event in nature is all comprehended and described in the meaningless succession of symbols.

Making sequences of symbols that are not significant but rigorously logical is far more difficult than it sounds. It is far more difficult than ordinary reasoning, because the mathematician cannot call up familiar words or sights to guide him and give him "intuition." Choosing his dark path, he usually cheats a little and starts out with concrete ideas that he generalizes into pure abstraction only gradually. Then, having once abandoned all recourse to familiar notions from the world of reality, he has to move cautiously. Above all, he has to make his logic foolproof. In doing this, mathematicians have learned to be intensely introspective about their mental processes and wary about their use of words. How introspective and word-wary is well illustrated by the fact that a massive treatise now being prepared by an international group of mathematicians who call themselves "Monsieur Bourbaki" devotes two hundred pages simply to defining the word "one."

By having the words and common sense weeded out of it, mathematics has grown far more general and pragmatically useful than it used to be. Theorems developed in the approved modern manner apply, at their best, not only to this universe but to all possible universes. On the other hand, the old hope that man will discover the final master formula explaining the whole of creation has either vanished altogether or faded into the distant future. This is partly because most of the equations hitherto fitted to nature have turned out to be only very exact approximations and partly because in 1931 a twenty-five-year-old Austrian, Kurt Goedel, published one of the most marvelous and revolutionary proofs in the history of mathematics. Goedel proved that all the possible theorems of mathematics can never be deduced from a finite number of assumptions. No matter how many assumptions have been made already, mathematicians can always make more and from them derive new truths —meaningless symbolic truths, of course, but unless the universe proves finite in both time and extent, there is no assurance that these truths cannot be given meaning someday and interpreted to shed new light on the cosmos.

The kind of ultimate barrier to total understanding implicit in Goedel's proof is reminiscent of one of the basic physical findings of quantum mechanics. This is Heisenberg's uncertainty principle, which says that a scientist cannot find out both where a subatomic particle is and where it is going without making it go somewhere else instead. The reason for Heisenberg's principle is simply that you can't "look" at something—measure its precise place and speed and direction—without subjecting it to a tiny amount of energy that changes its future whereabouts. It is as if you wanted to know where a rat was heading in a dark room. Shine a flashlight on the rat, and you frighten it into going somewhere else. You could use radar on the rat, of course, and he would never be any the wiser, but in the world of the atom, electrons are equally sensitive to all kinds of radiation and indeed to any kind of probe at all. Predicting the futures of electrons or other subatomic particles can only be done as insurance actuaries predict the futures of human beings: by calculating probabilities and estimating what will happen to the average —the average man or the average particle.

These two discoveries, Heisenberg's principle and Goedel's proof, are barriers that human beings can never hope to vault. Fortunately, they are neither of them very severe limitations to a scientist of spirit and imagination. Goedel's proof only says to the mathematician that he will never run out of lands to explore. The universe is composed of an infinite or nearly infinite number of energy quanta, and in post-Goedelian mathematics every new number larger than the numbers investigated already is a proposition in itself—a proposition from which a new law can be constructed and a new truth discovered. Heisenberg's principle only says to the physicist that he can never cut and dry an experiment beyond predicting what is probable. The improbable may still happen; for instance, the physicist may be thrilled and confounded to see a table levitate because all the particles in it happen improbably to move in the same direction at the same time.

Both barriers leave the scientist with a residual world beyond certainty in which to exercise his metaphysical imagination. Beyond the barrier of Goedel's proof are very big numbers, and very big numbers of particles. Beyond the barrier of the Heisenberg principle lie many of the exact mechanisms and processes of atoms—all the things which happen so fast that they can never be detected, according to the Heisenberg principle, without being found out as mere figments of the detection process itself.

The prohibitions laid down by Goedel and Heisenberg are basic to all the sciences. But every science also has barriers of its own, some of which may turn out to be equally insurmountable. In astronomy the expansion of the universe may make it impossible for stargazers to see beyond a certain limit where the galaxies are receding from the telescope at the speed of light. In biology there is a less insurmountable but more exasperating barrier in the fact that every living thing has a living container. Break the skin or the cell wall—lift the living hood to get at the engine inside—and the biologist has changed the organism and possibly changed the particular piece of mechanism he wants to investigate. But these are only examples. Whenever the investigator probes small things he finds that his own presence is a great obstacle, and whenever he grapples with immensities he finds himself frustrated and fascinated by imponderables.

Indeed, science *is* very difficult. It is also very young. For every wonder it has performed, it holds promise of doing millions more. In the next century it will undoubtedly deluge the world with new ideas. Finding that nature is not mathematics and that mathematics has nothing to do with words has freed scientists to use words and concepts without compunction as a form of stimulus—a way of getting started on something new and a crutch to help in thinking abstractly.

The freedom to use words poetically as images or metaphors rather than as literal truths even permits a kind of intellectual poaching from one scientific specialty to another. The words of information theory, for instance, developed to assist in thinking about electronic circuits, calculators, telephone switchboards, and such, have proved a tremendous impetus to biophysics and biochemistry. One may read articles about "the information content" of a cell's nucleus or the means of "information storage" in the blood in scientific magazines almost any month.

Poached concepts and words have proved so pregnant when they turn up in new and surprising contexts that more and more scientists are willing to think verbally and straightforwardly when they can. Some of the purest theoreticians, of course, still insist that all mental models, words, and pictures are unnecessary and misleading. But it is the gossip of history that many of the most abstract advances in physics started when someone opened his eyes and mind in unsophisticated innocence on a specific problem. Newton is supposed to have thought about falling apples, and Einstein appears to have begun his work with elementary considerations about flashes of lightning beside a railroad track. Later on in the creative process, of course, the specific is generalized in mathematics and purged of the dross of words. The final results may be so far from the original words or any familiar concept whatsoever that decades may elapse before they can be interpreted. It seems to be true, though, that one theory is not usually replaced by another better one until the first has accumulated around it a rich body of interpretative lore—words, pictures, metaphors, similes—which enables some innovator to rethink the premises in a vivid human way. Most good scientists tend to agree with the mathematical physicist Hermann Weyl that the imperative preceding any sort of scientific originality is: "Think concretely."

Obviously the interplay between the scientist and the layman should be important to both of them. The layman has to know about scientific advances to keep up with the world in which he finds himself. But the scientist has to return his findings periodically to the fount of common language and culture from which they sprang. He can get new ideas from the figures of everyday speech and he can clarify old ideas by having to explain them concretely. Of course the senator may bridle if the scientist smiles, but the friction is healthy and helpful. Nature's mute language is her own fractious, perplexing self, and science must avail itself of every means of expression and inspiration if it is to use nature and control her as fully as possible.

• *Questions for Study*

1. According to Bergamini, what is the difference between scientific and non-scientific ideas? What does Bergamini mean when he says that early in the century "scientists were beginning to suspect that nature did not speak in human accents"?

2. Explain the ways in which Bergamini's view of science qualifies Huxley's comparatively simple view of scientific method and the relationship between the layman and the scientist?
3. What are the implications of Heisenberg's principle and Goedel's proof?
4. Compare and contrast the views of language in this selection with those of C. S. Lewis concerning emotional language in "At the Fringe of Language."

ROBERT W. KING

•

TECHNOLOGY AND SOCIAL PROGRESS

I

An industrial society represents a vast team, not of humans alone, but of humans affiliated with machines.

That the machines are intended to save labor, enrich living and facilitate the making of more machines need not engage us here.

Rather let us consider that machines are stubborn and unyielding. They are not to be cajoled or coerced. Herein they differ, of course, from human beings, for human beings have always yielded, and presumably always will yield when enough pressure is brought to bear upon them. It follows that as mankind amalgamates itself more and more into a machine society it will be the human elements who will make the essential accommodations and adjustments. The human units who, individually, are the temperamental and unpredictable partners to the union will do the bidding of their mechanical servants.

What, for instance, is a modern manufacturing establishment but a miniature society in which the humans aliment and groom the machines?

From *Political Science Quarterly*, Volume LXXVI, No. 1 (1961). Reprinted by permission of the *Political Science Quarterly*.

The nature and quality of the factory's product are fixed by the machines, with the human complement an accessory whose idiosyncrasies and vagaries are but handicaps, unavoidable nuisances, that the institution would gladly be rid of if it could. Likewise, by legal concept, the factory—the corporation—is a composite citizen, a being of steadfast purpose whose conduct is accountable in spite of the uncertain behavior of its operatives.

And as nations, generally, develop technological competence and pull more abreast of one another in respect to their industrialization their problems of compatible and efficient articulation, their concern with the over-all welfare, will, like the factory's, approach as a limit an affair of balance between inanimate agglomerations, the human temperaments and emotions playing but an insulated part.

Nor will international issues escape this refining and smoothing-out process. They will become less the kind of issues that carry emotional charges, more the kind that involve concrete and factual knowledge, and therefore invite logical and candid approach. For such, in general, are the questions associated with technology and industry; and as these spheres of activity influence human relationships more positively, both domestic and international politics will respond by demanding that they, too, be dealt with in a matter-of-fact fashion.

Take, for example, the nuclear bomb. Here is a technological achievement whose call upon the world is mandatory, not simply petitionary. It offers no quarter, no hint of option. Its inflexible demand is for the outlawing of war. In respect to it nations have no choice but to circumscribe their erstwhile range of sovereignty. The single alternative is virtual extinction. Such a situation being quite new in the history of mankind, the past provides no hint as to what collective human behavior to expect. But even among those individuals who fully comprehend the crisis there are probably few who really fear that common sense will lose the day. When the great renunciation comes, if come it does, it will mark an outstanding spiritual victory for technology as being the agency to abruptly force consummation of a goal, and attainment of an ideal, where a millennial-long appeal to the brotherhood of man has consistently failed.

II

"Nature is commanded by obeying her." The observation is Francis Bacon's, and the social and political ferment now arising throughout the world suggests that mankind everywhere is bent upon reaping all the material rewards that may inhere in complete obedience.

With physical man or, as we might better denote him, technological man, so firmly seated in the saddle and virtually certain to guide social developments for years to come, what can be said of the world's probable spiritual gain or loss since the driver's chief concern will be for material gain? Many are asking this question and as eminent an authority on human conduct as Arnold Toynbee voices his pessimism, at least to the extent of advising a change of approach. In his *Historian's Approach to Religion* he states as his verdict that the time has come for us "to wrench ourselves out of the seventeenth century mathematico-physical approach which we are still following and make a fresh start from the spiritual side." And he adds that such a spiritual approach "is now, once again, the more promising of the two."

Upon examination, however, science and its close kin, technology and industrial development, are seen to offer very significant spiritual values, though premonitory fears are no doubt natural enough in view of the upheaval in thinking brought about by the destructiveness of the atomic bomb. And to suggest—as above—that the time is probably at hand when the bomb will be regarded as a great spiritual force may come as a shock rather than as assurance to many people. Nevertheless, the application of scientific knowledge to everyday life has already proved so productive of material aids and conveniences—to say nothing of medical blessings—that scarcely a nation but is beginning to think in terms of an intensive technological future. We may compare ourselves to children in a dream toyland of such wondrous size that, if we but search, the answer to every material wish will be found.

Or consider some of the recent devices of solid state physics in which the functional leverages of single atoms are so great that they seem to take on almost macroscopic rôles. Through such developments important uses have been found for properties of matter and laws of Nature which appear to have had no slightest evolutionary function, but have lain dormant from the beginning of time. Our physical environment with its complement of ninety odd chemical elements, which eons ago ushered in the dawn of life, and in succeeding ages nurtured the varied sequences of living forms, is now proving itself a partner to man's highest intellectual efforts. He and the material world about him bear in their respective natures the desire for and the means of satisfying an extravagantly complex existence. These two sets of attributes, human on the one hand and material on the other, suggest a deep unity or propinquity in Nature: the obverse and reverse aspects of a single and undissociable principle of life; an affinity which seems to decree that where uses of material existence are possible a user shall in time appear.

With such relationships in mind it is hard to accept without reservations the admonition Toynbee and many others voice. Or, turning to a bizarre sort of extreme, it is equally unconvincing to picture our human kind as glorified bower birds bent chiefly upon gratifying an extravagant urge to adorn their nests with glittering assortments of spangles. Each of these derogatory appraisals of science and technology seems inappropriate in the light of the well-nigh boundless areas of congruence which we discover between man's desires and tastes on the one hand and the agreeable adaptiveness of our physical environment on the other. It can scarcely be that mankind, in accepting Nature's bounty, stands to lose his spirituality in a maze of mechanism. Even should the future hold in store other situations more or less akin to the atomic bomb in cataclysmic possibilities, they will make new and perhaps greater demands upon the human virtues of self-control and due regard for others.

III

In so far as technology fixes man's future course in Nature he must travel a largely predetermined corridor of indefinite length—a corridor walled by the physical and chemical properties of matter. From this corridor he cannot stray except in thought, and what it offers to one portion of mankind it offers to all, for actually technology recognizes no national boundaries; it is unaware of race or culture, and the language of science comes about as naturally to one people as to another.

This suggests a unification of human purposes and interests so fundamental that its full significance may be difficult for us to grasp. In a word, the world's conglomerate of peoples seems on the verge of exchanging their diversity of backgrounds, physical and cultural, for a common point of view, a common objective, and a more or less common milieu. The promise is of a new and universal culture arising to bind mankind as never before. Much as the butterfly, after emerging from its chrysalis, expands and tests its wings for flight, all races and nations, in their ardent espousal of technologically directed industry appear to be awaiting a common signal to slough off most of their outmoded ideological differences—encumbrances inherited from an uncomprehending past—and assume instead a unanimity of outlook and purpose that will be totally new in the world, and no doubt as revolutionary as it will be new.

The mutualities of human conduct, arising thus and coming to link mankind in a new brotherhood, will not be of knowledge per se; but they will be the far stronger bonds comprised by like desires and similar industrial objectives and problems. The pursuit of knowledge alone has failed signally to bring peoples and nations together, but worldwide industrialization, rooted in technology, seems likely to succeed, and at a

rapid pace. In contrast to mere knowledge, the consequences of technology are so far-reaching and their counsels speak so feelingly that they
promise to reconstruct life patterns generally and, in the process, make
them much more alike the world around.

IV

One of the important humanitarian by-products of technology is the
greater dignity and value that it imparts to human labor. In highly
mechanized industry there is no essential difference between white and
black, between Brahmin and untouchable, Moslem and Christian; they
are equally useful and hence equally valuable, for in the industrial
society individual productivity fixes the size of the pay check and this,
ever so steadily and sometimes not unobtrusively, fixes social status.

And there is another reason why the onward sweep of industry will
level caste systems and erode away social stratification. Mass production
is not possible without mass consumption, which is but another way of
saying that everyone must consume to the limit of his purchasing power,
and keep on doing so continuously. Here personal pride plays an important economic rôle. Social repression and discrimination can have no
lasting place in a social order intent upon encouraging ready and enthusiastic buyers. Pride, self-respect and desire of possession go hand in
hand and to ensure mass consumption they must be fostered at every
opportunity. Ready testimony comes from current advertising techniques
as we see them practised here at home—testimony which is spontaneous
and unpremeditated, and hence such that it can be taken at face value.
Its manifest aim is to puff up the ego of the individual consumer by
appealing to his pride, appearance, health, good taste—even on occasion
to his intelligence—while promoting the vision that he has the unique
opportunity to get in stride with an élite procession marching onward into
a materialistic paradise.

In brief, it needs no emphasis that in lands where human labor is
the least productive—China, India, the Arab states, pre-revolutionary
Russia will serve as examples—the least regard for human life is to be
found as well as deeply rooted social discrimination. In technologically
backward lands the pitiable status of the human being contrasts sharply
with that now prevailing in the West, where the earning power and the
economic importance of workers generally have risen to levels that would
have been regarded as fabulous even a century ago. Thus technological
man, by virtue of his improved industrial status, stands forth as a more
substantial political entity than ever the rank and file of workers have
stood before.

The relationship is twofold. On the one hand, labor is now valuable enough to justify economically its being conserved and provided with working conditions that are consistent with efficient production; on the other, the margin of productivity and profit in the economy as a whole has expanded to such a level that the entrepreneur is able to afford the humanitarian benefits which his moral sense, and the moral sense of society, have all along hinted at.

It follows that even such a political structure as the monolithic state will, under an expanding internal economy, tend in the direction of relaxed controls. The worker's initial lot as a serf under the party cannot remain his permanent lot. As factories and industries grow and shelves fill with consumer goods, the erstwhile serf must be induced to play the rôle of spender and consumer; until, when the tide runs full in this new and final direction, and pressure is no longer upon the creation of capital goods but upon the consumption of what has been mass-produced, the state finds that it must give priority to full and steady employment. As we know from our domestic experience this requires a widening diversity in most lines of production and service together with the stimulus of changing styles. "The changes progressively taking place . . . tend to bring out into stronger relief the importance to man and society of a large variety of types of character, and giving full freedom to human nature to expand itself into innumerable and conflicting directions." These words, though they were written many years ago by John Stuart Mill to epitomize the political basis for individual liberty, pretty well set the sights for any industrial society which is bent upon maintaining full employment and mass production as coequals. They suggest the extent to which, as an economy evolves, political regimentation must yield to the release and exploitation of individual differences. In fact, according to good report, Russian industrialism has already advanced to such a level that the Soviet hierarchy seems much more mindful of its subjects as indispensable consumers to whom a growing freedom of choice must be accorded.

V

The argument above outlined—and it is but the barest outline—brings us to envisage the world as poised at the threshold of an era in which the most dynamic social and political forces will be of technological origin. Republics, democracies, limited monarchies, together with socialist and communist states will, under the impetus of technology, find themselves facing similar social and industrial problems; and this fact, when joined with the fundamental sameness of human nature the world over, suggests the approach of generally similar social conditions and, in consequence, a recourse to generally similar legislative responses. "Steam is almost an Englishman," observed Emerson a century ago. "I do not know but that they will send him to Parliament to make the laws." And what, in Emerson's day steam seemed capable of, is far outmatched in our day by the electron. Never heretofore has mankind kept intimate company with so commanding and so uniting a creature.

In a word, the basic aim of every national program of industrialization is to gratify its public and cater to its yearning for a higher material standard of living. And every actual advance, every new goal envisaged, but reaffirms the fact that implicit in each such program is the democratic principle that the state is made for man, not man for the state. This is the great humanistic message of technology; for it, above all other agencies, is the fulfiller of political dreams. Each national program of progressive industrialization must, in due course, include the guarantee that as a higher economic stage is reached it will be more humanitarian. Viewing the present promise of a world-enveloping sweep of technology, and bearing in mind what it has already accomplished in limited areas toward the liberalization of mankind, one finds it difficult if not, indeed, impossible to hold to the view that there can inhere and endure in what we commonly label communism an effective threat to dominate and regiment the world.

What we chiefly witness in those countries now communistic is the functioning of a political device that is extremely well suited to surmounting the hurdles interposed by their lack of free capital and trained labor. Their peoples, thirsting for the material benefits which more developed countries have attained, see no political alternative to some form of state planning and control (call it communism or not) that will regiment workers and credits alike to the end that their collective technological metamorphosis will be as rapid as possible.

VI

A task we face—and by "we" I mean chiefly those who are citizens of the more developed nations—is, therefore, to set aside attitudes and suspicions that we inherit from the past, and prepare to greet and measure up to a uniquely different future. If the statistician is correct in his estimate that the Russian economy has grown one or two per cent faster than that of the United States during recent years, it is a welcome fact. It means that the Russian people are that much nearer to being ruled by the inanimate and steadfast machine, not by an unpredictable dictator. And there is much for us to do if we are to measure up to such a future.

Of major importance is a viable and forward-looking plan for the distribution of the essential raw materials of the earth. Industrialization can spread and become universal only as all peoples can find access to quire into the prevalence of suitable sites for biological operations. The initial question is not whether such sites are presently inhabited. First we ask: Are there other habitable celestial bodies—bodies that would be hospitable if life were there?

It will clarify the discussion if we start with two routine reminders: (1) by life we mean what here we terrestrials recognize as life—a biochemical operation involving carbon and nitrogen and making use of water in the liquid state (other kinds are imaginable; e.g., one where silicon replaces carbon, or where sulphur's participation is like that of oxygen. Such is imaginable, but unlikely); and (2) Mars and Venus are therefore the only other planets of our solar system that are at all suitable for living organisms. The evidences are good that Martian life is low and lichen-like, if it exists at all, and the surface of Venus is an unsolved problem, with the odds against living organisms because of the lethal chemistry of the atmosphere.

Life as we know it on the earth has wide adaptability; but there are limits, and one of them is the heat and radiation near a star's surface, where the molecules constituting protoplasm would be dissociated.

In our consideration of the spread of life throughout the universe, we must therefore immediately drop all thoughts of living organisms on the millions of radiant stars, on meteors or on comets. We are therefore left with the planets neither too near their stars nor so remote from them that the cold is unrelieved. They should not be too small to hold an oxygen atmosphere, must have salutary waters, agreeable rocky crusts and orbits of low eccentricity. Highly eccentric orbits would bring their planets too near the star and then too far out. The resulting temperature oscillations would be too much for comfort, perhaps even too much for the origins and persistence of early life.

We must always remember that our Sun is a very ordinary sort of star. One hundred thousand of the brightest million stars are essentially identical with the Sun. Let us suppose that only one star in a thousand has a planetary system. Personally I would think that one in fifty would be a better estimate. But to be conservative, we say that only one out of a thousand stars has a planetary system, and then assume that but one out of a thousand of those stars with systems of planets has one or more planets at the right distance from the star to provide the water and warmth that protoplasm requires. (In our solar system we have two or three planets in such an interval of distance.) Further let us suppose that only one out of a thousand of those stars with planets suitably distant has one planet large enough to hold an atmosphere. (In our system we have at least seven planets out of nine with atmospheres.) That will reduce our suitable planets to a one in a billion chance. Then let us make

vital natural resources upon somewhat equal terms. The need in this respect is imperative and calls for prompt and progressive statesmanship. A question so important to the future welfare of the world could well be brought before the United Nations. Fortunately science is doing much to assist the have-little nations; the rôle of substitutes and alternatives is expanding daily. But it still remains a fact that the terrestrial distribution of minerals represents, as it were, but a single throw of the geological dice, thereby leaving to human ingenuity the arranging of an harmonious give and take among the nations.

• *Questions for Study*

1. King's is one of several essays in this anthology which attempt to forecast future conditions on the basis of present achievement and current directions. Compare King's considerations of the future with those of Marx and Engels, Galbraith, Shapley, and others.
2. Many people fear technology and believe that further industrialization will make man conformist and ant-like. What is King's view of this fear and this belief? Is he too optimistic? Does he offer convincing evidence to support his position?
3. By what method is this essay organized? Comment on King's style.

HARLOW SHAPLEY

•

COMING TO TERMS
WITH THE COSMOS

The goal of this writing is to present some information and ideas, new and old, bearing on the position of mankind in the universe of physics and sensation. It is an essay on orientation.

To postpone a possible depression about our role or function in the stellar universe, and to evade for a time the heavier implications of man's physical position, we could first emphasize the good features of life under the present constellations. We might introduce this essay in an optimistic vein, since later there will be time and need for a more somber look.

It is a good world for many of us. Nature is reasonably benign, and good will is a common human trait. There is widespread beauty, pleasing symmetry, collaboration, lawfulness, progress—all of them qualities that appeal to man-the-thinker if not always to man-the-animal. When not oppressed by hunger or cold or man-made indignities, we are inclined to contentment. . . .

But rather than a lighthearted and somewhat evasive view of our situation and responsibilities, it would be more in keeping with what lies ahead to adopt from the beginning the attitude of mature inquirers, and confront the cosmic facts squarely and fully: small but magnificent man face to face with enormous and magnificent universe.

For the sake of simplicity, we are tempted to put all the world of physics and perhaps all the biological world into the framework of four properties. They are, of course, space, time, matter, and energy. May there be others, perhaps some of even superior importance? In particular, is there one other property of the material world that is essential to make the universe go? To put the question in personal terms: If you were given the four basic entities and full power, opportunity, and desire, could you construct a universe like this one out of space, time, matter, and energy? Or would you require a fifth entity?

We seem to belabor this mystical fifth entity. That it exists, we can hardly doubt. Is it a master entity, perhaps more basic than space and matter and possibly including them—something quite unlike the four named above? Is it indispensable?

Some readers may be thinking of the word and concept God, but we should not be hasty in such a deep and critical matter. Let us not use up that important and comprehensive concept for only a part of the universe, or for something already comprehensible to primitive us.

An elementary reason for a reconsideration of mankind as a world factor lies in the recognition in recent years of the "displacement" of the Sun, Earth, and other planets from a central place, or even a significant place, in the sidereal universe—in the placing of the observer in a very undistinguished location in a faint spiral arm of an ordinary galaxy.

This reason is elementary but momentous, for it concerns the replacement of the earlier *geocentric* and *heliocentric* theories of the universe by the *eccentric* arrangement that now we all accept. By this move we have made a long forward step in cosmic adjustment—a step that is unquestionably irreversible. We must get used to the fact that we are peripheral,

that we move along with our star, the Sun, in the outer part that is one among billions of star-rich galaxies.

Man may be something very special, something superior. I hope he is. But certainly it is not in his location in space, or not in his energy content or chemical composition. He is no standing in the four basic material entities—space, time, ma Nothing unique and worthy of boast in his size, activity, con his epoch in cosmic chronology. He is of course an intricate ing phenomenon, but we should get sentimental about him w

There should be, however, nothing very humiliating ab terial inconsequentiality. Are we debased by the greater s sparrow, the larger size of the hippopotamus, the keener he dog, the finer detectors of odor possessed by insects? We c adjusted to all of these evidences of our inferiority and mai ing of importance and well-being. We should also take the stride.

Provided as we are with new and basic data on the universe, we moderns could and should now interpret the w more circumstantial and rational than it could be interpret or Lucretius, or Spinoza, or Locke, or Pascal, whose cosn geocentric or heliocentric and limited. We have gone far, ve accumulation of verifiable facts. There will be, if we remair return. We must henceforth live with our scientific acc amount of skepticism about details, no sweeping denials o no distortion of the recent revelations of science can erase t progress. Wishing will not revive the dear, dead hypotheses.

The prophets of ancient Israel gloried at times in the of the universe, which of course, in their time, was cent Those days, however, were scientifically very early and c perhaps more than a third of the way back to the beginn cultures. What the inquiring mind has since uncovered wo incredible if revealed to the ancient prophets. Their vision see, myopic. Reverence then had to be supported with i superstition. To be reverent now, we have no need of sup Deeper thoughts will surely come, wider spread of the se preciation of the functioning of the human brain, higher men participating in the greatest operation of nature—a cosmic dimensions that might simply be called Growth.

We should turn our attention to the possible existen spread of protoplasm throughout stellar spaces and cos can no longer be content with the hypothesis that living of this Earth only. But before we ponder on the life spr

one other requirement of our suitable planet: The chemical composition of air and water must be of the sort that would develop the naturally arising complex inorganic molecules into the organic. Perhaps that happens but once in a thousand times?

Assembling all four of the one-to-a-thousand chances (we are making it as hard as possible to find other habitable planets), we come to one star out of a million million. Where does that high improbability of proper planets leave us? We get a hundred million planetary systems suitable for organic life. This number is a minimum, and personally I would recommend its multiplication by at least a thousand times, possibly by a million times.

Exactly where these other life-bearing planets are we cannot now say; perhaps we never can, lost as they are in the glare of their stars, isolated as we are in space, and equipped with sounding apparatus that is still, we hope, primitive. Nor can we say what kind of organisms inhabit these other worlds. Are they people like us? Are they only plants, animals, and the simpler of noncellular organisms (protista)? Or are there perhaps other highly developed animate kingdoms, neither plants nor animals, nor in between?

If a mature tree would at times pull up its roots and stroll away to a more nutritious locality, or if an animal should give up its mobility at times, put down roots and feed itself through the soil and the material provided by photosynthesis, we would be astonished. But stranger operations are already known to occur in the lower life of the earth's biology. Chlorophyll, carotin, and xanthophyll may not be the only means of capturing the sun's radiant energy. Our yellow star radiates the wave lengths that we have grown to need. Redder and bluer suns would generate and cooperate with life forms that prosper in radiation emanating from redder and bluer sections of the spectrum. Their chemical energy converters may not even resemble our chlorophyll.

Although the life on what we shall call Planet X, an unidentified high-life planet, is a matter for loose conjecture, we should naturally expect it to resemble in many ways some of the myriad life forms on the earth. A mixture of pure chemical elements will always under the same physical conditions, produce the same result, whether it be an odor, an explosion, a color. Perhaps we should expect that a mixture of starshine, water, carbon, nitrogen, and other atoms, when physical conditions are fairly similar, will everywhere produce animals that are much alike in structure and operation and plants that have certain standard behaviors, notwithstanding great morphological differences. If we should visit a planet essentially identical with ours in mass, temperature, age, and structure, we would probably not find the biology queer beyond comprehension. We might find it no more peculiar than we would find the biology if we were transported on our own planet into Carboniferous times, or taken back just 150,000,000 years when the great lizards ruled the land and sea, and the birds, mammals, and flowering plants were not yet far developed.

Judged by current standards, the early philosophical and theological contemplators of the origin of life were not very successful in convincing themselves or others. A century ago, using biblical argument and metaphysical vocabularies, they fought wordy battles, against the biologists, who resorted to observations—to those lances that so easily penetrate the fondly held theological shields. The biologists in fact changed the problem from the misty mystery of the origin of self-conscious man to the clean-cut general question of the origin and nature of all life, of monkeys and mice, of algae and oaks, of everything that crawls, flies, swims, breathes, and metabolizes. As supernaturalism retreated a bit, many scientists overcorrected, unfortunately, and embraced a sterile God-excluding mechanistic philosophy.

What should be the rational response of man to his current acquaintance with these matters?

What does our new knowledge mean with respect to the prevalent religious teachings?

If care is taken to cope with the natural regressions that often ensue from static conformity, we shall continue to evolve with the rotating of the planets and the radiating of the suns. We grow naturally with the passage of time, as do the animals and plants. They also make the effort, through adjustments and improvements, to survive and grow. The tempo of their evolution, however, is often even slower than ours.

But we can consciously speed the development. It is not growth in size, or strength, or longevity, but growth primarily in the qualities that we associate with mind, a development that includes those fine indefinables—heart and spirit. And therein lies the nucleus of our cosmic ethic. The evidence clearly shows that we have the potentiality not only of conforming to the cosmic theme of Growth, but we can perhaps elaborate or revise some of the natural rules. Indeed, each day can and should compete with all the yesterdays of the species.

We have by implication suggested that the Omnipotence (shall we say Nature?) which looks after us has very much else to do. But before we turn to such contemplations, I should like to comment on the tools of comprehension.

The most important aid to the human mind in the understanding of the universe, both the microcosmos and the macrocosmos, is the electromagnetic spectrum, as currently exploited. The major part of our knowledge of the universe has in the past come through information provided by one sense organ alone—that of vision. Our eyes are, however, sensitive only in a small segment of the long radiation spectrum—they are sensitive from the violet to the red—much less than two octaves. But with a suddenness unequaled in the development by artifice of sense-organ spread, we have now learned to explore Nature with radiations extending over a range of more than fifty octaves, a range from the cosmic rays of less than a billionth of an inch in wave length, through gamma rays, X-rays, and the ultraviolet, up to the blue-to-red radiation our eyes record; and then from red to heat waves to radio and on to electric wave lengths measured in miles. We know and measure and use these off-color radiations not directly with the retinas of our eyes, as we do with light, but with artifacts, with the retinas, we might say, of photographic plates, Geiger counters, and photo cells.

The eyes and other sense organs arose naturally to serve animals in the practical problems of existence, not for use in profound researches into the nature and operations of the universe. Practical existence had not until recently included the thirst for "impractical" knowledge.

It happens that the range of human vision from violet to red covers that part of the radiation spectrum where the Sun's light is most intense. In fact, there is not much solar intensity in the short waves of X-rays or the long waves of radio.

If there are animals with vision on a planet near a hotter, bluer star than the Sun, for instance Rigel in Orion, they probably are more sensitive than we are to light in the bluer section of the spectrum; and near a cooler, redder star, like Betelgeuse, more sensitive to reddish light.

A fact worth emphasizing at this point is that man is blind except to a narrow range in the electromagnetic spectrum. To feed himself, to dodge or overcome his enemies, and to find his mate, he has had little need of the solar radiation with wave lengths like those that activate our radios; and since the atmosphere, as it has developed on the Earth has through its ozone blockage shut off the ultraviolet, he, as an animal, has also had no practical need for the short-wave end of the spectrum.

As an organism ambitious to know, and know deeply, he is rather primitive in his senses, if not in sense. (Our primitivism in body anatomy is, of course, generally recognized.) Every human sense receptor, except possibily that concerned in tone discrimination, is outdone by the corresponding receptor of one animal or another—by the hawk's vision, the dog's hearing, the insect's smelling. Some stars have enormously strong magnetic fields; ours a weak one, and we have no recognized sense receptor whatever for magnetism.

But these sensory limitations, and the resulting failure to comprehend fully much of Nature, may be only a local deficiency. On the basis of the new estimates of the great abundance of stars and the high probability of millions of planets with highly developed life, we are made aware—embarrassingly aware—that we may be intellectual minims in the life of the universe. I could develop further this uncomfortable idea by pointing out that sense receptors, in quality quite unknown to us and in fact hardly imaginable, which record phenomena of which we are totally ignorant, may easily exist among the higher sentient organisms of other planets.

Sometimes we suspect the existence on this planet of senses other than those we recognize in ourselves, among animal and plant forms—not merely extended ranges of hearing or of vision or smell, but entirely different responses. The bees and ants respond, as we do not, to polarized light; the birds in migration—to what? And there are those among us who dream of vestigial or embryonic senses hovering about the human psyche.

Rather than dwell on these probabilities, let us note simply that anthropocentric religions and philosophies, which have so often been conspicuously Earth-bound and much tangled up with the human mind and human behavior, have in these present days an opportunity for aggrandizement through incorporating a sensibility of the newly revealed cosmos. If the theologian finds it difficult to take seriously our insistence that the God of humanity is the God of gravitation and the God of hydrogen atoms, at least he may be willing to consider the reasonableness of extending to the higher sentient beings that have evolved elsewhere among the myriads of galaxies the same intellectual or spiritual rating he gives to us.

You may say that these are but speculations, insecurely founded, and that you choose to believe and reason and worship otherwise. And I must reply that you should follow your inclination. But you are invited to think seriously of the cosmic facts. The new discoveries and developments contribute to the unfolding of a magnificent universe; to be a participant is in itself a glory. With our confreres on distant planets; with our fellow animals and plants of land, air, and sea; with the rocks and waters of all planetary crusts, and the photons and atoms that make up the stars—with all these we are associated in an existence and an evolution that inspires respect and deep reverence. We cannot escape humility. And as groping philosophers and scientists we are thankful for the mysteries that still lie beyond our grasp.

There are those who would call this attitude their philosophy, their religion. They would be loath, I hope, to retreat from the galaxies to the earth; unwilling to come out of the cosmic depths and durations to concern themselves only with one organic form on the crust of one small planet, near a commonplace star, at the edge of one of the galaxies. They would hesitate to retreat to that one isolated spot in their search for the Ultimate. May their kind increase and prosper!

• *Questions for Study*

1. What does Shapley mean by the "geocentric" and "heliocentric" theories of the cosmos? How did these theories affect man's view of himself? How does Shapley's view of man depend upon "the eccentric arrangement" and upon his picture of the cosmos? What is the significance of the title of the essay?
2. What might the effects of our new knowledge be upon religious teachings?
3. By what steps does Shapley conclude that there are a "hundred million planetary systems suitable for organic life"? Is his evidence convincing? Why is it difficult for the lay reader to attempt to disagree with him?
4. What does Shapley say about man's senses and their limitations?

LANCELOT HOGBEN

•

MATHEMATICS,

THE MIRROR OF CIVILIZATION

Two views are commonly held about mathematics. One comes from Plato. This is that mathematical statements represent eternal truths. Plato's doctrine was used by the German philosopher, Kant, as a stick with which to beat the materialists of his time, when revolutionary writings like those of Diderot were challenging priestcraft. Kant thought that the principles of geometry were eternal, and that they were totally independent of our sense organs. It happened that Kant wrote just before biologists discovered that we have a sense organ, part of what is called the internal ear, sensitive to the pull of gravitation. Since that discovery, the significance of which was first fully recognized by the German physicist, Ernst Mach,

Reprinted from *Mathematics for the Million* by Lancelot Hogben. By permission of W. W. Norton & Company, Inc. Copyright 1937, 1940. 1943 and 1951 by W. W. Norton & Company, Inc the geometry which Kant knew has been brought down to earth by Einstein. It no longer dwells in the sky where Plato put it. We know that geometrical statements when applied to the real world are only approximate truths. The theory of Relativity has been very unsettling to mathematicians, and it has now become a fashion to say that mathematics is only a game. Of course, this does not tell us anything about mathematics. It only tells us something about the cultural limitations of some mathematicians. When a man says that mathematics is a game, he is making a private statement. He is telling us something about himself, his own attitude to mathematics. He is not telling us anything about the public meaning of a mathematical statement.

If mathematics is a game, there is no reason why people should play it if they do not want to. With football, it belongs to those amusements without which life would be endurable. The view which we shall explore is that mathematics is the language of size, and that it is an essential part of the equipment of an intelligent citizen to understand this language. If the rules of mathematics are rules of grammar, there is no stupidity involved when we fail to see that a mathematical truth is obvious. The rules of ordinary grammar are not obvious. They have to be learned. They are not eternal truths. They are conveniences without whose aid truths about the sorts of things in the world cannot be communicated from one person to another. In Cobbett's memorable words, Mr. Prynne would not have been able to impeach Archbishop Laud if his command of grammar had been insufficient to make himself understood. So it is with mathematics, the grammar of size. The rules of mathematics are rules to be learned. If they are formidable, they are formidable because they are unfamiliar when you first meet them—like gerunds or nominative absolutes. They are also formidable because in all languages there are so many rules and words to memorize before we can read newspapers or pick up radio news from foreign stations. Everybody knows that being able to chatter in several foreign languages is not a sign of great social intelligence. Neither is being able to chatter in the language of size. Real social intelligence lies in the use of a language, in applying the right words in the right context. It is important to know the language of size, because entrusting the laws of human society, social statistics, population, man's hereditary make-up, the balance of trade, to the isolated mathematician without checking his conclusions is like letting a committee of philologists manufacture the truths of human, animal, or plant anatomy from the resources of their own imaginations.

You will often hear people say that nothing is more certain than that two and two make four. The statement that two and two make four is not a mathematical statement. The mathematical statement to which people refer, correctly stated, is as follows:

$$2 + 2 = 4.$$

This can be translated: "to 2 add 2 to get 4." This is not necessarily a statement of something which always happens in the real world. The illustration (Fig. 1) shows that in the real world you do not always find that you have 4 when you have added 2 to 2. To say $2 + 2 = 4$ merely illustrates the meaning of the verb "add," when it is used to translate the mathematical verb "+". To say that $2 + 2 = 4$ is a true statement is just a grammatical convention about the verb "+" and the nouns "2" and "4." In English grammar it is true in the same sense to say that the plural of "mouse" is "mice," or, if you prefer it "add mouse to mouse to get mice." In English grammar it is untrue to say that the plural of "house" is "hice." Saying "$2 + 2 = 2$" is false in precisely the same sense. A slight change in the meaning of the word "add," as used to translate "+", makes it a perfectly correct statement about the apparatus in Fig. 1. Such changes of

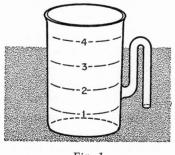

Fig. 1

In the real world you do not always find that you have got FOUR, *when you add* TWO *and* TWO.
Try filling this with water. Its laws of "addition" would be:

$$1 + 0.1 = 2$$
$$1 + 0.2 = 3$$
$$1 + 0.3 = 2$$
$$2 + 0.2 = 2 \text{ etc.}$$

The dot is put in to show that the kind of addition used here is not the kind of addition (+ without a dot) which applies to a vessel which cannot leak, and is so large that it cannot be filled.

meaning are confusing. The object of grammar is to control the freedom of words so that there is no congestion of the intellectual traffic. As a statement about the real world, saying that the British Houses of Parliament are in Glasgow, is a plain lie. As a statement of grammar, it is a true example of how the plural of "house" is formed. If a British Radical member said that the Hice of Parliament were treating the unemployed of Glasgow with shameless frivolity, he might convey a profound and important truth about the real world to a few bright people. As a statement of grammar, it would be false. Many would miss the point and wonder whether he were certifiable. Unlike Mr. Prynne, who understood grammar, he would fail to advance the liberties of the people.

We must not be surprised if we find that the rules of mathematics are not always a perfect description of how we measure the distance of a star, or count heads in a population. The rules of English grammar are a very imperfect description of how English is used. The people who formulated them were preoccupied with translating the bible and other classical texts. So they were over-anxious to find exact equivalents for the peculiarities of Greek and Latin. They were like the first zoologists who used words for the limbs and organs of the human body, when describing the peculiar anatomy of the insect. The English grammar taught in English schools is rather primitive zoology. Also it is essentially a description of the habits of speech prevailing in the English professional class, from which writers of books on grammar are drawn. When the American from New England says "gotten," he is using what was the correct past participle of the strong verb "to get" in *Mayflower* times. When the English labourer says "we be going," he is correctly using one of the three original verbs which have been used to make the roots of the modern mixed verb "to be." When he says "yourn," he is using one of two once equally admissible and equally fashionable forms introduced by analogy about the time when Chaucer wrote the *Canterbury Tales*. To say that "are" and "yours" are grammatically correct is merely to say that we have agreed to adopt the habits of the more prosperous townspeople. When Mr. Shaw is dead, and hence a topic for grammarians, we shall say that "dont" is the correct way to write "do not." Almost certainly we shall soon admit "it is me" as correct grammar. The rules of mathematical grammar also change. In modern vector analysis the rules for using "+" are not the rules we learned at school.

If we can unearth milestones of man's social pilgrimage in the language of everyday life, it is much more easy to do so when we study the grammar of mathematics. The language in which people describe the different *sorts* of things there are in the world is vastly more primitive and more conservative than the *size* languages which have been multiplied to cope with the increasing precision of man's control over nature. In the world which is open to public inspection, the world of inorganic and organic nature, man was not compelled to enlarge the scope of language to describe any new *sorts* of phenomena between 2000 B.C. and the researches of Faraday and Hertz, the father of radio. Even electric and magnetic attractions were recognized as a special sort of thing before there were any historians in the world. In the seventh century B.C. Thales recorded the attraction of small particles to a piece of amber (Greek "electron") when rubbed. The Chinese already knew about the lodestone or natural magnet. Since about 1000 B.C., when some men broke away from picture writing or script like the Chinese which associates sounds with picture symbols, and first began to use an alphabet based purely on how words sound, there has only been one conspicuous invention introduced for describing the qualities of things in the world. This was made by biologists in the eighteenth century, when the confusion existing in the old herbals of medicinal plants forced them to invent an international language in which no confusion is possible. The clear description of the immense variety of organic beings has been made possible by the deliberate introduction of unfamiliar words. These words, like "Bellis perennis," the common daisy, or "Pulex irritans," the common flea, are taken from dead languages. Any meaning for which the biologist has no use lies buried in a social context forgotten long ago. In much the same way the North Europeans had borrowed their alphabet of sound symbols from the picture scripts, and buried the associations of distracting metaphors in the symbols used by the more sophisticated people of the ancient world.

The language of mathematics differs from that of everyday life, because it is essentially a rationally planned language. The languages of size have no place for private sentiment, either of the individual or of the nation. They are international languages like the binomial nomenclature of natural history. In dealing with the immense complexity of his social life man has not yet begun to apply inventiveness to the rational planning of ordinary language when describing different kinds of institutions and human behaviour. The language of everyday life is clogged with sentiment, and the science of human nature has not advanced so far that we can describe individual sentiment in a clear way. So constructive thought about human society is hampered by the same conservatism as embarrassed the earlier naturalists. Nowadays people do not differ about what sort of animal is meant by Cimex or Pediculus, because these words are only used by people who use them in one way. They still can and often do mean a lot of different things when they say that a mattress is infested with bugs or lice. The study of man's social life has not yet brought forth a Linnaeus. So an argument about the "withering away of the State" may disclose a difference about the use of the dictionary when no real difference about the use of the policeman is involved. Curiously enough, people who are most sensible about the need for planning other social amenities in a reasonable way are often slow to see the need for creating a rational and international language.

The technique of measurement and counting has followed the caravans and galleys of the great trade routes. It has developed very slowly. At least four thousand years intervened between the time when men could calculate when the next eclipse would occur and the time when men could calculate how much iron is present in the sun. Between the first recorded observations of electricity produced by friction and the measurement of the attraction of an electrified body two thousand years intervened. Perhaps a longer period separates the knowledge of magnetic iron (or lodestone) and the measurement of magnetic force. Classifying things according to size has been a much harder task than recognizing the different sorts of things there are. It has been more closely related to man's social achievements than to his biological equipment. Our eyes and ears can recognize different sorts of things at a great distance. To measure things at a distance, man has had to make new sense organs for himself, like the astrolabe, the telescope, and the microphone. He has made scales which reveal differences of weight to which our hands are quite insensitive. At each stage in the evolution of the tools of measurement man has refined the tools of size language. As human inventiveness has turned from the counting of flocks and seasons to the building of temples, from the building of temples to the steering of ships into chartless seas, from seafaring plunder to machines driven by the forces of dead matter, new languages of size have sprung up in succession. Civilizations have risen and fallen. At each stage a more primitive, less sophisticated culture breaks through the barriers of custom thought, brings fresh rules to the grammar of measurement, bearing within itself the limitation of further growth and the inevitability that it will be superseded in its turn. The history of mathematics is the mirror of civilization.

The beginnings of a size language are to be found in the priestly civilizations of Egypt and Sumeria. From these ancient civilizations we see the first-fruits of secular knowledge radiated along the inland trade routes to China and pushing out into and beyond the Mediterranean, where the Semitic peoples are sending forth ships to trade in tin and dyes. The more primitive northern invaders of Greece and Asia Minor collect and absorb the secrets of the pyramid makers in cities where a priestly caste is not yet established. As the Greeks become prosperous, geometry becomes a plaything. Greek thought itself becomes corrupted with the star worship of the ancient world. At the very point when it seems almost inevitable that geometry will make way for a new language, it ceases to develop further. The scene shifts to Alexandria, the greatest centre of shipping and the mechanical arts in the ancient world. Men are thinking about how much of the world remains to be explored. Geometry is applied to the measurement of the heavens. Trigonometry takes its place. The size of the earth, the distance of the sun and moon are measured. The star gods are degraded. In the intellectual life of Alexandria, the factory of world religions, the old syncretism has lost its credibility. It may still welcome a god beyond the sky. It is losing faith in the gods within the sky.

In Alexandria, where the new language of star measurement has its beginnings, men are thinking about numbers unimaginably large compared with the numbers which the Greek intellect could grasp. Anaxagoras had shocked the court of Pericles by declaring that the sun was as immense as the mainland of Greece. Now Greece itself had sunk into insignificance beside the world of which Eratosthenes and Poseidonius had measured the circumference. The world itself sank into insignificance beside the sun as Aristarchus had measured it. Ere the dark night of monkish superstition engulfed the great cosmopolis of antiquity, men were groping for new means of calculation. The bars of the counting frame had become the bars of a cage in which the intellectual life of Alexandria was imprisoned. Men like Diophantus and Theon were using geometrical diagrams to devise crude recipes for calculation. They had almost invented the third new language of algebra. That they did not succeed was the nemesis of the social culture they inherited. In the East the Hindus had started from a much lower level. Without the incubus of an old-established vocabulary of number, they had fashioned new symbols which lent themselves to simple calculation without mechanical aids. The Moslem civilization which swept across the southern domain of the Roman Empire brought together the technique of measurement, as it had evolved in the hands of the Greeks and the Alexandrians, adding the new instrument for handling numbers which was developed through the invention of the Hindu number symbols. In the hands of Arabic mathematicians like Omar Khayyám, the main features of a language of calculation took shape. We still call it by the Arabic name, algebra. We owe algebra and the pattern of modern European poetry to a non-Aryan people who would be excluded from the vote in the Union of South Africa.

Along the trade routes this new arithmetic is brought into Europe by Jewish scholars from the Moorish universities of Spain and by Gentile merchants trading with the Levant, some of them patronized by nobles whose outlook had been unintentionally broadened by the Crusades. Europe stands on the threshold of the great navigations. Seafarers are carrying Jewish astronomers who can use the star almanacs which Arab scholarship had prepared. The merchants are becoming rich. More than ever the world is thinking in large numbers. The new arithmetic or "algorithm" sponsors an amazing device which was prompted by the need for more accurate tables of star measurement for use in seafaring. Logarithms were among the cultural first-fruits of the great navigations. Mathematicians are thinking in maps, in latitude and longitude. A new kind of geometry (what we call graphs in everyday speech) was an inevitable consequence. This new geometry of Descartes contains something which Greek geometry had left out. In the leisurely world of antiquity there were no clocks. In the bustling world of the great navigations mechanical clocks are displacing the ancient ceremonial function of the priesthood as timekeepers. A geometry which could represent time and a religion in which there were no saints' days are emerging from the same social context. From this geometry of time a group of men who were studying the mechanics of the pendulum clock and making fresh discoveries about the motion of the planets devised a new size language to measure motion. Today we call it "the" calculus.

For the present this crude outline of the history of mathematics as a mirror of civilization, interlocking with man's common culture, his inventions, his economic arrangements, his religious beliefs may be left at the stage which had been reached when Newton died. What has happened since has been largely the filling of gaps, the sharpening of instruments already devised. Here and there are indications of a new sort of mathematics. We see a hint of it in social statistics and the study of the atom. We begin to see possibilities of new languages of size transcending those we now use, as the calculus of movement gathered into itself all that had gone before.

• Questions for Study

1. In what ways does Hogben's essay supplement Bergamini's "The Language of Science"? Which is more interesting and entertaining? Why? Which is more informative?
2. What is Hogben's purpose in describing the nature of mathematics? According to Hogben, why is our language an inadequate instrument for mathematical investigation?
3. What is meant by the sentence "The history of mathematics is the history of civilization"? How might an artist, an economist, or a psychologist object to this generalization?

HENDRIK WILLEM VAN LOON

·

HEINRICH SCHLIEMANN

I hope you won't mind a slight detour before we get to ancient Hellas, but it is a necessary detour if we want to be fully prepared for what awaits us in the country of Pericles and Phidias. I want to say something about my old friend "serendipity." You will find that strange-looking word in the dictionary. It occurred originally in a story mentioned by Horace Walpole, the English wit and connoisseur, who died in 1797. The title of the novel was *The Three Princes of Serendip*, which was the old name for Ceylon. These three young men were forever making discoveries by "accidents and sagacity" of things for which they were really not looking at all. Since then, serendipity came to mean "the faculty of making happy and unexpected discoveries by accident."

The career of Heinrich Schliemann is one of the best examples of serendipity that has ever come to my notice. As a child he listened spellbound to the stories about the Trojan War, which his father, a poor north German minister, read to him. He made up his mind that some day he would go forth to discover the site of ancient Troy. He realized, however, that such an expedition would cost a lot of money, and so first of all he determined to get rich.

He left the paternal roof as soon as he was old enough to do so, and apprenticed himself to a grocer in a near-by village. But weighing cheese and prunes was not a very lucrative business. He therefore decided to try his luck in South America, and shipped as a cabinboy. His ship was wrecked before it had reached the shores of that fabulous land of the Incas, and Schliemann found himself in Amsterdam working as an assistant bookkeeper for a firm of Dutch merchants.

His evenings he spent learning languages. Before he got through he

From *The Arts*, New York: Simon and Schuster, Inc., 1937. Reprinted by permission of the Margot Johnson Agency.

knew eight of them and knew them well. On account of his familiarity with Russian his employers sent him to St. Petersburg. There he set himself up as an importer of indigo. When the Crimean War broke out in 1854 he took on several military contracts and made an outrageous profit. Not yet satisfied with the results, he went to California during the gold rush and became an American citizen.

Finally in 1868 he decided that he had money enough to start upon his real life task. After a trip around the world he landed in Constantinople, bribed all the Turkish officials whose help he might possibly need, and went forth to a certain hill called Hissarlik, which was situated not far from the Hellespont but on the Asiatic side of these famous straits and where, so he was convinced, he would find his beloved Troy.

Soon it became clear that this crazy German had guessed right. That low hill, to which nobody had paid any attention for almost two thousand years except a few goatherds and their nimble charges, had once upon a time been one of the most important trading centers of the ancient world.

Unfortunately Schliemann was not a trained archaeologist. In his eagerness to get results and to locate the palace of Priam, he dug his way straight through the remnants of the Troy of the Homeric days and uncovered several villages which were so much older than the historic Troy that they had already been in ruins when Achilles and Agamemnon visited this spot to avenge the theft of the lovely Helen, twelve hundred years before the beginning of the Christian era.

Schliemann, like all men with a fatal hobby, refused to consider the possibility of error. He proudly proclaimed to all the world that the problem had been solved and that Troy at last had been given back to the world. This might have led to a bitter dispute between the amateur and the professionals, but at that moment the Turkish officials made an end to all further dispute by telling Schliemann to leave the country. They were dissatisfied with their bribes. The foreigner had promised them gold. Where was the gold?

It was there but it lay much higher up in those strata through which Schliemann had so unceremoniously dug his way in his hurry to get at the real thing. For the moment, at least, there was no further chance to ransack the mound of Hissarlik, and so Schliemann paid his native workingmen, shook the dust of Asia Minor from his feet, and made for the mainland of Greece.

In the central part of Argolis, in the northeast corner of the Peloponnesus, there stood the ruins of an ancient city called Mycenae. It was widely known for the gigantic size of the blocks that had been used for the walls of its citadel and the enormous piece of carved stone over the entrance gate, which showed the figures of two lions, reminiscent of the sort of wild animals the Babylonian sculptors used to carve. No one had ever explored these ruins very seriously until Schliemann made his appearance. He began to dig near the Lion Gate and at once he discovered something very rare, a series of shafts in which the people were buried standing up instead of lying down. These graves had been arranged in a circle and they had never been touched. Not only were the bodies themselves intact but none of the gold and silver that had been buried with the corpses had been stolen. This could only have happened if the city of Mycenae had been attacked so suddenly and unexpectedly that none of the inhabitants had been able to buy their lives by telling their captors where they could find a treasure.

Some ten years later (in 1885), after a second visit to Troy and an attempt to discover the palace of Odysseus in Ithaca, Schliemann tackled the problem of Tiryns. This was another city in the Peloponnesus and a spot of such great antiquity that it was supposed to have been the site whence Hercules had embarked on his career as the major miracle worker of Greek mythology. Here, in Tiryns Schliemann uncovered a complete palace that also showed traces of going back to the pre-Homeric period of Greece.

He then turned his attention to Crete, which was known to have been settled at a much earlier date than the Greek mainland. But here, once again, the desire for graft on the part of the local Turkish officials prevented him from doing the work he had in mind. And so this curious creature, this strange mixture of war profiteer and daydreamer, gold miner, and explorer, died and undoubtedly started digging for a pre-paradisean civilization before he had been in heaven for more than half an hour.

Schliemann had made some very serious mistakes. But when he departed this life in the year 1890, the calendar of Greek history had been pushed back by fully seven hundred years. Best of all, this self-taught German had made the learned world realize that there was a great deal more to the civilization of that particular part of the world than most of the professors had even begun to suspect.

Until then it had been customary to begin the history of art in Europe with that of the Greeks. Now it was shown that the Greeks, far from being the first to appear upon the scene, had been among the last to arrive and that the Aegean Sea had been a center of trade and art and of a very high degree of culture thousands of years before the Athenians laid the cornerstone of their Acropolis.

I often listen to the complaint of the younger generation that this is a dull world because everything has already been done. If anybody wants a job that will keep him busy for the rest of his days, he might devote his attention to the history of the Aegean Sea. For the problems connected with the civilization of these waters, which for so many centuries served as the connecting link between East and West, are still far from solved. And they are not of local interest, either, but touch every part of the Western World. For example, just what sort of people were the first to occupy all this territory, once it had become habitable, and whence had they come? It is only through their art that we shall ever come near a satisfactory answer.

The artists of what we now call the Minoan Age, the artists of Crete in the twentieth century before our era, had a great gift for depicting animal life with all that vivacity and all that power of scrupulous observation which were so typical of the paintings we have found in the caves of prehistoric Europe. But thousands of years (it may be as many as seven or eight thousand) separated the paintings of the caves of Altamira from those in the palaces in Cnossus. What had happened to these cave dwellers during those seventy or eighty centuries? When a change in the climate of central Europe forced them to leave their old home, had they taken to sea and had they finally found a new home among the islands of the Aegean, the last bits of European land before they must touch the shores of a hostile Asia? Or again, how about these mysterious cyclopean walls of Mycenae and Tiryns and several other deserted strongholds on the Greek mainland?

When I first learned my Greek history, forty years ago, I was taught that those walls had been built by the earliest invaders of the Greek peninsula, long before the coming of the real Greeks, and that therefore they had been called cyclopean walls after the Cyclopes, the one-eyed giants who, Homer tells us, used to eat their human prey while still alive. Today we know that these walls, far from being very old, were merely part of a comparatively recent form of architecture which shows considerable similarity to the methods employed by the builders of the menhirs and dolmens of the Atlantic coast in Europe and of Stonehenge in England.

Is there any connection between the two? We would very much like to know. Is Cyprus, as the name seems to suggest, the earliest "copper island" from which the rest of the prehistoric world got its copper? What were the ceremonial and artistic relations between Egypt and Crete during the centuries when Cnossus was the most important center of civilization of the ancient world (during the period, roughly speaking, from 2500 till 1500 B.C.)? Finally, who exactly were those newcomers who almost overnight destroyed this flourishing empire and destroyed it so completely that for almost five hundred years we lost all trace of the original population?

Once more we must confess that we do not know, though we would dearly love to, for the Cretans of thirty centuries ago had so many things in common with us of today that we have a much greater feeling of kinship for their statues and their paintings and their jewelry than for those of the Egyptians or the people of Mesopotamia.

These early Aegean sea rovers must have had a great sense of order and comfort. Their palaces were well lighted and decently aired, in complete contrast to the royal residences of Thebes and Babylon and Nineveh, which were as dusty as those of Queen Elizabeth or Louis XIV of France. Their public buildings had drains and running water and an installation for heating the premises. We have found arrangements by which they could hoist people from one floor to the next— a sort of primitive elevator for the benefit of the aged. Furthermore, there were bathrooms inside the houses and sliding doors between the different apartments and there were also separate quarters where the royal secretaries could do their work without being disturbed by the other menials.

The wheel, at the time of the Minoan civilization, had been in common use in Egypt and Chaldea for at least a thousand years. Carriages (which incidentally were not introduced into Scotland until the middle of the eighteenth century) were not only used for purposes of driving but also apparently for racing. Like ourselves, these people were devotees of all sorts of sport and they went in quite seriously for dancing and boxing and wrestling and (as one would have expected in the land of the Minotaur) also for bullfighting.

The form of government under which they lived was not the democratic one which afterwards was practiced by the Greeks and which was so sadly responsible for their ultimate collapse and loss of liberty. The early Aegean nations were ruled by kings. As we have found practically no statues of soldiers but on the other hand a large number of laws engraved on stone tablets, these potentates seem to have tried to maintain themselves by means of an efficient civil service rather than by violence. This may account for a certain air of something that reminds us quite distinctly of the art which forty years ago was known as *fin de siècle,* the art of the end of the nineteenth century. The last forty years of that century, too, were an era when a great many people felt convinced that the age of sweet reason had at last made its appearance and that armies and navies could now be discarded as unpleasant survivals from the days of the Middle Ages. The Great War gave them their answer. The present dictatorships continue that answer. And the rather effeminate civilization of the "end of the century" has been smashed to pieces.

Judging by their art, it is more than likely that the people of Crete had landed in exactly the same sort of blind alley where all effort was lamed by the thought that sheer intellectuality would eventually cure the world of all its ills. This may seem far-fetched to you, but wait until you see some of these late Cretan products. You will then understand what I mean.

It was not until the year 1900 that Sir Arthur Evans began to excavate the ruins of Cnossus. Since then we have learned so much about Cretan antiquities that we are now able to follow the development of this Aegean civilization quite accurately.

First of all, there was a slow growth of almost a thousand years. This was the Early Minoan Age from 3000 to 2000 B.C., during which this civilization gradually spread from island to island.

Next came the Middle Minoan Age (from 2000 B.C. or thereabouts to 1500 B.C.) during which Crete was the center of this civilization and Cnossus the London of this island empire.

Then came the Late Minoan Age (1500 to 1000 B.C.) during which the island culture established itself firmly on the mainland and, marked by some characteristics that make us differentiate it as Mycenaean civilization, spread its art all over the Greek peninsula.

And then, as has so often happened under similar circumstances, it appeared that the colonies in these little settlements in the wilderness of a distant land were of tougher fiber than the rather blasé young men and women at home. Until finally a place like Mycenae, a mere hick town that had begun its career as a small Cretan trading post, was able to conquer its former rulers and in turn change the island of Crete into a colony of its own.

Thereupon art, which invariably follows the full dinner pail, hastily moved from the island to the mainland and enjoyed a new lease on life, bursting forth into a great many new forms, such as pottery and metalwork and ornaments of silver and gold, which from then on were spread all over the Mediterranean Sea, from Spain to Phoenicia and from Egypt to Italy.

And then?

Then we suddenly lose track both of the Cretans and the Mycenaeans and for almost five hundred years the people of the Aegean Sea go through a period of obscurity not unlike that of those Dark Ages which followed in the wake of the downfall of the Roman Empire.

But how could such vast and distant citadels as those of Tiryns and Mycenae be overrun and destroyed by an enemy unless that enemy was possessed of much better weapons than the defenders? The answer is that the newcomers, although complete and unmitigated barbarians from an artistic point of view, were probably much better soldiers than their opponents. The business of war was as important to them as the business of living beautiful and artistic lives had been to their former oppressors. Furthermore, as we have reason to believe, these new arrivals had originally come from the north, from the valley of the Danube, and there they had learned how to make excellent swords and lance points from those ironmasters who had been working their primitive little furnaces in that part of the world ever since prehistoric days.

Homer does not bear this out, but Homer was a poet, not an exact historian. According to him, the original inhabitants of Greece had been called the Achaeans and they had lived somewhere in the north of Europe, perhaps in the land of the Scythians, the ancestors of the present Cossacks. But whoever they were and whether they were called Achaeans or not, these intruders completely overthrew the civilization of the Aegean Sea, as it then survived among the fortified towns of the mainland. They must have done this with great brutality and quite unexpectedly. For otherwise they would never have overlooked the gold that lay hidden in those curious shaft graves which, almost three thousand years later, were found still quite intact by our friend, Herr Schliemann.

After this surprise attack, what ever became of the Aegean civilization that had first of all moved from the islands to the mainland? It was forced to go back whence it had come. The few people who survived this wholesale slaughter escaped to the islands of the Aegean, as fifteen hundred years later the Italians from the mainland were to flee to the islands of the Adriatic and there found the mighty city of Venice that they might be safe from the Goths and the Vandals and the Huns and all the other marauding tribes from the east. And gradually these refugees picked up the odds and ends of their former mode of living. The fishermen once more caught their fish, the bakers once more baked their bread, the potters returned to their wheels, the jewelers began to engrave their cameos, the goldsmiths dreamed of the time when they should once more hammer away at their little bits of precious metal.

Meanwhile, on the mainland, the new masters were trying to feel happy among the unaccustomed splendors of these ancient palaces (no temples could here be desecrated, as the Mycenaeans and their neighbors seem to have got along quite happily without any definite places of worship), and now and then they must have noticed that they were lacking something which the former occupants had had in rich abundance. Gradually, too, both the victor and the defeated must have felt the need of re-establishing some sort of commercial relations. For commerce, being part of the natural order of things, can never be easily suppressed, no matter how hard all sorts of governments may try to do so. The barbarian, plagued by his wife who wanted to know why she and her children could not enjoy all the advantages these Mycenaean women had enjoyed, must have sent to the nearest island for a few artisans and architects and bronze workers, for a few people who could teach him those crafts of which he was completely ignorant but which filled his simple soul with awe and that of his wife with envy.

At first these craftsmen may have hesitated to go. But they had to live and so they ventured back to the mainland. Once it was proved that they ran no unusual risks, others followed their example.

Such events do not happen from one day to the next. They take a lot of time. In this case, they took almost five hundred years. But then at last we find ourselves face to face with an art which was no longer either Aegean or Minoan or Mycenaean, but which was definitely Greek.

• Questions for Study

1. How effective is Van Loon's use of the word "serendipity" in describing Schliemann's efforts? Considering Van Loon's account of Schliemann's life, can you say that qualities other than serendipity played a part in his success?
2. What stylistic effects are created by such phrases as "this crazy German," "people were buried standing up instead of lying down," and "take a lot of time"? Would you call Van Loon's style generally informal? What effects are created by his tendency to ask questions and leave them unanswered?
3. The account of Schliemann's life is quite brief and the details are highly selective. Suggest some of the ways in which a biographer, doing a full length portrait of Schliemann, might develop Van Loon's material.

WILLIAM D. MCELROY

•

THE PROMISE OF THE SEA

Man's dominion of the earth ends at the shorelines of the land he inhabits. Beyond his terrestrial kingdom—a meager one-third of the planet —lie the vast, unconquered oceans. The sea is a world unto itself: In its protective depths live ninety per cent of the earth's different kinds of animals; it produces all its own food—about ten billion tons of organic carbon a year, only a tiny fraction of which is harvested by man; it claims inorganic riches which stagger the imagination—enough gold, for instance, to make every man on earth a millionaire.

Fear and ignorance have kept man from this alien world of the sea. Throughout history, from Odysseus to Piccard, the sea has been, first and foremost, the province of men of rare courage. Not until great sea explorers crossed frontiers and conquered ignorance and superstition did others venture across the oceans or into its depths. As familiarity grew, man learned the commercial and military importance of the sea, and these in turn spurred greater mastery of the sea. As elsewhere, necessity became the mother of invention.

To the curious and the courageous, the sea still presents the challenge of the unknown, for ignorance is still the distinguishing characteristic of man's relation to the sea. But now, more than ever, necessity goads us onward in our exploration of the sea. We now have submarines capable of steady submergence for many months holding missiles capable of destruction many times greater than that wrought by World War II. For strategic reasons, therefore, we need urgently to learn more about the topography of the ocean bottom, about deep ocean currents, temperature, density, and so forth.

Quite apart from the threat of war, another necessity presses us to

From *Johns Hopkins Magazine*, May–June 1961. Reprinted by permission of *Johns Hopkins Magazine* and of the author.

learn to master the sea. That necessity is basic to life itself: food. The lives of two-thirds of the world's people are wholly dictated by that basic necessity; they are oppressed by hunger and by the weakness and disease which hunger generates.

Out of the sea we can extract the food to relieve the hunger of these millions of people and give dignity to their lives. We *must* turn to the sea, because the bounty of the land has limits. And in some places— significantly, places where malnutrition is most chronic—the limits have been reached.

It is true that a lot more food than we are currently producing can be raised on the land. It is estimated that an additional one billion acres of land, though largely inferior to present cultivated land, can be put to agricultural use. Theoretically, the yield from this land can match the high yield per acre of present day Western Europe, though in practical terms, this will be a fantastically costly enterprise. This would be a level of productivity twice the present world average.

A rate of increase in agricultural production of two per cent per year is quite practical (four per cent per year is possible), so that doubling of productivity can be achieved within fifty years. But two per cent is barely ahead of the rate of population increase in the world, and may in fact fall behind it. Add to this the consideration that per capita consumption of food must increase in a number of areas of the world, and that industrial and urban civilization will crowd the agrarian, and it is obvious that we must squeeze an even higher yield from the land to feed the world population fifty years from now.

Surely the saturation point of land agriculture will have been reached a century from now; most likely it will occur sooner. The day is not far off when we must turn to the sea for a large part of our nourishment.

But in fact, the crisis is more immediate. Essentially the problem of today's hunger is not one of production, but of distribution. In many areas of chronic malnutrition, the saturation point of land agriculture is near. In China, two-thirds of the land is desert or mountain territory, unadapted to agriculture. The Chinese population is crowded into the relatively fertile eastern part of the country on farms which average 4.18 acres (compared to the average of 157 acres in the United States). Here they scratch a bare subsistence from the soil—whenever famines, floods, or locust plagues do not destroy the crops. The diet is almost entirely rice. There are few grazing animals on this precious land, since the conversion of vegetable calories into animal calories is far too costly; the recovery in milk, for example, is 15 per cent; in eggs, 7 per cent; and in beef, only 4 per cent.

Ironically, the Chinese population is concentrated close to the sea, where the animal proteins they so sorely lack could be easily fished from the waters. Moreover, a great reservoir of nutrients to enrich their soil lies in the sea, but China's impoverished medieval economy makes little use of these riches.

Similarly, protein starvation plagues areas of Latin America, South Africa, India, and Indonesia—and all of these areas are close to the oceans of the world. They present a startling contrast with Japan, which, though not agriculturally self-sufficient, has by far the largest fishing industry in the world. Significantly, 45 per cent of the proceeds from that industry go into fertilizers for land farming. In addition, Japan has pioneered in the cultivation of certain algae as human food.

For the sake of the billion and a half who are hungry, we need urgently to turn to the sea. We need the foods the oceans can provide directly; we need the mineral salts and organic nutrients to enrich the earth's soil; and we need fresh water extracted from the sea to irrigate our parched, unused land.

Some of the barriers to fuller exploitation of the sea have been merely economic. There are regions of the sea where fish abound but no fishing boats scoop them up. Countries like India lack the capital to develop an efficient, large-scale fishing industry. Desalination of ocean water is practicable; several processing plants have already been built in this country, but they have been costly to build and the yield is still fairly expensive—about a dollar per thousand gallons.

Nonetheless, the greatest barrier is still our ignorance. We simply do not know enough about the sea as it is, much less how to manipulate and use it efficiently.

Like the land, the sea is varied. It has rich and fertile pastures and "dry" deserts. The life of the sea is subject to disease, depredation, erosion, and weather. There are seasonal changes and yearly cycles, which sometimes alter drastically. A species of fish suddenly changes its migratory habit. Why? We do not know. With respect to the sea, we are in the position of early man, who hunted and foraged on the land and accepted, because he had to, the conditions he met. We do not know how to enrich the "soil" of the sea, how to prevent fluctuations in abundance, how to combat marine diseases, how to practice selective breeding and develop the best species of marine life. As Lionel Walford has pointed out, "We are too ignorant of the sea and its resources to know how to intervene to the degree possible in farming. We cannot do what agriculturists do; we cannot manipulate the environment. Nor will we until we have acquired a great deal more knowledge than we now have."

The information we must gather will have to be *basic* knowledge about the sea; the practical knowledge cannot be attained without it. We must know the environment before we can manipulate it. And there are as many different aspects to the problem as there are "branches" to the broad science called oceanography: physical, chemical, meteorological, zoological, bacteriological, and so forth.

Where do we start? The chain of life in the sea begins with the tiny plant organisms, called phytoplankton, which form the "grass" of the sea. The phytoplankton are consumed by tiny animal organisms, called zooplankton; both, in turn, are consumed by larger forms of marine life. Smaller fish are eaten by larger carniverous fish and sea mammals—and so on, up through the blue whale, which consumes a huge diet of zooplankton. Lastly, animal wastes which decompose and oxidize provide nutrition for the phytoplankton, and the cycle begins again.

A single copepod, one of the many kinds of zooplankton, may consume more than 120,000 plant organisms in a day. There is, of course, some energy loss in the process; a further loss occurs when the copepod is eaten by a larger animal, and so on up the ladder; by the time a fish has fattened himself to a size suitable for human consumption, an enormous output of basic energy by phytoplankton has been expended. Fortunately, these organisms multiply prodigiously under favorable conditions. One diatom may have 100 million descendants in thirty days.

Like the green plants on the land, phytoplankton, in the presence of sunlight and chlorophyll, use carbon dioxide and water to build nourishing carbohydrates from their own molecules and to release free oxygen— thus providing animal life its basic fuels. This process of photosynthesis is complex and mysterious; we do not yet understand it well enough to duplicate it in the laboratory, but we do know a great deal about its essential ingredients.

In addition to supplies of water (which, it is safe to say, will never be exhausted in the sea), photosynthesis requires sunlight. For this reason, plant life in the sea exists in a thin layer at the surface—seldom deeper than two hundred feet, and never deeper than six hundred feet. Temperature also influences photosynthesis. The other essential ingredients are carbon dioxide and the organic and inorganic nutrients in the sea water, which the phytoplankton use to reproduce themselves and to manufacture the complex chlorophyll molecule, the indispensable catalyst in the photosynthetic reaction. The range of elements used by these simple organisms is impressive. In addition to the common "building blocks" of organic compounds—carbon, oxygen, hydrogen, and nitrogen —these phytoplankton use phosphorus, calcium, copper, zinc, and a number of other elements. Recent studies have also shown that they need certain vitamins and amino acids.

Obviously, if there were no movement in the sea, the plant life would quickly use up all the nutrients near the surface and die. Fortunately, the sea is never still. Winds, temperature changes, and deep-sea currents induce turbulence, or upwelling, which draws the nutrient-rich deep waters toward the surface to replenish the "soil." In coastal waters, where movement occurs regularly and where land erosion provides rich nutrients, the sea is a rich pasture. Most of the important commercially interesting marine life is harvested in coastal waters or in off-shore waters not far from land. In many other areas, where movement is sluggish or where nutrients are sparse, the sea is a desert.

There are a number of problems which must be mastered before the deserts of the sea can be made fertile and the rich pastures made even more productive. We must learn, for example, which species of plankton are most favorable to the growth of commercially important marine life. These will vary with the climate of the oceans.

Some species, we know, are downright harmful. The "red tide" of the Gulf of Mexico, which poisons fish and piles them up on the beaches as thickly as one hundred pounds per foot, is caused by the sudden and mysterious "population explosion" of a certain dinoflagellate. Obviously, to discourage the growth of these harmful organisms and to encourage the growth of the best ones, we must know *how* they grow. And we are far from having that knowledge.

In the regions where upwelling is sluggish, we must learn how to speed it up. Scientists have suggested a number of ways to do this. One proposal is a floating chain, to which are attached huge metal flaps; deep currents would cause the flaps to wave, inducing motion all the way to the surface. Another proposal is a nuclear reactor, deep in the water, generating heat to force water upward by convection. These are some of the imaginative suggestions, but none has yet been tried.

Nor do we yet know enough about the topography of the ocean bottom or the action of deep-sea currents to use natural endowments to assist future efforts at artificial upwelling.

As selective breeding must be practiced with the simpler organisms, it must also be practiced with higher species. The kingdom of the sea must be divided into those species which are commercially useful (a far greater number than we are presently using), those which contribute to the growth of useful species, and those which play no useful part or are harmful. We must learn what habitats are best suited for the growth of the best species, and then learn how to create those habitats and hold them constant. At the same time, we must control the habitat in such a way as to discourage the growth of harmful species.

The problem is like that of growing a field of plump tomatoes with the best fertilizers while inhibiting the growth of weeds which choke the tomato plants. The difference, of course, is that we know a lot more about tomatoes and weeds than we do about fish.

But the minute we begin to tamper with the sea we raise a host of further problems. Despite the vastness of the oceans and their varied environments, there is a delicate balance to the life cycle of the sea. It cannot be disrupted at any one point without important consequences at all other points.

Fishermen know that underneath a thick patch of a certain kind of algae, herring will be scarce. For some reason, the fish run away from these too-rich waters. Nature sees to it that the algae growth is controlled and the plants consumed for good use, but if man were to enter the scene and promote the growth of the algae far beyond Nature's bounds, the consequences could be disastrous.

There may be another danger in thickening the carpet of plankton at the surface. As the density increases, the sun penetration diminishes, and the layer becomes thinner. Since the world of the sea is roughly divided into horizontal layers, each dependent upon the others but with definite boundaries for marine life within each layer, a disruption of the top layer can seriously affect all beneath it.

Again, there may be a danger if we begin, as some have proposed, to mine organically concentrated deposits of metals from ocean water on a large scale, for we may rob phytoplankton of valuable nutrients.

There is also reason to believe that wherever we tamper with the energy and matter exchange at the surface or change the upwelling rates in the ocean depths, we will affect the earth's weather patterns on a vast scale. Hopefully, we can enrich the seas and improve our weather at the same time, but we have no guarantee that the two considerations work to mutual advantage.

The very complexity of these problems underscores the need to attack oceanographic research on a broad front. Geophysicists, chemists, bacteriologists, and innumerable others must provide pieces to the huge puzzle before mankind can begin intelligent and safe, large scale farming of the sea.

As a footnote, it is worth mention here that, in one manner, mankind has already begun tampering with the sea with greater haste than his present knowledge warrants. In the last decade we have dumped about 10,500 curies of radioactive wastes off the Atlantic coast and about 14,000 curies off the Pacific coast. Weapons tests have deposited more than two million curies of strontium-90 in the sea. As consumption of radioactive materials increases, especially with the advent of nuclear powered ships, the rate of disposal in the sea will rise sharply. By all our calculations, the present rate of disposal seems safe, even arch-conservative when matched against current British practice, which permits disposal of wastes through a three-mile pipeline directly into the Irish Sea at a maximum of 10,000 curies per month.

But our calculations have been based on limited information—insufficient to permit a great increase in the rate of dumping contaminants in the sea. Not enough is known about ocean currents to know where and how fast the contaminants travel through the water from disposal sites. Not enough is known about man's radioactive tolerance, both pathologically and genetically; almost nothing is known about the limits for all forms of marine life. Nor is enough known about the ability of marine organisms to absorb certain isotopes into their own structure to high concentration; clearly, some of these could be dietary hazards to man.

If we continue to limit ocean dumping to low-level wastes, and if the wastes were to disperse evenly throughout the vast ocean waters, the effects would probably remain negligible even if the dumping rate were increased many times over. But radioactive wastes obviously are not evenly distributed, and do create local, short-term problems. A number of scientists, including members of the staff of the Chesapeake Bay Institute of Johns Hopkins, are studying these problems, but a great deal more research will have to be done before the hazards are eliminated. As one of them has said, "The situation is urgent but not hopeless. There is time to make up our deficiences, but no extra time."

Experts agree that we have lagged in our study of the sea. We know more about the far side of the moon than we do about many regions of the oceans. By one estimate, it would take thirty-four research ships working ten years just to fill the gap in our knowledge of the physical structure of the oceans. And physical oceanography is but one aspect of the broad problem of understanding the sea and turning that knowledge to good use. Much of the work to be done will be accomplished in quiet and undramatic ways in laboratories far from the shorelines.

The Committee on Oceanography of the National Academy of Sciences, of which Harrison Brown is chairman, has recommended "at least a doubling of basic research activity during the next ten years" by the United States. A bill to sponsor a comprehensive ten-year program of oceanographic research was introduced in the Senate last year by Warren G. Magnuson, and the bill follows closely the studied recommendations of the N.A.S. committee. Hearings on the Magnuson bill are still in progress.

"For the first time in history," Arnold Toynbee has written, "mankind has dared to believe that the benefits of civilization could be made available to the entire human race." If the increased effort in oceanographic research is forthcoming, as it must be forthcoming, we may see the day when the sea is mastered, hunger is conquered, and dignity is granted to the lives of every human being.

Only then will man's kingdom encompass the whole planet.

• *Questions for Study*

1. McElroy is trying to popularize a difficult scientific subject, and he wants to persuade us of its significance. How effectively does he use language that a layman would understand? How can his use of trite expressions in certain parts of the essay be justified?
2. How do comparison and contrast aid McElroy to develop his essay? What specifically are his arguments concerning the importance of the sea? Which do you consider the most important? Why?
3. In what ways is the sea hostile to man? In what respects do man's activities affect the content of the sea?

INDEX